RESEARCH
METHODS
IN APPLIED
SETTINGS

RESEARCH
METHODS
IN APPLIED
SETTINGS

AN INTEGRATED APPROACH TO DESIGN AND ANALYSIS

SECOND EDITION

JEFFREY A. GLINER
Colorado State University - Fort Collins

GEORGE A. MORGAN
Colorado State University - Fort Collins

NANCY L. LEECH
University of Colorado - Denver

Routledge
Taylor & Francis Group
New York   London

Routledge
Taylor & Francis Group
270 Madison Avenue
New York, NY 10016

Routledge
Taylor & Francis Group
27 Church Road
Hove, East Sussex BN3 2FA

Library of Congress Cataloging-in-Publication Data

Gliner, Jeffrey A.
   Research methods in applied setttings : an integrated approach to design and analysis / Jeffrey A. Gliner, George A. Morgan, Nancy L. Leech. -- 2nd ed.
        p. cm.
   Includes bibliographical references and indexes.
   ISBN 978-0-8058-6434-2 (hardback)
   1. Social sciences--Research. I. Morgan, George A. (George Arthur), 1936- II. Leech, Nancy L. III. Title.

H62.G523 2009
300.72--dc22   2008046239

**Visit the Taylor & Francis Web site at
http://www.taylorandfrancis.com**

**and the Psychology Press Web site at
http://www.psypress.com**

Contents

Section III Sampling, Measurement, and Data Collection

Section IV   Data Analysis and Interpretation

Section V   Evaluating and Writing Research Reports

Appendices

Preface

In this second edition of *Research Methods in Applied Settings: An Integrated Approach to Design and Analysis*, we continue to promote our philosophy of an integrated approach to quantitative research methods and to the selection and interpretation of data analyses. Our book provides guidance for graduate students in the applied behavioral sciences about planning and conducting a research project, including collecting and analyzing data and writing a research report. The target disciplines include education, allied health, psychology, and other applied behavioral science areas.

Overview of the Content

The table of contents shows the 27 chapters divided into five sections: (I) Introductory Chapters; (II) Quantitative Research Approaches, Questions, and Designs; (III) Sampling, Measurement, and Data Collection; (IV) Data Analysis and Interpretation; and (V) Evaluating and Writing Research Reports. Although we have organized the chapters in a logical order, we also wanted the sections and chapters to "stand alone" as much as possible. This required some repetition, or at least brief redefinition of terms at various points in the text. Thus, the reader should have some flexibility to skip chapters or read them in a different order. For example, the first section in Chapter 27, "Anatomy of an Article," might be part of an early lecture to introduce students to what might be expected when reading a journal article.

We continue to believe that all phases of the research process are *interdependent*. Many authors treat the different parts of their research methods books as essentially unrelated. No time is this more obvious than when viewing the curriculum of a typical graduate program where a course in research methods is separate from a course in measurement and statistics is taught as though it had no relation to research design. We continue to make a strong case that in any quantitative research study, the research design guides the data analysis and that the two should not be viewed as totally different content areas, to be taught in two different courses. We have had so many experiences where students have a good grasp of statistics but have no idea why a particular analysis is used for a particular design. However, this is not a statistics book so there are few formulas or computations. We have tried to make this book student friendly as well as sophisticated, partly by being consistent and clear in terminology and partly by organizing the material so that the various chapters are consistent and fit together logically.

We have found in our approach to teaching research methods that students become confused due to inconsistent terminology. Perhaps the most common example is the confusion created by the terms *selection* and *assignment*. Traditionally, research texts have interchanged the two terms so that students cannot tell the difference between *selection* into the study, an external validity issue, and *assignment* to groups, an internal validity issue. Another example is the term *validity*. Is this a term to be used only when assessing a measurement tool, or does it apply to the evaluation of the design of a study, or to the whole study? We are reminded of Bruce Thompson's frequently repeated, intentionally facetious remark at his many national workshops: "We use these different terms to confuse the graduate students." For these reasons we have tried to present a semantically consistent and coherent big picture of what we call research approaches (e.g., experimental, quasi-experimental) and how they lead to three basic kinds of research questions (difference, associational, and descriptive), which, in turn, lead to three kinds or groups of statistics with the same names. We realize that these and other attempts to develop and use a consistent framework are both nontraditional and somewhat of an oversimplification. However, we think the framework and consistency pay off in terms of student understanding and ability to actually design research and use statistics to help answer research questions.

Distinctive Features

An important feature of the book is the emphasis on students becoming good *consumers of research* by helping them analyze and evaluate research articles. Chapters 23 and 24 bring together many points from earlier chapters into an integrated framework for the analysis and evaluation of research articles using eight rating scales to evaluate research validity and the validity of a whole study.

A second feature is that the text has a large number of *diagrams* and *tables* that summarize various topics and show in a different way topics that are often confusing or prove difficult to learn well enough to apply. Visual learners especially may appreciate the figures and tables.

A third feature of the book is the division of all quantitative research questions (and we think qualitative research as well) into five categories that we call *research approaches*: *randomized experimental, quasi-experimental, comparative, associational,* and *descriptive*. Complex studies may use more than one of these approaches; for example, "survey" studies often have descriptive as well as comparative and associational research questions.

This categorization of research or, more accurately, of research questions into one of five approaches has been helpful for several reasons. One is with regard to discussions of *cause and effect*. We feel that causal questions can be appropriately answered only with well-controlled randomized experiments and to a lesser extent with the quasi-experimental approach. Neither the comparative *nor* the associational approach is well suited to deal with cause and effect.

Another reason that our classification of research approaches is helpful is that one can follow the research process from *purpose* through *question/hypothesis* to *data analysis*. For example, in general, the randomized experimental, quasi-experimental, *and* comparative approaches use what we call *difference inferential statistics*, such as the *t* test or analysis of variance, whereas the associational approach uses *associational inferential statistics*, such as correlation and multiple regression. We realize that all parametric inferential statistics are relational (special cases of canonical correlation), but we think that it is helpful educationally to make the aforementioned distinction, which is consistent with our framework for research approaches as well as most basic statistics books.

A fourth feature of the book is what we call the *design classification* based on the three major types of design: *between groups, within subjects,* and *mixed* designs. These general classifications apply to the comparative approach as well as to the experimental and quasi-experimental approaches, which have been more traditional. We show that although these three types of approaches use the same general type of statistics (e.g., analysis of variance,

ANOVA), the specific statistics for between-groups designs are different from those for within subjects and from those in mixed designs. We also point out that the associational approach uses a different set of statistics, but the data resemble the data in a within-subjects design. Thus, a distinctive feature of the book is our emphasis on the integration of design and the selection of data analyses techniques.

Although our backgrounds are in education and psychology, we have worked and taught research courses in applied departments including occupational therapy, education, human development and family studies, and consumer science and merchandising as well as psychology. Also, we have had in our classes students from business, music therapy, social work, and communication disorders, to mention a few of the more common areas. Thus, we feel that we have a good grasp of the types of research problems faced by master's and doctoral students in these diverse areas and have designed a book that we feel is user friendly as well as sophisticated.

Major Changes from the First Edition

- The biggest change is the inclusion of a third author, Nancy Leech. Professor Leech is currently teaching quantitative and qualitative research methods in a graduate program of education. Her expertise in the area of measurement, including reliability and validity, is especially valuable in keeping up with the changes put forth by the American Psychological Association (APA) and the American Educational Research Association (AERA).

- Null hypothesis significance testing (NHST) continues to be an area of controversy for researchers and statisticians. We felt that the importance of this topic should be addressed by adding a second chapter ("Making Inferences from Sample Data II: The Evidence-Based Approach") on statistical inference. In this new chapter we emphasize the reporting of confidence intervals and effect sizes. We also discuss the important role that meta-analysis has come to play in all scientific disciplines.

- In keeping with our philosophy that students should know how to evaluate *all* aspects of a research study, we divided our framework for evaluating research into two separate chapters ("Evaluating Research Validity: Part I" and "Evaluating Research Validity: Part II"). In addition, we added a following chapter that demonstrates our evaluation framework with five sample articles that were introduced in Chapter 1 and used in a number of other chapters to illustrate the concepts discussed in those chapters.

- The order of the chapters has been changed somewhat; for example, the chapters on measurement reliability and validity (now separate chapters) and an overview of data collection techniques have been moved up to Chapters 11–13. The chapter on measurement validity has been extensively rewritten to be consistent with the current APA/AERA/National Counsel on Measurement in Education (NCME) standards.

- There are fewer chapters dealing with inferential statistics and their interpretation. Chapters 20–22 provide an updated introduction to inferential statistics, how their selection is related to the design of the study, and how to interpret the results, using not only NHST but also effect sizes and confidence intervals.

- Because clinicians and others working in applied settings are increasingly expected to base their treatments/interventions on scientific evidence, we have added a chapter on evaluating evidence for evidence-based practice.
- Chapter 7 ("Nonexperimental Approaches and Designs") is now a separate chapter, including a brief introduction to qualitative research approaches.
- Chapter 2 ("Planning a Quantitative Research Project"), Chapter 15 ("Practical Issues in Data Collection and Coding"), and Chapter 27 ("Writing the Research Report") provide practical advice about conducting research and are largely new to this edition.

Feedback that we have received from students and colleagues, especially those who have used our text to teach their research classes, leads us to continue to believe that we have a good text on research methods that will help graduate students understand, evaluate, and conduct research, topics which are often unnecessarily frightening to students in applied fields.

Learning Tools and Instructional Aids

This book has a number of features to help students understand, evaluate, and conduct research projects. Each chapter ends with a summary, lists of key terms and key distinctions, and several application problems based on material discussed in the chapter. The *key concepts* are defined in the *Glossary* (*Appendix C*) and are identified in the chapter either in a section heading or in bold type. The *key distinctions* lists should help students focus on terms that are important to distinguish or contrast. *Appendix B*, "Confusing Terms," also is designed to help students identify partially similar terms (e.g., *random* assignment and *random* sampling) that need to be distinguished. *Appendix B* also identifies different terms for similar concepts (e.g., dependent variable and outcome variable) that are used interchangeably in the research literature and in this book. These features should help alleviate the semantic confusion mentioned earlier.

Appendix A provides a short list of books and articles that we have found especially useful to students as they learn about and implement research projects. *Appendix D* provides templates and examples of how to write research problems and five types of research questions; the five sample articles, which are described and evaluated throughout the text, are used to illustrate how to write research questions. *Appendix E* lists the 19 questions that we use in our comprehensive evaluation of research articles. Finally, *Appendix F* provides information and examples of tables and figures in APA format. The appendices are intended to provide practical advice to new researchers.

The Instructor's Resource material is housed on a password-protected website at http://www.psypress.com/applied-settings. It is intended to help faculty members who use the text with their classes. An additional resource that instructors and students may find useful is the 4Researchers website (http://www.4Researchers.org), funded by the National Institute of Mental Health. This site provides more than 250 interviews with respected experts, including practical advice about research design, statistics, and career advancement.

Acknowledgments

Chapters 20–24 in the current book expand on and reprint several tables, figures, and some text from Morgan, Gliner, and Harmon's (2006) *Understanding and Evaluating Research in Applied and Clinical Settings* (ISBN 0-8058-5331-6) published by Lawrence Erlbaum Associates, now under the Routledge/Taylor & Francis Group. We also acknowledge that some tables, figures, and text in Chapters 14 and 27 and in Appendix F are reprinted from Leech, Barrett, and Morgan's (2008), *SPSS for Intermediate Statistics* (ISBN 13-978-0-8058-6267-6) or from Morgan, Leech, Gloeckner, and Barrett's (2007) *SPSS for Introductory Statistics* (ISBN 978-0-8058-6027-6). We thank our colleagues Karen Barrett and Gene Gloeckner for use of those materials. Information about these books can be found at http://www.researchmethodsarena.com.

We would like to thank several reviewers, Marty Drell, Mina Dulcan, Brian Isaacson, Kenneth Solberg, Cherng-Jyh Yen, Kimberly S. Maier, Jie Hu, and Nancy L. Leech, for their reviews of this and earlier versions of this material. Several colleagues, Karen Atler, Robert Fetsch, Gail Gliner, Orlando Griego, Helena Kraemer, David MacPhee, Maura MacPhee, Jerry Vaske, and Ray Yang, also provided helpful comments on earlier versions. Many current and former students provided suggestions for improving the manuscript at several points in its development; we especially want to recognize Joan Anderson, Shelly Haddock, Lori Teng, Mei-Huei Tsay, and Sue Tungate. We owe special thanks to Gene Gloeckner, Andrea Fritz, and Kathryn Kidd, who carefully read the current manuscript and made useful suggestions; Kathryn also wrote the new application problems and Appendix C (Glossary) for this edition. Don Quick wrote Appendix F ("Making APA Tables and Figures"); his technical help and that from Ian Gordon were critical. Our word processors, Alana Stewart and Sophie Nelson, were especially helpful in producing the tables, figures, and manuscript.

Finally, we want to thank our spouses, Gail, Hildy, and Grant, for their support during the writing of this book and over the years.

JAG, GAM, NLL

Section I

Introductory Chapters

1

Definitions, Purposes, and Dimensions of Research

In this chapter, we discuss definitions and several purposes of research. Then, we describe important dichotomies or dimensions along which research studies vary. Next, we provide an overview of our general framework for describing types of quantitative research that we call approaches. Finally, we describe briefly five studies that serve as examples for each of the five research approaches. The sample studies will be used in this and several later chapters to illustrate research concepts and how to evaluate research.

Definitions of Research

What is research? Many definitions have been given. Two examples are (1) a systematic method of gaining new information and (2) a persistent effort to think straight. The definition utilized by government agencies for the purpose of federal regulation and the protection of human participants is the systematic collection of data that develops or contributes to generalizable knowledge. Such data are intended to be published, are part of a thesis or dissertation, are presented to the public, or are developed for others to build on. (The ethical and practical issues of the review of human research are discussed in Chapters 14 and 15.)

Smith (1981), in an old but still useful definition, suggests that the term *research* be equated to **disciplined inquiry,** which

> ... must be conducted and reported so that its logical argument can be carefully examined; it does not depend on surface plausibility or the eloquence, status, or authority of its author; error is avoided; evidential test and verification are valued; the dispassionate search for truth is valued over ideology. Every piece of research or evaluation, whether naturalistic, experimental, survey, or historical must meet these standards to be considered disciplined. (p. 585)

Smith's definition of disciplined inquiry is worth considering in some detail. The term *inquiry* implies a systematic investigation, which is certainly a part of any definition of research. Regardless of the particular research paradigm to which the investigator adheres, there must be underlying guidelines for how the research is to be carried out. The focus of this book is on quantitative methods, so most of our discussion will be about that research strategy.

Notice that the definition of disciplined inquiry states that the research must be *conducted* and *reported* so it can be carefully examined. The conducted part of the definition implies that the research must be carried out. Designing research serves no useful purpose if it is not actually performed. Also, the research must be reported—that is, published in a journal or at least delivered as a talk at a professional meeting. This dissemination function is important if the research is to be examined by others in some detail. Unless the research is conducted and reported, it cannot be evaluated or replicated to determine whether, given similar circumstances, others would come to the same conclusion as the investigators.

Finally, this definition refers to the fact that the research must stand on its own merit. It should not matter who performed the research, how eloquently it might be described, or even the nature of the problem. If the research has been carried out systematically, following guidelines within a particular research paradigm, and disseminated within a particular discipline, then that research could be tested or verified by others. While there have been numerous attempts to define research, we feel that this definition includes the key elements of the concept.

Purposes of Research

Why do we do research? What is it that we want to find out? Some questions from education that have been addressed with research studies are as follows:

- Does class size affect student outcomes?
- Is cooperative learning more successful than individualized learning?
- Do students with special needs do better if mainstreamed into the school system?

Some questions that need to be addressed in allied health fields are as follows:

- Does a particular treatment work?
- Are certain characteristics of therapists more effective than others?
- Is supported employment more successful for community integration than sheltered work?

There are many purposes for carrying out research. The rationale for learning about research will be divided into two general purposes: (1) increasing the knowledge base of the discipline; and (2) increasing your self-knowledge as a professional consumer of research to understand new developments within the discipline.

Increasing the Knowledge Base of the Discipline

This purpose of research, discovery of new knowledge, can take many directions; three of them are discussed here.

Theory Development

Research can support the theoretical basis of the discipline. A **theory** presents interrelated concepts, definitions, and propositions that provide a systematic view of phenomena and identify relationships among variables. For example, purposeful activity is a construct within the theory of occupation in the field of occupational therapy. The theory states that if the activity is "purposeful," the individual performing the activity will be more invested in the activity and perform better. Studies to test this theory might use the following research design. Two groups are formed through **random assignment**, which means that a table of random numbers, or perhaps a coin toss, is used to *assign* each participant to either the *experimental* or *comparison* group. One group (comparison group) receives a condition of exercise (e.g., jumping in place). The other group (experimental group) also jumps in place, but this is done with a jump rope and the goal or purpose of doing it well. At the end of some given time period, the two groups are measured on performance, satisfaction, or motivation. If, as the theory predicted, the exercise-with-purpose condition was better than the exercise-without-purpose condition, the result would provide some support for the theory.

Practical Application

A second approach to increasing knowledge within the discipline involves providing evidence for the *efficacy* of a curriculum, a therapeutic technique, or administrative change when there may not be a theory that would predict the results. For example, one could compare the effectiveness of two approaches to teaching students. After randomly assigning students to one of two curriculums, both groups are assessed on several outcome measures such as achievement tests. This type of study is typically used to test the effectiveness of different therapeutic or curricular interventions. Notice that the design of this study and the prior one are similar, but the purposes are somewhat different.

Development of Research Tools

A third approach to increasing knowledge within the discipline involves *creating methods* to assess behaviors. For example, researchers could develop a new standardized testing procedure and set of tasks to assess mastery motivation in young children. The procedure could be designed to be useful for typically developing children and also for children who are at risk for developmental problems. To compare children with different ability levels, an individualized approach to measuring mastery motivation could be developed. This approach could vary the difficulty of the task in accordance with the child's ability level so that each child is given tasks that are moderately difficult. Each child's motivation is assessed with tasks, from several graded sets of similar tasks that are found to be challenging but not too difficult or too easy. *Evidence for the validity* or usefulness of these mastery task measures could be confirmed in several ways. For example, groups of children (e.g., those who are at risk) who had been predicted to score lower on mastery motivation measures could be compared with a group of typically developing children.

Increasing Your Self-Knowledge as a Professional

For most students and professionals, the ability to *understand* and *evaluate* research in one's discipline may be more important than personally making a research contribution to the profession. Dissemination of new knowledge occurs for the professional through an exceptionally large number of journals, workshops, and continuing education courses as well as popular literature such as daily newspapers. Today's professional cannot simply rely on the statements of a workshop instructor or newspaper to determine what should or should not be included for future intervention in the classroom, clinic, or community. Even journal articles need to be scrutinized for weak designs, inappropriate data analyses, or incorrect interpretation of these analyses. The current professional must have the research and reasoning skills to be able to make sound decisions and to support them. In addition, research skills can make the professional in education or therapeutic sciences a better provider because she knows how to examine her own school, classroom, or clients and note if improvement in various areas has occurred.

Because conducting research (making a contribution to the profession) and understanding the research of others are important, this book provides a framework and advice for doing both. Suggestions for designing a study, collecting data, analyzing data, and writing about the results are spread throughout the book. A framework for understanding and evaluating research is introduced later in this chapter and amplified in Chapters 23–25.

Research Dichotomies

Now, we discuss briefly six contrasts or dichotomies that can be used to describe research: (1) theoretical versus applied; (2) laboratory versus field; (3) participant report versus researcher observation; (4) quantitative/postpostivist versus qualitative/constructivist philosophical or *theoretical framework*; (5) quantitative/objective versus qualitative/subjective data and data collection *methods*; and (6) quantitative/statistical versus qualitative/descriptive data *analysis*.

Although some studies fit well into one end of each dichotomy, other studies are mixed. For example, some studies have both *participant reported* and *researcher observed* measures. Some studies use both *qualitative* and *quantitative* methods and data.

Theoretical Versus Applied

Most social science disciplines perform research with some application in mind. The goal of the research is directed toward some specific, practical use, such as treatment, learning enhancement, or evaluation. Some theoretical research is performed in which there may or may not ever be an application of the knowledge gained. Most of the research projects we examine in this book are at the applied end of this dimension. Nevertheless, all studies have or should have some theoretical or conceptual framework and be based on previous research literature, even if the primary purpose is applied. The five sample studies described later in this chapter meet these criteria for applied research because they have a conceptual framework and describe how the current study fits with past research literature.

Laboratory Versus Field

A second dichotomy for describing a research study is the setting. The term *field* could mean a clinic, school, work setting, or home. Laboratory implies a controlled, structured setting that is not where the subjects or participants usually live, work, or receive therapy. In the social and allied health sciences, a laboratory most often refers to a room with a video camera and microphones (i.e., a somewhat unnatural setting). Social science disciplines usually perform research that is slanted toward the field end of the dimension to be more *ecologically valid*, but laboratory settings provide better control over *extraneous variables*. Sometimes testing of participants, to obtain the dependent variable measures, is done in a controlled laboratory-type setting, as are some studies of young children's play behavior.

Studies conducted in classrooms or in the participants' homes would be called field settings, as would studies in which teachers or workers were in their offices. Occasionally, one study will utilize both a field setting (e.g., home) and a laboratory observation.

Participant Report Versus Researcher Observation

In some studies the participants report to the researcher (in writing or orally) about their attitudes, intentions, or behavior. In other studies, the researcher directly observes and records the behavior of the participants, for example, children's play behavior or a physical exam of a patient. Sometimes instruments, such as standardized tests or heart rate monitors, are used by researchers to "observe" the participant's functioning. For example, achievement tests could be used in a study rather than asking participants to rate how much they thought they had learned.

A large amount of research in the applied social sciences and education relies on reports by the participants using interviews or questionnaires. For example, quality of life could be reported by participants. Such participant reports are always influenced by the fact that the participants know they are in a study; they may want to please the researcher; or they may want to hide, have forgotten, or do not really know things. For these reasons, many investigators prefer researcher observed behavioral data even though these data also have potential limitations. On the other hand, sensitive, well-trained interviewers may be able to establish enough rapport with participants to alleviate some of the biases inherent in self-reports.

Quantitative Versus Qualitative Philosophical Paradigms

This is the most confusing and controversial dichotomy, because it deals with philosophical or paradigm differences in the approach to research. This philosophical dichotomy (sometimes called **positivistic** versus **constructivist**),[1] has had a major impact on how research methods courses are taught in the United States, especially in the discipline of education. Sometimes, this dichotomy has created an either/or mindset with qualitative and quantitative research methods courses taught separately. In the postpositivist/quantitative framework, a specific plan is developed prior to the study. In the constructivist/qualitative approach, less structure is placed on the use of specific guidelines in the research design. However, there are general guidelines to be followed in qualitative research.

What is a **paradigm**? The term, coined by Kuhn (1970), has been defined and used several ways in educational research (Morgan, 2007). One interpretation of paradigm is *the beliefs members of a scientific community share*. Others refer to a paradigm as a system of ideas or a systematic set of beliefs, together with their accompanying methods. In our view, a paradigm is a way of thinking about and conducting research. It is not strictly a methodology, but more of a *philosophy* that guides how the research might be conducted. More importantly, a paradigm determines the types of questions that are legitimate and in what context they will be interpreted.

The approach of this book is within the framework of the postpositivist paradigm; thus, it mainly focuses on quantitative methods. We feel that a textbook emphasizing the quantitative approach to research has several advantages. First, to date, the majority of research performed in the social sciences, education, and allied health disciplines has used a quantitative methodology. Thus, it is critical for students in these disciplines to be able to understand and build on these studies for future research. Second, and perhaps more importantly, we feel that quantitative randomized experiments are the most appropriate methodology for answering questions about whether an intervention or new treatment causes an improved outcome. We feel that a big advantage of the quantitative approach is that results from many studies can be combined to produce a large body of evidence toward answering questions that may not be answered in a single study. However, the constructivist paradigm provides us with useful tools, including types of data collection, data analysis, and interpretation methods.

Quantitative/Objective Versus Qualitative/Subjective Data and Data Collection

Students sometimes confuse the paradigm distinction just presented (quantitative versus qualitative philosophies) with *type of data* and *data collection techniques*. Quantitative data are said to be "objective," which implies that the behaviors are easily classified or quantified, either by the participants themselves or by the researcher. Some examples are demographic variables such as age and gender, scores on an achievement test, and time to recovery. The data usually are gathered with some sort of instrument (test, physiological device, or questionnaire) that can be scored reliably with relatively little training. The scores on multiple choice exams and quizzes are examples of quantitative data and a quantitative data collection technique.

Qualitative data are more "subjective," which indicates that they could be interpreted differently by different people. Some examples are *perceptions* of pain, *feelings* about work, and *attitudes* toward school. Usually these data are gathered from interviews, observations, or narrative documents such as biographies. These types of data are also gathered in studies that are mainly quantitative, but in that case researchers usually would translate such perceptions, feelings, and attitudes into numbers. For example, participants' subjective feelings of mental health or quality of life can be converted into numerical ratings or scores. In studies that are philosophically qualitative, on the other hand, researchers usually would not try to quantify such subjective perceptions: The data are kept in text form and analyzed for themes. We believe that the approach in this book is useful for dealing with both qualitative/subjective *data* and quantitative/objective *data*.

Note that a researcher could be philosophically postpositivist, but the data could be subjective and qualitative. In fact, this combination is quite common, especially when participants' behavior is observed. On the other hand, a researcher may embrace the constructivist paradigm, and some of the supporting data may be quantitative or objective. Thus, the type of data and even data analysis are not necessarily the same as the research paradigm.

It is important to point out that studies done within *both* the quantitative/postpositivist paradigm and the qualitative/constructivist paradigm use interview and observational methods and both are interested in objective as well as subjective data. However, studies done from the constructivist viewpoint usually include *open-ended* interviews, observations, and narrative documents, such as diaries. Studies done mainly from the postpositivist viewpoint most commonly include *structured* interviews (or questionnaires), observations, and documents such as school or clinic records. We describe data collection methods in more detail in Chapter 13.

Quantitative/Statistical Versus Qualitative/Descriptive Data Analysis

Finally, we discuss a sixth dichotomy about how data are analyzed. The interpretation and understanding of quantitative data analysis is a major theme of this book. It is dealt with in detail in Chapters 16–22, which discuss many of the most common inferential statistics and show how they are related to the approaches and designs discussed in Chapters 4–7. Qualitative data analysis involves various methods for coding themes and assigning meaning to the data, which are usually words or images. This book does not deal very much with qualitative coding or data analysis techniques such as content analysis. Studies that use a constructivist framework rarely include inferential statistics, although sometimes the descriptive statistics discussed in Chapter 10 are used.[2]

Relationships Among the Six Dichotomies

Certain of the six dichotomies tend, in common practice, to go together. For example, applied research tends to be done in field or natural settings, often using participant reports. Constructivist research is almost always conducted in the field. On the other hand, theoretically oriented research tends to be done in the lab, using researcher observations.

However, there is *not a necessary association* among *any* of these six dimensions. For example, applied research can be done in either the lab or field, using either observation or participant reports and can be either postpositivist/quantitative or constructivist/ qualitative. As mentioned already, both postpositivist and constructivist researchers utilize interviews and observations so these methods are not restricted to one paradigm, type of data, or type of data analysis.

The Mixed Methods or Pragmatic Approach

Philosophically the postpositivist and constructivist paradigms are quite different, yet the two may be found together in one research study. When the two paradigms are blended so that one paradigm sets the stage for or leads to the other paradigm the approach is called **mixed methods**. (When the two approaches are included in the same study but are discussed separately this is not considered a mixed methods approach, but rather two methods are being used.) *The Handbook of Mixed Methods in Social and Behavioral Research* (Tashakkori & Teddlie, 2002) describes several strategies for such *mixed methods* approaches to research.

Morgan (2007) and Onwuegbuzie and Leech (2005) advocate a **pragmatic approach** as a new guiding paradigm for social and therapeutic science research methods, both for research that combines qualitative and quantitative methods and as a way to focus attention on methodological rather than philosophical concerns. Research conducted from the pragmatic approach utilizes exploratory and confirmatory methods (instead of qualitative or quantitative methods), which increases the options for researchers in regard to data collection methods, data analysis tools, and interpretations.

Research Types or Approaches

Now, we describe our general framework for quantitative research, which we call *approaches*, and then we describe briefly five studies that are used in this and later chapters as examples, especially for demonstrating how to evaluate a research study. These studies were selected to illustrate certain key concepts and issues, not because they were especially strong or weak. All studies, including our own, have weaknesses as well as strengths. There are almost always trade-offs made in conducting research so that few, if any, studies are strong in all aspects of their design.

In this book, all quantitative research is divided into three main types that we call *experimental*, *nonexperimental*, and *descriptive*. The first two types of research each have two approaches as shown in the following paragraphs. Unfortunately, some researchers use somewhat different terminology so we have a section at the end of the chapter labeled "Different Terms for Similar Concepts." This section and the terms in our "key concepts" and "key distinctions" should help focus on important terms and keep them straight.

Experimental Research

1. The *randomized experimental approach* has *random assignment* of participants to the intervention and comparison groups and an *active* or manipulated *independent variable*.[3] The scores of the groups on the *dependent variables* are compared.

2. The *quasi-experimental approach* has an *active independent variable* but *without random assignment* of participants to groups. Again, an experimental or intervention group is compared to a control or comparison group of participants.

Nonexperimental Research (Sometimes Called Observational Research)

1. The *comparative approach* also makes a comparison of a few groups on the dependent variables. However, the groups are based on an *attribute independent variable*, such as gender. In that case, males are compared with females.

2. The *associational approach,* sometimes called correlational, has two or more usually continuous variables for the same group of participants, which are related or associated. For example, an achievement test is correlated with family income. Again, the independent variable is an attribute rather than active.

Descriptive Research

We use the term *descriptive approach* to refer to research questions that use only descriptive, not inferential, statistics. **Descriptive statistics**, such as averages and percentages, summarize data from the current sample of participants without making inferences about the larger population of interest. In the descriptive approach no formal comparisons or associations are made. *Qualitative research* could be classified as one type of descriptive research using this definition and framework. This distinction between what we call the descriptive approach and the other four approaches is unusual, but we think it is educationally useful, in part, because the term *descriptive* is used in a consistent way.

It is important to note that most studies, especially complex ones, use more than one of these approaches because "approaches" really refer to *types of research questions*, not necessarily whole studies. A single study usually has more than one research question; for example, "survey studies" often have descriptive as well as comparative *and* associational research questions. Experimental studies often also include an important attribute independent variable such as gender and, thus, include a comparative question. Of the hundreds of studies that we have evaluated, all fit into *one or more* of these five categories based on their research questions and data analysis. Chapter 4 describes these approaches in more detail.

There are several reasons to categorize research questions into one of the five approaches. First, we feel that questions of *cause and effect* can be answered best with well-controlled randomized experiments and to a lesser extent with the quasi-experimental approach. Neither the comparative nor the associational approach is well suited to demonstrate cause and effect, but we realize that some statistics, such as linear regression or structural equation modeling, may provide some evidence for causality from nonexperimental studies. If a study is nonexperimental or descriptive, it rarely provides strong information about cause and effect, but it may provide suggestions about related variables, effective clinical practice, and *possible* causes.

Second, our classification of research approaches and Figure 1.1 should help the reader follow the research process from the *general purpose* of the research to the type of *research question* or hypothesis. For example, the *experimental, quasi-experimental,* and *comparative approaches*

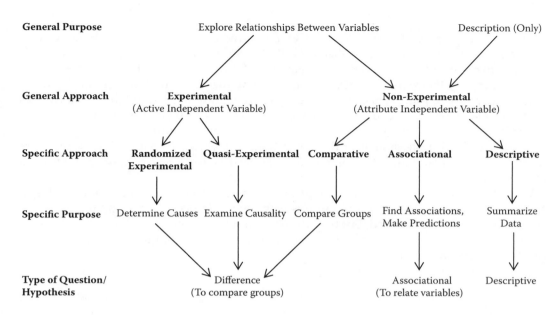

General Purpose   Explore Relationships Between Variables   Description (Only)

General Approach   **Experimental** (Active Independent Variable)   **Non-Experimental** (Attribute Independent Variable)

Specific Approach   **Randomized Experimental**   **Quasi-Experimental**   **Comparative**   **Associational**   **Descriptive**

Specific Purpose   Determine Causes   Examine Causality   Compare Groups   Find Associations, Make Predictions   Summarize Data

Type of Question/ Hypothesis   Difference (To compare groups)   Associational (To relate variables)   Descriptive

FIGURE 1.1
Schematic diagram of how the general type of research question corresponds to the purpose and approach of the study.

typically compare two or a few groups. On the other hand, the *associational approach* typically associates or relates variables for participants in a single group. The *descriptive approach* summarizes data using *descriptive statistics* such as averages, percentages, and various graphs.

Sample Studies

In this section, we describe briefly five studies, one for each of the five approaches just introduced. Here we focus on why we classified the study as indicated and point out the key independent and dependent variables. In several later chapters these studies, and others, are used to illustrate important concepts to discuss the research validity evaluation framework that we recommend.

Study 1: A Randomized Experiment

The purpose of this study (Schellenberg, 2004) was to test the hypothesis that music lessons enhance the intellectual abilities and educational achievement of 6-year-old children. The *active independent variable* in this study was the type of lesson. There were four types or *levels* of this independent variable: standard keyboard music lessons, Kodály voice music lessons, drama lessons, or no lessons. The two music lesson groups were considered *experimental* or intervention conditions, and the drama and no lessons groups were considered the *comparison* or *control groups*. (Chapter 3 discusses variables and their levels in more detail.) The 144 children were *randomly assigned* to one of the four groups. Because there was an active independent variable and the participants were randomly assigned to each group, the approach was *randomized experimental*.

The *dependent* or *outcome variables* were IQ (measured by the Wechsler Intelligence Scale for Children, WISC-III, IQ scales; Wechsler, 1991), educational achievement (measured by the Kaufman Test of Educational Achievement, K-TEA; Kaufman & Kaufman, 1985), and parent ratings of their child's behavior (measured by the Behavioral System for Children, BASC; Reynolds & Kamphaus, 1992). These are frequently used standardized measures with considerable evidence to support *measurement reliability* and *measurement validity*.

The lessons (intervention) were given in small groups of six children each over a 36-week period by trained professionals at the Royal Conservatory in Toronto. All children were tested both before and after the intervention. Thus, this was a *pretest–posttest, randomized experimental design*.

We discuss aspects of the method and the results more in later chapters, but it will suffice here to say that the two music groups (combined) gained more on IQ than the two comparison groups combined, but they didn't gain reliably more on educational achievement. The drama group improved in adaptive social behavior, but the other three groups did not change on this variable.

Study 2: A Quasi-Experiment

This study titled "The Value of Time Limits on Internet Quizzes" (Brothen & Wambach, 2004) evaluated the effect of putting a time limit on "take home" quizzes. Two sections of a psychology class were used as participants. The study is considered quasi-experimental because, although there was an active independent variable, the students were *not randomly assigned* to the two groups (timed quizzes versus untimed). The *active independent variable* was whether there was a time limit for students when they took a quiz. One section of the course had a 15-minute time limit, and the other section had no limit. The authors theorized that if students knew they would have a time limit, they were more likely to study the material before starting the quiz rather than starting the take home quiz and then looking up the answers. The *dependent variables* were the students' scores on the regular exams and also how long they spent on the quizzes. Students who had a time limit on the quizzes did better on the exams and took less time on the quizzes.

Study 3: A Nonexperimental Study Using the Comparative Approach

DiLorenzo, Halper, and Picone (2004) compared older (60–85 years old) and younger (29–59 years old) persons with multiple sclerosis (MS) on physical functioning, mental health, and quality of life. The *independent variable*, age, is an *attribute* that for this study had two levels: older or younger. There were many *dependent or outcome variables* that fell into the three broad categories of physical functioning, mental health, and quality of life. The approach was considered comparative because the main independent variable, age, was an attribute and had only a few levels or groups (younger and older) that were compared on each of the dependent variables. Although the older patients had poorer physical functioning, they were not different from the younger MS patients on mental health and perceived quality of life when length of illness was controlled.

Study 4: A Nonexperimental Study Using the Associational Approach

Zamboanga, Padilla-Walker, Hardy, Thompson, and Wang (2007) conducted a study about academic background and course involvement as predictors of exam performance in a university psychology class. The study is considered to be associational because there was no active independent variable or treatment, and both independent and dependent variable scores vary widely from low to high so they are essentially continuous. Two of the key *attribute independent* or predicted variables were ACT college entrance scores and frequency of attendance at the course lectures. The *dependent* or outcome variable was total exam performance, the average of the students scores on the four exams. Both ACT and attendance were related to and, thus, could be used to predict total exam score.

Study 5: A Purely Descriptive Study

This study by Wolfe et al. (2006) described the results of 112 interviews about the use of antiretroviral therapy in AIDS patients. There was *no independent variable* reported in this study because all of the participants had been offered the therapy and because its effects were not assessed in this report. Likewise, *no comparisons* or *associations* between variables were reported. What was asked and reported were various aspects (variables) of the sample such as age, gender, and education. The key outcome variables were who, if anyone, they disclosed their illness to and perceived social effects of their illness (how it had affected their social relationships, ability to work, and fear of loss of employment). Most of the participants had kept their illness secret from the community, and many felt that it affected their social relationships and ability to work. About 25% feared loss of employment. Although only the tabulated quantitative findings were reported in this article, the structured interview questions were supplemented by qualitative or open-ended questions for all 110 participants.

Summary

We equate research and "disciplined inquiry," which must be conducted and reported so that it can be carefully examined. Inquiry is a systematic investigation of a matter of public interest. All research must be conducted and reported so that it can be tested and verified by others.

There are two main purposes of research: (1) to increase knowledge within one's discipline; and (2) to increase knowledge within oneself, as a professional consumer of research. To increase knowledge within a discipline, research may expand the theoretical basis of the discipline, test the effectiveness of practical applications, or develop research tools. Research skills are necessary for one to be able to examine and evaluate the existing research in one's discipline.

Six research dichotomies are discussed: (1) theoretical versus applied; (2) laboratory versus field; (3) participant report versus researcher observation; (4) quantitative/ postpostivist versus qualitative/constructivist philosophical or theoretical framework; (5) quantitative/objective versus qualitative/subjective data and data collection methods; and (6) quantitative/statistical versus qualitative/descriptive data analysis. Although qualitative data are often collected within the constructivist paradigm, that is not exclusively the case. Furthermore, qualitative data and data analysis can be used within the postpositivist paradigm. The six dimensions or dichotomies are somewhat related in practice, but conceptually they are independent. This means that it is possible for a study to fit any combination of these six dichotomies.

Philosophically the postpositivist and constructivist paradigms are quite different, yet the two may be found together in one research study. When the two paradigms can be blended so that one paradigm sets the stage for or leads to the other paradigm the approach is called mixed methods. The pragmatic approach is a new approach that shows promise for social and therapeutic science research that combines qualitative and quantitative methods focusing on methodological rather than philosophical concerns.

We categorize research questions into five types or approaches: randomized experimental, quasi-experimental, comparative, associational, and descriptive. The approach and the independent variable and dependent variables for each of five sample studies were described briefly.

Key Concepts

The concepts and distinctions listed next are discussed in this chapter, and the concepts are defined in the glossary. It will help you learn the material if you understand the meaning of each concept and can compare and contrast the concepts listed under key distinctions.

Associational approach

Comparative approach

Descriptive approach

Disciplined inquiry

Mixed methods

Pragmatic approach

Quasi-experimental approach

Random assignment

Randomized experimental approach

Theory and theory development

Key Distinctions

Active independent variable versus attribute independent variable

Independent or predictor variable versus dependent or outcome variable

Laboratory versus field research

Postpositivist versus constructivist paradigm/theoretical framework

Producing knowledge versus understanding research as a consumer

Quantitative versus qualitative data analysis

Quantitative versus qualitative data and data collection

Participant report versus researcher observation

Theoretical versus applied research

Different Terms for Similar Concepts

Active independent variable ≈ manipulated ≈ intervention ≈ treatment

Associational approach ≈ correlational ≈ survey

Attribute independent variable ≈ measured variable ≈ individual difference variable

Comparative approach ≈ causal comparative ≈ ex post facto

Comparison group ≈ control group

Continuous variable ≈ normally distributed ≈ interval scale

Dependent variable ≈ DV ≈ outcome ≈ criterion

Descriptive approach ≈ exploratory research

Difference questions ≈ group comparisons

Independent variable ≈ IV ≈ antecedent ≈ predictor ≈ presumed cause ≈ factor

Levels (of a variable) ≈ categories ≈ values ≈ groups

Measurement reliability ≈ reliability ≈ test, instrument, or score reliability

Measurement validity ≈ test, instrument, or score validity ≈ validity

Nonexperimental research (comparative, associational, and descriptive approaches; some writers call all three descriptive) ≈ observational research

Randomized experiment ≈ true experiment ≈ randomized clinical trial ≈ randomized control trials ≈ RCT

Research validity ≈ validity of the whole study

Application Problems

The application problems at the end of each chapter require you to apply the information from in the chapter and sometimes from preceding chapters. If you learn to apply the material, you will become a good consumer of research and a better researcher.

1. The chapter introduced several research dichotomies (i.e., theoretical versus applied, laboratory versus field, participant-report versus researcher observation, and quantitative versus qualitative paradigms). Identify the appropriate end of each of the six dichotomies for each of the following examples. (Remember that some research projects might use both ends. For instance, many projects incorporate both quantitative and qualitative data collection methods; others may use both participant-report and observational measures.)

    a. To improve therapy, a researcher was interested to know if there were differences in the physiological arousal of men and women during arguments. She recruited 30 couples and asked them to come to the Happy Family Counseling Center. Couples were comfortably seated in an attractively decorated room. The researcher placed heart rate and blood pressure monitors on each person in the couple. They were then instructed to identify and discuss a problem area in their relationship for 20 minutes. The researcher recorded the heart rate and blood pressure for each individual to determine if there were differences between men and women in her sample.

b. A researcher was interested in learning which characteristics of marriages were based on equality to help couples adjust. She also wanted to learn what the benefits and costs of equality were for women and men. She interviewed couples in their home for 3 hours, asking them open-ended questions about previous relationships, about their marriage, about the evolution of their attitudes, feelings, and behaviors, and about descriptions of how they handled conflict, intimacy, children, jobs, and lifestyle issues. To analyze the data, she coded the conversation according to common themes that emerged from the interviews.

c. A model was developed to explain a family's response to a stressful event. More specifically, the model was developed to explain a family's adaptation over time given several variables such as the nature and degree of a stressor and the family's resources. A researcher is interested in determining if this model applies to a particular catastrophic event—the loss of one's home to an environmental catastrophe. The researcher recruits families from a town that recently experienced an earthquake. Members of these families are asked to complete questionnaire measures of particular variables (e.g., family resources, perceptions of the stressor event); these measures have been used in prior research about the model.

2. A researcher was interested to learn how the work environment influences employees' experience of work–family conflict, or the degree to which their work responsibilities impinged on their home responsibilities and vice versa. The researcher gained permission from several company presidents to collect data from company employees.

   a. Describe how the researcher might proceed if this were field research. What if it were done in a laboratory?

   b. How might the researcher use qualitative data collection methods to gain information? How might she use quantitative data collection methods?

   c. Describe how she might use participant-report measures to gather certain information? What about observational methods?

   d. Would this research be applied or theoretical?

3. A researcher is interested to learn the qualities of and strategies used by dual-earner couples who are successful in balancing work and family responsibilities. He asks each member of the couple to complete several measures of variables that they believe will be particularly relevant, such as creativity, optimism, and self-esteem. He also plans to interview each couple to learn about their strategies for balancing work and family. These interviews will begin with the question: "What is it about you or your life that you believe most leads to your success in balancing work and family?"

   a. Which of the aforementioned methods for collecting data is quantitative? Which is qualitative?

   b. If the researcher uses qualitative methods of data analysis for the interview, how might they conduct this analysis?

4. A recently hired president of a university is committed to increasing the number of minority students who graduate with their bachelors' degrees. The president calls to arrange a meeting with you. In this meeting, the president explains that she wants you "to do some research on this topic." She explains that she is aware of other universities that have set and achieved this goal in prior years. She is also aware that this university has developed several programs in prior years in the effort to reach this goal. She wants you to provide her with information that will help her design specific initiatives that are most likely to produce the results she wants. Is the president asking you to be a consumer or producer of knowledge? What kind of skills must she believe that you have?

Notes

1. Although we believe that the term *positivist* is not an accurate label for most quantitative social scientists, the term is commonly used by qualitative/constructivist writers when describing researchers who use quantitative methods. Instead of referring to positivists, Phillips and Burbules (2000) call this paradigm *postpositivist,* and so do we. Likewise, the term *constructivist* may not be the best identifier for what is often called the *naturalist* or *qualitative* paradigm, but, again, it helps make important distinctions.
2. Note that some research methods texts use the phrase *qualitative data analysis* to mean the analysis of categorical or nominal data, including inferential statistics such as chi square.
3. A *variable* is a characteristic of a person or situation that has two or more values (it varies) *in a study*. An **active independent variable** is one such as a treatment, workshop, or other intervention that is given to one group of participants and withheld or given in another form to another group. An **attribute independent variable** is one that is not given or withheld in the study. It is a measure of a characteristic or attribute of the person or his or her situation. The **dependent variable**s in a study are the outcome; they are presumed to measure the effect of the independent variable (and, thus, to depend on it).Variables are discussed in more detail in Chapter 3.
4. Terms are listed alphabetically. The term we use most often is listed on the left. Similar terms (indicated by ≈) used by other researchers or by us are listed to the right.

2

Planning a Quantitative Research Project

Quantitative research begins with a step-by-step plan of how the research will be conducted. This plan becomes the map of how the study will take place. Thus, it is extremely important to consider all aspects of the research study, from beginning to end, when organizing the research plan. This chapter outlines the quantitative research plan, using Figure 2.1 as a guide. Specific chapters that present information on each of the steps of the plan are delineated in the figure. The present chapter focuses on steps 1 and 2 in the figure: the research problem and literature review. The other steps in the figure are discussed in depth in later chapters.

Overview of the Steps in the Research Plan

One of the hallmarks of quantitative research is *a priori planning*, which means that a plan is made prior to the study. The steps of the plan for a quantitative research study are basically linear; thus, the first step is completed before going on to the next. Traditionally, the quantitative process is based on the scientific method, which includes 10 steps relevant for education, health, and human service disciplines. These steps, shown in Figure 2.1, are discussed briefly:

1. The first step involves identifying the **research problem**. This initial stage involves choosing a question that has the potential to become a researchable project. Where does the problem come from? For many, especially those in applied disciplines, the problem often comes from a *clinical situation*. Will a particular type of therapy lead to improvement? Will adaptive technology increase communication skills? Will a particular assessment yield the information I need? Another place from which research problems may arise is the *previous literature*. A published study may help to formulate questions leading to a new study.

2. The second step is to conduct a review or synthesis of the literature relevant to the research problem. The last part of this chapter discusses the **literature review**.

3. Next, the researcher develops hypotheses or research questions. In essence, this involves reducing the research problem to specific research hypotheses or questions that are *testable*. This step is discussed in Chapter 3.

4. The next step is developing a research approach (e.g., randomized experimental) and design that allows the investigator to test the hypotheses. The major focus of the research design is to allow the investigator to control or eliminate variables that are not of direct interest to the study but might affect the results. The design allows the investigator to directly test or answer the research question. Approaches and designs, briefly discussed in Chapter 1, are discussed in detail in Chapters 4–7.

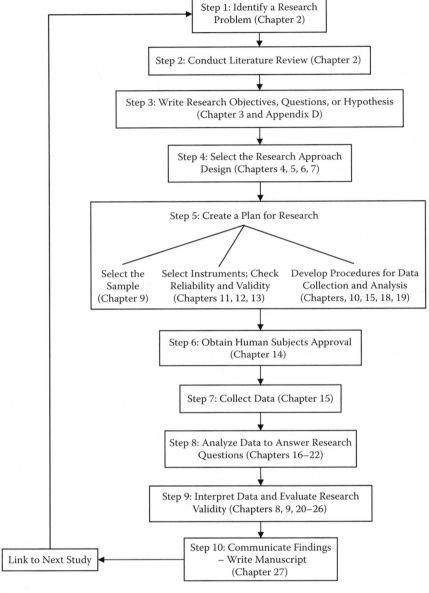

FIGURE 2.1
Steps in the research process for a quantitative study and the chapters that present information on the topic.

5. Next, create a plan for conducting the research, which includes selecting the sample, selecting or developing the instruments, and developing procedures for data collection and analysis.

6. Approval from the human subjects Institutional Review Board (IRB) must be obtained prior to data collection. This is discussed in Chapter 14.

7. The next step involves data collection. Researchers attempt to collect data in an unbiased and objective fashion. In the traditional method, the scientist does not examine the data in detail until the study has been completed (see Chapter 15).

8. The data, which are usually numbers, are then analyzed using inferential statistics as discussed in Chapters 16–22.

9. The next step involves making inferences or interpretations from the data. These interpretations are based on the statistical analyses related to the hypotheses or research questions as discussed in Chapters 20–22. The validity of the methods and analyses are evaluated using the information in Chapters 8, 9, and 23–26.

10. Finally, the findings must be communicated to the profession via a published manuscript or professional presentation as discussed in Chapter 27.

This example of the research process is in the form of a feedback loop. After the last step, a new research question is asked. If the hypothesis was confirmed, then a new question could be asked toward gaining additional information. If the hypothesis was not confirmed, the new question may be a modification of the original question, or the methodology might be altered to readdress the original question.

It should be noted, however, that quantitative research often varies somewhat from this idealized format. That is, in practice, the scientific approach is *not as deductive* (literature/theory → deduce hypotheses → test hypotheses) *or as rigid* as implied by the 10 steps. For example, interesting findings that were not based on the original hypotheses often emerge during the project or at the data analysis stage.

The first two steps—(1) identifying a research problem; and (2) conducting a literature review—are discussed in this chapter. The remaining steps are discussed in more detail in the next chapter and throughout this book. For each step, the specific chapters that discuss the topic are specified in Figure 2.1. Creswell (2009) provides a useful discussion of the research process for both quantitative and qualitative research.

Research Problems

The research process begins with a problem. What is a *research problem*? It is usually a sentence or *statement about the relationship between two or more variables*. Some studies such as the Wolfe et al. (2006) AIDS study (see Chapter 1) are purely descriptive and do not *formally* examine the relationship among the several variables in the study. It is important to point out that almost all actual research studies have more than two variables. Kerlinger (1986) suggests that prior to the problem statement "… the scientist will usually experience an obstacle to understanding, a vague unrest about observed and unobserved phenomena, a curiosity as to why something is as it is" (p. 11).

Three Sample Research Problems

Next, each of the three authors of this text describes the process that they experienced in formulating a research problem. When deciding on a dissertation topic, N. L. L. was interested in what makes a counselor "good" in the perception of clients:

> At the time, I was working as a supervisor of master's degree students who hoped to become counselors. There was anecdotal information available from clients about counselors in the field: Some were considered excellent and received many referrals, other counselors were considered marginal, and then a few were considered not good. How

these differences between counselors were identified was not apparent. After looking into the literature, I found very little extant research on the topic; in fact, there was so little research that the problem would need to start with *what is the definition of "good" when it comes to counselors?*

After doing much reading, I realized that I was mainly interested in how potential clients chose a counselor. Once again, there was very little research in this area. I did find literature on willingness to seek counseling. The research in this area had been conducted mostly with undergraduate students. I thought it would be interesting to find out the level of willingness to seek counseling for counselors in training. There was an existing model in the literature that explained most of the variance of willingness to seek counseling for undergraduates; I wondered if this model would fit for counselors in training. Thus, my examinations into the research lead me to the research problem of *Does Cramer's (1999) model of willingness to seek counseling fit for counselors in training?*

Another example comes from J. A. G. who was working in the area of environmental physiology:

I was to give a talk at the Federation of American Societies for Experimental Biology. There were many well-known scientists at my talk, and I was nervous to say the least, especially because I felt that others in the audience knew more about my topic, regional distribution of blood flow during alcohol intoxication, than I. During the talk immediately preceding mine, a colleague sitting next to me asked how I felt. I answered that I felt fine but took my pulse and found my heart to be beating at a rate of about 110 beats per minute, considerably above my normal resting heart rate of 60 beats per minute but similar to my rate after moderate exercise. I wondered if this could be a healthy response. I first formulated my problem as *could a high heart rate in the absence of exercise be normal?*

Next, I found numerous studies that examined heart rate under conditions producing anxiety. The heart rate could get exceedingly high, much higher than mine had been. None of the previous studies examined the metabolic requirements (e.g., oxygen uptake and cardiac output) under these anxiety situations. On the other hand, several studies had examined metabolic requirements on heart rate during exercise. These studies considered elevated heart rate following exercise to be normal, since the heart must deliver an increased amount of oxygen to the tissues under higher metabolic demands. The problem now became a general question: *If we measured the metabolic demands of a situation under anxiety would it be similar to a situation under exercise?*

Now an obstacle became clear. How could we create two situations, one under anxiety and one under exercise that yielded similar heart rates? In order to remove this barrier, we decided to use a *within-subjects design*, where each participant took part in all conditions of the study. First we could determine the heart rate and metabolic requirements under an anxiety-provoking situation (e.g., prior to giving a talk). Next we could have the participant exercise on a treadmill at a workload high enough to give us a heart rate identical to that experienced under anxiety, and we could also measure metabolic requirements.

Now we could state our problem as *how are heart rate and metabolic requirements related under conditions of anxiety?* Our next step would be to change the problem statement into a prediction statement or *hypothesis* that could be directly tested.

The third example is a research problem faced by G. A. M. and his colleagues who were studying the motivation of infants to solve problems:

We had observed that infants who were born prematurely and also those who had been abused or neglected seemed to have lower motivation to master new skills and seemed to get less pleasure from trying. This clinical observation raised several issues. First, *could the motivation of preverbal infants be measured?* Achievement motivation in adults and older children had been assessed from stories they told in response to ambiguous pictures. Some other method would need to be developed for infants. Second, was it really the case that premature and abused or neglected infants were less motivated to master tasks? The second part of the research problem might be phrased as *is there a relationship between prematurity, abuse, or neglect and mastery motivation?*

Sources of Research Problems

The examples just discussed illustrate four common sources of research problems: *the existing research literature, theory, personal experience,* and *clinical observation.* The last two assume knowledge of the literature and theory in the field and the ability to relate it to the experiences or observations. Often experiences at work or school can be the source of a research problem, if you know what questions are unanswered at present and how to translate your unrest about incongruous phenomena into a testable research problem.

An important distinction that is sometimes confusing to students is that the word *problem* might convey the false impression that a research problem is the same as a personal or societal problem. These types of problems, however, *may lead to* research problems and questions or hypotheses that can be answered by collecting and analyzing data. For J. A. G. to worry that he would be nervous during his presentation is not a research problem. Likewise, for G. A. M. to be concerned about the apparent low mastery motivation of abused or neglected children is a societal but not a research problem.

One of the first steps in the research process is to read the *research literature* on and around the topic of interest so that you will be able to identify gaps in knowledge. We provide some advice about conducting the literature review later in this chapter.

Another source for research problems is *theory.* Kerlinger (1986) suggested that a **theory** explains natural phenomena, which is a goal of science, and he defined it as, "A theory is a set of interrelated constructs (concepts), definitions, and propositions that present a systematic view of phenomena by specifying relations among variables, with the purpose of explaining and predicting the phenomena" (p. 9). Most researchers suggest that a theoretical orientation should be presented at the beginning of an article as the basis for understanding the rest of the article, but we do not believe that a theory *must* be a part of the article; instead, explanation, rationale, or point of view could be substituted and satisfy, to some extent, the same purpose as theory. However, none of these concepts are as strong as a theory. A number of books deal extensively with the role of theory in research, but we have chosen to emphasize research design and how it influences data analysis and the interpretation of results.

The issue in contemporary social and health science research is not so much whether theory is important and how it should fit into an article but how important should theory be in designing research. We agree that theory is important and that the value of the results of a study depend, in part, on whether they support some theory.

Identifying Research Problems in the Literature

All published studies start with a research problem. Unfortunately, in many published research studies, the research problem is difficult to identify in one sentence or paragraph. It is common for authors to allude to the problem instead of outright stating the problem. Furthermore, due to the pressure to integrate extant literature into introductions of research studies, many times it is impossible to discern how a research problem was identified; often, the research problem appears to have emerged from the existing literature based on how the information is presented.

Some authors clearly delineate the research problem as well as state how the problem came to their attention. For example, in the sample quasi-experimental study introduced in Chapter 1, Brothen and Wambach (2004) begin their article by discussing Internet quizzes and the different ways students prepare to take them. The authors include their personal experience using Internet quizzes in their classes. This leads the reader to think the research problem stemmed from personal experience. The authors clearly state their research problem as, "If instructors deliver computerized quizzes via the Internet instead of in a computerized classroom, how are they to encourage their students to use the quizzes as an opportunity for feedback?" (p. 62).

Another example of a research problem apparently stemming from personal experience is from Landrum and Mulcock (2007). These authors state their research problem as the following: "As the undergraduate psychology major continues to grow in popularity, the challenge to provide accurate advising information to large numbers of students also continues to grow" (p. 163).

Characteristics of a Good Research Problem

In addition to being grounded in the empirical (data-based) and theoretical literature and examining relationships between two or more variables, there are several other characteristics of a good problem. As indicated already, it should hold the promise of filling a *gap in the literature* or providing a *test of a theory*.

A good research problem should also be *stated clearly and unambiguously*, indicating the variables to be related. Often research problems start out too broadly or vaguely stated. Appendix D provides several examples and templates for writing good research problems. Problems also should imply several research questions. Appendix D also provides examples of research questions in formats that are consistent with the framework of this book (see especially Chapter 3, which also provides some examples of research questions).

As just implied, a good research problem should be *testable* by empirical methods; it shouldn't be just a statement of your moral, ethical, or political position. You should be able to collect data that will answer the research questions.

Of course, the methods used must be *ethical* and consistent with the guidelines spelled out in Chapter 14. The problem also needs to be *feasible,* given your resources and abilities. Finally, it is desirable, especially for graduate students, to choose a problem that is of *vital interest to you* so that you can sustain the motivation to finish, often a difficult thing to do.

Another way of deciding on a good, appropriate research problem for a thesis or dissertation is to examine where it would lie on several dimensions. We provide three different dimensions on which to examine research problems.

Broad Versus Narrow

Previously, we stated that research problems often start out too broad. For example, "What factors cause low mastery motivation" is too broad and probably not a feasible problem. Remember that your time and resources are limited so practicality requires that you limit the scope of your problem. It is also important to realize that science progresses in small steps. Even big, well-funded research projects often raise more questions than they answer and usually address only a limited piece of a broad research problem. On the other hand, you don't want the problem to be too narrow. For example, usually it should deal with more than a single, limited research question and two variables. (See Appendix D for examples of research problem statements.)

Widespread Versus Limited Interest

It might seem that you would want as many people (scholars and the public) as possible to be interested in your research. Certainly *you* should be interested, and it is a good strategy to pick a problem that is of interest to your advisor. You will get more and better feedback from your advisor and committee if they have interest in and knowledge about the area. It is also desirable to choose a topic that is of widespread interest, but some topics become almost faddish and have so many studies about them that it is hard to make a contribution. If you choose a topic that is currently very popular, it is also important to find recent unpublished literature by attending conferences, searching the Web and ERIC documents, and writing researchers who have recently published in the area to see if they have something new. It is hard to find gaps in the literature of a currently popular topic because a lot of work still may be in progress. This point overlaps with the next.

Well-Researched Versus Unknown Territory

It is exciting to think that you might be the first one to explore an area. However, if that is the case, one might wonder why it is unexplored. Is the topic of very limited interest, as discussed already? Are there practical, ethical, or financial reasons? Is the topic too specialized or narrow? Of course, there are interesting and important topics that are relatively unexplored and are not faced with these objections, but they are not easy to identify. Quantitative researchers tend to place considerable emphasis on finding gaps in the literature so they tend to study relatively well-researched areas. Qualitative researchers, on the other hand, place less emphasis on finding literature ahead of time and tend to explore less well-researched topics, seeing where their observations lead them.

Review of the Literature

Of all the steps in the research process, reviewing the literature is one of the most important due to it being the fundamental step that can ensure a rigorous and meaningful research design and results (Boote & Beile, 2005). Research reviews are necessary in the research process for a number of reasons, including to (1) identify gaps in the literature; (2) help to select appropriate methods for your specific topic; and (3) describe the inferences that have come from past research. This list is not exhaustive, as literature reviews can assist researchers in multiple domains to conduct rigorous, important, and meaningful research.

It is important to remember that research literature reviews are not without bias. When conducting reviews, researchers choose what journals to read, how many studies to read, and on which research studies to focus. Furthermore, researchers evaluate each study as to its importance and rigorousness. According to Dellinger (2005), "A review of the literature tells the researcher's own story about what was deemed valid, worthwhile, meaningful, and valuable in a set of studies and how those studies fit together" (p. 44). Thus, it is necessary to keep in mind that your bias as a researcher will influence your literature review.

Definition of the Literature Review

There are many definitions of a literature review. Most definitions are not comprehensive; thus, we agree with the definition of literature review from Onwuegbuzie, Collins, Leech, Dellinger, and Jiao (2005, p. 7):

> We define the literature ... as an interpretation of a selection of published and/or unpublished documents available from various sources on a specific topic that optimally involves summarization, analysis, evaluation, and synthesis of the documents. The literature review interpretation results from systematic study of these sources culminating in qualitative and/or quantitative measurement of the quality, characteristics, and validity of the body of reviewed sources.

This definition of a literature review is beneficial due to its emphasis on summarization, analysis, evaluation, and synthesis. Each of these needs to be used when conducting a literature review. It is not enough to just summarize the literature; researchers need to read the existing literature with a critical eye and to analyze and evaluate the literature. Furthermore, literature reviews are not annotated bibliographies. Many students confuse annotated bibliographies with literature reviews. A literature review is more than just a list and summary of the existing literature; it requires a synthesis of the literature. This last aspect of the process can be daunting for some students. Reading published literature reviews can assist novice researchers to learn how to do the synthesis.

Sources to Use in Literature Reviews

When conducting a literature review, it is important to use all existing literature in the topic area. Unfortunately, to accomplish this, researchers usually need to employ multiple databases. Additionally, all literature should be *considered* for inclusion, including published and unpublished work. Many dissertations and conference presentations are not published but can assist researchers in increasing their understanding of what topics are currently being studied and what methods have been recently been drawn upon.

Although all types of literature should be explored, caution should be used when selecting literature for *inclusion* in your final review. The most trustworthy information usually can be found in journal articles that have been refereed (reviewed for suitability for publication in a particular journal) by peers in the field. Some sources may have suspect information. For example, the Internet includes many helpful and trustworthy websites, yet it also includes information that can be incorrect. It is helpful to check who the author of the source is (e.g., a website created by a professor affiliated with a research university probably would be more trustworthy than one created by a beginning student). Also, check to see if the sources have been reviewed by someone other than the author.

There are other important considerations when deciding what literature to include in your final review. Whenever possible, use the *primary source* rather than a secondary source. An example of a *secondary source* would be a textbook that cites a research study. If you want to cite the research study, you need to read the actual research article and cite it, not the textbook. Reading the primary source is important because secondary source authors might have misinterpreted an article they cite. Occasionally, the primary source will not be available because it is out of print or in a foreign language. In that case, note that the study is reported "as cited in ___."

It is important when conducting a literature review for a research study that the sources used be empirical, evidence-based research. There are many published articles, books, magazines, and so forth that publish information about the author's opinions, thoughts, and ideas, and these opinions might not have been based on well-designed, empirical research. For example, a junior high principal may have had to change students' schedules from a traditional one (e.g., seven classes each day) to a block schedule (e.g., five classes a day, with different classes offered on different days). The next year, the principal notices that the test scores have improved for his school. He then writes about this "finding," and it is published in a journal for school administrators. The problem is that there is not strong evidence that the change from a traditional format to a block scheduling format is *the reason* or cause for the change in test scores. Using this type of literature can be misleading. If the article does not have reasonably complete sections describing the methods and results, it is not an empirically based research article. If there is a description of the methods and results, one still needs to evaluate the quality (i.e., validity) of the design and analysis. We discuss these issues extensively in later chapters.

It is always important to include a literature review when writing a proposal or a research paper. Dissertations and theses usually have an entire chapter devoted to the literature review, and these reviews are most commonly comprehensive, including all the key literature related to the topic and often providing a historical review.

In journal articles, literature reviews are usually short, due to the page or word restrictions of the journal. It is common for researchers to have conducted extensive reviews of the literature prior to a study (e.g., to identify gaps in the literature). Yet in the presentation of the research in a journal article, only the most pertinent and recent literature is included. For example, in our sample associational study (#4) by Zamboanga, Padilla-Walker, Hardy, Thompson, and Wang (2007) all the cited research was published within the past 8 years and was summarized in about 700 words (two to three typed pages). Yet another example is Schellenberg (2004), our sample randomized experiment. Except for mention of a few classic articles, the literature about music and intelligence was condensed to about 1,000 words and to articles published within 10 years preceding the study.

Hart (2001), Locke, Spirduso, and Silverman (2007), and Fink (1998) provide additional information about reading and understanding research and conducting literature reviews.

Summary

This chapter presents an overview of 10 steps and a flow chart (Figure 2.1) for planning and conducting a quantitative research study. The steps in Figure 2.1 include the following:

1. Identify a research problem.
2. Conduct a research literature review.
3. Write research questions or hypotheses.
4. Select the research approaches and specific design.
5. Create a plan for conducting the research. This includes plans for: selecting the sample, selecting or developing the instruments, and developing procedures for data collection and analysis.
6. Obtain approval from the human subjects IRB.
7. Collect the data.
8. Analyze the data.

9. Interpret the data.
10. Communicate the findings.

The focus of this chapter was on steps 1 and 2. Later chapters discuss each of the other eight steps in detail. Next we described the process each author went through in developing a research problem that we have studied. This was followed by a broader discussion of several sources of research problems: literature, personal experience, clinical observation, and theory. Next we described characteristics of a good research problem: testable, ethical, feasible, and of vital interest to you as well as the discipline. Finally, we discussed research literature reviews, what they are, what types of sources to use, and some issues and examples.

Key Concepts

Characteristics of good research problem

Literature review

Research problem

Sources of research problems

Sources for literature reviews

Steps in planning research

Theory

Key Distinctions

Broad versus narrow research problems

Existing literature versus personal experience versus clinical observation

Literature review versus annotated bibliography

Primary source versus secondary source

Well-researched versus unknown territory

Widespread versus limited interest

Application Problems

1. What is the purpose of the literature review in a research study?
2. Why is it important to use primary sources rather than secondary sources in the literature review?

3. List three sources for the literature review—what are the advantages and disadvantages of each?

4. Why should the researcher be cautious about using Web sources in the literature review?

5. Why is it important to link theory to the research problem?

6. In this chapter, the authors each describe the process they went through to identify a research problem. For one of these three research problems, answer each of the following:

   a. Is this a broad or narrow research problem? Explain.

   b. Is this research problem of widespread or limited interest? Explain.

   c. What topics in the literature might the researcher want to explore? Explain.

   d. Rate the stated research problem on the different characteristics of a good research problem—support your answer.

7. For one of the five sample studies described in Chapter 1, answer each of the following:

   a. Is this a broad or narrow research problem? Explain.

   b. Is this research problem of widespread or limited interest? Explain.

   c. What topics in the literature might the researcher want to explore? Explain.

   d. Rate the stated research problem on the different characteristics of a good research problem—support your answer.

Section II

Quantitative Research Approaches, Questions, and Designs

3

Variables, Research Questions, and Hypotheses

The research process begins with an issue or problem of interest to the researcher. Usually the **research problem** is a statement that *asks about the relationships between two or more variables*. However, some research problems are purely descriptive and describe one variable at a time. Yet almost all research studies have *more* than two variables. In this chapter, we discuss variables—including the difference among independent, dependent, and extraneous—research questions, and hypotheses.

Variables

Key elements in a research problem are the variables. A **variable** is defined as a characteristic of the participants or situation for a given study that has different values. A *variable must vary or have different values in the study*. For example, *gender* is a variable because it can have two values, female or male. *Age* is a variable that can have a large number of values. *Type of treatment/intervention* (or *type of curriculum*) is a variable if there is more than one treatment or a treatment and a control group. The *number of days to learn something* or *the number of days to recover from an ailment* are common measures of the effect of a treatment and, thus, are also variables. Similarly, *amount of mathematics knowledge* is a variable because it can vary from none to a lot.

However, if a concept has only one value in a particular study, it is not a variable; it is a constant. Thus, ethnic group is not a variable if all participants are European American. Gender is not a variable if all participants in a study are female.

In quantitative research, variables are defined operationally and are commonly divided into **independent variables** (active or attribute), **dependent variables**, and **extraneous** (or control) **variables**. Each of these topics is dealt with briefly in the following sections.

Operational Definitions of Variables

An operational definition describes or *defines a variable in terms of the operations or techniques used to make it happen or to measure it*. When quantitative researchers describe the variables in their study, they specify what they mean by demonstrating how they measured the variable. Demographic variables like age, gender, or ethnic group often are measured simply by asking the participant to choose the appropriate category from a list.

Types of treatment (or curricula) are usually operationally defined much more extensively by describing what was done during the treatment or new curriculum. Likewise, abstract concepts like mathematics knowledge, self-concept, or mathematics anxiety need to be defined operationally by spelling out in some detail how they were measured in a particular study. To do this, the investigator may provide sample questions, append the actual instrument, or provide a reference where more information can be found.

Independent Variables

There are two types of independent variables: **active** and **attribute.** It is important to distinguish between these types when we discuss the results of a study. As presented in more detail in Chapter 4, an active independent variable is a necessary but not sufficient condition to make cause and effect conclusions.

Active or Manipulated Independent Variables

An active independent variable is a variable, such as a workshop, new curriculum, or other intervention, at least one level of which *is given to a group of participants, within a specified period of time during the study.* For example, a researcher might investigate a new kind of therapy compared with the traditional treatment. A second example might be to study the effect of a new teaching method, such as cooperative learning, on student performance. In these two examples, the variable of interest is something that is *given to* the participants. Although active independent variables are *given* to the participants in the study, they are not necessarily given or manipulated *by the experimenter.* They may be given by a clinic, school, or someone other than the investigator, but from the participants' point of view, the situation is manipulated.

Our definition of an active independent variable requires the treatment to be given *after* the study is planned so that there could be, and usually is, a **pretest.** If some sort of event that resembles an intervention or treatment happened *in the past,* before the study was planned, we do *not* consider the variable active. This type of study is considered *ex post facto,* or after the fact. (See Chapter 7 for more discussion of ex post facto studies.)

Randomized experimental and *quasi-experimental* studies, as described in Chapters 1 and 5, have an active independent variable. Ex post facto studies are considered to be nonexperimental.

Attribute or Measured Independent Variables

The term *independent variable* is not restricted to those variables that are manipulated or active. We define an **independent variable** broadly to include any predictors, antecedents, or *presumed* causes or influences under investigation in the study. Attributes of the participants as well as active independent variables fit within this definition.

The values of an **attribute independent variable** are *preexisting attributes of the persons or their ongoing environment* that do not change *during the study.* For example, level of parental education, socioeconomic status, gender, age, ethnic group, IQ, and personality characteristics are attributes of participants that could be used as attribute independent variables. Studies with only attribute independent variables are called **nonexperimental** studies.

For the social sciences and education, attribute independent variables are especially important. For example, type of disability may be the major focus of a study. Type of disability certainly qualifies as a variable because it can take on different values even though they are not *given* during the study. For example, cerebral palsy is different from Down's syndrome, which is different from spina bifida, yet all are types of disabilities. People already have defining characteristics or attributes that place them into one of two or more categories. Disabilities and other characteristics of the participants that existed before the study are considered to be attributes.

Type of Independent Variable and Inferences About Cause and Effect

When we analyze data from a research study, the statistical analysis does not differentiate whether the independent variable is an active independent variable or an attribute independent variable. However, although most statistics books use the label *independent variable* for both active and attribute variables, there is a crucial difference in interpretation.

A major goal of scientific research is to be able to identify a causal relationship between two variables. Demonstrating that a given intervention or treatment causes a change in behavior or performance is extremely important for researchers in applied disciplines. *Only the approaches that have an active independent variable (randomized experimental and, to a lesser extent, quasi-experimental) can provide data that allow one to infer that the independent variable caused the change or difference in the dependent variable.*

In contrast, a significant difference between persons who differ on an attribute independent variable (e.g., gender or ethnicity) should *not* lead one to conclude that the attribute independent variable *caused* the scores on dependent variable to differ. Thus, this distinction between active and attribute independent variables is important because terms such as *main effect* and *effect size* used in this and most statistics books might lead one to believe that if you find a significant difference, the independent variable *caused* the difference. Causal terms such as *influence, determine,* or *effect* can be misleading when the independent variable is an attribute.

Although nonexperimental studies (those with attribute independent variables) are limited in what can be said about causation, they can lead to solid conclusions about the differences between groups and about associations between variables. Furthermore, *if the focus of research is on attribute independent variables, a nonexperimental study is the only available approach.* For example, if a researcher is interested in learning how boys and girls differ in learning mathematical concepts, the variable of interest would be the attribute independent variable of gender. Therefore, a conclusion that any difference is *caused by* gender is incorrect.

Levels or Values of the Independent Variable

It is crucial to understand the difference between a variable, such as gender, and the levels (values of the variable), such as male or female. Several other terms, *values, categories, groups,* or *samples,* are sometimes used interchangeably with the term *levels,* especially in statistics books. Suppose that an investigator is performing a study to investigate the effect of a treatment. One group of participants is assigned to the treatment group. A second group does not receive the treatment. The study could be conceptualized as having one independent variable (*treatment type*), with two levels or values (*treatment* and *no treatment*). The independent variable in this example would be classified as an active independent variable. Now, suppose instead that the investigator was interested in comparing two different treatments and a third no-treatment group or control group. The study would still be conceptualized as having one active independent variable (*treatment type*), but with three values or levels (the two treatment conditions and the control condition). This variable could be diagrammed as follows:

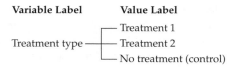

In this example, Treatment 1, Treatment 2, and the control group are different from each other, but there is no presumed order to their difference. However, the levels could be ordered such as a high-, medium-, and low-intensity treatment. An independent variable with a few ordered levels could be diagrammed as follows:

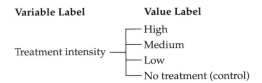

As an additional example, consider *gender,* which is an attribute independent variable with two values, *male* and *female.* It could be diagrammed as follows:

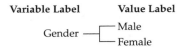

Note that each variable has a **variable label,** and the levels or values, which are often discrete categories, have **value labels** (e.g., male and female). It is especially important to know the value labels when the variable is **nominal**—that is, when the values of the variable are just names and, thus, are not ordered.

More Than One Independent Variable

It is common for a study with an active independent variable such as a treatment to include gender, or another attribute, as a second independent variable. When more than one independent variable is included in a study, the investigator is usually interested not only in the effect of each independent variable by itself but also in the *interaction* between the two independent variables. We discuss variables, levels, and interactions in more detail in later chapters because most published studies and theses have more than one independent variable. Studies with two independent variables are called *two-factor* or *factorial* designs.

Dependent Variables

The **dependent variable** is assumed to *measure or assess the effect of the independent variable.* It is thought of as the *presumed outcome or criterion.* Dependent variables are often test scores, ratings on questionnaires, readings from instruments (e.g., electrocardiogram, galvanic skin response), or measures of physical performance. Our discussion of measurement in Chapter 10 focuses on the dependent variable. Dependent variables, like independent variables, must have at least two values; most of the dependent variables discussed in this book have *many levels, varying from low to high.*

Extraneous Variables

These are variables (also called control variables or, in some designs, covariates) that are *not of interest in a particular study but could influence the dependent variable* so they need to be ruled out or controlled. Environmental factors (e.g., temperature or distractions), time of day, and characteristics of the experimenter, teacher, or therapist are some possible extraneous variables that might need to be controlled. Sometimes such variables are "controlled" using random assignment as discussed in Chapters 4 and 5. Other times statistics, as discussed in Chapter 22, are used to control extraneous variables.

Ordered Versus Unordered/Nominal Levels of Variables

An important thing to know about a variable is whether the levels are *unordered* categories or whether they are ordered from low to high. Remember that within any study a variable must vary; that is, it must have two or more different values.

Most of our previous examples (e.g., gender, treatment type) of independent variables had levels or categories that were not ordered. The categories in such variables were essentially labels or names, and the variables are said to be **nominal** variables. For example, the independent variable gender has two, unordered levels: female and male. In a study, all the participants of a given level of a nominal variable are treated as if they are the same, and all are assigned the same label and the same value. For example, when gender is a variable all females are considered the same, are labeled "female," and in our diagram were assigned a value of 2. All males are for this purpose the same and were assigned the value of 1. However, these categories are nominal, not ordered, so you should not consider females to be more (or less) than males, only different.

On the other hand, **ordered variables** have a set of values that vary from low to high within a certain range (e.g., a 1-to-7 rating of satisfaction), such that a larger value of the variable indicates more of it than a smaller value of the variable. Often there is an assumption that there *are* or *could* be an infinite set of values within the range; if so the variable is considered to be *continuous*. Weight and time to finish a task are continuous variables, but many ordered variables have only a few levels or categories, such as high, medium, and low. We expand on this introduction to measurement in Chapter 10.

Other Considerations About Variables

For the most part, the studies we discuss have *independent variables* that have a few levels and *dependent variables* that have many ordered levels. However, in the associational approach, discussed in Chapters 4 and 7, both independent and dependent variables usually have many ordered levels. There are some studies in which the independent variables have many levels and the dependent variable has two or a few levels, and there are even studies where both variables have only a few levels. We discuss these different combinations of independent and dependent variables and how they are analyzed later in the book.

Some variables (e.g., knowledge of mathematics or self-concept) could be either the independent variable or dependent variable (or even an extraneous variable), depending on the study. These variables are usually a *changeable* characteristic of the participant (like an attitude or personality characteristic).

Individual participants usually do *not* vary on a characteristic or variable; it is the group that must have more than one value (e.g., some men and some women). However, in some studies, participants may change over time or due to an intervention. In these studies there are *repeated measures* of the same variable (e.g., a pre- and a posttest on math knowledge).

Groups or Sets of Variables

In analyzing research articles, it is of utmost importance to distinguish between variables and the levels of variables. Sometimes this distinction can be difficult because in complex studies researchers have many variables that often are grouped into what might be called *sets* of similar variables. For example, the variables age, gender, education, and marital status could be grouped together and referred to collectively in an article as demographics. Similarly, Graduate Record Examination (GRE) verbal, quantitative, and writing scores could be called Graduate Record Exams scores. Confusion arises if one *mistakenly* assumes that the sets or groups of variables (demographics or GRE scores) are the variables and the actual variables (e.g., age, gender, GRE verbal) are the levels.

How can one avoid this confusion? Thoughtful reading is the key, but some tips may help. Remember that a variable has to have at least two levels, but a level or category is a single value.[1] Thus, if something *can vary* from low to high (e.g., age or GRE verbal) or has two or more nominal values (e.g., gender), it has to be a variable, not a level.

Research Hypotheses and Questions

Research hypotheses are predictive statements about the relationship between variables. **Research questions** are similar to hypotheses, except that they do not make specific predictions and are phrased in question format. For example, one might have the following research question: "Is there a difference in students' scores on a standardized test if they took two tests in 1 day versus taking only one test on each of 2 days?" A hypothesis regarding the same issue might be, "Students who take only one test per day will score better on standardized tests than will students who take two tests in 1 day." In a given study, a researcher presents a general research problem and then specific research hypotheses, or research questions, which have been generated from the research problem and can be tested statistically.

We divide research hypotheses and questions into three broad types—**difference, associational,** and **descriptive**—as shown in the middle of Figure 3.1. This key figure also shows the general and specific purposes and the general types of statistics for each of these three types of research questions. This key figure, or part of it, appears in several chapters because of its applicability throughout the book.

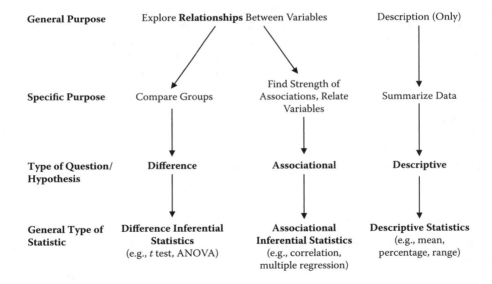

FIGURE 3.1
Schematic diagram showing how the purpose and type of research question correspond to the general type of statistic used in a study.

Difference Research Questions

For these questions, we compare scores (on the dependent variable) of two or more different groups, each of which is composed of individuals with one of the values or levels on the independent variable. This type of question attempts to demonstrate that groups are not the same on the dependent variable.

Associational Research Questions

Here we associate or relate two or more variables. This approach usually involves an attempt to see how two or more variables covary (i.e., higher values on one variable correspond to higher, or lower, values on another variable for the same persons) or how one or more variables enables one to predict another variable.

Descriptive Research Questions

These are not answered with inferential statistics (which make inferences about a larger group, *the population*, from the group we studied, called the *sample*). Descriptive questions ask for a summary description of the current data, without trying to generalize to a larger population of individuals.

Figure 3.1 shows that both difference and associational questions or hypotheses explore the relationships between variables; however, they are conceptualized differently, as is described shortly.[2] Note that difference and associational questions differ in specific purpose and the kinds of statistics they use to answer the question.

Difference Versus Associational Inferential Statistics

We think it is educationally useful to divide inferential statistics into two types corresponding to difference and associational hypotheses or questions.[3] Difference inferential statistics (e.g., *t* test or analysis of variance [ANOVA]) are *used for approaches that test for differences between groups.* Associational inferential statistics *test for associations or relationships between variables* and use, for example, correlation or multiple regression analysis. We use this contrast between difference and associational inferential statistics in Chapter 4 and later in this book (Chapters 20–22) when we discuss how to interpret statistics.

Table 3.1 provides the general format and one example of a basic difference question, a basic associational question, and a basic descriptive question. Remember that research questions are similar to hypotheses, but they are stated in question format. We recommend the question format for the descriptive approach or when one does not have a clear directional prediction. (More examples are given in Appendix D.) As implied by Figure 3.1, it is acceptable to phrase any research question that involves two variables as whether there is a relationship between the variables (e.g., is there a relationship between *gender* and *math achievement* or is there a relationship between *anxiety* and *GPA*?). However, phrasing the question as a difference or association is preferable because it helps one choose an appropriate statistic and interpret the result.

Complex Research Questions

Some research questions involve more than two variables at a time. We call such questions and the appropriate statistics *complex*. Some of these statistics are called *multivariate*

TABLE 3.1

Examples of Three Kinds of Basic Research Questions/Hypotheses

---

1. Basic difference (group comparison) questions
- Usually used for randomized experimental, quasi-experimental, and comparative approaches.
- For this type of question, the groups of individuals who share a level of an active independent variable (e.g., intervention group) or an attribute independent variable (e.g., male gender) are compared with individuals who share the other levels of that same independent variable (e.g., control group or female gender) to see if the groups differ with regard to the average scores on the dependent variable (e.g., aggression scores).
- Example: Do persons who experienced an emotion regulation intervention differ from those who did not experience that intervention with respect to their average aggression scores? In other words, will the average aggression score of the intervention group be significantly different from the average aggression score for the control group following the intervention?

2. Basic associational (relational) questions
- Used for the associational approach, in which the independent variable is usually continuous (i.e., has many ordered levels).
- For this type of question, the scores on the independent variable (e.g., anxiety) are associated with or related to the dependent variable scores (e.g., GPA).
- Example: Will students' degree of anxiety be associated with their overall GPA? In other words, will knowing students' level of anxiety tell us anything about their tendency to make higher versus lower grades? If there is a negative association (correlation) between anxiety scores and grade point average, those persons who have high levels of anxiety will tend to have low GPAs, those with low anxiety will tend to have high GPAs, and those in the middle on anxiety will tend to be in the middle on GPA.

3. Basic descriptive questions
- Used for the descriptive approach.
- For this type of question, scores on a single variable are described in terms of their central tendency, variability, or percentages in each category/level.
- Example: What percentage of students make a B or above? What is the average level of anxiety found in 9th grade students? The average GPA was 2.73, or 30% had high anxiety.

---

in other texts, but there is not a consistent definition of multivariate in the literature. We provide examples of how to write certain complex research questions in Appendix D, and in Chapter 22, we introduce two complex statistics: *multiple regression* and *factorial ANOVA*.

Five Sample Research Studies

In Chapter 1, we described five sample studies, including the research problem and the key independent and dependent variables. That section of Chapter 1 should be reread now. Given our current discussion of variables, several additional points can be made. Note that several of the studies, including the music intervention experiment (Schellenberg, 2004) and the comparative study of older and younger multiple sclerosis (MS) patients (DiLorenzo, Halper, and Picone, 2004) had several dependent variables. This is quite common in published articles. Note that the associational study (Zamboanga, Padilla-Walker, Hardy, Thompson, & Wang, 2007) also had several independent or predictor variables (e.g., several academic background variables and course involvement).

Summary

A research problem is a statement that asks whether there is a relationship between two, or likely more than two, variables. A variable is a characteristic of the participants or situation of a given study that has different values or levels. There are three main types of variables:

1. Independent variables, which are the *presumed* causes, influences, or antecedents in the study. We differentiated two types of independent variables:

   a. Active independent variables, which are variables that are given to the participants, usually for some specified time period during the study.

   b. Attribute independent variables, which are observed or measured characteristics of the participants or environment that either *was not* or *cannot* be manipulated by the investigator.

2. Dependent variables, which are the outcomes and are presumed to depend on the level of the independent variable.

3. Extraneous variables are not of interest in this study, but they could influence the dependent variable and therefore need to be controlled.

If everyone in a study is the same on a given characteristic, that characteristic is *constant, not a variable*, in the study. For example, in a study of 9-year-old boys' learning of mathematics in one of two curricula, the participants' age and gender (9-year-old boys) are not variables.

The distinction between the variable and the levels, values, or categories of a variable is important. The variable itself is given a name that encompasses all the levels or categories (e.g., treatment type, gender, or ethnicity). The levels are the names of the specific categories or groups or values (e.g., experimental versus control, male versus female, Asian versus African versus European). In this context, level does not necessarily imply order; one level is not necessarily higher or lower than another. Variables can have either nominal (unordered) levels or categories or have ordered levels that vary from low to high.

Some variables (e.g., knowledge of mathematics or self-concept) could be either the independent variable or dependent variable (or even an extraneous variable), depending on the study. These variables are usually a changeable characteristic of the participant (e.g., an attitude, personality characteristic); if one of these is used as the independent variable, it is an attribute independent variable.

Individual participants do *not* have to vary on a characteristic or variable—it is the group that must have more than one value (e.g., some men and some women). In some studies there are *repeated measures* of the same variable (e.g., a pre- and a posttest on math knowledge), and individuals *may* change over *time* in a longitudinal study.

The research problem is usually stated more broadly than the research hypotheses or questions. Most studies have several hypotheses or questions that indicate predicted or possible relationships between variables. In Chapter 4 we describe six specific types of research questions and five types of research approaches that form the basis for an understanding of research design and data analysis.

Key Concepts

Operational definition
Pretest
Research hypotheses
Research problem
Research questions
Variable

Key Distinctions

Active versus attribute independent variable
Basic versus complex research questions (and statistics)
Independent versus dependent versus extraneous variable
Levels of one variable versus a set or group of variables
Ordered versus unordered or nominal variables
The variable (itself) versus levels or values of the variable

Application Problems

For each research hypothesis (1–9), provide the information requested in a–g:

- a. Name the independent/antecedent/predictor variable.
- b. Name the dependent/outcome variable.
- c. Give an operational definition of each variable. If active, how might the independent variable be manipulated? If an attribute, how will the attribute be measured? How will the dependent variable be measured?
- d. Is the independent variable active or an attribute?
- e. How many levels of the independent variable are there?
- f. Are the levels ordered or nominal?
- g. Is the population of interest named? What is it?

1. Family conflict is associated with absenteeism rates in clerical workers.
2. A workshop on visual imagery improves memory in college students.
3. The number of faculty members at a committee meeting is related to the length of the meeting.

4. The amount of child abuse is related to the age of parents when they married.

5. Voters' political party is related to their attitude toward gun control.

6. Whether a pregnant woman's diet was high, medium, or low in folic acid affects the birth weight of her child.

7. Students given an exercise program have reduced levels of stress.

8. The gender of the instructor is related to students' evaluation of the instructor.

9. Participation in an anxiety reduction workshop is related to test performance.

10. Compare the terms *active independent variable* and *attribute independent variable*. What are the similarities and differences?

11. What kind of independent variable (active or attribute) is necessary to infer cause?

12. What is the difference between the independent variable and the dependent variable?

13. Compare and contrast associational, difference, and descriptive types of research questions.

14. Write both a research question and a corresponding research hypothesis regarding variables of interest to you but not used in the chapter. Is it an associational, difference, or descriptive question?

15. Using one or more of the following variables, *religion, achievement test,* and *anxiety*:

   a. Write an associational question.

   b. Write a difference question.

   c. Write a descriptive question.

Notes

1. In some cases a level may be a range of values (e.g., ages 21–30), but in these cases the values in a given range are treated as if they were all the same (e.g., young adult or given a single group code such as 3).

2. This similarity is in agreement with the statement by statisticians that all common parametric inferential statistics are relational. We use the term associational for the second type of research question rather than relational or correlational to distinguish it from the *general purpose* of both difference and associational questions/hypothesis, which is to study relationships. Also we want to distinguish between correlation, as a specific statistical technique, and the broader type of associational question and that group of statistics.

3. We realize that all parametric inferential statistics are relational so this dichotomy of using one type of data analysis procedure to test for differences (when there are a few values or levels of the independent variables) and another type of data analysis procedure to test for associations (when there are continuous independent variables) is somewhat artificial. Both continuous and categorical independent variables can be used in a general linear model approach to data analysis. However, we think that the distinction is useful because most researchers utilize the dichotomy in selecting statistics for data analysis.

4

Research Approaches

This chapter serves two related purposes. First, we expand on the Chapter 1 discussion of *research approaches*, comparing and contrasting the five approaches: randomized experimental, quasi-experimental, comparative, associational, and descriptive. Our discussion of the approaches emphasizes the extent to which they can provide evidence that the independent variable *caused* any observed change or difference in the dependent variable. In Chapter 8, we focus on the concept of *internal validity*, which depends on the approach and the strength of the research design. Internal validity indexes the extent to which the relationship between the independent and dependent variable is a causal one. Thus, the discussion of internal validity follows directly from the discussion of the extent to which a research approach can provide evidence about cause and effect.

Overview of the Research Approaches

The general purpose of all research studies, except descriptive, is to *look for relationships* between variables (see Figure 4.1, which is Figure 3.1 expanded). As mentioned in Chapter 1, we divide approaches to research into three general or broad types: experimental, nonexperimental, and descriptive. The **experimental approach** has an *active independent variable* such as an intervention, new curriculum, or treatment. The **nonexperimental approach** has an *attribute independent variable* and includes survey and observational research. The **descriptive approach** does not have an independent variable. We use the label descriptive approach to indicate studies that only describe the current sample rather than that use inferential statistics to test hypotheses about a larger population of interest.

Next, as shown in Figure 4.1, we divide the experimental approach into two *specific approaches* (i.e., randomized experimental versus quasi-experimental), and we also divide the nonexperimental approach into three specific approaches (i.e., comparative versus associational versus descriptive). All the specific approaches *except the descriptive* seek to find *relationships* among variables; they differ in terms of purposes and in what kinds of hypotheses/research questions that they help answer.

Figure 4.1 also indicates the *specific purpose* for each of the five approaches. Notice that the randomized experimental approach is the best suited to determine causes. The quasi-experimental approach, at best, provides good clues about causes. The statement that the independent variable *caused* a change in the dependent variable is not appropriate if the approach was either comparative or associational.

In the sections that follow we expand the discussion of the utility of these five approaches to produce conclusions about cause and effect. We also examine the similarities and differences

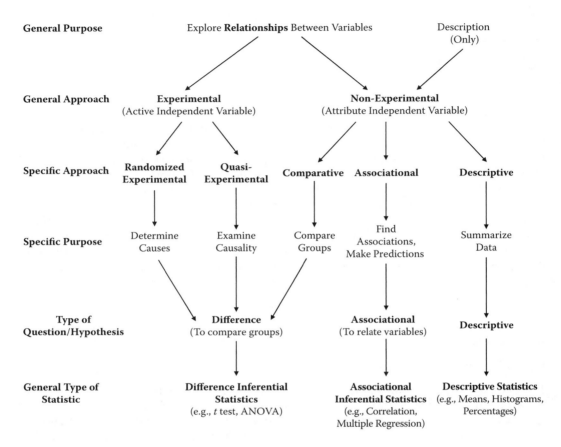

FIGURE 4.1
Schematic diagram showing how the general type of statistic and hypothesis/question used in a study corresponds to the purposes and the approach.

between each of the five approaches. Figure 4.2 presents information about the five research approaches in a different way than Figure 4.1 and provides distinguishing criteria.

Note that the comparative and associational approaches are the same in many respects. Neither has an active independent variable or random assignment to groups. These nonexperimental approaches *usually* differ in the number of levels of the independent variable and the type of statistics used.

In the associational approach, the independent variable is *assumed to be continuous.* That is, it *has many ordered levels*/categories. We consider an approach to be associational if the independent variable has five or more *ordered* categories. However, there are associational statistics that can be used when there are a few levels of the independent variable.

In the comparative approach (and also the two experimental approaches), the independent variable usually has two to four levels so that two to four groups of participants are compared. However, sometimes, the comparative approach is used when there are more than four levels of the independent variable, especially if it is nominal/not ordered, such as when five or more ethnic groups are compared.

Criteria	Randomized experimental	Quasi-experimental	Comparative	Associational	Descriptive
Random assignment of participants to groups by investigator	Yes	No	No	No (only one group)	No groups
Independent variable is active	Yes	Yes	No (attribute)	No (attribute)	No independent variable
Independent variable is controlled *by the investigator*[a]	Usually	Sometimes	No	No	No
Number of levels of the Independent variable[b]	Usually 2–4	Usually 2–4	Usually 2–4	Usually 5 or more ordered levels	No independent variable
Relationships between variables or comparison of groups	Yes (comparison)	Yes (comparison)	Yes (comparison)	Yes (relationship)	No

[a] Although the control of the delivery of the independent variable *by the investigator* is a desired quality of randomized experimental and quasi-experimental designs, it is not sufficient for distinguishing between them.

[b] This distinction is made for educational purposes and is only "usually" true.

FIGURE 4.2
A comparison of the five basic quantitative research approaches.

Research Approaches With an Active Independent Variable

The Randomized Experimental Approach

For a research approach to be called randomized (or true) experimental, two criteria must be met. The key criterion is that the researcher must *randomly assign participants to groups* or conditions. (We use the word *condition* in addition to *group* because under certain circumstances a group can undergo both the control and intervention conditions.) Random assignment of participants to groups is what differentiates randomized experiments from quasi-experiments (Figure 4.2) and is often difficult to achieve. Much applied research involves intact groups, such as classrooms or rehabilitation settings, and it is usually not possible to change those settings. Thus, research with existing classes or groups is considered quasi-experimental, *not* randomized experimental.

The second criterion for the randomized experimental approach, also satisfied by quasi-experiments, is that the *independent variable* must be *active* as defined in the last chapter. In addition, as shown in Figure 4.2, the researcher usually is able *to control the independent variable* in randomized experiments. In other words, the researcher can decide exactly *what* the treatment will be and *when* and to *whom* it will be given. However, this third criterion is not absolute. In all random experiments there is an active independent variable and the participants are randomly assigned to groups, but in some cases the experimenter does not control the delivery of the treatment.

Random Assignment

What is random assignment, and why is it so important? The concept of randomness implies that there is no bias. When the investigator randomly assigns participants to groups, it means that each participant has an *equal chance* to be in either the intervention group or the control group. Random does *not* mean haphazard or any old way, as it sometimes does in popular language. One could use a computer-generated random number table or a method such as the one described in the next paragraph to randomly assign participants to groups.

For example, suppose there are to be 60 participants in a study, with 30 persons in each of two groups. The investigator takes 60 pieces of paper and places a 0 on half of the pieces and a 1 on the other half. Then, the investigator places all 60 pieces of paper in a bowl and shakes the bowl to mix up the pieces of paper. Now, when each participant comes in for the study, the investigator reaches into the bowl and pulls out a piece of paper. If the paper has a 0 on it, the participant is assigned to the control group. If the paper has a 1 on it, the participant is assigned to the intervention group. (It is important in this situation that the investigator does *not* put the piece of paper back into the bowl after each participant's assignment is made.) This procedure continues until all 60 participants have been assigned to either the intervention or control groups.

After random assignment, but prior to the intervention, it is assumed that the participants in the two groups are equivalent *in all other respects*, including demographic characteristics. In fact, if the dependent or outcome variable were measured *before* the intervention the two groups should not differ significantly. In the practical situation, two relatively small groups, as in the previous example, probably would not be exactly equal. The concept of randomness only makes things equal in the long run, with relatively large numbers of participants in each group. However, after random assignment, even if the two groups are not exactly equal, the differences between them are considered to be unbiased.

Random Selection or Sampling

It is very important to understand the difference between random sampling and random assignment. The concept of *random* or *unbiased* is, of course, common to both and to several other phrases, such as *random order*, which we discuss in later chapters. **Random sampling**—also called random *selection of participants* from the population—if done in a study comes before *random assignment to groups* in the procedure. As we see in Chapter 9, random selection has to do with how some persons in the whole population of interest are selected to become participants in the study, not how they get into experimental or control groups.

A randomized experiment may or may not use random selection or sampling. Although a study with a weak sampling procedure can still be a randomized experiment, its *overall* quality will be reduced as discussed in Chapters 23 and 24. It is also true that inferential statistics assume that the sample studied is a random sample of the population of interest. If it is not, the statistical results may be misleading. Nevertheless, a randomized experiment does *not* necessarily involve random sampling.

An Example

Consider a study to increase functioning of persons who had spinal cord injuries. Using participants at the rehabilitation center where she worked, the researcher randomly *assigned* participants to one of two groups (Note that this was not random *sampling*). One group (intervention) received the therapy. A second group (control) did not receive the therapy. The dependent variables were measured after 12 weeks using a test and strength measures.

Is this study a randomized experiment? The first criterion, random assignment of participants to groups, was satisfied. The study satisfied the second criterion because the independent variable was *active* (intervention). The researcher also decided what the treatment would be and which group should get the treatment, so she had control over the independent variable. Thus, the study was a randomized experiment.

This sample study used one of several specific experimental designs, the pretest–posttest control group design, which is described in Chapter 5. What this specific experimental design has in common with the others and what distinguishes it from the other four research approaches described in this chapter is shown in Figure 4.2.

The Quasi-Experimental Research Approach

The **quasi-experimental** research approach is similar to the randomized experimental approach but fails to satisfy the condition of random assignment of participants to groups. In these designs, for example, participants are already in intact groups, such as two different classrooms, prior to the study.

Note in Figure 4.2 that quasi-experimental designs have an *active independent variable* with a few (usually 2 to 4) levels and also *involve a comparison* between, for example, an intervention and a control condition. However, there is a word of caution about the active independent variable. In the randomized experimental approach, the researcher usually has control over the independent variable in that he or she determines the contents and timing of the intervention, and the intervention can be randomly assigned to the experimental group and the nonintervention can be randomly assigned to the control group. The *strength* of the quasi-experimental design is based, in part, on how much control the investigator actually has in manipulating the independent variable and deciding which group will receive which treatment. In Chapter 5 we illustrate how control of the independent variable affects the strength of the quasi-experimental design. The strength of the design influences how confident we can be about whether the independent variable was *the cause* of any change that took place in the dependent variable.

We divide the quasi-experimental approach into four categories: (1) quasi-experiments with major limitations; (2) pretest–posttest designs; (3) time-series designs; and (4) single-subject designs. We discuss these designs in more detail in Chapters 5 and 6.

Research Approaches With Attribute Independent Variables

The associational and comparative approaches are similar in that they study attribute independent variables and do not use random assignment, and the investigator does not have control over the independent variables. Because they do not have an active independent variable (intervention), we call the comparative and associational approaches **nonexperimental**. Neither approach provides evidence that the independent variable is the *cause* of differences in the dependent variable. Most nonexperimental research includes both comparative and associational *research questions*, which also are used in "survey" and "observational" research. We use the term *nonexperimental* because survey and observational refer to *data collection techniques* (discussed in Chapter 13) rather than designs or approaches.

Surveys (questionnaires) and observations are often, and mostly, used in nonexperimental research, but they can be, and sometimes are, used to collect data for experiments.

The Comparative Research Approach

The comparative approach differs from the randomized experimental and quasi-experimental approaches because the investigator *cannot randomly assign participants* to groups and because there is *not an active independent variable*. Figure 4.2 shows that, like randomized experiments and quasi-experiments, comparative designs usually have a few categories of the independent variable and make comparisons between groups. Studies that use the comparative approach examine the *presumed* effect of an *attribute independent variable*. These attributes could be demographic variables such as age, gender, or ethnicity. Or, they could compare a few groups based on personality characteristics (e.g., high versus low trait anxiety), type of disability, or previous experiences such as the type of school (e.g., private, public, charter) that students attended.

Summary of the Three Approaches That Compare Groups

In each of the three previous approaches (i.e., randomized experimental, quasi-experimental, and comparative), a comparison of two or more levels/groups composing the independent variable were compared in terms of the dependent variable. Regardless of whether the independent variable was active or attribute, it had a few levels, usually less than five. For example, in the sample experimental study, the participants either received therapy or did not; thus, these are the two levels of the independent (treatment) variable. Likewise, in a comparative study the participants could be divided into two groups, older or younger, with age being the independent variable. Studies that compare groups can have more than two categories (e.g., two treatments and a control or four age groups). Furthermore, the categories can be ordered (e.g., high, medium, low) or not ordered (e.g., three nominal categories like Protestants, Catholics, and Jews).

The Associational Research Approach

Now, we consider an approach to research where the independent variable is usually continuous or has a number of ordered categories, typically five or more. Suppose that the investigator is interested in the relationship between age and self-concept in children. Assume that the dependent variable is self-concept and the independent variable is age. If the participants were divided into a few age groups such as "young," "middle-aged," and "older" we would still consider the research approach to be comparative. On the other hand, in the typical associational approach the independent variable age, such as actual age in years, is treated as *continuous*. In other words, all participants are in a single group measured on two continuous variables: age and self-concept. Even if there is a strong relationship between these two variables, one cannot conclude that age *causes* high self-concept.

The Basic Descriptive Research Approach

The descriptive approach, discussed in more detail in Chapter 7, is different from the other four approaches in that only one variable is considered at a time so that no comparisons or relationships are made. This lack of comparisons or relationships is what distinguishes the descriptive approach from the other four (Figure 4.2). Of course, the descriptive approach does not meet any of the other criteria such as random assignment of participants to groups.

Most research studies include some descriptive questions (at least to describe the sample). However, it is rare these days for published quantitative research to be purely descriptive; we almost always examine several variables and their relationships. On the other hand, political polls and consumer surveys are sometimes interested only in describing how voters as a whole react to an issue or what products consumers in general will buy. Exploratory studies of a new topic may just describe what people say or feel about that topic. Furthermore, qualitative/constructivist research may be primarily descriptive in this sense.

Summary Diagrams for the Five Approaches

Figure 4.3 includes schematic diagrams illustrating each of the five approaches. These diagrams present the information in Figure 4.2 in a somewhat different way. They also serve as a preview of Table 5.2, in the next chapter, which diagrams the designs for the several different specific randomized experimental and quasi-experimental *designs*.

For explanatory purposes, each of the five approaches is shown in Figure 4.3 as having a very small sample of six participants. In the randomized experimental approach, this sample is divided randomly (R) into experimental (E) or comparison (C) groups, whereas in the quasi-experimental and comparative approaches the sample is divided *nonrandomly* (NR) into groups. In the associational approach, the sample is *not* divided; each participant has a score (S) on the attribute independent variable such as age in years and also a score (O) on the dependent variable. In the basic descriptive approach, the sample is not divided, and there is no independent variable.

The right-hand column for all five approaches shows the dependent variable (O), which is an observation or score. In the three approaches that compare groups and in the descriptive approach, the O's are a summary measure such as the average for the group. For the associational approach, the dependent variable for each participant is a separate measure such as a self-concept score.

Combinations of Research Approaches

It is important to note that *most studies are more complex* than implied by the previously given examples, in part because the approach is based really on the *research question*. Almost all studies have more than one research question and, thus, may use more than one of the given approaches. For example, it is common to find a study with one active independent variable (e.g., type of treatment) and one or more attribute independent variables (e.g., gender). This type of study combines the randomized experimental approach (if the participants were randomly assigned to groups) and the comparative approach. We discuss studies with two (or more) independent variables or factors in later chapters. Many studies include associational, comparative, and descriptive research questions. As mentioned already, most studies also have some descriptive questions so it is common for published studies to use three or even more of the approaches.

Summary

Figure 4.1 and Figure 4.2 summarize most of the key points made in this chapter. Note that the top row of Figure 4.1 lists two general purposes of quantitative research: discovery

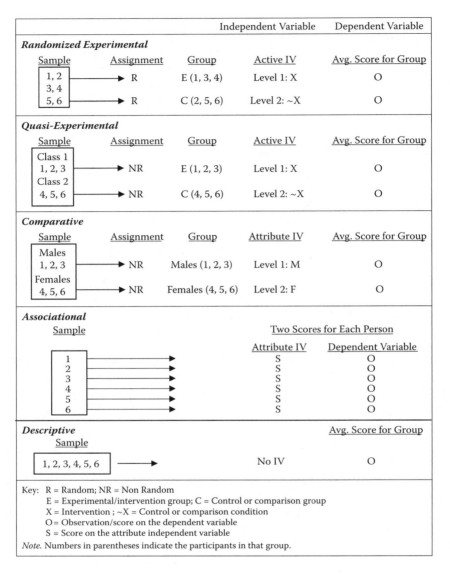

FIGURE 4.3
Schematic diagrams of the five research approaches.

of relationships and description. Remember that Chapter 3 began with a definition of a research problem as a question about the *relationship* between two or more variables. This is the broad sense in which all the approaches, except the descriptive, seek to establish relationships between variables.

In terms of more specific purposes, you can see from Figure 4.2 that the randomized experimental approach is the only one whose purpose is to determine or identify causes; however, quasi-experiments help us examine possible causes. Both the comparative approach and the quasi-experimental and the randomized experimental approaches enable us to compare groups. Thus, all three of the approaches on the left side of Figure 4.1 use difference questions or hypotheses (as discussed in Chapter 3) and inferential statistics

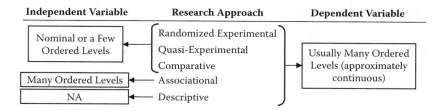

FIGURE 4.4
Most common types of variable for the independent and dependent variables within each of the five research approaches.

that test for differences between groups (e.g., *t* tests, analysis of variance). Note that there is no distinction between the *statistics* used in experiments to determine causes and those used in comparative studies that tell us only that there is a difference between groups, *not about causal* effects.

The specific purpose of the associational approach includes finding associations, relating variables, and also making predictions from the independent or predictor variables to scores on the dependent or criterion variables. Although somewhat of an oversimplification, the associational approach usually uses a different type of hypothesis (associational) and different inferential statistics (correlation and multiple regression) than do the comparative, quasi-experimental, and randomized experimental approaches.

Figure 4.4 provides some of the information in Figure 4.2 in a different way. It brings together the discussion of ordered versus nominal variables from Chapter 3 with the discussion of the five approaches in this chapter. A continous independent variable is a characteristic only of the associational approach. However, as shown in Figure 4.4, typically all the quantitative approaches have dependent variables that are continous or have many ordered levels such as scores varying from very low to very high.

In the next three chapters, we discuss in more detail the various quasi-experimental and randomized experimental designs (Chapter 5), single-subject quasi-experimental designs (Chapter 6), and then nonexperimental (comparative, associational, and descriptive) approaches (Chapter 7).

Key Concepts

Cause or inferring causation
Continuous variable
Normal variable
Research validity

Key Distinctions

Active versus attribute independent variable
Difference versus associational versus descriptive research questions and statistics

Experimental versus nonexperimental research approaches

Random versus nonrandom assignment

Random assignment of participants to groups versus random selection of participants to be included in a study

Randomized experimental versus quasi-experimental versus comparative versus associational versus descriptive approach to research

Relationships between/among variables versus description of a variable

---

Application Problems

1. Listed below are some differences among the five approaches to research. Match the description (A–E) that best fits the type of approach (a–e). Explain.

   a. Experimental   A. Compares groups
   b. Quasi-experimental   B. Asks questions that describe the data
   c. Comparative   C. Examines causality
   d. Associational   D. Associates the many levels of one variable with the
                               many levels of another
   e. Descriptive   E. Randomized assignment, tries to determine causality

   Which research approach best describes the following five scenarios (2–6)? Why?

2. A researcher wants to know if drinking caffeine helps students get better grades on a math exam. He randomly assigns students to two groups—one that he gives caffeine to drink and one he does not. He gives each subject a math exam.

3. A study is done to investigate type of classroom seats and test performance. The subjects are from two English classes at a local high school. One class is assigned to meet in a room with pillows on the floor for seats. The other class is to meet in a traditional classroom.

4. A grade school teacher is interested in whether more males or females use their left hand as their dominant hand. She asks her class of 28 students to write down whether they are right- or left-handed.

5. A study is done to analyze whether a high level of stress (measured on a 0–100 scale) is related to a high level of loneliness (measured on a 0–100 scale).

6. You are interested in comparing the effects of two different types of therapy, music therapy and occupational therapy, on pain perception in people with chronic arthritis.

7. You have two different rehabilitation settings at your disposal. Describe how a randomized experimental design would differ from a quasi-experimental design.

5

Randomized Experimental and Quasi-Experimental Designs

In Chapter 3 we introduced two types of independent variables: active and attribute. We also described how an independent variable has different values, which we called *levels.* In addition, we described the dependent variable as the outcome measure or criterion of the study. How participants become assigned to the levels of the independent variable, in part, determines the type of quantitative research approach, which was the topic of Chapter 4. It is worth going back to Chapter 4 and reviewing Figure 4.1 to examine the relationship between type of independent variable and type of quantitative research approach. The randomized experimental and quasi-experimental approaches have an active independent variable, whereas the comparative and associational approaches have an attribute independent variable.

In this chapter we introduce the concept of research design. We discuss **specific research designs**, which are the designs described in this chapter and summarized in Figure 5.1 at the end of the chapter. These designs describe specific types of randomized experimental and quasi-experimental research approaches. A specific research design helps us visualize the independent variables of the study, the levels within these independent variables, and when measurement of the dependent variable will take place.

Both randomized experimental and quasi-experimental approaches have an active independent variable, with at least one level being some type of intervention or manipulation given to participants in the experimental or intervention group. Usually there is a comparison or control condition/treatment, which is given as another level of the independent variable. There can be more than two levels or groups. Unfortunately, in some poor quasi-experimental designs there is only one level so no comparisons can be made. Before discussing specific designs, we introduce some terminology to help conceptualize each design.

Design Terminology

R = random assignment to the group

NR = nonrandom assignment to the group

O = observation of the dependent variable

X = intervention (one level of the independent variable)

~X = no intervention or the usual intervention (another level of the independent variable)

E: = experimental or intervention group[1]

C: = control or comparison group[2]

M = matching

Quasi-Experimental Designs with Major Limitations

The three quasi-experimental designs discussed in this section all have serious flaws so they are referred to as *preexperimental* designs. Unfortunately, these designs are relatively common, especially in applied research. Sometimes these types of designs are used due to inadequate preplanning of the design leading to unanticipated problems. Other times it isn't feasible to have a comparison group or a pretest.

One-Group Posttest-Only Design

An example of this design, often referred to as the *one-shot design,* would be an evaluation of a new curriculum in a school system. The investigator introduces the curriculum (X) and then decides that it might be useful to determine if it is working. At the end of the semester, the investigator uses some form of measurement (O) to determine the students' response to the new curriculum. The design is shown as follows:

$$NR \quad\quad E: \quad\quad\quad\quad\quad\quad X \quad\quad O$$

This diagram and those that follow indicate a time sequence. First, all participants are assigned to the intervention group; this is, of course, nonrandom. Then the treatment and, finally, a posttest take place. The problem with the design is it does not satisfy even the minimum condition for a research problem, which is investigation of a relationship or comparison. Note that the intervention is not a variable because there is only one level. Does the one-group posttest-only design have any value? If nothing else, it provides pilot (a common term to indicate exploratory) data for a future study. The investigator could compare the results with data from an earlier group or from the same group at an earlier time. However, if this were done, the design would no longer be a one-group posttest-only design.

One-Group Pretest–Posttest Design

The one-group pretest–posttest design can be shown as follows:

		Pretest	Intervention	Posttest
NR	E:	O_1	X	O_2

The operations for this design are that, after all participants are assigned to the experimental group, an observation in the form of a pretest is given. Then the intervention is given, and, finally, a second observation in the form of a posttest is recorded. This design is typical when exploring a new intervention for community-based programs. For example, a community might be interested in increasing safety-based activities such as using bicycle helmets. The intervention (independent variable) might be an advertising campaign designed to demonstrate the positive safety effects of bicycle helmets for bicyclists. The dependent variable could be change in attitude about safety. Since there is no control group, the only comparison would be from the pretest to the posttest.

The problem with the one-group pretest–posttest design is that there is *no comparison with a second group.* Instead, the only comparison in the one-group pretest–posttest design is between the pretest and the posttest within the same group. Because there is no comparison group, it is not possible to conclude that any change from pretest to posttest is due to the intervention and not due to other extraneous variables. See Chapter 8 for discussion of this problem, which is called a threat to internal validity.

Extraneous *environmental events* are a possible threat to internal validity in this design because the lack of a control group prevents the investigator from knowing, for example, whether other activities at the same time as the intervention might be producing the facilitation. *Maturation* is a possible threat to internal validity because the students are getting older and may be better coordinated and stronger at the same time as the intervention. *Carryover effects* are a possible problem in this design because taking the pretest could influence the posttest. In this sample, *equivalence of the groups* would have been a problem if there had been some control-group children who didn't drop out. Even if the intervention group had *initially* (at the pretest) been similar to the control group, the high dropout rate (called *attrition* or experimental mortality by Shadish, Cook, & Campbell, 2002) would likely have meant that the groups who took the posttest had different characteristics.

Improving This Design

In some cases it is impractical or even unethical to have a comparison group that does not receive the treatment. When that happens, several things could be done to improve the design. Sometimes it is possible to make several pretest and posttest assessments as discussed later in this chapter under *single-group time-series designs*. Also, there may be the possibility of using one of the single-subject designs described in Chapter 6.

Another possibility, when it is not practical or ethical to have a group that does not get the planned treatment, is to use the **wait-list comparison-group design**. In this design all participants eventually receive the treatment, but some, preferably a random half, are assigned to a waiting list. They are assessed when they first enter the study and twice more later: once after waiting the same length of time it took for the intervention to be completed and again after receiving the intervention. A diagram of the wait-list comparison-group design can be shown as follows:

Immediate Intervention Group	O_1	X	O_2		
Wait-List Group	O_1	~X	O_2	X	O_3

This design is practical only when the intervention is relatively brief, a few months at most, and when it is ethical and practical to expect potential participants to wait for the opportunity to receive the treatment.

If one *cannot* find an acceptable comparison group for the one-group pretest–posttest design, increasing the number of dependent variables is another option that can help in interpreting the results. One could use a measurement tool that has several domains—for example, scholastic competence, athletic competence, and behavioral conduct. Not all of these measures would be expected to improve due to the intervention. One could *predict* which measures should change due to the intervention and which wouldn't be expected to change. If only the predicted measures changed, then more confidence could be placed in the intervention as being responsible for changes in those measures. The addition of several outcome variables to the one-group pretest–posttest design is sometimes called the *nonequivalent dependent variables design* (Shadish et al., 2002).

Posttest-Only Nonequivalent Groups Design

This design is the third common type of quasi-experimental design with major limitations. It can be diagrammed as follows:

$$NR \quad E: \quad X \quad O$$
$$NR \quad C: \quad {\sim}X \quad O$$

Because there is *no random assignment* to groups and *no pretest*, it is impossible to determine how similar the groups were prior to the treatment. As an example of this type of design, an investigator is interested in a program to reduce falls in the elderly. One group of participants (the intervention group) receives a Tai Chi program known to increase balance in the elderly. Other participants (the comparison group) do not receive the Tai Chi program. At the end of the study, both groups perform on an instrument to measure balance. It is likely that those in the Tai Chi group chose to participate in the program and that those in the second group were participants who did not sign up for the training. We call this problem *assignment bias* because it is the result of nonrandom assignment to groups, not selection or sampling. The problem occurs because participants who chose or volunteered to participate in the intervention group may be different in terms of motivation, health, and many other characteristics from those in the comparison group.

Improving This Design

If at all possible, there should be a pretest of the dependent variable given to both groups. Then the design would be changed to a better, but still weak, *pretest–posttest nonequivalent comparison group design* as discussed in the next section. The problem is that even if the groups were initially (at pretest) the same in terms of balance, they might well differ on other variables such as motivation, current health, and demographics.

A common attempt to improve this design, when a pretest is not possible or wasn't done, is to see if the groups differ on demographic or other available information. Often this checking is done after the fact. Finding no statistically significant group differences on, for example, gender, ethnicity, or social class provides some support that the groups are similar, as was the case in our sample study 2 (Brothen & Wambach, 2004). However, "not significantly different" is not the same as equivalent, and, more importantly, one can never measure all of the possible crucial participant characteristics.

Better Quasi-Experimental Designs

Pretest–Posttest Nonequivalent Comparison Group Designs

The pretest–posttest designs within the quasi-experimental approach are usually referred to as nonequivalent comparison group designs. The procedure is diagrammed as follows:

$$NR \quad E: \quad O_1 \quad X \quad O_2$$
$$NR \quad C: \quad O_1 \quad {\sim}X \quad O_2$$

Notice that there is *not random assignment* of the participants to the two (or more) groups in this design. The sequential operations of the nonequivalent comparison group design are as follows. First, measurements are taken on two different groups prior to an intervention. Then, one group receives the intervention, and the other group does not receive the intervention. At the end of the intervention period, both groups are measured again to determine if there are differences between the two groups.

The design is considered to be *nonequivalent*. Even if the two groups have the same mean score on the pretest, the groups could be different on some important characteristics that have not been measured. These variables may interact with the treatment to cause differences between the two groups that are not due strictly to the intervention. For example, in our balance study in the last section, the groups could well differ on motivation. In addition, one group may not have had the same proportion of males or ethnic minorities as the other group, or the groups may have been different in their level of education or some other important personality characteristic. The researchers cannot know or equate all the possible variables that could affect the outcome or dependent variable.

We have classified the pretest–posttest nonequivalent comparison group design into three *strengths* of quasi-experimental design. They look alike, as shown previously, when diagrammed, but they vary in how the participants got into the groups or conditions and in how much control the investigator has over the independent variable. We now describe examples of strong, medium strength, and weak pretest–posttest quasi-experimental designs. We provide the following example, which will help to distinguish strong, moderate, and weak quasi-experimental approaches from each other *and* from the two most frequently used randomized experimental approaches. Thus, we use this example frequently throughout the rest of the chapter.

The National Science Foundation (NSF) and other federal agencies were interested in increasing the number of teachers in the areas of mathematics and science. It was proposed that if classes at the college level were taught in an inquiry-based manner (student centered and with a focus on understanding), student attitudes and interest about the subject matter would increase, and ultimately more students would consider a career in teaching. In our example we consider college algebra as the subject matter course. The independent variable for our example is type of teaching, with two levels: inquiry-based and traditional. The dependent variable is attitude toward mathematics or a mathematics performance test. The dependent variable would be given at the start and at the end of the semester. In our example there are two college-level algebra classes at the same university.

Strong Pretest–Posttest Quasi-Experimental Designs

In the strong quasi-experimental approach, the students were not randomly assigned to the classes. Perhaps some chose the class based on time of day, whereas others did not give a preference. However, in the strong quasi-experimental approach, the investigator has control over the independent variable and can **randomly assign the treatment** (inquiry based) to one (intact) classroom and the traditional approach to the other. The strength of this quasi-experimental design is that it is quite similar to a random experimental design except that *participants* have not been randomly assigned to groups or conditions. In some intact situations, such as classrooms within a single school, the assignment of students to different classrooms may be almost random (i.e., there was no intentional bias introduced in the assignment); in those cases, the strong quasi-experimental design is almost equivalent to a randomized experimental design.

TABLE 5.1

Issues That Determine the Strength of Quasi-Experimental Designs

Strength of design	Random assignment of *treatments* to intact groups	Participant characteristics likely to be similar
Designs with major limitations		
Very weak	No	No, because no comparison group or no pretest
Pretest–posttest nonequivalent designs		
Weak	No	Not likely, because participants decide which group to join (self-assign to groups)
Moderate	No	Maybe, if participants did not self-assign to groups and no known assignment bias
Strong	Yes	Maybe, if participants did not self-assign to groups and no known assignment bias

Is this study a randomized experiment? There was an active independent variable. The researcher had control over who received the independent variable; he randomly *assigned the treatment* to one class, and the other class did not get the intervention. However, the researcher was not able to randomly assign *participants* to groups so this was not considered a randomized experiment. Not satisfying this condition may or may not be a major problem, depending on how students got into each class. If assignment to classes was unbiased and similar to chance, the study could be considered almost as strong as a randomized experiment. On the other hand, if there was some systematic reason for students being in one class rather than another (e.g., preference for teacher or time of day), then there is a bias in the methodology, and all conclusions must take this bias into consideration.

Table 5.1 summarizes the two issues that determine the strength of a quasi-experimental design: control over the independent variable (indicated by random assignment of *treatments* to intact groups) and equivalence of participant characteristics. Remember there is *no* random assignment to the groups in *any* quasi-experimental design, so the groups are never totally equivalent.

Even if the intact groups vary in important ways, if there are a large enough *number* of available groups (e.g., class sections), random assignment of the treatments to half of the groups is equivalent to random assignment of participants.[3] However, except in some national studies, it is usually not possible to include more than a few classes (or clinics), so it is important that they be similar if the design is to be considered a strong quasi-experiment.

Moderate-Strength Quasi-Experimental Designs

This design involves less control by the investigator over the independent variable, and, as in all quasi-experiments, the participants were not randomly assigned to groups. The moderate-strength quasi-experimental design fits between the weak quasi-experimental design and the strong quasi-experimental design based on how similar the groups were prior to the intervention. In this design, participants do *not* decide (self-assign) which group they will be in based on knowledge of the intervention. That is, they do not volunteer to be in the study because they want to receive that specific treatment, workshop, and so forth. The group they are in is intact before the study due to other factors, which presumably are not related to the intervention. Examples of these factors include students scheduling classes due to availability or people choosing hospitals due to geographical convenience. The critical difference between this version of the design and strong quasi-experiments is that the investigator is not able to *randomly assign the treatment* to certain groups because the investigator takes advantage of a situation where it is known ahead of time that one group (e.g., school or hospital) is scheduled to receive the intervention (or new curriculum) and another group will not receive the intervention.

Returning to our previous example of a study on the effects of inquiry-based learning, suppose that the same two classes were used, with one class receiving the inquiry-based approach and the other class receiving the traditional approach. Thus, the independent variable and dependent variable are the same. However, in the present example (moderate-strength approach) the researcher cannot randomly assign treatments to the classrooms.

Did the study meet the criteria for a randomized experiment? Although there was an active independent variable (teaching approach), the investigator did not randomly assign *participants* to classes. The classes were intact prior to the intervention. Did the investigator have *control over* which class received the intervention? No, in this example, the investigator could not *randomly assign the treatment* to one class and no treatment to a second class. Instead, the classes were selected because the researcher knew that one class was going to receive the inquiry-based approach and the other class was going to receive the traditional approach. This design is not as strong as the previous design because, in this case, the investigator could not randomly assign the intervention. The instructors had already decided which approach they would use.

The relative strength of this design rests on whether students in the class that received the intervention were different from students in the class that did not receive the intervention. If there is no reason to suspect bias relative to the dependent variable, then the design is almost as strong as the strong pretest–posttest quasi-experiment. On the other hand, the design is weaker if there is some reason to believe that there is bias in which group received the treatment or differences, such as previous performance differences or mathematics background.

Weak Quasi-Experimental Designs

This design occurs when one tries to evaluate an intervention where participation is voluntary. It has some of the problems mentioned earlier for the quasi-experiments without a pretest. As in all quasi-experiments, the researcher cannot randomly assign participants to groups. In fact, in this example, participants *choose* whether to get the intervention; that is, they *assign themselves* to the groups. A related problem is that the researcher does not have control over the independent variable and cannot randomly assign the treatment to one of the groups. The participants presumably chose to be in a particular group to receive a particular intervention or treatment.

Again we return to our example on inquiry-based instruction. In the weak quasi-experimental approach, students sign up to be in the inquiry-based class or the traditional class because they know ahead of time that is how the course will be taught. Thus, selection to the class is biased. Because at least one group has volunteered, the researcher cannot randomly assign the inquiry-based approach to one class and the traditional approach to the other class. Therefore, any eventual difference between the class that received the intervention and the class that did not receive the intervention must be tempered by this potential bias.

Time-Series Designs

A second general category of better quasi-experimental designs is called time-series designs. Like all quasi-experimental designs, there *is* no random assignment of *participants* to groups. The two most common types of time-series designs are *single-group time-series designs* and *multiple-group time-series designs* (see Shadish et al., 2002). Within each type of time-series design there are *temporary treatment* and *continuous treatment* designs.

Single-Group Time-Series Designs

The logic behind these designs, and all time-series designs, involves convincing others that a baseline (i.e., several pretests) is *stable* prior to an intervention so that one can conclude that the change in the dependent variable is due to the intervention and not other environmental events. For example, consider the one-group pretest–posttest design, which we discussed as a quasi-experimental design with major limitations.

The one-group pretest–posttest design can be viewed as follows:

		Pretest	Intervention	Posttest
NR	E:	O_1	X	O_2

The problem with this design is that if there is a change from the pretest to the posttest score, it is not known whether the change was due to the intervention or some other event that could have happened at the same time. Now, suppose we add several earlier observations (pretests 1, 2, and 3, every 2 months prior to the study). Suppose also that there was little change observed among pretest 1, pretest 2, and pretest 3 prior to the intervention. But after the intervention, a change was observed in the posttest. This design would be more convincing if even more observations took place prior to the introduction of the independent variable and still no change had occurred. It is common in time-series designs to have multiple measures before and *after* the intervention, but *there must be multiple* (at least three) *pretests to establish a baseline.*

The single-group time-series design with temporary treatment is diagrammed as follows:

$$\text{NR} \qquad \text{E:} \qquad O_1 \, O_2 \, O_3 \, O_4 \, XO_5 \, O_6 \, O_7 \, O_8$$

An example of this single-group time-series design could involve a company that was interested in the effects of a workshop on being a team player. Observations would take place prior to the workshop on some relevant measure, such as cooperative interactions. The workshop is given after four baseline measures, each a week apart, on cooperative interactions. The workshop is a temporary intervention, and observations are recorded immediately after the intervention and at three later times. One would expect that if the workshop was successful, there would be an immediate increase after the intervention relative to the preceding baseline periods, and the effects might or might not be long lasting.

The single-group time-series design with continuous treatment is a variant of the design with temporary treatment. This design is diagrammed as follows:

$$\text{NR} \qquad \text{E:} \qquad O_1 \, O_2 \, O_3 \, O_4 \, XO_5 \, XO_6 \, XO_7 \, XO_8$$

An example of this type of design might be a school implementing a new curriculum. Observations of the old curriculum might take place with standardized reading scores from previous semesters. These same measurements would be examined during the new curriculum intervention. The new curriculum is not a temporary intervention like a workshop but takes place continuously until replaced. This design is especially popular when there are student records with many repeated measures that can be used for observations and when it is not possible or practical to have a control group.

Multiple-Group Time-Series Designs

These time-series designs are similar to the single-group time-series designs but are *stronger* by adding a comparison group that receives the same number of measurements made but does not receive the intervention.

The multiple-group time-series design with temporary treatment is diagrammed as follows:

$$\text{NR} \quad \text{E:} \quad O_1\, O_2\, O_3\, O_4\, XO_5\, O_6\, O_7\, O_8$$
$$\text{NR} \quad \text{C:} \quad O_1\, O_2\, O_3\, O_4\, {\sim}XO_5\, O_6\, O_7\, O_8$$

We provide an example of this type of design by extending our workshop example from the single-group time-series design. Suppose that the company that is trying to promote cooperation through the team player workshop establishes a comparison group by examining cooperative interactions among workers who did not attend the workshop. Or, a more common occurrence would be to examine workers at a similar company (or perhaps another branch) who did not receive the workshop.

The multiple-group time-series design with continuous treatment is the final time-series design that we discuss. This design can be diagrammed as follows:

$$\text{NR} \quad \text{E:} \quad O_1\, O_2\, O_3\, O_4\, XO_5\, XO_6\, XO_7\, XO_8$$
$$\text{NR} \quad \text{C:} \quad O_1\, O_2\, O_3\, O_4\, {\sim}XO_5\, {\sim}XO_6{\sim}X\, O_7\, {\sim}XO_8$$

If we return to our school curriculum example, the single-group time-series design with continuous treatments could be extended to the multiple-group time-series design with multiple treatments by adding a comparison group, perhaps from another school district. This comparison group would receive just the traditional curriculum.

Conclusion

Time-series designs (especially single-group time-series designs) have become important designs in educational settings, where it is often not practical to introduce a control group. The key advantage of such a time-series design, in contrast to the one-group pretest–posttest quasi-experimental design, is the use of repeated observations or records that provide a degree of assurance that changes are not due to other environmental events or maturation. Another type of quasi-experimental time-series design is the single-subject design. However, because of several unique features the single-subject design is discussed in some detail in the next chapter.

Randomized Experimental Designs

In the first part of this chapter, we discussed quasi-experimental designs and some of their weaknesses. Remember that both quasi- and randomized experimental designs have an active independent variable, but in randomized designs the *participants* are randomly assigned to the experimental and control groups. Random assignment of participants to groups should eliminate bias on *all* characteristics *before* the independent variable is introduced. This elimination of bias is one necessary condition for the results to provide convincing evidence that the independent variable caused differences between the groups on the dependent variable. For cause to be demonstrated, other biases in environmental and experience variables occurring during the study also must be eliminated.

For ethical reasons, often it is not possible for the control group to receive no treatment at all, but it may be difficult to decide which type of comparison group is best. For randomized experiments, we label all such options the *control treatment*. A placebo or no treatment at all group is especially problematic in situations where the participants are patients with some sort of problem or illness. It is not ethical for them to receive no treatment at all or a placebo so they usually receive the standard or typical treatment.

Controlling for No-Treatment Effects

Where ethical and possible, the addition of a third (or more) level to experimental studies, where two different interventions are compared, will make the results easier to interpret. For example, a study could compare two types of enrichment programs. Although participants were randomly assigned to groups to produce good internal validity, the results would be hard to interpret if the study did not include a control group that did not receive any enrichment. In that case, the study could only compare which of the programs worked better, but there would be no way to evaluate whether either program was better than no program at all. Had they added a third level or group, which had not received any program, the interpretation would have been improved. Similarly, if you started with a new program and a control/no program group, you would obtain additional information if you added a group with an alternative/or traditional program.

Next, we discuss five specific types of randomized experimental designs. For each we describe and diagram the design and present some of the advantages and disadvantages. The diagrams and discussion are limited to two groups, but remember that more than two groups may be used with any of these designs. There could be more than one type of intervention or more than one type of comparison group. The experimental group receives the intervention, and the "control" groups receive the standard (traditional) treatment, a placebo, or another (comparison) treatment.

Posttest-Only Control-Group Design

The posttest-only control group design is diagrammed as follows:

R   E: X   O
R   C: X   O

The sequential operations of this design are to randomly assign participants to either an intervention or control group (remember that more than two groups may be used with any of the randomized or quasi-experimental designs); then the intervention group receives the intended intervention and the control group receives a different intervention, or no intervention, or the usual treatment/curriculum. If two different interventions are used, this design would be called a *posttest-only comparison group design*. At the end of the intervention period, both groups are measured using some form of instrumentation (dependent variable) relevant to the study.

To demonstrate the posttest-only control group design we return to our investigation of the inquiry-based teaching approach and college algebra. All students who signed up for college algebra were randomly assigned to one of the two classes. Then, one class was randomly assigned to the inquiry-based condition and the other class to the traditional teaching approach. At the end of the 15-week session, both classes were tested on an attitude about mathematics inventory.

The key point for the posttest-only control group design is the random assignment of participants to groups. One can assume that if participants are assigned randomly to either one or the other class, the two classes were essentially equivalent *prior* to the intervention on all relevant variables including demographics and the dependent variable. Therefore, if there are differences on the dependent measure following the intervention, it can be assumed that the differences are due to the intervention and not due to differences in participant characteristics.

Does random assignment of participants to groups always make the groups equivalent? With at least 30 participants in each group or a homogeneous sample of participants, the investigator can be quite confident that random assignment will yield equivalent groups. However, with smaller numbers in the sample, or very heterogeneous participants, less confidence can be placed in random assignment providing equivalent groups. In the latter cases, a different experimental design, the pretest–posttest control group design, is suggested.

Pretest–Posttest Control Group Design

The pretest-posttest control group design is diagrammed as follows:

$$R \quad E: \quad O_1 \quad X \quad O_2$$
$$R \quad C: \quad O_1 \quad {\sim}X \quad O_2$$

The sequential operations of the pretest–posttest control group design are as follows. First, participants are randomly assigned to groups. Then, each group is pretested on the dependent variable. The intervention group then receives the intervention; the control group receives the traditional treatment. Because of the ethical reasons previously mentioned, the control group participants may drop out of the study or not try hard to do well on the posttest. Thus, it is uncommon and usually not desirable for the control group to receive nothing at all, especially if they have some problem or if the time between pretest and posttest is long. After the intervention period, both groups are measured again on the dependent variable (posttest).

The pretest–posttest control group design is the most common randomized experimental design, as in our sample study 1 (Schellenberg, 2004). Any time a treatment is compared with a control group across two time periods, usually pretest and posttest, this is the design that is used. It is randomized experimental because the participants are randomly assigned to groups prior to the initial measurement (pretest) period. The reason for using this design compared with the posttest-only control group design is to check for equivalency of the groups before the intervention. On the other hand, the problem with using a pretest is that it could bias the participants as to what to expect of the study and influence them in some way; that is, there could be *carryover effects*. This is especially likely when the intervention is brief. The investigator must weigh the advantages of giving a pretest—that is, gaining information about the equivalency of groups with the disadvantage of possibly biasing the posttest. In our previous example, the dependent variable was an attitude scale, which could alert students to what might be expected from the intervention. The pretest–posttest control group design would be a better choice if the dependent variable was performance change.

Often, the decision about which type of randomized experimental design to use is made by the sample size. If each group is at least 30 participants after random assignment, the researcher may choose to use the posttest-only control group design, because with that number of participants it is expected that the concept of randomness should work well and the groups would be expected to be equivalent. On the other hand, if each group has only 10 participants and the participants are heterogeneous, then the pretest–posttest control group design is probably best because it is possible that random assignment did not make the groups equivalent and further statistical adjustment (e.g., analysis of covariance) may be necessary.

Solomon Four-Group Design

One method of dealing with the possible effect of the pretest in the randomized experimental approach is to include an intervention and a control group that receive the pretest and an intervention and a control group that do not receive the pretest. This randomized experimental design, called the Solomon four-group design, appears as follows:

$$
\begin{array}{ccccc}
R & E_1: & O_1 & X & O_2 \\
R & E_2: & & X & O_2 \\
R & C_1: & O_1 & {\sim}X & O_2 \\
R & C_2: & & {\sim}X & O_2
\end{array}
$$

The sequential operations of the Solomon four-group design are as follows. First, participants are randomly assigned to one of the four different groups. Then, two of the groups (E_1 and C_1) are measured on the dependent variable (pretest). The other two groups (E_2 and C_2) do not receive a pretest. Then two groups (E_1 and E_2) receive the intervention. One group that receives the intervention was pretested (E_1), and one group that receives the intervention was not pretested (E_2). In addition, two groups do not receive the intervention: one that was pretested (C_1) and one that was not pretested (C_2). Therefore, the Solomon four-group design allows the investigator to test the effects of a pretest in addition to testing the effects of the intervention. However, to determine the effects of the pretest on the posttest, the investigator must double the number of participants, which is not worth the cost and effort in most situations, so this design is rarely used.

Randomized Experimental Design With Matching

The next specific experimental design, which is commonly used, is one where participants are matched on some characteristic prior to the introduction of any of the conditions of the study. The characteristic that is used for the match must be related to the dependent variable; otherwise, matching is a waste of time and results in a loss of power. The sequential operations of the experimental design with matching are as follows. First, the investigator measures all of the participants on some characteristic (variable) that appears to be related to the dependent variable. For example, intelligence or grade point average (GPA) would probably be related to a dependent variable of school achievement. Next, if the independent variable has two levels, the investigator divides all of the participants into pairs of participants based on their scores on the intelligence test. (If there were three levels or groups, the participants would be divided in triads.) The idea is to have pairs that are as close as possible on the variable of intelligence. For example, if there were six participants with IQ scores of 122, 110, 99, 102, 113, and 120, then the three pairs would be 122 with 120, 113 with 110, and 102 with 99. After all pairs are formed, the investigator *randomly assigns* one member of each pair to the intervention group and the other member of the pair to the control group. The key to the randomized experimental design with matching is to make it as if the two participants are identical (at least as far as the characteristics of interest). Therefore, it is as though one participant is receiving both conditions of the study, even though there are actually two different participants in each pair. This design is illustrated as follows:

$$
\begin{array}{llcc}
\text{M R} & \text{E:} & \text{X} & \text{O} \\
\text{M R} & \text{C:} & \sim\text{X} & \text{O}
\end{array}
$$

Within-Subjects Randomized Experimental (or Crossover) Design

In the simplest case, this design has two levels and can be shown as follows:

		Condition 1	Test	Condition 2	Test
R	Order 1	X	O_1	$\sim$X	O_2
R	Order 2	$\sim$X	O_1	X	O_2

The participants are randomly assigned to order 1 (which receives the experimental condition first and then the control condition) or to order 2 (which receives the control condition and then the experimental). The approach is considered randomized experimental if the participants are assigned randomly to order 1 or order 2. If the order for each participant is not determined randomly, the approach is quasi-experimental. This type of design is frequently used in studies in which participants are asked to evaluate diets, exercise, and similar events assumed from previous research *not* to have *carryover effects*. The strength of this design is that participants act as their own control, which reduces error variance. However, this design has problems if there are carryover effects from the experimental condition. Furthermore, one must be extremely cautious with this design when comparing a new treatment with a traditional treatment. The problem, often referred to as *asymmetrical transfer effects*, occurs when the impact of one order (perhaps the traditional treatment before the new treatment) is greater than the impact of the other order (new treatment before the traditional treatment).

Summary

Figure 5.1 is a summary schematic diagram of the main types of experimental designs discussed in this chapter. Many possible variants of these designs are discussed in Shadish et al. (2002). We divide Figure 5.1 into three sections: quasi-experimental designs with major limitations, better quasi-experimental designs, and randomized experimental designs, which are sometimes called true-experimental designs.

Random assignment of participants to groups is what differentiates randomized experiments from quasi-experiments. We have discussed the strengths and weaknesses of each design. Randomized experimental designs provide the best information about whether the independent variable caused changes in the dependent variable. The quasi-experimental designs with major limitations are missing a comparison group, a pretest, or both, so by themselves they provide little support for the effectiveness of the intervention. Quasi-experimental designs, if the experimental and comparison groups are very similar, provide some support for the causal effect of the intervention.

Key Concepts

    Multiple-group time-series designs
    One-group posttest-only design
    One-group pretest–posttest design
    Pretest–posttest randomized experimental control group design
    Pretest–posttest nonequivalent comparison group designs
    Posttest-only randomized experimental control group design
    Posttest-only nonequivalent group design
    Randomized experimental design with matching
    Single-group time-series designs
    Solomon four-group design
    Specific research designs
    Wait-list comparison group design
    Within-subjects randomized experimental (crossover) design

Key Distinctions

    Quasi-experimental versus randomized experimental designs
    Assignment of participants to groups: random assignment versus nonrandom assignment
    Random assignment of *treatments* versus random assignment of *participants*
    Weak versus moderate strength versus strong pretest–posttest (better) quasi-experimental designs

	Assign.	Grp.	Pre.	I.V.	Post.
Quasi-experimental designs with Major Limitations					
One-group posttest-only design	NR	E:		X	O
One-group pretest-posttest design	NR	E:	O	X	O
Posttest-only nonequivalent groups design	NR	E:		X	O
	NR	C:		~X	O
Better Quasi-experimental designs					
Pretest-posttest nonequivalent	NR	E:	O	X	O
comparison-group designs	NR	C:	O	~X	O
Single-group time-series designs					
With temporary treatment	NR	E:	OOO	X	OOO
With continuous treatment	NR	E:	OOO	XOXO	XOXO
Multiple-group time-series designs					
With temporary treatment	NR	E:	OOO	X	OOO
	NR	C:	OOO	~X	OOO
With continuous treatment	NR	E:	OOO	XOXO	XOXO
	NR	C:	OOO	O O	O O
Randomized experimental designs					
Posttest-only control-group design	R	E:		X	O
	R	C:		~X	O
Pretest-posttest control group design	R	E:	O	X	O
	R	C:	O	~X	O
Solomon 4-group design	R	E_1:	O	X	O
	R	E_2:		X	O
	R	C_1:	O	~X	O
	R	C_2:		~X	O
Randomized experimental design with matching	M R	E:		X	O
	M R	C:		~X	O

		Order	Post 1		Post 2
Within-subjects or crossover design	R	E_1	X	O	~X	O
	R	E_2	~X	O	X	O

Notes: Assign. = assignment of participants to groups (NR = nonrandom, R = random, M R = matched then randomly assigned). Grp. = group or condition (E: = experimental, C: = control or comparison). Pre. = pretest (O = an observation or measurement; a blank means there was no pretest for that group). I.V. = active independent variable (X = intervention, ~X = control, comparison or other treatment). Post. = posttest (O = a posttest observation or measure).

FIGURE 5.1
Summary of specific designs for experiments and quasi-experiments.

Application Problems

For each of the three scenarios (1–3), identify:

 a. The independent variables. For each, state whether it is active or attribute.
 b. The dependent variables.
 c. The specific design name (e.g., posttest-only control group design). If the approach is quasi-experimental, evaluate its strength.

 1. You are a researcher in science education who is interested in the role of diagrams in instruction. You wish to investigate whether using diagrams in place of text will facilitate comprehension of the principles and concepts taught. To do so, you have developed a 12th-grade physics unit that incorporates the liberal use of diagrams. You plan to compare student's knowledge of physics before and after the instructional unit. You will teach one of your classes using the diagram unit and the other using the text-only unit.

 2. The purpose of this study was to determine whether type of class could alter attitudes toward persons with disabilities. Two classes at a large university were studied. One class, "Survey of Human Disease," placed emphasis on specific diseases and handicapping conditions. The emphasis was on how these conditions differed from each other. The other class, "Handicapped Individual in Society," placed emphasis on abilities and did not address how handicapping conditions were different for this study. A total of 20 different volunteers from each class served as subjects for this study. At the end of the first semester, all subjects were tested on the Attitude Toward Disabled Persons Scale (ATDP).

 3. A researcher wants to study the effects of social worker support on homeless peoples' job attainment. There are two similar mission sites. A social worker spends a month at one of the sites, but not the other. The people at the sites did not differ in average age, gender, and education. At the end of a year, she collects the following data on the two groups from labor department records for the previous 2 *years*: monthly totals of the number of days of employment.

 4. Explain the rationale for a randomized experimental design with matching.

 5. Health educators administering a large wellness program are interested in whether structured classes or support groups seem to have the greater influence on "healthy" attitudes toward food. Individuals voluntarily sign up for either the classes or the support groups. Their plan is to randomly select 30 participants from the classes and 30 from support groups and (with their permission) to administer an eating attitudes instrument as a pretest and as a posttest to assess change in attitudes over time. One of the health educators expressed the concern that taking the eating attitudes test prior to the course would have an effect on posttest scores because participants will already be familiar with items on the instrument and may attempt to provide the "socially desirable" response. Practice effects would be an issue. What could they do to address this?

6. Describe how a researcher could explore the impact of a new curriculum on attendance:

   a. Using a single group time-series design.

   b. Diagram the design and give the specific design name.

   c. Why is a time-series design stronger than a similar design that is not a time-series design?

7. Subjects are matched in pairs on key attribute variables of test scores and age, and then the children in each matched pair are randomly assigned to one of two groups, one receiving the intervention and one receiving no intervention. What specific type of experimental design is this? Explain.

Randomized experimental with matching

Notes

1. To simplify the examples in this chapter we have described designs with only one intervention group and one control group. However, it is common to have more than two groups.

2. In quasi-experiments, it is better to use the term *comparison group* rather than *control group* because, especially with poor and weak quasi-experiments, there is little that is "controlled." For similar reasons, quasi-experiments are labeled "nonequivalent group designs."

3. These designs, common in epidemiological research, are referred to as *cluster random assignment designs*. The intact units, such as hospitals or schools, are treated as the participants.

6

Single-Subject Designs

In this chapter, we describe **single-subject designs**, a subcategory of quasi-experimental time-series designs that can be used with one or a few participants. These single-subject designs have many of the characteristics that govern traditional time-series designs with groups of participants. They have numerous repeated measures on each participant and the initiation and withdrawal of treatment. Traditionally, the data from single-subject designs had infrequently been analyzed using statistical methods, and when those methods were applied, they were often unique to these designs. Recently, there have been increased efforts to apply statistical analyses to single-subject designs, and some of these analyses have used more traditional statistics. In addition, efforts have been made to combine results from different single-subject studies on a similar topic into a meta-analysis to increase generalizability. The topic of single-subject designs is quite complex and contains too much material to be covered completely in a single chapter. For those interested in a complete treatment of the topic, we suggest the text by Kazdin (1982). For a clinical perspective on single-subject designs, Ottenbacher (1986) and Skinner (2005) are recommended. For excellent reviews of the evaluation of single-subject designs, we recommend Franklin, Gorman, Beasley, and Allison's (1997) treatment of the visual analysis and Gorman and Allison's (1997) treatment of the statistical analysis.

Single-subject designs became prominent in the field of psychology in the 1960s, resulting in two journals: *Journal of the Experimental Analysis of Behavior* and *Journal of Applied Behavior Analysis*. The rationale for single-subject designs is explained as follows. In a traditional study using groups, 10 participants might be assigned to receive the treatment, and 10 participants do not receive the treatment. At the end of a particular time period, a comparison is made between the two groups to determine if the treatment was successful. If the group that receives the treatment performs significantly better than the group that does not receive the treatment, then a judgment is made that the treatment was successful. Note that only one treatment was given one time to 10 participants, and no treatment was given to the other 10 participants. Participants were measured prior to the intervention and after the intervention. Now consider a situation where one participant (or sometimes as many as three or four participants) receives the same treatment 10 times, and, in addition, the treatment is withdrawn over 10 different times to the same participant. Each participant would be measured 20 times. If each time the treatment was given, an increase in the desired behavior occurred and, each time the treatment was withdrawn, the desired behavior failed to occur, one could conclude that the treatment was successful in increasing the desired behavior. Since reliability of research results is what is desired for all disciplines, these early efforts of single-subject designs are admirable.

We describe single-subject designs as time-series designs where an intervention (active independent variable) is given to very few participants, four or fewer. In most situations, the independent variable is initiated and withheld numerous times throughout the study. In some situations, *multiple-baseline* single-subject designs for example, the removal of the independent variable is not necessary for a study to be included as a single-subject design.

Single-subject designs are quasi-experimental designs because they include an active independent variable but there is no random assignment of participants to different treatments.

Single-subject designs should not be confused with *case-study* designs, which fall under qualitative research methods, where descriptions of participants in natural settings are the rule. Case studies often are used to describe an unusual case or to provide more descriptive evidence to support a quantitative study such as a program evaluation.

In this chapter we introduce and provide examples for three types of single-subject designs: (1) *ABAB* or *reversal designs*; (2) *multiple-baseline designs*; and (3) *alternating treatment designs*. We describe each design. Next, we discuss the methods of observation and the length of measurement periods in single-subject designs. Then, we discuss the analyses of these types of designs. Last, we discuss meta-analysis and the generalizability of single-subject designs.

Reversal Designs

Reversal designs, often referred to as *ABAB* designs, are the original single-subject designs and are still the most common type of single-subject design. In these designs, the first *A* stands for the baseline period, where the participant is observed for a number of time periods. The key here is that the participant is observed until the baseline is relatively flat or stable. This is a large departure from traditional group designs, where the amount of time allotted to the experimental and control treatments is decided prior to the study. In single-subject designs, the investigator plots the data for each measurement period on graph paper to determine if the behavior during baseline (or treatment) is increasing, decreasing, or leveling off. The first *B* period refers to the first intervention period. After the baseline has leveled off or stabilized, the investigator initiates the treatment or active independent variable. Again, the investigator plots the data from each session to determine the effect of the treatment.

One should not stop here because there has been only one baseline and one treatment phase (*AB* design). With an *AB* design, it is difficult to know whether it is the treatment or some other variable that is making the difference. Therefore, once the treatment data appear to level off (relatively flat line) the investigator withdraws the treatment, and initiates a second *A* phase. The investigator observes this phase for several periods (three at the minimum) until the behavior levels off. Then the investigator initiates the second *B* or treatment phase. This completes the minimum reversal design, with two *A* or baseline phases and two *B* or treatment phases. It should be noted that having two *A* and two *B* phases does not eliminate all extraneous variables and that the more *A* and *B* phases inserted, the more convincing is the design of the study, similar to any time-series design.

What should happen in a typical *ABAB* single-subject study? Figure 6.1 demonstrates a single-subject *ABAB* design. One would expect that during the initial baseline period (*A*) there may be some fluctuation of responding, but after the first few periods, the participant's responses (dependent variable) should stabilize or level off. During the initial treatment period (*B*), behavior should increase (or decrease if the treatment is designed to reduce an undesirable behavior, e.g., aggression). One would expect this behavior to continue to increase up to a point and then to level off. Next, during the withdrawal of the treatment (second *A* period), the expectation is that performance will decrease (although perhaps not as low as the first *A* period) and then will begin to stabilize. When the stabilization has

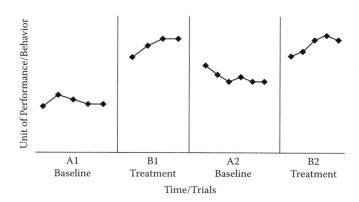

FIGURE 6.1

Hypothetical data for an *ABAB* single-subject quasi-experimental design.

occurred, the reintroduction of the treatment (second *B* period) takes place, and performance should increase above that of all of the preceding phases.

While the previous paragraph spells out the ideal results of an *ABAB* single-subject design, things rarely happen exactly as planned. Perhaps the most common problem involves stabilization of performance for each phase of the study. First, it often takes time to get a stable baseline. How long should the investigator wait until the baseline stabilizes? Usually, the baseline should stabilize within five or six periods. If the performance is still quite irregular (i.e., high one day and low the next), then the investigator should look for external influences to explain why the participant is performing so irregularly. Sometimes, it just takes a little while to habituate to the setting. Other problems that may interfere with stabilization may involve reactivity to the measure of performance. If the measure of performance requires that an observer be present, this may cause reactivity by the participant.

Although stabilization of the initial baseline is a common problem in *ABAB* designs, a second problem is related to treatment withdrawal. Many single-subject designs institute a treatment that has a permanent effect. If this is the case, then in the second baseline (*A*) phase, one would expect that there might be little or no drop in performance. If there is no drop in performance, then the expectation is an increase in performance in the second intervention (*B*) phase to a level substantially higher than that of the first intervention (*B*) phase.

The *ABAB* single-subject reversal design does not necessarily mean that there should be only two baseline phases and two intervention phases. Most *ABAB* designs use at least three *A* and three *B* phases, whereas many use quite a few more. Actually, using only two *A* and two *B* phases is the minimum that could pass for a single-subject study. Additional *A* and *B* phases make the study more convincing, ruling out the influences of extraneous variables. In addition, the investigator is not limited to just the phases of *A* and *B*. Consider a situation where after the initial *A* phase, the investigator initiates a treatment in the *B* phase. However, the treatment fails to increase performance above that observed during the baseline period. If this were a traditional between-groups type of design, the investigator would be stuck with a study that failed to demonstrate a successful intervention. Instead, in a single-subject design, the investigator could modify the treatment and introduce it (*C*) after the *B* phase. Thus, the design might be something like *ABCAC*. It is important to remember that a strength of single-subject designs is their flexibility. Just

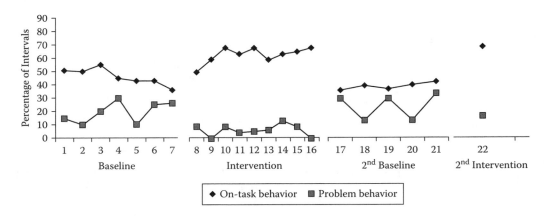

FIGURE 6.2
Results showing the effects of the intervention on problem and on-task behavior.

as the number of sessions making up any particular phase is not predetermined, it is not predetermined that there be only *A* and *B* phases.

An example of a reversal design with two baseline periods and two intervention periods can be seen in Figure 6.2 (data modified from Dunlap, Foster-Johnson, Clarke, Kern, & Childs, 1995), which shows data for one participant who had severe disabilities. The study examined two dependent variables at the same time: on-task behavior and problem behavior. The baseline periods consisted of standard outcomes, whereas the intervention periods consisted of functional outcomes. Notice that during the baseline period, the on-task behavior is somewhat higher than the problem behavior and that both are level for the most part. During the first intervention phase, the on-task behavior increases, and then levels off, whereas the problem behavior is uniformly low. In the second baseline period, the on-task behavior has decreased to that seen near the end of the initial baseline period, and the problem behavior has increased to about that seen in the initial baseline period. During the second intervention, which had only one session, the on-task behavior increased, and the problem behavior decreased below the average of the previous period. We return to Figure 6.2 when we discuss evaluation of single-subject designs.

Multiple-Baseline Designs

Multiple-baseline single-subject designs were introduced more recently than reversal designs. There were two major reasons for the introduction of multiple-baseline designs. First, in clinical situations the removal of treatment often was considered unethical, especially if the treatment appeared successful. Second, many of these studies were being performed when the patient, in one form or another, was responsible for the payment of the treatment. In **multiple-baseline designs**, in the initial stages of the study, as many as three baselines may be recorded simultaneously. These baselines may represent responses of three different *participants*, responses of three different *behaviors* of the same participant, or the responses of the same participant in three different *settings*. The key to multiple-baseline single-subject studies is that the investigator intervenes at a randomly selected time and observes the effect on only one of the baselines while the other two baselines should be unchanged. This type of design eliminates the possibility that some other external event was responsible for altering behavior because it would affect all participants, settings, or behaviors, not just one.

Multiple Baseline Across Subjects Designs

The most common multiple-baseline design is multiple baseline across subjects. Its popularity is partially due to the ease of completing this type of study, especially in a clinical setting. The procedure for carrying out this type of design is as follows. Initially, the investigator selects three (or perhaps four) different participants for the study. All three participants are observed concurrently in a baseline phase, and their responses for each baseline period are plotted on a graph (Figure 6.3). Next, the investigator gives the intervention to one of the participants while continuing to obtain a baseline on the other two participants at the same time. After a given number of periods, the intervention is started with the second participant and continued with the first participant while a baseline is continued for the third participant. Again, after a number of baseline periods, the intervention is started with the third participant and continued with the first two participants.

An example of a multiple-baseline design across subjects can be seen in a study by Bambara and Ager (1992), who examined the frequency of self-directed leisure activities in three adults with moderate developmental disabilities. The intervention was self-scheduling. The study was similar to that shown in Figure 6.3. The first participant, P1, had a baseline of 3 weeks and then received the intervention. Meanwhile, participants P2 and P3 continued to be in the baseline condition. After 3 more weeks, P2 started the intervention while P3 continued the baseline condition. Finally, P3 received the intervention. A potential problem for this design is *contamination* if the second or third participant learns about the intervention from the first participant while he or she is still in their baseline phase. Such contamination could affect participants' behavior.

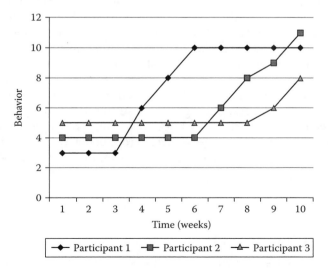

FIGURE 6.3
Hypothetical data for a multiple-baseline across-subjects design.

Multiple Baseline Across Behaviors Design

This second type of multiple-baseline design is less popular than the multiple baseline across subjects design, especially in clinical settings. The procedure for this type of design is that three different behaviors of the same participant are targeted for change by the investigator. Instead of recording baseline data for three different participants as in multiple baseline across subjects designs, baselines for three different behaviors are recorded concurrently. Then, an intervention is started with one of the behaviors while baselines continue to be recorded on the other two behaviors. Next, the second behavior is targeted with an intervention while the first behavior continues with the intervention. Last, the third behavior is targeted with an intervention while the other two behaviors continue to receive the intervention.

For this type of design to be successful, one must assume that the treatments affect each targeted behavior independently. In other words, when one behavior is being treated, it is important that the other behaviors are not affected. On the other hand, if treating one behavior affects the second behavior, then the design will not be successful because all behaviors will change at the same time. For example, in the field of occupational therapy, where most treatments are assumed to be holistic, it is difficult to find behaviors that would be increased or eliminated by treatments that are independent of each other. On the other hand, the prominent use of operant conditioning techniques in the field of special education makes this type of design ideal because specific behaviors can be targeted without affecting other behaviors.

Multiple Baseline Across Settings Design

This type of multiple-baseline design is similar to the multiple baseline across behaviors single-subject design. Usually a single participant is used in the study. However, in multiple baseline *across settings* studies, a single behavior is usually targeted, but in at least three different settings. The procedure for this type of design is that baseline responses are collected on one participant in three different settings. For example, one setting might be the therapist's office or clinic. A second setting might be at the participant's home. The third setting might be at the participant's school. After a number of baseline periods, intervention could begin at the clinic. During this time, baseline responses at school and at home would still be recorded. Next, after a few periods, intervention might start at home. Meanwhile, no intervention would be attempted at school. Last, the intervention at school would be tried. The multiple baseline across settings single-subject design suffers from some of the same problems as the multiple baseline across behaviors design. For the design to be successful, one would expect changes in responding in each setting to be independent of each other. However, realistically, a therapist would hope that treatment would generalize across settings, just as it might be expected to generalize across behaviors. If this is the expectation, then multiple baseline across behaviors and settings are probably not good designs to use.

Alternating Treatment Designs

A third commonly used single-subject design is the alternating-treatment design. The term *multielement design* also is used to describe this design. The purpose of this design is to compare the impact of two different treatments within the single-subject design framework. The procedure for this design is to establish a baseline on each participant and then to introduce the first treatment. Once the responses to this treatment become stable, the first treatment is discontinued and a second treatment is introduced. After response stabilization, the second treatment is discontinued and the first treatment is reinstated. The two treatments continue to be alternated until definitive response patterns to each treatment can be discerned. The more phases for each treatment, the fewer data points are required for each phase (Ottenbacher, 1986). Some studies do not implement a baseline prior to the introduction of the treatment. However, Ottenbacher pointed out that a baseline phase helps to demonstrate the impacts of the treatments.

One method to strengthen the alternating treatment design is to counterbalance the order of the treatments among the different participants. Specifically, after baseline, the first participant would get treatment one and then treatment two, whereas the second participant would get treatment two and then treatment one. The major disadvantage of this design, similar to all within-subject/repeated measures designs, is carryover effects, which is a good reason to counterbalance the order. Once a treatment is discontinued there may be transient or permanent changes to the participant that could influence responses to the second treatment. Therefore, the design is more applicable for demonstrating the impacts of treatments that do not have permanent or lasting effects.

Flexibility and Random Assignment in the Three Designs

Of the three types or categories of single-subject designs already discussed, the reversal design is the most flexible. If one treatment is not working, why not modify the treatment? More important, a carefully performed reversal single-subject design pays close attention to stable baselines. The investigator has the flexibility to wait within a particular phase of the design until the response is stable. Alternating-treatment designs also have considerable flexibility to wait for a stable baseline but suffer from carryover effects. Multiple-baseline designs, on the other hand, have much less flexibility when planned properly. The key to a strong, well-planned multiple-baseline design is deciding ahead of time, through random assignment, which of the three participants, behaviors, or settings will get the intervention first and when the treatment will begin for each participant, behavior, or setting. Random assignment of the schedule of treatment to a particular participant, behavior, or setting means that the intervention must go ahead, even if the baseline is not yet stable, while baselines of other participants, behaviors, or settings might be quite stable. The random assignment to a particular schedule lends credibility to the design, but it reduces flexibility considerably. A further problem with random assignment might be that a particular order of interventions with behaviors or settings might be considered advisable. For example, if one is planning a multiple behavior across settings design using clinic, home, and school, it is doubtful that home or school would be planned as a target setting before the clinic. However, random assignment precludes this from happening.

These strengths and weaknesses of the different types of single-subject designs are based on how much confidence one can have that the intervention (independent variable) caused a change in the dependent variable. Of the three types of single-subject designs previously described, the multiple-baseline category appears to be the most convincing. This is because the random assignment to treatment schedules, if adhered to, rules out many of the influences from extraneous variables. The other two categories of single-subject designs—reversal designs and alternating-treatment designs—also might rule out extraneous variables, but this is contingent upon the number of reversals that occur, especially because the number of reversals is not specified ahead of time.

Measurement and Data Analysis

Measurement Periods and Instruments

The number of measurement periods may change between one phase and another in a reversal design. One should wait until each phase is stable before initiating or withdrawing treatment. This adds to the flexibility of the design. On the other hand, each measurement period (session) must be the same length of time. Responses cannot be recorded on a participant for 1/2 hour one day and 1 hour on the next day. This invalidates the design, because the number of responses per period or session would have no meaning for comparison.

A second measurement issue to consider when performing single-subject designs is that the type of instrument selected could seriously compromise the study. Each session must yield a score or a number of responses. If there are a limited number of responses per session, then the instrument may not be sensitive enough for the study. There are two popular types of measures (dependent variables) used in single-subject designs: paper–pencil tests and behavioral observation.

Paper–Pencil Tests

These types of instruments often are standardized. However, if a decision is made to use a standardized instrument such as a paper-and-pencil test, then the length of the instrument and how often it could be used must be determined so that the participant does not get bored or become unreliable in responding. Typically, paper-and-pencil tests are used only once a week and usually in conjunction with some other measure such as observation.

Behavioral Observation

Observation of the participant's behavior is probably the most common form of measure in single-subject designs. Certain rules should be followed when observation is used.

1. It is best to have the observer be someone different from the teacher, parent, or therapist.
2. It is best to have the observer be as discrete as possible (e.g., passive observer who is another student in the classroom, or an observer watching through a one-way mirror.).
3. The critical responses to be judged should be well defined *prior* to the study.
4. More than one judge should be used to record the responses.
5. Interrater reliability should be carried out among judges prior to the study.

Evaluation of the Results of Single-Subject Designs

The early studies using single-subject designs, especially those performed with rats or pigeons typically had very stable baselines and intervention periods. In addition, the number of baseline and intervention periods far exceeded those that are used in studies with humans, especially clinical studies. For aforementioned reasons, the early single-subject studies did not use statistical analysis to convince the appropriate audience that interventions were successful. Instead, the investigators believed that the graphic displays were convincing.

Visual Analysis of Single-Subject Designs

When visually exploring a single-subject graph, the key is to look for patterns in the data, especially as the phases change from baseline to intervention and back to baseline. Three general criteria are used for visual inspection of single-subject designs. These criteria relate to the (1) *variability of the data* points within a phase; (2) the *gain or loss (level)* from phase to phase; and (3) the *rate of change (slope)* in gain or loss within a phase and between phases.

The criterion of **variability** for visual analysis of single-subject designs refers to the spread of the data points within any particular phase. If one looks within any particular phase, a line could be fit through the points in the phase. The amount of distance the points fall from that line is a good measure of the *variability* within the phase. For example, we can see in Figure 6.4 that the second baseline phase shows a large amount of variability for the *problem* behavior yet very little variability for the on-task behavior because the points are much closer to the dashed line for problem behavior.

Gain or loss from phase to phase is labeled **level,** or *change in level.* As in any of the visual criteria for evaluating single-subject designs, one must be careful how level is defined. Early definitions (Kazdin, 1982) refer to level as the change from the last measurement in a phase to the first measurement in the next phase. This definition of level can be misleading because the first data point (or any single data point) in a phase may not be representative of the whole phase. It appears that what most researchers refer to as level is the mean or average level within a phase. (However, median level also has been used and would be better if there is an extreme score.) Level provides the investigator with an indication of how much of a gain or loss occurred due to the intervention, and change in level between phases can be easily assessed by subtracting the average of the data points between two phases. Figure 6.4 shows the *mean level* of each of the first three phases with the best flat or stable line through the points within each phase.

Unfortunately, it is uncommon for data points to fall along a flat or stable line within each phase. Thus, the assessment of level is often complicated because the best-fit line to the data points may have an increasing or decreasing angle or slope, as shown in Figure 6.5.

Slope or change in slope is the third common criterion used in the visual evaluation of single-subject designs. **Slope** refers to the angle of the data points within a particular

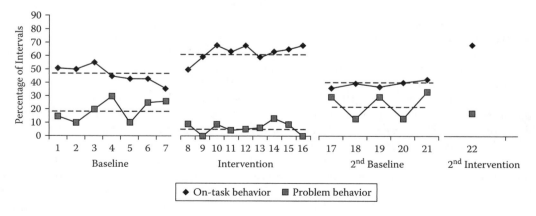

FIGURE 6.4
Mean level within each phase for on-task and problem behaviors.

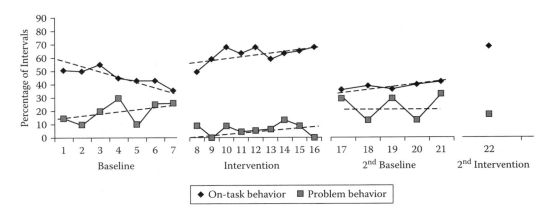

FIGURE 6.5
Best-fit lines for on-task and problem behaviors with each phase.

phase. In other words, if one were to fit a line through the data points in any particular phase, this would describe the slope of that phase. The best-fit dotted lines in Figure 6.5 indicate the slopes for each phase. Slope is an important criterion to consider when visually examining single-subject designs because it is common to have a situation where the baseline phase is increasing or decreasing and the intervention phase also is increasing or decreasing, but at a sharper angle, indicating that the intervention is in fact effective. How the slope is determined is one of the problems in the visual analysis of single-subject designs. Although it is often the case that slope is assessed by visually fitting the line, more acceptable methods might be a line fit through least squares regression (see Chapter 22) or a split-middle procedure using medians. For either of these methods to be successful, a considerable number of data points must be present.

Statistical Analysis of Single-Subject Designs

Single-subject studies with humans, especially reversal designs, usually have fewer baseline and intervention periods than animal studies. In addition, the baseline periods often are shorter and less stable. Perhaps an even greater problem for visual analysis of single-subject designs is *serial dependency* (Parsonson & Baer, 1992). Since single-subject designs are repeated measures or within-subjects designs—that is, the participant gets measured numerous times—a problem arises that each data point is usually not independent from the previous or following data point. In other words, if one knows the value of a particular data point, the value of the next data point could be predicted. It appears that serial dependency may cause inconsistency in agreement on the effect of the intervention in single-subject designs. Considering all of these problems, there has been an increasing emphasis given to using some form of statistical analysis in addition to visual analysis. Therefore, investigators using these designs have resorted to statistical tests to determine if interventions have made a difference.

Kazdin (1982) discussed the use of traditional statistical tests, such as a t test to compare the difference between a baseline and intervention period, or a single-factor analysis of variance to compare all phases of an *ABAB* design. However, he also cautioned that these tests should not be used if serial dependency existed. Kazdin suggested the use of time-series designs when serial dependency problems existed. However, the requirement of at least 20 data points per phase brings these types of analyses for human single-subject designs into question because it is seldom possible to have that many data points. (See McCleary & Welsh, 1992, for a more detailed description of time-series analyses in single-subject designs.) Nonparametric tests such as the Mann-Whitney *U* Test, the Fisher Exact Test, and the Sign Test also have been suggested when the data are not normally distributed (see Chapter 10 for discussion of the normal curve).

Randomization tests also have been suggested for use in analysis of single-subject designs. These tests, because of their inherent simplicity and that they do not require the assumptions of parametric tests such as the *t* test or *F* test, should be appealing to single-subject designs. Levin, Marascuilo, and Hubert (1978) demonstrated the simplicity of this type of procedure for an *ABAB* design. As we stated earlier, in the traditional reversal design with only two baseline phases and two intervention phases, the results that would be expected are as follows. The lowest level of response would be expected in the first baseline phase. The next lowest level of response would be expected in the second baseline phase. The first intervention phase should have a higher level of responding than either of the two baseline phases. The highest level of responding should be the second intervention phase. This could be depicted as $A1 < A2 < B1 < B2$. If one were to hypothesize this outcome and the results did, in fact, occur in this order, then the probability of this occurrence is 1 in 24, or about .05. The idea is that there are four factorial possible outcomes of two *A* phases and two *B* phases, that is, $4 \times 3 \times 2 \times 1$ possibilities, which equal 24. In addition to the predicted outcome there are 23 others, such as $A1 > A2 > A3 > A4$. While this has been a demonstration of a ranking procedure, randomization designs are typically used with the actual data. (See Edgington, 1992, for a more in-depth analysis). Interestingly, randomization statistics applied to single-subject designs apparently have not had the appeal that was expected.

Generalization and Meta-Analysis of Single-Subject Designs

The problems in generalization for single-subject designs are obvious. The random selection of one participant, or even a small number of participants, is unusual because the participants are usually selected because of some particular behavioral or physical problem. What eventually works for one client/participant may not work for another.

To solve some of the external validity problems created by single-subject designs and to increase the scope of knowledge of different intervention areas, attempts have been made to combine the results of single-subject studies performed on a similar topic. To combine studies, an effect size from each study is computed and then averaged among all of the studies. An effect size is typically a numerical value representing the strength of the relationship between the intervention (independent variable) and measure (dependent variable). This averaging of effect sizes across studies results in a meta-analysis, which is described in more detail in Chapter 17. However, for now, it is important to point out some of the major issues when combining single-subject studies for meta-analysis.

The first, and perhaps largest, problem is that there does not appear to be an agreed upon effect size among single-subject studies (Gliner et. al., 2004). For example, three major meta-analyses that have been performed with single-subject studies, Scruggs and Mastropieri (1994), Stage and Quiroz (1997), and Swanson and Sachse-Lee (2000), all used different indexes of effect size. Recent studies describing strengths and weaknesses of different effect sizes have not been conclusive (Campbell, 2004; Parker & Brossart, 2003; Parker et. al., 2005). Of interest, it appears that more than one effect size, such as both change in level and change in slope, may be necessary to effectively describe the effects of an intervention in a single-subject study.

A second issue when combining single-subject studies involves the types of single-subject designs that can be combined; that is, can the results of reversal designs be combined with the results of multiple-baseline designs? Another issue involves combining single-subject studies with group studies. The effect sizes in single-subject studies appear to be larger and unrepresentative of those found in group designs. While combining the results of single-subject designs appears to have problems, the large number of previous studies and the use of sophisticated statistical techniques make this an exciting area for the future of single-subject designs.

Summary

We described single-subject designs as a subcategory of quasi-experimental time-series designs that can be used with very few participants. Using very few participants increases the flexibility of the design and leads to completely different methods of data analysis. These single-subject designs use numerous repeated measures on each participant and the initiation and withdrawal of treatment.

We introduced three major types of single-subject designs—*ABAB* or reversal designs, multiple-baseline designs, and alternating-treatment designs—and provided examples. The *ABAB* design is the most flexible design but often takes longer to carry out and is dependent on stable baselines. Multiple-baseline designs are easier to carry out, but to ensure the strength of the design random assignment to a particular intervention time period must be instituted. This reduces flexibility in multiple-baseline designs.

The methods of measurement for single-subject designs are usually observation and paper-and-pencil tests. We discussed their strengths and weaknesses. Two types of evaluation of single-subject designs are visual analysis and statistical analysis. One must be cautious when interpreting the results from a single-subject design study, especially with respect to generalization.

Key Concepts

Behavioral observations

Level

Multiple-baseline designs

Paper–pencil tests

Reversal designs

Slope

Variability

Key Distinctions

Level versus slope versus variability

Multiple-baseline designs: across subjects versus across behaviors versus across settings

Reversal designs versus multiple-baseline designs

Single-subject designs versus traditional group designs

Application Problems

1. A clinician has been reading about behavioral techniques useful with young children. She has been referred several children (ages 4–5) with biting behaviors and wishes to conduct a single-subject design to test the effectiveness of this new behavioral treatment. How might she do this as a:

   a. Reversal design (*ABAB*)?

   b. Multiple baseline across subjects design?

   c. Alternating-treatment design?

2. A student in teacher X's class has been very disruptive in class. The child's parents report that this behavior also has been seen at home and in the after-school day care center. The school counselor designs an intervention and institutes a multiple baseline across settings design to test the intervention. Teacher X, the parents, and the day care instructor all implement the treatment and serve as observers of the behavior. Discuss the various problems with this design. How might the counselor improve the design to address the problems?

3. Compare and contrast the multiple-baseline designs (across subjects, across behaviors, and across settings). How are extraneous variables ruled out in each of the three designs?

4. A dietician in a wellness clinic returns from a workshop with a new intervention for motivating healthy eating. He wishes to test this intervention against his current intervention for effectiveness. He also wishes to test both interventions for those overweight (and trying to lose) and for those working to maintain their current weight. (He wishes to see which intervention is most effective with which group.)

   a. How might he design this as a single-subject design?

   b. What are some of the issues regarding influences of extraneous variables?

   c. How long should he make his measurement periods?

5. An *ABAB* reversal design is considered to be more flexible than multiple-baseline designs. Why?

6. What are the advantages of selecting a multiple-baseline across-subjects design compared with a reversal design?

7. An investigator performs a multiple baseline across subjects design. He has three participants in the study, labeled A, B, and C. All three participants will receive the

same treatment. After observing the participants for 5 days, the researcher decides to start the treatment with participant B since her baseline was the most stable. After 3 more days, treatment is instigated with participant C since his baseline is more stable than participant A. After 6 more days, treatment is started with participant A. What are the advantages and disadvantages of this method of deciding the order of treatment?

8. You are conducting a study to determine the effects of a specific treatment using a single-subject design. You decide to use a reversal design (*ABAB*). After five sessions, a stable baseline was established (phase A). You introduce your treatment during phase B, and after eight sessions there has been no increase on your measure. You decide to modify your treatment and introduce the new treatment as phase C. After five sessions you notice an increase easily visualized on your graph. What should be your next steps (phases) to rule out the influences of extraneous variables?

9. The following single-subject study is an *ABA* design. Cathy was having a difficult time succeeding at her mail-sorting job. Her job coach decided to try a new cueing system with Cathy, which involved verbal redirects when Cathy's attention would get off her work. For the baseline period, the job coach counted how many letters Cathy could sort in 15 minutes. After eight measurement periods, Cathy had a stable baseline. Her job coach then instituted the verbal redirects and measured Cathy for eight more measurement periods. After this, the job coach stopped the redirects and measured Cathy for the last eight measurement periods. The measures for each section are listed as follows:

A	B	A
50	65	60
60	70	65
35	70	65
45	75	70
50	80	70
45	80	65
50	85	60
50	90	65

a. Graph the measurements.

b. Describe how variability, level, and slope relate to the graph.

c. Form a conclusion about the study.

10. The following single-subject study is an *ABAB* design. Brad is a young man with mental retardation. An occupational therapist (OT) has been assigned to assist Brad in learning his job. He is at risk of losing his job because he is forgetting to do certain tasks on a regular basis. The OT decides to try a self-monitoring checklist with Brad to see if that will help him keep track of his duties. For 2 work weeks the OT monitors Brad's work, counting how many assigned tasks Brad completes without cueing. At the end of 2 weeks, she decides to start Brad with a checklist and to count his task completion After 8 work days, Brad seems to be fairly stable in his work routine. The OT then removes the checklist and monitors Brad for 10 more work days and counts his task completion. After this

period, the OT reinstates the checklist. The measures for each section are listed as follows:

A	B	A	B
11	17	14	19
12	18	13	20
13	16	14	22
11	18	15	21
12	17	13	23
9	18	13	22
10	18	14	21
11	17	13	22
12		12	23
9		13	23

a. Graph the measurements.
b. Describe how variability, level, and slope relate to the graph.
c. Form a conclusion about the study.

7

Nonexperimental Approaches and Designs

These approaches can be differentiated from the experimental approaches because in the nonexperimental approaches, there is no active independent variable (intervention), and the researcher does not manipulate or control the independent variable. Thus, nonexperimental approaches focus on *attribute independent variables*. Recall from Chapter 3 that attribute independent variables are characteristics that the participants bring with them to the study and are not controlled by the researchers.

Three nonexperimental approaches use quantitative methods. In addition, there are qualitative nonexperimental approaches. The *quantitative nonexperimental approaches* or designs are associational, comparative, and descriptive. The *qualitative nonexperimental approaches* or designs consist of phenomenological, grounded theory, ethnographic, case study, and narrative research approaches. Each of these approaches is described in this chapter.

Quantitative Nonexperimental Research Approaches

In this section, each of the three quantitative research approaches is discussed. We also include comparisons of these approaches with the experimental and quasi-experimental approaches discussed in Chapters 4–6.

Contrasting the Approaches

Figure 7.1 contrasts key elements of the *descriptive, associational*, and *comparative* research approaches with the *randomized experimental* and *quasi-experimental* research approaches discussed in Chapter 5.[1] This figure shows that in several ways the associational and comparative approaches are similar; for example, they study attribute independent variables and do not use random assignment, and the investigator does not have control over the independent variables. Because there is no treatment or intervention, we call them **nonexperimental approaches**. Most survey-type research includes comparative and associational as well as descriptive research questions so it is common for one study to use all three of these approaches. None of these approaches provide good evidence that the independent variable is the *cause* of differences in the dependent variable.

Figure 4.1 provided a somewhat different comparison of the approaches showing how they differ in terms of specific purpose, type of research question, hypothesis, and typical type of statistic used. Differences among the three nonexperimental approaches in these respects are discussed in the following sections.

Criteria	Descriptive	Associational	Comparative	Quasi-experimental	Randomized experimental
Random assignment of participants to groups by investigator	No groups	No (only one group)	No	No	Yes
Independent variable is active	No Independent variable	No (attribute)	No (attribute)	Yes	Yes
Independent variable is controlled *by the investigator*	No	No	No	Sometimes	Usually
Number of levels of the Independent variable	No Independent variable	Usually 5 or more ordered levels	Usually 2–4 levels	Usually 2–4 levels	Usually 2–4 levels
Relationships between variables or comparison of groups	No	Yes (relationship)	Yes (comparison)	Yes (comparison)	Yes (comparison)

FIGURE 7.1

A comparison of the five basic quantitative research approaches.

The Basic Descriptive Research Approach

In basic descriptive research questions, only one variable is considered *at a time* so that no statistical comparisons or relationships are made. Of course, descriptive studies almost always include several variables. We restrict the term **descriptive research** to research questions and studies that use only descriptive statistics, such as averages, percentages, histograms, and frequency distributions, which are not tested for statistical significance with inferential statistics.

Also, it is common for the methods section of studies to include some complex descriptive analyses such as cross-tabulation tables to illustrate, for example, how many participants of each gender fall into each of several age groups. Such descriptive tables are not analyzed with inferential statistics. Figure 7.1 shows that this lack of statistical comparisons or relationships is what distinguishes this approach from the other four. Of course, the descriptive approach does not meet any of the other criteria such as random assignment of participants to groups.

Most research studies include some descriptive questions (at least to describe the sample), but few quantitative studies stop there. In fact, it is rare these days for published quantitative research to be purely descriptive. We almost always examine several variables and test their relationships with inferential statistics that enable us to make inferences about the larger population from our sample of participants (see Chapter 16 for an introduction to inferential statistics). However, political polls and consumer surveys are sometimes interested in describing only how voters *as a whole* react to an issue or what products consumers in general will buy. Exploratory studies of a new topic may just describe what people say or feel about that topic. Furthermore, qualitative/constructivist research may be primarily descriptive, providing an in-depth description of a topic or phenomenon. Five qualitative approaches are described briefly later in this chapter.

An example of a descriptive study is the AIDS study by Wolfe et al. (2006), which was introduced briefly in Chapter 1. In identifying this study as a descriptive study, several things were considered. Although the participants were recruited from several clinics, they were considered in this study to be members of a single group, AIDS patients. There is no independent variable such as clinic site or gender used to split the group for further analysis. The dependent variables used to describe the whole group included age, gender, level of education, disclosure, and social effects of having AIDS. Finally, the analyses included only descriptive statistics such as percentages of the entire group on each of these variables. No comparisons or relationships using inferential statistics were used. Thus, this study falls within the scope of the descriptive approach.

The Associational Research Approach

Now, we would like to consider an approach to research where the independent variable is often continuous or has many ordered categories, typically five or more. Suppose that the investigator is interested in the relationship between giftedness and self-concept in children. Assume that the dependent variable is self-concept, and the independent variable is giftedness. If children had been divided into gifted versus not gifted, or high, average, and low gifted groups, which are a few ordered categories, the research approach would be the comparative approach. On the other hand, in the typical **associational approach** the independent variable, giftedness, would be *continuous* or have at least five ordered levels. In other words, all participants would be in a single group measured on two continuous variables: giftedness and self-concept. A *correlation coefficient* could be performed to determine the *strength* of the relationship between the two variables (see Chapter 10 and 21). Even a very strong relationship between these variables does not justify the conclusion that high giftedness causes high self-concept. Although correlation is the typical statistic, it is not the only statistic used so it is better to have a more generally applicable label (i.e., associational). We discuss the complex (more than one independent variable) associational approach and some statistics used with it in some detail later in the text. However, we want to mention here that *multiple regression* is a common complex associational statistic that is used when the question is whether some combination of several independent variables predicts the dependent variables better than any one predictor alone. For example, multiple regression is used by schools and companies to determine the best combination of entrance or application factors, such as test scores, grades, and recommendations, to predict success in college or on the job.

It is arbitrary whether a study is considered to be comparative or associational. For example, a continuous variable such as age can always be divided into a small number of levels such as young and old. However, we make this distinction for two reasons. First it is unwise to divide a variable that potentially has many *ordered* levels into just a few because information is lost. For example, if the cut point for "old age" was 65, persons 66 and 96 would be lumped together, as would persons 21 and 64, and persons 64 and 65 would be in different age groups. Yet persons aged 64 and 65 are likely to be similar, and persons 21 and 64 are likely to be different. Second, different types of statistics are *usually*, but not always, used with the two approaches.

An example of a study from the associational approach can be found in Zamboanga, Padilla-Walker, Hardy, Thompson, and Wang (2007). In this study the researchers were attempting to predict student performance based on a number of attribute independent variables. The predictors (i.e., independent variables) are attributes, because they all are variables that the researcher did not control, including year in school, attendance, ACT scores, and prior grade point average (GPA). The most striking aspect of the Zamboanga et al. study that identifies it as using the associational approach is the number of levels of the independent variables. Almost all of these variables have five or more ordered levels. The dependent variables were total examination performance, lecture-based questions exam score, and text-based questions exam score. The participants, students in an undergraduate course, were analyzed as one group.

The Zamboanga et al. (2007) study is a complex associational study because there were multiple independent and dependent variables. However, one can see from each pair of independent and dependent variables (e.g., ACT scores and total examination performance) that the approach is associational because the independent variable, ACT, and the dependent variable, total examination performance, have many ordered levels.

The Comparative Research Approach

The comparative approach differs from the randomized experimental and quasi-experimental approaches because the investigator *cannot randomly assign participants* to groups and because there is *not an active independent variable*. Figure 7.1 shows that, like randomized experiments and quasi-experiments, comparative designs usually have a few categories of the independent variable and make comparisons between groups. Studies that use the comparative approach examine the *presumed* effect of an *attribute independent variable*.

An example of the comparative approach is a study that compared two groups of children on a series of performance tests. One group of children with cerebral palsy was compared with a second group of children who did not have such motor problems. Notice that the independent variable in this study was an attribute independent variable with two levels: with motor problems and without motor problems. It is not possible for the investigator to randomly assign participants to groups or to *give* participants the independent variable. Thus, the independent variable was not active. However, the independent variable did have only a few levels or categories, and a statistical comparison between the two groups could be made.

Note that comparative studies do not meet the criteria for attributing causality because it is impossible to control for all the other variables that are extraneous to the study. For example, we might compare the achievement of 10-year-old children who had *previously* attended Head Start with others who had not. These two groups of children might differ in many ways (e.g., education, ethnic group, economic status) in addition to achievement. A good comparative study would try to control for some of these by matching or some other technique, but we could never be certain that the groups were equivalent in all respects as we could be if random assignment to groups were possible. Thus, we should not state in our conclusions that this experience *caused* any differences in performance that were found. If the results are statistically significant, we would be able to say that there were significant differences between the children who had experienced Head Start and those who didn't, but we should not conclude that Head Start caused the difference. Note that the design in this example is sometimes called *ex post facto* because the effect of the independent variable, Head Start experience or not, was studied later, "after the fact."

The study by DiLorenzo, Halper, and Picone (2004) also used the comparative approach. The participants were split into two age groups: those who were 60 years of age or older and those who were under 60 years of age. Of course, the researcher could not randomly assign participants to be older or younger. The independent variable, age group (either >60 or <60 years old) is a preexisting attribute and is not controlled by the researcher. The independent variable had only a few levels—in this case two—that were compared. The dependent variables are the physical health, sexual satisfaction, social support, mood disturbance, depression, and activities of daily living, all assessed from a clinical telephone interview. Thus, this study was used to help answer a research question about the differences between younger and older persons with multiple sclerosis (MS).

You might ask, "Why conduct a comparative study if we cannot make conclusions about what caused what?" In part the answer is that if you are interested in attribute independent variables, you have no other choice than a nonexperimental (comparative or associational) approach. Attributes, in general, cannot be given or manipulated in a study. Some attributes, such as self-confidence or anxiety, do vary from time to time, or situation to situation, so they could be active or manipulated variables. However, in recent years it is usually considered unethical to do so. Thus, with some exceptions, we must use the comparative approach if we want to study an attribute of participants.

Studies With More Than Two Levels of the Independent Variable

In the comparative approach (as well as in the randomized experimental and quasi-experimental approaches), it is often desirable to have more than two groups (i.e., more than two levels of the independent variable). An example from the *comparative* approach would be a study that compared three groups: 1st-, 3rd-, and 5th-grade students, on some aspect of cognitive development. Again, this study does not meet the requirements for a randomized experimental or quasi-experimental study because the independent variable is an attribute of the students and was not manipulated. Note that the independent variable (grade in school) in this case has three ordered levels.[2]

It is also possible to compare a relatively large number of groups/levels (e.g., 5 or even 10) if one has enough participants so that the group sizes are adequate (e.g., 20 or more in each). However, having more than four groups is atypical except when the independent variable is *nominal* (unordered). If there are five or more *ordered* levels of the independent variable we recommend the associational approach that was discussed in the previous section.

Determining the Complete Relationship

A reason for having more than two levels to a single attribute independent variable is to determine more precisely a relationship between the independent and dependent variables. An example involves the relationship between task difficulty and mastery motivation. Mastery motivation, the dependent measure, was defined as persistence at a task. Task difficulty was the independent variable. If the study had used only very easy and very difficult tasks, the investigators might have found no difference in persistence as shown in the following graph:

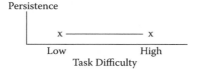

It would appear that task difficulty did not affect persistence, or that there was no relationship between task difficulty and persistence. Now consider the relationship when another level (medium difficulty) was added to the independent variable. A more complete relationship is described in the following graph:

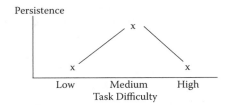

Notice that adding the third level indicates that there is an inverted U relationship between difficulty and persistence. Persistence increases as difficulty increases, up to a point, but then is lower as difficulty gets high. Had the medium difficulty condition not been included, the actual relationship between task difficulty and persistence would have been missed.

Although it is often considered desirable to add a third or more level to a single independent variable that does not change the general design classification. A study that has two levels is a **single-factor** (one independent variable) design with two levels. If we add a third (or more) level, it would still be a single-factor design; there are just more levels or groups to compare.

Conceptual Diagram of the Three Quantitative Nonexperimental Approaches

Figure 7.2 is a schematic diagram of the procedure used for each of the three nonexperimental approaches. This figure shows how in the comparative approach a small sample of six participants might be divided nonrandomly into groups. In the associational and

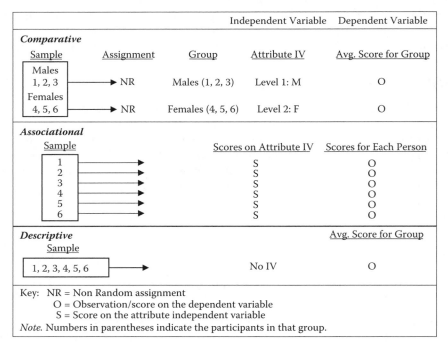

FIGURE 7.2
Schematic diagrams of the three nonexperimental research approaches.

descriptive approaches, all the participants are in a single group. Note that the descriptive approach does not have an independent variable.

An Expanded View of the Five Quantitative Approaches

Most published studies are more complex than illustrated in Figure 4.3 and Figure 7.2. We previously discussed the reasons for having more than two levels or groups in a comparative (or experimental) study. Published studies also often have more than one independent variable and frequently use more than one of the five approaches.

Basic and Complex Research Questions

Remember that the approaches are based on the **research questions** that are asked in a given study. Difference research questions are used in the randomized experimental, quasi-experimental, and comparative approaches. Associational research questions are found in studies that use the associational approach. We further delineate difference and associational research questions into basic and complex questions. Basic research questions are used in studies with one independent variable, whereas complex research questions are answered in studies using two or more independent variables.

Table 7.1 presents the six types of research questions and the number of variables considered with each. This table expands the overview of research questions presented in Chapter 3 to include both basic and complex questions of each of the three types: *descriptive, difference,*

TABLE 7.1

Summary of Types of Research Questions

Type of research question
1. **Basic descriptive questions:** one variable.
2. **Complex descriptive questions**: two or more variables, but no use of inferential statistics.
3. **Basic/single-factor difference questions:** one independent and one dependent variable. Independent variable usually has a few levels (ordered or not).
4. **Complex/multifactor difference questions:** three or more variables. Usually two or a few independent variables and one or more dependent variables considered one at a time.
5. **Basic associational questions:** one independent variable and one dependent variable. Usually at least five *ordered* levels for both variables. Often they are continuous.
6. **Complex/multivariate associational questions:** two or more independent variables and one dependent variable. Usually five or more ordered levels for all variables, but some or all can be dichotomous variables.

and *associational.* Note that Appendix D presents examples of each of these six types of research questions and the statistics that are typically used with each type of question.

Combinations of Research Approaches

Most studies have more than one hypothesis or research question and may use more than one of the research approaches. It is common to find a study with one active independent variable (e.g., treatment) and one or more attribute independent variables (e.g., gender). This type of study combines the comparative approach with the randomized experimental approach (if the participants were randomly assigned to groups) or with the quasi-experimental approach (if there was nonrandom assignment.) Most "survey" research studies include both the associational and comparative research questions, and most, using any of the other four approaches, also have some descriptive questions, at least to describe the sample. Thus, it is common for published studies to use a combination of three or even more of the approaches.

Qualitative Nonexperimental Research Approaches

There are numerous qualitative approaches to research: The number depends on which author you consider. For example, Tesch (1990) outlined 28, Miller and Crabtree (1992) delineated 18, and Denzin and Lincoln (1994) specified nine approaches. Fortunately, Creswell (2007) simplifies this by describing five main qualitative approaches based on common types of research conducted in the behavioral, social, and health science arenas: (1) phenomenological; (2) grounded theory; (3) ethnographic; (4) case study; and (5) narrative. Each of these five qualitative approaches is discussed, and an example of a study illustrating each type of approach is presented.

All of these qualitative approaches are considered nonexperimental because it would be uncommon for them to have an active independent variable (i.e., intervention) and rare for random assignment to be used. The use of inferential statistics with a qualitative approach also would be rare, but some types of descriptive statistics such as tables and percentages might be presented.

Although qualitative approaches are outside the scope of this book, they are described here so that the reader can put them in perspective. In addition, a *pragmatic approach* to research would lead a researcher to use whatever techniques seemed most useful to address the research problem of interest. Unfortunately for researchers wanting to use methods from both qualitative and quantitative approaches, qualitative/constructionist researchers have developed different terminology so it is hard to apply the vocabulary described in most of this book to these approaches.

The qualitative approaches discussed in this section are most similar to the descriptive approach already described, but the descriptions in these approaches would likely be in verbal rather than numerical form and would be presumed to provide a richer and more nuanced description of the phenomenon. Some comparisons between groups or associations among variables might be made, but it is unlikely that they would be done using inferential statistics. However, similar data collection techniques, such as interviews and observations, could be used in these qualitative approaches and in the quantitative approaches. Chapter 13 discusses this overlap.

The Phenomenological Research Approach

The **phenomenological approach** helps researchers to understand the meaning participants place onto, for example, events, phenomenon, and activities. This approach answers questions that begin with "how" and "why." Mainly, through interviews—although documents and observations sometimes are used—information is gleaned from participants. The goal of studies conducted through the phenomenological approach is to be able to explain the essence of experiences lived by the participants.

An example of a study that could be conducted from the phenomenological research approach is how teachers in an urban middle school feel about the new administration. The researcher plans to interview the teachers in the school, hopefully to better understand and describe their perceptions.

The Grounded Theory Research Approach

The **grounded theory approach** was developed by Glaser, Strauss, and Corbin (Corbin & Strauss, 2008; Glaser, 1978; Glaser & Strauss, 1967; Strauss, 1987). The goal of the grounded theory approach is to generate theory from data collected from participants. A common focusing question used in grounded theory studies is, "What is the theory that can be induced from the data?" Studies accomplished with the grounded theory approach focus on the process, actions, or interactions experienced by 20–60 participants. Interviews are the primary means of collecting data.

Using grounded theory, a researcher would first identify the research problem, for example, why do clients chose a specific provider? Next, because the goal of grounded theory is to generate a theory, it is important for the researcher to assess through a literature review if a theory already exists. The researcher would then interview clients to ascertain their thought process regarding choosing a provider. From analysis of the data, the researcher would hope to identify a theory to answer the research problem.

The Ethnographic Research Approach

Ethnography is a research approach which evolved from anthropology and sociology. Studies conducted through the **ethnographic approach** describe a group of individuals who share the same culture. A common focusing question in studies done with the ethnographic approach is, "What is the culture of this group of people?" To collect data, researchers immerse themselves in the culture, using observations, interviews, and documents to understand the culture.

Most commonly, ethnographies are conducted with cultures different than the researchers. Qualitative researchers do not agree on a definition of *culture*. In our opinion, as long as the researcher can define the culture under study, the study can be considered an ethnography. For example, a researcher may be interested in the gang culture in a large city. The researcher identifies a gang, observes and interviews the members, and then analyzes the data. It is common for ethnographies to take a considerable amount of time as there can be many facets to a given culture. The hope is that the researcher will be able to better understand the culture of the participants.

The Case-Study Research Approach

Yin (2008) is the father of the qualitative case-study research approach. Some (e.g., Stake, 2005) believe case studies are not a methodology but a description of what will be studied.

Others, such as Creswell (2007) and Yin believe case studies are a methodology. The goal of the **case-study approach** is to develop deep understanding of a case or cases. *Cases* are defined by the researcher but must be bounded by time, place, or context. Multiple types of data are necessary when using the case-study approach: documents, archival records, interviews, direct observations, participant observations, and physical artifacts. Case studies can be explanatory, exploratory, or descriptive.

For example, a researcher may be interested in office politics at a specific office. First the researcher would need to identify the "case." In this example the researcher might choose, as boundaries for the case, the supervisor and all his or her supervisees. Thus, the participants would be all the employees under a specific supervisor. Next, the researcher would need to collect as much data as possible to understand the case. This means that everything within the case can be considered as opportunities for data, including interviews and focus groups, paper work (i.e., documents), observations *of* participants and observations made *by* the participants, and physical artifacts (e.g., worn spaces on the carpet identifying walking patterns throughout the office).

The Narrative Research Approach

According to Creswell (2007) the **narrative research approach** explores the life of an individual. Yet some studies conducted with the narrative research approach explore multiple people with shared experiences. Most commonly, with the narrative research approach interviews and documents are the means of data collection. The goal of this approach is to identify and report stories from the participants.

An example of narrative research would be a researcher who is interested in learning more about someone who is running for president of the United States. In this situation, the researcher would request participation from the candidate and then would interview the candidate, as well as analyze pertinent documents. The goal of this research would be to tell a story that reflects the candidate's perceptions, thoughts, and experiences.

Summary

Figure 7.1 and Figure 7.2 summarize the key points made in the quantitative section of this chapter. Note that there are two general purposes of quantitative research: discovery of relationships and description. Remember that Chapter 2 began with a definition of a research problem as a question about the relationship between two or more variables. This is the broad sense in which all the approaches, except the descriptive, seek to establish relationships between variables.

Both the comparative approach and the quasi-experimental and the randomized experimental approaches enable us to compare groups. In terms of more *specific purposes,* the randomized experimental approach is the only one whose purpose is to determine or identify causes; however, quasi-experiments help us examine possible causes. Thus, all three of these approaches use difference hypotheses (as discussed in Chapter 3) and inferential statistics that test for differences between groups (e.g., *t* tests and analysis of variance).

Note that there is no distinction between the *statistics* used in experiments to determine causes and those used in comparative studies that tell us only that there is a difference between groups.

The specific purpose of the associational approach includes finding associations, relating variables, and also making predictions from the independent/predictor variables to scores on the dependent/criterion variables. Although somewhat of an oversimplification, the associational approach uses a different type of hypothesis (associational) than the comparative, quasi-experimental, and randomized experimental approaches.

The five qualitative approaches have substantive differences. The phenomenological research approach focuses not on the life of an individual but on understanding a concept or phenomenon. The grounded theory approach leads to the development of substantive theory. The ethnographic research approach leads to a portrait of a cultural group or people, that is, the recording of human behavior in cultural terms. The case-study approach involves the in-depth study of a case with clear boundaries (i.e., context- or time-bound case). And finally, the narrative approach focuses on the life of individuals. There are some similarities among the five qualitative research approaches. All five approaches focus on understanding participants and their perceptions. Furthermore, all five of the qualitative approaches often use interviews as a means of data collection. Chapter 13 discusses interviews and other data collection techniques, pointing out that they can be used by both qualitative and quantitative researchers.

Key Concepts

Basic or single-factor quantitative approaches

Case-study qualitative approach

Ethnographic qualitative approach

Grounded theory qualitative approach

Narrative qualitative approach

Phenomenological qualitative approach

Research questions

Key Distinctions

Active versus attribute independent variable

Difference versus associational versus descriptive research questions

Experimental versus nonexperimental research approaches

Comparative versus associational versus descriptive approach to research

Relationships between or among variables versus description of a variable

Application Problems

1. Describe each of the following and provide an *original* example of each:
   a. Descriptive research approach.
   b. Comparative research approach.
   c. Associational research approach.
2. Compare and contrast experimental versus nonexperimental approaches.
3. What do we mean by qualitative nonexperimental research approaches?
4. Can a researcher combine approaches? Explain your answer. Give an original example to illustrate.

Choose which quantitative research approach best describes the following three scenarios. Describe why. Also identify the independent and dependent variable.

5. A grade school teacher is interested in whether more males or females use their left hand as their dominant hand. She asks her class of 28 students to write down whether they are right- or left-handed. *descriptive*
6. A study is done to analyze whether a high level of stress (measured on a 0–100 scale) is related to a high level of loneliness (measured on a 0–100 scale). *Assoc.*
7. You are interested in the relationship between regions of the United States (Northeast, Southeast, Midwest, Rocky Mountain West, and the West Coast) and body mass index. *Comparative*

Notes

1. Figure 7.1 is the same as Figure 4.2, except the nonexperimental approaches are placed on the left of the figure in the order they are discussed in this chapter. It is repeated here because it is important for understanding the three nonexperimental approaches. The nonexperimental approaches are placed on the left of the figure in the order they are discussed in this chapter.
2. This type of study is called *cross-sectional*, versus *longitudinal*, because different children are assessed at each age. If children had been followed from 1st grade through 5th grade the study would be a longitudinal one.

8

Internal Validity

One of the main objectives of this book is to help students evaluate the quality or merit of a study. **Validity** is the general term most often used by researchers to judge quality or merit. The term validity is used in several somewhat different ways so we have used modifiers to indicate what aspect of validity is being discussed and to help keep the several aspects clear. Four uses of the term validity are shown in Figure 8.1. Notice that research validity is the broadest term and is based on the other three. This chapter discusses *causation* and *internal validity*, which are dependent in good part on the type of approach and design, as discussed in Chapter 4 through Chapter 7. Remember that randomized experiments are the most likely to provide evidence that the independent variable caused changes in the dependent variable.

Before examining internal validity in depth, we discuss the criteria for inferring that one variable caused another to change. Then, we note that the evaluation of internal validity has two major dimensions: (1) equivalence of the groups on participant characteristics; and (2) control of extraneous experiences and environment variables. Next, we describe how to evaluate the internal validity of a study on these two dimensions. Finally, we discuss the traditional "threats" to internal validity and how each of them fits into the two major dimensions.

Identifying Causal Relationships

A major goal of scientific research is to be able to identify a causal relationship between variables. However, there is considerable disagreement among scholars as to what is necessary to prove that a causal relationship exists. Most scientists subscribe to a probabilistic statement about the causal relationship between two variables. Researchers note that even if they cannot identify *all* the causes or the most important causal factor of an outcome, they can identify a particular variable as one (or a partial) cause, when the approach was a well-controlled randomized experiment.

Three criteria for causality are necessary for postulating that an independent variable caused a change in a dependent variable. First, the independent variable *must precede* the dependent variable. Second, the independent variable *must be related* to the dependent variable. And third, there must be no other variables that could explain why the independent variable is related to the dependent variable.

Let's reexamine the sample studies initially described in Chapter 1 to see if they met these three criteria. In the randomized experiment (Schellenberg, 2004), the sequence of the study was, *first*, the random assignment of participants to one of four groups; there were two music treatments (keyboard or voice lessons), a drama lessons group, and a control (no lessons) group. *Next*, the treatment, type of lesson, was given, and, *finally*, the dependent

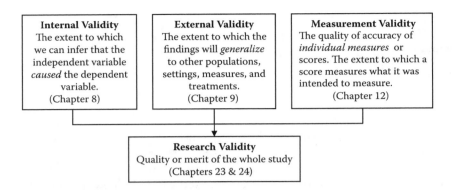

FIGURE 8.1
Four uses of the term *validity* and where they are discussed.

variables, IQ and achievement, were measured. Thus, the independent variable (type of lesson) did precede the dependent variable, satisfying this first criterion. Was there a relationship between the independent variable and the dependent variable? The results showed a statistically significant improvement in IQ among the groups at the end of the study. Therefore, the researcher satisfied the second criterion for stating that the independent variable was a cause of the change in a dependent variable. Were extraneous variables ruled out? The researcher *randomly assigned* participants to the four groups so the groups were *presumed* to be equal prior to the introduction of the intervention, and the groups were treated identically during the study except for whether they were given the music lessons. If there was a change in the dependent variable for the groups that received the music lessons and no change for the groups that did not receive the music lessons, it would be difficult to postulate that some other variable was responsible for any change in the dependent variable. Thus, all three criteria for identifying a casual relationship were satisfied.

In purely descriptive studies there is no independent variable and no attempt to find relationships (casual or otherwise) between variables so the issue of casual relationships is not relevant. The quasi-experimental, comparative, and associational approaches all attempt to identify relationships between variables. In published studies, these three approaches usually satisfy the second criterion; the independent variable is related to the dependent variables. The first criterion, the independent variable precedes the dependent variable, also is often met, especially in quasi-experiments. However, when the approach is comparative or associational the sequential order may not be clear. In Chapter 7 we used the example of studying the relationship between giftedness and self-concept; it would be difficult, if not impossible, to know whether children's high self-concept preceded or followed their being gifted. Likewise, in a study of the relationship between the extent of a parental practice, such as spanking, and amount of child aggression, we usually assume that parent behavior preceded and caused the child's behavior, but the reverse is possible and there may be reciprocal effects. The third criterion for causation, ruling out *other* possible explanations, is never possible in the comparative and associational approaches and is problematic in all but the strongest quasi-experiments. However, some things can be done to control for extraneous variables.

In this chapter we show that the degree to which a study meets the three conditions for inferring causation is based on the strength of the design and internal validity. In the next section we define internal validity, discuss how it is related to the issue of causation, and describe how to evaluate it.

Evaluating Internal Validity

What Is Internal Validity?

Cook and Campbell (1979) defined **internal validity** as "the approximate validity with which we can infer that a relationship is causal" (p. 37). Internal validity depends on the strength or soundness of the design and influences whether one can conclude that the independent variable or intervention *caused* the dependent variable to change. Although internal validity is often discussed with respect to randomized and quasi-experiments, we think the concept also applies to research with attribute independent variables (i.e., to nonexperimental studies).

We group issues relevant to the evaluation of internal validity into two main types: (1) equivalence of the groups on participant characteristics (e.g., equivalence of the intervention and comparison groups *prior to the intervention*); and (2) control of extraneous experience and environmental variables. In this section, we discuss these two aspects of internal validity and how to evaluate them.

Equivalence of Groups on Participant Characteristics

In research that compares differences among groups, a key question is whether the *groups* that are compared are *equivalent in all respects* prior to the introduction of the independent variable or variables. Using the randomized experimental approach, equivalence is approximated through random assignment of participants to groups, if there are at least 30 in each group. Random assignment, which is characteristic of randomized experiments but not quasi-experiments, is the best way to ensure equivalent, or at least unbiased, groups. However, in quasi-experimental, comparative, associational and descriptive research, random assignment of participants to groups has not or cannot be done.

Equivalence of Groups in Quasi-Experiments

Methods such as random assignment of *treatments* to similar intact groups, matching, or checking for pretest similarity of groups after the study are attempts to make the groups similar. Even if one or more of these methods to achieve group equivalence is done, total equivalence can *never* be achieved unless there was random assignment of participants to groups. That is why the specific quasi-experimental designs described in Chapter 5 are labeled *nonequivalent groups designs*. (Even in randomized experiments there may be some pretest differences, but they will be due to chance, not bias.)

Equivalence of Groups in Comparative Studies

Groups based on attributes (e.g., age, gender, diagnostic category, and giftedness) are seldom close to equivalent on *other* participant characteristics. For example, older persons are more likely to have physical ailments, slower reaction times, and more varied experiences than younger persons. These other uncontrolled characteristics lead to problems in internal validity. Several techniques can be used to make the groups more similar, at least on some key variables, but they never produce equivalence on all important variables.

DiLorenzo, Halper, and Picone (2004), in our sample comparative study, used analysis of covariance (ANCOVA), a statistical technique used to adjust the dependent variable scores so that the groups would be more nearly equivalent. In the DiLorenzo et al. study, they used duration of illness as the covariate to partially control for group differences on that important variable. Because the older group had been ill longer than the younger group, ANCOVA helped to adjust statistically for length of illness differences between the groups.

Matching of participants on characteristics other than the independent variable is another method of approaching participant or group equivalence. This technique is especially popular in the comparative approach, where a "diagnostic group" is compared with a "typical" group. For example, a study might compare persons with multiple sclerosis to an equal number of persons without the diagnosis to assess motor and intellectual functioning. Before the study, they could match the participants on age, gender, and education. If participants are not different with the exception of the diagnosis, then the authors could conclude that differences between the two groups *might* be attributed to the disease.

Often in comparative studies, investigators check *after* the study is over to see how well matched the groups were with respect to demographic measures collected during the study. If the groups are similar, *some* degree of internal validity is shown.

Equivalence in Associational Studies

If the research approach is *associational*, there is only one group. Thus, it might seem that equivalence of the groups would be not applicable. However, we think that it is important to emphasize that the associational approach does not provide evidence of causation no matter how strong the statistical association.

We propose that in the associational approach, equivalence of participant characteristics comes down to the question of whether those who score high on the independent variable of interest are similar to those participants who score low in terms of *other attributes* that may be related to the dependent variable. For example, if the independent variable was education and the dependent variable was later income, we should not interpret a high correlation as indicating that more education *causes* a higher income. It is likely that the highly educated participants may differ from the less educated in terms of other possible causal factors such as IQ, parents' education, and family social status. If the high scorers are not equivalent to the low scorers in terms of such variables, the researcher could statistically control for some, but never all, of the variables on which the high and low participants are unequal. This is one method of achieving some degree of internal validity within the associational research approach.

Although the comparative and associational approaches are limited in what can be concluded about causation, they can lead to strong conclusions about the differences between groups and about associations between variables. Furthermore, if the focus of the research is on an attribute independent variable, nonexperimental approaches are the *only* ones available. The descriptive approach, as we define it, does not attempt to identify causal relationships or, in fact, any relationships. It focuses on describing and summarizing variables.

Control of Extraneous Experience and Environment Variables (Contamination)

This dimension of internal validity includes the effects of extraneous (variables other than the independent or dependent variables) experiences or environmental conditions *during* the study. Thus, we have called this internal validity dimension *control of extraneous experience and environment variables*. Cook and Campbell (1979) addressed this problem, in part, when discussing threats to internal validity that random assignment does not eliminate. Many of these problems occur because some participants gain information about the purpose of the study while the study is taking place.

One aspect of this dimension has to do with whether extraneous variables or events *affect one group more* than the other. For example, if students learn that they are in a control group, they may give up and not try as hard, exaggerating differences between the intervention and control groups. Or the opposite could occur: Students in the control group might overcompensate, eliminating differences between the two groups.

In the associational approach, the issue is whether the experiences of the participants who are high on the independent variable are different from those who are low on the independent variable. Control of extraneous experiences and the environment depends on the specific study, but it is generally better for randomized experiments and for studies done in controlled environments such as laboratories or inpatient facilities.

Rating the Two Dimensions of Internal Validity

A good study should have moderate to high internal validity on both dimensions of internal validity (equivalence of groups on participant characteristics and control of extraneous experience/environment variables). If not, the author should, at the very least, be cautious about saying that the independent variables influenced, impacted, or *caused* the dependent variables to change.

To evaluate internal validity, we use the two rating scales in Figure 8.2. The key to obtaining a high rating on the first scale is random assignment of participants to the groups (e.g., experimental and comparison groups). If random assignment was not or could not be done, were there attempts to make the groups similar or at least to check their similarity after the study? Good retention (a low attrition or dropout rate during the study) is also part of this first rating as is whether the attrition was similar for the groups.

Randomized experimental designs conducted in a laboratory usually control experiential and environmental variables well and would receive high ratings on the second rating scale. However, in quasi-experimental designs, and especially in the comparative and associational approaches, such experiences may be inadequately controlled.

Traditional Threats to Internal Validity

Shadish, Cook, and Campbell (2002) proposed a long list of "threats" to research validity. The labels of these threats are confusing and more complex than necessary for an understanding of internal validity. Another issue with the *threats to internal validity* is that they only emphasize design problems that might result. In other words, the threats tell you what is wrong. They do not necessarily provide advice about how to correct the problem.

On the left hand side of Table 8.1 there is a list of threats to internal validity as described by Shadish et al. (2002). We have added a column for our suggested names, and we show how these threats fit into the two main types of threats already described and rated in Figure 8.2.

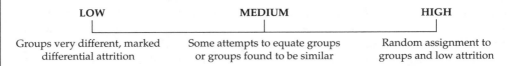

INTERNAL VALIDITY

Equivalence of Groups on Participant Characteristics

Based rating on:

a) Were the participants randomly assigned to the groups?

b) If not, were there adequate attempts to make groups similar (e.g., ANCOVA) or *check* similarity on a *pretest*?

c) If no randomization, were there adequate attempts to make groups similar or check similarity on *other key variables*?

d) Was retention during the study high and similar across groups?

LOW	MEDIUM	HIGH
Groups very different, marked differential attrition	Some attempts to equate groups or groups found to be similar	Random assignment to groups and low attrition

Control of Experiences and Environment Variables (Contamination)

Base rating on:

a) Was the study conducted in a controlled environment (e.g., a lab)?

b) Were extraneous variables that could affect one group more than the others controlled? Did the groups have the same type of environment?

c) Was there a no-treatment group (placebo) or usual-treatment group?

d) Were extraneous variables that could affect all groups and obscure the true effect controlled?

e) Were attempts to reduce other extraneous influences adequate?

LOW	MEDIUM	HIGH
Extraneous variables not controlled, no comparison group (field setting)	Attempts to control experiences and environment	All extraneous variables controlled, eliminated, or balanced (controlled lab)

FIGURE 8.2
Rating scales to evaluate the internal validity of a study.

TABLE 8.1

Threats to Internal Validity

Shadish et al. (2002)	Our terms
	Equivalence of groups
Statistical regression	Use of extreme groups
Attrition or mortality	Participant dropouts or attrition during the study
Selection	Bias in *assignment* to groups
	Control of extraneous variables
Maturation	Changes due to time or growth and development
History	Extraneous environmental events
Testing	Repeated testing, carryover effects
Instrumentation	Instrument or observer inconsistency
Additive and interactive threats	Combinations of two or more threats
Ambiguous temporal precedence	Did the independent variable actually occur before the dependent variable?

Shadish et al.'s (2002) Threats Related to Equivalence of Groups

Statistical Regression

Sometimes the purpose of a quasi-experimental study is to benefit a particular group that, before an intervention, is well above or below average (i.e., the design uses *extreme groups*). For example, children who score in the lowest 10% on some measure might be compared with a nonclinical group. What can happen is that the scores from the low group improve relative to the scores on the pretest even without the intervention. Because these scores were low to start with, children may move or "regress" toward the mean of all scores due to measurement error or unreliability in the dependent variable. Note that reliability is always less than perfect. Because the pretest is used in the screening, only children who score low on the pretest are selected to be in the "clinical" or extreme group. However, because there is measurement error, some of the students selected to be in this extreme group probably were having a "bad day" and should not actually or usually be that low. Hence, when tested a second time (posttest), their "true score" is more apt to be reflected, and it would *seem to be* an increase from the pretest. However, the investigator would not know whether the posttest score was due to the intervention or the statistical problem of regression to the mean. In a classic article, Campbell and Kenny (1999) discussed regression artifacts due to selecting extreme groups and several other related problems.

Attrition (Previously Called Mortality)

This threat refers to participants' *attrition from the study*. Problems are created if the percentage of participants who drop out is large, if there is differential loss between or among groups, or both. High attrition (dropouts) could lead to a biased posttest score, especially if either the intervention or the control condition prompts participants to drop out. For example, if the intervention is found by participants to be onerous or not effective, they may quit the study. On the other hand, if participants know they are in the control condition and feel cheated, they may withdraw. Attrition is also a potential problem in comparative and associational studies where participants are followed longitudinally over time. Attention to participants' needs and maintaining frequent contact with them can be helpful in reducing attrition.

Selection Bias

We call this threat *participant assignment bias* because the problem arises from how participants were assigned to a particular group (comparison or intervention), not from how they were selected (sampled) from the population. Problems are created when participants are not randomly assigned to groups, even if a pretest suggests that the groups are similar. The extent of this problem, however, depends on whether there was biased selection/assignment of participants into the groups. There is usually some bias in quasi-experiments; the comparative and associational approaches, by definition, have biased groups.

Shadish et al.'s (2002) Threats to Control of Experiences and the Environment

Maturation

The internal validity threat called maturation happens when participants in the study *change as a function of time*, such as from the pretest to the posttest in the case of randomized experimental and quasi-experimental research. Some of these changes could be due to growth, but other changes are not due to physical maturation. For example, psychiatric patients may get better over time without any treatment. The maturation threat can make it difficult to determine whether it was the intervention or something else related to time that led to the difference in the dependent variable.

History

This threat, which we call *extraneous environmental events*, occurs when something other than the independent variable happens between the pretest and the posttest, especially if it happens to only one group. Consider a situation in which you are interested in the effect of a particular type of curriculum, but during the period that your intervention is taking place, students are exposed to information on the merits of your method. Because of the extraneous environmental events threat, it cannot be concluded it was your method and only your method that made the difference in the study.

Testing

This threat most often occurs when the investigator uses *repeated testing* or a pretest and a posttest in the study and the two are identical or similar, resulting in a possible *carryover* from the pretest that might alert the participants about the study and how they should behave. Or, if the study involves learning, the pretest may include information that is on the posttest. It would be difficult to separate what was learned from the pretest from what was learned from the intervention.

Instrumentation

When using the same pretest and posttest in a research design, it is possible that there could be *inconsistency* and the scoring of the test may change, especially if the interval between the pretest and the posttest is relatively long. For example, there could be a *calibration drift* in an instrument that is used to record reaction time or physiological measures, such as heart rate. Even slight changes will prevent the investigator from concluding whether the change was due to the intervention or to the change in calibration. A common problem involving the instrumentation threat is when the pretest and posttest measurements involve raters. It is not uncommon for people to change their criteria over time. Even worse, one or more of the raters may leave the study and have to be replaced with different raters. Repeatedly establishing high interrater reliability is one method of circumventing this problem.

Additive and Interactive Threats

The impact of any one of the preceding threats can be added to one or more of the other threats. Or the impact may depend on (i.e., interact with) the level of another threat. Thus, combinations of the threats can be a problem.

Ambiguous Temporal Precedence

Remember that the first criterion for determining cause is that the independent variable (intervention) must *precede* the dependent variable (outcome or posttest). Occasionally this is unclear in quasi-experiments; it is often a problem in associational studies and sometimes is a problem in comparative studies. For example, if an associational study found a relationship between maternal depression and infant mastery behavior, it would not be clear which variable came first. The authors might assume that maternal depression influenced child behavior, but it is plausible that infants who don't seem to be developing well could cause an increase in mothers' depression. The effect may actually be bidirectional or cyclical. When the temporal order of the variables is unclear, causation can not be established and internal validity should be rated as low.

Other Threats That Random Assignment Does Not Eliminate

Most of these threats occur because of *contamination*. Participants in different groups communicate or gain information intended for another group while the study is taking place. As mentioned earlier, if participants learn that they are in a control group, they may become *resentful* or *demoralized* and not try as hard, exaggerating differences between the intervention and control groups. Or the opposite may occur, and persons in the control group may *overcompensate* or imitate the experimental group, eliminating differences between the groups.

Likewise, *expectation effect,* sometimes called Hawthorne effects, might make the treatment appear more powerful than if the patients in the intervention condition did not expect good results from a new treatment. One method of preventing expectation effects is to design the study so that the participants don't know (i.e., they are *masked*) whether they are receiving a treatment. Use of a *placebo* (no-treatment) *control group* can help the researcher estimate and control for *no-treatment effects*. Participants in a placebo group may improve somewhat because they know that they are in a study that *might* be helpful to them. Use of a placebo control group is possible in some studies, but it raises ethical questions. So, "treatment as usual" for the control group may be a good alternative as long as the participants in the control group do not think they are missing out.

Observer or experimenter bias is another problem; this can be dealt with by "double masking," that is, making both the participant and the tester or evaluator unaware of who is receiving the intervention. Masking of the treatments from the evaluator is often difficult with behavioral interventions, but, at the least, the evaluator should not be someone who has a stake in the success of the treatment.

Summary

The focus of this chapter is on internal validity, which is the extent to which we can infer that a relationship is casual. There are three criteria for inferring a casual relationship. First, the independent variable must *precede* the dependent variable. Second, the independent variable must be related to the dependent variable. Third, there must be no other variables that could explain why the independent variable is related to the dependent variable. We describe two main dimensions used to evaluate internal validity: (1) the equivalence of the groups on participant characteristics (e.g., equivalence of the intervention and control groups *prior to the intervention*); and (2) control of extraneous experience and environmental variables. The chapter concludes with a discussion of the traditional threats to internal validity and how they fit into our two main evaluative dimensions.

Key Concepts

Cause or inferring causation
Control of extraneous experience/environment variables
Equivalence of groups on participant characteristics
Internal validity
Traditional threats to internal validity
Validity

Key Distinctions

Internal validity versus research validity

Application Problems

1. Match each research example with the traditional threat to internal validity that it contains. How could the design be modified to reduce the threat in each example?

   a. Maturation
   b. History or environmental events
   c. Repeated testing
   d. Instrumentation
   e. Selection (assignment)
   f. Mortality or attrition
   g. Statistical regression

   _C_ A control group takes a pretest about social studies knowledge. Some of them are intrigued and decide to read up on the topic before the posttest.

   ____ The research assistants become bored and don't do their observations as carefully near the end of the study.

   _E_ An experiment is conducted to assess a new history teaching method. School districts that volunteer serve as the experimental group and those that don't volunteer serve as the control group.

   _F_ A researcher is interested in the long-term effects of an election on the political attitudes of voters. Prior to the election, the views of 100 voters are assessed. Afterward the researcher is able to reassess the attitudes of 74 voters.

   _b_ An event other than the manipulation of the independent variable occurs between the pretest and the posttest.

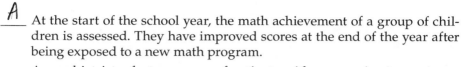

_A_ At the start of the school year, the math achievement of a group of children is assessed. They have improved scores at the end of the year after being exposed to a new math program.

_____ A psychiatrist selects a group of patients with very serious symptoms. After 1 month of therapy, the patients have markedly improved.

Using this chapter and Chapter 4, answer the following for studies 2–5:

  a. What research approach was used?

  b. Evaluate internal validity by (a) rating the equivalence of the groups on participant characteristics; and (b) evaluating the control of extraneous experience and environmental variables.

2. Researchers were interested in effects of different types of television programming on the aggressive behavior of preschool-aged children. Children from a preschool were randomly assigned to spend 30 minutes viewing one of two different types of television programming. One group watched violent animated cartoons such as Power Rangers, and in an adjacent room the other group watched programming that modeled prosocial behavior such as Barney. During the hour after the viewing, aggressive acts initiated by individual children from both viewing groups were counted by observers. They compared the two groups on number of aggressive behaviors.

3. In this study, the researchers were interested in comparing the way three types of reinforcement affected the conditioning of children to use the word _they_ when making up sentences. Subjects were brought to the lab and then randomly assigned to three groups: (1) Children in the "material" reinforcement condition received an M&M candy immediately after using the word _they_ at the beginning of a sentence; (2) Children assigned to the praise condition were reinforced by the experimenter's saying _good_; and (3) Children in the symbolic reinforcement condition were simply given a plus mark.

4. A professor wants to know whether student anxiety (on an anxiety inventory with scores from 1 to 10) influences test performance scores on the midterm exam.

5. The organizers of a required week-long graduate course were interested in which one of two teaching/training approaches was most effective. Two sections of the course (on trauma assessment and intervention) were taught. One teacher used a traditional structured didactic approach. The other teacher used a new approach/ curriculum, incorporating a high proportion of experiential components. One section met in the afternoon and the other section in the morning. Students could sign up for either session. However, the instructors were unknown to the students, and the students had no prior awareness of the differing approaches/curriculums. The sections were of equal size and the students were demographically similar. Students were pretested to assess their prior knowledge, and at the end of the course students were tested on the content of the course.

Section III

Sampling, Measurement, and Data Collection

9

Sampling and Introduction to External Validity

What Is Sampling?

Sampling is the process of selecting *part* of a larger group of participants with the intent of generalizing from the **sample** (the smaller group) to the **population** (the larger group). To make valid inferences about the population, we must select the sample so that it is representative of the total population.

Political pollsters and market researchers have developed and refined the process of sampling so that they are usually able to estimate quite accurately the voting or purchasing intentions of the population of the United States from samples as small as several hundred participants. We are all familiar with public opinion and voting surveys, usually done by telephone interviewers who may use random-digit dialing techniques to select the persons whom they choose to call. If the questions are clear and the participants answer them truthfully and accurately, a random sample of approximately 1,000 participants is enough to predict, within ±3%, what the whole population of the United States would say or feel about a certain issue.

You may be familiar with the Nielsen television ratings, which are based on information gathered about the TV viewing of a few thousand representative households. These ratings are then extrapolated to indicate the percentage of the total TV viewing population of the United States that would have watched a certain show, and this determines advertising rates. A similar Nielsen system was developed to assess the specific shopping behaviors of a sample of American consumers who actually scanned the bar codes on the items they purchased so that Nielsen could report information to manufacturers not only about the number and types of items purchased but, perhaps more importantly, also about profiles of the people who were doing the buying.

With a few notable exceptions, these modern survey techniques have proven to be useful and accurate in predicting or reporting information about the attitudes and behaviors of the American public. Historically, however, there have been a number of examples of major miscalculations that can be traced in part to inadequate sampling techniques. One of the often cited examples is that of the grossly erroneous prediction, by a *Literary Digest* poll and based on a very large sample of several million respondents, that Franklin Roosevelt would lose the 1936 presidential election, when, in fact, he won by a landslide. One of the problems with this poll was that the sample was selected from automobile registrations, telephone directories, and other related sources. This led to oversampling of affluent and higher educated individuals who were not representative of the voting public, especially during the middle of the Great Depression. In addition, only about 20% of the selected sample actually returned their questionnaires. This example illustrates the point that the representativeness of the sample is more important than its size, not only for marketing or election purposes but for academic research as well. Fowler (2009) and Fink (2009) are good sources of information about sampling and survey research methods.

Advantages of Sampling

Selecting less than the total population is an advantage for researchers for several reasons. First, it is *less expensive* to interview, observe, or send surveys to a smaller group of people than to a large number. Second, it clearly takes less time to study a sample of participants than it would to study a whole population, especially if the people are observed or interviewed individually. Third, better *quality* control can be obtained if one has a reasonable amount of time to devote to the assessment of each participant rather than trying to spread oneself too thin over a larger group.

Key Concepts of Sampling

To have an understanding of sampling as it actually takes place in the research reported in the social science and education literature, key concepts must be defined. Figure 9.1 helps to visualize several of these key concepts and the relationships among them.

- *Participants, cases, or elements:* These are the people or objects or events that are of interest in a particular study. In the social sciences the participants are usually individual people, but they also could be groups of people such as married couples, siblings, families, teams, and schools. Although less common, the cases could be animals, such as white rats, or events, such as television programs or car accidents. In Figure 9.1, high school teachers are the participants.

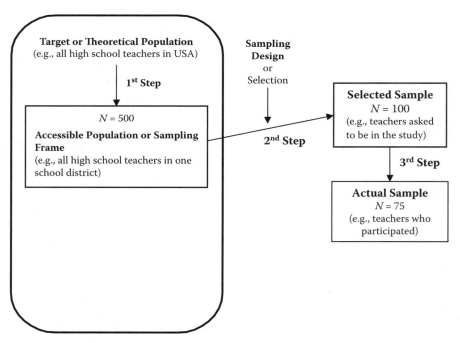

FIGURE 9.1
Schematic diagram of the sampling process.

- *Theoretical or target population:* This includes all of the participants of theoretical interest to the researcher and to which he or she would like to generalize. Examples of theoretical populations are as follows: all high school teachers in the United States (Figure 9.1), all 3rd-grade children in the United States, all Hispanic males in the Southwest, or all women over 80 in the world. It is rarely possible to study or even to sample such large target or theoretical populations for both economic and practical reasons. We usually do not have access to such broad groups, especially if we are attempting to observe or measure them in a face-to-face situation. Unfortunately, the theoretical population is usually *not* specified in published research articles. One has to infer it from the context and any generalizations made in the results and discussion.

- *Accessible population* (sometimes called the survey population and frequently called the *sampling frame*): As the name implies, the accessible population is the group of participants to which the researcher has access, perhaps through a telephone directory or membership list. The accessible population also might be an organization or group such as a class to which the researcher has entry. Examples of accessible populations might be the 3rd graders in a particular school or school district, Hispanic men who belong to certain fraternal organizations in selected cities in the Southwest, or couples who are on a mailing list developed by an international marketing firm. In Figure 9.1, the accessible population is all high school teachers in the district to which the researcher had access.

- *Selected sample:* This is the smaller group of participants selected from the larger accessible population by the researcher and *asked* to participate in the study. The selection can be performed in a number of different ways as described under types of sampling. The point here is that the selected sample is composed of the participants that the researcher has selected, but not everyone in this sample necessarily participates in the study. In Figure 9.1, the selected sample is the 100 teachers asked to participate in the study. In some cases, the accessible population may be so small or defined so narrowly that it is not necessary to sample the participants. Rather, *every* participant in the accessible population is asked to participate in the study. However, even though no actual sampling was done, this type of selected sample is called a **convenience sample**, unless the accessible population is representative of the theoretical population.

- *Actual sample*: These are the participants that complete the study and whose data are actually used in the data analysis and in the report of the study's results. The ratio of the size of the actual sample to the selected sample is known as the **response rate**. In Figure 9.1, the actual sample is 75 teachers, and the response rate is 75% (75/100). A low response rate (perhaps less than 50%) will usually lower the quality of the sample, especially if the persons who responded are different in important ways from those who didn't respond. Thus, in evaluating research it is important to know the response rate and to know whether the responders were similar to nonresponders.

There are many reasons that participants in the selected sample do not end up in the actual data for the study. Some decline to participate, perhaps, by not returning the researcher's questionnaire or by telling the phone interviewer that they do not wish to participate. Others have moved or are not able to be reached on the telephone. Still others return a partially completed questionnaire, provide answers that are judged to be suspect, or, perhaps, drop out in the middle of the study.

Steps in Selecting a Sample

There are many ways to select a sample from a population. The goal is to have an actual sample that is *representative* of the target or theoretical population. A **representative sample** is a sample that represents the population—that is, it is a small replica of the population. It has, on all of the key variables, the same *proportions* as in the whole population (e.g., 52% female, 48% male). A representative sample is most likely obtained using the techniques described as *types of probability sampling*.

Obtaining a representative sample is not easy because things can go wrong at a number of steps of the research process. Figure 9.1 shows the concepts we previously described and also the *three steps* (shown with arrows) from the theoretical population to the actual sample.

1. The *first step* is from the theoretical population to the accessible population. It may be that the accessible population or sampling frame is not representative of the theoretical population. This is a common problem because researchers often do not have access to the geographical, socioeconomic, or other range of participants to which they would like to make inferences or generalizations. Often, especially, if participants need to be measured via face-to-face contact, we are limited to a specific location and to groups that are available to us such as persons in a certain school, hospital, or organization.

2. The *second step* in the sampling process is called the *sampling design* or selection of participants. This step, between the accessible population and the selected sample, is the step that is usually described in the methods section of articles and is the step over which the researcher has the most control. We expand on this step in the next section, types of sampling.

3. The *third step* takes place between the selected sample and the actual sample. The problem here is that participants may not respond to the invitation to participate or may drop out of the study so that the actual sample may be considerably smaller than the selected sample; that is, there is a low response rate. The actual sample may be unrepresentative of the selected sample. This is often a problem with mailed surveys, especially if the survey is sent to busy people such as small business owners. In these cases, less than 25% of the questionnaires may be returned. Thus, even if the selected sample was quite representative of the theoretical population, the actual sample may be unrepresentative.

Sampling Designs

The **sampling design** is the procedure or process used to select the sample. There are two general types of sampling design: probability and nonprobability sampling techniques.

Probability sampling involves the selection of participants in a way that is nonbiased. In a probability sample every participant or element of the population has a known, nonzero probability of being chosen to be a member of the sample.

In **nonprobability sampling** there is no way of estimating the probability that each participant has of being included in the sample. Therefore, *sampling bias* is usually introduced. Nonprobability samples are used when probability samples, which rely on random or systematic selection of participants, are not feasible. The advantages of nonprobability samples are economy and convenience. In fact, most published studies in the social sciences and education use nonprobability sampling or the entire accessible population, if it is small. These samples may be useful in examining the relationship between variables or the differences between groups, but they are clearly not the best way to describe or make generalizations about the whole population.

Types of Probability Sampling

As stated already, in probability sampling, every participant or element in the population has a known, nonzero chance of being selected. When probability sampling is used, inferential statistics enable researchers to make an estimate of the extent to which results based on the sample are likely to differ from what we would have found by studying the entire population. Four types of probability sampling are now described briefly.

Simple Random Sampling

The best known and most basic of the probability sampling techniques is the simple random sample, which can be defined as a sample in which all participants or elements have an equal and independent chance of being included in the sample. If we put 100 pieces of paper (numbered from 1 to 100) in a hat, shake the hat, and draw out 10, without replacing them, this would approximate a simple random sample. In such a sample each participant has an equal and independent chance of being selected or picked as one of the 10 persons to be asked to participate in the study. This type of probability sample will produce a representative sample if the number of participants selected is relatively large. However, if the number selected is small, like the 10 numbers drawn from the hat, the sample might not be a small replica of the total population.

In an actual research study we would draw or select our random sample using a random number table or computer generator of random numbers rather than selecting numbers out of a hat. The way this would work is that all of the possible participants in the accessible population or sampling frame would be listed and numbered from 1 to 900, assuming that there are 900 participants in the accessible population. Then, if we decided to select a sample of 90, we would start by unsystematically picking a starting point in the random number table and proceeding in a systematic and planned manner down the rows (or across the columns) to select the first 90 nonrepeated numbers listed in the random number table.

Table 9.1 is an example of a *small* part of a random number table. (Complete tables can be found in most statistics books.) For this example, we want to select numbers from 001

TABLE 9.1

A Small Section of a Random Number Table

55515	81899	04153	79401
46375	81953	etc.	etc.
15792	35101		
37824	etc.		
11508			
37449			
46515			
30986			
63798			

to 900. We would need three digits so one could use, for example, the three right-hand columns in the set of random numbers. Let's say we started by nonsystematically picking the number 11508, which is about halfway down the left-hand set of five-digit numbers. The three right-hand digits are 508, so the first participant to be selected would be number 508, the second participant would be number 449, and the third 515. However, we would skip number 986 because that number is outside the range of 1 to 900 in your sampling frame. We would continue down the list skipping numbers larger than 900 and any that had already been picked until we had selected 90 of the original 900 potential participants for this simple random sample.

Although the simple random sample is the prototype of a probability sampling method, it is used infrequently, in part because it may be time consuming to number the entire list, if it is long. Also, many times there is no list of the population of interest. A more frequent equivalent of the simple random sample is systematic sampling with a random start, which is discussed next. To use either sample random or systematic random sampling, the population has to be finite, and there has to be a list or directory of persons in the population.

Systematic Random Sampling

To obtain this type of sample, we would start by using the random number table to select a number between 1 and 10 if, as in the previous example, we have decided to select a one-tenth sample of the population. If we randomly selected the fourth person on the list as the first participant, then we would systematically select every tenth participant, starting from the fourth. Thus, the sample would include the 4th, 14th, 24th, 34th, etc. person on the list and would include 90 participants. Many research books warn against systematic samples if a list is ordered in some way, especially in a reoccurring pattern, that will have a differential effect on the resulting sample depending on where one started. For example, if we had a list of 90 youth soccer teams, each of which had 10 players, and their goalie was always the fourth person listed for each team, the previous example, starting randomly with number four, would select only goalies for this 90-person sample (or no goalies if the random start had begun at a different number). Thus, we should examine the list with the interval (e.g., 10) to be used in mind. However, this is rarely a problem, and in almost all cases a systematic sample with a random start will produce the equivalent of a simple random sample.

Stratified Random Sampling

Strata are variables (e.g., race, geographical region, age, gender) that could be used to divide the population into segments. If the researcher is knowledgeable about these dimensions and assumes that they are important in obtaining a representative sample, the strata can be used to obtain a *stratified random sample*. (Also, they are used in specifying the quotas in a *quota sample*.)

Thus, if some important characteristics of the accessible population or sampling frame are known ahead of time (i.e., are noted on the sampling frame), then we can reduce the sampling variation and increase the likelihood that the sample will be representative of the population by stratifying the sample on the basis of these key variables. In our previous example, let's suppose that we wanted to be sure that a representative number of goal keepers were chosen as part of the sample. We would use a stratified random sampling technique. The list or sampling frame would be rearranged so that all the goalies were listed together, and then one tenth of them would be selected randomly using either a simple random sampling technique or a systematic sampling technique with a random start. The same techniques could be used for selecting a sample from each of the other positions. Stratifying ensures that the sample contains exactly the proportion of goalies (one tenth) as in the overall population.

When participants are geographically spread across the country (or a state), it is common to stratify based on geography so that appropriate proportions of the selected sample come from the different regions of the country or state. It is also common to stratify on the rural, suburban, and urban characteristics of the sample if these are identifiable in the sampling frame.

We now describe two more complex types of sampling. The first is a variant of the stratified sampling procedure just described, and the second is a multistage sampling procedure designed to make sampling geographically diverse participants more practical.

Stratified Sampling With Differential Probabilities of Selection

Sometimes stratified sampling will lead to one or more sizable groups of participants and one or more very small groups of participants. For example, if we wanted to compare various ethnic groups, the number of Hispanics, African Americans, and especially Asian Americans and Native Americans would be quite small in a moderate-sized sample that was representative of the total population of the country. If we wanted to compare different ethnic groups, it is desirable to have the groups equal or at least of a substantial size (maybe 30 or more). Therefore, one might want to *oversample* the minority group members to have enough in each group to make reasonable comparisons with the Caucasian or White sample.

In our example of the soccer teams, the goalies would be similar to minority ethnic group members in that, if we did a one-tenth sample of the 90 goalies, we would end up with a sample of only nine goalies, which is too small for reasonable comparisons with the group of nongoalies. We might, for example, want to sample half of the 90 goalies to get a large enough sample to compare.

However, we should be *cautious*. If we draw conclusions later about a total population from the sample, we need to *statistically adjust for the fact that some groups have been oversampled*. That is, if we were interested in the hand–eye coordination of soccer players, we could not just take the average of the hand–eye coordination of the oversampled goalies and of the nongoalies. We would have to weight the goalies less so that the overall average coordination score would not be distorted by the fact that there were five times as many goalies in our sample as would be representative of the population.

Cluster (Random) Sampling

Cluster sampling is a two-stage sampling procedure that is especially useful when the population is spread out geographically or there is no single overall list of individuals in the accessible population. **Clusters**, sometimes called sampling units, are collections or groups of potential participants that do not overlap. The individual participants within a given cluster are usually geographically grouped together. Clusters include towns, schools, or hospitals that are important. For *cluster probability sampling* the researchers need a list of such clusters. The basic strategy is to *first* select specific clusters (groups of participants) using a probability sampling method such as simple random sampling. Then, as a *second stage*, select *all* or randomly select a specific proportion of participants from the clusters.

Take, for example, the situation where we are interested in sampling one tenth of the students from a fairly large number of schools. The task of going to each of, for example, 150 schools and selecting 1 of every 10 students would be difficult in terms of time and expense. A less expensive alternative would be to *select randomly* 1 of 10 schools (i.e., 15) and then to *select all* of the students in those 15 schools as the one-tenth sample. There are, of course, various combinations of the proportions that one might be selected on the first step and on the second step. However, a common strategy, as just described, is to randomly select just enough geographically compact clusters (e.g., schools or communities) so that one will have the needed number of participants if one selected all of the students in the selected clusters and did not select any students from the other schools. Some precision in sampling is sacrificed because the sample of schools, even if randomly selected, could be unrepresentative of the larger population of schools, but often cost considerations outweigh this, hopefully minor, loss in precision.

Concluding Comments on Probability Sampling

Figure 9.2 provides diagrams of the five probability sampling methods that we just described. Notice that all of them involve randomization at some point in the process of selecting participants. However, they differ in whether the accessible population is stratified in some way (indicated by horizontal lines) and in what proportion of a stratum or cluster is selected. The numbers in the boxes represent a single potential participant and his or her subject number. Of course, such samples are usually much larger than shown here. These diagrams do not include all of the possible combinations of the four main sampling strategies but give a good idea of the methods used by researchers who attempt to obtain a representative sample and high *population external validity*. With a probability sample, descriptive statistics from the sample also can describe the population. However, with stratified sampling with different proportions, one would need to weight the results appropriately to describe the population.

Types of Nonprobability Sampling

Nonprobability samples are ones in which the probability of being selected is unknown, often because there is no sampling frame or list of the members of the accessible population. Time and cost constraints also lead researchers and pollsters to use nonprobability samples. Although nonprobability samples may appear similar to probability samples in the demographics of the selected participants, the results can be distorted, and the assumptions of probability theory and sampling error are no doubt violated. The first type of nonprobability sampling, *quota sampling*, is often used by public opinion pollsters, political pollsters, and market researchers because the resulting samples look representative of the population and the cost of obtaining the data is considerably less than would be required to obtain a probability sample.

Quota Sampling

In quota sampling, the investigator sets certain parameters or quotas for hired interviewers to follow, but some degree of latitude or discretion is allowed in the selection of the actual participants. For example, the interviewer may be directed to certain zip codes (or telephone exchanges) that may have been chosen randomly. Then the interviewer is asked to find and interview a certain number of participants within each zip code (or telephone exchange). There may well be further restrictions such as obtaining certain proportions of men and women or having younger and older participants, but the actual participants are selected by the interviewer because they are home and willing to participate when asked.

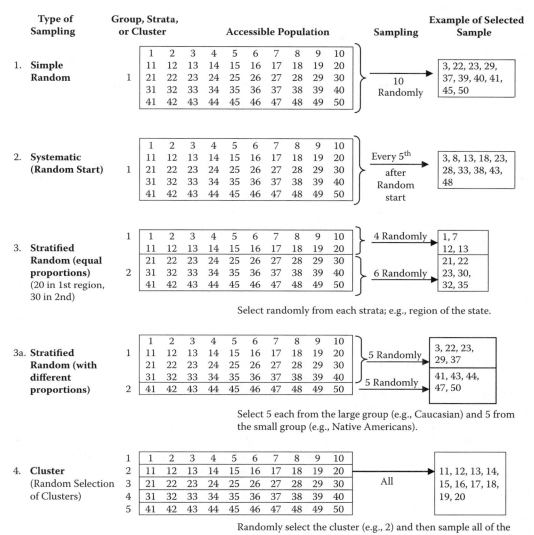

FIGURE 9.2
Schematic diagrams of five probability sampling methods for a sample of 10 from an accessible population of 50.

The technique saves money in part because participants who are not available are not called back. A problem is that people who aren't home much or don't answer the phone are underrepresented. Furthermore, in house-to-house surveying, the interviewer may be tempted to skip certain households—for example, those that are located on upper floors, that are in dilapidated condition, or that have a barking dog.

Purposive Sampling

This type of sampling seems to be especially confusing to students and new researchers because the term is similar to purposeful sampling, which is a term used in qualitative research. However, in *quantitative* survey research, the term *purposive sampling* means that the participants are hand picked from the accessible population so that they presumably will be representative or typical of the population. This technique is sometimes used by political pollsters who have information about previous elections that indicates which voting districts seem to be typical in forecasting how people in larger entities, such as the state, will vote. The interviewer then polls people in that district to make extrapolations and generalizations about the larger unit.

A purposive sample is much like a quota sample in that one must be able to identify several key characteristics of the population. Take the soccer sample as an example: If we wanted to know how players evaluated the fairness or the quality of the referees, we might purposively select players who were on teams that were about average in terms of wins, losses, and goals. Or we might select some players that did well in terms of competition, some that did about average, and some that did poorly. As another example, perhaps one would ask teachers to select children who were felt to be representative of the class. However, unless more detailed instructions were given, it might turn out that the teachers tend to select children that they, perhaps unconsciously, felt would make them or the school look good rather than selecting representative children.

We would *not* consider it purposive sampling if teachers were asked to identify children with, for example, dyslexia, or if a social service agency was asked to identify family caregivers of Alzheimer's patients in their files. Selecting such specific groups is similar to what is called *screening* or the use of *inclusion* or *exclusion criteria*. Sometimes researchers exclude households that do not have participants of the desired types. The sampling would be purposive only if, *given* that dyslexic children (or of family caregivers of Alzheimer's patients) was the population of interest, one attempted to pick typical or representative cases from that population.

As an aside, if the selection of participants to be contacted is done using probability techniques such as random digit dialing, and we screen out participants who do not fit the selection criteria, we would still end up with a probability sample. However, if we select cases from the accessible population purposefully, not randomly or systematically, the resulting sample will be a nonprobability sample. Like quota sampling, purposive sampling is an attempt to make the sample representative of the population, but it will probably not achieve the goal of complete representativeness.

A purposive sample is different from a convenience sample in that at least an attempt has been made to select participants so that they are representative of that accessible population, not just ones that are convenient and available.

Purposeful Sampling

This is the term used in qualitative research for the types of sampling that are often conducted. The idea is to intentionally or purposefully select individuals (or documents, events, or settings) so that they will best help the investigator understand the research problem. How does the researcher decide or know whether the sample is the best to help understand the problem or research question? Qualitative researchers state that they carefully select participants who are "information rich." In the qualitative literature a number of strategies have been used to purposefully select participants and research sites. These strategies vary widely from *maximum variation sampling*, intended to get multiple perspectives on the topic, to *extreme or deviant case sampling*, intended to study particularly troublesome or enlightening examples. Such purposeful sampling, like purposive and quota sampling, make an attempt to identify participants to fit certain criteria.

Convenience Sampling

Unfortunately, this is probably the most common sampling method used in student projects, including theses and dissertations. Also, it is often used by researchers in experimental laboratory studies and by researchers with limited resources available for sampling. As the name implies, the participants are selected on the basis of convenience rather than making a serious attempt *beforehand* to select participants that are representative of the theoretical population. Examples of convenience or *accidental sampling* are as follows: the use of students in one's class, the use of passersby at a certain point (e.g., the student center, a mall), members of certain clubs or church groups, volunteer teachers or students in a school, or employees of a company who happen to be willing to cooperate. Researchers *later* may examine the demographic characteristics of their convenience sample and conclude that the participants are similar to those in the larger population. This does *not* mean that the sample is, in fact, representative, but it does indicate an attempt by the researcher, at least after the fact, to check on representativeness.

There are two ways by which the term convenience sample is used. First, whenever the *accessible population* is not representative of the *theoretical population* (step 1 in Figure 9.1), the result is called a convenience sample, even if all the members of the class, club, or clinic were assessed. Second, the sample is also one of convenience if the participants are volunteers or selected (step 2) from the population in a nonprobability manner, as described in the previous paragraph.

Snowball Sampling

Snowball sampling is a modification of convenience or accidental sampling that is used when the participants of interest are from a population that is rare or at least whose members are unknown to you. These might be persons with unusual attributes, beliefs, or behavior patterns and that do not belong to known groups with identifiable lists of members, for example, self-cured drug addicts. What is done is find a few participants that meet the characteristics and then ask them for references or names of other people they may know who fit into the same category. Then, these other people are asked for additional references and so forth—thus, the name *snowball sampling*. This is clearly a convenience or accidental sample. Sampling similar to this is sometimes used by constructivist/qualitative researchers.

Why Are Nonprobability Samples Used So Frequently?

In addition to the cost and time efficiency advantages already mentioned, there appear to be other reasons for using nonprobability samples. First, it may not be possible to do a probability sample of the participants. This is true for student researchers and others on limited budgets who cannot afford the costs of purchasing a mailing list or postage or of travel to interview geographically diverse participants.

Perhaps most importantly, some researchers, especially those using controlled laboratory and experimental designs, are *not* primarily interested in making inferences about the population from the descriptive data, as is the case in survey research. These researchers are more interested in whether the experimental treatment has an effect on the dependent variable, and they assume that if the treatment is powerful, the effect will show up in many kinds of participants. In fact, the use of nonhuman animals in medical and behavioral research assumes that we can generalize some types of results to humans from other species.

In other types of research, the investigator is primarily interested in the relationship between variables and may assume that the relationship will hold up in a wide variety of human participants. Thus, some say, perhaps inappropriately, that it is not necessary to have a representative sample of the population to make generalizable statements about the *relationship* between two or more variables. Implicitly, many researchers seem to believe that *external population validity*, (discussed later in this chapter), which is directly related to the representativeness of the sample, is less important than internal validity, as discussed in Chapter 8.

Aspects of a Study That Lead to an Unrepresentative Sample

As a summary, we would like to describe some of the things that lead to a sample that is unrepresentative of the target population.

1. First, there is selection of an accessible population or sampling frame (step 1 in Figure 9.1) that is not representative of the target or theoretical population but is picked for its *convenience*. With this kind of accessible population, for example, schools in a certain city in an unrepresentative part of the country, the sample would not be representative of the theoretical population even if it was chosen randomly from this accessible population.

2. Of course, the obvious way to obtain an unrepresentative sample is to use a *non-probability sampling* design or method (step 2). If participants in an accessible population, such as a school or clinic, are asked to or allowed to volunteer (self-select) to be in the study, an unrepresentative (convenience) sample will result. This type of unrepresentative sample is unfortunately common.

3. If there is a poor *response rate*, (step 3), the representativeness of the sample is likely to be compromised. The response rate is the number of people interviewed or responding divided by the total number of people sampled. This denominator includes all the people who were selected but did not respond for a variety of reasons: refusals, language problems, illness, or lack of availability. However, usually the response rate does *not* include those who were *screened* out because they (a) did not fit the *exclusion criteria*; (b) did not have a working telephone; (c) or whose questionnaire was returned because it was not deliverable. The effect of nonresponses on the results of the survey depends on both the percentage of people who are not responding *and* also on the extent to which those who didn't respond are biased in some way—that is, different from the rest of the sample who did respond.

4. **Attrition** (*after* step 3), sometimes called *experimental mortality*, occurs when selected participants initially agree to participate but then *drop out during* the study. High attrition for the whole sample will produce a problem for the representativeness of the sample. In addition, if attrition is high for certain groups but not others, it can produce a nonrepresentative sample. For example, if an intervention turned out to be unpleasant or irritating to males but not to females, there might be a much larger percentage of males who would drop out during the study and, thus, lead to a biased sample of males, even if everything up to that point had been based on probability sampling. Attrition also produces a sampling problem if participants in a *placebo control group* drop out because they perceive that they are not benefiting from the study, or, on the other hand, if participants in the experimental group experience negative side effects from the intervention and drop out.

How Many Participants?

One of the most often asked questions is, "How many participants do I need for this study?" The answer can be quite complex, but we give some general guidelines here. One part of the answer depends on the people you ask and what discipline they come from. National opinion surveys almost always have about a thousand participants, whereas sociological and epidemiological studies usually have at least several hundred participants. On the other hand, psychological experiments and clinical trials in medicine with 10 to 20 participants *per group* are common, and in some clinical areas and education, single-subject designs are often used. To some extent these dramatic differences in sample sizes depend on differences in types of designs, measures, and statistical analyses, but they also seem to be based in good part on custom.

Some authors suggest that the sample be as large as is feasible for the investigators and their budget. Other things being equal, it is true that a larger sample will be more likely to detect a significant difference or relationship and lead to the rejection of the null hypothesis. However, two points should be made.

First, *representativeness is a more important consideration than sample size.* If the sample is not representative of the population, it can be huge and still give misleading results. For example, remember that there were 2.5 million respondents to the 1936 *Literary Digest* poll that predicted the defeat of Roosevelt instead of his landslide victory.

Second, very large samples will detect differences or relationships that may have little practical or societal importance (see Chapter 17). If we are trying to *describe a population* with a statistic such as the mean or percentage, we want to be as accurate as possible. In that case a large (usually >500) sample, if appropriately drawn, will reduce the sampling error. However, in most social science and educational research we are not interested in describing the population. Rather, we want to identify the key factors that may influence the dependent variable or help us predict it. We have relatively less interest in finding factors that account for very small percentages of the variance. Thus, in some ways a large sample can be detrimental to identifying important results. For example, with 500 participants, a large proportion of correlations probably will be statistically significantly *different from zero*, but some of them may account for less than 1% of the variance and, thus, not be of much practical importance.

Thus, the size of the sample should be large enough so one does not fail to detect important findings because the sample was too small, but a large sample will not necessarily help one distinguish between the merely *statistically significant* and the *practically or clinically important* findings. This key point raises the issue of *statistical power* that we discuss in more depth in later chapters.

For now we only mention a guideline that historically had been used: A study should include a minimum of 30 participants. Thus for associational (one group) designs, one might have as few as 30 participants, but for comparative, quasi-experimental, and experimental designs one should have a total of 30 participants. The rationale was that a distribution of the dependent variable with at least 30 participants was a good approximation of the normal curve. However, a total of 30 participants in a study with at least two groups is not usually large enough to yield the desired power (reject the null hypothesis when it should be rejected).

In Chapter 16, we address the topic of *power* and how to calculate it, which is the technically correct way to plan ahead of time how many participants are needed to detect a result of a certain effect size. There are several classic books about how to determine the needed power based on the sample size and the effect size. Kraemer and Thiemann (1987), in *How Many Subjects,* provide a relatively easy way to find the needed sample size. Cohen (1988), in *Statistical Power Analysis for the Behavioral Sciences,* is a standard reference book even today.

External Validity

In this chapter and several to follow we again discuss aspects of **research validity**, the validity or quality of a whole study. In Chapter 8, we introduced *internal validity,* the validity related to the design of the study. Research validity also depends on sampling. Now we discuss *external validity,* an aspect of research validity that depends in part on the quality of the sample.

External validity deals with generalizability—that is, the extent to which samples, settings, treatment variables, and measurement variables can be generalized beyond the study. External validity does not depend on internal validity. For example, it might be suggested that because the study had poor internal validity (a weak design), then external validity also *must* be poor. However, external validity should be judged separately, before the fact, and not be based on the internal validity.

Evaluating External Validity

Questions dealing with the external validity of a study are based on the principle that a good study should be rated high on external validity, or, if not, the author should at least be cautious about generalizing the findings to other measures, populations, and settings. Figure 9.3 provides scales to rate each of two main aspects of external validity: *population external validity* and *ecological external validity.*

Population External Validity

This first aspect of external validity is a selection problem that involves how participants were selected to be in the study. Were participants randomly selected from a particular population, or were they a convenience sample? As discussed earlier in this chapter, most quantitative studies in the social sciences have *not* used random selection of participants and, thus, are not high on population external validity. However, the issue of population external validity is even more complex than an evaluation of the sampling design (i.e., it is more than step 2, how the sample was selected from the accessible population).

The important question is whether the actual sample of participants is representative of the theoretical or target population. To evaluate this question, it is helpful to identify the (1) apparent theoretical population; (2) accessible population; (3) sampling design and selected sample; and (4) actual sample of participants that completed participation in the study. It is possible that the researcher could use a random or other probability sampling design but has an actual sample that is not representative of the theoretical population, due either to a low response rate or to the accessible population not being representative of the theoretical population. The latter problem seems almost universal, in part due to funding and travel limitations. Except in national survey research, we almost always start with an accessible population from, for example, the local school district, community, clinic, or animal colony.

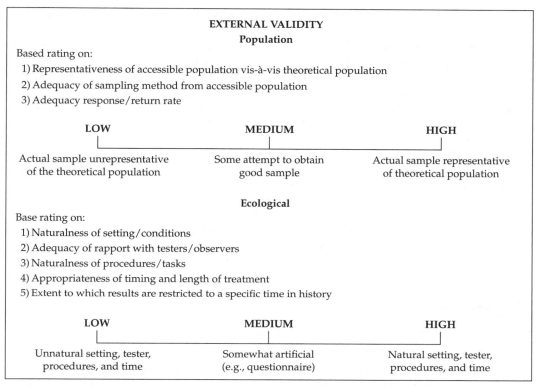

EXTERNAL VALIDITY
Population

Based rating on:

1) Representativeness of accessible population vis-à-vis theoretical population
2) Adequacy of sampling method from accessible population
3) Adequacy response/return rate

LOW	MEDIUM	HIGH
Actual sample unrepresentative of the theoretical population	Some attempt to obtain good sample	Actual sample representative of theoretical population

Ecological

Base rating on:

1) Naturalness of setting/conditions
2) Adequacy of rapport with testers/observers
3) Naturalness of procedures/tasks
4) Appropriateness of timing and length of treatment
5) Extent to which results are restricted to a specific time in history

LOW	MEDIUM	HIGH
Unnatural setting, tester, procedures, and time	Somewhat artificial (e.g., questionnaire)	Natural setting, tester, procedures, and time

FIGURE 9.3
Evaluating the external validity of the findings of a study.

Ecological External Validity

A second aspect of external validity is called ecological validity. It has to do with whether the conditions, settings, times, testers, or procedures are representative of natural conditions and so forth and, thus, whether the results can be generalized to real-life outcomes. Obviously, field research is more likely to be high on ecological external validity than laboratory procedures, especially if they are highly artificial. We would rate most of the self-report measures, especially questionnaires, to be somewhat artificial because they are not direct measures of the participants' actual behavior in a typical environment.

For example, there would be a problem with ecological validity if 6- to 12-month-old infants were tested for fear of strangers in an unnatural setting like a lab playroom with a male stranger who approached and picked up the baby in a short series of predetermined steps. In the name of experimental control, one might not attempt to have the stranger's behavior be contingent on the baby's. This procedure, and even the existence of fear of strangers, could be questioned by researchers who might show that a slower, more "natural" approach by a female stranger would produce almost no crying or attempts to get away from the stranger. Of course, the determinants of infant fear are complex, but the key point here is that studies in a controlled laboratory setting are usually low on ecological validity. Lab researchers usually trade ecological validity for better control of the environmental and independent variables. That is, they try to enhance internal validity.

As another example of a problem in ecological validity, if an educator is interested in the effect of a particular teaching style on student participation, the classroom should be similar to that of a normal classroom. Similarly, if the investigator asked students to come at night for the study, but these students normally attended class during the day, then there is a problem with ecological external validity. The investigator must ask if some representative method was used for selection of the setting and time. Or was a convenience method used?

For high ecological validity, an intervention should be conducted by a culturally appropriate intervener (teacher, therapist, or tester). And it should last for an appropriate length of time, given the planned use of the intervention.

Finally, there is the question of whether the study is specific/bound to a certain time period or whether the results will be applicable over a number of years. Attitudes about certain topics (e.g., school vouchers) may change over a relatively short number of years so that results may not be generalizable even a few years after the study.

Sampling and the Internal and External Validity of a Study

We discussed the internal and external validity of a study and noted that external validity is influenced by the representativeness of the sample. Much of this chapter has been about how to obtain a representative sample and what problems may arise in the process of sampling. Figure 9.4 is similar to Figure 9.1 but expands it on the right side to show how the *actual sample* could be divided into three groups. How this is done (randomly or not) affects the *internal validity of a study but does not directly affect external validity*, the sampling design, or the type of sampling. Thus, a study, as is the case with many randomized experiments, may have a small convenience sample and still have high internal validity because random assignment of participants to groups eliminates many threats to internal validity.

Figure 9.4 is a schematic diagram that extends Figure 9.1 to show how assignment and selection have different effects on internal and external validity even though both are performed with a random procedure. *Random selection*, or sampling of who is asked to participate in the study, is important for high external validity. On the other hand, *random assignment*, or placement of participants into groups, is important for high internal validity. This distinction, which is often confused or misunderstood, is an important one in terms of evaluating the quality of a research study and its internal and external validity.

Summary

Sampling is the process of selecting part of a larger group (the accessible population) with the intent of generalizing from the smaller group (the sample) to the population. We identified two kinds of population (theoretical or target versus accessible), and we discussed difficulties in obtaining an accessible population that is representative of the theoretical population of interest. Sampling (the sampling design) is the method used to select potential participants (the selected sample) from the accessible population. Several

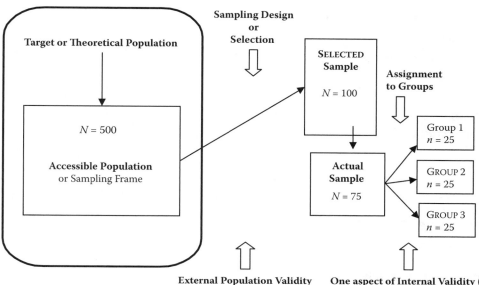

FIGURE 9.4
Random sampling versus random assignment to groups and their relationships to external and internal validity.

good sampling designs (probability sampling) were discussed; these include simple random, systematic with a random start, stratified, and cluster sampling. Several common but less desirable sampling methods (quota, purposive, and convenience) were also described. Finally, we discussed external validity and how to evaluate two of its major components, population external validity and ecological external validity. Random selection of participants is useful to produce high population external validity, whereas random assignment of participants to groups is important for high internal validity.

Key Concepts

Attrition

Clusters

External validity

Participants, cases, or elements

Population

Representative sample

Research validity

Response rate

Sampling

Sampling design

Strata

Key Distinctions

External validity versus internal validity

Population versus sample

Population external validity versus ecological external validity

Probability sampling versus nonprobability sampling

Purposive sampling versus purposeful sampling

Quota sampling versus convenience sampling

Random sampling versus random assignment

Selected sample versus actual sample

Simple random versus systematic random versus stratified random versus cluster (random) sampling

Stratified sampling with equal versus differential proportions

Target or theoretical population versus accessible population

Different Terms for Similar Concepts

Accessible population ≈ population

Actual sample ≈ sample

Participants ≈ cases ≈ elements

Probability sampling ≈ representative sampling

Sampling design ≈ sampling ≈ sample selection

Theoretical population ≈ target population

Application Problems

1. A researcher distributed questionnaires (surveys) to all employees of a municipal agency to obtain feedback regarding their jobs at this particular agency. Of 720 questionnaires distributed, 605 completed, usable surveys were returned. In this project what was (a) the target population?; (b) the accessible population?; (c) the selected sample?; and (d) the response rate? Was any sampling done? Evaluate the external population validity overall.

2. The Fort Choice municipal agency was interested in employee feedback. A decision was made to survey a representative sample of employees. The units comprising the agency ranged from very small, 14 to 18 employees, to fairly large units of more than 100 employees. The researchers wanted to be certain that all units were represented in proportion to their size in the survey. What kind of sampling approach might they use?

3. The county office on aging is interested in the perceived needs of older adults in their service area. A telephone survey is planned. A systematic random sample of 25% older adults with birth dates prior to 1938 is generated from voter registration lists. Describe how this would be done and then discuss the strengths and weaknesses of the external validity of this approach.

4. A researcher is interested in studying men and women's reactions to a violent crime show on national TV.

    a. Describe an appropriate probability sampling technique she might use.

    b. What are some problems that might affect external validity?

5. A researcher has a limited research budget, so he decides to look only at the high schools within a Midwestern community of 50,000 people. There are three high schools. He makes a list of all the students for each grade level (8th–12th). He randomly samples 10 students from each of the grade levels at each school (150 students total). Name and critique the sampling used in this study.

6. A researcher decides to do a laboratory experimental study of sleep deprivation on math performance. He randomly assigns students from his convenience sample to two groups. One group is kept awake all night and given a math test in the morning. The other group is allowed to sleep as long as they want before they take their math test in the morning. Critique this study on the basis of ecological validity.

7. Dr. G. is evaluating a large government grant. The purpose of the grant is to revise how mathematics and science education courses are taught at the community college and university level. There are 20 community colleges and 10 universities involved with the grant, each with one science education course. Describe how you would carry out the procedure for a 50% sample:

    a. simple random sample.

    b. stratified random sample.

    c. cluster sample.

10

Measurement and Descriptive Statistics

This chapter focuses on measurement, which provides rules about assignment of numbers and symbols to the levels of variables, and on descriptive statistics, which summarize and describe data from a sample without making inferences about the larger population from which the sample data were drawn. We begin by providing a brief overview about the normal or bell-shaped curve. As you will see throughout the chapter and in later ones, whether the responses or scores on a variable are distributed normally is important in the selection of appropriate statistics. Thus, understanding what is meant by normally distributed (or normal) data is important for measurement and for the use of appropriate descriptive statistics and graphs.

Overview of the Normal Curve

Figure 10.1 is an example of a normal curve. The normal curve, which is often referred to as a bell-shaped curve, was derived theoretically through the use of calculus. The curve is an idealized frequency distribution, with the horizontal axis (x axis) below the curve representing scores or responses on an ordered variable that varies from very low (−3), through average (0), to very high (+3). The vertical axis (y axis) or height of the curve represents the number of participants who had a particular score or response. The normal curve provides a model for the fit of the distributions of many of the dependent variables used in the behavioral sciences. Examples of such variables are height, weight, IQ, and many other psychological variables. Notice that for each of these examples, most people in the population would fall toward the middle of the curve, with fewer people at either extreme. If the mean or average height of men in the United States were 5'10", the number of men who were 5'10" would be shown by the hump shown in the middle of the curve. The number of men taller than 5'10" would be shown by the heights of the curve to the right of the middle, and these numbers would decrease as height goes up. So very few men would be 7 feet tall or more. Conversely, the numbers at each height shorter than 5'10" would be shown to the left of the middle and would decrease with few men shorter than 5 feet tall.

We discuss additional properties of the normal curve and its importance for understanding statistics later in this chapter.

Measurement

Measurement is the assignment of numbers or symbols to the different levels or values of variables according to rules. To understand variables, it is important to know their level

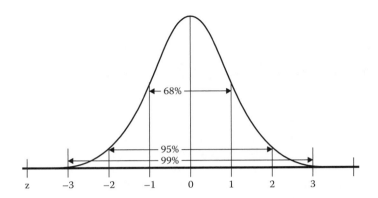

FIGURE 10.1
Frequency distribution and probability distribution for the normal curve.

of measurement. Depending on the level of measurement of a variable, the data can mean different things. For example, the number 2 might indicate a score of two; it might indicate that the participant was a male; or it might indicate that the participant was ranked second in the class. To help understand these differences, types or levels of the measurement of variables have been identified. It is common and traditional to discuss four levels or scales of measurement (*nominal, ordinal, interval,* and *ratio*), which vary from the lowest unordered level (nominal) to the highest level (ratio).[1]

The Traditional Levels or Scales of Measurement

Nominal Scales/Variables

This is the lowest or most basic level of measurement in which the numerals assigned to each mutually exclusive category stand for the *name* of the category but have *no implied order* or value.

Ordinal Scales/Variables (i.e., Unequal Interval Scales)

In ordinal scales there are not only mutually exclusive categories, as in nominal scales, but also the categories are ordered from low to high in much the same way that one would *rank* the order in which horses finished a race (i.e., first, second, third, … last). In the traditional definition of an ordinal scale, one knows the order from lowest to highest (or most preferred) on a dimension, but the intervals between the various ranks are not equal. For example, the second place horse may finish far behind the winner but only a fraction of a second in front of the third-place finisher. Thus, in this case there are unequal intervals among first, second, and third place, with a very small interval between second and third and a much larger one between first and second.

Interval and Ratio Scales or Variables

Not only do the **interval scales** have mutually exclusive categories that are ordered from low to high, but also the categories are equally spaced, that is, have equal intervals between them. Most physical measurements (e.g., length, weight, and dollars) have equal intervals between the categories and are called **ratio scales** because they have, in addition, an absolute or true zero, which means in the previous examples, no length, no weight, or no money. Few psychological scales have this property of a true zero, and, thus, even if they are very well-constructed equal interval scales, it is not possible to say that one has no intelligence or no extroversion or no amount of an attitude of a certain type. The differences between interval and ratio scales are not important for us because all of the types of statistics can be done with interval data. The traditional position is that if the scale has equal intervals, it is not necessary to have a true zero.

Difficulty Distinguishing Between the Traditional Scales

It is usually fairly easy to tell whether categories or levels of a variable are ordered—that is, whether they vary from low to high. Thus, one can readily distinguish between nominal and ordinal data. This distinction makes a lot of difference in what statistics are appropriate, as we shall see.

However, it is considerably less clear how to distinguish between ordinal and interval data. While almost all *physical* measurements provide either ratio or interval data, the situation is less clear with regard to psychological measurements. When we measure characteristics such as attitudes, often we are not certain whether the intervals between the ordered categories are equal, as required for the traditional identification of interval level variables. Suppose we have a five-point scale on which we are to rate an attitude about a certain statement from strongly agree as 5 to strongly disagree as 1. The issue is whether the intervals between a rating of 1 and 2, or 2 and 3, or 3 and 4, or 4 and 5 are all equal or not. *Some researchers* could argue that because the numbers are equally spaced on the page and because they are equally spaced in terms of their numerical values, the participants will view them as equal intervals, and, thus, they will have psychologically equal intervals. However, especially if the in between points are labeled (e.g., "strongly agree," "agree," "neutral," "disagree," and "strongly disagree"), it could be argued that the difference, for example, between strongly agree and agree is not the same as between agree and neutral. This contention would be hard to disprove, so many *other researchers* would argue that such a five-point scale is *ordinal* rather than *interval* level.

Furthermore, some questionnaire or survey items have responses that are clearly unequal intervals. For example, let's take the case where the participants are asked to identify their age as one of five categories: "less than 21," "21–30," "31–40," "41–50," and "51 or older." It should be clear that the first and last categories are much larger in terms of number of years covered than the three middle categories. Thus, the age intervals would not be equal. Another example of an ordered scale that is clearly not interval would be one that asked how frequently participants do something. The answers go something like this: "every day," "once a week," "once a month," "once a year," and "once every 5 years." The categories become wider and wider and, therefore, are not equal intervals. There is clearly much more difference between 1 year and 5 years than there is between 1 day and 1 week.

These four levels have been discussed in most statistics and research methods textbooks, and they have been used to indicate the level of measurement necessary to compute certain statistics. In general, the mean, standard deviation, and parametric inferential statistics, such as the *t* test, are said in such textbooks to require at least *interval* level measurement for the variables. However, we have found the distinction between the traditional *ordinal* and *interval* levels somewhat confusing to apply, and statisticians have argued that this traditional distinction is not necessary to use parametric statistics, if the data are approximately normally distributed (Gaito, 1980, 1986; Velleman & Wilkinson, 1993). Thus, we

TABLE 10.1

Our Recommended Measurement Terms Compared With the Traditional

Our term	Our definition	Traditional term	Traditional definition
Nominal	Three or more *unordered* categories	Nominal	Two or more *unordered* categories
Dichotomous	Two categories, either ordered or unordered	NA	NA
Ordinal	Three or more *ordered* levels, but the frequency distribution of the scores is *not* normally distributed	Ordinal	*Ordered* levels, in which the difference in magnitude between levels is not equal
Approximately normal	Many (at least five) *ordered* levels or scores, with the frequency distribution of the scores being approximately normally distributed	Interval and ratio	**Interval:** *ordered* levels, in which the difference between levels is equal, but there is no true zero **Ratio:** *ordered* levels; the difference between levels is equal, and there is a true zero

describe, in the next section of this chapter, a somewhat different classification of levels of measurement that we think is more useful and easier to understand.[2]

Our Categorization of Levels of Measurement

We believe that the concepts *nominal, dichotomous, ordinal,* and *approximately normally distributed* (which we call *normal* data) are more useful than the traditional measurement terms for the selection and interpretation of statistics. In part, this is because as mentioned earlier statisticians disagree about the usefulness of the traditional levels of measurement in determining appropriate selection of statistics. Furthermore, our experience is that the traditional terms are frequently misunderstood and applied inappropriately. Table 10.1 compares the traditional terms to our terms and provides summary definitions.

Nominal Variables

This level is the same as the traditional nominal scale of measurement, except that we include only variables that have *three or more unordered* categories. For example, single people might be assigned the numeral 1, married persons might be coded as 2, and divorced persons could be coded as 3. This does not imply that a divorced person is higher than a married one or that two single persons equal one married, or any of the other typical mathematical uses of the numerals. The same reasoning applies to other nominal variables such as ethnic group, type of disability, or section number in a class schedule. In each of these cases, the categories are distinct and nonoverlapping but not ordered; thus, each category in the variable ethnic group is different from each other, but there is no necessary order to the categories. The categories could be numbered 1 for Asian American, 2 for Latin American, 3 for African American, and 4 for European American or the reverse, or any combination of assigning a number to each category. What this implies is that the numbers used for identifying the categories in a nominal variable must not be treated as if they were numbers that could be used in a formula, added together, subtracted from one another, or used to compute an average. Average ethnic group makes no sense. However, if one asks a computer to compute average ethnic group, it will do so and provide meaningless information. The important thing about nominal scales is to have clearly defined, nonoverlapping, or mutually exclusive categories that can be coded reliably by observers or by participant self-report.

Qualitative or constructivist researchers rely heavily, if not exclusively, on nominal variables and on the process of developing appropriate codes or categories for behaviors, words, and so forth. Qualitative coding may seem different because it is much more detailed and because it is unusual to assign numerals to the various categories. Although using qualitative (nominal) data does dramatically reduce the types of statistics that can be used with data, it does not eliminate the *possible* use of statistics to summarize data and make inferences. Therefore, when the data are nominal, one's research may benefit from the use of appropriate statistics. Later in this chapter we discuss the types of descriptive statistics that are appropriate for nominal data.

Dichotomous Variables

A dichotomous variable, one with only two levels or categories (e.g., Yes or No, Pass or Fail) is sometimes assumed to be nominal. While some such dichotomous variables are clearly unordered (e.g., gender) and others are clearly ordered (e.g., math grades—high or low), all dichotomous variables form a *special case*. Statistics such as the mean or variance would be meaningless for a three or more category nominal variable (e.g., ethnic group or marital status, as described already). However, such statistics *do have meaning* when the data are dichotomous, that is, have only two categories. For example, if the average gender was 1.55 (with males = 1 and females = 2), then 55% of the participants were females. Furthermore (as we show in Chapter 22) for multiple regression, dichotomous variables, called "dummy" variables, can be used as independent variables along with other variables that are normally distributed. It turns out that dichotomous variables can be treated, in most cases, as similar to normally distributed variables.

Ordinal Variables

These variables have three or more ordered categories or levels, and the responses are *not normally distributed*. This level of measurement is similar to the traditional ordinal scale of measurement discussed earlier. However, we emphasize that when the frequencies of scores from a sample of participants are plotted they do *not* look like the bell-shaped or normal distribution of the scores shown in Figure 10.1.

Normally Distributed Variables

Not only do these variables have mutually exclusive categories that are *ordered* from low to high, but also the responses or scores are at least *approximately normally distributed* in the population from which the sample was selected. An assumption of many parametric inferential statistics, such as the *t* test, is that the dependent variable is normally distributed. Normality is also important for the appropriate use of several common descriptive statistics discussed later in this chapter (e.g., mean and standard deviation).

Confusion About Terms

Unfortunately, the literature is full of confusing terms to describe the measurement aspects of variables. *Categorical* and *discrete* are terms sometimes used interchangeably with *nominal*, but nominal is more appropriate because it is possible to have ordered, discrete categories.

TABLE 10.2

Correspondence of Measurement Terms

Our measurement term	Other somewhat similar terms
Dichotomous	Binary, dummy variable, two categories
Nominal	Unordered, qualitative, names, categorical,[a] discrete[a]
Ordinal	Unequal intervals, ranks, discrete ordered categories
Normal (approximately normally distributed)	Continuous, equal intervals, interval scale, ratio scale, quantitative scale (in SPSS), dimensional

[a] However, ordinal variables and even normally distributed variables, sometimes have discrete categories.

TABLE 10.3

Characteristics and Examples of Variables at Each Level of Measurement

	Nominal	Dichotomous	Ordinal	Normal

Characteristics	3+ levels
	Not ordered
	True categories
	Names, labels
		2 levels
		Ordered or not
			3+ levels
			Ordered levels
			Unequal intervals
			  between levels
			Not normally distributed
				5+ levels
				Ordered levels
				Approximately
				  normally distributed
				Equal intervals
				  between levels

Examples	Ethnicity Religion Curriculum type Hair color	Gender Math grades (high versus low)	Most ranked data Race finish (1st, 2nd, 3rd)	Test scores GRE scores Height IQ

Continuous, dimensional, and *quantitative* are terms that appear in the literature for ordered variables that vary from low to high. Many such variables are assumed to be normally distributed.

These terms and their relationships to the terms nominal, dichotomous, ordinal, and normally distributed are sometimes used inconsistently. Table 10.2 clarifies these somewhat overlapping and confusing terms. Nominal variables have discrete, unordered categories. Ordinal and even normally distributed variables also can use discrete categories or scores such as 1, 2, 3, 4, 5; however, with ordinal and normal level measurement, the categories are ordered. Researchers differ in the terminology they prefer and on how much importance to place on levels or scales of measurement, so all of these terms and others mentioned in textbooks and articles are commonly seen.

Table 10.3 provides a review of the concept of levels of measurement of a variable. We point out here that it is *always* important to know the levels of measurement of the *dependent variable* in a study. Also, when the *independent variable* is an attribute, a judgment about the level of measurement should be made. Usually, with an *active independent* variable the categories of the independent variable are nominal, but in certain cases (treatment dosages, e.g., no drug, 10 mg, 20 mg, and 30 mg) an active independent variable could be ordinal or even normally distributed.

An example that illustrates three levels of measurement and may be helpful is based on an afternoon at the horse races. The numbers worn by the horse represent a nominal scale. Although the numbers correspond to the gate in which the horse starts the race, their function for the spectator is to identify the *name* of the horse in the racing form. The betting is based on an ordinal scale: whether the selected horse comes in first, second, or third (i.e., win, place, or show). It does not matter if the horse wins by a nose or by 10 lengths, a win is a win. Thus, these ranks form an ordinal scale. However, the money people might receive from all the bets that day might be normally distributed. A few people probably win a lot, many break even or lose a little, and a few lose a lot. More details and examples of approximately normally distributed data are presented later in the chapter.

Descriptive Statistics and Graphs

Descriptive Graphs

Frequency distributions indicate how many participants are in each category; they are useful whether the categories are ordered or unordered. If one wants to make a graph or diagram of a frequency distribution there are several choices, including frequency polygons, histograms, and bar charts. **Frequency polygons** and **histograms** (shown in Figure 10.2) connect the points between the categories, so they are best used with normally distributed (normal) data. Frequency polygons should *not* be used with nominal data because in that case there is no necessary ordering of the points.

Thus, for variables (e.g., ethnic group, school curriculum, or other nominal variables) it is better to make a **bar graph** (or chart) of the frequencies (Figure 10.3). The points that happen to be adjacent in a frequency distribution are not by necessity adjacent.

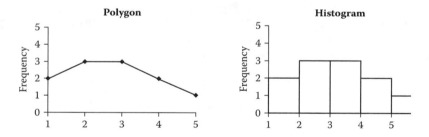

FIGURE 10.2
Sample frequency polygon and histogram for the same-ordered, normal-level data.

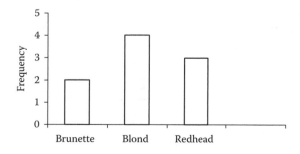

FIGURE 10.3
Sample frequency distribution bar chart for the nominal scale of hair color.

Measures of Central Tendency

The three main measures of the center of a distribution are the mean, median, and mode. As you can see from Table 10.7 near the end of the chapter, any of these measures of central tendency can be used with normal data. The mean, median, and mode are all the same and in the center of the distribution when the data are normally distributed.

The **mean** or arithmetic average takes into account all of the available information when used to compute the central tendency of a frequency distribution. Thus, the mean is usually the statistic of choice if *one has normal data*.

The **median** or middle score is an appropriate measure of central tendency for ordinal-level data. The median may be a better measure of central tendency than the mean under certain circumstances, namely, when the frequency distribution is skewed markedly to one side. For example, the median income of 100 mid-level workers and a millionaire is substantially lower and reflects the central tendency of the group better than the mean income, which would be inflated in this example and for the country as a whole by a few people who make very large amounts of money.

Finally, the **mode**, or most common category, can be used with any kind of data but generally provides the least precise information about central tendency. One would use the mode as the measure of central tendency if there is only one mode, if it is clearly identified, and if you want a quick noncalculated measure.

Calculation of the Mean

We demonstrate here the calculation of the mean because of its common use in both descriptive and inferential statistics. The formula for the population mean, μ, is the same as the formula for the sample mean, M. To calculate the mean or *average* of a set of numbers, we add or sum (Σ) the numbers (X) and then divide by the number of entries (N). X refers to individual scores (often referred to as raw scores).

The formula for M (the mean of the sample) is

$$M = \frac{\sum X}{N}$$

where X is the individual or raw scores in the sample, and N is the number of scores in the sample.

Suppose that 10 people took a test and the scores were arranged from highest to lowest. We want to know the mean of the 10 scores. The scores are shown in Table 10.4 in the column labeled "Test Score."

We calculate the mean using the previous formula.

$$M = \frac{\sum X}{N}$$

$$M = \frac{700}{10}$$

$$M = 70$$

TABLE 10.4

Scores for 10 Participants on Form B

Participant ID number	Test score
1	93
2	85
3	82
4	77
5	75
6	66
7	63
8	62
9	54
10	43
	$\Sigma = 700$

Thus, the mean or average test score is 70. Because the scores are arranged from highest, as participant number 1, to the lowest, it is quite easy to determine the median score. If there had been an odd number of persons, the median would be the middle score. Because there are 10 (an even number) participants, the median is halfway between the fifth (75) and sixth (66) persons' scores (i.e., 70.5). Note that the median is similar but not the same as the mean in this case. There is no clear mode in this example because each participant has a distinct score. The mode is more useful when the data are nominal or dichotomous, there are relatively few categories, and there are a larger number of participants.

Measures of Variability

Variability describes the spread or dispersion of the scores. In the extreme, if all of the scores in a distribution are the same, there is no variability. If they are all different and widely spaced apart, the variability will be high. The **standard deviation**, the most common measure of variability, is appropriate only when one has normally distributed data.

For ordinal data the interquartile range, the distance between the 25th and 75th percentiles, is the best measure of variability. With nominal data one would need to ask how many different categories are there and what are the percentages in each.

Calculation of the Standard Deviation

The formula for the standard deviation of the sample is

$$SD = \sqrt{\frac{\sum x^2}{N-1}}$$

Because it is common in both descriptive and inferential statistics, we show how to calculate the standard deviation. Notice in the formula that the numbers that we square and add are not raw scores (*X*) but *deviation scores* (*x*). To compute the deviation scores, we subtract the mean from each raw score because the standard deviation is a measure of how scores vary about the mean. Now we calculate the standard deviation using the same sample of 10 scores that we used to compute the mean in the previous section.

TABLE 10.5

Calculation of the Standard Deviation

ID#	X	M	x	x^2
1	93	70	23	529
2	85	70	15	225
3	82	70	12	144
4	77	70	7	49
5	75	70	5	25
6	66	70	−4	16
7	63	70	−7	49
8	62	70	−8	64
9	54	70	−16	256
10	43	70	−27	729
Total				2086

We start by creating Table 10.5 using the scores (X) from the test. First, subtract the mean, 70, from each of the raw scores. These deviation scores can be seen under the column x. If we added these scores, the total would be zero. (The sum of the deviations around the mean always equals zero.) Next we square each of the deviation (x) scores, which gives us the scores in column x^2. Then we add the scores in column x^2, which is 2,086. Note when you square a minus number (e.g., −8), the square is a positive number (64). Next, we divide this sum by the number of participants minus one and take the square root to arrive at the standard deviation.

The calculation of the standard deviation is as follows:

$$SD = \sqrt{\frac{\sum x^2}{N-1}}$$

$$SD = \sqrt{\frac{2086}{9}}$$

$$SD = \sqrt{231.78}$$

$$SD = 15.22$$

Thus, the standard deviation is 15.22. The fact that few of the scores are close to the mean of 70 indicates that there is quite a bit of variability in this sample. We discuss more about the interpretation of the standard deviation later in this chapter in the section about areas under the normal curve.

Measures of Association Between Two Variables

Scatterplots

A scatterplot (Figure 10.4 and Figure 10.5) provides a visual picture of the correlation. Each dot or circle on the plot represents a particular individual's score on the two variables, with one variable being represented on the x axis and the other on the y axis. A **scatterplot** is a plot or graph of two variables that shows how the score for an individual

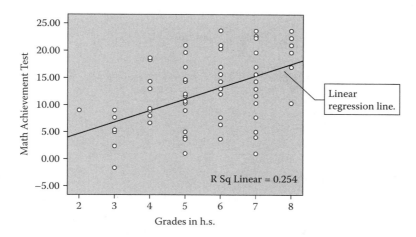

FIGURE 10.4
Scatterplot of math achievement with high school grades.

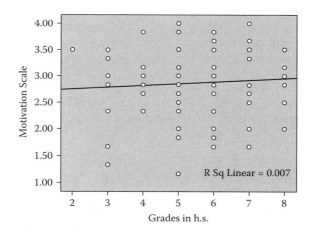

FIGURE 10.5
A scatterplot showing a very weak linear correlation.

on one *variable associates with his or her score on the other variable.* When the plotted points are close to a straight line (the *linear regression line*) from the lower left corner of the plot to the upper right as in Figure 10.4, there is a relatively high *positive correlation* (e.g., +.5) between the variables. When the linear regression line slopes downward from the upper left to the lower right, the correlation is *high negative* (e.g., −.5). For correlations *near zero* (as in Figure 10.5), the regression line will be close to flat with many points far from the line, and the points will form a pattern more like a circle or blob than a line or oval.

In both Figure 10.4 and Figure 10.5, the scatterplots show the best fit for a straight (linear) regression line (i.e., it minimizes the squared differences between the points and the line). Note that for Figure 10.4 (grades in high school with math achievement), the points fit the line pretty well; $r^2 = .25$, and, thus, r is .50. Figure 10.5 shows that grades in high school and motivation are only weakly correlated; the points do not fit the line very well ($r^2 = .007$, $r = .08$).

TABLE 10.6

Sample Cross-Tabulation Table

Variable	*n*	Gender	
		Males	Females
Geometry			
Taken	36	24	12
Not taken	39	10	29
Totals	75	34	41

Pearson and Spearman Correlations

The **Pearson product moment correlation** is a bivariate parametric statistic used when both variables are ordered and approximately normally distributed. When the data are ordinal or when other assumptions are markedly violated, one should use a nonparametric equivalent of the Pearson correlation coefficient. One such nonparametric, ordinal statistic is the **Spearman rho.**

Both Pearson and Spearman correlations can vary from –1.0 (a perfect negative relationship or association) through 0.0 (no correlation) to +1.0 (a perfect positive correlation). Note that +1 and –1 are equally high or strong, but they lead to different interpretations. A high *positive correlation* between anxiety and grades would mean that students with higher anxiety tended to have high grades, those with lower anxiety had low grades, and those in between had grades that were neither especially high nor especially low. On the other hand, if there were a high *negative correlation,* it would mean that students with high anxiety tended to have low grades; also, high grades would be associated with low anxiety. With a *zero correlation* there are no consistent associations; a student with high anxiety might have low, medium, or high grades.

Cross-Tabulation Tables

This type of table is designed to show the association between two nominal or dichotomous variables. Remember, nominal variables are variables that have distinct *unordered* levels or categories; each participant is in only one level (a person is either male *or* female). Cross-tabulation tables also can be used with ordered variables but are less appropriate if either variable has three or more *ordered* levels. Table 10.6 shows the cross-tabulation of gender with whether students took geometry in high school for a group of 75 former students. It is evident that a higher proportion (24 of 36) of males took geometry; only 10 of 39 females did. Thus, there seems to be an association between gender and taking geometry. In Chapter 21, we discuss the chi-square statistic to test whether this association is statistically significant—that is, whether one can be confident that the apparent association is not due to chance. Chapter 21 also discusses how to interpret the statistical significance of correlation coefficients.

More on the Normal Curve

The Normal Curve as a Probability Distribution

While the normal curve often is conceptualized as a frequency distribution, for our purposes, it is more important as a *probability* distribution. Visualize that the area under the normal curve is equal to 1.0. Therefore, portions of this curve could be expressed as fractions of 1.0. For example, if we assume that 5'10" is the average height of men in the United States, then the probability of a man being 5'10" *or taller* is .5. The probability of a man being over 6'5" or less than 5'5" is considerably smaller. It is important to be able to conceptualize the normal curve as a probability distribution because statistical convention sets acceptable probability levels for rejecting the null hypothesis at .05 or .01. As we shall see, when events or outcomes happen very infrequently, that is, only 5 times in 100 or 1 time in 100 (way out in the left or right tail of the curve), we wonder if they belong to that distribution or perhaps to a different distribution. We come back to this point several times later in the book.

Properties of the Normal Curve

The normal curve has five properties that are always present:

1. The normal curve is unimodal. It has one "hump," and this hump is in the middle of the distribution. The most frequent value is in the middle.
2. The mean, median, and mode are equal.
3. The curve is symmetric. If you folded the normal curve in half, the right side would fit perfectly with the left side; that is, it is not *skewed*.
4. The range is infinite. This means that the extremes approach but never touch the *x* axis.
5. The curve is neither too peaked nor too flat, and its tails are neither too short nor too long; it has no *kurtosis*. Its proportions are like those in Figure 10.1.

Areas Under the Normal Curve

All normal curves, regardless of whether they are narrow or spread out, can be divided into areas or units in terms of the standard deviation. Approximately 34% of the area under the normal curve is between the mean and one standard deviation above or below the mean. If we include both the area to the right *and* to the left of the mean, 68% of the area under the normal curve is within one standard deviation from the mean, as was shown in Figure 10.1. Another approximately 13.5% of the area under the normal curve is accounted for by adding a second standard deviation to the first standard deviation. In other words, two standard deviations to the right of the mean account for an area of approximately 47.5% of the curve. And two standard deviations to the left *and* two to the right of the mean make up an area of approximately 95% of the normal curve. If we were to subtract 95% from 100% the remaining 5% relates to the probability or *p* value of 0.05 conventionally established for statistical significance, as we see in Chapter 16. Values not falling within two standard deviations of the mean are relatively rare events.

Using our previous example of the ID test score shown in Table 10.5, note that 7 of 10 (70%) scores fell between 55 and 85, which are approximately one standard deviation below and above the mean of 70. All the scores were within two *SD*s. These percentages are about what one would expect if the scores were normally distributed.

The Standard Normal Curve

All normal curves can be converted into standard normal curves by setting the mean equal to zero and the standard deviation equal to one. Since all normal curves have the same proportion of the curve within one standard deviation, two standard deviations, and so on of the mean, this conversion allows comparisons among normal curves with different means and standard deviations. The normal distribution curve shown in Figure 10.1 has the standard normal distribution units underneath. These units are referred to as *z* **scores**, which indicate the number of standard deviation units that a person's score deviates from the group mean. In our example, the student who had 93 on the test would have a *z* score of +1.51 (93 − 70 ÷ 15.22), whereas the student who scored 43 had a *z* = −1.77. A valuable characteristic of *z* scores is that they allow you to compare scores on different tests. For example, a student with an exam score of 80 (in a class whose mean was 70 and *SD* was 5) has *z* score of +2.0 and did relatively better than the student in Table 10.5 who had a test score of 93 and *z* = 1.51.

Another important use of the standard deviation and the standard normal curve has to do with the strength or size of the relationship between variables. Statisticians refer to this as the **effect size**. In Chapter 17 we discuss various effect size measures and how to interpret them. For now, we want to point out that the most common effect size measures are similar to *z* scores in that they are expressed in standard deviation units. For example, *d* = 0.5 means that on average the intervention group performed one half a standard deviation better than the comparison group. This common metric is useful in comparing the size or strength of the effect across several different studies.

Levels of Measurement and Descriptive Statistics

Table 10.7 summarizes whether and how a number of common descriptive statistics and plots should be used if the data (i.e., dependent variable) were nominal, dichotomous, ordinal, or normally distributed. For example, *frequency distributions* are appropriate for all four levels of measurement but most useful with nominal, dichotomous, and ordinal data. With nominal data the order in which the categories are listed is arbitrary. With ordinal and normally distributed data the order of the categories would be invariant. For normally distributed data the frequency distribution would look similar to the normal curve in Figure 10.1.

As discussed earlier and summarized in Table 10.7, certain types of plots and descriptive statistics should *not* be used with certain levels of data. For example, frequency polygons and histograms should not be used if the data are nominal as indicated by "No" in Table 10.7. In some cases graphs or statistics are okay (indicated in the table by "OK") but are not the best use. For example, histograms can be used with ordinal data but are more appropriately used if the data are normally distributed.

Other things being equal, one would obtain more sound results using normally distributed data than ordinal, and ordinal would be better than nominal measurement. However, sacrificing reliability or validity (Chapters 11 and 12) to have a higher level of measurement would mean that you would have greater accuracy or power to get the wrong answers! As we see in later chapters, if reliable and valid data are normally distributed, more powerful inferential statistics are available to test our hypothesis.

TABLE 10.7

Selection of Appropriate Descriptive Graphs and Statistics

	Nominal	Dichotomous	Ordinal	Normal
Graphs				
Frequency distribution	Yes[a]	Yes	Yes	OK[b]
Bar chart	Yes	Yes	Yes	OK
Histogram	No[c]	No	OK	Yes
Frequency polygon	No	No	OK	Yes
Central tendency				
Mean	No	OK	Of ranks, OK	Yes
Median	No	OK = Mode	Yes	OK
Mode	Yes	Yes	OK	OK
Variability				
Range	No	Always 1	Yes	Yes
Standard deviation	No	No	Of ranks, OK	Yes
Interquartile range	No	No	OK	OK
How many categories	Yes	Always 2	OK	Not if truly continuous
Shape				
Skewness	No	No	Yes	Yes
Association				
Pearson correlation	No	OK	OK	Yes
Spearman correlation	No	OK	Yes	OK
Cross-tabulation	Yes	Yes	OK	OK
Scatterplot	No	No	OK	Yes

[a] Yes means a good choice with this level of measurement.
[b] OK means OK to use, but not the best choice at this level of measurement.
[c] No means not appropriate at this level of measurement.

Summary

This chapter provides an overview of levels of measurement and how they influence the appropriate use of statistics. We divide variables into four types or levels: dichotomous, nominal, ordinal, and normally distributed. Dichotomous variables have only two levels; nominal have three or more unordered levels. Ordinal variables have three or more ordered levels, but the frequency distribution of responses is not normal. Finally, normally distributed variables have at least approximately a normal (bell-shaped) frequency distribution. Properties of the normal curve were discussed because many statistics assume that responses are normally distributed, and many behavioral variables are distributed at least approximately normal. Three of the many ways of plotting frequency distributions (histograms, frequency polygons, and bar charts) were described and illustrated. Similarly, measures of central tendency (mean, median, and mode) were described, as were measures of variability (range, standard deviation, interquartile range, and number of categories) and measures of the association between two variables (scatterplots, correlation, and cross-tabulation). Finally, recommendations about the appropriate use of various descriptive statistics and graphs or plots were presented.

Key Concepts

Correlation

Cross-tabulation

Interquartile range

Normal distribution and normal curve

Scatterplot

Skewness

Standard deviation

Standard normal curve

z scores

Key Distinctions

Histogram versus frequency polygon versus bar chart

Mean versus median versus mode

Nominal versus dichotomous versus ordinal versus normal levels of measurement

Ordered versus unordered categories or levels of a variable

The traditional nominal versus ordinal versus interval scales of measurement

Application Problems

1. Describe our four levels of measurement (nominal, dichotomous, ordinal, normal); provide an original example for each.
2. How are our levels of measurement similar and different from the traditional ones?
3. Why is it important to know/determine the level of measurement for your data?
4. Which measures of central tendency are appropriate to use with data at each of our levels of measurement?
5. For the examples that follow, state the level of measurement and your reasoning or justification:
   a. Urban, suburban, rural
   b. Young, middle aged, old
   c. 15, 16, 17, 18, 19, 20, 21 … years
   d. Strongly agree, agree, neutral, disagree, strongly disagree
6. Both dichotomous variables and nominal variables are categorical. Why is it informative to calculate the mean with a dichotomous variable but not with a nominal variable?

7. How does the normal curve differ from the standard normal curve?

8. The following scores were recorded from students in a statistics class. Determine the mean, median, mode, and standard deviation.

    89, 93, 81, 93, 73, 93, 85, 89, 75, 85, 90, 70

9. A student in a large undergraduate class (approximately 500 students) scores one standard deviation above the mean on her first midterm. Her score is higher than what percentage of the class?

10. Another student in this same class scores two standard deviations below the mean. What percentage of students has a higher score? What is this student's z score?

Notes

1. Unfortunately, the terms *level* and *scale* are used several ways in research. Levels refer to the categories or values of a variable (e.g., male or female); level can also refer to the four different types of measurement (e.g., nominal, ordinal). These several types of measurement also have been called *scales of measurement*. Scale is also used to describe questionnaire items that are rated from strongly disagree to strongly agree (Likert scale) and for the sum of such items (summated scale).
2. This alternative categorization was proposed to us by Helena Chmura Kraemer, professor of biostatistics at Stanford, (personal communication March 16, 1999).

11

Measurement Reliability

In this chapter and the next we discuss the reliability and validity of individual measurements or scores from an instrument. The quality of a study depends, in part, on the quality of the design (internal validity) and of the sample (population external validity) as discussed in Chapters 8 and 9. Study quality also depends on the consistency (measurement reliability) and accuracy (measurement validity) of the specific instruments, as discussed in this chapter and Chapter 12. In Chapters 23 and 24, we show how these four quality indicators (and others) can be used to evaluate the overall quality of a study.

Measurement Reliability

What is **reliability**? When a person is said to be reliable, we have certain conceptions about that person. For example, the person always shows up for meetings on time; therefore, he is a reliable person. Or, the person always gets the job done; therefore, she is a reliable person. When we use tests or other instruments to measure outcomes, we also need to make sure that these instruments provide reliable data. Cronbach (1990) said that reliability refers to consistency of a series of measurements. According to Thompson (2003), reliability is a property of scores and is not immutable across all conceivable uses of a given measure. The importance of reliability for research methods cannot be overstated. If our outcome measure does not provide reliable data, then we cannot accurately assess the results of our study. Hence, our study will be worthless.

An Example

To understand the importance of measurement reliability and its underpinnings, it is best to start with an example. A researcher is interested in determining if quality of life for persons with cognitive disabilities can be increased through a recreational support program. To determine if the intervention (recreational support program) works, he designs a randomized experiment using a pretest–posttest control group design, where one group receives the intervention (X) for 6 months and the other group does not receive the intervention (~X). Both groups receive the pretest with an instrument that measures quality of life and then after the 6-month period receive the same instrument on the posttest. As in earlier chapters, the design can be shown as follows:

$$R \qquad O_1 \qquad X \qquad O_2$$
$$R \qquad O_1 \qquad \sim X \qquad O_2$$

The researcher will measure quality of life (dependent variable) with a particular measurement tool, which we call the Quality of Life (QOL) inventory. He will measure both the intervention and control groups on the QOL prior to the intervention and then again after the period of the intervention. Therefore, each participant in the study will obtain a score on the QOL prior to the intervention and after the intervention period. If the QOL inventory has a range between 0 and 100, then each participant will receive both a pretest score and a posttest score within this range. He hopes, and thus hypothesizes, that the posttest scores in the intervention group are higher than those of the control group. Because of the random assignment, the groups should be equivalent initially. As we have seen in Chapters 5 and 8, this design is a strong one in terms of internal validity. However, it is possible that the study is weak in other respects. For example, population external validity could be low if the participants were unrepresentative of the theoretical population. The issue to consider here is whether the QOL inventory will measure quality of life consistently (reliably) in this study with this group of participants.

Test Scores

We call any score that we obtain from any individual on a particular instrument an **observed score.** One of the participants named Jones is in the intervention group. If Jones scores 49 on the pretest of the QOL, then Jones's observed score is 49. If we were to give Jones the QOL a second time, his observed score probably will be different from 49. It might be 53 or 43. If we gave the QOL to Jones a third time, the score probably will be different from either of the scores received from previous administrations of the test. Since Jones's score will not be the same each time we give the QOL, and, since we must give Jones a second QOL *after* the intervention, how will we know if the change in Jones's score from pretest to posttest is due to the intervention or perhaps due to something else? Stated another way, how do we know whether the change in Jones's score is due to systematic variation (variation due to the intervention) or unsystematic variation (variation due to other factors). To understand our problem, we must consider classical test theory, true scores, and error.

According to classical test theory:

$$\text{Observed score} = \text{True score} \pm \text{Error}$$

Thus, an *observed* score is made up of a **true score** and **error**. Because classical test theory is a hypothetical theory, we can never know a person's true score. We will know only their observed score. Furthermore, because all measurement usually includes some error, we cannot assume that the observed score is the same as the true score. If we could subtract the true score from the observed score, we could determine how much of the score is due to error. We never actually know the amount of the observed score that is due to the true score and the amount of the observed score that is due to error. If we were to measure the person thousands of times and take the average of all of those measurements, then the average score would be very close to the individual's true score. Unfortunately, we rarely measure a person more than a couple of times on any given instrument.

Since we rarely measure a person multiple times with any instrument, the researcher may have trouble in his study. Again, the problem is that if he is trying to assess the change due to his intervention, he will need to measure each participant more than one time. Let's suppose that Jones's QOL score increases from 49 (pretest) to 53 (posttest). How do we know whether this increase is due to an increase in Jones' true score (systematic variation) or merely to an increase due to error (unsystematic variation)? The solution to the problem is to choose a test that produces scores that have high reliability. We have not considered specific methods of determining reliability at this point, but we have stated that reliability is a measure of consistency. How does reliability relate to observed scores and true scores? **Measurement reliability** is expressed as a coefficient. The reliability coefficient is the *ratio of the variance of true scores to the variance of observed scores* (Ghiselli, Campbell, & Zedeck, 1981). In other words, the higher the reliability of the data, the closer the true scores will be to observed scores. Now, given what we know about observed scores, true scores, and error, we should consider correlation coefficients.

Standard Error of Measurement

When selecting a test, one of the most important questions to ask, in addition to reliability and validity information, is what type of variability of performance we might expect. In the previous chapter we discussed the standard deviation as an index of variability and also introduced the normal curve. Both of these and information on reliability are needed when we consider the standard error of measurement. The **standard error of measurement** allows us to establish a range of scores (i.e., confidence interval) within which should lie a performer's true score. Confidence intervals are difficult to understand and often misinterpreted but very important for understanding research results. In Chapter 17 we examine confidence intervals in some depth.

First let's look at the formula for the standard error of measurement; then we will provide an example to help explain the concept. The formula for the standard error of measurement is

$$s_m = s\sqrt{1-r}$$

where
  s = standard deviation of the test
  r = the reliability coefficient for the test

We start with an intelligence test like the Wechsler Adult Intelligence Scale (WAIS), which has a known standard deviation of 15. Let's say that the reliability coefficient is, on average, .92. What will be the standard error of measurement? Fitting these numbers into the equation, the standard error of measurement (s_m) is 4.24. A given individual takes the test and scores 110 (which is the person's observed score). From our earlier introduction to classical test theory, this *observed score* is equal to a *true score* plus *error*. We do not know (nor will we ever know) the individual's true score. Therefore, we can estimate the range in which a person's true score may fall from a single test. To do this, we use the standard error of measurement and set a confidence interval around the observed score. The size of this confidence interval will depend on how sure we want to be that the true score fits within this interval. In most cases we want to be at least 95% sure (two standard deviations). Therefore, we set up a 95% confidence interval around the observed score. To do this, we multiply our standard error of measurement times the z score representing two standard deviations from the mean on a normal curve. This z value is 1.96 (Figure 10.1). Therefore, 4.24 times 1.96 gives us a value of 8.32. We can conclude that our true score falls within the 95% confidence interval of 110 ± 8.32 or between 101.68 and 118.32. A brief explanation of the 95% confidence interval is that if the test were given to the same person a large number of times, 95% of the confidence intervals would contain the true score.

The standard error of measurement illustrates the importance of the reliability coefficient. Suppose that in the illustrated example our reliability coefficient was .65. Our standard error of measurement would now be 8.87. We multiply this value times 1.96 to establish our confidence interval. Our confidence interval is 110 ± 17.39, or between 92.61 and 127.61. The precision of our estimate of the true score has *decreased* substantially due to a low reliability coefficient.

Correlation Coefficient

We can conceptually discuss reliability as some form of consistency. However, when evaluating scores from an instrument it is important to be able to express reliability in some numerical form. This allows us to compare different scores from instruments on properties of reliability. The measure most often selected to evaluate reliability is referred to as a **correlation coefficient**. As discussed in Chapter 10, a correlation coefficient is usually expressed as the letter *r* and indicates the strength of a relation. The values of *r* range between −1 and +1. A value of 0 is viewed as no relation between two variables or scores, whereas values close to −1 or +1 are viewed as very strong relationships between two variables. A strong negative relationship, often referred to as an inverse relationship, indicates that the *higher* the score is on one variable or test, the *lower* the score is on a second variable or test. On the other hand, a strong positive relationship indicates that people who score high on one test also will score high on a second test. *To say that scores from a measure are reliable, one usually would expect a coefficient between +.7 and +1.0.* Others have suggested even stricter criteria. Reliability coefficient of .70 to .80 are somewhat lower than is desirable so psychometricians suggest that reliability coefficients of about .8 are acceptable for research but that ones .9 or more are necessary for measures that will be used to make decisions about individuals, using instruments such as IQ tests, the GRE, the SAT, and those for personnel decisions. However, it is common to see published journal articles in which one or a few reliability coefficients are below .7 but usually .6 or above. Note that although correlations of −.7 to −1.0 indicate a strong (negative) correlation, they are totally unacceptable with regards to reliability. Such a high negative correlation would indicate that persons who initially score high on the measure later score low and vice versa. A negative reliability coefficient probably indicates a computational error or terrible inconsistency.

Methods to Assess Measurement Reliability

There are many methods used to assess measurement reliability. Here, we discuss eight types of measurement reliability: (1) test–retest; (2) parallel forms; (3) internal consistency measured through split-half methods; (4) internal consistency measured through Kuder-Richardson 20; (5) internal consistency measured through Cronbach's alpha; (6) interrater (interobserver) measured through percentage agreement methods; (7) interrater (interobserver) measured through intraclass correlation coefficients (ICCs); and (8) interrater (interobserver) measured through the Kappa statistic. We also briefly discuss generalizability theory and item response theory (IRT). For more detail on each method of determining measurement reliability, including formulas, we recommend Anastasi (1988) and Nunnally and Bernstein (1994).

For many published measures, more than one reliability coefficient has been obtained. However, when choosing a measure, the investigator needs to make sure of the following criteria:

- Past reliability of the data produced by the instrument is high (e.g., above .80) or at least marginally acceptable (e.g., above .60).
- The length of time that had been used to establish the test–retest reliability is similar to the length of time to be used in the study. It should be noted that as the length of time increases between administrations, the reliability usually decreases.
- The sample that had been used to determine reliability of the instrument is similar to the sample that will be used in the current study.

Furthermore, it is important to note that two reliability coefficients need to be reported: (1) reliability coefficients cited in the literature prior to data collection for the study; and (2) the reliability coefficients estimated with the data from the study. Some of the methods of assessing reliability are common for published measures; these (i.e., test–retest reliability, parallel forms) are cited as previously reported reliability coefficients. Other methods (i.e., internal consistency, interrater reliability) can be cited as previously reported reliability coefficients and also as reliability coefficients estimated with the data from the study.

Test–Retest Reliability

Test–retest reliability is one of the most common forms of reliability (Daniel and Witta, 1997). Cronbach (1990) refers to this coefficient as a coefficient of stability. Test–retest reliability is easy to understand. If a test produces reliable scores, then if it is given more than once to the same person, that person's scores should be very close, if not equal. If the researcher wants to obtain test–retest reliability on his QOL instrument, he would find a sample of persons who were not participants in the experiment previously described but who would fit his target population. He would administer the QOL to this sample, and at a later date (at a date that would approximate the interval of the intervention) he would administer the QOL to the same sample. Then he would determine the reliability coefficient based on the scores of the two administrations using a correlation between the two sets of scores. If the reliability coefficient is relatively high (e.g., above .80), then he would be satisfied that the QOL has good test–retest reliability. On the other hand, if the reliability coefficient is below .70, then he may need to reconsider the QOL as a measure that produces reliable scores of quality of life.

Certain considerations must be taken into account to determine test–retest reliability. The first point is that test–retest reliability is *not established during a study*. The test–retest reliability coefficient must be established ahead of time, prior to the study, using a period of time when little related to the substance of the instrument should be happening between the two administrations of the instrument.[1] Even if **test–retest** reliability has already been established for the instrument of choice, the investigator needs to determine some type of reliability for the present study.

Parallel Forms Reliability

One of the problems of using the same instrument for the pretest and the posttest of a study is that participants may use the knowledge gained on the pretest to alter the posttest score. This problem, often referred to as testing, or carryover effects, creates significant problems for the investigator because it becomes impossible to determine if the change in scores is due to the intervention or to knowledge obtained on the pretest. One way of avoiding the pretest problem is to create a design without a pretest (e.g., the posttest-only control group design). However, that design can be used only if the investigator can randomly assign participants to groups. A quasi-experimental approach is more likely in applied settings, where the investigator will need to use a pretest.

To counteract the testing problem, some tests have a second or parallel form that could be used as a posttest in place of the instrument used for the pretest. A parallel form can be created by simply reordering the items or by writing new items that are similar to the existing items. It is important that the two forms have similar content. Parallel forms reliability (i.e., the coefficient of equivalence) involves establishing the relationship between the two forms of the same test. This type of reliability is easy to establish, since it involves having a sample of participants take the two forms of the same instrument with very little time elapsed between the two administrations. Then, similar to test–retest reliability, a correlation coefficient is determined for the two sets of scores. Again, a reliability coefficient of at least .80 would be expected for parallel forms reliability.

Internal Consistency Reliability

Often, in addition to obtaining test–retest reliability, or parallel forms reliability, the researcher wants to know that the instrument is consistent among the items; that is, the instrument is measuring a single concept or construct. Rather than correlate different administrations of the same instrument, the investigator can use the results of a single administration of the instrument to determine internal consistency. The most common methods of determining internal consistency are the split-half method, the Kuder-Richardson (K-R 20) method, and Cronbach's alpha. The last two methods are often referred to as interitem reliability and can be used only when one has data from several items that are combined to make a composite score.

Split-Half Methods

These methods of obtaining internal consistency reliability involve correlating two halves of the same test. The term split-half is a general term to describe a number of different methods of correlating one half of the test with the second half of the test. For example, one could correlate the first half of the test with the second half of the test, or compare the odd items with the even items. A third and highly recommended method is to random sample half of the items of the test and correlate them with the remaining items. Regardless of how the test is split, it is important that the two halves are similar in content and difficulty.

One of the problems with obtaining split-half reliability is that when dividing the test into two halves, the number of items is reduced by 50% compared with test–retest reliability or alternative forms reliability. This reduction in size means that the resulting correlation coefficient will probably *underestimate* reliability. Therefore, once the reliability coefficient is established by calculating the correlation coefficient, r, it is necessary to adjust the size of the r by using the Spearman-Brown formula.[2] For example, if you compute the correlation coefficient between the first and second halves of your test, and it equals .7, the Spearman-Brown formula would estimate the reliability of the scores when using the entire test to be approximately .82.

Kuder-Richardson 20 (K-R 20)

If the instrument that is being used is intended to measure a single theme or trait, it is desirable to determine how all of the items are related to each other. If each item is scored dichotomously, such as pass/fail, true/false, right/wrong, then *K-R 20* is an appropriate method of determining interitem reliability.

Cronbach's Alpha

If each item on the test has multiple choices, such as a Likert scale, then **Cronbach's alpha** is the method of choice to determine interitem reliability. Alpha also is appropriate for dichotomous items, so it can be used instead of the K-R 20. Cronbach's alpha is the *most commonly used index of reliability* in the area of educational and psychological research (Daniel and Witta, 1997).

It should be noted that measures of interitem reliability, especially Cronbach's alpha, are often seen when reading a research article. The reason for this, as stated earlier, is that it takes only one administration of the instrument. More important, though, is that alpha is related to the validity of the construct being measured. One of the problems with Cronbach's alpha is that while it is a measure of internal consistency, it does not necessarily measure homogeneity, or unidimensionality. In other words, people often determine Cronbach's alpha and assume that since it is at a high level (e.g., .85), the test is measuring only one concept or construct. Unfortunately, as pointed out by Schmitt (1996), even though the overall item correlations may be relatively high, they could be measuring more than one factor or dimension. This can lead to problems, because one of the assumptions of using Cronbach's alpha as an index of reliability is that it is measuring only one construct. We caution that when reporting reliability, if only Cronbach's α is provided, without information indicating that there is only one underlying dimension, or another index of reliability, then reliability has not been adequately assessed.

Cronbach's alpha was reported in the study by Zamboanga, Padilla-Walker, Hardy, Thompson, and Wang (2007). For the exam performance, Cronbach's alpha was calculated for "the lecture-base exam items (α = .77; $n = 40$, 20% of all test items) and ... all exclusively text-based questions (α = .73; $n = 44$, 22% of all test items)" (p. 159). These Cronbach's alpha values are lower than our suggested .80 but are high enough for these items to be considered internally consistent.

Interrater (Interobserver) Reliability

The previous methods to establish reliability were accomplished by examining scores on some instrument. However, sometimes the measurement tool is observation performed by judges. When observation is the method of collecting data, then reliability must be established among the judges' scores to maintain consistency. This type of reliability is referred to as interrater reliability. Although there are numerous ways to determine this form of reliability, the common theme is that two or more judges (observers) score certain episodes of behavior and some form of correlation is performed to determine the level of agreement among the judges.

Percentage Agreement Methods

These methods involve having two or more raters, prior to the study, observe a sample of behaviors that will be similar to what would be observed in the study. It is important for the two raters to discuss what they will be rating (i.e., the construct of interest) to agree on what each rater believes is an instance of the construct. Suppose that rater A observes 8 occurrences of a particular behavior and rater B observes 10 occurrences of the same behavior. A percentage is then computed by dividing the smaller number of observations by the larger number of observations of the specific behavior. In this case, the percentage is 80.

One of the problems with this method is that although both observers may agree that a behavior was elicited a particular number of times, this does not mean that each time the behavior occurred that both judges agreed. For example, suppose that the behavior of cooperation was the dependent variable for a study. Prior to the study, two judges were to observe a classroom of students for particular instances of cooperation. One observer (judge) said that there were eight examples of cooperation. A second observer said that there were 10 examples of cooperation. The percentage agreement would be 8 divided by 10, or 80%. However, it is possible that the eight instances observed by one judge were not the same instances observed by the second judge. The percentage would be inflated in this particular instance.

Using a point-by-point basis of establishing interrater reliability, each behavior would be rated as an agreement or disagreement between judges. The point-by-point method would be easiest to perform if the behavior is on a tape that could be played for the judges. To calculate percentage agreement in the point-by-point method, the number of agreements between the two judges would be divided by the total number of responses (agreements plus disagreements). A problem with this method is that it ignores chance agreements when few categories are used. An additional problem with these percentage agreement methods is that they are most suited to situations with only two raters.

Interrater reliability was used in Penningroth, Despain, and Gray (2007). First, one person rated all the tests. Then, a second author independently scored 30 (9%) of the exams, 15 pretests and 15 posttests. Reliability was high for both pretest $r = .93$, and posttest, $r = .94$. This is a good example of using interrater reliability as it is not necessary for both raters to rate all the observations after achieving a high reliability coefficient.

Intraclass Correlation Coefficients (ICCs)

Often, when performing a study using observations of behavior as the dependent variable, more than two observers are needed. **Intraclass correlation coefficients** allow the researcher to calculate a reliability coefficient with two or more judges. For an excellent review of ICC type methods, including Kappa, see Bartko and Carpenter (1976). One criterion that must be satisfied to use the intraclass correlation coefficient is that the behavior to be rated must be scaled at an interval level. For example, each rater might be rating instances of cooperation on a 1–5 scale. These ICCs are computed using analysis of variance methods with repeated measures to analyze interrater reliability.[3] (We discuss repeated measures analysis of variance in Chapter 21 of this book.) A second advantage of the ICC method of computing interrater reliability is that if the judges are selected randomly, then the researcher can generalize the interrater reliability beyond the sample of judges that took part in the reliability study.

Kappa

A method of calculating intraclass correlation coefficients when the data are nominal is the **Kappa** statistic. Similar to ICC, Kappa can be computed with two or more raters. Kappa can validate that the agreement exceeds chance. While the data for using Kappa are often dichotomous (e.g., present or absent), it is not uncommon to have more than two nominal categories.

Generalizability Theory, Item Response Theory, and Reliability

The methods that we have discussed to assess reliability are based on classical test theory. A major problem with classical test theory is that measurement error is considered to be a single entity, which does not give the researcher the information necessary to improve the instrument. *Generalizability theory,* an extension of classical test theory, allows the investigator to estimate more precisely the different components of measurement error. In its simplest form, this theory partitions the variance that makes up an obtained score into variance components, such as variance that is attributable to the participants, to the judges (observers), and to items. *Item response theory* allows the researcher to separate test characteristics from participant characteristics. This differs from both classical test theory and generalizability theory by providing information about reliability as a function of ability rather than averaging overall ability levels. Nunnally and Bernstein (1994) and Strube (2000) provide more complete discussions of these topics.

Summary

We have discussed different methods of assessing reliability. While each method gives some measure of consistency, not all provide the same measure of consistency. It is up to the consumer to be aware of how reliability was established before using a particular instrument. To say that an instrument produces reliable scores has relatively little meaning. Each statement of reliability must specify the type of reliability and the strength of the reliability coefficient.

Typically, if one does not create the instrument but uses an instrument already published, then reliability indices should have been established. The most common places to find studies of the reliability of the instrument are in the instrument manual, which is often referred to in the journal publication that introduced the instrument. The instrumentation section of any research article that used the particular instrument also should provide information about the reliability of that instrument. It is always important to report reliability for the data from the present study. Since reliability is a function of the data, the reliability coefficients most likely will be different from one administration to the next.

Measurement reliability is an exceptionally important issue for research in applied settings. Many of the issues are beyond the scope of the present text. For those interested in measurement reliability in more depth, especially for constructing an instrument, we recommend the texts of Cronbach (1990) and Crocker and Algina (2006). Table 11.1 provides a summary of the concepts covered in the preceding sections.

TABLE 11.1

Measurement Reliability

There is reliability of:

a. *Participants' responses*
   1. *Test–retest reliability*—Stability over time
   2. *Parallel forms reliability*—Consistency across presumably equivalent versions of the instrument
   3. *Internal consistency*—Items that are to be combined are related to each other
b. *Observers' responses*
   4. *Interrater reliability*—Different observers or raters give similar scores

Note: Reliability means stability or consistency of scores, observations, or ratings.

Key Concepts

Cronbach's alpha

Correlation coefficient

Error

Intraclass correlation coefficients

Kappa

Kuder-Richardson 20

Observed score

Percentage agreement methods

Split-half methods

Standard error of measurement

True score

Key Distinctions

Measurement reliability versus measurement validity

Test–retest versus parallel forms versus interval consistency versus interrater evidence for measurement reliability

Application Problems

1. A researcher is interested in determining if therapists interrupt female clients more than male clients. He has obtained videotapes of 30 therapy sessions and plans to count the number of times the therapist interrupts female and male clients. The researcher hires a graduate student to count the occurrence of interruptions on all the tapes. The researcher then hires another graduate student to count the occurrence of interruptions on 12 of the tapes. Why did the researcher hire the second graduate student? What type of evidence for reliability is the researcher concerned with? What statistical procedure might the researcher best use to determine this type of reliability?

2. A researcher has developed a measure of anxiety. She plans to use the measure for the first time to determine if learning about stress reduction techniques will influence anxiety levels. She gives her anxiety measure to her undergraduate psychology class and teaches them stress reduction techniques. The next day, she gives her anxiety measure again. She is excited to report that her test–retest reliability is very high (.98). You realize that she does not understand test–retest reliability fully. What recommendations would you make to her about how to appropriately establish test–retest reliability?

3. What is the appropriate method (if any) for determining internal consistency reliability for the following measures?

   a. A 10-item measure of locus of control scored with true or false.

   b. An 80-item measure of intimacy scored with a five-point Likert scale.

   c. A one-item measure ("Whose career is given more priority between you and your spouse?") of relative career priority between spouses.

4. Researchers are presented with a new form of intelligence test to use with elementary age children in the United States. The test has been pilot tested with great excitement in several Western states. Colorado researchers would like to have more information before piloting the instrument. They have been informed that the standard deviation is 15 and the reliability coefficient is on the average, .74. What is the standard error of measurement? Why is it useful to know this? How would this be measured?

5. An instrument of support was used to measure perceived support from coworkers in a mental health institution. Participants responded to four items on a seven-point Likert-like scale. Cronbach's alpha for the (support) scale was .79. What does this mean?

6. Gliner has developed a multiple-choice test called, "I want to get into grad school real bad" to make the selection process easier. (Also, if enough other schools are interested, he might make some money.) He wants to determine evidence for *reliability*.

   a. Describe at least three methods that he could use to assess reliability.

   b. After studies on reliability have been performed, Gliner concludes that the test is reliable. What, if anything, is wrong with this statement?

Notes

1. This is especially important regarding experiments and for areas such as child development, where rapid growth during the interval between the two administrations of the instrument could alter test–retest reliability.

2. The Spearman-Brown formula is most commonly used to determine reliability of a test if more items were to be added or subtracted.

3. While it appears that intraclass correlation coefficients are used most commonly for interrater reliability, especially in rehabilitation literature, these same methods can be used for test–retest reliability and internal consistency reliability (Shavelson, 1988).

12

Measurement Validity

In this chapter we discuss measurement validity. Measurement validity is concerned with establishing evidence for the use of a particular measure or instrument in a particular setting with a particular population for a specific purpose. We use the term measurement validity; others might use terms such as *test validity, score validity,* or just *validity.* We use the modifier *measurement* to distinguish it from internal, external, and overall research validity (discussed in Chapters 8, 9, 23, and 24) and to point out that the scores provide evidence for validity; *it is inappropriate to say that a test is "valid" or "invalid."* Thus, when we address the issue of measurement validity with respect to a particular test, we are addressing the issue of the evidence for the validity of the scores on that test for a particular purpose and not the validity of the test or instrument.

Scores from a given test might be used for a number of purposes. For example, specialty area scores on the Graduate Record Examination (GRE) might be used to predict first-year success in graduate school. However, the scores could also be used as a method to assess current status or achievement in a particular undergraduate major. Although the same test is used in both instances, the purpose of the test is different, and thus the evidence in support of each purpose could be quite different.

Reliability or consistency is necessary for measurement validity. However, an instrument may produce consistent data (provide evidence for reliability), but the data may not be valid. For example, one could construct a device to measure students' jumping distance and then use the scores as measures of research knowledge. Suppose the participants consistently jump similar lengths, thus giving evidence of reliability. Yet the data would not be considered valid, as the data are not giving information regarding research knowledge. This is an extreme example, yet it shows the importance of using measures appropriately to obtain valid data.

In research articles, there is usually more evidence for the reliability of the instrument than for the validity of the instrument because evidence for validity is more difficult to obtain. To establish validity, one ideally needs a "gold standard" or "criterion" related to the particular purpose of the measure. To obtain such a criterion is often not an easy matter, so other types of evidence to support the validity of a measure are necessary.

From 1966 until 1999, the Standards for Educational and Psychological Testing (referred to also as Standards) included the so-called trinity view of validity, which categorized validity into three types: content validity, criterion-related validity (including concurrent and predictive methods), and construct validity. However, the 1985 Standards warned that the use of the labels (content, criterion, and construct) should not lead to the implication that there were three distinct types of validity. Increasingly, validity has been conceptualized as a unitary concept; many types of evidence should be gathered to help assess validity for a given set of data. During the 1980s and 1990s, the process of accumulating evidence in support of validity began to be emphasized.

TABLE 12.1

Comparison of 1985 Standards with 1999 Standards

1999 Standards	1985 Standards
Evidence based on content	Content-related evidence
Evidence based on response processes	Construct-related evidence
Evidence based on internal structure	Construct-related evidence
Evidence based on relations to other variables	Criterion-related evidence and construct-related evidence
Evidence based on consequences	None

The current Standards (American Educational Research Association, American Psychological Association, & National Council on Measurement in Education, 1999) described validity as "the degree to which evidence and theory support the interpretations of test scores" (p. 9). The standards go on to say that "the process of validation involves accumulating evidence to provide a sound scientific basis for the proposed score interpretations. It is the interpretations … that are evaluated, not the test itself" (p. 9).

Note that the current Standards (American Educational Research Association et al., 1999) are different from earlier versions of the Standards and most previous discussions of this concept. Goodwin and Leech (2003) published a useful summary of the changes with recommendations for teaching measurement courses. In this chapter, we examine validity from the perspective of the new standards. We think it is important to understand the earlier methods of determining measurement validity, often referred to as the trinity conception of measurement validity (i.e., content, criterion, and construct validity). However, all of these former methods are subsumed under the new standards. Table 12.1 demonstrates the differences between the old and new standards. We present the five broad types of evidence to support the validity of a test or measure that emerged from the 1999 Standards. These five types of evidence for validity are (1) content; (2) response processes; (3) internal structure; (4) relations to other variables; and (5) the consequences of testing. Note that the *five types of evidence are not separate types of validity* and that any one type of evidence alone is insufficient. Validation should integrate all the pertinent evidence from as many of the five types of evidence as possible. Preferably, validation should include some evidence in addition to content evidence, which is probably the most common and easiest to obtain.

Introduction to Validity from the 1999 Standards

As previously mentioned, in 1999, the Standards for understanding measurement validity changed. Table 12.1 should help you to understand the relationship between the trinity view of validity and the current evidence-based assessment of validity.

Evidence Based on the Content of the Measure

Content evidence refers to whether the content that makes up the instrument is representative of the concept that one is attempting to measure. Does the instrument accurately represent the major aspects of the concept and not include material that is irrelevant to it? For example, Fisher (1995) constructed an instrument called the Assessment of Motor and Process Skills (AMPs). One of the most important contributions of the instrument is that it has ecological soundness. Fisher has participants choose to perform "everyday" tasks from a list of possible tasks that require motor and process skills. If Fisher asked participants to stack blocks or perform other artificial types of motor tasks, then her test would not have strong content validity, even though the artificial tasks involved motor activity. Her test has strong evidence based on the content of the measure not only because the tasks involve motor and process activity but also because they are representative of the types of tasks that a person would do in everyday life. This type of evidence is important for almost all measures and is based on a logical analysis of the content of the measure.

There is no statistic that demonstrates evidence based on the content of the measure. Instead, the process of establishing this type of evidence usually starts with a definition of the concept that the investigator is attempting to measure. A second step is a literature search to see how this concept is represented in the literature. Next, items are generated that might measure this concept. Gradually, this list of items is reduced to form the test or measure.

One of the main methods of reducing items is to form a panel of experts to review the items for representativeness of the concept. Because this type of evidence depends on the logical, but subjective, agreement of a few experts, we consider it necessary but not sufficient evidence. The experts review the measure for clarity and fit with the construct to be measured. Goodwin and Leech (2003) indicated that the experts also are often asked to review the measure for possible bias (e.g., gender, culture, age). It is important to examine whether an unfair advantage can be given to certain subgroups because the test measures either more than intended (*construct-irrelevant components*) or less (*construct underrepresentation*) than intended. An example of a *construct-irrelevant component* would be a measure that includes terms that are not understood by the test takers, which, in turn, cause the scores to be lower than they should be. *Construct underrepresentation* occurs when aspects of a construct are not included in the construct itself.

Evidence Based on Response Processes

Goodwin and Leech (2003) pointed out that in the 1985 edition of the Standards, evidence based on response processes, was included under construct-related validity. Evidence based on response processes is defined as the extent to which the types of participant responses match the intended construct. For example, with self-report measures of constructs we need evidence that respondents are not just giving socially desirable answers. Another example would be students taking a multiple-choice math test. The teacher hopes the students are using analytical math skills in answering the questions, not multiple-choice test-taking skills (i.e., if you don't know, answer "B"). This sort of evidence can be gathered by observing examinees as they perform tasks and by questioning participants to identify their reasons for providing certain answers.

In addition to examining the responses of the participants, this type of evidence for validity could include an examination of the responses of observers, raters, or judges to determine whether they are using the appropriate criteria. This type of response process evidence is the extent to which raters are influenced by irrelevant factors in making their judgments.

Evidence Based on Internal Structure

This type of evidence, like that based on response processes, was originally placed in the trinity conception under construct validity. Evidence from several types of analysis, including factor analysis and differential item functioning (DIF), can be useful here. The Standards (American Educational Research Association et al., 1999) said:

> Analyses of the internal structure of a test can indicate the degree to which the rela-
> tionships among test items and test components conform to the construct on which the
> proposed test score interpretations are based. The conceptual framework for a test may
> imply a single dimension of behavior, or it may posit several components that are each
> expected to be homogeneous, but that are also distinct from each other. For example,
> a measure of discomfort on a health survey might assess both physical and emotional
> health. The extent to which item interrelationships bear out the presumptions of the
> framework would be relevant to validity. (p. 13)

Most surveys have an overall construct to be measured; in this example, the construct was
discomfort. Many times, the overall construct will have subconstructs; multiple areas that
combine to measure the overall construct. In this example, the subconstructs were physical health and emotional health. **Factor analysis** can provide evidence based on internal
structure when a construct is complex and several aspects (or factors) of it are measured.
If the clustering of items supports the theory-based grouping of items, factorial evidence
is provided. Therefore, from this example, a factor analysis would help us identify if the
data supported the two subconstructs by indicating if the respondents answered similarly
to the questions for physical health. A factor analysis also would show if the respondents
answered similarly to the questions for emotional health. For more explanation on factor
analysis, please see Chapter 15.

Note that a high **Cronbach's alpha** (see Chapter 11) is incorrectly assumed to provide
evidence that a measure contains only one dimension or construct; it is possible to have
a high Cronbach's alpha and be measuring multiple dimensions; thus, Cronbach's alpha
should not be relied on to assess evidence based on internal structure.

Evidence Based on Relations to Other Variables

This category of evidence is the most extensive, including the categories of criterion-related
validity and much of what was included under construct validity. **Constructs** are hypothetical concepts that cannot be observed directly. Intelligence, depression, mastery motivation, and anxiety are all constructs. Although we cannot observe a construct directly,
most of us agree that these constructs can be inferred from observable behaviors. For
example, we cannot directly observe anxiety, but under certain circumstances we may
observe anxious behaviors, such as sweating or pacing, that are specific to a particular
context, such as immediately before an important examination. In addition, we often infer
a construct from self-reports on an inventory or from an interview. Such self-reports can
be useful, but it is prudent to be cautious about accepting them as evidence for validity. It
is common to create instruments to measure particular constructs (e.g., an inventory that
measures state anxiety or a test that measures intelligence).

When applying evidence based on relations to other variables to an instrument, there is
a requirement that the construct the instrument is measuring is guided by an underlying
theory. Often, especially in applied disciplines, there is little underlying theory to support
the construct. As Cronbach (1960) pointed out, "Sometimes the test is used for a long time
before any theory is developed around it" (p. 121). Nevertheless, construct validation is
a process (relatively slow process) where the investigator conducts studies to attempt to
demonstrate that the instrument is measuring a construct.

Test-Criterion Relationships

This refers to correlating the instrument to some form of measurable external or outside
criterion. A common example involves instruments that are intended to select participants

for admission to a school or occupation. Two types of evidence for **criterion validity** are called *predictive* and *concurrent*.

Predictive-Criterion Evidence

When we try to determine how someone will do in the future on the basis of his or her performance on a particular instrument, we are usually referring to predictive evidence. Tests such as the SAT and the Graduate Record Examination (GRE) are examples of instruments that are used to predict future performance. If the SAT provided good predictive evidence, then students who score high on this test would perform better in college than those who do not score high. The criterion in this case would be some measure of how well the students perform in college, usually grades during their first year.

To establish predictive evidence in the previous example, high school students would take the SAT. Then, when they are finished with their freshman year of college, correlations would be established between their high school SAT scores and college grades. If the correlation is high, then predictive evidence is good. If the correlation is low, then the test has problems for prediction of future performance. A problem with predictive evidence is that often not all of the participants who were evaluated on the original instrument can be evaluated on the criterion variable. This is especially the case in selection studies. For example, we may have SAT scores for a wide range of high school students. However, not all of these students will be admitted to college. Therefore, our criterion variable of first-semester college grade point average (GPA) not only will have fewer participants than our predictor variable but also will represent a more homogeneous group (only those admitted to college). Therefore, the range of scores of those who could participate in the study on both the predictor and criterion variables is restricted, thus decreasing confidence in our predictive evidence.

A second drawback with predictive evidence is that the researcher must wait until those who were tested initially can be measured on the criterion. Sometimes this wait could take years. Sometimes this type of evidence is found retrospectively. For example, students who are in college are asked what their SAT scores were and what their current GPA is, and these two variables are correlated.

Concurrent-Criterion Evidence

Similar to predictive evidence, concurrent evidence also examines the relationship between an instrument and an outside criterion. However, sometimes it is too expensive to wait between the time that the test was taken and the measurement of the criterion. For example, suppose that we want to see whether a statewide standardized test is a good indicator of a student's learning. To determine concurrent evidence, we could take students' test scores and correlate them with end-of-year test scores or grades. If there is a high correlation, we can have some confidence that the state assessment test is measuring the students' knowledge. Additionally, concurrent evidence is appropriate when a test is proposed as a substitute for a criterion measure (perhaps one that is more expensive or takes longer to administer). The test developer hopes that the less expensive or time-consuming measure will provide very similar information and, thus, a high correlation with the criterion (Cronbach, 1990).

Concurrent evidence also can be obtained by substituting another instrument for the criterion, especially if it is difficult to measure the criterion. For example, the AMPs (Fisher, 1995) was compared to the Scales of Independent Behavior in adults with developmental disabilities (Bryze, 1991). However, the instrument substituted for the criterion can never be more valid than the criterion. One must be cautious when substituting an instrument for a criterion, since in many cases the substituted instrument has not been validated against the criterion of interest. This is often the case with therapeutic or educational outcomes. Perhaps more importantly, if another instrument is substituted for the criterion, what size correlation would be expected? If the correlation coefficient is quite large (e.g., .8 or .9), then your instrument is not providing different information from the criterion instrument. If the correlation is too small, then your instrument is measuring a different construct than the criterion instrument.

The major drawback to criterion validity is the problem of identifying and then being able to measure a suitable criterion. For example, admission to medical school programs in the United States is difficult because of the large number of applicants for the limited number of positions. To select successful applicants, criteria such as grades and achievement tests often are used. Students (especially those who are not admitted) might complain that high grades do not make a person a good physician. Could one create an admission test that would predict becoming a good physician? Consider the problems of defining and measuring the criterion of what makes a good physician. The difficulty of identifying good, measurable criteria for many complex concepts was one of the key reasons for developing other methods to provide evidence for validity.

Convergent and Discriminant Evidence

Convergent evidence is determined by obtaining relatively high correlations between a scale and other measures that theory suggests would be positively related. To demonstrate construct validity, one develops hypotheses about what the instrument should predict (*convergent evidence* or validity) if it is actually measuring the construct. On the other hand, discriminant evidence is provided by obtaining relatively low relationships between a scale and measures that the theory suggests should not be related. Discriminant evidence also can be obtained by comparing groups that should differ on a scale and finding that they do, in fact, differ.

The Standards (American Educational Research Association et al., 1999) provide a good example of convergent and discriminant evidence based on relationships among variables:

> Scores on a multiple-choice test of reading comprehension might be expected to relate closely (convergent evidence) to other measures of reading comprehension based on other methods, such as essay responses; conversely, test scores might be expected to relate less closely (discriminant evidence) to measures of other skills, such as logical reasoning. (p. 14)

Validity Generalization

The other main type of evidence discussed under the category of evidence based on relationships to other variables is validity generalization. The Standards describe this type of evidence as raising the important issue in educational and employment settings of the degree to which criterion-related evidence of validity can be generalized to a new situation. Unfortunately, in the past, relationships of a test with similar criteria often varied substantially from one situation to the next. Thus, as in meta-analysis, "statistical summaries of past validation studies in similar situations may be useful in estimating test-criterion relationships in a new situation. This practice is referred to as the study of validity generalization" (American Educational Research Association et al., 1999, p. 15).

Validity generalization can be viewed as taking information regarding a test's validity (e.g., the GRE) and extrapolating the findings to another group. For example, test administrators might find that students taking the GRE do well under certain circumstances. Based on this information, the test administrators might decide the GRE can be used under the same conditions with students who have learning disabilities.

Evidence Based on Consequences of Testing

Goodwin and Leech (2003) stated that this type of evidence for validity, which was new to the 1999 Standards, includes both positive and negative anticipated and unanticipated consequences of measurement. The Standards (American Educational Research Association et al., 1999) stated:

> Tests are commonly administered in the expectation that some benefit will be realized from the intended use of the scores. A few of the many possible benefits are selection of efficacious treatments for therapy, placement of workers in suitable jobs, prevention of unqualified individuals from entering a profession, or improvement of classroom instructional practices. A fundamental purpose of validation is to indicate whether these specific benefits are likely to be realized. (p. 16)

This type of evidence was added to the standards in 1999 to assist researchers in considering how the use of measures negatively and positively affects the respondents.

Measurement Validity—An Example

Several types of evidence were provided by Morgan et al. (1993) for the Dimensions of Mastery Questionnaire (DMQ), which was designed to measure five aspects of mastery motivation. *Factor analysis* supported the grouping of items into these five appropriate clusters, providing some evidence based on internal structure. Overall DMQ scores were related to infant persistence at behavioral tasks, providing *convergent evidence*, and maternal ratings of normally developing infants were higher than maternal ratings of at-risk and delayed infants, providing some *discriminant evidence*. If infants both were correctly identified as being at risk for later mastery problems and obtained appropriate early intervention, the consequences of using this questionnaire for such a purpose would be positive. Notice that three different types of validity evidence were used to support the DMQ. It is unrealistic for any instrument or test to expect validity evidence from all possible methods, but, as mentioned earlier, it is highly desirable to have more than one type of evidence.

Evaluation of Measurement Validity

Our suggestions about how to evaluate the strength of the support for measurement validity depends on the type of evidence. Evaluation of evidence based on content, response process, internal structure, and consequences of testing is subjective and depends on logical judgments by the researcher or other experts.

Evaluation of evidence based on relationships (often correlations) with other variables also requires a judgment because there are no well-established rules or even guidelines. Our suggestion is to use Cohen's (1988) guidelines for interpreting effect sizes, which are measures of the strength of a relationship. In Chapter 17, we describe several measures of effect size and how to interpret them. For evaluating statistical evidence for validity, the correlation coefficient (r) is the most common statistic (correlation is described briefly in Chapter 10 and in more detail in Chapter 21). Cohen suggested that generally, in the applied behavioral sciences, $r = .5$ could be considered a large effect, and in this context we would consider $r = .5$ or greater to be strong support for measurement validity. In general, an acceptable level of support would be provided by $r > .3$, and some weak support might result from $r > .1$, assuming that such an r was statistically significant (see also Chapter 23's discussion of measurement validity). However, for concurrent, criterion evidence, if the criterion and test being validated are two similar measures of the same concept (e.g., IQ), the correlation would be expected to be very high, perhaps .8 or .9. On the other hand, for convergent evidence, the measures should not be that highly correlated because they should be measures of different concepts. If the measures were very highly related, one might ask whether they were really measuring the same concept.

Summary

Table 12.2 summarizes much of the preceding material, including the main types of evidence and a summary of what evidence would support the validity of the measure. An instrument is not valid or invalid; however, there may be various degrees of support for its use with particular populations for particular purposes. The strength of the evidence for the measurement validity of the measures is extremely important for research in applied settings because without measures that produce data that have strong evidence for validity the results of the study can be very misleading. Validation is an ongoing, never fully achieved, process based on integration of all the evidence from as many sources as possible.

Key Concepts

Evidence for validity based on content

Evidence for validity based on response processes

Evidence for validity based on internal structure

Evidence for validity based on relations to other variables

Evidence for validity based on consequences

Key Distinctions

Criterion-related evidence: predictive versus concurrent

Measurement reliability versus measurement validity

Measurement validity versus research validity

TABLE 12.2

Evidence for Measurement Validity

Type of Evidence	Support for validity depends on ...
Evidence based on content: All aspects of the construct are represented in appropriate proportions.	Good agreement by experts about the content and that it represents the concept to be assessed
Evidence based on response processes: Participants' responses match the intended construct.	Evidence that participants and raters are not influenced by irrelevant factors like social desirability
Evidence based on internal structure: Relationships among items on the test consistent with the conceptual framework.	Meaningful factor structure consistent with the conceptual organization of the constructs
Evidence based on relations to other variables.	
Criterion-concurrent: Test and criterion are measured at the same time.	The effect size of the relationship[a]
Criterion-predictive: Test predicts some criterion in the future.	The effect size of the relationship[a]
Convergent: Based on theory, variables predicted to be related are related.	The effect size of the relationship[a]
Discriminant: Variables predicted not to be related are not related.	The effect size of the relationship[a,b]
Validity generalization: Results using the measure generalize to other settings.	Supportive meta-analytic studies
Evidence based on consequences: Conducting the test produces benefits for the participants.	Evidence that positive consequences outweigh unexpected negative ones in terms of the outcomes of, for example, therapy or job placement

[a]　The strength or level of support for validity (weak, medium, strong) could be based on Cohen's (1988) effect size guidelines, with the qualifications noted in the text.

[b]　Depending on the data, the appropriate strength of association statistic will vary.

Application Problems

1. A researcher is interested in the influence of marital equality on marital satisfaction. In reading the literature, she learns that many variables (or factors) have been used to operationally define equality, such as shared decision-making power between spouses, fair division of labor, and equal access to finances. She decides to include several of these factors in her measure of equality. Is the researcher concerned with reliability or validity as she makes decisions about the best way to measure equality? What kind of reliability or validity is she principally concerned with? In analyzing her data, how might she determine if the variables she measured were related to her independent variable?

2. Gliner developed a multiple-choice test called, "I want to get into grad school real bad" to make the selection process easier. (Also, if enough other schools are interested, he might make some money.) After he determines evidence for *reliability*, he wants to assess evidence for validity. Gliner conducts a predictive validity study. He gives his test to all students admitted to the graduate program in 1988. Five years later, he sends each student a one-item questionnaire. The question asks, "How much money do you make per year?" The correlation between scores on the Gliner test and salary level is .70. Therefore, Gliner suggests that the test be used in the future for applicants.

a. What are some of the problems encountered with the way Gliner established validity evidence?
b. How could Gliner have obtained validity information using concurrent validity?
c. When compared with predictive validity, what are the advantages and disadvantages of concurrent validity?

13

Types of Data Collection Techniques

Overview

There are many types of techniques and instruments used to collect data. Some research methods books have a number of chapters, each focusing on a different technique or tool such as interview, questionnaire, projective techniques, tests, or observations. Because this book focuses on research design and the resulting data analysis, we have chosen to de-emphasize our treatment of data collection techniques. In addition, this book is designed for a broad audience of students in the many disciplines related to education, applied health sciences, and applied social sciences. Because each of these fields has its preferred data collection techniques, we have focused on what is in common across these disciplines. In this chapter we provide a broad context for thinking about data collection techniques and some sources where you may go to learn more about the specifics of developing or evaluating a questionnaire, interview, or other data collection technique.

As pointed out in Chapter 1, we conceptualize research approaches as being approximately orthogonal or unrelated to the techniques of data collection. Thus, in theory at least, any type of data collection technique could be used with any approach to research. It is true that some types of data collection are more commonly used with the randomized experimental or quasi-experimental approaches. Others are more common with the comparative or associational approaches, and still others are more common in qualitative research.

Table 13.1 gives an approximation of how common each of several data collection techniques are within each of these three major groupings of research approaches. Note that we have ordered the data collection techniques along a dimension from researcher-observed reports at the top to self-report measures. The observer report end includes observations and physiological recordings that are assumed to be less influenced by the participants' desire to look good or to answer in a socially desirable way. Of course, even these measures are not free of the effects of such factors if, as is usually the case, the participants realize that they are being observed or recorded. At the other end of the scale are measures based on self-reports of the participants, such as interviews, questionnaires, focus groups, attitude, and personality scales. In these cases, the responses are clearly filtered through the participants' eyes and are probably heavily influenced by factors such as social desirability and answering in acceptable ways. In the middle we have put several types of measures that are undoubtedly influenced by the participants' conscious or unconscious need to look good but are, perhaps, less susceptible to such factors. In standardized achievement and aptitude tests, for instance, people do as well as they can in figuring out the correct answer. With archival documents and content analysis, the data are gathered from records made for another purpose so there may be less built-in bias.

TABLE 13.1

Data Collection Techniques Used by Specific Research Approaches

	Quantitative research		Qualitative research
Data collection techniques	Experiments and quasi-experiments	Comparative, associational, and descriptive approaches	
Researcher-observed measures			
Physiological recordings	++	+	–
Physical trace measures	+	–	+
Coded observations	++	++	++
Narrative observations	–	+	++
Participant observations	–	+	++
Tests and Documents			
Standardized tests	+	++	–
Archival measures/documents	–	+	++
Content analysis	–	+	++
Self-Report Measures			
Summated attitude scales	+	++	–
Standardized personality scales	+	++	–
Questionnaires/surveys	+	++	+
Interviews	+	++	++
Focus groups	–	+	++

Note: Symbols in the table indicate likelihood of use.
++ Quite likely.
+ Possibly.
– Not likely.

The concern about the filtering of participants' answers through perhaps faulty memories or in terms of socially desirable responses has led quantitative researchers, especially those who tend to use the randomized experimental and quasi-experimental approaches, to be suspicious about the validity of the self-report instruments. Thus, when using self-report measures you should always be prepared to provide evidence supporting their validity, as discussed in Chapter 12. Of course, some self-report information such as gender and other simple questions of fact that are not sensitive or controversial are usually accepted at face value. On the other hand, observer reports are not necessarily valid measures of what they are intended to assess. One issue that is often pointed out by qualitative researchers is that cultural biases may lead observers to interpret their observations in inappropriate or ethnocentric ways.

Recommendations for further reading about data collection techniques are provided in the references cited in the chapter. In general, it is advisable to select instruments that have been used in other studies if they have been shown to produce reliable and valid data with the types of *participants* and *for the purpose* that you have in mind. *Tests in Print* provides references to thousands of published educational, psychological, and business instruments that are available for purchase or use. The *Mental Measurements Yearbooks* (1938–present) provide summaries and reviews of a large number of published instruments, including aptitude, intelligence, and achievement tests and also personality and vocational inventories or scales. Similarly, *Test Critiques* annually publishes norms, reliability, and validity data, as well as practical applications in a user-friendly style. It covers the most frequently used psychological, educational, and business-related instruments. Note that the use of the term *tests* in those resources is broader than used in this book. *Tests*, as in *Test Critiques*, refers to a broad range of data collection techniques; not just ones with correct answers, and are similar to our term *standardized*. Textbooks on testing and measurement (e.g., Anastasi & Urbina, 1997; Thorndike, 2004) also provide information on a wide variety of types of standardized instruments. The relevant research literature is a good source for instruments that one might use.

Of course, you may not be able to find an instrument that suits the goals of your research. This is especially likely if you are interested in attitudes or knowledge about a *specific* topic, issue, or program. In this case you may decide to construct a *questionnaire* or *interview* to assess what your participants know about or how they perceive the topic. Dillman (2007), Fowler (2009), Salant and Dillman (1994), and Czaja and Blair (2005) provide useful advice about developing and using interviews and questionnaires.

Standardized Versus Investigator-Developed Instruments

Standardized instruments are ones that have resulted from careful preparation and cover topics of broad interest to a number of investigators. They are usually published and often copyrighted. Reference books such as *Mental Measurement Yearbook* and *Test Critiques* provide evaluative descriptions and review of many published instruments designed to assess abilities, achievement, personality, and attitudes. These instruments usually have a manual that includes norms used to make comparisons with some broader sample than is usually used in a single study, and they commonly include information about reliability and validity.

Investigator-developed measures are ones developed by a researcher for use in one or a few studies. Such instruments also *should be* carefully developed, and they should provide at least basic evidence of **reliability** and **validity** of the data that have been collected in the article or report of the study in which they were used. However, there usually is no separate manual or materials available for others to buy or use.

Although some instruments, such as personality measures and attitude measures, are developed by investigators or teachers for one-time use in a specific study, many standardized measures are available, and, in general, it is wise to use them if the data that have been collected with the measure have good reported reliability and validity and cover the concept that you intend to measure. Questionnaires and interviews are usually developed by an investigator for one-time use in a particular study on a specific topic. However, some questionnaires and interviews are used in a number of studies, often to assess the same issue at different times; for example, there is an annual survey of entering college freshmen that has asked many of the same questions for a number of years.

Researcher-Observed Measures

Direct Observation

As noted already, many researchers prefer systematic, direct observation of behavior as the most accurate and desirable method of recording behavior, especially the behavior of children. The following discussion of observations deals with what is often called "**direct observation**" in which the investigator trains observers to observe and record the behaviors of the participants in the study. Indirect observations are used when the investigator interviews or otherwise questions untrained observers, such as parents or teachers, about participants (e.g., children) that they know well. Indirect observation could also include questionnaires or interviews because the participants often are asked to report about their own behavior. Now we discuss several other dimensions on which observational techniques vary.

Naturalness of the Setting

The setting for the observations can vary from natural environments (e.g., a school, playground, park, or home) through more controlled settings (e.g., a laboratory playroom designed to look like a living room) to highly artificial laboratory settings (e.g., used in a hospital or physiological laboratory). In Chapter 9 we discussed the issue of ecological validity, one aspect of which was the naturalness of the setting. Although natural settings have ecological validity, they usually sacrifice some degree of control and the opportunity to present stimuli in a systematic way. Furthermore, equipment such as video cameras and computer-based observational aids are much more difficult to use in a natural setting. Note that in qualitative research, observations are commonly conducted in natural settings. In quantitative research the whole range of settings is used, but some researchers using the quantitative framework prefer laboratory settings.

Degree of Observer Participation

This dimension varies from situations in which the observer is a participant (preferred by researchers using the qualitative framework) to situations such as public places in which the observer is entirely unobtrusive. Most observations, however, are done in situations where the participants know that that observer is observing them and have agreed to it. It is common for such observers to attempt to be as unobtrusive as possible by sitting off to one side or observing from behind a one-way mirror in a laboratory.

Amount of Detail

Observations also vary on this dimension, which goes from global summary information (e.g., overall ratings based on the whole observation period) to moment-by-moment records of the observed behaviors. Obviously, the latter provides more detail, and it requires considerable preparation and training of observers. Moment-by-moment observations may use codes for various behaviors that can be recorded either with paper and pencil or with some aid such as a computer or dictating machine. Detailed records also can be narrative records in which the observer dictates or attempts to write down everything that happens in sequential order.

Breadth of Coverage

This dimension varies from observational schemes that attempt to record as much as possible about an event or a person's environment to, on the other hand, very specific observations of one or a few types of behavior, such as aggressive incidents or task-directed behaviors. Qualitative observations usually attempt to provide a holistic or overall narrative of the situation.

Tests and Documents

Tests Contrasted With Other Measures

Although the term *test* is often used quite broadly to refer to a wide range of aptitude, personality, and attitude measures, we define the term more narrowly. By a test we mean a set of problems with right or wrong answers. The score is based on the number of correct answers that the person had.

Standardized Tests

In *standardized tests* there is a specific procedure to follow to administer the test. With many standardized tests, the scores are translated into some kind of normed score that can be used to compare the participants with others who have taken the test. These tests are referred to **norm referenced tests**. The scores may be provided in terms of percentile ranks or may be on some well-established metric in which the mean and standard deviation are known. For example, the Graduate Record Examination (GRE) scores were originally normed so that 500 would be the mean and 100 would be the standard deviation. IQ tests were normed so that 100 was the mean and 15 was the standard deviation. An alternative to norm referenced tests is called **criterion referenced tests**. These tests examine how well the student or participant has learned a specific skill (the criterion). Such tests measure a student's achievement without comparing it with the scores of other test takers. This kind of test is often used in schools but is less commonly used in research.

Most standardized tests are said to be objective because there is little disagreement about the scores obtained from them due to the consistency in the administration of the measure. There may be disagreement about how to interpret the results, but if a machine or an untrained assistant can score the test or other measure, the measure would be said to be objective. Multiple-choice tests and rating scales are said to be objective; essay tests and projective techniques are less objective because the scores are influenced by the judgment of the scorers.

Achievement Tests

Most research about the effectiveness of instructional methods uses achievement as the dependent or outcome variable. Thus, achievement tests are widely used in educational research as well as in schools. Such tests measure the mastery or achievement of students in some area related to what they should have learned in school. Achievement tests are available for individual school subjects such as biology or history, and they are also available in comprehensive batteries that measure broad areas of achievement such as verbal or quantitative. For example, the California Achievement Test (CAT) contains tests in the area of reading, language, and arithmetic. When selecting an achievement test, you need to be careful that it provides reliable data and is appropriate for measuring the aspect of achievement in which you are interested. The test also must show reliability and validity evidence of the current data to be included in the study. Thus, if you are using a particular ethnic group or students with developmental delays, you need to be sure that the test is appropriate for that sample. If these criteria are met, then there are advantages in the use of a standardized instrument. In addition to saving time and effort, the results of your study can be compared with those of others using the same instrument.

When the available tests are not appropriate for the objectives of your study, you may have to construct your own test. It is better to do so than to use an inappropriate test just because it is available. If you do develop your own test, you should be careful in preparing it so that you determine the reliability and validity of the data collected with it before using it. Refer to the books on tests and measurement mentioned already (e.g., Thorndike, 2004) if you decide to develop your own achievement test.

Performance and Authentic Assessments

Although most common achievement tests are paper-and-pencil tests of the type just described, a researcher may want to measure actual performance—that is, what an individual can do rather than what he or she knows. **Performance assessment** has become a popular alternative to traditional tests. In such an assessment, the investigator observes an individual's performance on a certain task and then judges the product based on some criteria. Performance assessments are common in such areas as art, music, or science where the individual is expected to be able to do or produce something such as a painting, recital, or research report.

Some performance assessments are referred to as **authentic assessments**, but not all performance assessments are authentic in the sense that they are "real-life" assessments. To be considered authentic, the tasks should be high on ecological validity as discussed in Chapter 9. That is, they might include such things as an actual job interview, an individual or group research project, or a report. Performance and authentic assessments provide a way to measure abilities and skills that are not easily assessed by paper-and-pencil tests. However, they take much more time and expense to administer and score.

Aptitude Tests

Aptitude tests in the past were often called *intelligence tests*, but this term is less often used now because of controversy about the definition of intelligence and to what extent it is inherited. Performance on such aptitude tests is partly dependent on genetic background and partly dependent on environment and schooling. Aptitude tests, as contrasted to achievement tests, are intended to measure more general performance or problem-solving ability. These tests attempt to measure the participant's ability to solve problems and to apply knowledge in a variety of situations. Researchers and educators have found aptitude tests to be generally useful for the purpose of predicting school success and as an independent variable that must be controlled in educational studies. The many aptitude tests that are available can be divided into those that must be administered individually and those that can be used with groups.

The most widely used individual intelligence tests are the Stanford-Binet and the Wechsler tests. The Stanford-Binet test produces an *intelligence quotient* (IQ), which is derived by dividing the obtained mental age (MA) by the person's actual or chronological age (CA). The Stanford-Binet gives a general measure of intelligence and does not attempt to provide measures of separate abilities. There are several age versions of the Wechsler intelligence scales; each provides two scores for each person, verbal and nonverbal IQ. A trained psychometrician must give these individual intelligence tests to one person at a time, which is expensive in both time and money.

Group aptitude tests, on the other hand, are more practical for use in school systems and in research where group averages are to be used. There are now many group aptitude tests available, identified in the *Mental Measurements Yearbook* or *Test Critiques*.

An example of an aptitude test used in a research study can be found in our sample study 1 (Schellenberg, 2004). Here, the author used the Wechsler Intelligence Scale for Children as a dependent or outcome variable in the music intervention study. This scale measures the intelligence of children.

Documents

A common method for collecting data is through documents. Documents include items such as historical records, newspapers, and student files. Any information that is collected regarding a participant (e.g., grade point average) that is not obtained directly from the participant, but through records or documents can be considered document data. The advantage to using documents is that usually the information is more accurate. For example, requesting a student's transcript to find out his or her GPA would give the exact GPA, opposed to asking the student, who might round his or her GPA or give an inflated value. The downside to using documents is that their use can be time consuming for the researcher, and obtaining consent from the participants to examine documents can at times be difficult.

Landrum and Mulcock (2007) provide an example of using documents in research. In this study, data were obtained from the college Registrar regarding the participants' major, whether they had graduated, in what subject they had majored, and course grade.

Self-Report Measures

Standardized Personality Inventories

Personality inventories present the participant with a collection of statements describing behaviors or patterns of behaviors. The participants are then asked to indicate whether the statement is characteristic of their behavior by checking yes or no or by indicating how typical it is of them. Usually there are a number of statements for each characteristic measured by the instrument. Some of these inventories assess only one trait; for example, authoritarianism is measured by the *California F Scale* and anxiety is measured by the *State Trait Anxiety Scales*. Other personality inventories, such as *Cattell's 16 Personality Factor Questionnaire*, measure a number of traits. Some inventories measure characteristics of persons that one might not strictly consider to be personality. For example, the *Strong Interest Inventory* is used primarily to assess vocational interests. Other inventories measure temperament (e.g., *Child Temperament Inventory*), behavior problems (e.g., *Child Behavior Checklist*), or motivation (e.g., *Dimensions of Mastery Questionnaire*). Notice that these personality instruments have various labels (e.g., scale, inventory, questionnaire, or checklist).

These measures are said to be standardized because they have been administered to a wide variety of respondents and because information about these norm groups and about the reliability and validity evidence of past data collected is usually provided in the manual for the inventory. It is also possible for an investigator to develop a measure of some aspect of personality specifically for a particular study. As with other measures, reliability and validity need to be addressed.

Paper-and-pencil inventories have the advantages of being relatively inexpensive to administer and objective to score. However, there are disadvantages mostly related to the problem of validity. We should mention here that the validity of a personality inventory depends not only on respondents' ability to read and understand the items but also on their understanding of themselves and their willingness to give frank and honest answers. Although personality inventories, especially the more carefully developed and standardized ones, can provide useful information for research, there is clearly the possibility that they may be superficial or biased.

Another major type of personality assessment is the *projective technique*. These measures are not frequently used in educational and social science research because they require an extensively trained person to administer and score. Thus, they are expensive. Projective techniques ask the participant to respond to unstructured stimuli like ink blots or ambiguous pictures. They are called projective because it is assumed that the respondent will project his or her personality or motivation into their interpretation of the stimulus.

Attitude Scales

Summated (Likert) Attitude Scales

Many personality inventories use the same summated method to be described here, but Likert (1932) initially developed this method as a way of measuring attitudes about particular groups, institutions, or concepts. Researchers often develop their own scales for measuring attitudes or values, but there are also a number of standardized scales to measure certain kinds of attitudes like social responsibility. There are several approaches to measuring attitudes. We describe only the summated Likert scales and the *semantic differential* scales.

The term *Likert scale* is used in two ways: (1) for the summated scale to be discussed next; and (2) for the individual items or rating scales from which the summated scale is computed. Likert items are statements about a particular topic, and the participants are asked to indicate whether they strongly agree, agree, are undecided, disagree, or strongly disagree. The summated Likert scale is constructed by developing a number of statements about the topic, usually some of which are clearly favorable and some of which are unfavorable. These statements are intended to provide a representative sample of all possible opinions or attitudes about the subject. These statements are then presented to a group of participants who are asked to rate each statement from strongly disagree to strongly agree. To compute the summated scale score, each type of answer is given a numerical value or weighting, usually 1 for strongly disagree up to 5 for strongly agree. When computing the summated scale, the negatively worded or unfavorable items need to be reversed in terms of the weighting; in that case strongly disagree is given a weight of 5 and strongly agree is given a weight of 1. Consider the following three items from a social responsibility scale:

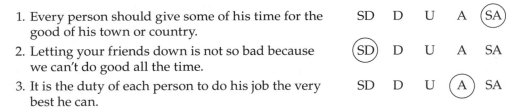

1. Every person should give some of his time for the good of his town or country.   SD   D   U   A   (SA)

2. Letting your friends down is not so bad because we can't do good all the time.   (SD)   D   U   A   SA

3. It is the duty of each person to do his job the very best he can.   SD   D   U   (A)   SA

As shown, a person with a highly favorable attitude about "social responsibility" might circle SA for the first item, SD for the second item, and A for the third item. His or her summated score would be 5 for the first item, 5 for the second item (after it is reverse coded), and 4 for the third item, or 14. You should be able to see that the summated scores could range from 3 for someone who is very low on agreement with the three *attitude of social responsibility* items to a maximum of 15 for someone who is most highly positive in terms of this attitude.

Data collected with summated rating attitude scales, like all the other data collection tools discussed in this chapter, need to be investigated for reliability, as discussed in Chapter 11. Internal consistency would be indicated if the various individual items correlate with each other, indicating that they belong together in assessing this attitude. Validity would be assessed in the ways detailed in Chapter 12 by seeing if this summated scale can differentiate between groups thought to differ on this attitude or by correlations with other measures that are assumed to be related to this attitude. The construction of summated scales (for attitude or personality measurement) is discussed in depth by Spector (1992).

Semantic Differential Scales

Another approach to measuring attitudes is the semantic differential scale developed by Osgood, Suci, and Tannenbaum (1957). This measure is based on the assumption that concepts or objects have what is in addition to the denotative (or dictionary) meaning for individuals. Connotative meaning has to do with surplus meaning or what the concept or object suggests or connotes to the participant.

Semantic Differential scales are adaptable and relatively easy to construct, if one wants to know how participants feel about concepts such as *site-based management, ADA requirements*, or *organized religion*. Participants are asked to rate the concept on each of a set of bipolar adjective pairs, which Osgood et al. (1957) found formed three clusters or factors: (1) *evaluative*, with adjective pairs such as good–bad or valuable–worthless; (2) *potency* pairs such as strong–weak or large–small; and (3) *activity* pairs such as active–passive or fast–slow. The evaluative cluster is used most often in research. The semantic differential scales are scored much like the summated rating scales just discussed. The rating for each item is given a score, usually from 1 to 7. If the positively connoted term is on the left, the score would be reversed. If the positive term is on the right, no reversal would be done. Then the score for each item on a scale (e.g., evaluative) would be added or summated.

Questionnaires and Interviews

These two broad techniques are sometimes called *survey research methods*, but we think that is misleading because questionnaires and interviews are used in many studies that would not meet the definition of survey research. In survey research a sample of participants is drawn (usually using one of the probability sampling methods discussed in Chapter 9) from a larger population. This sample is asked a series of questions related to a topic about which they should have some knowledge or attitude. The intent of surveys is to make inferences describing the whole population, so the sampling method and return rate are very important considerations, as discussed in Chapter 9.

Questionnaires and interviews used in surveys are usually developed by the investigator for one-time use in a particular study. However, sometimes the same or similar questions are asked on a number of occasions to assess changes in attitudes, product preferences, or voting preferences over time. *Questionnaires* are any group of written questions to which participants are asked to respond in writing, often by checking or circling responses. *Interviews* are a series of questions presented orally by an interviewer and are usually responded to orally by the participant. Both questionnaires and interviews can be highly structured with close-ended questions in which the possible answers are specified and the participants merely pick one of the provided responses. However, it is common for interviews to be more open ended, allowing the participant to provide detailed answers to questions that do not lend themselves to short answers.

Questionnaires

There are three basic ways to gather information with a questionnaire: mailed questionnaires, Internet, and directly administered questionnaires.

Mailed Questionnaires

In this case, names and addresses of persons in the population must be assembled. Then, a sample from this population is selected using one of the techniques described in Chapter 9. When the accessible population is small, all persons may be sampled. This group is then mailed a questionnaire with a cover letter and a stamped, return-addressed envelope. Reminder post cards or duplicate copies of the questionnaire are often sent to nonrespondents or, if respondents are not specifically identified, to all persons who initially received the questionnaire. Compared with interviews, mailed questionnaires are relatively cost effective because they require little time to administer on the part of the investigators and do not require hiring of persons to administer the instrument. Information can be obtained relatively rapidly (i.e., in a few weeks), but a poor response rate is often obtained because of the impersonality and likely lack of rapport with the investigator. Dillman (2007) is a good source to use for mailed questionnaires.

Internet Questionnaires

Internet questionnaires are the newest and becoming one of the most commonly used type of questionnaire. With Internet questionnaires, the questionnaire is set up on the Internet, usually with an online survey program (e.g., Survey Monkey, http://www.surveymonkey.com). Participants can be selected through multiple techniques: existing groups (e.g., courses or clubs), email lists, and list serves, just to name a few. There are many advantages to using Internet questionnaires. Respondents, if they have a computer, can complete the survey in their own home while taking their time and having privacy. Contacting respondents is cheaper than mailing the questionnaires through the post office. Furthermore, the data can be sent directly to a data file, which can reduce or even eliminate data entry errors. There are a few negative aspects to using Internet questionnaires. The respondents must have access to a computer. If the survey is long, the respondents can easily close the survey window and not submit their responses. Finally, the most significant drawback to using Internet questionnaires is that the data collected with many of the Internet programs are not anonymous or confidential, as IP addresses attach themselves to the data. Dillman (2007) is a good source to use for Internet questionnaires.

An example of using the Internet to administer surveys is found in Brothen and Wambach (2004), our sample quasi-experiment on the effects of time limits on Internet quizzes. These authors sent the participants, who were students in a class, the survey via WebCT, an online course resource (Edutools, 2002).

Directly Administered Questionnaires

In this technique, the questionnaire is usually administered to a group of people who are assembled in a certain place for a specific purpose such as a class or a club meeting. It is also possible to directly administer a questionnaire in a one-on-one, face-to-face situation such as giving a questionnaire to the mother of a young child while testing the child, but this is relatively uncommon. The main advantage of this technique is that a high response rate is usually obtained, especially if the participants are expected to be in that location anyway. On the other hand, the sample is unlikely to be a probability sample from a desired target population, in part because some percentage of potential participants probably will not attend the class or meeting. This can be a serious problem in college classrooms. This technique can be quite cost effective if it requires only one or few administrations of the questionnaire and if the administrator's time is not considered or does not have to be paid.

An example of a directly administered questionnaire comes from Landrum and Mulcock (2007). In this study, the authors collected data from students enrolled in courses via a questionnaire. The students were given time to complete the survey during class. This is a common method for collecting data, as it ensures a higher response rate than for mailed or Internet questionnaires.

Types of Questionnaire Items

Salant and Dillman (1994), Cazja and Blair (2005), and DeVellis (2003) provide excellent sources for persons who want to develop and conduct their own questionnaire or structured interview. They describe four types of question structure for questionnaire and *interview* items: open-ended, partially open-ended, close-ended unordered choices, and close-ended ordered responses. Each of these types of items has advantages and disadvantages, as discussed next.

Open-ended questions do not provide choices for the participants to select. Instead, each participant must formulate an answer in his or her own words. Although this type of question requires the least effort to write, it has several major drawbacks. Open-ended questions are demanding for the participants, especially if the responses have to be written out or are on issues that the person has not considered recently or at all. Open-ended questions can produce many different responses with only a few mentions of each topic. This type of question might provide comparable information across a sample because people who did not think to mention an answer might have done so if they had been given choices from which to select. Finally, the responses to open-ended questions require considerable time to code and prepare for entry into a computer. However, there are a number of advantages that make open-ended questions useful in certain circumstances, especially if the investigator did not have enough knowledge before the study to make good close-ended questions. Sometimes open-ended questions require a simple straightforward answer such as the person's date of birth or favorite class. In these cases developing a list of possible responses is wasteful of space. Open-ended questions are more often successfully used in interviews than in questionnaires.

Partially open-ended questions usually provide several possible answers and then have a space for other responses or comments. This can be useful, but our experience is that participants usually do not use the spaces, and not much additional information is provided.

Close-ended unordered items are commonly used when answers to a question fit nominal categories that do not fall on a continuum. Participants are asked to choose among these discreet categories and select which one best reflects their opinion or situation. In some cases, the person is allowed to check all categories that apply, but then the question actually becomes a series of yes/no questions with each response category being scored later as if it were a separate question. If it is not possible to have a complete list of possible answers, a partially open-ended question may be used.

Finally, **close-ended questions with ordered choices** are common on questionnaires and are often similar to the individual items in a personality inventory or a summated attitude scale. These questions may in fact be single Likert-type items in which a statement is made and the respondent is asked to rate one or a series of items from strongly disagree to strongly agree. A number of other types of items with ordered choices are possible (see Salant and Dillman, 1994).

Interviews

Two main types of interviews are telephone and face to face. *Telephone* interviews are almost always structured and usually brief (i.e., less than half an hour). This technique is commonly used by survey researchers to obtain a quick, geographically diverse, or national sample. Groves et al. (1988) provide in-depth information for telephone interviews.

An example of using the telephone to collect data is DiLorenzo, Halper, and Picone (2004), our sample comparative study of younger and older persons with multiple sclerosis (MS). Because part of their sample consisted of participants who were nonambulatory, using telephone calls for data collection allowed the researchers to reach a larger sample.

Face-to-face interviews, on the other hand, can vary from what amounts to a highly structured, oral questionnaire with close-ended answers to in-depth interviews, which are preferred by qualitative researchers who want to get detailed responses from the participants. Telephone and structured face-to-face interviews are usually coded on the spot. The categories are often close-ended so that the interviewer needs only to circle the chosen response or fill in a brief blank. In-depth interviews are usually tape-recorded and then later transcribed so that the participant's comments can be coded later. All types of interviews are relatively expensive because of their one-on-one nature. In-depth interviews are even more expensive because of training, transcription, and coding costs. Fowler and Mangione (1990) provide an excellent source for standardized interviewing.

An example of an interview being used to collect data can be found in Wolfe et al. (2006), our sample descriptive study. The authors used both structured questions as well as open-ended questions to interview people living with HIV. Due to the sensitive nature of the topic of HIV, using interviews to collect the data most likely helped put the respondents at ease with the questions.

Focus Groups

Focus groups are like interviews, but relatively small groups of, perhaps, 8 to 10 people are interviewed together. Such groups may stimulate peoples' thinking and elicit ideas about a specific topic. They have been used by businesses to learn how customers will react to new products and by political campaigns to test voter opinions about a topic. Nonprofit agencies may also use focus groups to identify the perceptions and ideas of potential or actual participants in a program or a service. Focus groups can provide an initial idea about what responses people will give to a certain type of question. This can be helpful in developing more structured questionnaires or interviews. Krueger and Casey (2000) provide an excellent source for researchers who plan to use focus groups.

Summary

This chapter provides an overview of many of the techniques or methods used in the applied behavioral sciences to gather data from human participants. Most of the methods are used in quantitative, qualitative, and mixed methods research but to different extents. In qualitative research more open-ended, less structured data collection techniques are preferred than in quantitative research, but this distinction is not absolute. Direct observation of participants by the researcher is common among experimental research and qualitative research; it is less common in survey research where self-report interviews and questionnaires are used extensively. It is important that investigators use instruments that provide reliable and valid data for the population and purpose for which they will be used. Standardized instruments usually have manuals providing norms and indexes of reliability and validity from data collected in the past. However, if the populations and purposes on which these data are based are different from yours, it may be necessary for you to develop your own instrument or, at least, to provide evidence of reliability and validity for the data you have collected.

Key Concepts

Direct observation

Focus group

Naturalness of the setting

Participant observation

Performance and authentic assessment

Semantic differential scales

Reliability and validity of the measures

Standardized tests

Standardized personality inventories

Summated (Likert) attitude scales

Key Distinctions

Achievement tests versus aptitude tests

Data collection techniques (methods) versus research approaches

Norm references versus criterion referenced tests

Open-ended versus closed-ended questions

Questionnaire question/item versus research question

Questionnaire versus interview

Researcher report measures versus self-participant report measures

Application Problems

1. A researcher designed a measure of work satisfaction. Part of this measure is included in the table. Shown are pairs of words that indicate how people feel about their work. Consider each of the word pairs and circle the number that best indicates how YOU feel about your job/work in general. What kind of attitude scale is this? How would you score it if a person circled 5, 2, and 6?

Boring	1	2	3	4	5	6	7	Interesting
Enjoyable	1	2	3	4	5	6	7	Miserable
Useless	1	2	3	4	5	6	7	Worthwhile

etc.

2. Table 13.1 gives an approximation of how common each of the several data collection techniques are within each major grouping of research approaches.
   a. Why would physiological recordings be most common for experiments and quasi-experiments?
   b. Why would self-report measures be most commonly used with comparative, associational, and descriptive approaches?
   c. Why is it that standardized tests, summated attitude scales, and standard personality scales are unlikely to be used in qualitative research?

3. Indicate whether the following questions are open-ended or partially open-ended, or close-ended ordered, or close-ended unordered items. Discuss the pros and cons of formatting question as shown or in another way.
   a. What is your date of birth? _____
   b. Do you provide special care to anyone who is ill, handicapped, or elderly?
      No _____
      Yes _____
      Please explain: _____
   c. For which of the following areas of expenditure do you have the highest priority?
      Defense _____
      Education _____
      Health and welfare _____
      Other. Please specify:
   d. What type of work schedule best describes your work situation?
      _____ Standard full time (8 a.m. to 5 p.m.)
      _____ Flexible work hours
      _____ Compressed week
   e. Which best describes the kind of building in which you live?
      _____ A mobile home
      _____ A one-family house detached from any other
      _____ A one-family house attached to at least one other house
      _____ An apartment building
   f. Please describe the qualities of your favorite teacher.

4. Your colleague is interested in learning if parenting style influences adolescent delinquency. He asks for your opinion about whether he should use a questionnaire or interview format to collect his data. What do you tell him are the pros and cons of each?

5. A researcher is interested in the degree to which therapeutic alliance (or, the strength of the relationship between client and therapist) affects the therapeutic outcome (or, the success of therapy.)

   a. If the researcher observes the sessions from behind a one-way mirror and rates therapeutic alliance on a Likert scale, what kind of measure is this?

   b. If the researcher asks the client to report his or her perception of alliance using a Likert scale, what kind of measure is this?

   c. What are the benefits and drawbacks of each?

6. What is the difference between a research question and a questionnaire or item? Provide two examples of each.

14

Ethical Issues in Conducting the Study

Throughout this book, we have been discussing the principles of applied behavioral research. In this chapter, we discuss ethical principles of human research and a variety of ethical issues related to the various steps in the process of doing research, including obtaining approval from institutional review boards (IRBs).

Ethical Principles in Human Research

Historical Overview

There have been ethical problems regarding the treatment of human subjects throughout history, but we begin our summary with the Nazi *research* atrocities of 1933–1945. In contrast to the rest of this book, we used the phrase *human subjects* rather than *participants*. The latter is a relatively recent change that emphasizes the collaborative and voluntary relationship of investigator and participant. The Nazi research atrocities were experiments conducted by respected German doctors and professors on concentration camp inmates that led to their mutilation or death. Although it is tempting to think that these atrocities could be blamed on prison guards, soldiers, or rogue scientists, the evidence indicates otherwise (e.g., Pross, 1992). Not only were many of these doctors respected, but Germany also had more advanced moral and legal regulations concerning consent and special protections for vulnerable subjects than any other country at that time (Young, 1999). As a result of the trial of these doctors, the *Nuremberg code* was prescribed by an international court in 1947. Its first principle stated that voluntary consent of human subjects is absolutely essential. Principles 2 through 8 dealt with experimental design and the risks and benefits of the research. Principle 9 stated the subject's right to refuse to participate or continue, and principle 10 dealt with the investigator's obligation to stop the experiment when continuing it would likely lead to harm.

Lest we think that ethical problems with human research have been confined to Nazi Germany, some examples of American research are cited briefly. In 1963 mentally impaired children from the Willowbrook State School in New York were given live hepatitis A virus. Their parents were not adequately informed and were even coerced into volunteering their children for the study.

The Tuskegee syphilis study, which began in 1932, continued until it became public knowledge in 1972 (Heller, 1972). The study involved several hundred poor African American men in Alabama who were studied but not treated over a 40-year period, even though antibiotics were available and commonly used to treat syphilis for more than 25 years of the study. The long-term effects of this study include mistrust and suspicion of medical research and of doctors in general in the African American community.

Serious ethical concerns were, however, not confined to the biomedical sciences. Milgram (1974) conducted a series of well-known experiments on obedience that sparked ethical debate both inside and outside of the behavioral sciences. His intent to perform these experiments was based on his dismay at the effects of blind obedience to Nazi commands in World War II. Milgram decided that it was important to study the psychological mechanism that linked blind obedience to destructive behavior. He wanted to know how far ordinary adults will go in carrying out the orders of a seemingly legitimate authority. In his experiments, he deceived subjects into believing that they would be giving painful electric shocks to a third person, the "learner," when the "learner" made a mistake on a particular task. The results were startling. A great many of the "teachers," who were the actual subjects in the study, obeyed without hesitation the experimenter's urging to continue to increase the presumed level of the shocks, no matter how much the learner pleaded and screamed. Milgram was especially surprised that none of the subjects refused to apply the shocks or dropped out of the study. The learner in these studies was a confederate of Milgram's, and no actual shocks were transmitted by the teacher. Nevertheless, concerns about the studies and the use of deception have continued to this day. Milgram defended his work as showing that remarkable obedience was seen time and time again at several universities where the experiment was repeated. He emphasized the willingness of adults to go to almost any lengths when commanded by an authority. He did fully debrief the subjects and provided an opportunity for a friendly reconciliation with the presumably shocked learner, who was shown not to have received any actual electric shocks. Furthermore, he sent follow-up questionnaires to the former subjects and found that less than 1% regretted having participated in the study. In spite of this, it is doubtful that institutional review boards would allow this kind of study today because subjects were tricked into participating in a study that they probably would find unacceptable if they had understood it correctly.

If you think that ethical problems with regard to research have been confined to experimental studies, Humphreys's (1970) research on the "tea room" trade indicates some of the issues potentially raised by participant observations and qualitative methodology. For this study of male homosexual behavior, Humphreys received a prestigious award. He used considerable deception and violated the subjects' privacy by surreptitiously noting the license plates of men he knew had had fellatio in public restrooms. Humphreys then obtained their addresses from the Division of Motor Vehicles to obtain interviews with them while pretending to be a health service worker. He suspected that the men would not grant an interview if they had known his real purpose because most of the men were married and lived with wives who would not have approved of this behavior.

In 1974 the Department of Health, Education and Welfare published regulations on the protection of human subjects. It mandated that there be institutional review boards at each research institution accepting federal funding to determine whether subjects were placed at risk and, if so, whether the risks so outweighed the benefits and importance of the knowledge to be gained that the subjects should be allowed to accept these risks. The guidelines also mandated that effective informed consent be obtained from participants in research.

The Belmont Report: Principles and Norms

In a report called the Belmont Report, the National Commission for the Protection of Human Subjects of Biomedical and Behavioral Research (1978) identified three ethical principles and guidelines for the protection of human subjects.

Respect for Persons

This principle incorporates two ethical convictions. First, participants should be treated as autonomous agents, which means that the individual is capable of deliberating and making individual decisions and choices. Second, persons with diminished autonomy, such as children, developmentally delayed persons, prisoners, and persons with emotional disorders, are entitled to special protection.

Beneficence

Researchers should not harm participants, and good outcomes should be maximized for the *participants* as well as for science and humanity. This principle requires maximizing the potential benefits and minimizing the risks.

Justice

Research should not be exploitative, and there should be a fair distribution of risks and benefits. For example, those who bear most of the risks should benefit the most from the research. Participants should not be selected merely on the basis of convenience.

Voluntary Informed Consent

Informed consent is the procedure by which persons choose whether they wish to participate in a study. Consent is an ongoing process and may be withdrawn at any time during the study. The Belmont Report discusses three aspects of informed consent.

Information

The information provided to participants should fully disclose the research procedure, purpose, risks, and anticipated benefits, including what a reasonable volunteer would want to know before giving consent. The information must be in language that the participants can understand, and efforts should be made to check that it is understood, especially when risks are involved.

Comprehension

The participants should have the legal capacity and the ability to understand the information and risks involved so that they can make an informed decision. Some participants (e.g., children) are not legally qualified to make decisions of consent for themselves, so others must make the decision for them. This is usually the parent or guardian, but the child also must *assent* to the procedure. Comprehension also may be impaired in mentally retarded or emotionally disabled persons. To the extent possible, these persons should be allowed to assent or not, but a third party (e.g., the legal guardian) should be chosen to act in their best interest.

Voluntariness

The third aspect of informed consent means that the participant freely, without threat or undue inducement, has decided to participate in the study. There should not be any element of deceit, constraint, or coercion. Persons in authority can elicit unjustifiable obedience from children and even from well-educated adults. Also voluntariness is reduced when the research offers financial or other inducements that the potential participants would find hard to refuse.

A number of aspects of the consent process should be considered. *Rapport* should be achieved, not only because participants are more likely to cooperate but also because it can strengthen the ecological validity of the study. It is important that the researcher not rush through the consent aspect of the study or give the impression that consent is unnecessary. Developing trust and understanding personal and cultural situations is important, especially for community-based research done in cultures that are different from the researcher's. The research also should be relevant to the concerns of the research population and explained in those terms.

The issue of who should provide the consent is easy when the potential participant is an adult who has the capacity to consent. The issue is less clear for those with diminished capacity and children. We should not automatically assume that parental or guardian consent is sufficient, although in most cases it should be. In some situations there may be a conflict of interest. For example, poor parents offered large payment for their children's participation might not have the interest of the child foremost.

How is consent obtained? IRBs require a formal signed consent form, except in certain situations specified in the federal regulations. A signed consent form may be omitted when adult subjects who have the legal capacity to consent can easily refuse by discontinuing a phone call with an interviewer or by not returning the survey that was received in the mail. It is important, however, that the interviewer or questionnaire cover letter describe the purpose of the research and any risks involved and state that participation is voluntary. Returning the survey or answering the questions is the subject's way of *implying consent*.

Privacy

Much of behavioral research involves asking participants to reveal some aspects of their behavior or attitudes. **Privacy** refers to participants' concern about controlling access to information about themselves. Voluntary informed consent involves the participant agreeing to reveal certain aspects that may have been private previously. If participants feel that privacy is being invaded or confidentiality will not be maintained, answers that they provide may be distorted and, therefore, give misleading or false information. The essence of privacy is that the participant is free to choose the extent to which his or her attitudes, beliefs, and behaviors are to be shared with or withheld from others. There is always the potential for a conflict between the right of privacy and the goal of the research.

If the data are anonymous, the participant may be more willing to share. It is important to make a distinction between *confidentiality* and *anonymity*. **Anonymous** means that the participant's name and other identifiers, such as social security or school ID number, are not known and cannot be deduced by the researcher or others. In many studies the data cannot be anonymous because the researcher sees the participants face to face or must know their identity to match information about them from different sources. In all cases it is important that the data remain **confidential**. That is, there is an agreement that private information will remain private to the researcher, and the participant will not be identifiable in the reports or in conversations with persons outside of the research team.

Sensitive researchers will be very careful not to invade the privacy of participants, and IRBs are typically alert to this issue. This implies that fully informed voluntary consent will be obtained ahead of time and that the researcher will assure confidentiality of the data. The participants can then decide whether to participate. Participants who view the research as an invasion of privacy may feel some subtle pressure to participate, but then they may distort answers. Thus, both to be sensitive to the participant's concerns and to obtain the best data, it is important to consider whether participants view the research as an invasion of privacy. To learn about the privacy interests of your research population, you should ask persons who are members of the population whether they might find your questions an invasion of privacy.

Assessment of Risks and Benefits

Probably the most important concern about research ethics is that the individuals not be harmed by serving as participants in the study. **Risk** refers both to the probability of harm and to the magnitude and type of harm. There are many possible harms and benefits that need to be taken into account. Psychological and physical pain or injuries are the most often discussed, but other risks, such as legal, economic, or social (e.g., embarrassment, stigmatization, or invasion of one's privacy), should be considered.

Although it is rare to attempt to quantify the *risks and benefits* of a particular research study, there should be a systematic assessment of these factors. The Belmont Report states that the assessment of whether the research is justifiable should reflect at least five considerations:

1. Brutal or inhumane treatment is never justified.
2. Risks should be reduced to those that are necessary and consideration given to alternative procedures that would reduce risks.
3. When research involves risks of serious harm, review committees should be very careful that the benefits justify those risks. For example, in medical research, an unproven treatment may promise significant benefits even though there are risks of serious side effects.
4. When vulnerable populations are involved, the appropriateness of using them should be demonstrated.
5. Relevant risks and benefits must be fairly explained in the informed consent procedure and form.

In addition to minimizing the risks, it is important for researchers to *maximize the benefits*. This may be relatively easy to do in community-based and medical research where some clear benefit to the individual participants is envisioned. However, beforehand such benefits are only anticipated or predicted, or else there is no need for the study.

It is less easy to achieve benefits for the participants in survey research and certain kinds of laboratory experiments. Nevertheless, researchers must think about the issue of maximizing benefits and do this in a realistic manner, which avoids false promises or grandiose claims about benefits to science and society. Benefits to participants could include an informative debriefing, workbooks or materials, a chance to share concerns or interests with the researcher, and, in some cases, the effects of the experimental treatment. Benefits to the community, but not necessarily the participants, could include improved relationships with a university, more understanding about the problems under study, materials such as books, special training, and the prestige of being associated with the program and university.

If participants have a good research experience (e.g., they are treated with respect and provided with results to validate their contribution), this increases the likelihood of future participation. Conversely, bad experiences predispose subjects to not participate in another study, resulting in their not benefiting from other new treatments. This would be a travesty and is perhaps the most significant risk of "benign" social research.

Ethical Issues in the Sample Selection

In Chapter 9, we described the process of selecting a sample of potential participants from what is usually a much larger theoretical population. Several strategies for selecting the sample and several obstacles to obtaining a representative sample were discussed. We pointed out that *external population validity* depends both on the representativeness of the accessible population and on the representativeness of the actual sample of those participants who agreed to participate and completed the study.

Cooperating Agencies

To obtain a broad and, hopefully, representative *accessible population*, it is often necessary to make arrangements with other agencies or institutions such as school districts or clinics. These organizations must be convinced of the importance and benefits of the research and that any potential risks are minimal. If the agency has an IRB, that IRB will need to review the project or may decide to exempt it. If the organization does not have an IRB, you need to assure your IRB that the project is acceptable to the cooperating agency. A person authorized to obligate the agency could write a letter to your IRB stating support for the project and the extent of any assistance. Developing and maintaining contacts can be a time-consuming aspect of research that needs to be planned and budgeted. There are also ethical issues to be considered in regard to collaborating agencies. What benefits will they and their students/clients gain? Will the agency benefit but the students/clients be exposed to some potential risk or loss of privacy? Your IRB will no doubt consider these issues and possible conflicts of interest.

A variant of this is what is called "brokered" data. In this case the researcher lacks access to a given population and the broker (e.g., school principal or clinic director) may not allow the researcher to actually collect the data because of concern about privacy. The agency may be willing to collect the data for the researcher or at least to hand out anonymous questionnaires to their clients and ask them if they would be willing to respond. It is considered a breach of patient–provider confidentiality to allow an outside researcher full access to medical files or even a list of patients to contact directly. Contact or file review should be done by the health-care provider or school. Because clinics and schools are busy, they may not have time to contact clients or review files. This has led to a fair amount of tension between the outlined principles of recruitment ethics and the desire to obtain complete data and a representative sample. A low response rate and, likely, an unrepresentative sample will be created if the clinic or school announces the study and leaves it up to potential participants to contact the researcher.

Response Rate

Another issue with regard to response rate is the need to balance obtaining a high response rate with respect for persons who decide not to take part. It is okay to try to convince potential participants of the importance and value of their contribution; you may remind them that they forgot to answer a mailed survey. You can also offer incentives, but you must stop before becoming coercive or offensive. This may be especially a problem with telephone surveys, in part because hired interviewers may go too far unless properly trained. Remember that well-constructed short questionnaires are more likely to be responded to than poorly worded, long, or open-ended ones. Participants are often more willing to verbally answer questions or be interviewed than to write answers to questions.

Dropouts

In multisession and longitudinal research, there is the additional issue of maintaining the consent and cooperation of the participants. In these kinds of research it is important that participants do not drop out of the study unnecessarily. Any coercion to continue is unacceptable. Therefore, developing good rapport and maintaining good sensitive relationships with the participants and their needs will often forestall such dropouts. If the participants are to be rewarded for their participation, it may be possible to partially back load the prorated payments so that completion of the study is rewarded. However, the IRB will have to approve any such arrangements, and they must not seem coercive or unfair to participants who desire to leave the study midway.

Ethical Issues and the Methods Section

Ethical Issues in the Design

It is important to carefully and ethically plan the research design and also the data analysis before data collection begins. Statisticians are frequently frustrated when an inexperienced researcher comes to them with a pile of data and asks for it to be analyzed. All too often the design or instruments were not carefully planned, and, thus, the appropriate analysis cannot be performed. When this happens, participants' time may well have been wasted, which is unethical.

Qualitative researchers say that their design is emergent rather than preplanned. We believe that this apparent dichotomy between qualitative and quantitative research paradigms is relative, more one of degree than absolute. Qualitative researchers need to have a good idea about their research questions and at least a good indication of the literature related to those questions. They would be unwise to embark on a major study without a good idea about how they were going to analyze the data. It is true that after doing a few interviews or observations they may discover that their original research questions were not the most interesting ones or did not elicit the information they sought. Then they may decide to reformulate the questions to ask future participants. This is also true, to a lesser extent, of quantitative research. All good research should begin with pilot testing to ensure that the design and instruments are appropriate and will work well to answer the research questions. If it is discovered that the procedures or questions are not the most appropriate, a new sample to assess the new questions should be obtained.

Deception

Certain ethical issues are more likely to arise with some types of design than others. For example, deception is more likely to occur in experimental research, but qualitative and survey research can be misleading if the participants are not fully informed of the researcher's purposes and procedures. *Deception* involves a misrepresentation of facts, by commission, which occurs when the researcher gives false information about the study. If the investigator does not fully inform the subjects about the important aspects of the study or its goals, omission or *concealment* has occurred.

Until recent years, social psychological research relied heavily on deception because it was assumed that information about certain topics, such as conformity or obedience, would be unobtainable without deception due to participants' defensiveness, embarrassment, or fear of reprisal. The classic Milgram (1974) studies on obedience to authority, which we described briefly at the beginning of this chapter, would pose two problems today. First, it is now typical for research participants, especially college students, to assume that deception *will* occur, and they are likely to alter their behavior based on that assumption. Second, institutional review boards probably would not allow such research because deception should not encourage participants to act in ways that *they*, the participants, would find unacceptable. It is usually indefensible for deception to trick people into behaviors that they would have found unacceptable if they correctly understood the research. IRBs place a greater emphasis on truly informed consent and respect for autonomy.

Deception may be allowable under certain circumstances but is restricted by IRBs in recent times. Are there alternatives to deception in research? Simulations, which are mock situations, are being used effectively to explore social behavior. Ethnographic or participant observation methods are used increasingly to study real behavior, often in a community-based setting. Ethical and practical considerations have led researchers to provide fully informed consent procedures and to rely on rapport and trust rather than cleverness or deception, as was the case in the Milgram (1974) obedience studies. Also participants may be asked to agree (consent) that the researcher may conceal some important parts of the procedure. There is now evidence that most subjects will participate in research with the understanding that some details must be withheld until after the study. Of course, they are guaranteed a full debriefing. After the debriefing, participants may be offered an opportunity to withdraw their data from the study. If the participants trust the researcher to keep their data confidential, few are likely to withdraw at this point.

There are deep differences among the members of the research community about the ethics of deception. Some are strongly against it, and others believe that it is the only viable way to study certain types of social behavior. There are two points on which we hope all can agree. First, some important behaviors vanish under obvious scrutiny, and, thus, concealment or deception is sometimes necessary. Second, the more objectionable forms of deception are unnecessary and should not be used.

Debriefing

Debriefing is a good practice for most studies and is almost always necessary for deception studies. In addition to discussing the goals of the study and reasons for the deception, it is desirable to provide some evidence about the deception. In the case of false feedback about test performance, participants could be given their own unscored tests in a sealed envelope just as they had submitted them. It is important to try to eliminate any residue of generalized mistrust on the part of the participants. If the researcher detects any undesirable emotional results of the research, he or she should attempt to restore participants to a frame of mind at least as positive as that with which they entered the study.

However, there are certain cases where it might be better *not* to dehoax or debrief the participant because such debriefing may be harmful. For example, if a researcher was to study dishonesty, it may be better not to point out to participants that their behavior during the study was dishonest. At any rate, debriefing should be done without demeaning the participants' behavior or attitudes. The institutional review board will no doubt require this issue to be thought through carefully and may place requirements on the researcher with regard to the type and extent of debriefing.

Experimental Research

It is the nature of experimental designs (randomized experimental and quasi-experimental approaches) that some or all of the participants are given an intervention or treatment that may be medical, psychological, or educational. With these interventions, there is always the possibility of potential harm. Physical harm is much more likely with medical interventions than with educational or psychological ones, but less tangible harm is possible with all interventions. For example, the participants in the new curriculum group may learn less than they would have if they had stayed in the traditional curriculum. Or certain kinds of training may require the participants in the intervention group to be more open and self-disclosing than they might otherwise prefer. If there is potential risk of harm, due to the intervention, it should be minor, reversible, short duration, and negated as much as possible.

We have described some difficult issues regarding the control group in earlier chapters about experimental designs. For example, if a new treatment is found to be highly advantageous, it may be unethical to withhold it from the control group. It would be desirable to offer it to the control group. In some cases, this can be done by having a *wait-list control group* that receives the treatment after a period of delay presumably equal to the time that the intervention group was given the treatment. It may be necessary for an investigator to budget the costs of providing treatment to the control group at a later date.

In earlier chapters, we discussed the design advantages of having a no-intervention or placebo control group. If a placebo control group was used, a "natural state argument" would need to be made to the IRB. The reasoning is that untreated participants are not being denied a benefit they already have but are merely being left in their natural state. This argument is severely undercut if the control group has a disease or has come in for and does not receive treatment.

Nonexperimental and Qualitative Research

As mentioned earlier, ethical problems are not confined to experimental research. For example, survey research has potential ethical issues related to coercing subjects to participate. In addition, certain types of information obtained from surveys could distress participants or be detrimental economically to them if they were identified by their employers or by other persons with power. So care must be taken. This issue applies to *qualitative* research as well. In fact, long quotes gathered in qualitative studies may be identifiable because they may include unique or personal information recognizable by others. In these cases, such information would have to be altered or deleted from the research report.

Animal Research

There is a separate set of issues related to research with nonhuman animals. Because this book deals almost exclusively with human research, we discuss only animal research here briefly. It is important to note that the National Institutes of Health has published information about appropriate use of animals in research, and most universities have a separate internal review board to consider use of animals in research. Principles in animal research involve the training of the personnel conducting the research and handling the animals, the nature of the research and procedures, the facilities used to feed and house the animals, the methods used to transport them, and the justification for the number and species to be used. Clearly, experiments should be conducted to avoid all unnecessary suffering and harm to the animals.

Ethical Issues in the Selection or Development of the Instruments

As discussed in the last chapter, it is necessary for a valid and ethical study to have high-quality data collection instruments. Therefore, selecting or developing instruments with strong evidence supporting measurement reliability and validity is both a practical and ethical issue. In general, an inexperienced researcher should use already developed, standardized instruments whenever there are appropriate ones available. Remember that reliability and validity reside not in the instruments themselves but in their use for certain *purposes* with certain types of *participants*. You should consider whether commonly used instruments are appropriate if your population is an unusual or vulnerable one. Even well-established instruments should be pilot tested to be sure that the instrument is appropriate and does not raise ethical issues.

Ethical Issues in the Procedure for Data Collection

Institutional review boards are sensitive to issues surrounding the procedure that is used for data collection. We have already discussed the issue of deception; if it is needed it should be fully explained and justified. The procedure section of a proposal and, especially, the human research protocol should spell out the procedures that will be used to obtain consent from the participants. This and other materials that the IRB will probably want to review are described in the section of this chapter on obtaining approval of the IRB.

In funded research projects it is common to pay subjects something to participate in the study, especially if their involvement requires them to come into a laboratory or is time consuming. Even for brief or easy tasks it may be desirable to consider tokens of appreciation such as a small toy for child participants or a pen or a dollar for other participants. Such inducements are designed to increase the response rate. However, the IRB will *not* consider them to be "benefits" to the participants. Payments or other inducements should not be so high that they seem to be coercive. For example, the payment for poor people or students should not be so high that they would find it hard to refuse. Similarly, prisoners should not be promised privileges that would lead them to agree to do harmful procedures.

Confidentiality

As mentioned earlier, it is an important part of the research procedure to ensure confidentiality for each participant. This is a two-part issue: (1) Only those on the research team should be able to match the participants' identities with their responses, if such a match is necessary; and (2) the identity of specific participants, if known, is not revealed. This proscription not only applies to written reports but also means that the team will not talk about specific participants in public (e.g., the restroom, lunchroom, or hall). Focus groups pose special confidentiality problems because even though the researcher instructs other participants in the group about confidentiality, they may not heed it.

Confidentiality also may be important to the groups (e.g., school, hospital, company) from which the sample is drawn. It is common practice and often necessary that the identity of such groups be disguised in a report. In fact, some Native American tribes require that they only be referred to by general geographic region to avoid stigmatizing tribal members.

Usually the issue of confidentiality arises when the researcher is aware of the participants' identities and has agreed to keep them confidential. Certain procedures eliminate or minimize the link between identifiers and the data and, therefore, help to assure confidentiality. For example, one can assure that participants' names are not put on transcriptions of audio tape recordings, questionnaires, or data forms. Participants can be identified by a code (but never their social security numbers) that is kept locked in a different place from the data. If vignettes or other descriptions are provided in a write-up, characteristics such as occupation, city, or ethnic background should be changed. Audiotapes or videotapes should be stored in a locked place and viewed only in places that provide privacy from unintended visitors. Tapes and master lists of names can be destroyed after the report has been accepted for publication or the graduate project approved. The methods used to preserve confidentiality should be identified in the consent process so that the prospective participants can be assured that information will be kept confidential.

In cases where the research data are *anonymous* to the investigators, the issue is different. For example, if demographic or other potentially identifying data are obtained from an anonymous survey, the researcher needs to be careful that results are not presented in a way that someone familiar with the institution from which participants were drawn would be able to deduce the identity of participants. For example, if a company had only one or a few minority workers, the confidentiality of their responses would be jeopardized if the average of their responses were presented in a report. Ensuring that the report does not unintentionally reveal identities is, of course, important in all research.

Approval from the Institutional Review Board

IRBs and How They Work

An IRB or human subjects committee is a group that reviews proposals for studies with human participants *before* the research can begin. Sieber's (1992) book *Planning Ethically Responsible Research: A Guide for Students and Internal Review Boards* is a helpful guide. The committee is mandated by federal regulations to protect human subjects and to decide whether the research plan has adequately dealt with ethical issues related to the project. IRBs were the result of the kinds of ethical problems that we mentioned at the beginning of this chapter. The board or committee consists of five or more members who have varying backgrounds; they include members of the broader community as well as scholars from a variety of areas within the university or research institution. The committee meets periodically, often monthly, to review research protocols for projects proposed by scholars and students at the institution.

All research at the institution that systematically collects data and is intended to develop generalizable knowledge must be reviewed, unless it meets the exemption criteria that some institutions allow. In practice this means that any research project that is intended to be published in a journal, book, or as a dissertation or thesis must be reviewed. Data gathered for administrative purposes and classroom demonstrations are not reviewed. Many institutions do not review research done as part of a course and not intended to be published, but the instructor and student should nevertheless follow the ethical principles described in this chapter. The government also allows certain types of research, for example, anonymous questionnaires on noncontroversial topics and research dealing with methods of instruction in schools to be "**exempt**." However, many university IRBs require that *all* proposed research projects should be submitted to them, and then they (the IRB) decides whether it will be exempt. Exempt status may mean only that there is a less intensive review, which will not have to wait until the next full committee meeting, but the research protocol and also periodic reports on progress may be required.

Usually **pilot testing**, which involves trying out procedures or fine-tuning a questionnaire with a few acquaintances or knowledgeable persons in the field, does not require IRB review. However, **pilot studies** in which data are collected (and analyzed) from participants like those to be used in the research do require IRB review.

IRBs have been controversial with some researchers who viewed them as obstacles to good scientific research. This is partly due to pressures to meet deadlines, which can lead to miscommunication and misunderstandings. The federal regulations require institutions to develop policies in keeping with the regulations but that reflect community standards. Thus, it is likely that each institution may have somewhat different policies and could make different decisions about the same protocol. For these reasons, it is desirable for students to discuss their research with knowledgeable people at their institution, such as experts in the content area and experienced researchers, to be aware of potential ethical issues. It is also desirable to talk with people about the procedures of the local IRB and whether feedback from IRB staff or members can be obtained in advance. This may save a considerable amount of time and frustration. Students should be aware of the policies and procedures of the institutional review board at their university. Often the administrator or a member of the board is willing to discuss ethical issues related to a project with the researcher before the protocol is submitted.

The Research Protocol

The research protocol is a short version of your research proposal focusing on the research problem or objectives, the participants, procedures to be followed, risks, benefits, consent procedures, and confidentiality. Your local IRB probably will provide a detailed list of questions that they want to have answered as part of the protocol. Usually you will include brief but specific answers to these questions in the text of the protocol. Although some of the answers may be condensed versions of your proposal, others (e.g., statements of risks and benefits) may have to be expanded from what you have in your proposal. In addition, you will probably have to include several of the following attachments:

- Advertisements or posters.
- Telephone scripts or other recruitment scripts.
- Consent forms, including parental permission and child assent, or cover letters if written consent is not required. (Most IRBs have a sample consent form, which indicates necessary and suggested wording.)
- Letters of agreement or an IRB approval from cooperating organizations, perhaps on their letterhead with original signatures.

- Instruments (evidence of permission for use may be required if the instrument is copyrighted).
- Debriefing materials.
- Principal investigator's resume.
- A copy of the full research proposal or at least the method section.

The protocol and attachments are submitted to the IRB for their consideration and, one hopes, approval. The protocol should remind the researcher of the elements that are essential for scientifically and ethically sound research.

Institutions are legally responsible for research conducted by faculty and students, and so are the researchers and advisors. Thus, the protocol must reflect what is actually done in the research. If the researcher decides to change the procedure or the instruments, approval must be obtained from the IRB.

In addition to a complete discussion of the risks and benefits including inducements and an analysis of the risk/benefit ratio, there should be a complete discussion of the characteristics of the participants and the consent and confidentiality procedures. In terms of the participants, information about their ethnic background, gender, age, and state of health should be given, and, if vulnerable populations are included, their use should be justified. If cooperating organizations or institutions are used to gain participants, written approval must be obtained. It is desirable to provide a rational for the number of participants to be included using a *power analysis* as discussed in Chapters 9 and 16.

The consent procedures and methods used to assure confidentiality need to be spelled out in the protocol. The procedures should indicate how, where, and by whom informed consent will be acquired and how any debriefing will be conducted. The actual consent form should be attached to the protocol. If consent is implied by returning a mailed questionnaire or verbally, as in the case of a telephone interview, the cover letter or script detailing the procedures must be provided.

Potential Problems With Research Protocols

IRBs frequently encounter certain types of problems. Sometimes students or inexperienced researchers will not have adequate help in preparing the protocol. If that is your case, you should consult other experienced researchers or the IRB administrator. Watch for training classes that the institution might provide, and check other informational resources such as the IRB Web page.

Some student IRB protocols devote a lot of space to the importance of the research but fail to describe the methods and procedures in enough detail or specificity. For example, the consent procedure needs to be spelled out clearly, as does the research design and the procedures for recruiting and retaining participants.

Some researchers exaggerate potential benefits or downplay risks that the IRB may identify. In addition to physical risks, there can be risks to employment, advancement, reputation, and financial standing. Emotional distress also can be a significant risk. Researchers need to be clear that they are sensitive to the issues of coercion and *dual-role relationships*—that is, when a researcher is also the teacher or supervisor of the potential participants. The researcher, whose intention is to help persons with some kind of problem or handicap using an intervention, also needs to be sensitive to the possibility that identifying them as participants in the intervention may in fact stigmatize them. Every effort should be made to be sensitive to this sort of situation and to ensure the privacy of such individuals.

Ethical Issues With Regard to the Data Collection

As with the other steps in the research process, a number of ethical issues arise during the data collection and analysis phases of research. Some of them involve the treatment of participants and have already been discussed (e.g., sensitivity to participants' privacy concerns, confidentiality, or debriefing). Another set of ethical issues has to do with the integrity of the data collection, recording, and analysis. We turn now to these issues.

Integrity of the Data

It should be obvious, that researchers should not fabricate data or falsify results in their reports. And if researchers discover significant errors in their published data, they should correct them. Unfortunately, such scientific misconduct has occurred too often. Altman and Hernon (1997) described more than 60 publicly discussed cases of publications that involved fabricated, falsified, or plagiarized data. Altman and Hernon stated that they discuss only a fraction of the cases in which scientific misconduct was determined. They note that although medicine has the most cases, the problem is spread across many disciplines, including psychology, history, and chemistry. Whole issues of journals in sociology, business, and medicine have been devoted to discussions about misconduct and professional ethics.

Fabrication (i.e., making up the data or results) and **falsification** (i.e., changing data or results) are clearly unacceptable but, hopefully, are relatively rare. However, there are other behaviors that may be due to carelessness, bias, or an unwise decision that cause problems for the integrity of the data and for the inferences made from these data. Some error in observing, recording, and entering data may be an inevitable byproduct of using humans (versus electronic recording devices) in these roles, but good research will minimize such errors. Careful training of observers and other assistants can help. Checking data to be sure they were recorded and entered correctly can help as, in some cases, can the use of computers to reduce possible errors in transcribing data. Thus, carefulness is as important as honesty if the collected data are to be meaningful.

Qualitative researchers have pointed out that inquiry is always value laden and is never completely objective. Thus, the perspectives that one brings to the research are bound to influence not only the selection of the problems, variables, and methods used but also the coding and categorization of the data and how they are interpreted. This is true, but much can and should be done to minimize the effects of the researcher's biases. First, one can acknowledge biases and try to figure out how they might influence the data collection, coding, and analysis. Checking the reliability of coding is desirable but not enough, especially if the other coders have similar biases or were trained by the same researcher. Again, care to minimize the effects of avoidable bias may be as important as honesty for good research.

There are many choices to be made in conducting research. Financial and other constraints result in necessary choices that weaken a study in some way to strengthen it in other ways. For example, there is almost always a trade-off between internal and external validity; that is, good control tends to make things artificial. However, researchers also make unnecessary bad choices, some of which are ethically questionable. One example is the investigator who eliminates participants from the study for unexplained reasons. As we already discussed, participants must be given permission to withdraw at any time, so that it is a valid reason for the data to be excluded. But if participants do not perform in the expected manner, that is not a valid reason. Another example would be changing the length of the study or overruling supposedly independent raters. Any such changes need to be justified and should not be because the data turned out in the "wrong" way.

Summary

This chapter discusses ethical problems and principles. First, we gave a brief historical overview of ethical problems in the treatment of human subjects. Next, we reviewed the broad policies related to voluntary informed consent, privacy, and assessments of risks and benefits. Then, we moved step by step through the research process, discussing ethical issues dealing with sampling, planning the design, selecting instruments, planning the procedure, obtaining approval from the IRB, and collecting data.

Key Concepts

Assent by children

Beneficence

Consent

Data fabrication and falsification

Deception

Debriefing

Informed consent

Institutional review board (IRB)

Justice

Masked (blind) review

Privacy

Research protocol

Respect for persons

Response rate

Key Distinctions

Confidential versus anonymous

Pilot testing versus pilot studies

Risks versus benefits

Application Problems

1. What is the purpose of the IRB? When is a researcher required to obtain IRB approval?

2. List each of the three ethical principles/guidelines for the protection of human subjects. Give an *original* example for each.

3. What are the three aspects of informed consent? Give an original example for each.

4. What is the difference between anonymity and confidentiality?

5. Explain the issue of assessing risk versus benefit in research.

6. Name three ethical issues in sample selection, and give an original example for each.

7. What is deception in research? Is deception ever acceptable? Explain.

8. Name two ethical issues with data integrity. Give an original example for each.

9. A researcher interested in juvenile probation services has developed a tool to measure the degree to which a juvenile is at risk for repeated offenses (scale indicates low risk, medium risk, or high risk). The researcher reviewed initial case records of all new probationers for a 6-month period and applied the scale to each case. He then followed the probationers for an additional 6 months to determine whether the probationers were arrested for additional offenses.

    a. What ethical issues does this researcher face?

    b. How would the researcher address each ethical issue from (a)?

10. A researcher has been consulted by a continuing education program offering English language classes to immigrants who speak little or no English. The program has two different curricula and wishes to know which is more effective.

    a. What ethical issues does this researcher face?

    b. How would the researcher address each ethical issue from (a)?

11. Read the following scenario, and then answer the questions that follow:

    Dr. Jones, of the College of Education at Major University, is interested in the emotional health of children. She wants to study the emotional well-being of children raised in a traditional "religious school" setting. She hypothesizes that these children will be emotionally "stronger" than the general national norms. Because Dr. Jones serves on the Board of Directors for the school, the principal, Sister Mary, readily agrees. Dr. Jones may meet with the 5th graders and can interview all 20 students about their family attitudes toward alcohol, tobacco, drug use, and their resistance to violence. She also knows of a standardized instrument of emotional health. Sister Mary determines that the assessment of the children's emotional health will be useful information for the school to have in the students' records, so students will be told the interviews are part of the class. Because it is part of the class assignment, there is no need to especially inform the parents. Besides, notices sent to parents never come back when they are sent out in lunch boxes anyway! The 20 students are about evenly split between boys and girls, three Cuban students attend, and the rest are Caucasian. Along with the standardized psychological instrument, she should be able to "snapshot" the children reasonably well and differentiate well-being by gender, ethnicity, and family attitudes.

    a. Who are "the players" (both apparent and not apparent), and what might be their issues?

b. Which Belmont Report principles (respect for person, beneficence, or justice) pertain, and how?

c. What questions might an institutional review board have about this project?

d. Should the project be approved as currently proposed?

e. How could the project be redesigned to address some of the IRB's concerns?

In the scenarios in Problems 12 and 13, what ethical issues were violated?

12. A researcher is interested in chocolate consumption and reaction time. She randomly assigns 16 students to either an experimental or control group. The students are told that as part of their final grade in the course, they must be a subject in the study. After giving eight of the students five candy bars each to eat (while she sits and watches to ensure they eat all of them), she gives all 16 students a test for reaction time. When the students have completed the test, she allows them to leave.

13. At a large university a researcher wants to find out if graduate students have better decision-making skills than undergraduates. The researcher tells 30 graduates and 30 undergraduates that he will give them $50 each if they complete a difficult decision task. After the results were tabulated, the researcher posts the students' social security numbers and decision-making score on her door so the students can know how they did on the task.

14. Scientists are interested in the causes of violent behavior. Why do some individuals who appear to have experienced a "normal" childhood exhibit very violent behavior, with little or no remorse? The researchers hypothesized innate brain physiology differences. The warden agreed that all male prisoners from a high security prison in a southern state who had committed a violent crime and who had no evidence of childhood abuse or neglect would be included in the study. A demographically similar (e.g., age, ethnicity, family background) sample of males was selected from that state's general population to serve as a comparison group; 40% of them agreed to participate (and were compensated $200). There were 28 individuals in the prisoner group and 30 in the noncriminal community group. Brain scans were done on all participants, and then comparisons were made between the two groups.

a. Discuss the ethical issues involved in this study.

b. Discuss population validity issues from the information provided.

c. Discuss issues of ecological validity.

15

Practical Issues in Data Collection and Coding

In this chapter, we provide a brief review of the initial steps in a research project before focusing on (1) getting data ready (coding and checking) to enter into a spreadsheet; (2) defining and labeling variables; (3) entering the data appropriately; (4) checking to be sure that data entry was done correctly without errors; and (5) computing composite rating scales. Much of this chapter is adapted from Morgan, Leech, Gloeckner, and Barrett (2007).

Initial Steps in the Research Process

Planning the Study, Pilot Testing, and Data Collection

Planning the Study

Research starts with identification of a problem and questions or hypotheses. It is also necessary to plan the research approach and design before selecting the data collection instrument (Chapter 13) and beginning data collection.

Selecting or Developing the Instruments

If there are appropriate instruments available and they have been used with a population similar to the intended population, it is usually desirable to use these instruments. However, sometimes it is necessary to modify an existing instrument or develop a new one. For this chapter, we provide an example of a short questionnaire to be given to students at the end of a course. Therefore, to simplify our introduction to data coding, we focus on this instrument. However, in studies that use the randomized experimental, quasi-experimental, or comparative approaches, coding into treatment and control groups also would be undertaken. Questionnaires or surveys are only one way to collect quantitative data. Structured interviews, observations, tests, standardized inventories, or some other type of data collection method also could be used. If established instruments are used, the literature will provide some evidence for reliability and validity.

Refining Instruments and Procedures

It is always desirable to try out (pilot test) an instrument and its accompanying directions with, at the very least, a few colleagues or friends. This is especially the case if the instruments, procedures, or population are ones that haven't been used before in this combination.

Pilot participants should be asked about the clarity of the items and whether they think any items should be added or deleted. Feedback can be used to make modifications in the instrument before beginning a formal pilot study. **Content validity** also can be checked by asking experts to judge whether your items cover all aspects of the domain you intend to measure and whether they are in appropriate proportions relative to that domain.

When possible, a formal **pilot study** should be conducted with a sample similar to the one planned for use later. This is especially important if the instrument is going to be used with a population different from the one for which it was developed or on which it was previously used. The data collected from a formal pilot study can provide evidence about the reliability and validity of the data in this context with the planned population. Again, if the instrument or procedures are changed after the pilot study, these data should *not* be combined with the data from the actual study.

Data Collection

The next step in the research process is to collect the data. There are several ways to collect questionnaire or survey data (e.g., telephone, mail, or email). The Salant and Dillman (1994) guidebook *How to Conduct Your Own Survey* provides considerable detail on the various methods for collecting survey data and potential issues to consider.

Raw data should be checked after it is collected, even *before* it is entered into the computer. It is important to be sure that the participants marked their score sheets or questionnaires appropriately; also, it is necessary to see if there are double answers to a question (when only one is expected) or answers that are marked between two rating points. If this happens, a consistent rule needs to be applied (e.g., "use the average"). Thus, data need to be "cleaned up," making sure they are clear, consistent, and readable, before entering them into a data file or spreadsheet. This does *not* mean that it is okay to change or alter the data.

Let's assume that the brief questionnaire shown in Figure 15.1 was given to a class of students who completed them and turned them in at the end of the class. If the questionnaire is intended to be *anonymous*, it would not include an ID number, but after collecting the questionnaires the researcher would number the forms so that the data entry could be checked later. Then the researcher is ready to begin the coding process, described in the next section.

Var. No.	Please circle or supply your answer	ID_____	Variable Name
		SD enter # SA	
1	1. I would recommend this course to other students	1 2 3 4 5	Recommen
2	2. I worked very hard in this course	1 2 3 4 5	Workhard
3	3. My college is: Arts and sciences = 1 Business = 2 Engineering = 3		College
4	4. My gender is	M = 0 F = 1	Gender
5	5. My GPA is	enter # with 2 decimals	GPA
	6. For this class, I did: (check all that apply)	blank checked	
6	The reading	= 0 = [1]	Reading
7	The homework	= 0 = [1]	Homework
8	Extra credit	= 0 = [1]	Extracrd

FIGURE 15.1
A blank survey showing how to code the data.

Data Coding, Entry, and Checking

Guidelines for Data Coding

Coding is the process of assigning numbers to the levels or values of each variable. Figure 15.1 is our example questionnaire. There are eight measures in the questionnaire. The questionnaire provides an example of the descriptive approach in that it is being used to describe how students feel about a particular course at the end of the course. In this case, the measures would provide information to the instructor about how students felt about, for example, the course, their major, and grade point average (GPA). However, this questionnaire also could be considered as an example of the comparative approach, with an attribute independent variable of gender (item 4) or college (item 3) and a dependent variable of item 1. Or, the questionnaire could be an example of the associative approach with an attribute independent variable of GPA (item 5) or an attribute independent variable of how hard the student worked (item 2) and a dependent variable of item 1.

Before starting the coding process, we present some guidelines or rules to keep in mind. These suggestions are adapted from rules proposed in Newton and Rudestam's (1999) useful book titled *Your Statistical Consultant*.

Each Level of a Variable Must Be Mutually Exclusive

That is, only one value or number can be recorded for each variable. Some questionnaire items, like our item 6 in Figure 15.1, allow for participants to *check more than one response*. In that case, the item should be divided into a separate variable for each possible response *choice* (checked or not), with one value of each variable corresponding to yes (i.e., checked = 1) and the other to no (not checked = 0). For example, as shown in Figure 15.1, item 6 becomes variables 6, 7, and 8.

Usually, items should be phrased so that persons would logically choose only one of the provided options, and all possible options should be provided. A category labeled "other" may be provided in cases where all possible options cannot be listed, but these "other" responses are usually quite diverse and, thus, are usually not very useful for statistical purposes.

Each Variable Should Be Coded to Obtain Maximum Information

Categories or values should not be collapsed when coding is set up. If needed, the computer could be used to do it later. In general, it is desirable to code and enter data in as detailed a form as available. Thus, actual test scores, ages, GPAs, and so forth should be entered if they are known. It is good practice to ask participants to provide information that is quite specific. However, care should be taken not to ask questions that are so specific that the respondent may not know the answer or may not feel comfortable providing it. For example, more information will be obtained by asking participants to state their GPA to two decimals (Figure 15.1) than if they were asked to select from a few broad categories (e.g., less than 2.0, 2.0–2.49, or 2.50–2.99). However, if students don't know their GPA or don't want to reveal it precisely, they may leave the question blank or write in a difficult-to-interpret answer.

For Each Participant, There Must Be a Code or Value for Each Variable

These codes should be numbers, except for variables for which the data are missing. We recommend using blanks when data are missing. SPSS, for example, is designed to handle blanks as missing values. However, sometimes there is more than one type of missing data, such as items left blank and those that had an inappropriate or unusable answer. In this case numeric codes such as 98 and 99 could be assigned to them, but the computer program must be told that these codes are for missing values or they will be treated as actual data.

Coding Rules Must Be Applied Consistently for All Participants

This means, for example, that if a decision is made to treat a certain type of response as missing for one person, the decision must be the same for all other participants.

High Numbers (Values or Codes) Should Be Used for the "Agree," "Good," or "Positive" End of a Variable That Is Ordered

Sometimes questionnaires use 1 for "strongly agree" and 5 for "strongly disagree." This is not wrong as long as it is clear and consistent. However, there will be less confusion when interpreting results if high values have positive meaning. Some questionnaires have both positively and negatively worded items. In Chapter 13, we demonstrated how to reverse the coding for some of the items so that all the items to be combined had a high score for the positive end of the scale.

All Data Should Be Numeric

Even though it is possible to use letters or words as data, for data analysis it is generally not desirable to do so. For example, we could code gender as M for male and F for female, but to do most statistics, the letters or words would have to be converted to numbers. It is usually easier to do this conversion before entering the data into the computer. Figure 15.1 shows that we decided to code females as 1 and males as 0. This is called **dummy coding**. In essence, the 0 means "not female." We could have, of course, coded males as 1 and females as 0, or we could have coded one gender as 1 and the other as 2. However, it is crucial to be consistent in coding (e.g., for this study, all males are coded 0 and females 1) and to have a record and at least one duplicate for how the coding was done. Such a record is called a **codebook** or dictionary.

Each Variable for Each Case or Participant Must Occupy the Same Column in the Spreadsheet or Data Editor

For almost all statistical analyses, it is important that data from each participant occupies only one line (row), and each column must contain data on the same variable for all the participants. The data editor should have the variable names that are chosen at the top of each column. If a variable is measured more than once (e.g., pretest and posttest), it will be entered in two columns with somewhat different names like *mathpre* and *mathpost*.

Some decisions will need to be made about how to code the data, especially data that are not already in numerical form. When the responses provided by participants are numbers, the variable is said to be "self-coding." The number that was written, circled, or checked can just be entered. On the other hand, variables such as *gender* or *college* in Figure 15.1 have no intrinsic value associated with them. Figure 15.1 shows the decisions we made about how to number the variables, to code the values, and to name the eight variables. Each of the questionnaires needs to be numbered to later check the entered data against the questionnaires.

Check the Completed Questionnaires for Problems

For each type of incomplete, blank, unclear, or double answer, a rule needs to be made for what to do. As much as possible, these rules should be made before data collection, but there may well be some unanticipated issues. It is important that the rules be applied consistently for all similar problems so as not to bias the results.

In this section, we identify several types of possible participant responses on questionnaires that need to be clarified. Copies of the questionnaires for six students that posed such problems are shown in Figure 15.2. We discuss each of these issues and how we might decide to handle them. Of course, some reasonable choices could have been different from ours. We have written our decisions in numbered callout boxes in Figure 15.2, and discuss them next.

1. For Participant 7, the *GPA* appears to be written as 250. It seems reasonable to assume that this student meant to include a decimal after the 2, so we could enter 2.50. We could instead have said that this was an invalid response and coded it as missing. However, missing data create problems in later data analyses, especially for complex statistics. Thus, we want to use as much of the data provided as is reasonable. The important thing here is that all other similar problems *must* be treated the same way.

2. For Participant 8, two colleges were checked. We could have developed a new legitimate response value (4 = other). Because this fictitious university requires that students be identified with one and only one of its three colleges, we have developed two missing value codes. Thus, for this variable, we used 98, for multiple checked colleges or other written-in responses that did not fit clearly into one of the colleges (e.g., history and business). We treated such responses as missing because they seemed to be invalid or because we would not have had enough of any given response to form a reasonable size group for analysis. We used 99 as the code for cases where nothing was checked or written on the form. Having two codes enables us to distinguish between these two types of missing data. Other researchers (e.g., Newton & Rudestam, 1999) recommended using 8 and 9 in this case, but we think that it is best to use a code that is very different from the "valid" codes so that they stand out visually in the spreadsheet and will lead to noticeable differences in the descriptive statistics if they are not coded as missing values.

3. Also, Subject 8 wrote 2.2 for his *GPA*. It seems reasonable to enter 2.20 as the *GPA*.

4. We decided to enter 3.00 for Participant 9's *GPA*. Of course, the actual *GPA* could be higher or, more likely, lower, but 3.00 seems to be the best choice given the information, "about 3 pt," provided by the student.

5. Participant 10 answered only the first two questions, so there were lots of missing data. It appears that he or she decided not to complete the questionnaire. We made a rule that if three out of the first five items were blank or invalid, we would throw out that whole questionnaire as invalid. In a research report, it should be stated how many questionnaires were thrown out and for what reasons. Usually no data

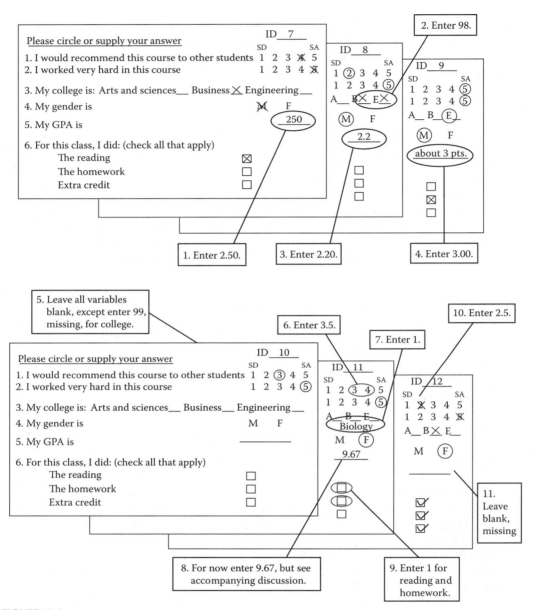

FIGURE 15.2

Completed survey with callout boxes showing how we handled problem responses.

would be entered from that questionnaire. To demonstrate how to code someone's *college* if it were left blank, we did not delete this participant at this time.

6. For Participant 11, there are several problems. First, she circled both 3 and 4 for the first item; a reasonable decision is to enter the average or midpoint, 3.50.

7. Participant 11 has written in "biology" for *college*. Although there is no biology college at this university, it seems reasonable to enter 1 = arts and sciences in this case and in other cases (e.g., history = 1, marketing = 2, or civil = 3) where the actual college is clear. See the discussion of issue 2 for how to handle unclear examples.

8. Participant 11 appears to have entered 9.67 for the *GPA*, which is an invalid response because this university has a four-point grading system (4.00 is the maximum possible *GPA*). To show you one method to check for errors that have been entered into the computer, we entered 9.67. Of course, it would have been better to have identified problems like this and have entered a blank for missing/invalid data.

9. It seems reasonable to assume that a circled box should be coded as if it was checked so we entered 1's for reading and for homework for Participant 11. Also, we entered 0 for extra credit (not checked) as we would do for all the boxes left unchecked by other participants (except Subject 10). Even though this person circled the boxes rather than putting X's or checks in them, her intent is clear.

10. We decided to enter 2.5 for Participant 12's X between 2 and 3, as we had decided for subject 11.

11. Participant 12 also left *GPA* blank, so we left it blank, the usual missing value.

After rules have been created and decisions have been made on how to handle each problem, these rules and decisions must be clarified to the persons who will enter the data. A common procedure would be to write the decisions on each actual questionnaire, probably in a different color.

Defining and Labeling the Variables

The next step is to name and label the variables. It is common to give the variables short **variable names,** as shown in Figure 15.1, for example, *recommen* for item 1, "I would recommend this course to other students." For item 2, we named it *workhard*. In computer programs, such as SPSS, one also can give each variable a longer **variable label** such as the one in quotes for item 1. We named the third variable *college*. It is especially important to label the **levels** or **values** of nominal variables such as *college* so that there isn't confusion later. Note that in Figure 15.1 we gave the value label of *1* to students in the *arts and sciences college*; we used 2 for business; and 3 for engineering. Remember that we decided to use *98* for other or *multiple answers* and *99* for when the student left it blank. *It is essential*, if numbers are used for missing values, that the computer is instructed that such numbers (e.g., 98 or 99) should be considered missing, not actually 98 or 99. It should be realized that the researchers have made decisions that another researcher could have done differently. For example, one could have used 1 instead of 3 for the engineering college so it is important to clearly and consistently label the values.

The next step is to label gender and its levels (1 = female, 0 = male, as shown in Figure 15.1). Question 6 was divided into the three variables related to the parts of the class that a student completed. In Figure 15.1 the **Names** of these last three variables were *reading, homework*, and *extracrd*. The **variable labels** could be *I did the reading, I did the homework*, or *I did extra credit*. The **value labels** were 0 = not checked/blank and 1 = checked.

Displaying the Dictionary or Codebook

After the variables have been defined and labeled, a codebook or dictionary of the variables should be printed. The **codebook** is a complete printed record of the names and labels for each variable and of the values and value labels for the levels of at least the nominal and dichotomous variables.

	Recommen	Workhard	College	Gender	GPA	Reading	Homework	Extracrd
1	3	5	1	0	3.12	0	0	1
2	4	5	2	0	2.91	1	1	0
3	4	5	1	1	3.33	0	1	1
4	5	5	1	1	3.60	1	1	1
5	4	5	2	1	2.52	0	0	1
6	5	5	3	1	2.98	1	0	0
7	4	5	2	0	2.50	1	0	0
8	2	5	98	0	2.20	0	0	0
9	5	5	3	0	3.00	0	1	0
10			99					
11	3.5	5	1	1	9.67	1	1	0
12	2.5	5	2	1		1	1	1

FIGURE 15.3
A sample data entry spreadsheet.

Entering and Checking the Data for Errors

After defining and labeling the variables, the next task is to enter the coded and cleaned-up data into a computer spreadsheet from the questionnaires. Most computer spreadsheets are prenumbered down the left-hand column (Figure 15.3). These numbers correspond to the identification number the researcher put on each questionnaire. The data for each participant's questionnaire go on one and only *one line across* the page with each column representing a variable from the questionnaire. Next, the data should be typed in the computer spreadsheet. Figure 15.3 shows the data for 12 student participants, including IDs 7–12, which had the problems shown in Figure 15.2 and discussed previously.

Before any analysis is performed, the data on the questionnaires need to be compared with the data entered into the computer. If there is a large amount of data, a sample of the participants can be checked, but it is preferable to check all of the data to be sure that they were entered correctly. If errors are found in the checked sample, all the entries should be checked and errors corrected. In the next section, we show one way to double check for certain kinds of serious data entry errors.

Descriptives and Data Checking

To get a better "feel" for the data and to check for some types of errors, we recommend computing basic descriptive statistics. Frequency distributions, especially for nominal, dichotomous, and ordinal data, provide a useful way to get a feel for the data and spot certain errors. Computing the minimum and maximum values for all participants on all variables with a computer program will provide a compact output to make an initial examination of the data. Because the mean (average) provides meaningful information for all types of

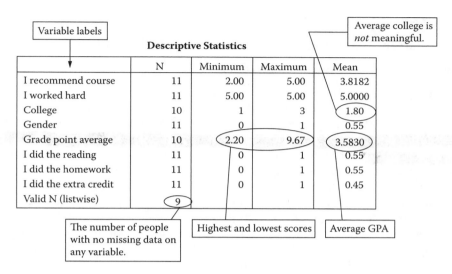

Descriptive Statistics

Variable labels

Average college is *not* meaningful.

	N	Minimum	Maximum	Mean
I recommend course	11	2.00	5.00	3.8182
I worked hard	11	5.00	5.00	5.0000
College	10	1	3	1.80
Gender	11	0	1	0.55
Grade point average	10	2.20	9.67	3.5830
I did the reading	11	0	1	0.55
I did the homework	11	0	1	0.55
I did the extra credit	11	0	1	0.45
Valid N (listwise)	9			

The number of people with no missing data on any variable.

Highest and lowest scores

Average GPA

FIGURE 15.4
SPSS output using descriptive statistics to check data entry.

variables except nominal ones with three or more categories, we also requested the mean in Figure 15.4. (It shows these descriptive statistics computed with the SPSS program.)

Next, for each variable, we compare the minimum and maximum scores shown in the figure with the highest and lowest *appropriate* values in the codebook. If any entered data are either higher (e.g., 9.67 for GPA) or lower than those specified in the codebook, those errors should be found in the data set and corrected before doing any more statistics.

In Figure 15.4, we indicate the key things we can learn from this output by circling them and adding some comments. Of course, these circles and callout information boxes would not show up on the actual computer printout.

This output shows, for each of the eight variables, the number (*N*) of participants with no missing data on that variable. The output also shows the *Minimum* and *Maximum* score that any participants had on that variable. For example, no one circled a 1, but one or more persons circled a 2 for the *I recommend course* variable, and at least one person circled 5. Notice that for *I worked hard*, 5 is both the minimum and maximum so all students rated themselves working hard, a 5. This item is, therefore, really a constant and not a variable; it will *not* be useful in statistical analyses. Figure 15.4 also provides the **Mean** or average score for each variable. Notice the mean for *I worked hard* is 5 because everyone circled 5. The mean of 1.80 for *college*, a nominal (unordered) variable, is nonsense, so it can be ignored.

However, the means of the dichotomous (two level) variables can be interpreted meaningfully. For *gender, I did the reading,* and *I did the homework,* the means were all .55 indicating that in each case 55% chose the answers that corresponded to 1 rather than 0 (i.e., female for gender and "yes" for doing the reading and homework). However, 45% said they did the extra credit because the mean was .45.

The mean *grade point average* was 3.58, which is an error because the output shows a maximum *GPA* of 9.67, which is not possible at this university. Thus, the 9.67 for participant 11 is an invalid response. The questionnaires should be checked again to be sure there wasn't a data entry error. If, as in this case, the form says 9.67, it should be changed to blank, the missing value code.

Data Reduction: Applying Measurement Reliability and Validity

Reasons to Reduce the Number of Variables

This section provides examples of two complex descriptive statistics that are commonly found in journal articles to help researchers reduce a large number of related questions or items to meaningful composite variables, also called aggregated or summated scales. The most important reason for reducing the number of measures in a survey or questionnaire is data analysis. If the measure, such as a questionnaire, has 15 items, comparisons between the treatment and control group would require 15 statistical tests. Although the computer could easily perform 15 comparisons, a problem results because the 15 items are most likely *not independent* from each other; that is, many of the items are measuring similar concepts. Performing this many statistical tests inflates the significance level such that comparisons between groups on many items might yield statistically significant results when, in fact, they are not statistically significant. Therefore, when the researcher has a dependent variable such as a test, survey, or questionnaire, with numerous items, it is important to reduce the number of items so that they can be analyzed statistically. Two methods to reduce these items are to (1) add the items of a scale to produce a composite rating scale; and (2) reduce the items of a scale to a few variables through exploratory factor analysis. The statistics discussed here that are used to help accomplish these two alternatives are Cronbach's alpha and exploratory factor analysis (EFA). They are often discussed in the method section of an article when researchers describe the reliability and validity of their measures or the development of composite scores.

Here we provide examples of how a researcher might meaningfully condense the number of variables and provide evidence for reliability and validity of the new measures. First, we discuss the use and interpretation of one common measure of reliability: Cronbach's alpha. Then, we discuss exploratory factor analysis, which is used to prepare a large data set for more efficient inferential analyses of the research questions in a study. The primary examples cited in this chapter are based on a data set, which is described, analyzed, and interpreted in a textbook, *SPSS for Intermediate Statistics,* by Leech, Barrett, and Morgan (2008), some of which is reprinted here.

Assessing Internal Consistency Reliability With Cronbach's Alpha

Several types of statistics, especially correlations, are used to assess support for reliability, but in this chapter we discuss only Cronbach's coefficient alpha, which is probably the most commonly reported measure of reliability. Alpha is a measure of the **internal consistency reliability** of a composite or summated scale. It is typically used when the researcher has several Likert-type items (ratings from *strongly disagree* to *strongly agree*) that are summed or averaged to make a composite score or summated scale. Alpha is based on the average correlation of each item in the scale with every other item. In the behavioral science literature, alpha is widely used because it provides a measure of reliability that can be obtained from a single testing session or one administration of a questionnaire.

Leech et al. (2008) computed three alphas to provide evidence for the internal consistency reliability of each of three mathematics attitude scales (motivation, competence, and pleasure.) The motivation scale score was composed of six items that were rated on four-point Likert scales, from very atypical (1) to very typical (4). Did these items go together (intercorrelate) well enough to add them together for use as a composite variable labeled

TABLE 15.1

Interitem Correlation Matrix for the Motivation Scale Items

	item 1 motivation	item 4 reversed	item 7 motivation	item 8 reversed	item 12 motivation
1. Practice math until do well	1.00	—	—	—	—
4. (Don't) give up easily	.25	1.00	—	—	—
7. Prefer to figure out problems without help	.46	.55	1.00	—	—
8. (Do) keep at it long if problem challenging	.30	.58	.59	1.00	—
12. Try to complete math even if it takes long	.18	.38	.34	.40	1.00
13. Explore all possible solutions	.17	.32	.36	.31	.60

TABLE 15.2

Item–Total Statistics for the Motivation Scale Items

	Corrected item-total correlation	Cronbach's alpha if item deleted
Practice math until do well	.38	.80
(Don't) give up easily	.60	.75
Prefer to figure out problems without help	.68	.72
(Do) keep at it long if problem challenging	.63	.74
Try to complete math even if it takes long	.52	.77
Explore all possible solutions	.48	.77

motivation? That is, what is the internal consistency reliability of the math attitude scale labeled *motivation*?

Table 15.1 lists the items included in this motivation scale, their labels, and a matrix showing the interitem correlations of every item in the scale with every other item. Note that items 4 and 8, which were negatively worded in the questionnaire, were reversed (e.g., 4 = 1, 3 = 2) before alpha was computed. This is necessary for alpha to be computed correctly. Note also that some of the correlations are high; for example, items 12 and 13 were correlated .60. Other pairs of items had a weak positive association; for example, items 1 and 13 were correlated only .17.

Table 15.2, labeled "Item–Total Statistics," provides two pieces of information for each item in the scale—the *corrected item–total correlation* and *Cronbach's alpha*—if that item was deleted. The former is the correlation of each specific item with the sum/total of the *other* items in the scale. If this correlation is moderately high (say, .40 or above) the item is probably at least moderately correlated with most of the other items in the proposed scale and will make a good component of this summated rating scale. Items with lower item–total correlations (such as item 1) do not fit into this scale as well, psychometrically. If the item–total correlation is negative or too low (less than .30), the researchers should examine the item for wording problems and conceptual fit, and they may want to modify or delete such items. The right-hand column describes what the alpha would be if an item were deleted. This can be compared with the alpha for the scale with all six items included, which was .79. Deleting a poor item usually will make the alpha increase. However, such a deletion probably will make only a small difference in the alpha, unless the item–total correlation is near to zero (or negative). Deleting an item has more effect if the scale has only a few items because alpha is based on the number of items as well as their average intercorrelations.

As with other reliability coefficients, alpha should be above .70; however, it is common to see journal articles where one or more scales have somewhat lower alphas (e.g., in the .60–.69 range), especially if there are only a small number of items in such a scale. A very high alpha (e.g., greater than .90) probably means that the items are somewhat repetitious or that there may be more items in the scale than are really necessary for a reliable measure of the concept for research purposes.

A common error is to compute a *single* overall alpha when there are several scales such as motivation, competence, and pleasure. The overall alpha is appropriate only if the researcher intends to compute an overall summated scale, such as overall math attitude, and such an overall scale is meaningful conceptually. Frequently, and in this example, there was no plan for an overall score. In our example, three separate alphas (one each for motivation, competence, and pleasure) but not an overall alpha were computed and reported. Leech et al. (2008) wrote, for the method section, the following sentences about the reliability of the motivation scale and the other two scales:

> To assess whether the six items that were summed to create the motivation score formed a reliable scale, Cronbach's alpha was computed. The alpha for the six items was .79, which indicates that the items form a scale that has reasonable internal consistency reliability. Similarly, the alpha for the competence scale (.80) indicated good internal consistency, but the four item alpha (.69) for the pleasure scale indicated minimally adequate reliability. (p. 53)

Exploratory Factor Analysis

Exploratory factor analysis is a method that is used to help investigators represent a large number of relationships among *normally distributed* variables in a simpler (more parsimonious) way. This approach has the computer specify groups or sets of items that "hang together." Factor analysis results suggest that all the items studied can be grouped into one or several sets of items that are correlated for the participants. A related approach is *confirmatory factor analysis,* in which one tests very specific models of how variables are related to underlying constructs (conceptual or latent variables). It is not discussed here but is, along with EFA, in Thompson (2004).

In **exploratory factor analysis**, one postulates that there is a smaller set of unobserved (latent) variables or constructs that underlie the variables that actually were observed or measured. There are a number of somewhat different ways of computing factors for factor analysis; one of these methods, *principal axis factor analysis,* was used to describe EFA for this chapter. SPSS and many research textbooks call all of these methods, including principal components analysis, "factor analysis," and the results are often quite similar.

Usually, the larger the sample size, especially in relation to the number of variables, the more reliable the resulting factors. Factor analysis seeks to explain the correlation matrix, which would not be a sensible thing to do if all the correlations hover around zero.

Using Exploratory Factor Analysis to Provide Evidence for Measurement Validity

In Leech et al. (2008), a principal axis factor analysis on the mathematics attitude variables was performed. Factor analysis was appropriate because the authors believed that there were three latent variables underlying the variables or items measured: *motivation, competence,* and *pleasure.* They wanted to see if the items that were written to index each of these constructs actually did "hang together." That is, they wished to determine empirically whether participants' responses to the motivation questions were more similar to each other than to their responses to the competence or pleasure items. In Chapter 12, we mentioned that one method to provide support for measurement validity was to look for evidence of *internal structure* consistent with one's theory.

Factor analysis programs generate a number of tables depending on which options are chosen. One such table, a *correlation matrix*, would show how each of the 14 items was associated with each of the other 13. Some of the correlations were high (e.g., +.60 or −.60), and some were low (i.e., near zero). High correlations indicate that two items are associated and will probably be grouped together by the factor analysis.

In this example four factors had *eigenvalues* (a measure of explained variance) greater than 1.0, which is a common criterion for a factor to be useful. When the eigenvalue is less than 1.0, this means that the factor explains less information than a single item would have explained. Most researchers would not consider the information gained from such a factor to be sufficient to justify keeping that factor. Thus, if the researchers had not specified otherwise, the computer would have looked for the best four-factor solution. Because the authors believed there were three constructs and specified that they wanted only three factors, three were "retained."

The authors used an **orthogonal rotation** called *varimax*. This means that the final three factors would be as uncorrelated as possible with each other. As a result, we can assume that the information explained by one factor is independent of the information in the other factors. Rotation makes it so that, as much as possible, different items are explained or predicted by *different* underlying factors, and each factor explains more than one item. This is a condition called *simple structure*. Although this is the *goal* of rotation, in reality, this often is not fully achieved. One usually examines the rotated matrix of factor loadings to see the extent to which simple structure is achieved.

Within each factor (to the extent possible), the items are sorted from the one with the highest absolute **factor weight** or **loading** for that factor to the one with the lowest loading on that first factor. Loadings resulting from an orthogonal rotation are correlation coefficients of each item with the factor, so they range from −1.0 through 0 to +1.0. A negative loading just means that the question needs to be interpreted for that factor in the opposite direction from the way it is written. For example, "I am a little slow catching on to new topics in math" has a negative loading on the competence factor, which indicates that the people scoring higher on this item see themselves as *lower* in competence. Usually, factor loadings lower than .30 or .40 are considered low, which is why the authors didn't print (suppressed) such loadings in Table 15.3. On the other hand, loadings of .40 or greater are typically considered acceptably high. This is just a guideline; however, setting the criterion higher than .50 would be unusual.

Every item has a weight or loading from every factor, but in a "clean" factor analysis almost all of the loadings beyond +.40 or −.40 in the rotated factor matrix would be in only one column or factor. Notice in Table 15.3 that two items (*prefer to figure out problems without help* and *feel happy after solving a hard problem*) have loadings above .40 or two factors. This is common but undesirable, in that one wants only one factor to predict each item.

Leech et al. (2008) wrote about this factor analysis:

> Principal axis factor analysis with varimax rotation was conducted to assess the underlying structure for the fourteen items of the Math Motivation Questionnaire. Three factors were requested, based on the fact that the items were designed to index three constructs: motivation, competence, and pleasure. After rotation, the first factor accounted for 21.5% of the variance, the second factor accounted for 16.6%, and the third factor accounted for 12.7%. The table (15.3) displays the items and factor loadings for the rotated factors, with loadings less than .40 omitted to improve clarity. (p. 65)

TABLE 15.3

Factor Loadings for the Rotated Factors

Item	Factor loading		
	1	2	3
Slow catching on to new topics	−.90		
Solve math problems quickly	.78		
Practice math until do well	.78		
Have difficulties doing math	−.57		
Try to complete math even if takes long		.72	
Explore all possible solutions		.67	
Do not keep at it long if problem challenging		−.62	
Give up easily instead of persisting		−.60	
Prefer to figure out problems without help	.41	.59	
Really enjoy working math problems			−.80
Smile only a little when solving math problem			.58
Feel happy after solving hard problem	.49		−.54
Do not get much pleasure out of math			.52
Eigenvalues	3.02	2.32	1.78
Percent of variance	21.55	16.62	12.74

Note: Loadings <.40 are omitted.

The first factor seems to index competence; it included the first four items in the first column. The first and fourth items indexed low competence and had negative loadings. The second factor, which seemed to index motivation, was composed of the five items with loadings in the second column of the table. "I prefer to figure out the problem without help" had its highest loading on the second factor but had a cross-loading over .40 on the competence factor. The third factor, which seemed to index low pleasure from doing math, comprised the four items with loadings in the third column. "I feel happy after solving a hard problem" had its highest loading from the pleasure factor but also had a strong loading from the competence factor. One of the 14 items did not load above .40 on any of the three factors so it was deleted.

In the next section, we discuss how a researcher might use the results of a factor analysis to aggregate (sum or average) the items that have high loadings for each factor and use these composite variables in further research. The implication is that each composite variable is an index of a separate underlying construct such as motivation, competence, or pleasure when studying mathematics.

Developing Summated or Aggregated Scales

It is common for a researcher to develop a smaller number of new variables from an initially larger number of items such as the 14 Likert-type ratings we designed to measure attitudes about mathematics motivation, competence, and pleasure. Figure 15.5 shows a schematic flow chart of a method that researchers can use to help decide which items to combine or summate and how to check the internal consistency reliability of the resulting summated scales. In our example, we could use this method to develop three summated scales. As illustrated earlier in this chapter, three Cronbach's alpha would be used to check the reliability of each of the three initially planned scales: competence, motivation, and

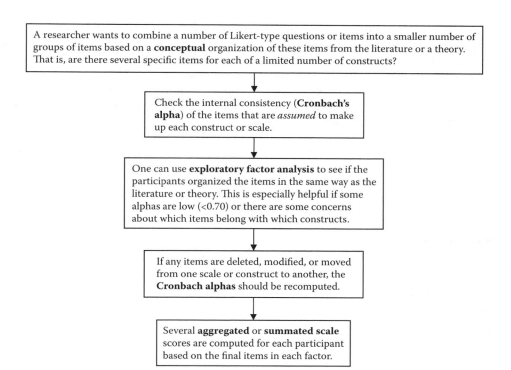

A researcher wants to combine a number of Likert-type questions or items into a smaller number of groups of items based on a **conceptual** organization of these items from the literature or a theory. That is, are there several specific items for each of a limited number of constructs?

Check the internal consistency (**Cronbach's alpha**) of the items that are *assumed* to make up each construct or scale.

One can use **exploratory factor analysis** to see if the participants organized the items in the same way as the literature or theory. This is especially helpful if some alphas are low (<0.70) or there are some concerns about which items belong with which constructs.

If any items are deleted, modified, or moved from one scale or construct to another, the **Cronbach alphas** should be recomputed.

Several **aggregated** or **summated scale** scores are computed for each participant based on the final items in each factor.

FIGURE 15.5

Schematic diagram of a strategy for making multiple-item summated or composite scales when there are a number of Likert-type items that the researcher thinks can be reduced to a smaller number of conceptually meaningful scales (variables).

pleasure. EFA could be used if one or more of the alphas were low or if a check was needed to determine whether the 14 items should be grouped in the way initially predicted. EFA could help reduce the 14 items to a smaller number of meaningful groups or sets of items. One would specify the number (3 in this case) of factors to be used when the researcher has a conceptual plan, as Leech et al. (2008) did for the three mathematics attitude scales. Then if any items were deleted or moved from one scale to another, the alphas should be recomputed for the revised grouping of items.

Finally, the items in each group or scale should be summated or averaged to form new composite variables. In our example, each participant's score on the four competence items would be summed to form a new composite competence variable for each person. Likewise, scores on the five motivation items would be summed, and the four low pleasure items would be summed. Now, each participant would have three new variables or measures that would be used in later inferential data analyses *instead of* their scores for the 14 original items.

Summary

In this chapter, we started with a brief review of the process of planning and pilot testing the procedure and instruments. Next, there was an extended discussion of seven guidelines or rules for coding the data to prepare it for entry into a computer database. This was followed by an example of a brief questionnaire, which produced a variety of difficult to code responses, and our suggestions about how to handle such problematic responses. Once the participants' responses are coded, the researcher sets up a computer database and enters the coded data using designated variable names and values. Before doing any data analyses to help answer the research questions or hypotheses, the data should be carefully checked to make sure it was entered accurately. The chapter concludes with extended examples of the use of Cronbach's alpha and factor analysis to make composite or summated scales. Alpha also is used to check the internal consistency reliability of a multiple item rating scale. Factor analysis is used to reduce a relatively large number of questions to a smaller number of scales, which can then be computed by summing or averaging several related items.

Key Concepts

Cronbach's alpha
Coding
Factor analysis
Pilot study

Key Distinctions

Measurement reliability versus measurement validity
Variable labels versus value labels

Application Problems

1. What steps or actions should be taken after you collect data and before you run the analyses aimed at answering your research questions or testing your research hypotheses?

2. Are there any other rules about data coding of questionnaires that you think should be added? Are there any of our "rules" that you think should be modified? Which ones? How and why?

3. Why would you print a codebook or dictionary?

4. What problems with completed questionnaires were identified? How would you decide to handle the problems and why?

5. If the university in the example allowed for double majors in different colleges (such that it would actually be possible for a student to be in two colleges), how would you handle cases in which two colleges are checked? Why?

6. (a) Why is it important to check your raw (questionnaire) data *before and after* entering them into a computer?; and (b) What are ways to check the data before entering them? After entering them?

7. Provide another example of how you might use Cronbach's alpha and factor analyses to reduce 20 items on a questionnaire to four new variables.

Section IV

Data Analysis and Interpretation

16

Making Inferences from Sample Data I:
The Null Hypothesis Significance Testing Approach

Rarely are we able to work with an entire *population* of individuals. Instead, we usually study a *sample* of individuals from the population. Hopefully, if our treatment is successful, we can *infer* that the results from our sample apply to the population of interest. While we refer here to implementation of a treatment and thus the use of either the randomized experimental or quasi-experimental approaches, inferential statistics also are appropriate for the comparative and associational approaches. Inferential statistics involve making inferences from *sample statistics*, such as the sample mean (*M*) and the sample standard deviation (*SD*) to *population parameters* such as the population mean (μ) and the population standard deviation (σ). When we refer to sample statistics, we use italicized Roman letters (our alphabet); when we refer to population parameters, we use Greek letters.

We start our discussion with an example and then offer two approaches to reporting the outcomes of statistical tests: the null hypothesis significance testing (NHST) approach (this chapter) and the evidence-based approach (Chapter 17). The NHST approach is discussed first, in considerable detail, because historically it has been the generally accepted method to guide inferences from data analysis and is still the dominant approach to reporting outcomes from statistical tests. However, there is considerable controversy about the role of NHST and whether its use should be continued in the social sciences and education, especially in its present form. We discuss these very important issues at the end of this chapter on the NHST approach.

An Example

Suppose we are interested in the relationship between exercise and quality of life in depressed adolescents. A reasonable *general hypothesis* is that depressed adolescents who exercise regularly will have higher quality-of-life scores than those who do not exercise regularly. Inferential statistics provides us with a way to make a judgment about the relationship between exercise and quality of life in depressed adolescents. We start by operationalizing our variables. The *independent variable*, exercise, has two levels: either use of a stationary bicycle 45 minutes per day (5 days per week for 6 weeks at a work load of 50% of maximum capacity) or no prescribed exercise. The *dependent variable*, a Quality of Life inventory (QL), is an indicator of quality of life and is measured as a score between 1 and 100. To add support for our hypothesis, we would expect that 36 participants who exercise will have a higher quality-of-life index than 36 who do not exercise regularly.

The Null Hypothesis (H_0) and Alternative Hypotheses (H_1)

The NHST approach begins by reformulating our general hypothesis into two statements or hypotheses, the null hypothesis (H_0) and the alternative or research hypothesis (H_1).

These hypotheses can be shown as follows:

$$H_0: \mu_I = \mu_C \qquad H_1: \mu_I > \mu_C$$

where

μ_I = Intervention group population mean

μ_C = Control or comparison group population mean

In our example, the *null hypothesis* states that the mean QL of the population of those who will receive the intervention will be equal to the mean QL of the population of those who will not receive the intervention. If the null hypothesis is true, the intervention of exercise has not been successful in providing a better quality of life. The *alternative hypothesis* states that the mean QL of the population of those who receive the intervention will be greater than the mean QL of the population of those who will not receive the intervention. If the null hypothesis is false, or rejected, the intervention of exercise has been successful in altering quality of life. According to NHST, the goal of the research is to reject the null hypothesis in favor of the alternative hypothesis.

Note that we have stated the null hypothesis as a "no difference" null hypothesis; that is, that there is no difference between the population means of the treatment and control groups. However, especially in practical applications, the null hypothesis could be stated as *some amount* of *difference* between the means of the two populations. For example, we could say that to reject the null hypothesis the treatment group would have to exceed the control group by an amount necessary to make a *functional* difference. This is referred to as a **non-nil null hypothesis**. Unfortunately, most statistical computer packages are not set up to facilitate non-nil null hypothesis testing, and it has not been widely used in the research literature.

Directional Versus Nondirectional Alternative Hypotheses

For our alternative hypothesis we specified that the intervention population mean will be higher (or lower if we were measuring depression and predicting it to decline) than the control group population mean. This is a *directional hypothesis* and is just one method of expressing the alternative hypothesis. Another choice is to specify the alternative hypothesis as nondirectional. A prediction is made that the intervention will be significantly different from the control, but we are not sure of the direction of this difference. A *nondirectional alternative hypothesis* is often used when comparing two different treatment methods. Directional alternative hypotheses are used most often when comparing a treatment to a control condition.

While it may appear that choosing a directional or nondirectional hypothesis is arbitrary, two things are important. First, the type of alternative hypothesis selected should be based on literature or theory. When there is previous research to support the intervention, a directional hypothesis should be used. Sometimes there is not strong support for the intervention. This could be due to conflicting reports from previous studies or to very little research performed with the intervention. In these cases a nondirectional alternative hypothesis should be used. Second, there are statistical consequences. There is less **statistical power** attached to the nondirectional type of hypothesis. This means it is more difficult to reject the null hypothesis (assuming it should be rejected) when using a nondirectional hypothesis. However, if a directional alternative hypothesis is selected, and the result is a statistically significant difference in the opposite direction, the only acceptable conclusion is a failure to reject the null hypothesis.

Three Ways to State the Alternative Hypothesis

Specifying our alternative hypothesis in the exercise example as the intervention population mean will be higher than the control group population mean is just one method of expressing the alternative hypothesis. Actually there are three choices. One choice is to specify the *alternative hypothesis as nondirectional*. This is expressed as

$$H_1: \mu_I \neq \mu_C$$

This indicates that the intervention is predicted to be significantly different from (i.e., unequal to) the control, but the direction of this difference is not specified. The other two choices for alternative hypotheses are *directional positive*:

$$H_1: \mu_I > \mu_C$$

and *directional negative* (intervention population mean will be smaller/less than the control population mean):

$$H_1: \mu_I < \mu_C$$

Because there are statistical consequences attached to the type of hypothesis that is selected, "there is no free lunch." We discuss this issue later in this chapter.

Theoretical and Accessible Populations

Now that we have stated the null and alternative hypotheses, we need to consider the population of interest for the exercise study. If we are interested in generalizing to all depressed adolescents, they would be our *theoretical or target population*. Perhaps a subset of all depressed adolescents, such as adolescent outpatients, is our theoretical population. However, we often have access only to depressed adolescents who visit one or two clinics in the community. Therefore, these available patients are our accessible population.

If the *accessible population* is not representative of the theoretical or target population of interest, the inference made from the sample will not be accurate about relationships in the theoretical population of interest. For example, in our sample study about the effects of an exercise intervention, perhaps the clinics that were used to obtain the accessible population of depressed adolescents had clients who were quite different from *all* depressed adolescents (e.g., in terms of social class or ethnicity). If so, the results of the study would apply only to the population from the accessible clinics, not to the broader population of interest. Unfortunately, such a difference between the theoretical and accessible population is a common problem for population external validity, as discussed in Chapter 9.

Also, there is an external validity problem with the interpretation if the *selected sample* is not representative of the *accessible population*. If, in our exercise study, the adolescents in the accessible clinics had been sampled by convenience rather than with probability (e.g., random) sampling, the 72 participants might have been very different from the others in the accessible population. For example, if only less severely depressed adolescents agreed to participate, the samples would not be representative of all adolescents seen at the clinic. If so, the results would generalize only to clients similar to those sampled, not the whole accessible population.

The Inferential Process

Figure 16.1 provides insight into the inferential process using our example. At the far left of the figure is a box representing the population. From the accessible population (depressed adolescents from the available community clinics) we sample or select, preferably randomly, 72 adolescents. This is step (a) in Figure 16.1. This step is best done by selecting names from a total list of accessible depressed adolescents in such a way that all available depressed outpatients have an *equal chance of being selected to be in our study (random selection)*. However, frequently the sample is one of convenience, not randomly selected.

In the next step (b), we assign participants to groups. We assign 36 patients to be in the exercise (intervention) group and 36 patients to be in the nonexercise (control) group. Again, it is best to use randomization, in this case *random assignment*, which implies that each patient has an *equal chance to be in either group*. If the participants cannot be randomly assigned, the approach, as discussed in Chapter 5, would be a quasi-experiment rather than a randomized experiment and a *pretest would be needed* to determine the similarity of the groups prior to the intervention.

Moving to the right in Figure 16.1, the next step (c) is to conduct the study. The intervention group (one level of the independent variable) exercises on a stationary bicycle for 45

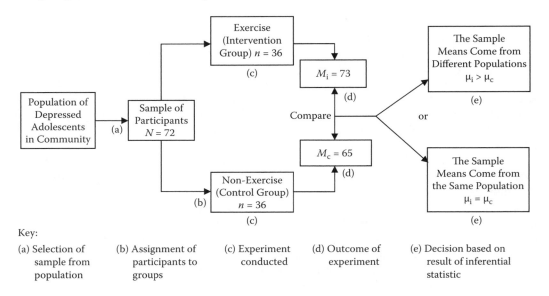

FIGURE 16.1
Schematic diagram of the process of making an inference about the difference between two groups.

minutes per day, 5 days per week, for 6 weeks. The control group (the other level of the independent variable) continues with its usual daily activities for the next 6 weeks.

After 6 weeks we ask the participants to complete the Quality of Life inventory (step d); the QL scores are the dependent variable. Assume that we find the mean of the QL scores of the intervention group is 73 and the mean of the QL scores of the control group is 65. Then the mean of the intervention group is higher, seeming to support our hypothesis that exercise increases quality of life for depressed patients. From these results, can we reject our null hypothesis (that there is no difference between the exercise and no exercise conditions) and support the alternative hypothesis (that the exercise condition will increase quality of life)? Before we make this decision, the results of a second study will be informative.

To illustrate a key issue involved in deciding whether to reject the null hypothesis, imagine that we did a similar study. In our new study, we use the same number of participants (also depressed adolescents), the same method of sample selection, and random assignment to groups. However, in this new study, neither group is instructed to exercise for 6 weeks. At the end of the 6-week period we measure the mean quality of life of both groups. Will the means be identical? It is unlikely that the means will be identical because there are individual differences among the members of each sample. Because we are not measuring the whole population, only two samples from the population, we would expect the means to be different due to random fluctuation. That is, even without introducing a treatment and even if the two samples were equivalent in other characteristics, we would expect the two means to be somewhat different. Therefore, we need to use inferential statistics to help make the proper decision about the null hypothesis.

Now back to our original study. After performing the proper statistical test (a *t* test for independent samples for this example), we can make one of two conclusions. On the one hand, we could conclude that the intervention group mean is significantly greater than the control group mean. In other words, we could conclude that the intervention group mean represents the mean of a population of participants with a higher quality of life, and the control group mean comes from a different population of participants with a lower quality of life. This conclusion defines a **statistically significant difference** and is shown in the upper box of column e in Figure 16.1.

A second conclusion could be that there is no difference between the two means. This is shown in the box in the lower portion of the right-hand column (e) of the figure. In other words, the difference between the means was simply due to random fluctuation. This latter conclusion would imply that the two groups come from the same underlying population and that this amount of exercise does not make a difference in quality of life for depressed adolescents as defined for our study.

Which conclusion do we make? How much of a difference between the two means is needed before we can conclude that there is a statistically significant difference? Inferential statistics provide us with an outcome (a statistic) that helps us make an informed decision about how much of a difference is needed. Even after performing inferential statistical procedures on our data, we are still making a decision with some degree of uncertainty.

We stated that there were two possible decisions that could be made based on our sample data. Either we would reject the null hypothesis and conclude that the two groups come from two different populations, or we would *not* reject the null hypothesis and conclude that the groups come from the same population. The decision to reject or not reject the null hypothesis is determined by subjecting our sample data to a particular statistical test. *An outcome that is highly unlikely (i.e., one that results in a low probability value) if the null hypothesis was true will lead us to reject the null hypothesis.* Most social science researchers and journals establish this probability value as 5 times in 100, or .05. An outcome that is more likely (probable) will result in a failure to reject the null hypothesis.

Results From a Statistical Test

Now we examine the results from a statistical test applied to the data from our example. An independent samples *t* test was selected to test for statistical significance. (See Chapter 19 for a discussion of the rationale for the selection of this test in this situation.) The independent samples *t* test yielded a value of 2.10 with an associated probability (*p*) value of .04 for a nondirectional hypothesis, or .02 for the directional hypothesis that we originally proposed. Assuming we had established an alpha level (significance level) before the study of 0.05, our *p* value is *less* than the significance level. Therefore, we can conclude that our result is statistically significant and reject the null hypothesis of no difference between our intervention and control conditions. Another way to state this outcome is that the two groups represent two different populations, one that underwent the intervention and one that did not receive the intervention.

Type I and Type II Errors

Although inferential statistics inform us of the decision we should make (i.e., to reject or not reject the null hypothesis), there is still a possibility that the decision may be incorrect. This is because our decision is based on the *probability* of a given outcome. The statistical value we obtain is associated with a particular probability. While calculations performed on the example led us to reject the null hypothesis in favor of an alternative hypothesis, there is a possibility that we were in error. In other words, the null hypothesis may be true. Although inferential statistics inform us to either reject or not reject the null hypothesis based on our sample data, either the decision can be correct *or* it can be in error.

Anytime we conduct a study based on *sample data*, four outcomes are possible. Two of the outcomes are correct decisions and two of the outcomes are errors.

Correct Decisions

1. We do *not reject* the null hypothesis when it is true and should not be rejected. That is, there really is *no* difference in the population.
2. We *reject* the null hypothesis when, in fact, it is false. That is, there really is a difference in the population.

Errors

1. We *reject* the null hypothesis when, in fact, it is true. This is called a **Type I error**.
2. We do *not reject* the null hypothesis when it is false. This is called a **Type II error**.

We are never sure if the decision we have made is actually true in the population (i.e., correct) because we are basing our decision on sample data. Figure 16.2 is a flow chart that shows the process that leads to the four outcomes (in shaded boxes) that can result from the decision to reject or not reject the null hypothesis based on the results of a statistical test of sample data.

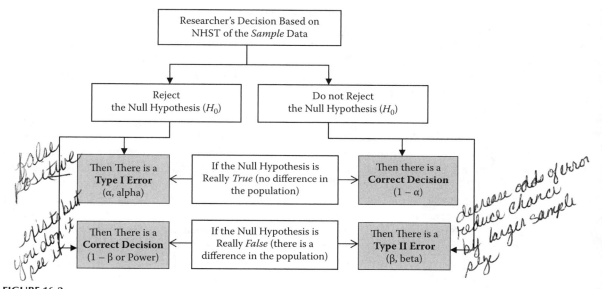

FIGURE 16.2

Flow chart showing the four possible outcomes (two correct and two errors) that could result from a decision to reject or not reject a null hypothesis.

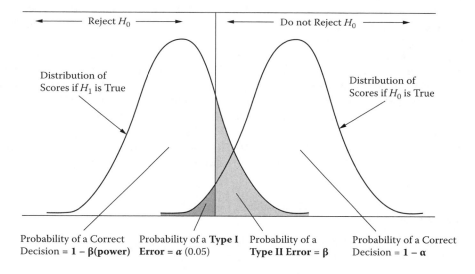

FIGURE 16.3

Type I and Type II errors related to the null and alternative population distributions. (Adapted from Loftus, G. R., & Loftus, E. F., *Essence of statistics*, Monterey, CA, Brooks/Cole, 1982, p. 225. With permission.)

Figure 16.3 (adapted from Loftus & Loftus, 1982, p. 225) helps us to conceptualize the four possible outcomes that we have just discussed. The figure is based on testing a directional negative hypothesis (i.e., a lower score on the dependent variable is expected). The curve on the right represents the population distribution if the null hypothesis is true. The curve on the left is one possible representation of the population distribution under the alternative hypothesis if the null hypothesis is false (i.e., if H_1 is true). The line drawn perpendicular to the x axis represents the .05 decision point or significance level. We establish this level *prior* to the study. It is customary to decide that any difference between our two sample means that is large enough to yield a statistical outcome that could occur less than 5 times in 100 (α = .05), if the null hypothesis is true should result in a rejection of the null hypothesis. Sometimes researchers use a significance level of 0.01 which is more conservative (more difficult to reject the null hypothesis) than 0.05. This is especially true if there are several treatments in the study.

The curve on the *right* represents the population distribution *if the null hypothesis is true*. Most of the area under this right-hand curve (95%) is to the right of the .05 decision point or vertical statistical significance level line. Only a small portion (5%) of the area is to the left of the statistical significance line. We call the portion to the left of the statistical significance line **alpha (α)**. This also refers to the probability of making a **Type I error** (see also Figure 16.2.) Therefore, in the present example, since the area under the curve to the left of the significance level line is 5%, the probability of a Type I error (α) is .05. The remaining portion of the curve (the part of the curve to the right of the significance line) is the probability of making a correct decision; this is $1 - \alpha$. Since we are dealing with the population distribution associated with the null hypothesis, a correct decision would be to not reject the null hypothesis, assuming it is true. In our present example, the probability of making a correct decision to not reject the null hypothesis is .95 ($1 - \alpha = 1 - .05 = .95$).

The curve on the left in Figure 16.3 represents the population distribution related to the *alternative hypothesis*, if it is true. The area of this curve to the right of the statistical significance line is called **beta (β)**. It is relatively small but usually not as small as alpha. Beta depicts an area of the alternative hypothesis curve associated with **type II error**. The area depicted for β provides the probability of making the error of not rejecting the null hypothesis when it is false or should be rejected. The area of the alternative hypothesis curve that falls to the left of the significance line is the probability of making a correct decision. Because it deals with the alternative hypothesis curve, this correct decision is to reject the null hypothesis when it is false, that is, when it should be rejected. The probability of making this correct decision is $1 - \beta$. Since our goal in research usually is to reject the null hypothesis in favor of an alternative hypothesis, the area or probability $1 - \beta$ is very important. We would like to increase this area as much as possible. Because of its importance, $1 - \beta$ is called **power**. We discuss power in more detail later in this chapter. Again, Figure 16.2 and Figure 16.3 summarize our discussion of Type I and Type II errors.

Statistical Decision Making

We return now to directional and nondirectional alternative hypotheses. Remember that earlier in the chapter we stated that there are statistical consequences associated with the type of alternative hypothesis selected. If we hypothesize a *directional negative alternative hypothesis*, it would be conceptualized similar to Figure 16.3. The distribution of scores under the alternative hypothesis is to the left of the distribution of scores under the null hypothesis. If, as in Figure 16.3, we establish our significance level, α, at .05, then a statistical outcome to the *left* of this .05 value would result in a rejection of the null hypothesis.

A similar conceptualization would result for an *alternative hypothesis that is directional positive*, like our example with exercise and depressed adolescents. In that example, the alternative hypothesis curve would be to the right of the null hypothesis curve, and a statistical outcome that is to the *right* of the .05 value would result in a rejection of the null hypothesis.

Now, suppose instead that our *alternative hypothesis is nondirectional*, as seen in Figure 16.4. We would have two distributions of scores under the alternative hypothesis.

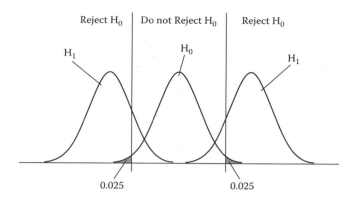

FIGURE 16.4
Alternative nondirectional hypotheses.

One distribution would be to the right of the distribution of scores under the null hypothesis, and the other distribution would be to the left of the distribution of scores under the null hypothesis. If we keep our significance level at .05, then it would mean that to reject the null hypothesis in either direction, the statistical outcome would have to exceed the .025 level rather than the .05 level. Therefore, it is more difficult to reject the null hypothesis using a nondirectional hypothesis. However, a critical mistake is less likely. In other words, if a directional alternative hypothesis is selected, and the result was a significant difference in the opposite direction, a conclusion of failure to reject the null hypothesis or no significant difference must be made. It should be noted that, because we are using both ends, or *tails*, of the distribution under the null hypothesis when stating a nondirectional hypothesis, a test of this hypothesis is referred to as a **two-tailed test**. When using a directional hypothesis, the test is called a **one-tailed test**.

A final key point on the philosophy of hypothesis testing is that when the null hypothesis is not rejected, it is *never actually accepted*. The correct conclusion is that the null hypothesis is not rejected. Though one may question the difference between the terms *accept* and *not reject*, the problem with the former is that there could be many reasons why our study did not result in rejection of the null hypothesis. Perhaps another more powerful or better designed study might result in a rejection of the null hypothesis. When we fail to reject the null hypothesis, we are just saying that we don't have enough evidence to conclude that the two samples are from the same population. This is not the same thing as concluding that the two samples are definitely from the same population.

Understanding and Assessing Statistical Power

We now return to the concept of statistical power mentioned earlier. Power from a statistical point of view is defined as the probability of rejecting a false null hypothesis. Power implies a correct decision, so it should be maximized. In other words, if we set our alpha level at the conventional .05 or the less conventional .01, what is the probability of rejecting the null hypothesis assuming it is false?

We return to Figure 16.3, which shows two normal curves representing both the population distribution if the null hypothesis is true (H_0) and the population distribution if the alternative hypothesis (H_1) is true (the null hypothesis is false). We are interested in the area of the distribution of the alternative hypothesis that is *not shaded*—that is, the probability of rejecting a false null hypothesis, or power $(1 - \beta)$. What most researchers really want to know is will they have enough power in their study to allow for a fair test of the null hypothesis. Ideally, power should be a value of .80.[1]

We can determine how much power $(1 - \beta)$ is present using power charts, or a computer program, if we know the size of the sample, the significance level (α) and an estimate of the effect size of the relationship. For example, suppose a study is proposed to determine the effect of reform teaching on mathematics achievement in college students. A faculty member has volunteered to teach two different sections of linear algebra. She will teach one section in a reform manner and the other section in the traditional manner. The class size of the reform section is 24, and the class size of the traditional section is 28. She sets her alpha level prior to the study at .05 for a nondirectional hypothesis. Now she knows her sample size and alpha level. What is the estimated effect size? The effect size is the strength of the relationship between the independent and dependent variables. We discuss effect size more in Chapter 17 and discuss how it is computed in Chapter 20. However, for current purposes, typically the investigator specifies an effect size as small, medium, or large. For example, a small effect size would be around 0.20 standard deviations difference between the intervention and control means, a medium effect size would be around 0.50 standard deviations between the intervention and control means, and a large effect size would be about 0.80 standard deviations between the intervention and control means. How does the researcher know what effect size to estimate? The best estimate would be from previous studies in this area. If previous studies investigating the relationship between reform teaching and achievement demonstrated medium effect sizes, then an estimate of effect size for her study might be 0.50. Now that the researcher knows sample size, estimated effect size, and significance level for her study, she can use Table 16.1 to determine her power (from Cohen, 1988).

Notice that this particular power table (Table 16.1) is for an independent samples t test with an α of .05 two tailed (nondirectional hypothesis). Above the left-hand column in the table is the letter n, which stands for the number of participants in each group. As we go down column n, we see that the sample size increases from 10 to 100. Since our two groups are not equal in size, we take the average of the two, which is 26. We use that as an estimate of our sample size in each group. Across the top of the table is the letter d (effect size), which has a separate column for each effect size from .1 to 1.2. We locate the effect size column of .50, the estimate of our predicted effect size. Then, we find where the effect size column of .50 intersects the sample size row of 26. The number at this point is our power. In our example, the power would be .42. This is less than an ideal level of power, so the researcher would like to have more power in her study.

How Can We Increase Power?

To increase power in our research situation, we need to decide which things we can control and which we cannot control. Control in this situation is relative. We present several ways to increase power, from what is usually least appropriate to most appropriate and controllable.

One possible way to increase power is to change alpha (α). In Figure 16.3 one can visualize that if α was set at a lower significance level, power would be decreased (i.e., if α were set at .01, the cutoff point would be moved to the left). On the other hand, if α was set at a higher level (e.g., .10), then power would be *increased*. However, as we increase alpha, we

TABLE 16.1

Power for a Two-Tailed t Test at Alpha = .05

n	.10	.20	.30	.40	.50	.60	.70	.80	1.00	1.20
10	06	07	10	13	18	24	31	39	56	71
11	06	07	10	14	20	26	34	43	61	76
12	06	08	11	15	21	28	37	46	65	80
13	06	08	11	16	23	31	40	50	69	83
14	06	08	12	17	25	33	43	53	72	86
15	06	08	12	18	26	35	45	56	75	88
16	06	08	13	19	28	37	48	59	78	90
17	06	09	13	20	29	39	51	62	80	92
18	06	09	14	21	31	41	53	64	83	94
19	06	09	15	22	32	43	55	67	85	95
20	06	09	15	23	33	45	58	69	87	96
21	06	10	16	24	35	47	60	71	88	97
22	06	10	16	25	36	49	62	73	90	97
23	06	10	17	26	38	51	64	75	91	98
24	06	10	17	27	39	53	66	77	92	98
25	06	11	18	28	41	55	68	79	93	99
26	06	11	19	29	42	56	69	80	94	99
27	06	11	19	30	43	58	71	82	95	99
28	07	11	20	31	45	59	73	83	96	99
29	07	12	20	32	46	61	74	85	96	99
30	07	12	21	33	47	63	76	86	97	*
31	07	12	21	34	49	64	77	87	97	
32	07	12	22	35	50	65	78	88	98	
33	07	13	22	36	51	67	80	89	98	
34	07	13	23	37	53	68	81	90	98	
35	07	13	23	38	54	70	82	91	98	
36	07	13	24	39	55	71	83	92	99	
37	07	14	25	39	56	72	84	92	99	
38	07	14	25	40	57	73	85	93	99	
39	07	14	26	41	58	74	86	94	99	
40	07	14	26	42	60	75	87	94	99	
50	08	17	32	50	70	84	93	98	*	
60	08	19	37	58	77	90	97	99		
80	10	24	47	71	88	96	99	*		
100	11	29	56	80	94	99	*			

* Power values in the column below this point are greater than .995.

Source: Adapted from Cohen, J., *Statistical Power Analysis for the Behavioral Sciences*, Hillsdale, NJ, Lawrence Erlbaum Associates, 1988. With permission.

also increase the probability of a type I error. More importantly, we really should not set alpha at a level higher than .05. The reason for this is mostly convention. Few research journals and, hence, our colleagues will accept a research publication with alpha established higher than .05, except, perhaps, in a clearly exploratory small sample study.

A second method to increase power involves formulation of hypotheses. When we use a *t* test, we have the option of formulating a directional or nondirectional hypothesis. Choice of a *directional* hypothesis will increase power because the alpha level is increasing from, for example, .025 to .05. Had we proposed a directional hypothesis in our teaching example, our power would have increased from .42 to about .55. Similarly, when one has more than two groups in a single-factor design, the option of using planned comparisons as opposed to a single-factor analysis of variance is another way to increase power through the use of hypothesis formulation (see Keppel, 1991).

A third general method to increase power is to decrease variability or error variance. Though there are many methods to decrease variability, we suggest two here. One method to decrease variability is to make sure that the groups in the study are homogeneous. A second strategy to decrease variability is to make sure that the dependent measure has a high level of reliability. Whenever possible, a measurement instrument should be selected that has been standardized and shown evidence of good reliability. Measures that have low evidence of reliability increase within-group variability.

Finally, sample size is the element over which we usually have the most control in increasing power. Note that an increase in total sample size (N) usually reduces variability. Returning to Table 16.1, our power table, we can see that an increase in participants will increase power. If we increase our sample size to 40 participants in each group, our power would be .60. If we have 80 in each group, power would be .88. It is important to remember all of the methods to increase power because there are many situations, such as program evaluations, where there are limits on obtaining participants. Also, there may be diminishing returns after a certain sample size is achieved.

Problems With Null Hypothesis Significance Testing

We have just discussed the process of null hypothesis significance testing, which has been an integral part of all inferential statistics (e.g., *t* test, correlation, chi-square) in the biological, behavioral, and social sciences for much of the past century. For years, researchers have questioned the use of NHST, but the intensity of objection has increased recently (e.g., Finch, Thomason, & Cumming, 2002). Although literally hundreds of articles address the topic across multiple disciplines, two excellent texts about this issue are worth considering (Harlow, Mulaik, & Steiger, 1997; Kline, 2004). The major criticisms of NHST appear to be both philosophical and a misinterpretation of statistical significance.

Philosophy of Science Criticism

One criticism of NHST is that it does not promote good scientific knowledge and understanding because scientific knowledge is not based on the results from a single study. Instead, replication of findings is the hallmark of science. When we engage in NHST, we end by making a dichotomous decision: reject or do not reject the null hypothesis. Often, when the null hypothesis is *not* rejected, the study does not get published due to a bias against publishing statistically nonsignificant findings. Or worse, the study gets published, but continued research on the problem is dropped because it appears that the intervention does not work. In discussing the decision to reject the null hypothesis or not, Schmidt and Hunter (1997) say:

> But in fact no such dichotomous decision need be made in any individual study. Indeed, it is futile to do so, because no single individual study contains sufficient information to support a final conclusion about the truth or value of a hypothesis. Only by combining findings across multiple studies using meta-analysis can dependable scientific conclusion be reached.... From the point of view of the goal of optimally advancing the cumulation of scientific knowledge, it is best for individual researchers to present point estimates and confidence intervals and refrain from attempting to draw final conclusions about research hypotheses. These will emerge from later meta-analyses. (p.52)

Confusion About the Meaning of Statistical Significance

The second general criticism, misunderstanding of what statistically significant results tell us, can be seen as follows. From our earlier example with depressed adolescents, a test of statistical significance, such as a t test, was performed to determine if the two groups, exercise and nonexercise, were statistically different from each other. The results of that statistical test are provided in the form of a probability value or p value. Conventionally, if the p value was less than .05 (5 times in 100), the two groups were considered to be statistically significantly different from each other. What, however, does the p value really tell us? What most of us *think* it tells us is the probability of a true null hypothesis. Thus, we think a p value of less than .05 tells us that less than 5 times in 100 the null hypothesis is true. Unfortunately, *this is not the case* as Cohen (1994) points out:

> What's wrong with NHST? Well, among many other things, it does not tell us what we want to know, and we so much want to know what we want to know that, out of desperation, we nevertheless believe that it does! What we want to know is "Given these data what is the probability that the H_0 (null hypothesis) is true?" But ... what it tells us is "Given that H_0 is true, what is the probability of these (or more extreme) data?" These are not the same, as has been pointed out many times over the years. (p. 997)

This **inverse probability fallacy** shows us the confusion with the p value. What we would like the p value to tell us is the conditional probability $p(H/D)$. In other words, what is the probability that the null hypothesis (H) is true, given our data (D)? The data from our example would be the difference between the means of the exercise and nonexercise groups. However, what p actually tells us is the conditional probability $p(D/H)$. In other words, what is the probability of the data (the difference between means of the two groups), given the null hypothesis is true? Therefore, when a p value is provided after a statistical test, it tells us only the probability of the data (the present difference between means or a larger difference) *assuming a true null hypothesis* and nothing more. While some might argue that since the probability of the data are highly unlikely, assuming a true null hypothesis, the null hypothesis cannot be true. However, one never knows the probability of the null hypothesis being true.

To show that these two conditional probabilities are not the same, consider a more practical example from the field of rehabilitation. First, consider the conditional probability that one might have a spinal cord injury due to an automobile crash. *Given* one has a spinal cord injury, the probability that it was *due to a car crash* is relatively high. Over 50% of all spinal cord injuries are due to car crashes. However, the inverse of that situation—the likelihood that, *given* one is in a car crash, the probability that the crash will result in a spinal cord injury—is quite low. There are hundreds of different outcomes from car crashes, of which spinal cord injury is a relatively rare occurrence.

Further Complications of NHST

In addition to the inverse probability fallacy, there are several other complications from using NHST. Kline (2004) lists 13 fallacies associated with the use of NHST. Schmidt and Hunter (1997) list eight objections to NHST. Nickerson (2000) lists 11 misconceptions associated with NHST. We discuss the most common of these objections, which we call complications of using NHST.

The first complication is the observation that *the null hypothesis is rarely true*; there is almost always *some* difference between the means of the two populations of interest. It then becomes merely a matter of having enough participants in the study to demonstrate this difference statistically. This is especially problematic with the comparative and associative research approaches when making comparisons within nonexperimental settings. Since there is no possibility of random assignment to groups or conditions, the probability of a true null hypothesis is small.

The second complication involves the statement of the null hypothesis as a *nondirectional hypothesis* and follows from the first complication. If there are enough participants, it becomes especially easy to find a statistically significant difference since the difference between the intervention and control conditions could either be positive or negative.

The third complication of NHST involves statistical significance as a *dichotomous decision*. Using an artificial "cut point" of .05 (or .01) to determine statistical significance implies that outcomes are dichotomous, significant, or not significant rather than continuous. Certainly a finding with a p value of .06 should add almost as much supporting evidence for a hypothesis as finding p values of .05 or .04.[2]

The fourth complication (*strength of relationship*) of NHST is the confusion that the smaller the p value (e.g., .01 versus .05), the stronger the relationship in the study. This is not the case because the larger the sample, the smaller the p value. However, if the sample size is constant, as it often is in a given study, the smaller the p, the larger the effect size. As stated earlier, the p value only demonstrates the probability of the outcome, given a true null hypothesis. To know the strength of the relationship in a study, one must compute the *effect size* as discussed in the next chapter.

The fifth complication is the confusion between statistical significance and *substantive* or *clinical importance*. A statistically significant result doesn't demonstrate the importance of the difference between groups because it doesn't tell us the strength of the relationship or anything about other key factors contributing to substantive importance such as cost or side effects. A statistically significant finding only indicates that it is unlikely that there is no difference between the groups.

Improvements to NHST

Null hypothesis significance testing could be strengthened by addressing some of the criticisms stated already. For those who advocate the use of NHST, the null hypothesis of no difference (the nil null hypothesis) should be replaced by a null hypothesis specifying some nonzero value based on previous research (Cohen, 1994). Thus, there would be less chance that a trivial difference between groups would result in a rejection of the null hypothesis. If a null hypothesis of no difference is used, the alternative hypothesis should be directional because at least the outcome would have to be in the hypothesized direction (i.e., greater than or less than). This would help to minimize a trivial outcome often associated with a large sample size. If the alternative hypothesis is nondirectional, then any difference, regardless of direction, could be statistically significant.

Therefore, for NHST to be made more acceptable, the following are necessary. First, the researcher must propose one or a limited number of specific hypotheses. In the detailed example in this chapter, we put forward a hypothesis that introduction of an exercise program would result in an increase in quality of life among depressed adolescents. Second, a large, accessible population should exist from which the researcher will have the option to draw a random sample large enough to have adequate *power* (i.e., the probability of declaring a result "statistically significant" when the null hypothesis is false). Third, the researcher must have a measure (dependent variable) that has strong psychometric properties, such as sufficient evidence of measurement reliability and validity. Perhaps more importantly, the measure must have some degree of clinical or practical validity. This means that the researcher should know how much of a difference between M_I and M_C would produce a clinically significant change in the quality of life of the participants. It is also desirable to test the *non-nil null hypothesis* that the difference between M_I and M_C is equal to or greater than this clinically significant amount.

Therefore, prior to collecting any data, the researcher should have a specific hypothesis, a representative accessible population, an adequately sized sample, and a clinically valid measure. In addition, the researcher must have a sound methodological approach for carrying out the study. This includes appropriate choices of how many participants will be sampled, how they will be sampled, how they will be assigned to groups, how the data will be analyzed, and an established level of statistical significance, alpha, usually set at .05. However, these steps are hard to achieve, as discussed in the next chapter.

Summary

In this chapter we discussed the null hypothesis significance testing approach to reporting the outcomes of statistical tests. Attention was given to setting up the null and alternative hypotheses, to the different types of alternative hypotheses (directional and nondirectional), and to the inferential process associated with NHST. An example was provided to help illustrate the inferential process. Type I and Type II errors were explained with accompanying figures. Statistical power is the probability of making a correct decision so, ideally, it should be .80 or better. A chart was provided to illustrate that power depends on the sample size, effect size, and alpha. Several methods for increasing power were described. Finally, criticisms of NHST were described, and possible improvements to NHST were offered.

Key Concepts

Alternative hypotheses

Inferential process

Inverse probability fallacy

Non-nil null hypothesis

Null hypothesis significance testing (NHST)

Power

Statistical significance

Key Distinctions

Directional versus nondirectional alternative hypotheses

Type I versus Type II errors

Application Problems

For problems 1–4, provide nondirectional and directional alternative hypotheses.

1. There is no difference between reform teaching methods and traditional teaching methods in students' mathematics achievement data.

2. There is no difference between supported employment and sheltered work in successful community participation.

3. There is no difference between exercise and no exercise in cardiovascular health.

4. There is no difference between students who perform well and students who do not perform well on teacher evaluations.

For problems 5–8, describe in words the type I error, the type II error, and the two correct decisions.

5. A study is performed to determine if reform teaching methods are better than traditional teaching methods.

6. A study is performed to determine if people in supported employment participate more in the community than people in sheltered workshops.

7. A study is performed to determine if those who exercise have lower resting heart rates than those who do not exercise.

8. A study is performed to determine if students with high grades give better teacher evaluations than students with low grades.

9. What are two general problems with null hypothesis significance testing? How can these problems be alleviated?

10. For each of the five example studies in Chapter 1, answer the following:
    a. What would be a null hypothesis?
    b. What would be a possible alternative hypothesis?

11. A school psychologist is interested in testing a new intervention for bullying behaviors in elementary school boys.
    a. What would be her null hypotheses?
    b. What would be an alternative *directional* hypothesis?
    c. What would be an alternative *nondirectional* hypothesis?
    d. How might she reduce Type I error?
    e. What could she do to reduce Type II error?

For questions 12, 13, and 14 use Table 16.1.

12. A researcher feels that certain modifications to her treatment will result in added benefits to patients. A study is set up to compare the modified treatment (intervention group) to the original treatment (control group). Previous research using the original treatment has demonstrated effect sizes of about .70. The researcher is willing to accept power of .60. How many participants will she need in each group?

13. A colleague has just performed a study. A *t* test had failed to demonstrate a significant difference between his treatment and control groups. The effect size was .4. He had 15 participants in each group. How much power did he have in this study? What was the probability of a type II error?

14. A graduate student is planning her study. She has the cooperation of enough undergraduates to form two groups of 30 students in each group. She would like to have power of .70. To obtain a statistically significant outcome, how large of an effect size will she need?

15. One method of gaining power is to reduce error variance. How is this accomplished without increasing sample size?

16. You have been asked to evaluate a program that advocates joint protection techniques for persons with arthritis. The program is relatively small, and you have only 18 participants in each group. What reasonable steps should you take to maximize power without increasing sample size?

Notes

1. Keppel (1991) suggests that most methodologists in the behavioral sciences appear to agree on this level of power, assuming that type I errors are more serious than type II.

2. The adoption of an alpha of .05 dates back to the early 1900s, when agricultural scientists wanted to set a low level for the Type I error so that they could be quite sure that their recommendations would lead to improvements.

17

Making Inferences from Sample Data II: The Evidence-Based Approach

The evidence-based approach to reporting the outcomes of statistical tests is about the reliability of findings. The key to this approach is the accumulation of evidence through multiple studies investigating the same or similar hypotheses. Sophisticated statistical methods that might be applied to a single study are not necessary. *Underlying the evidence-based approach is the knowledge that a single study is not sufficient to use as evidence to substantiate a hypothesis or theory.* In the social or applied sciences and in the discipline of education, there is a tendency to try new interventions based on minimal evidence such as that derived from a single study. However, if we examine the discipline of clinical medicine, we would be horrified if the medication we were taking or the surgical technique applied were based on a single study. Instead, we assume that the judgments made by medical practitioners are based on multiple, well-designed studies that demonstrate reliable interventions.

Problems With Considering Only a Single Study

In the previous chapter we discussed some of the problems involved with null hypothesis significance testing (NHST). All of these problems, such as the limitations of the p value, the concept of rejecting a null hypothesis that could already be false, and the confusions around statistical significance apply to the single study. Added to these problems is the failure to obtain a random sample from the target population and a large enough sample to provide adequate statistical power. Often single studies are not well designed and, at best, are based on quasi-experimental approaches. Unfortunately, even when single studies are well designed (random assignment of participants to groups), they are most often performed with convenience samples. In addition, measurement error in a single study is always a possibility, even when reliability and validity evidence for the instrument appear adequate. All of these problems can lead to either Type I or Type II errors.

In the rest of this chapter, we discuss three methods underlying the evidence-based approach to the interpretation of research results. These methods use (1) confidence intervals; (2) effect sizes; and (3) meta-analysis.

Confidence Intervals

A primary problem with NHST involves the interpretation of a statistically significant difference in the form of an all-or-none decision. Findings from a single study are interpreted as significant or not significant rather than the acknowledgment that statistical significance implies a probability of uncertainty. In addition, when we dichotomize statistical significance in this way, we become removed from the actual data of our study. One important procedure of the evidence-based approach is the creation of *confidence intervals*.

The concept of confidence intervals is difficult to understand even for experienced researchers, leading to it being reported infrequently in the research literature, especially in the behavioral sciences. In the following paragraphs we attempt to clear up many of the misconceptions associated with confidence intervals.

We start by examining the terms *point estimate* and *intervals* with an example common to most of us: *How hot do you think it will be tomorrow?* One could watch the weather news for tomorrow's forecast. Suppose the forecaster predicts a high temperature of 84 degrees. This exact number is a **point estimate**. It uses a specific number to estimate the temperature. While this number might be a good estimate, so might the numbers 83 degrees or 85 degrees. If you were asked on a scale of 1 to 100 how sure you were that the high temperature would be *exactly* 84 degrees, you would probably respond with a relatively low number, perhaps below 50. Now, what if the question was rephrased to ask you how sure you were of obtaining a high temperature between 80 degrees and 88 degrees? This is an *interval* of 8 degrees. Your rating of "sureness" would probably increase substantially, perhaps as high as 90 out of 100. What if the interval were increased to between 70 degrees and 95 degrees? Your "sureness" rating might be as high as 99 out of 100 that the high temperature for tomorrow will be within that interval. From the example we want to emphasize the following: First, as we went from a single data point or point estimate to a relatively small interval estimate and then to a larger interval estimate, our "sureness" of what the actual value might be *increased*. Second, as we went from a point estimate to a larger range of values and larger intervals, the *preciseness* of information *decreased*. In other words, as the interval becomes larger, there is less useful information.

Now, let's return to the example from the previous chapter (Chapter 16) that examined an exercise intervention to increase quality of life in depressed adolescents. From Figure 16.1 we see that the average difference in scores on the Quality of Life Inventory between the two groups, Exercise Group and Control Group, is eight points (73–65). This value of eight points is a *point estimate*, similar to what we discussed in the previous paragraph. Remember that the point estimate in this situation has been determined from two samples of participants. It is an *estimate* because we do not know the actual difference on the Quality of Life Inventory between a *population* of depressed adolescents who exercise and those who do not exercise. Thus, we use the difference between the *sample* means as the point estimate in this example.

Now, instead of performing an independent samples *t* test to determine if the two groups are statistically significantly different as we did in the previous chapter, the evidence-based approach calls for the construction of an interval around the point estimate, called a **confidence interval**. The confidence interval is a range of the dependent variable scores that *should contain the true population difference between means*. To construct this confidence interval (see Chapter 20 for a more detailed example on the computation of a *t* test, confidence interval, and effect size from the same data) we use the same information that was used to perform the independent samples *t* test, the difference between the means, the number of participants, and the standard deviations from each sample. However, rather than establishing a significance level (α) of .05, we typically establish the confidence interval at 95%. We could establish a confidence interval at 99% or 90% but a 95% confidence interval is the most commonly used. Using the example from Chapter 16, one might compute a 95% confidence interval. Let's say it is between .42 and 15.28.

Interpreting the Confidence Interval

Now the fun begins. As we stated earlier, there are many misconceptions about what a *single* confidence interval tells us. From the example in Chapter 16, our 95% confidence interval is between .42 and 15.58. Is our true population difference between means within this interval? We do not know for certain. If we constructed an infinite number of studies using the same exercise and nonexercise conditions, the same measure, and the same sample size and computed a 95% confidence interval for each study, exactly 95% of the intervals would contain the true population difference between means, and 5% would not contain this value. *Be careful here.* First, this does *not* mean there is a .95 probability that the true population difference between means is within our interval. Second, if we could create an infinite number of confidence intervals, 95% would contain the true population difference between means, but all the intervals of these confidence intervals would not be the same. They would not all be between .42 and 15.28.

So, one might ask why we construct confidence intervals instead of performing a statistical test? Confidence intervals are part of a long-range approach to performing research. Remember, the evidence-based approach discourages making decisions based on a single study. Instead, it encourages replication of studies as its basis. While constructing a confidence interval for a single study only provides the point estimate and the 95% interval, the size of the interval tells the researcher how much of the estimate might be due to sampling error. Figure 17.1 shows a hypothetical example of confidence intervals derived from 10 different studies that used the same independent and dependent variable as in our exercise and quality-of-life example. Also included in the figure are the values of the independent samples t test for each study and whether the null hypothesis would be rejected (nondirectional, $p < .05$).

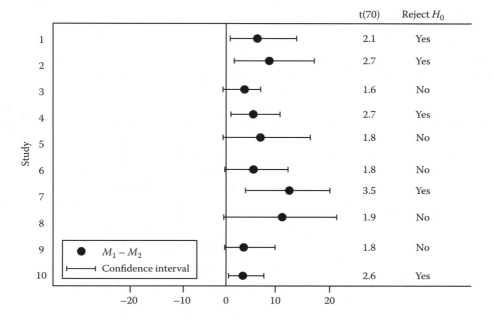

FIGURE 17.1
Hypothetical replications of 10 studies with exercise and depressed adolescents. (Data are from Kline, R. B., *Beyond Significance Testing*, Washington, DC, American Psychological Association, 2004, p. 74.)

The confidence intervals for the 10 studies range from a little less than 0 to 20.8. The average of the difference between means of the exercise and nonexercise conditions for the 10 studies is 7.4, providing an estimate of the population mean difference. However, of the 10 hypothetical studies, 5 were *not* statistically significant. If only the five studies that demonstrated statistical significance were published, the average difference between means would be larger (8.2), yielding an overestimation of the true population value.

A Last Word on Confidence Intervals

It has been difficult for researchers to move away from reporting statistical significance from a single study. This is especially true when the information from a confidence interval seems so nonspecific. However, one can always make a decision about statistical significance from a confidence interval by observing whether zero is within the interval. If zero is contained in the interval, then the confidence interval indicates that the outcome is *not* statistically significant. In our example of exercise versus no exercise, zero is not in the confidence interval; therefore, we could conclude that the two groups were statistically significantly different at $p < .05$. We also would like to be able to say more about the confidence interval from an individual study. According to Kline (2004), "There is a kind of compromise language for describing traditional confidence intervals that 'splits the difference' between frequentist and subjectivist views of probability" (p. 30). Using Kline's terminology, we would say from our example that the unique interval .42 to 15.28 *estimates* the population mean difference with 95% confidence.

Effect Sizes

While confidence intervals always should be reported, regardless of whether one subscribes to the evidence-based approach or the hypothesis testing approach, they have limitations. We have already discussed problems of interpretation of confidence intervals. Perhaps a more important problem with confidence intervals for the evidence-based approach is that the dependent variable must be the same from study to study to compare the different intervals. Unfortunately, exact replications are not rewarded in academic institutions because, in part, there is a perceived lack of creativity in exact replication of someone else's work. Therefore, replications of previous work are likely to involve some alteration of the independent variable, the dependent variable, or both. A follow-up on our previous exercise study example might include a different type or amount of exercise or a different measure of quality of life. If a different measure of quality of life were employed with a different scale, then comparing a confidence interval from the previous study with this modified study would have little meaning. It should be noted that when clinical studies use a slightly different intervention but a standard dependent variable such as blood pressure, then confidence intervals from these studies are comparable. To solve this problem of using a different scale to measure the same construct, researchers have added a second strategy to the evidence-based approach: effect size.

A statistically significant outcome does not provide information about the strength or size of the outcome. Therefore, it is important to know, in addition to information on statistical significance, the size of the effect. **Effect size** is defined as the strength of the relationship between the independent variable and the dependent variable or the magnitude of the difference between levels of the independent variable with respect to the dependent variable. Statisticians have proposed effect size measures that fall mainly into three types or families: the *r* family, the *d* family, and measures of risk potency (see Grissom & Kim, 2005; Kraemer et al., 2003).

Standardized Versus Unstandardized Effect Size

When we discuss effect size in this text, we are referring to **standardized effect sizes**— that is, effect sizes that can be computed regardless of the specific measurement scale used in the study. For example, in our study investigating the effect of exercise with depressed adolescents (Chapter 16), the effect size could be expressed as an unstandardized effect size or a standardized effect size. The unstandardized effect size is just the difference between the means of the intervention and control group, which was 8. This unstandardized effect size does not have a lot of meaning by itself, unless we could compare it with studies that used a similar measurement scale (e.g., the Quality of Life Inventory). Thus, unstandardized effect sizes are sometimes found in medical interventions, where the dependent variable is change in blood pressure or level of low-density lipoprotein (LDL) cholesterol, which are common to many studies. However, in the social sciences it is quite common for different studies measuring a similar construct to use *different* measurement scales. To have a similar metric for comparison among these studies, effect sizes are standardized. In our present example, we compute a standardized effect size by dividing the difference between the intervention and control group means by the pooled standard deviation of the two groups. Then, the standardized effect size of our study can be compared to similarly computed effect sizes from other studies with different measurement scales.

Type of Effect Size

The r Family of Effect Size Measures

One method of expressing effect sizes is in terms of strength of association. The most well-known variant of this approach is the *Pearson correlation coefficient, r*. Using the Pearson *r*, effect sizes always have an absolute value less than or equal to 1.0, varying between −1.0 and +1.0 with 0 representing no effect and +1 or −1 representing the maximum effect. This *family* of effect sizes includes many other associational statistics such as rho (r_s), phi (φ), eta (η), and the multiple correlation (R). See Chapters 21 and 22 for discussion of these statistics and effect size measures. For a more detailed description of all effect size indices we recommend Grissom and Kim (2005).

The d Family of Effect Size Measures

The *d* family focuses on the magnitude of the difference that two levels of the independent variable have on the dependent variable rather than on the strength of association. One way that the effect size (*d*) is computed is by subtracting the mean of the comparison group from the mean of the intervention group and dividing by the pooled standard deviation of both groups. There are other formulas for *d* family effect sizes, but they all express effect size in standard deviation units. Thus, a *d* of .5 means that the groups differ by one half of a standard deviation. Using *d*, effect sizes can vary from 0 to infinity, but *d* is usually less than 1. The statistics that use *d* effect sizes are discussed principally in Chapter 20.

TABLE 17.1

Interpretation of the Strength of a Relationship (Effect Sizes)

General interpretation of the strength of a relationship	The *d* family[a] *d*	The *r* family[b]		Risk potency RD (%)
		r and φ	*R*	
Much larger than typical	>1.00[c]	>.70	.70+	>52
Large or larger than typical	.80	.50	.51	43
Medium or typical	.50	.30	.36	28
Small or smaller than typical	.20	.10	.14	11

[a] *d* values can vary from 0.0 to infinity, but *d* greater than 1 is uncommon.

[b] *r* family values can vary from 0.0 to +1.0 or –1.0, but except for reliability (i.e., same concept measured twice), *r* is rarely above .70. In fact, some of these statistics (e.g., phi) have a restricted range in certain cases; that is, the maximum phi is less than 1.0.

[c] We interpret the numbers in this table as a range of values. For example, *d* greater than .90 (or less than –.90) would be described as "much larger than typical"; *d* between, say, .70 and .90 would be called "larger than typical"; and *d* between, say, .60 and .70 would be "typical to larger than typical." We interpret the other numbers in these columns similarly.

Measures of Risk Potency

These measures are based on data with both dichotomous independent and dependent variables. There are many such effect size measures, usually expressed as ratios or percentages, including *odds ratios, relative risk,* and *risk difference.* Typically, the use of these effect size measures comes from a 2 × 2 contingency table and the chi-square test, discussed in Chapter 21, or from logistic regression analysis, mentioned briefly in Chapter 22.

To summarize, the *r* effect size is most commonly used when the independent and dependent variables are continuous. The *d* effect size is used when the independent variable is dichotomous and the dependent variable is continuous. Finally, risk potency effect sizes are used when the independent and dependent variables are dichotomous (binary). However, as demonstrated in Table 17.1, most effect sizes can be converted from one family to another.

Issues About Effect Size Measures

Unfortunately, there is little agreement about which effect size to use (e.g., see Rosenthal, 2001). Although *d* is the most commonly discussed effect size measure for experimental studies in the behavioral sciences and education, odds ratios and other risk potency effect sizes are most common in medical research. The *r* family effect sizes, including *r* and *R* (multiple correlation), are common in survey research using associational research questions.

Also, there is disagreement among researchers about whether it is best to express effect size as the unsquared or squared *r* family statistic (e.g., *r* or r^2). The squared versions have been used historically because they indicate the percentage of variance in the dependent variable that can be predicted or explained from the independent variables. However, Cohen (1988) and others argued that these usually small percentages provide an underestimated impression of the strength or importance of the effect. We, like Cohen, prefer to use the unsquared statistics as our *r* family indexes, but both are common in the literature.

Although statisticians have recommended for many years that researchers report effect sizes, relatively few researchers did so before 1999 when the American Psychological

Association (APA) Task Force on Statistical Inference stated that effect sizes *always* should be reported for primary results (Wilkinson & the Task Force on Statistical Inference, 1999). The fifth edition of the *Publication Manual of the American Psychological Association* (American Psychological Association, 2001) essentially adopted this recommendation of the task force, so currently most authors of articles in behavioral science journals discuss the size of the effect as well as whether the result was statistically significant. Effect sizes should be reported because, with large samples, one can have a very weak relationship (a small effect size), but it nevertheless can be statistically significant.

Later in this chapter, we show that knowing the effect size, or at least the information necessary to compute it, is important for *meta-analysis*, which combines all of the appropriate studies. Meta-analysis includes both the statistically significant studies and those not significant to compute an effect size across studies.

Interpreting Effect Sizes

In our example in Chapter 16 with depressed adolescents and quality of life, we found that there was a statistically significant difference between the exercise intervention group and the nonexercise control group. Furthermore, we found that the confidence interval did not contain zero, another method of determining statistical significance. However, statistical significance does not tell us about the strength of the relationship between exercise and the measure of quality of life. Therefore, we should compute an effect size to estimate the strength of this relationship. For our example, we would choose the *d* effect size because the independent variable was dichotomous and the dependent variable was continuous. It turns out that the *d* value for our example is approximately .5. What does this mean? How should it be interpreted?

Cohen (1988) suggested values for large, medium, and small size effects. Note that these guidelines are based on the effect sizes *usually* found in studies in the behavioral sciences and education. Thus, they do not have absolute meaning; large, medium, and small are only relative to typical findings in these areas. For that reason, we think it would be good practice to use "larger than typical" instead of large, "typical" instead of medium, and "smaller than typical" instead of small. Cohen's guidelines will not apply to all subfields in the behavioral sciences, and they definitely will not apply to fields, designs, or contexts where the usually expected effects are either larger or smaller. It is advisable for authors to examine the research literature to see if there is information about typical effect sizes on the topic and reconsider what are said to be small, large, and typical values. Table 17.1 provides guidelines for interpreting the size of the "effect" for five common effect size measures: *d*, *r*, φ, *R*, and risk difference.

Cohen (1988) provided research examples of what he labeled small, medium, and large effects to support his suggested *d* and *r* family values. Most researchers would not consider a correlation (*r*) of .5 to be very strong because only 25% of the variance in the dependent variable is predicted. However, Cohen argued that a *d* of .8 and an *r* of .5 (which he showed to be mathematically similar) are "grossly perceptible and therefore large differences, as (for example is) the mean difference in height between 13- and 18-year-old girls" (p. 27). Cohen stated that a small effect may be difficult to detect, perhaps because it is in a less well-controlled area of research. Cohen's medium size effect is "… visible to the naked eye. That is, in the course of normal experiences, one would become aware of an average difference in IQ between clerical and semi-skilled workers …" (p. 26).

Therefore, finding a *d* effect size of .5 in our example appears to indicate a medium or typical effect size. However, we must not interpret this effect size out of context. As a researcher, knowledge about this content area *prior* to conducting our study is a requirement. Hopefully, from previous research, effect sizes have been reported either for a single study or, even more useful, in meta-analyses. Having this information allows one to describe the effect size in context. It is possible that a large research base exists that suggests that a *d* effect size of .5 is quite large relative to previous findings in this area. Thus, to interpret *d* of .5 as typical in this context would be misleading.

Effect Size and Practical Significance

Because effect size indicates the strength of the relationship, it provides some relevant information about practical significance. Although some researchers (e.g., Thompson, 2002) consider effect size measures to be an index of practical significance, we think that effect size measures are not direct indexes of the importance of a finding. As implied earlier, what constitutes a large or important effect depends on the specific area studied, the context, and the methods. Furthermore, practical significance always involves a judgment by the researcher or the consumers (e.g., clinicians, clients, teachers, or school boards) of research that takes into account such factors as cost and political considerations. For example, the effect size of taking some medication (e.g., a statin) might be relatively small for heart attacks, but the practical importance could be high because preventing heart attacks is a life-or-death matter, the costs of statins are relatively low, and side effects are relatively uncommon. On the other hand, a therapeutic or curriculum change could have a large effect size but not be practical because of high costs or extensive opposition to its implementation.

Computation of Effect Sizes

There are two important points to remember about deriving effect sizes for individual studies. First, effect size indices can be computed from significance tests when the means and standard deviations of the measures have not been provided in the study. For example, if a study compared a treatment group with a control group and reported the results of a *t* test but did not report means and standard deviations, a *d* value could be computed from *t*. Second, effect size indices can be converted from one effect size to another. For example, if the researchers chose to use the effect size *d* as their effect size index for the meta-analysis, but a few studies to be included express effect size as *r*, then *r* can be converted to *d*.

Not only does the effect size indicate the strength of the relationship between the independent variable and the dependent variable, but *it also allows investigators to combine effect sizes from different studies even if different dependent variables were used*. This is a decided advantage over confidence intervals when combing evidence such as that used in meta-analysis, which we discuss next.

Meta-Analysis

Meta-analysis is a research synthesis of a set of studies that uses a quantitative measure, effect size, to indicate the strength of relationship between the treatment or other independent variables and the dependent variables. For the health-care professions, the internationally known Cochrane Collaboration publishes systematic reviews of the effects of health-care interventions (see Antes & Oxman, 2001). Not all research syntheses are meta-analyses. Often, the purpose of a **research synthesis** is to provide a description of a subject area, illustrating the studies that have been undertaken. In other cases, the studies are too varied in nature to provide a meaningful effect size index. The focus of this section, however, is on research syntheses that result in a meta-analysis.

One advantage of performing a meta-analysis includes the computation of a summary statistic for a large number of studies. This summary statistic provides an overall estimate of the strength of relationship between independent and dependent variables. Previously, research syntheses were divided into those studies that supported a particular hypothesis and those that did not support this hypothesis, making it difficult to form a conclusion. A second advantage of meta-analysis is that it provides evidence of the reliability of a research finding. Researchers have more confidence in the findings of multiple studies than in the results of a single study. A third advantage is that it takes into account studies that failed to find statistical significance and may not have been published perhaps because of a lack of statistical power (commonly from using a reduced sample size). A fourth advantage of meta-analysis is increased external validity. Many studies that are strong in internal validity (design characteristics) do not use a representative sample of subjects. This limits the generalization of results. However, including many studies increases the variation of the sample and strengthens external validity.

Although there are many advantages to meta-analysis, there also has been considerable criticism. The most frequent criticism of meta-analysis is that it may combine "apples and oranges." Synthesizing studies that might differ on both independent and dependent variables brings into question the usefulness of the end product. Furthermore, many studies have similar independent and dependent variables but differ in the strength of design. Should these studies be combined? Another criticism concerns small sample size. Introducing a large proportion of studies with inadequate statistical power into a meta-analysis could introduce bias into the overall effect size. Kraemer, Gardner, Brooks, and Yesavage (1998) demonstrated that the effect sizes generated from underpowered studies were likely to be poor estimates of the population effect sizes. Last, and perhaps most importantly, even though the statistics used in meta-analysis are quite sophisticated, the end product will never be better than the individual studies that make up the meta-analysis. We recognize that our discussion of meta-analysis is brief and recommend the text by Lipsey and Wilson (2000) as an introduction to meta-analysis. We recommend the edited text by Cooper and Hedges (1994) for the more sophisticated reader.

Criteria for Review

Although much of the focus of meta-analysis is on statistical procedures, perhaps the most important part of a meta-analysis is the planning of inclusion and exclusion criteria for selecting a study into the meta-analysis. These inclusion and exclusion criteria are often related to internal validity and external validity. Most researchers feel that meta-analyses composed of randomized control trials (RCT) represent the gold standard for clinical research. A randomized control trial is distinguished by random assignment of participants to treatment and comparison groups, creating an unbiased selection factor. However, there are some researchers who acknowledge the strengths of an RCT and its emphasis on internal validity but remind us of the importance of strong external validity. This is summarized in the following statement by Egger, Smith, and Schneider (2001):

> The patients that are enrolled in randomized trials often differ from the average patient seen in clinical practice. Women, the elderly, and minority ethnic groups are often excluded from randomized trials. Similarly, the university hospitals typically participating in clinical trials

differ from settings where most patients are treated. In the absence of randomized trial evidence from these settings and patient groups, the results from observational database analyses may appear more relevant and more readily applicable to clinical practice. (p. 213)

Statistical Computations for Individual Studies

Number of Effect Sizes

Each study in the meta-analysis should yield at least one effect size. It is not uncommon, however, to observe studies that compare a treatment group with a control group on many measures. An effect size could be computed for each measure of the study. However, when studies have more than one measure, the measures are usually related or correlated, and computing more than one effect size yields redundant information and gives too much weight to that particular study. Therefore, the researcher should select one representative measure from the study or use a statistical method to determine a representative measure. A common statistical method is to compute a weighted mean of the related measures of the study. However, there are more sophisticated methods for computing a representative effect size when there are correlated measures that make use of the strength of the correlations.

If the researcher is convinced that some of the measures in the study are representative of different constructs (i.e., independent of each other) more than one effect size may be computed from that study.

Weights

For the most part, each study included in the meta-analysis is based on a different sample size. Studies with larger sample sizes are likely to be better estimates of the population than studies with small sample sizes. Therefore, to take sample size into consideration when the effect sizes are averaged, a weight is computed for each effect size. Effect sizes also can be weighted by other important indices, such as quality of the study.

Computation of Combined Effect Size for Studies and Related Statistics

When all studies that meet the criteria for inclusion in the meta-analysis have been coded and effect size data entered, a *combined effect size* can be computed. Frequently there is an effect size computed for each construct. In addition to a mean effect size index computed for each construct, a confidence interval, usually 95%, also is obtained. Also, analyses are performed to test for statistical significance and to test for homogeneity as discussed next.

A common method of testing for *statistical significance of the mean effect size* is called the Stouffer method and is based on adding z values. This procedure, computation of a z value, is done for each effect size in the meta-analysis. An overall z value is obtained, yielding a corresponding p value. If the p value is less than .05, a statistically significant outcome is assumed. A significant outcome indicates that the effect size is significantly different from zero.

The second statistical analysis common to meta-analysis is the **test for homogeneity of the effect size** distribution. Is the mean effect size of a particular construct representative of the population effect size? How much variability should be expected around the mean effect size? The assumption is made that if the distribution is homogeneous, then the variability around the effect size is no greater than would be expected from sampling error (Lipsey & Wilson, 2000). However, if the variability around the mean effect size is large (effect size distribution is heterogeneous), then it appears that each effect size is not estimating a common population mean. To test for a homogeneous distribution, a common test used is the Q test. If Q is statistically significant, the null hypothesis of homogeneity is rejected and the researcher assumes a heterogeneous distribution.

Follow-Up Procedures

When a test for homogeneity of effect size distribution is statistically significant, the researcher can take a number of steps to explain the heterogeneity (Lipsey & Wilson, 2000).

Assume a Random Effects Model

Before undertaking the task of computing a meta-analysis, it is important to consider what generalizations will be made from the resulting effect size estimate. There are two models from which to choose, one with fixed effects and one with random effects. In a **fixed effects model**, the researcher is attempting to generalize only to studies that are the same as those included in the meta-analysis. The effect size generated from each study would be an estimate of the population effect size except for random error due to sampling variability. In other words, if each study had an infinite sample size, all of the studies would yield identical effect sizes. In the *random effects model*, there is random error due to subject-level sampling (similar to the fixed effects model) and also random error due to study-level sampling (problems in sampling of studies into the meta-analysis.) Study-level sampling variability could be due to differences in how therapeutic procedures were carried out or due to different settings of the study. The random effects model does not propose a single underlying effect size identical in all studies; instead, the effect sizes are presumed to be randomly distributed with the average as representative of these studies. When the test for homogeneity of effect size distribution is significant, *one possibility* is that the data fit a random effects model.

Identify Systematic Variability

The most common follow-up procedure when a test for homogeneity of effect size distribution is statistically significant is to attempt to identify the variability that is contributing to the heterogeneity. Most often, the researcher has in mind, prior to the meta-analysis, certain hypotheses about which variables might contribute to variability in the mean effect size. These variables (e.g., strength of research design, sample subgroups, gender) are usually referred to as *moderator* variables. In some cases, heterogeneity may be assumed, but introduction of moderator variables fails to be related to the mean effect size.

Meta-analysis is a valuable tool for both the researcher and the clinician. Summarizing the results of many studies as an effect size index provides important strength of relationship information. Caution always should be used concerning the types of studies that went into the meta-analysis; especially, one should be aware of design issues.

Summary

The evidence-based approach emphasizes the accumulation of evidence through multiple studies investigating the same or similar hypotheses. Problems with interpretation of results based on single studies were pointed out. Three methods used with the evidence-based approach are confidence intervals, effect size, and meta-analysis. Confidence intervals provide a good estimate of the amount of sampling error and are most useful in the accumulation of evidence when similar studies use the same dependent variable. Effect size provides an index of the strength of the relationship between the independent and dependent variables, and it is particularly important for meta-analysis where the dependent variables of the studies under consideration are usually different. Confidence intervals and effect size should be presented in a single study even if one subscribes to the hypothesis testing approach. Meta-analysis uses a quantitative measure, the overall effect size, to indicate the strength of relationship between an independent variable and dependent variable derived from a number of individual studies investigating similar purposes.

Key Concepts

Confidence intervals

Effect size

Fixed effects

Homogeneity

Meta-analysis

Point estimate

Research synthesis

Random effects

Key Distinctions

Effect size measures: *d* versus *r* versus risk potency

Fixed effects versus random effects

Meta-analysis versus research synthesis

Point estimate versus confidence interval

Practical significance versus statistical significance

95% confidence interval versus .05 statistical significance

Application Problems

1. Compare and contrast the evidence-based approach with the null hypothesis statistical testing discussed in Chapter 16.

2. Explain the difference between *point estimates* and *confidence intervals,* and give an original example to illustrate this difference.

3. When would you use each of the following?
   a. *r* effect size
   b. *d* effect size
   c. Risk potency effect size

4. Discuss the advantages and disadvantages of a meta-analysis.

5. Discuss the advantages and disadvantages of research synthesis.

6. What are fixed effects? Give an original example.

7. A group of social researchers is interested in the way local newspapers address crime and people of color, both victims and perpetrators. (For example, do they report in articles more crimes involving people of color as perpetrators? Do they indicate race when the perpetrator or victim is non-White?) There are 10 researchers involved in the study, each living in a different state. Over a 3-month period (1 week each month) each researcher will review three local newspapers in his or her state (one from a large urban area, one from a mid-size market, and one serving predominantly rural areas).
   a. Is this a meta-analysis or a research synthesis? Explain your answer.
   b. What would be the best method for measuring effect size? Support your decision.
   c. Which would be more important here: practical significance or statistical significance? Explain your response.

8. It is often stated that research studies in the social sciences are underpowered. How can meta-analysis improve the situation?

18

General Design Classifications for Selection of Difference Statistical Methods

In Chapter 5 we discussed specific experimental research designs, such as the posttest-only randomized experimental design and the nonequivalent pretest–posttest control group quasi-experimental design. These specific research designs help us visualize the operations of a study, especially with respect to internal validity. In the present chapter, we look at general design classifications, which are especially *important for determining the proper statistical approach* to be used in data analysis. In Chapter 19, we divide the selection of statistics used for data analysis into two general categories: *answering difference questions* and *answering associational questions*. Knowledge of general design classification is a prerequisite for selection of appropriate statistics to answer difference questions. Within the randomized experimental, quasi-experimental, and comparative approaches, all designs must fit into one of three categories (between groups, within subjects, or mixed) that we call *general design classifications*.

General Design Classifications

Between-Groups Designs

Between-groups designs are defined as designs where each participant in the research is in *one and only one* condition or group. For example, in a study investigating the effects of teaching style on student satisfaction, there may be three groups (or conditions or levels) of the independent variable, teaching style. These conditions could be traditional, inquiry based, and a combination of the two. In a between-groups design, each participant receives only one of the three conditions or levels. If the investigator found through a power analysis that 20 participants were needed in each group, then 60 participants would be needed to carry out the research. All 60 participants would be measured only *once* on student satisfaction, the dependent variable.

Within-Subjects or Repeated-Measures Designs

The second type of general design classification, within-subjects designs, is conceptually the opposite of between-groups designs. In these designs, each participant in the research *receives or experiences all of the conditions* or levels of the independent variable to complete the study. Using the previous example of the investigation of the effects of the independent variable, teaching style, on the dependent variable, student satisfaction, there still would be three conditions or levels to the independent variable, teaching style. These conditions again are traditional teaching style, inquiry-based teaching style, and a combination of the two. In a within-subjects design, each participant would experience and be measured for student satisfaction on all three conditions or levels of the independent variable. If the researcher found through a power analysis that 20 participants were necessary for each condition, only 20 participants would be needed to carry out the research, because each participant undergoes all three conditions of the independent variable in the research. Because each participant is assessed more than once (i.e., for each condition), these designs are also referred to as *repeated-measures* designs.

Within-subjects designs have appeal due to the smaller number of participants needed and to the reduction in error variance because each participant is his or her own control. However, within-subjects designs often may be less appropriate than between-groups designs because of the possibility of **carryover effects**. If the purpose of the study is to investigate conditions that may result in a long-term or permanent change, such as learning, it is not possible for a participant to be in one condition and then to "unlearn" that condition to be in the same previous state to start the next condition. Within-subjects designs may be appropriate if the effects of order of presentation are negligible, for example, when participants are asked to evaluate several topics. Order effects can be controlled by presenting the conditions to participants in different orders (e.g., in random orders or counterbalanced so that, for example, half receive condition *A* first and half receive condition *B* first). Also, whenever a study has a pretest and a posttest we have repeated measures and a within-subject design.

Mixed Designs

The previous two classifications have only one independent variable. A mixed design has at least *one between-groups independent variable* and at least *one within-subjects independent variable*; thus, it has a minimum of two independent variables.[1] A between-groups independent variable is any independent variable that sets up between-groups conditions. A within-subjects independent variable is any independent variable that sets up within-subjects conditions. Let's return to our example of investigating the effect of the independent variable, teaching style, on the dependent variable, student satisfaction. If teaching style is a within-subjects independent variable, as in the second previous example, we would additionally need a second independent variable that is a between-groups independent variable to complete the criteria for a mixed design. The second independent variable for this example could be the type of student in the class. Student type would be a between-groups independent variable, with two levels, traditional and nontraditional. Therefore, this example satisfies the criteria for a mixed design: two independent variables, with one a within-subjects variable (teaching style) and the other independent variable a between-groups variable (student type).

More Design Considerations

Number of Independent Variables

A mixed design must have a minimum of two independent variables: a between-groups independent variable and a within-subjects independent variable. Both between-groups designs and within-subjects designs also may have more than one independent variable (usually no more than three), although the minimum requirement for each of these designs is only one independent variable. If the researcher decides to use more than one independent variable in either a between-groups design or a within-subjects design, these additional independent variables also must be between-groups independent variables (in a between-groups design) and within-subjects independent variables (in a within-subjects design). Otherwise, the design would be called a mixed design.

Type of Independent Variable

Previously, all independent variables were described as *active* (i.e., the independent variable is manipulated or given to one group but not to a second group) or *attribute* (the investigator is interested in a quality that is a characteristic of one group of people that is not characteristic of a second group of people). In a *between-groups design*, the independent variable may be *either* an active or an attribute variable. Thus, between-groups designs can be found within the randomized experimental, quasi-experimental, or comparative approach. Examples of between-groups designs where the independent variable is active include interventions such as new teaching methods, new types of therapy, and workshops. Gender, giftedness, and type of disability are examples of attribute independent variables used in between-groups designs.

On the other hand, in a *within-subjects design*, the independent variable is usually active, and the participants are given both the intervention and comparison treatment or condition. Thus, the approach is usually randomized experimental (if the *order* of the conditions is randomized) or quasi-experimental. The reason within-subjects designs do not usually have an attribute independent variable is clearer if we consider an example of the relationship between learning disability, an attribute independent variable, and reading speed. A student cannot be both learning disabled and not learning disabled at the same time. Likewise, a person cannot be both female and male, so it is not possible in these comparative approach examples to use a within-subjects design. However, in some situations, there can be a within-subjects design using an attribute independent variable.

Three Within-Subjects Designs With an Attribute Independent Variable

These designs all use the comparative approach. The first situation occurs when participants' responses from several parts of a particular instrument, such as a test or questionnaire, are compared. For example, suppose an instrument provided separate scores for motor and mental skills. If the investigator is interested in comparing participants' motor scores with their mental scores, the design becomes a within-subjects design with two levels. The independent variable is *type of skill*, an attribute with two levels. A similar example of a within-subjects design with an attribute independent variable can be seen in a questionnaire study where the participants are asked to rate several aspects of their attitudes about something. Then these aspects are compared. For example, workers' perceptions on seven-point Likert scales of the *importance* of a salary increase versus extra vacation days could be compared.

A second case in which the independent variable in a within-subjects design is not active involves **matching** participants. Matching refers to a situation in which participants are combined into pairs (or triads) to make each member of the pair as much alike as possible on some measure relevant to the dependent variable.

Although we *do not usually recommend matching of participants as a common research strategy*, there are certain circumstances where the investigator may wish to match pairs of participants. These situations usually take place when the sample size is relatively small and heterogeneous with respect to the dependent variable. For example, a researcher might use matching to study quality-of-life issues for persons with developmental disabilities. Specifically, the researcher's interest is in determining if people who work in supported employment have higher quality of life than people in sheltered work. However, previous research has indicated that there is a relationship between intelligence and quality of life (the dependent variable for the study). Therefore, to eliminate the confounding effect of intelligence, the researcher uses a matching strategy. The intelligence level is determined for all of the participants who are in supported employment and for all of the participants in sheltered work. Matches (pairs of participants) are formed, one from supported employment and one from sheltered work, based on their intelligence level. The participant with the highest intelligence level from supported employment would form the first pair with the participant with the highest intelligence level from sheltered work. The participant with the next highest intelligence level from supported employment would be paired with the participant with the next highest intelligence level from sheltered work. This matching process would continue until, for example, 20 participants have formed 10 *pairs* of participants. Now the researcher has two groups, one with participants from supported employment and one with participants from sheltered work that are matched on intelligence. All participants can be given a quality-of-life inventory to determine if there are differences between those in supported employment and those in sheltered work

The important consideration for research designs using matching is that they change into the category of *within-subjects designs*.[2] Although participants are in one, and only one, group as demonstrated in the quality-of-life study just described, the design is not a between-groups design because the groups are not independent. The investigator matched the participants before analyzing the data. To understand matching conceptually, remember the definition of a within-subjects design: Each participant undergoes all conditions of the study. In the matching design, we are trying to make each pair of participants as though they were the same participant by matching on a criterion relevant to the dependent variable. For the first pair of participants, one participant is in the supported employment condition, and the other participant is in the sheltered work condition. However, from a statistical standpoint, it is as though the same participant was in both supported employment and sheltered work conditions. The lack of statistical independence would be obvious if the pairs of participants were twins or related, as discussed in the next section.

A third within-subjects design situation in which the independent variable is not active is when the members of the groups to be compared are related in some important way. The design is said to be *a related-samples* or *paired-samples* design. Obviously, identical twins should be treated statistically as if they were the same person, so one would use a within-subjects analysis. Perhaps less obvious, the same would be true for couples, parent and child, and teacher and student. These examples would be treated statistically as within-subjects designs. The reason that this classification as a within-subjects design is important is that different types of inferential statistics are appropriate for between-groups and within-subjects designs, as we see in Chapter 19.

Change Over Time (or Trials) as an Independent Variable

In within-subjects designs there can be a third type (neither active nor attribute) of independent variable, *change over time* or *trials*. This third type of independent variable is extremely important in randomized experimental and quasi-experimental designs because pretest and posttest are two levels of this type of independent variable. *Longitudinal studies*, in which the same participants are assessed at several time periods/ages, are another important case where change over time is the independent variable.

Consider the following study using a pretest–posttest control group design as described in Chapter 5. Participants are randomly assigned (R) to one of two groups: an intervention group (E), which receives a new curriculum; and a control group (C), which receives the old curriculum. Participants are measured prior to the intervention (O_1) and after the intervention (O_2), perhaps at the end of the semester. The design can be viewed as follows:

$$R \quad E: \quad O_1 \quad X \quad O_2$$
$$R \quad C: \quad O_1 \quad \sim X \quad O_2$$

It is a mixed design because there are two independent variables: a between-groups independent variable and a within-subjects independent variable. The independent variable, type of curriculum, is a between-groups independent variable because each participant experiences only one of the two curriculums. The other independent variable in this study, change over time, is a within-subjects independent variable because participants within each group were measured more than once in the study. This independent variable is referred to as change over time because the second measurement period took place at a later time than the first measurement period. Change over time is considered a third type rather than an active independent variable because change over time cannot be actively manipulated; the posttest always comes after the pretest.

Diagramming Designs

Between-groups, within-subjects, and mixed designs can be diagrammed to help visualize what is happening in the research. In addition, the method of diagramming that we recommend (based on Winer, 1962) *depicts how the data are entered into the computer* for statistical analyses.

Between-Groups Designs

These designs always have the data for a single subject or group placed *horizontally* into a row on the page and in the computer spreadsheet. Suppose that we have a between-groups design with two independent variables, teaching style and gender. Each independent variable has two levels (teaching style, traditional or inquiry based; and gender, male or female). Notice that we have simplified the diagram somewhat by including the names of the levels but not the variable name. Therefore, a diagram of the design would be as follows, assuming 40 participants were assigned to the four groups:

Traditional	Female (Group 1, $n = 10$)	O
	Male (Group 2, $n = 10$)	O
Inquiry based	Female (Group 3, $n = 10$)	O
	Male (Group 4, $n = 10$)	O

The four groups are as follows: (1) Traditional Female; (2) Traditional Male; (3) Inquiry-Based Female; and (4) Inquiry-Based Male. In this example, each participant in each group is observed or measured (O) once on the dependent variable, perhaps some measure of achievement.

Why don't we put the diagram into blocks as follows?

		Gender	
		Female	*Male*
	Traditional	(*n* = 10)	(*n* = 10)
Teaching Style			
	Inquiry based	(*n* = 10)	(*n* = 10)

One reason we don't use the block diagram method illustrated here is that it works well only as long as there are no more than two independent variables. When there are more than two independent variables, the third independent variable would have to be visualized on a third dimension. More importantly, the block diagram also does not represent the way the data would be entered into the computer for proper analysis. The following diagram partially illustrates the way the previous data would be set up for entering into the computer. (Only the first and last participants in each group of 10 are shown). Notice the similarity to the previous recommended diagram:

Participant No.	Teaching Style	Gender	Achievement
1	1	1	53
10	1	1	75
11	1	2	67
20	1	2	77
21	2	1	82
30	2	1	75
31	2	2	86
40	2	2	92

A third between-groups independent variable also can be diagrammed. Using our recommended format, let's add the independent variable age, with two levels, young and old. Since eight groups are needed to complete the design, we would need 80 participants to have 10 in each group. The diagram is as follows:

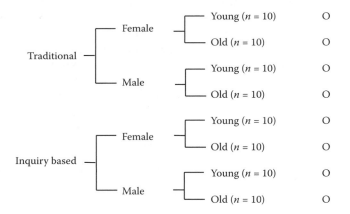

Within-Subjects Designs

In contrast to between-groups designs, within-subjects designs always are diagrammed using columns, and the data are entered into the computer that way for analysis. Suppose that we have a study that uses a within-subjects design. There are two independent variables, both within-subjects independent variables. The first independent variable is *change over time*, with two levels, pretest and posttest. The second independent variable is our teaching style independent variable, with two levels, traditional and inquiry based. However, because we have decided to make both independent variables be within-subjects independent variables, each participant must undergo all conditions of the experiment.

Note that the dependent variable (O) scores are what are entered in each column. The design is diagrammed as follows:

	Pretest Inquiry based (Condition 1)	Posttest Inquiry based (Condition 2)	Pretest Traditional (Condition 3)	Posttest Traditional (Condition 4)
($n = 10$)	O	O	O	O

In the design of this study, only 10 participants are needed to complete the study. However, each participant must undergo all four conditions.[3] As discussed earlier, this design is susceptible to carryover effects; the second teaching style may be affected by the first. Therefore, for half the participants, the researcher would probably present the traditional style first and then the inquiry style.

Mixed Designs

This type of design is diagrammed by combining both the between-groups design and the within-subjects design. A common example of a mixed design would be a research study to evaluate the effects of a new curriculum. The between-groups independent variable would be the curriculum, with two levels, new curriculum and old curriculum. The within-subjects independent variable would be time, with two levels, before the evaluation and after the evaluation. Because the diagram is relatively simple, we have included the variable name as well as the levels:

	Type of curriculum	Pretest	Posttest
(Group 1, $n = 10$)	1	O	O
(Group 2, $n = 10$)	2	O	O

Notice that each participant is in only one group, but all participants in each group are measured before the intervention and after the intervention.

Describing the Various Types of Design

Within the methods section of a research paper often there is a subsection designated *Design* or *Design/Analysis*. The purpose of this section is to identify the independent variables, dependent variables, and design in randomized experimental, quasi-experimental, and comparative studies. Because most journals will not allow for the space to diagram the design, the appropriate procedure is to describe the design in words and numbers. Designs are usually described in terms of (1) the general type of design (between groups, within subjects, or mixed); (2) the number of independent variables; and (3) the number of levels within each independent variable.

Single-Factor Designs

In either a between-groups design or a within-subjects design, if the design has only one independent variable it should be described as a *single-factor design*. (Factor is another name for independent variable.) For example, a between-groups design with one independent variable and four levels would be described as a single-factor design with four levels. If the same design was a within-subjects design with four levels, then it would be described as a single-factor repeated-measures design with four levels. Note that "between groups" is not stated directly in the first example, but it is implied because there is no mention in that example of repeated measures.

Between-Groups Factorial Designs

When there is more than one independent variable, then the levels of *each* independent variable become important in the description of the design. For example, suppose a design has three between-groups independent variables, and the first independent variable has two levels, the second independent variable has three levels, and the third independent variable has two levels. The design is written as a 2 × 3 × 2 factorial design. (Factorial means two or more independent variables.) Again, between-groups is not explicitly mentioned but is implied because there is no mention of repeated measures, as in a within-subjects design description. Since the design is a between-groups design, the number of groups needed to carry out the study is 2 multiplied by 3 multiplied by 2, or 12 groups.

Within-Subjects Factorial Designs

On the other hand, if the design is a within-subjects design with two independent variables, each with two levels, then it is described as a 2 × 2 within-subjects design or, more commonly, a 2 × 2 factorial design with repeated measures on both factors.

Mixed Designs

Such a design might have two between-groups independent variables with three and four levels, respectively, and have one within-subjects independent variable with two levels. It would be described as a 3 × 4 × 2 factorial design with repeated measures on the third factor.

Remember, when describing a design, that *each* independent variable is given one number, the number of *levels* for that variable. Thus, a design description with three numbers (e.g., 2 × 4 × 3) has *three* independent variables or factors, which have two, four, and three levels, respectively. A single factor design is specifically classified or described in words, as previously, and not with numerals and ×'s. Note that the *dependent* variable is *not* part of the design description, so it is not considered in this section. Table 18.1 provides examples of how to describe the between, within, and mixed designs for studies with one, two, and three independent variables.

TABLE 18.1

Examples of General Design Classifications

Single factor	**One independent variable**
Between	Single-factor design with ___ levels
Within	Single-factor repeated-measures design with ___ levels
Mixed	NA
Two factor	**Two independent variables**
Between	___ × ___ factorial design
Within	___ × ___ design with repeated measures on both factors
Mixed	___ × ___ (mixed) design with repeated measures
Three factor	**Three independent variables**
Between	___ × ___ × ___ factorial design
Within	___ × ___ × ___ design with repeated measures on all factors
Mixed	___ × ___ × ___ design with repeated measures on last (or last two) factors

Note: The dependent variable is not part of the design classification and, thus, is not mentioned. The number of levels for an independent variable is inserted in each blank.

Design Classifications of Specific Research Designs

Specific research designs are important for assessing internal validity; however, they do not help to determine selection of the proper statistical analysis. Any specific research designs also can be described using the general design classifications discussed in the previous section and Table 18.1. We provide three examples of how specific research designs fit into general design classifications: (1) the Solomon four-group design; (2) the pretest–posttest nonequivalent control group design; and (3) a within-subjects randomized experimental design.

Solomon Four-Group Design

Of particular interest is how this design, described in Chapter 5, fits into our general design classification of between-groups, within-subjects, or mixed designs. A first guess is that it seems to be a mixed design because at least two of the groups receive a pretest and posttest. However, closer examination of this design indicates that the investigator is really not interested in the pretest *scores*, only in the *effects that taking a pretest* has on the posttest. Therefore, the design is actually a between-groups design with two independent variables. Specifically, the design is a 2 × 2 factorial design. The two independent variables are pretest (yes or no) and intervention (yes or no), each with two levels. The design can be seen schematically as follows:

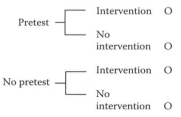

Pretest–Posttest Nonequivalent Comparison Group Design

This specific research design fits the general design classification for a mixed design. There are two independent variables. One independent variable is a type of intervention, a between-groups independent variable with two levels, treatment and no treatment. The second independent variable is change over time, a within-subjects independent variable with two levels, pretest and posttest. The design can be seen as follows:

	Pretest	I.V.	Posttest
Treatment	O	X	O
No treatment	O	~X	O

Notice that the randomized experimental pretest–posttest control group design has the same general design classification, mixed, as the pretest–posttest nonequivalent comparison group design, a quasi-experimental approach.

Within-Subjects Randomized Experiment

This design was also called a *crossover design* in Chapter 5. In the simplest case, this design has two levels and can be shown as follows:

	First	Posttest 1	Second	Posttest 2
R Group 1	X	O	~X	O
R Group 2	~X	O	X	O

The participants are randomly assigned either to group 1, which receives the experimental condition first and then the control condition, or to group 2, which receives the control condition and then the experimental. Remember that this design can have problems if there are carryover effects from the first condition to the second. The general design classification is considered to be mixed with change over time as a within-subjects independent variable and group (1 or 2) as a between-groups independent variable.

Figure 18.1, which is an expanded version of Figure 5.1, shows in the last column how each specific research design fits the general design classification. This classification (between groups, within subjects, or mixed) determines, in good part, the appropriate type of difference inferential statistic to use, as shown in the next chapter. For example, the one-group pretest–posttest *within-subjects design* would be analyzed using the paired samples *t* test rather than the independent samples *t* test, which would be used to analyze *between-groups designs* such as the posttest-only designs shown in Figure 18.1. Both *t* tests are discussed in Chapter 20. The two-factor Solomon four-group design and the mixed designs shown in Figure 18.1 could be analyzed with one of several two-way analyses of variance (ANOVAs). Chapter 19 describes which ANOVA is appropriate to use.

Summary

This chapter described the general design classifications of between-groups, within-subjects, and mixed designs. Remember that in *between-groups designs*, each participant is in only one

	Assign.	Grp.	Pre.	I.V.	Post.	Class.
Poor quasi-experimental designs						
One-group posttest-only design	NR	E:		X	O	None
One-group pretest-posttest design	NR	E:	O	X	O	Within
Posttest-only nonequivalent groups design	NR	E:		X	O	Between
	NR	C:		~X	O	
Quasi-experimental designs						
Pretest-posttest nonequivalent	NR	E:	O	X	O	Mixed
comparison-group designs	NR	C:	O	~X	O	
Single-group time-series designs						
With temporary treatment	NR	E:	OOO	X	OOO	Within
With continuous treatment	NR	E:	OOO	XOXO	XOXO	Within
Multiple-group time-series designs						
With temporary treatment	NR	E:	OOO	X	OOO	Mixed
	NR	C:	OOO	~X	OOO	
With continuous treatment	NR	E:	OOO	XOXO	XOXO	Mixed
	NR	C:	OOO	O O	O O	
Randomized experimental designs						
Posttest-only control-group design	R	E:		X	O	Between
	R	C:		~X	O	
Pretest-posttest control group design	R	E:	O	X	O	Mixed
	R	C:	O	~X	O	
Solomon 4-group design	R	E_1:	O	X	O	Between
	R	E_2:		X	O	2-factor
	R	C_1:	O	~X	O	
	R	C_2:		~X	O	
Randomized experimental design with	M R	E:		X	O	Within
matching	M R	C:		~X	O	

		Order		Post 1		Post 2	
Within-subjects or crossover design	R	E_1	X	O	~X	O	Mixed
	R	E_2	~X	O	X	O	

Notes: Assign. = assignment of subjects to groups (NR = nonrandom, R = random, M R = matched then randomly assigned). Grp. = group or condition (E: = experimental, C: = control or comparison). Pre. = pretest (O = an observation or measurement; a blank means there was no pretest for that group). I.V. = active independent variable (X = intervention, ~X = control or other treatment). Post. = posttest (O = a posttest observation or measure). Class. = classification (between, within, or mixed).

FIGURE 18.1
Classification of specific designs for experiments and quasi-experiments.

group or condition. In *within-subjects/repeated-measures designs,* on the other hand, each participant receives all the conditions or levels of the independent variable. In *mixed designs,* there is at least one between-groups independent variable and at least one within-subjects independent *variable. In classifying the design, the dependent variables are not considered.*

The diagrams, classifications, and descriptions presented in this chapter are for difference questions, using the randomized experimental, quasi-experimental, and comparative approaches to research. Appropriate classification and description of the design are crucial for choosing the appropriate inferential statistic.

Key Concepts

Between-groups designs
Carryover effects
Change over time
Matching
Mixed designs
Solomon four-group design
Within-subjects designs

Key Distinctions

Active versus attribute independent variable in within-subjects designs
Between-groups designs versus within-subjects designs versus mixed designs
General design classifications versus specific experimental and quasi-experimental designs
Single-factor versus factorial designs

Application Problems

1. Explain why the independent variables for a within-subjects design are not usually attribute independent variables.
2. Is change over time an active or attribute independent variable? Why? How used?
3. Give an example of a within-subjects/repeated-measure design, and diagram it.

For examples 4–7 answer the following:

    a. Identify the independent variables. For each, state whether it is active, attribute, or change over time

    b. Identify the dependent variables.

    c. Diagram the design.

    d. Identify the design classification (e.g., 4 × 4 factorial).

4. A researcher wanted to know if type of exercise and type of individual influences a person's willingness to stay in an exercise program. The researcher recruited 300 participants. The study included people considered young (20–35), middle-aged (36–50) and older (51–70); 150 were men, and 150 were women. Additionally, of the 300 participants, 100 were African American, 100 were Caucasian/Non-Hispanic, and 100 were Hispanic. The participants were randomly assigned to three different exercise regimes: (1) running in circles around a track; (2) swimming laps at an indoor pool; or (3) riding a bike in the Rocky Mountains. The regimes lasted for 2 months. At the end of the 2 months, the participants all completed the Willingness to Continue Exercising Regime Scale.

5. A humanities professor who was going to lead a year-long study abroad program wondered if travel experience had any impact on students' ability to understand and embrace diversity in others. At the beginning of the school year the professor gave all the students the Multicultural Acceptance Scale. This scale also was given at the end of the year when the students returned from abroad and 2 years later.

6. A dog trainer was interested in knowing whether her new aversive approach to obedience training was effective. She divided her new clientele into three different groups. The first group received traditional dog training, wherein good behavior is rewarded with praise and treats. The second group received the new aversive training, wherein nonconforming behavior was punished with temporary removal of water and food, slaps on the nose, and loud yelling by the trainer and the owner. Participants in the third group were the control and did not get any training for their dogs. Before the training and 3 months later the trainer rated the dogs from all three groups on a dog obedience scale.

7. An investigator was interested in two different cues that might be used in the reproduction of movement: (1) the initial position of the movement; and (2) the speed of the movement. In addition, she was also interested in how age affects reproduction of movement. Three groups of participants (40 participants per group) were in the study. These three groups were 7-year-olds, 11-year-olds, or adults. Each group was further randomly assigned to one of four conditions: (1) a fast movement with the initial position the same; (2) a slow movement with the initial position the same; (3) a fast movement with the initial position different; and (4) a slow movement with the initial condition different. The researcher measured the distance error from the target and the angle error.

Notes

1. Some introductory research design texts describe a mixed design as a design that has at least one active independent variable and one attribute independent variable. The problem with this characterization of a mixed design is that it could be confused with the mixed design as defined in this book, and then it would be incorrectly analyzed statistically because both independent variables are between-groups variables, which requires a different type of analysis of variance (ANOVA) than a mixed (between and within) design. To avoid confusion, a between-groups design with one active independent variable and one attribute independent variable could be referred to as a *generalized randomized blocks design* (Kirk, 1982). However, the proper data analysis does not distinguish between active or attribute independent variables, only that they are between-groups independent variables.

2. A name given to designs that involve matching subjects into pairs (or triads) and then randomly assigning one member of each pair to a particular group is a *randomized blocks design*. However, statistically these designs are analyzed similar to within-subjects designs.

3. In some cases the posttest for the first level (inquiry based) serves as the pretest for the second level (traditional) of one independent variable, necessitating only three observations.

19

Selection of Appropriate Statistical Methods: Integration of Design and Analysis

Choosing the proper statistical analysis may seem like a difficult task, considering the large number of possible choices. However, this task should be easier with knowledge of independent and dependent variables, research approaches, design classifications, and scales or levels of measurement. This chapter presents a series of decision steps and four tables that will help in making an appropriate choice of an inferential statistic. However, before presenting the decision tree and describing how to use the statistical selection tables, we review the concepts that are necessary for selecting inferential statistics.

Review of Concepts Necessary for Selecting Inferential Statistics

Research Approaches and Questions

In Chapter 4, we discussed five research approaches and three types of research questions. Figure 19.1, which is the same as Figure 4.1, is the key figure that presents the relationships among the five specific approaches, the three types of research questions and three types of statistics: difference inferential, associational inferential, and descriptive.

Difference Questions

The first three approaches (experimental, quasi-experimental, and comparative) all compare groups and test difference questions/hypotheses, as in our example of depressed adolescent teenagers and exercise (Chapter 16). These three approaches usually use the same types of statistics, which we call *difference inferential statistics*. Remember that difference statistics and questions are used to compare a few groups (e.g., males versus females, experimental versus control, or three curriculums) in terms of each group's average scores on the dependent variable (e.g., an achievement measure).

Associational Questions

Associational questions use the associational approach to research and what we call *associational inferential statistics*. The statistics in this group examine the association or correlation between two or more *variables*. If there is a positive association, persons who have high scores on one variable tend to have high scores on the second variable; those with low scores tend to be low on both variables. That is, high scores are associated with high, low with low, and medium with medium. On the other hand, if there is a negative association between the two variables, those with *low* scores on variable one tend to have *high* scores on variable two and vice versa. That is low scores are associated with high. If there is no

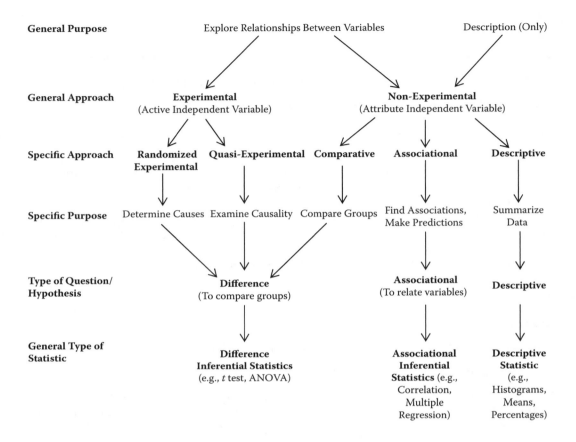

FIGURE 19.1
Schematic diagram showing how the general type of statistic and hypothesis/question used in a study corresponds to the purposes and the approach.

association, a prediction cannot be made of a person's score on the second variable from knowing the first. People who score high on the first variable might be high or low or medium on the second variable.

Descriptive questions and statistics were discussed in Chapter 10, so they will not be discussed in this chapter. It is worth noting that in several situations there *may be more than one appropriate statistical analysis*. One might assume, since the statistical formulas are precise mathematically, that this same precision applies to the choice of a statistical test. As we shall see, unfortunately, this is not always true.

Independent and Dependent Variables

We discussed variables in depth in Chapter 3. The independent variable is a *presumed* cause of changes in the dependent variable, although the moderate and weak quasi-experimental, comparative, and associational approaches do not provide good evidence about causes. We distinguished, in Chapter 3, between active/manipulated independent variables and attribute independent variables. Although this distinction is important for deciding whether the independent variable is a cause, it is relevant only for certain complex associational statistics (e.g., hierarchical multiple regression), which are, for the most part, beyond the scope of this book. Thus, we do not mention active and attribute independent variables again in this chapter. What *is* relevant for selecting statistics is the number of independent variables, levels within these independent variables, and measurement scale of the dependent variable.

Number of Independent Variables

The first question to be asked is whether there is one or more than one independent variable. If there is only one independent variable we call the design *basic (or single-factor* design, if answering a difference question). If there is more than one independent variable, the statistics are called *complex* (or *factorial* in the case of difference questions).

Number of Levels of the Independent Variable

A difference question is indicated when the independent variable has a few (i.e., two to four) levels. For example, do males and females or experimental and control groups differ on the dependent variable? However, if the independent variable has more than four *unordered* (nominal) levels one would usually still ask a difference question and compare the groups. For example, do six ethnic groups differ? Remember that there have to be at least two levels, or there is not a variable but rather a constant.

When the independent variable has five or more *ordered* levels, an associational question is asked, and an associational inferential statistic is used. Thus, if the independent variable is continuous (an infinite number of ordered levels within some range) or approximates a continuous variable (our guideline is five or more ordered levels), associational statistics are used. However, one can also ask an associational question when the independent variable is nominal. It should be noted that two variable associational inferential statistics (e.g., Pearson correlation) are *bidirectional*, so statisticians would say that there is no independent variable. However, because researchers usually have a causal relationship in mind, we suggest identifying one of the variables as the independent variable.

The *dependent variable* is also important for the appropriate choice of an inferential statistic. The primary issue is the level of measurement of the dependent variable, which we discuss following design classifications.

Design Classifications

Our discussion of design classifications in Chapter 18 is important background for selecting an appropriate statistic. The key issue for selecting an appropriate statistic is whether the classification is between, within, or mixed. These classifications apply only to the randomized experimental, quasi-experimental, and comparative approaches (i.e., to difference questions).

Between-Groups Versus Within-Subjects Single-Factor Designs

With one independent variable the design must be either between groups or within subjects because it takes at least two independent variables to have a mixed design. To use basic difference statistics, the information needed is whether the two or more groups or levels of the independent variable are independent of each other (a between-groups design) or related (within-subjects/repeated-measures designs).[1] In between-groups designs, each participant is in only one group, and participants are neither matched in pairs or triads nor related in some way such as couples, parent and child, or teacher and student(s). In within-subjects/repeated-measures designs, the participants are either assessed two or more times (repeated measures) or else two (or even three or more) of them are matched or paired up in some meaningful way. For statistical purposes, their scores are not independent (i.e., they are said to be related or correlated samples). These within-subjects designs use different statistics from the between-groups designs, as we will see.

Classification in Factorial Designs

When two or more independent variables, are present, there are three possible design classifications: all between groups, all within subjects, and mixed (between and within). It is important to understand this distinction to choose the appropriate complex difference statistic. As stated already, in between-groups designs, the *groups are independent*; each participant is assessed only once on any given dependent variable. In within-subjects designs, each person is assessed in every condition and so has a score in every cell in the design. In mixed designs, such as the pretest–posttest control group design, there is at least one between-groups variable and at least one within-subjects variable.

Levels of Measurement

For appropriate statistical selection, level of measurement is also important. Remember that *normally distributed* data were the highest level discussed in Chapter 10. Normal distributions are also an assumption of parametric statistics such as the *t* test, analysis of variance (ANOVA), and Pearson correlation. *Ordinal* data have three or more levels ordered from low to high (often ranks) but with unequal spaces between levels, and, more importantly for statistical selection, the data are not normally distributed. In contrast, *nominal* data have three or more *unordered* levels or categories.

For difference statistics, the variable whose level of measurement matters is the *dependent variable*. The independent variable can be nominal (e.g., ethnic groups) or ordered (e.g., low, medium, and high) but usually has fewer than five ordered levels. For associational statistics, the level of measurement for both or all variables needs to be determined.

Dichotomous variables form a special case as discussed in Chapter 10. Although dichotomous variables are in many ways like nominal variables, they can be used, especially as independent or predictor variables in multiple regression, as if they were normally distributed variables.

Statistical Assumptions

Every statistical test is based on certain assumptions. There are three general assumptions that need to be addressed for the use of parametric statistics (i.e., *t* test, ANOVA, Pearson correlation, multiple regression). There are more assumptions for complex statistics, which are beyond the scope of this book. One general assumption for parametric statistics assumes that the dependent variable comes from a *population* that is normally distributed. This is referred to as the assumption of **normality**. Often, there can be large violations of this assumption before the results are distorted; thus, the dependent variables used in parametric analyses only have to be approximately normally distributed.

A second assumption for parametric tests is that the variances of the groups must be equal. This assumption is referred to as **homogeneity of variance**. This assumption can be violated to some degree. However, when there are also unequal sample sizes, significantly unequal variances can lead to Type I errors (rejecting the null hypothesis when it should not be rejected), especially if the sample size of one group is exceptionally larger than the other groups. Some statistical programs (e.g., SPSS) have built-in corrections for violation of this assumption for some statistics. If one or both of these assumptions (normality or, especially, homogeneity) are *markedly* violated then the equivalent ordinal nonparametric test should be used.

The assumption of **independence** means that all of the participants within a particular group must be independent of each other. In other words, the score from one participant must not be influenced by or be contingent on the score of another individual. This assumption must *not* be violated when using either parametric or nonparametric inferential statistics. Remember that in between-groups designs, the participants in each group have to be independent (not matched or related) to those in the other groups.

Selection of Appropriate Inferential Statistics

How to Use the Statistical Selection Tables

Figure 19.2, as well as the following text, provides one method that can be used to help select the appropriate statistical test. The first step is to decide whether the research question or hypothesis is a *difference* one (i.e., compares groups) or an *associational* one (i.e., relates variables). To help decide whether to use a difference or associational statistic, we recommend that if the independent or predictor variable has five or more *ordered* levels/categories, the question should be considered an associational one.[2] If the *independent* variable has two to four categories it is usually better to treat the question as a difference one. However, if the independent variable has five or more nominal (i.e., *unordered* levels); one would usually

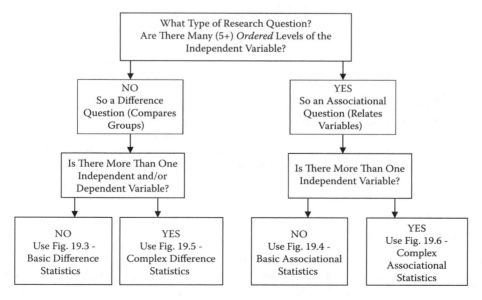

FIGURE 19.2
A decision tree to decide how to select the appropriate statistic.

	Scale of Measurement of **Dependent** Variable ⬇	COMPARE ⬇	One Factor or Independent Variable with 2 Categories or Levels/Groups/Samples		One Independent Variable 2 or More Categories or Levels or Groups	
			Independent Samples or Groups (**Between**)	Repeated Measures or Related Samples (**Within**)	Independent Samples or Groups (**Between**)	Repeated Measures or Related Samples (**Within**)
Parametric Statistics	Dependent Variable Approximates **Normal** Distribution Data and Assumptions Not Markedly Violated	MEANS	INDEPENDENT SAMPLES *t* TEST or ONEWAY ANOVA Ch. 20	PAIRED SAMPLES *t* TEST Ch. 20	ONEWAY ANOVA Ch. 20	REPEATED MEASURES ANOVA Ch. 20
Non Parametric Statistics	Dependent Variable Clearly **Ordinal** (Ranked) Data or Assumptions Markedly Violated	MEDIANS OR RANKS	MANN-WHITNEY Ch. 20	WILCOXON or SIGN TEST Ch. 20	KRUSKAL-WALLIS Ch. 20	FRIEDMAN Ch. 20
	Dependent Variable **Nominal** (Categorical) Data	COUNTS	CHI SQUARE Ch. 21 or FISHER'S EXACT TEST	MCNEMAR Ch. 20	CHI SQUARE Ch. 21	COCHRAN Q TEST

Notes: To select the appropriate statistic, locate a box based on a) the type of question, b) design, and c) scale of measurement. It is acceptable to use statistics which are in the box(es) **below** the appropriate statistic, but there is usually some loss of information and power. **It is not acceptable to use statistics above the appropriate box.**

• Related samples designs are also called repeated measures, matched or paired groups and are within-subjects designs
• Chi square tests for the independence of two variables. Frequency data or counts of the number of Ss in each cell or category are used rather than raw scores and means.
• ANOVA is Analysis of Variance.

FIGURE 19.3
Selection of an appropriate inferential statistic for basic, single-factor, difference questions or hypotheses (for experimental, quasi-experimental, and comparative approaches).

use difference inferential statistics and Figure 19.3. Difference questions lead to Figure 19.3 or Figure 19.5, and associational questions lead to Figure 19.4 or Figure 19.6.

The second step is to decide how many variables there are in the question. If there is only one independent variable, use Figure 19.3 or Figure 19.4, depending on how the first question was answered. If there is more than one independent (or dependent) variable in this analysis, use Figure 19.5 or Figure 19.6 depending on whether the research question is a difference or association question.

Basic Difference Statistics

If the question involves a *basic* or *single-factor* difference question, use Figure 19.3. To do so determine (1) the level of measurement of the *dependent* variable and whether assumptions are markedly violated; (2) how many levels/groups/samples are in the independent variable; and (3) whether the design is between groups or within subjects. The answers to these questions lead to a specific box and statistic in Figure 19.3. Notice that a decision

Level (scale) of Measurement of **Both Variables** ↓	RELATE ↓	Two Variables or Scores for the Same or Related Subjects
Variables are Both Normal Data and Other Assumptions Not Markedly Violated	SCORES	PEARSON *r* Ch. 21 or BIVARIATE REGRESSION Ch. 22
Both Variables at Least Ordinal Data	RANKS	SPEARMAN (Rho) or KENDALL'S TAU Ch. 21
One or Both Variables are Nominal Data	COUNTS	PHI Ch. 21 or CRAMER'S V

Note. As with Fig. 19.3, it is acceptable to use a statistic in a box below the appropriate statistic, but there will be some loss of power to detect an association from the top row to the second and a lot of loss from the second to the third row. It is **not acceptable** to use an ordinal or normally distributed statistic if even one variable is nominal.

FIGURE 19.4
Selection of an appropriate inferential statistic for basic, two-variable, associational questions or hypotheses (for the associational approach).

Dependent Variable(s) ↓	Two or More Independent Variables		
	All Between Groups	**All Within Subjects**	**Mixed (Between & Within)**
One Normally Distributed Dependent Variable	Factorial ANOVA Ch. 22	Factorial ANOVA with Repeated Measures on all Factors Ch. 22	Factorial ANOVA With Repeated Measures on Last or Last 2 Factors Ch. 22
Ordinal Dependent Variable	None Common	None Common	None Common
Nominal Dependent Variable	Log Linear	None Common	None Common
Several Normally Distributed Dependent Variables	MANOVA	MANOVA with Repeated Measures on all Factors	MANOVA With Repeated Measures on Last or Last Several Factors

FIGURE 19.5
Selection of the appropriate complex (more than one independent or dependent variable) statistic to answer difference questions/hypotheses (for the experimental, quasi-experimental, or comparative approaches).

that must be made is whether the independent variable has two versus two *or more* levels of the independent variable. One might ask why we bother to have a separate category for two levels when "two or more" includes two. Part of the answer is that the popular *t* test can be used only when there are two levels; the second part is that the *t* test can be used with a directional (one-tailed) hypothesis, whereas the alternative statistic, one-way

One Dependent Variable ↓	Several Independent Variables		
	All Normally Distributed	**Some Normal Some Dichotomous**	**All Dichotomous**
Normally Distributed (Continuous)	MULTIPLE REGRESSION Ch. 22	MULTIPLE REGRESSION Ch. 22	MULTIPLE REGRESSION Ch. 22
Dichotomous	DISCRIMINANT ANALYSIS Ch. 22	LOGISTIC REGRESSION Ch. 22	LOGISTIC REGRESSION Ch. 22

FIGURE 19.6
Selection of the appropriate complex associational statistic for the purpose of predicting a single dependent/ outcome variable from several independent variables.

ANOVA, is always two tailed. There is more on this topic in Chapter 20. Most of the statistics in Figure 19.3 are discussed, at least briefly, in Chapter 20. However, we have chosen to discuss chi-square in Chapter 21, and the Cochran Q test is not discussed because it is seldom used.

Remember that if assumptions of the parametric test (normality and homogeneity) are markedly violated, one should use the equivalent, ordinal nonparametric statistic (e.g., Mann-Whitney instead of the independent samples *t* test) or a corrected parametric test. The ordinal, nonparametric alternatives (used with highly skewed data) are listed right below the parametric test in Figure 19.3. Little power is lost using these tests so it is probably wise to use them when assumptions are markedly violated. It would also be legitimate to use the statistics in the bottom row (e.g., chi-square) if one had ordinal or nominal/ unordered data, but there is a major loss of power in doing that so it is not considered good practice. A principle in using Figure 19.3 and Figure 19.4 is that it is okay to use a statistic lower down a given column; a little power is lost going from the top to the second (ordinal) row. A lot of power is lost going from the second to the third row in the column. It is a serious error to use the wrong column—that is, within instead of between or vice versa. Another absolute violation that will produce meaningless results is to use a statistic from the top two rows in Figure 19.3 and Figure 19.4 (e.g., a *t* test or Mann-Whitney U) when one has a *nominal* (unordered) dependent variable. That is definitely wrong!

Basic Associational Statistics

If a *basic*, two-variable, associational question is asked, use Figure 19.4. Which row is used depends on *both* variables. If both are at least approximately normally distributed (and other assumptions are met), the Pearson product moment correlation would be used. If both variables are at least ordered and parametric assumptions are markedly violated, the Spearman rank-order correlation, Rho, would be used. If one or both of the variables are nominal, phi (if both variables have two levels, a 2 × 2 cross-tabulation) or Cramer's V for a larger cross-tabulation would be used. Figure 19.4 shows only two (phi and Cramer's V) of many associational statistics that provide information about the strength of the association between two variables, when one or both are nominal variables (e.g., ethnic group and voting preference). The use of nominal associational statistics is relatively uncommon in the literature so we do not discuss them in detail, but phi is discussed in Chapter 21. The Pearson, Spearman, and Kendall's correlations also are discussed in Chapter 21.

Complex Difference Statistics

If you ask a complex difference question (three or more variables) appropriate statistics are identified using Figure 19.5. To select the appropriate statistic, first decide whether the design classification is between groups, within subjects, or mixed. Then if there is one dependent variable and it is approximately normally distributed, the choice is one of three factorial ANOVAs. These ANOVAs are similar but have different formulas so it is important to know which one to use. Each of these three types of factorial ANOVA and analysis of covariance (ANCOVA) are discussed in Chapter 22.

Notice that, unfortunately, no common ordinal statistics are equivalent to the factorial ANOVAs. Log linear analysis is sometimes seen in the literature but is not discussed in this book. It is similar to a factorial ANOVA for nominal/categorical data and is somewhat similar to a complex chi-square.

The bottom row of Figure 19.5 shows three multivariate analyses of variance (MANOVAs) that parallel the three factorial ANOVAs but are used when one wants to analyze several normally distributed dependent variables together instead of one at a time. MANOVA also can be used instead of several one-way ANOVAs when there is one independent variable (single-factor design) and several dependent variables that are to be analyzed in one analysis rather than separately. Because of its complexity we do not discuss MANOVA further in this book.

Complex Associational Statistics

If a complex associational question (two or more *independent* variables) is asked, appropriate statistics are identified using Figure 19.6.

These complex associational statistics are discussed in Chapter 22. Notice that the left-hand column of Figure 19.6 is different from the other three tables in that ordinal and nominal levels of measurement are not listed. There are no common ordinal statistics similar to these. The top row lists multiple regression, which is used for cases in which two or more independent variables are used to predict a normally distributed dependent variable. Notice that multiple regression can be used both when the *independent* variables are normally distributed and when they are dichotomous. The assumption of normality for multiple regression is more complex than previously indicated; it would be helpful to check advanced statistics textbooks for discussion of the assumptions of multiple regression and other complex statistics. When to use discriminant analysis and logistic regression are indicated in Figure 19.6. Discriminant analysis is sometimes used when there are more than two levels of the dependent variable, but this makes the analysis and interpretation much more complex.

A Note About Best Practice

Occasionally a research article will be found in which a dichotomous *dependent variable* was used in a *t* test, ANOVA, or Pearson correlation. Because of the special nature of dichotomous variables, this is not wrong, as would be the use of a nominal (three or more unordered levels) dependent variable with parametric statistics. However, we think that it is a better practice to use the same statistics with dichotomous variables that are used with nominal variables. The exception is that it is appropriate to use dichotomous (dummy) independent variables in multiple regression and logistic regression (Figure 19.6).

Other Complex (Multivariate) Statistics

Four other complex associational statistics are seen in the literature. The most common is *factor analysis*, which is usually used to reduce a relatively large number of variables to a smaller number of groups of variables. These new composite variables are called factors or components. Factor analysis is discussed in Chapters 12 and 15.

Because they are very advanced statistics, the other three are not discussed in this book, but they are mentioned here. *Canonical correlation* is a correlation of a linear combination of several independent variables with a linear combination of several dependent variables. *Path analysis* is a multivariate analysis in which "causal" relationships among several variables are represented by figures showing the "paths" among them. *Structural equation models* (SEMs) are models that describe "causal" relationships among latent (unobserved) variables. Path analysis and SEM are related; both provide tests of the accuracy of the proposed model and both are said by proponents to provide evidence of causal linkages from nonexperimental designs. However, the American Psychological Association (APA) Task Force on Statistical Inference states, "The use of complicated 'causal modeling' software rarely yields results that have any interpretation as causal effects" (Wilkinson & the Task Force on Statistical Inference, 1999, p. 600).

The General Linear Model

Something that is not obvious from Figure 19.2 is that the broad question *of whether there is a relationship between variables X and Y can be answered two ways.* If both the independent variable and dependent variable provide approximately normally distributed data with five or more levels, the obvious statistic to use (based on Figure 19.2 and Figure 19.4) is the Pearson correlation, and that would be our recommendation. However, some researchers choose to divide the independent variable into two or several categories or groups such as low, medium, and high and then do a one-way ANOVA. Conversely, others who start with an independent variable that has a few (e.g., two through four ordered categories) may choose to do a correlation instead of a one-way ANOVA. Although these choices are not wrong, we do not think they are the best practice. We say this because, in the first example, information is lost by dividing a continuous independent variable into a few categories. In the second example, there would be a restricted range, which tends to decrease the size of the correlation coefficient.

In the previous examples we recommended one of the choices, but the fact that there *are* two choices raises a bigger and more complex issue that we have hinted at in earlier chapters. Statisticians point out, and can demonstrate mathematically, that the distinction between difference and associational statistics is an artificial one and that one-way ANOVA and Pearson correlation are mathematically the same, as are factorial ANOVA and multiple regression. Thus, the full range of methods used to analyze one continuous dependent variable and one or more independent variables, either continuous or categorical, are mathematically related (Keppel & Zedeck, 1989). The model on which this is based is called the *general linear model*; it is "general" in that the kind of independent variable is not specified. The idea is that the relationship between the independent and dependent variables can be expressed by an equation with terms for the weighted values of each of the independent or predictor variables plus an error term.

What this means is that if there is a continuous, normally distributed dependent or outcome variable and five or so levels of a normally distributed independent variable, it would be analyzed appropriately with either a correlation or a one-way ANOVA. A similar answer would be obtained with regard to the significance level. However, a large sample would be needed to have enough participants in each group for the ANOVA comparisons if there are more than four levels of the independent variable.

Although we recognize that our distinction between difference and associational parametric statistics is a simplification, we still think it is useful educationally. We hope that this glimpse of an advanced topic is clear and helpful.

Summary

This chapter serves as an introduction to selection of appropriate statistical methods. In the next three chapters we discuss conceptually, and in more depth, many of the statistical methods shown in Figure 19.3 through Figure 19.6. We take examples from journals that publish research in applied settings and demonstrate why the authors selected a particular statistical method. Our approach shows that the choice of a particular statistical method is directly related to the general design classification and the level of measurement. In addition, we discuss how the results of the statistical method were interpreted.

Selection of an appropriate statistic requires judgment as well as following the decision rules. This can be difficult, but this overview should provide a good foundation. A review of this chapter is helpful to decide on a statistic to use. It should provide a good grasp of how the various statistics fit together and when they should be used.

Key Concepts

Basic associational questions

Basic difference questions

Complex associational questions

Complex difference questions

Homogeneity of variance assumption

Independence assumption

Normality assumption

Key Distinctions

Basic associational questions versus basic difference questions

Complex associational questions versus complex difference questions

Homogeneity of variance assumption versus independence assumption versus normality assumption

Different Term for Similar Concept

Nonnormal distributions ≈ skewed distribution

Application Problems

1. How should you decide if your research is a difference question or an associational question?

2. How should you determine if you should use basic or complex statistical analyses?

3. In selecting a basic difference inferential statistic, when would one compare means? Medians? Counts? Explain.

4. A teacher ranked the 25 students in her Algebra 1 class from 1 = highest to 25 = lowest in terms of their grades on several tests. After the next semester, she checked the school records to see what grade the students received from their Algebra 2 teacher. The teacher asked, "Does final ranking of the students in Algebra 1 *influence* their grade in Algebra 2?" What is the appropriate statistical analysis? Explain. Why will the results, even if there is a very large effect size, not allow the teacher to answer the specific question that she asked? (Hint: See Chapter 4.)

For Problems 5–10, create an original example, and then use the figures in this chapter to arrive at the proper statistical analysis.

5. One independent variable, three levels, between groups, one ordinal nonnormally distributed dependent variable.

6. Two between-groups independent variables, each with three levels, one normally distributed dependent variable.

7. One between-groups independent variable, one repeated-measures independent variable, each with two levels, one normally distributed dependent variable.

8. One independent variable, two levels, repeated measures, one nominal dependent variable.

9. One independent variable, four levels, between groups, one nominal dependent variable.

10. Three normally distributed variables and one dichotomous independent variable, one normally distributed dependent variable.

11. The director of special education in a suburban school district wanted to compare two schools in terms of how English as a Second Language (ESL) students were performing in their respective schools. The independent variable was school, with two levels. Dependent variables included ESL students' standardized national test scores in each of the four subject areas. What type of statistic should be used in this study and why?

Notes

1. Note that in this sentence the word *independent* has two different meanings. The second usage, meaning "separate from, not related to, or not influenced by," is a key term in statistics and is an assumption of many statistical tests. Appendix B contrasts the several meanings of terms like *independent, random,* and *validity,* whose meanings, unfortunately, depend on the context. We have tried to be clear about the context.
2. The exception is that to assess the *strength* of the association between two nominal variables (the appropriate nominal associational statistic from Figure 19.4 would be used, that is, phi or Cramer's V).

20

Data Analysis and Interpretation— Basic Difference Questions

This chapter includes statistical tests that are used for designs that have one independent variable (factor) and one dependent variable. These statistical tests are used to answer basic difference questions (see Chapter 19 for decision guidelines on selection of such tests). Although many statistical tests are mentioned in this chapter, we pay particular attention to parametric tests that are commonly used in the literature. These tests are the *independent samples t test*, the *single-factor analysis of variance* (ANOVA), the *dependent or paired samples t test*, and the *single-factor repeated-measures analysis of variance*. All tests outlined in this chapter are commonly seen when a study uses the randomized experimental approach, quasi-experimental approach, or comparative approach.

Analyzing Single-Factor (Between-Groups) Designs With Parametric Statistics

There are three major assumptions underlying the use of the t test or ANOVA for independent samples that were discussed in Chapter 19: (1) *normality*; (2) *homogeneity of variance*; and (3) *independence*.

The t Test for Independent Samples

We start with single-factor between-groups designs performed on dependent variables that are normally distributed (often said to be interval or ratio scale). First, we discuss the independent-samples t test and then the single-factor or one-way ANOVA. For our discussion of the t test, we provide an example by Poirier and Feldman (2007).

Poirier and Feldman (2007) investigated the use of individual response technology (IRT) in a large introductory psychology course. Students were enrolled in one of two sections of an introductory psychology course. The section that incorporated IRT into lectures had 447 students. There were 418 students in the comparison section, which was traditional and did not use IRT. The two sections met back to back, and students had no knowledge prior to the beginning of the course that one would use IRT. Thus, bias based on selection of the intervention was not an issue. The design was quasi-experimental because participants were not randomly assigned to groups. At the end of the semester, IRT impact was assessed by comparing the students in each of the two courses on overall grade. Table 20.1 shows the means and standard deviations for each of the two groups.

The design for this study was a single-factor, between-groups design with two levels. The independent variable was receiving IRT with two levels: IRT and no IRT (traditional). The design was between groups because participants were in one and only one group, and

TABLE 20.1

Course Performance Data

	Traditional (*n* = 418)	IRT (*n* = 447)
Mean	82.72	84.03
Standard deviation	7.64	7.54

Source: Data are from Poirier, C. R., & Feldman, R. S., *Teaching of Psychology, 34*, 2007, 194–196.

participants were measured only once. The dependent variable (course performance as a percentage) was assumed to be normally distributed with equal variances. Therefore, the statistical choice for this study was an independent samples *t* test.

We express the results of the *t* test as follows. The differences between group means attained statistical significance: $t_{863} = 2.54$, $p = .01$. What does this mean? Conceptually, the *t* test and also the ANOVA (*F* test) are ratios of the variability between groups or conditions to the variability within the groups or conditions. What do we mean by the variability between groups and the variability within groups? In the *t* test, the variability between groups is determined from the difference between the mean of the IRT group and the mean of the traditional group. In the present study, the mean of the IRT group was 84.03, and the mean of the traditional group was 82.72. Therefore, the difference between the means was 1.31 percentage points in favor of the IRT group. The variability within groups or conditions is the variability among the individual participants within each group. One would expect there to be some variability among participants within groups because they are different individuals. Other variability might be due to errors made in measurement. The size of the variability within groups can be estimated from the standard deviations within each group, which are shown in Table 20.1. These standard deviations are used as part of the calculation of the within-groups variability. If there is a large amount of variability in performance among participants within a group, then the standard deviation will be large. On the other hand, if there is little variability, then the standard deviation will be small. Variability within groups is often referred to as error variance.

If the ratio just described is large (i.e., the variability between groups is several times greater than the variability within groups) and given a large enough sample, then it is likely that the result will be *statistically significant.* How does one know the result is statistically significant? To answer this question, we need to understand what is meant by statistical significance. When we use hypothesis testing (Chapter 16), we phrase our outcome in terms of the null hypothesis, which, in this case, is the hypothesis that there is no difference between the mean performance scores in the population of students who receive the IRT course and the mean in the population of students who receive the traditional course. Specifically, we state: If the null hypothesis were true, what is the likelihood that the outcome from the study could happen? If the likelihood was quite small, less than 5 times in 100, for example, *p* (the probability value) would be <.05, so we would reject the null hypothesis and provide support for the alternative or research hypothesis. (.05 is the most common significance level, but some researchers use a lower, more conservative level, such as .01, in part because they are less willing to take a chance that they will reject a null hypothesis that is true.). Using the Poirier and Feldman (2007) data, the computed probability was .01 that the outcome could happen if the null hypothesis was actually true. Therefore, they rejected the null hypothesis that there was no difference in performance scores between the population means of the two groups. It was concluded that the average performance scores in the population of IRT students is higher than the average performance scores of those in the traditional condition.

Poirier and Feldman (2007) stated the results of their comparison as $t_{863} = 2.54$, $p = .01$. The subscript number, 863, was the **degrees of freedom**, which refers to the number of independent pieces of information from the data collected in the study. In the independent samples t test, we find the degrees of freedom from the total number of participants minus 2. There were 865 participants in the study (447 in the IRT group and 418 in the traditional group). Thus, there are 863 degrees of freedom for the comparison.

As discussed in Chapter 17, it is not sufficient to state that the result was statistically significant and that the IRT group mean was higher than that of the traditional group. In addition, an *effect size* should be reported and interpreted, and, if possible, the practical or clinical importance of the finding should be noted. In the Poirier and Feldman (2007) study, a *d* family effect size was reported to be .17, which is quite small. Note that Table 17.1 shows that a *d* value of .2 is considered small or smaller than typical. Because of the large sample size, there was a strong possibility for finding a statistically significant difference, even though there was a small effect size.

The *t* Statistic, Confidence Intervals, and Effect Sizes

Now that we have discussed the *t* statistic, confidence intervals (CIs) (Chapter 17), and effect sizes (Chapter 17) it is instructive to demonstrate the differences among the three using the data from the Poirier and Feldman (2007) study (Table 20.1). First, we evaluate the *t* statistic. When computing the *t* statistic, we are dividing the difference between sample means by a measure of variability, the standard error of the difference between means. (A standard error is computed by dividing the standard deviation by the square root of the sample size). The information needed to compute the *t* test is provided in Table 20.1: the means of the two samples, the corresponding standard deviations, and the sample size for each group. While the denominator of the formula makes it a little difficult to compute with a hand calculator, especially if the sample sizes of the two groups are not the same, statistical computer programs are capable of performing the *t* test. The outcome of the test was statistically significant with a *p* value of .01.

$$t = \frac{\text{Difference between samples means}}{\text{Standard error of difference between means}}$$

$$t = \frac{M_I - M_C}{S_I S_C \times \sqrt{\dfrac{1}{n_I} + \dfrac{1}{n_C}}}$$

$$t = \frac{1.31}{.516} = 2.54$$

Next, using the same data provided by Poirier and Feldman (2007), we compute a 95% confidence interval. The information needed to compute the confidence interval is the same as that used in the *t* test. In addition, we need a value from a table of *critical values* of the *t* distribution, which can be found in any statistics book. With very large samples, such as in the Poirier and Feldman study, the critical value at .05 is 1.96.

Lower limit 95% CI = Difference between means − Estimated standard error of difference between means × Critical value

Upper limit 95% CI = Difference between means + Estimated standard error of difference between means × Critical value

Lower limit 95% CI = 1.31 − (.516)(1.96) = .29

Upper limit 95% CI = 1.31 + (.516)(1.96) = 2.32

Therefore, the 95% confidence interval for the Poirier and Feldman (2007) study is between .29 and 2.32. One could say with 95% confidence that the true population mean is within that interval. Notice that 0 is not within the confidence interval. This also is an indicator that there was a statistically significant difference at $p < .05$.

Last, we use the same data to compute effect size. In this case, since the independent variable was dichotomous and the dependent variable was continuous, we choose a d family effect size, as did Poirier and Feldman (2007). Notice that the denominator of the effect size formula is based on the standard deviation and not on standard error as in the t statistic and confidence interval.

$$d = \frac{\text{Difference between samples means}}{\text{Pooled standard deviations from both samples}}$$

$$d = \frac{M_I - M_C}{S_{\text{Pooled}}}$$

$$d = \frac{1.31}{7.58} = .17$$

Again, the effect size (.17), which is the strength of the relationship between the independent and dependent variable, was considered to be small, even though the difference between groups was statistically significant at .01. More than likely, this outcome was due to a large sample size.

Single-Factor ANOVA

The single-factor ANOVA (also called one-way ANOVA) is used for designs with one independent variable, between groups, and two *or more* levels. Similar to the independent samples t test, the single-factor ANOVA is performed on dependent variables that are normally distributed (often said to be interval or ratio scale). For our discussion of this analysis we provide an example by Herpertz et al. (2001).

Herpertz et al. (2001) investigated psychophysiological responses in boys with attention deficit hyperactivity disorder (ADHD) compared with boys with this disorder who also had conduct disorder (CD) (ADHD + CD). A third group of boys without ADHD served as a comparison or control group. Although the major focus of this study was psychophysiological differences among the three groups, other dependent variables, including IQ, were also of interest. For purposes of demonstration of the single-factor ANOVA, we use the IQ data shown in Table 20.2. Because Herpertz et al. had three groups in their study (ADHD, ADHD + CD, and control) and each participant in the study was in only one of the three groups and measured only once, the design was a single-factor between-groups design with three levels. The dependent variable, IQ, was considered to be normally distributed. Furthermore, because the groups differed on an attribute independent variable, the research approach to the study is considered comparative.

TABLE 20.2

IQ Data

	ADHD (n = 21)	ADHD + CD (n = 26)	Non-ADHD (n = 21)
Mean	95.71	93.50	110.24
Standard deviation	11.08	7.97	11.77

Source: Data are from Herpertz, S. C., Wenning, B., Mueller, B., Qunaibi, M., Sass, H., & Herpertz-Dahlmann, B., *Journal of the American Academy of Child and Adolescent Psychiatry, 40,* 2001, 1222–1230.

TABLE 20.3

Single-Factor ANOVA Source Table (Hypothetical)

Source	SS	df	MS	F
Groups	500	2	250	17.44*
Within subjects (error)	931.45	65	14.33	

$*p < .01$.
Source: Data are from Herpertz, S. C., Wenning, B., Mueller, B., Qunaibi, M., Sass, H., & Herpertz-Dahlmann, B., *Journal of the American Academy of Child and Adolescent Psychiatry, 40,* 2001, 1222–1230.

Because there are three groups or levels for this study, we could perform three independent samples *t* tests (comparing control with ADHD, ADHD with ADHD + CD, and ADHD + CD with control) to consider all possible paired comparisons. The problem is that the result of doing multiple *t* tests is that the probability of a type I error is increased substantially. This error occurs when the researcher incorrectly rejects the null hypothesis when it is true. If three separate *t* tests were performed in this situation, the significance level for each comparison should be reduced to approximately .017 (.05/3 tests) to keep the overall significance level at .05. This correction, called *Bonferroni,* divides the alpha level (usually .05) by the number of tests performed. Unfortunately, using the Bonferroni procedure reduces statistical power by changing the significance level (from .05 to .013 in this situation). The more appropriate statistical selection for a single-factor design with more than two levels is the single-factor ANOVA, which allows the researcher to test the null hypothesis at $p = .05$.

All ANOVA procedures have a **source table** that displays the results from the ANOVA. Although it is relatively rare for a source table from a single-factor ANOVA to be displayed in a journal article, source tables accompanying factorial designs are more common. Table 20.3 shows a *hypothetical* source table for the single-factor ANOVA from the Herpertz et al. (2001) data.

The single-factor ANOVA starts by dividing the sums of squares (*SS*) into a between-groups component and an error component. The degrees of freedom (*df*) for the independent variable, called groups, is the number of levels of the independent variable minus one. The *df* for the error term is computed by subtracting the *df* for the independent variable from the total *df*. The total *df* (not shown in the source table) is the number of participants minus 1. Each of the *SS* is divided by its corresponding *df* to obtain mean squares (*MS*). Thus, there will be two *MS* in the single-factor ANOVA. The *F* value, seen in the last column in Table 20.3, is obtained by dividing the *MS* for groups by the *MS* for error. As Table 20.3 shows, there is one *F* value in the source table.

Herpertz et al. (2001) performed a single-factor ANOVA on their IQ data and reported the results in a table. They reported an *F* of 17.44, which was statistically significant at *p* < .0001. Had they reported this result in the text, it would read as follows: A statistically significant difference was found among the three groups: $F(2,65) = 17.44; p < .0001$. Notice that there are two different degrees of freedom in the single-factor ANOVA. A total of 65 degrees of freedom are associated with the error variance, similar to the *t* test, and calculated by subtracting the number of groups (3) from the total number of participants (68). Two degrees of freedom are associated with between-groups variance, and they are calculated as the number of groups minus 1.

What does an *F* value of 17.44 mean? Herpertz et al. (2001) found, from a statistical table or their computer, that the probability (*p*) was less than .0001. In other words, the probability that the three different mean values could happen, assuming a true null hypothesis, was less than 1 in 10,000, or highly unlikely. Therefore, they rejected the null hypothesis of no difference among the three IQ population means. A statistically significant overall *F* value from an ANOVA reveals only that the population means are not equal. To determine which groups or conditions are significantly different from each other following a statistically significant *F*, a post hoc test must be performed.

There are numerous **post hoc test** alternatives from which to choose. The *Tukey honestly significant difference* (HSD) *test* is considered a middle-of-the-road test between liberal (e.g., the *Fisher least significant difference test* [LSD]) and conservative (e.g., the *Scheffé test* for all comparisons). Most statisticians believe that liberal tests, such as LSD or three *t* tests, allow too high a probability of making a type I error.

Herpertz et al. (2001) performed a post hoc test using the Tukey HSD procedure. The results of this test revealed that the non-ADHD (comparison) group IQ was statistically significantly higher than either the ADHD or ADHD + CD group. The ADHD group and the ADHD + CD group did not differ statistically significantly from each other on the dependent variable of IQ.

SPSS and other statistical computer packages provide an index of the *effect size*, eta^2, which corresponds to the overall *F* (Table 20.3). For our example, eta^2 is .35. Because eta^2 is similar to the squared correlation coefficient, this would imply that approximately 35% of the variance in the study is accounted for by the independent variable. However, we are usually more interested in the size of the effect for *pairs* of conditions or groups, so one would report *d* effect sizes for the pairs of means that were found to be statistically significant using the Tukey post hoc test. The ADHD versus non-ADHD and the ADHD + CD versus non-ADHD comparisons would have *d* values greater than 1.0 and thus would be very large, and probably clinically important, differences. It is important to point out that there is some disagreement about how *d* values should be computed in single-factor designs with more than two groups or levels and in factorial designs (Kline, 2004). The issue concerns the measure of variability. Should one use the pooled standard deviation from the two groups in the comparison (Hedges' *g*), or should one use the square root of the error term, mean square within subjects (Table 20.3), which is more conservative? We favor the former method.

Analyzing Single-Factor (Between-Groups) Designs With Nonparametric Statistics

Nonparametric analyses often are referred to as distribution-free analyses. Nonparametric tests are "free" of the equal variance and normal distribution assumptions. Actually, each nonparametric analysis has its own sampling distribution. Nonparametric tests should be used when the assumptions of the equivalent parametric statistic are markedly violated, but typically ordinal nonparametric tests are not quite as powerful.

There are many different nonparametric tests (see Siegel & Castellan, 1988). Both of the nonparametric tests discussed next begin by converting the data from all of the groups combined to ranks by ordering them from the smallest to the largest score, regardless of the particular group or condition. Once the data are ranked, the rankings are used in a formula. Usually this entails summing the rankings from each group. As one might expect, if the sums of the rankings are quite different between or among groups, then they are likely to be statistically significantly different. A computer program will indicate the probability, *p*, or the researcher can look up the result of the formula in a table and draw a conclusion using the same logic as the *t* test.

Mann-Whitney *U* Test for Independent Samples

The Mann-Whitney *U* test is performed when the design is a between-groups design with one independent variable and two levels. It is used when there has been a violation of the assumptions underlying the *t* test. The analysis yields a value for the *U* statistic and a *p* value associated with it. If the *p* value is less than the significance level of .05, the null hypothesis is rejected. Because there are only two groups or levels in a comparison, there is no need for a post hoc test following a statistically significant *U* value.

Kruskal-Wallis One-Way ANOVA by Ranks

This test is the nonparametric analog of the single-factor between-groups ANOVA. It is used when there is one independent variable with more than two levels, participants are in one and only one group, and there has been a violation of the assumptions for parametric statistics. The preliminary steps in the Kruskal-Wallis ANOVA are similar to those of the Mann-Whitney *U* test. Data are ranked from smallest to largest without respect to group. Then the ranks in each group are summed and applied to the Kruskal-Wallis formula.

The logic underlying the Kruskal-Wallis ANOVA is that if you had three identical distributions of scores and you selected three groups at random, one from each distribution, you would expect their ranks to be distributed equally under the null hypothesis. However, if the ranks were quite different for at least one of the groups, then the null hypothesis would be rejected. Similar to a single-factor ANOVA, a statistically significant Kruskal-Wallis test must be followed by a post hoc test. A common post hoc method for the Kruskal-Wallis ANOVA is to perform Mann-Whitney *U* tests for each pair of groups, but that is a liberal post hoc comparison, similar to doing three *t* tests after an ANOVA, so it would be prudent to use the Bonferroni correction.

Analyzing Single-Factor Repeated-Measures Designs with Parametric Statistics

The analyses discussed in this section are used in a design with one independent variable, with two or more levels or conditions, and participants are *measured under all conditions*. These designs are referred to as *within-subjects*, *dependent-samples*, or *repeated-measures designs*, and we use these terms interchangeably here. This means that participants undergo all conditions of the study or participants are matched on some variables assumed to be related to the dependent variable.

The types of research approaches used with single-factor, repeated-measures designs are often randomized experimental or quasi-experimental. The *comparative approach* can be used in a within-subjects design and analysis to compare participants who vary on an attribute independent variable if they are matched (e.g., pairs of students with and without ADHD matched on IQ and gender). The comparative approach also is used when a cohort of participants is followed longitudinally to study developmental change (i.e., they are assessed on the same measures two or more times without any planned intervention between assessments).

Now we discuss the *t* test for dependent samples and the single-factor repeated-measures ANOVA, which are used with single-factor within-subjects/repeated-measures designs.

The *t* Test for Dependent or Paired Samples

To facilitate our discussion of within-subjects designs, we provide an example of a quasi-experiment by Goddard (2003). The author taught a course called "Writing in Psychology" to improve students' writing skills. An attitude inventory and tests over American Psychological Association (APA) style and grammar were used to evaluate the impact of the course. For our example here, we focus on the results of the grammar test that was given to each student prior to the course and at the end of the course. This is an example of a single-factor repeated-measures (within-subjects) design with two levels. The independent variable was the impact of the course. The two levels were the pretest and the posttest. Since all students were examined twice, the design is a repeated-measures or within-subjects design. The dependent variable, the score on the grammar test, was assumed to be normally distributed. The maximum score that a student could achieve on this test was 33.

A paired or dependent *t* test was used to analyze the data. The selection of this statistical test follows from Chapter 19. The data from the grammar test can be seen in Table 20.4.

Goddard (2003) reported the results as follows: "A two tailed paired sample *t* test indicated that the difference was significant, $t(26) = -4.60$, $p < .001$" (p. 28). Notice that degrees of freedom (in parentheses) was only one less than the sample size. In a dependent samples *t* test, only one degree of freedom is lost from the total sample. The negative *t* value resulted because the posttest was subtracted from the pretest. No effect size was computed for this measure. Also, it should be noted that though an effect size can be computed for a dependent samples *t* test, a correlation coefficient must be obtained between the two measures (in this case between the pre- and postmeasures) as part of the analysis. This is different from computing the effect size from an independent samples *t* test, which could be done from the resulting *t* value.

TABLE 20.4

Course Performance Data (Grammar Test)

	Precourse (*n* = 27)	Postcourse (*n* = 27)
Mean	22.93	26.19
Standard deviation	5.25	4.06

Source: Data are from Goddard, P., *Teaching of Psychology,*
30, 2003, 25–29.

TABLE 20.5

Interest in Specialty Areas of Professional Psychology

	Counseling	Clinical	School	Forensic	Profiling
Mean	2.67	2.43	1.73	2.52	2.49
Standard deviation	1.14	1.04	1.08	1.14	1.27

Source: Data are from Stark-Wroblewski, K., Wiggins, T., & Ryan, J., *Journal of Instructional Psychology, 33,* 2006, 273–277.

Single-Factor ANOVA With Repeated Measures

The single-factor ANOVA with repeated measures is performed in designs with one independent variable, two or more levels, and the participants undergo all conditions or levels of the study. The dependent variable is distributed normally, and variances are similar for each condition. Consider an example by Stark-Wroblewski, Wiggins, and Ryan (2006) who assessed undergraduate student interest in and familiarity with five specialty areas in professional psychology. A total of 83 undergraduate students majoring in psychology rated their interest in and familiarity with subfields of psychology. The independent variable, subfields of professional psychology, had five levels: (1) counseling psychology; (2) clinical psychology; (3) school psychology; (4) forensic psychology; and (5) criminal profiling. To assess student interest, the dependent variable was a five-point Likert-type scale, ranging from 0 to 4, as follows: 0 = no interest, 1 = little interest, 2 = moderate interest, 3 = very interested, and 4 = interested enough to pursue a career in this specialty area. Students rated each subfield using the Likert scale. The design for this study was a single-factor repeated-measures design with five levels. The dependent measure was considered to be normally distributed and approximated an interval scale.

The data for this study can be seen in Table 20.5. A single-factor repeated-measures ANOVA was performed on the data. A statistically significant result was obtained: $F(4, 79) = 17.24, p < .001$. A statistically significant F indicates that there was at least one statistically significant difference for interest in specialty areas. The authors used a Bonferroni technique to make all pairwise comparisons among specialty areas. The Bonferroni technique is similar to performing t tests between each pair of disciplines. To control for making a Type 1 error for this many comparisons, the researcher typically divides the alpha (or significance level) by the number of comparisons (10 in this example). If the alpha level was established at .05 prior to the study, then each comparison would be tested at 0.005. The results demonstrated that there was statistically significantly greater interest in all of the disciplines compared to school psychology but no difference in interest among these other disciplines. Post hoc comparisons similar to those of the single factor between groups ANOVA could be performed following a statistically significant repeated-measures ANOVA, but the error term would be different (Keppel, 1991).

The assumptions of *independence, homogeneity of variance,* and *normality* discussed in the previous chapter also need to be considered for the t test for paired samples and the single-factor repeated-measures ANOVA. However, in addition to these assumptions, an additional assumption, sphericity, also must be considered for the single-factor repeated-measures ANOVA if it is applied to more than two groups. Conceptually, the **sphericity assumption** is satisfied when the correlations among the scores of the different levels are equal. In the Stark-Wroblewski et al. (2006) study, because there were five levels in the single-factor repeated-measures design, the correlation between, for example, counseling and clinical psychology must be similar to the correlation between counseling and school psychology, which must be similar to the correlation between clinical psychology and school psychology, and so on. If the assumption is violated, the type I error is inflated. However, most computer statistical programs have a correction for the violation of the sphericity assumption.

An overall effect size for the repeated-measures analysis of variance in the Stark-Wroblewski et al. (2006) study was reported: $eta^2 = .47$. This is a large effect size indicating the strength of relationship between interest and specialty.

Analyzing Single-Factor Within-Subjects Designs With Nonparametric Statistics

Nonparametric statistics are used with within-subjects/repeated-measures designs when one of the assumptions underlying use of parametric statistics has been markedly violated. We discuss briefly three nonparametric statistics.

Wilcoxon Signed Ranks Matched-Pairs Test

The Wilcoxon matched-pairs test is used in a design in which there is one independent variable, with two levels, and the participants undergo both conditions or pairs of participants have been matched on a relevant variable. The dependent variable data are ordinal (and not normally distributed), or there have been violations of assumptions of the *t* test for paired samples. For example, the Wilcoxon test could have been used instead of the paired-samples *t* in the Goddard (2003) study to compare the pretest and posttest if assumptions had been violated.

Friedman Two-Way ANOVA by Ranks

The Friedman test is used in a repeated-measures design when there is one independent variable, there are three or more levels, and the dependent variable is ordinal (and not normally distributed) or violations of ANOVA assumptions have occurred. Stark-Wroblewski et al. (2006), who assessed undergraduate student interest in and familiarity with five specialty areas in professional psychology, could have used the Friedman test. Because the Friedman test is carried out on data with more than two levels or conditions, a statistically significant result must be followed by some post hoc comparison to determine specific differences. The Wilcoxon test may be used as a post hoc test in this situation if the Friedman test is statistically significant. Note, however, that using the Wilcoxon test after the Friedman test is analogous to using the least significant difference test after an ANOVA; it is somewhat "liberal."

The McNemar Test

The McNemar test is used in designs similar to that for the paired *t* or Wilcoxon test, but the dependent variable is nominal or dichotomous. The McNemar test is similar to the chi-square test, which we discuss in Chapter 21, in that frequencies are the unit of measurement and they can be visualized in a cross-tabulation table. However, because each participant undergoes both conditions of the study, there are important differences from the chi-square test for independence. If the Goddard (2003) study had compared participants at pretest and posttest on the dichotomous measure of whether they improved, the McNemar test probably would have been used.

Advantages and Disadvantages of Within-Subjects Designs

Advantages of Within-Subject Designs

An obvious advantage of using a within-subjects/repeated-measures design is that fewer participants are needed in the study. If the Goddard (2003) study had used a between-groups design, a separate group of students would be needed, possibly doubling the number of participants in the study. The repeated-measures design saves time in recruitment of participants. Sometimes, if participants have characteristics that are not common, a repeated-measures design is more efficient. A more important reason for selecting a repeated-measures design is that variability among participants should be reduced. The statistical analysis of single-factor repeated-measures designs is usually a paired *t* test or repeated-measures ANOVA (previously discussed), which conceptually can be thought of as a ratio of the variability between groups to the variability within groups. When we perform a repeated-measures design, each participant undergoes all of the conditions. Therefore, it is expected that any changes from condition to condition are due to the nature of a particular condition (treatment) and not to variability among participants (error), because the same participant is experiencing each of the conditions. This reduction in error variance would increase the size of the *t* or *F* ratio and result in a greater probability of finding a statistically significant difference if one is actually there.

Disadvantages of Within-Subjects Designs

Although within-subjects/repeated-measures designs are advantageous in reducing error variance, there are two distinct disadvantages of using repeated-measures designs. First, repeated-measures designs (with the exception of matching) cannot be used in situations in which a lasting effect of a treatment might take place. The problem is often referred to as **carryover effects**. For example, studies of educational or psychological interventions would not use repeated-measures designs because once participants experienced the treatment conditions, they could not be expected to "unlearn" the treatment. Because of carryover effects, repeated-measures designs are not seen as frequently as between-group designs in the clinical literature.

One method of circumventing carryover effects while still gaining the advantage of reducing error variance is to use a **matching** procedure. Participants are grouped into pairs (dyads) or triplets (triads) on the basis of some characteristic that should be related to the dependent variable, for example, intelligence. After participants are matched, one of each pair is assigned (optimally randomly) to group *A* and the other to group *B*. Then the study is carried out. Conceptually, the idea of matching is to make each member of the pair or triad as though he or she was the same participant undergoing all conditions. Therefore, designs that use matching are considered to be within-subjects designs and use similar statistical procedures.

A second disadvantage of repeated-measures designs is that the degrees of freedom in the study are reduced. If one did a repeated-measures study with two conditions, it would take half as many participants to gather the same amount of data because each person would be measured twice. For example, consider a between-groups study that compares an intervention condition with a control condition, with 20 participants in each condition. Then, there are 40 participants, or 38 degrees of freedom ($df = [n_1 - 1] + [n_2 - 1]$) for an independent-samples t test. On the other hand, suppose that a repeated-measures design was used. There would be 20 participants in each condition, but because each participant undergoes both conditions, there would be only 20 participants. The degrees of freedom would be $n - 1$ or only 19; thus, statistical power is reduced. The decision of which type of design to use involves a trade-off between increased sample size (so increased df) with a between-groups design and reduced error variance with a within-subjects design.

Summary

In this chapter we discussed the application of appropriate statistical methods used to answer basic difference questions. In the first part of the chapter we addressed statistical analyses appropriate for between-groups designs. The second part of the chapter addressed statistical analyses for within-subjects or repeated-measures designs. Both sections are further divided into selection of appropriate parametric and nonparametric statistics based on the scale of the dependent variable and if certain assumptions had been satisfied. The emphasis of this chapter was on parametric statistics including the t test and analysis of variance. The t test is more commonly used when there is one independent variable with two levels because it gives the researcher the option of testing a directional hypothesis. When the independent variable has more than two levels, the ANOVA is the procedure of choice.

We also discussed nonparametric tests to answer basic difference questions. For between-groups designs these tests included the Mann-Whitney U test and the Kruskal-Wallis analysis of variance by ranks. For within-subjects designs we included the Wilcoxon test and the Friedman test. All of these nonparametric tests are used with ordinal data that are not normally distributed or with interval data converted to ranks because of violation of assumptions underlying parametric tests. We also mentioned the McNemar test, which is used in within-subjects designs with nominal data. Nonparametric tests are used less frequently than parametric analyses and usually are less powerful.

It should be noted that the suggestions we provided are guidelines, and, especially with respect to nonparametric analyses, there could be other appropriate choices. When selecting a particular statistical analysis, it is desirable to state an appropriate rationale. As a final word of caution, a statistically significant result is not necessarily a clinically significant result. Statistical significance just tells us that it is likely that there is some difference; it does not tell us about the size of the difference (effect) or whether it has clinical or practical importance.

Key Concepts

Analysis of variance (ANOVA)
Degrees of freedom
Carryover effects

Friedman test

Kruskal-Wallis analysis of variance by ranks

Mann-Whitney U test

Matching

McNemar test

Post hoc tests

Source table

Sphericity assumption

t test

Wilcoxon matched-pairs test

Key Distinctions

Between-groups designs versus within-subjects designs

Matching versus within-subjects designs

Parametric versus nonparametric statistics

Single-factor ANOVA versus Kruskal-Wallis ANOVA

Single-factor repeated-measures ANOVA versus Friedman test

t test for independent samples versus Mann-Whitney U test

t test for independent samples versus t test for paired samples

t test for paired samples versus single-factor repeated-measures ANOVA

t test for paired samples versus Wilcoxon matched-pairs test versus McNemar test

Application Problems

For questions 1–3, *select the proper statistical analysis* based on (a) whether the design is between groups, within subjects, or mixed; (b) number of levels of the independent variables; (c) the scale/level of measurement of the dependent variables; and (d) whether assumptions underlying parametric tests are violated.

1. A professor who taught statistics was curious to know about different methods of calculating the standard deviation. Specifically, he wondered which way was quicker: *the deviation method* or *the raw score* method. It just so happened that he had a class of 31 graduate students. He randomly assigned 16 students to the deviation method and 15 students to the raw score method and asked the students to keep track of how long it took (to the nearest minute) to determine the standard deviation for the problem.

2. At a clinic in the Rocky Mountains, a hand therapist was interested in determining the functional recovery of joint replacement surgery as opposed to two other more conservative treatments, steroids and splinting, on persons with rheumatoid arthritis. A total of 30 participants were randomly selected from a population of hand therapy patients. The participants were randomly assigned to one of three groups (10 participants in each). The groups were the surgery condition, drug condition, and the splint condition. After 6 months, all three groups were measured on a subtest of the Gliner Occupational Hand Recovery Index, an interval scale.

3. An investigator is interested in comparing successful employment due to different service delivery systems for persons with traumatic brain injury. One system ($n = 10$) was referred to as the cognitive delivery system (C). A second system ($n = 10$) was the emotional delivery system (E). A third system ($n = 10$) was the case management delivery system (CM). The investigator ranked the 30 subjects from 1 to 30 on how successful they were on their first job after recovery.

4. A therapist wanted to know if his special splint would increase the range of motion (ROM) in the wrist after a traumatic injury. He had eight patients wear the special splint and eight patients wear the standard splint. He predicted that his special splint would increase ROM (in degrees) at the end of the recovery period. He performed a *t* test for independent samples on the data and found a *t* value of 1.82. He went to a *t* table and found that this value was greater than the critical value for a *t* with 14 degrees of freedom (one tailed). He concluded that his special splint was statistically significantly better than the standard splint. What did he mean by statistical significance?

5. You have three independent groups, with 10 participants in each group ($n = 30$). These groups are labeled A_1, A_2, and A_3. The means of the three groups are 10, 14, and 20, respectively. You wonder if there is a significant difference for any of the possible comparisons.

   a. How many comparisons are there?

   b. If you use a *t* test to test each comparison, what danger do you run into?

   c. You decide to perform an analysis of variance on the data. The results are as follows. Fill in the rest of the table:

Source of variation	SS	df	MS	F
Between groups	320	$k - 1$		
Within subjects	1080	$n - k$		

   d. You find that the *F* is statistically significant. How do you determine which of the groups are different from each other?

6. The design is a single-factor (between-groups) design with two levels. The data are normally distributed. There are two analyses that can be performed.

   a. What are the two different types of analyses that can be used in this situation?

   b. When should each analysis be used and why?

For the following eight passages (questions 7–14), *select the proper statistical analysis* based on (a) whether the design is between groups or within subjects; (b) number of levels of the independent variables; (c) scale of measurement of the dependent variables; and (d) whether assumptions underlying parametric tests are violated.

7. A graduate seminar class has 10 students. The students are exposed to four different instructors, each instructor representing a different teaching style. At the end of the semester, each student is asked to rank the four instructors from 1 to 4 on class challenge. Are there significant differences among teaching styles?

8. A researcher hypothesized that applying splints over a 3-month period would significantly increase range of motion in patients who were quadriplegic. A random sample of 16 patients with this disability was selected. The patients were then matched on initial range of motion to form eight pairs. Then one participant of each pair was randomly assigned to the intervention group ($n = 8$) and the other randomly assigned to the control group ($n = 8$). The intervention group was splinted for 3 months, whereas the control group was not splinted. After 3 months, range of motion (which was normally distributed) was measured for each group, and they were compared.

9. An educator is interested in cooperative learning groups. She wonders if active participation increases if groups are facilitated by someone in this area. A study is conducted during two different class periods. In one class period, participants engage in cooperative groups without a facilitator. During a second class period she introduces a facilitator into the groups. One member of each group, unknown to other members, keeps track of active participation. After each class, participants are divided into whether they actively participated or did not actively participate.

10. A study is carried out to determine if a hands-on entrepreneurial curriculum for high school students will increase entrepreneurial skills. A total of 20 students were matched into 10 pairs based on gender and previous high school grades. One member of each pair was assigned to the intervention condition, the hands-on entrepreneurial curriculum. The other member of the pair was assigned to the traditional business class, where most of the activities involved students reading simulations and class discussions. At the end of the semester, each student was given an entrepreneurial skill score, on a 1-to-5 scale (5 = always, 4 = most of the time, 3 = sometimes, 2 = rarely, and 1 = never).

11. A researcher was interested in determining how to get people with arthritis to use joint protection techniques. She observed 20 people with arthritis in their home for one morning and found that 6 of 20 used joint protection techniques. She then gave a demonstration on joint protection to each participant. One month later she observed each of the participants again for one morning. She found that 16 of 20 people used joint protection techniques.

12. A graduate seminar class has 10 students. The students are exposed to four different instructors, each instructor representing a different teaching style. At the end of the semester, each student is asked to judge each teaching style as challenging or not challenging. Are there significant differences among teaching styles?

13. A study matched participants in pairs and then performed a *t* test for paired samples. What are the advantages and disadvantages of matching in this situation? (Hint: Consider degrees of freedom.)

14. Researchers performed a repeated-measures ANOVA to compare three matched groups. They also performed a post hoc test in the study. Explain why.

21

Analysis and Interpretation of Basic Associational Research Questions

In this chapter we discuss the selection and application of appropriate statistical methods to answer basic associational research questions. When we refer to basic research questions we are discussing analyses that have only one independent variable and one dependent variable. We examine in detail two very commonly used statistical tests: the *Pearson product-moment correlation coefficient, r,* and the *chi-square* (χ^2) *test for independence.* For the most part, the basic associational research approach examines the relation between two continuous variables (or at least ones that have many ordered levels) leading to a correlation coefficient. The most common correlation coefficient used to describe the relationships between two continuous variables is the Pearson product-moment correlation, which is represented by *r.* When one or both of the variables is not normally distributed or there are violations precluding the use of parametric statistics, the *Spearman correlation* or the *Kendall tau* (τ) is usually used.[1] However, when we examine the relationship between two variables that are dichotomous or nominal level, with a few nonordered categories, the Pearson chi-square (χ^2) test for independence is used.

In this chapter we also discuss common problems associated with the reporting and interpretation of correlation coefficients and the need to present effect sizes and confidence intervals. Also, we spend some time discussing the special case of the chi-square test with one degree of freedom because of its prominent use in medical research. Note that in Chapter 19 we included chi-square in Figure 19.3 as a difference inferential statistic that could be used for comparing two or a small number of groups of participants. Both difference and associational statistics examine the *relationship* between variables so chi-square could have been discussed in the current chapter or in Chapter 20 along with nonparametric statistics such as the Mann-Whitney test. When we discuss the relationship between two variables in the associational research approach, technically, neither variable is designated as independent or dependent because a correlation is bidirectional. However, researchers usually have some direction in mind so we continue to use the terms *independent* and *dependent* variable here.

Analyzing Continuous Variables With Parametric Statistics

Pearson Product-Moment Correlation

The Pearson product-moment correlation provides an index of the strength of the linear relationship between two continuous variables. The Pearson correlation assumes that the distribution of the dependent variable is normal, with equal variance for each value of the independent variable, and assumes that the independent variable also is normally distributed. The Pearson correlation is widely reported in the literature for evaluating measurement reliability where one might test the relationship between two administrations of the same instrument (test–retest reliability) or the relationship between two different observers (interrater reliability) and, for measurement validity, testing the relationship between an instrument and some external criterion (see Chapters 11 and 12). The Pearson correlation is expressed as a coefficient, *r*, which indicates the strength of the association or relationship between two variables. This coefficient has a range of –1 to +1. A positive relationship means that as scores on one variable increase, scores on the other variable also increase. If *r* is .5 or greater, it is usually considered to be a strong positive relationship, and *r* values that are below –.5 are considered to be strong negative or inverse relationships between the two variables. An inverse relationship means that a high score on one variable is associated with a low score for the same person on the other variable and vice versa. When the value of *r* is near zero, it indicates there is no relationship between the two variables; in this case, high scores on the independent variable are associated with high, medium, or low scores on the dependent variable. A zero or a low correlation means that the dependent variable cannot be predicted by knowing the scores on the independent variable.

A study by Zamboanga, Padilla-Walker, Hardy, Thompson, and Wang (2007) demonstrates the use of correlation coefficients. These authors were interested in predicting student class performance on lecture and text-based questions from student background and course involvement. To predict these outcomes, the authors used hierarchical linear regression analyses (Chapter 22). However, the authors provide, in a table, descriptive statistics and correlations among the variables to be used in the regression analysis. Although the authors included 10 different predictors in their study, for our purposes here, we look at four of their measures: (1) ACT scores; (2) prior grade point average (GPA); (3) lecture attendance; and (4) exam performance based on averaging scores on four exams.

There were 114 students in the study. Pearson correlation coefficients were obtained for all relationships among the four measures. Zamboanga et al. (2007) placed the results from their correlations in a table. However, had they reported a single correlation result in the text, such as the correlation between lecture attendance and exam performance, it would be written as follows: A statistically significant relationship between lecture attendance and exam performance was found: $r = .39$, $df = 112$, $p < .01$. The degrees of freedom for a Pearson correlation coefficient are the number of participants in the analysis minus 2. Again, degrees of freedom refer to the number of independent pieces of information from the data collected in the study and are closely associated with the number of participants with data on both variables. There were 114 participants so the degrees of freedom for this correlation were 112.

Statistical Significance

As with any inferential statistic, one must be cautious about the interpretation of statistically significant correlation coefficients. There is an inverse relationship between the number of participants in the study (degrees of freedom) and the size of the coefficient needed to obtain statistical significance. In other words, studies with a large number of participants might find statistically significant correlation coefficients, but they may be trivial. If we examine a table of critical values for the Pearson correlation, we find that with 114 participants in a study, a correlation of about .185 is all that is needed to obtain statistical significance at $p < .05$, given a nondirectional hypothesis or two-tailed test. Therefore, it is useful with correlation coefficients, as well as other inferential statistics, to obtain an index of effect size or confidence intervals.

TABLE 21.1

Correlations Among Variables Predicting Student Class Performance

	ACT	Prior GPA	Lecture attendance	Exam performance
ACT	—	.41**	.09	.53**
Prior GPA		—	.29**	.47**
Lecture attendance			—	.39**
Exam performance				—

**p < 0.01.

Source: Data are from Zamboanga, B. L., Padilla-Walker, L. M., Hardy, S. A., Thompson, R. A., & Wang, S. C., *Teaching of Psychology, 34,* 2007, 158–162.

Correlation Matrix

It is relatively rare to see only a single correlation coefficient or even two or three correlation coefficients in a study. When more than a few correlations are reported, correlation matrices commonly are used. A correlation matrix is a table of correlation coefficients that shows how all variables are related to each other.[2] Zamboanga et al. (2007) presented a correlation matrix in their study of all 10 variables. We show a correlation matrix (Table 21.1) for four of their variables studied.

A table displaying a correlation matrix has the variables ordered horizontally across the top row of the table and vertically down the first column of the table. In correlation matrices, the values usually are displayed in either the upper right corner or in the lower left corner of the table, but not both, which would be redundant because the same values would be present. To interpret a correlation matrix, one reads down the first column to find the variable of interest. Next, one proceeds across to find the other variable of interest. Where these two variables intersect is the correlation coefficient for the two variables. For example, the correlation for ACT and lecture attendance is $r = .09$; the correlation between ACT and exam performance is $r = .53$.

Although correlation matrices are common in journal articles, one should use caution in interpreting them because often statistically significant relationships may occur that were not originally hypothesized. To interpret these relationships outside of a theory or working hypothesis is often referred to as *"fishing" for statistical significance* and is not considered best practice.

Effect Sizes

A statistically significant outcome gives an indication of the probability that a result as extreme as this could happen, assuming the null hypothesis is true. It does not describe the strength of the relationship between the independent and dependent variables, which is what an effect size does. In other words, how much of the outcome can be predicted from knowing the value of the independent variable? One can calculate an effect size for every statistic. It is especially easy to perform this operation for a Pearson correlation because one effect size that is often used is r^2. This describes the amount of shared variance or the variance in the dependent variable that could be predicted from the independent variable. For example, in the Zamboanga et al. (2007) study, the r^2 for the correlation (.39) between lecture attendance and exam performance is .15. This would indicate that only 15% of the variance between the two measures was common to both. A total of 85% of the variance is unexplained. Note that r^2 for a correlation of .185, which would be statistically significant with $n = 114$, is .03; thus, only about 3% of the variance is shared.

There is a disagreement among researchers about whether to use r^2 or r as the measure of effect size. Cohen (1988) provided rough guidelines for interpreting the effect size of correlation coefficients. He considered Pearson r values around +.1 or –.1 to be weak relationships, values around +.3 or –.3 to be medium strength, and values of +.5 or –.5 or more to be strong. Even though a correlation (r) of .50 means that only 25% of the variance in the dependent variable can be predicted if the independent variable is known, Cohen argued that we could consider this a large effect because it is about as high as correlations between measures of *different concepts* get in the applied behavioral sciences.

Vaske, Gliner, and Morgan (2002) suggested that a more descriptive terminology would be that .1 is a *minimal relationship*, .3 is a *typical relationship* (one that is common for the behavioral sciences but could differ across disciplines), and .5 or more is a *substantial* (stronger than usual) *relationship* between two *different* concepts. We propose that correlations of these sizes be labeled *less than typical*, *typical*, and *greater than typical*, respectively, to emphasize that they are relative to literature in the field. When research is conducted in other fields, it can be helpful for the researcher to examine the literature to assess what would be considered typical in the specific field.

Confidence Intervals

Perhaps a better alternative to dealing with statistical significance and effect size (Chapter 17)—and one that is currently recommended by many methodologists—is to report the results from a correlation coefficient as a confidence interval. The reason for presenting a confidence interval is that showing a "statistically significant" r is showing only that it is nonzero. Thus a significant r may be completely trivial. A confidence interval delineates the magnitude and the error of estimation of r and is computed using the same information needed to determine statistical significance. Specifically, this information includes the value of r, the sample size used to determine r, and a table called the Fisher z transformation table. Zamboanga et al. (2007) might have stated the following as an example of a confidence interval: The 95% confidence interval for the relationship between lecture attendance and exam performance was between .23 and .54. In other words, they could be 95% confident that the actual (population) value of the relationship between the two variables would be found within this interval. (In Chapter 20, we illustrated how to compute the confidence interval for a t test.)

Using Nonparametric Associational Statistics

Spearman Rank-Order Correlation Coefficient and Kendall Tau Coefficient

When there are many ordered levels of both variables, one should use a nonparametric statistic if either the independent or dependent variable is ranked (or measured on an ordinal scale and not normally distributed) or if other assumptions underlying parametric associational statistics (linearity or equal variance) are violated. Two nonparametric statistics that are used to assess the relationship between ordered independent and dependent variables are the Spearman rank-order correlation (rho or r_s) and the Kendall tau (τ). The

Spearman correlation, the more common of the two, provides an index of the strength of a monotonic relationship (i.e., an increase in scores on one variable is accompanied by an increase or decrease in scores on the other variable, but this change in scores is not necessarily linear). Both the Spearman correlation and the Kendall tau are performed on ranked data rather than original scores. When the sample is relatively small and many of the rankings are the same for different participants (ties), the Kendall tau is the appropriate nonparametric choice.

Misleading Correlation Coefficients

Earlier, we discussed problems related to interpreting statistical significance and correlation coefficients. Other situations must be given attention that could lead to overestimation or underestimation of the correlation coefficient. A few common examples are as follows. (For a more in-depth explanation, see Shavelson, 1996). The first is referred to as restriction of the range. This occurs when the range of one of the variables used to compute the correlation coefficient is limited. This often happens with selected or homogeneous groups but also could happen if the scale of one of the variables has limited range. The result is usually a reduction in the size of the correlation coefficient. A second common example is when outliers, or extreme scores, occur in a relatively small sample. This can change the relationship between variables from linear to curvilinear or vice versa.

A third example occurs when samples from two different populations are combined. Fourth is the use of extreme groups. This happens when we perform correlations on participants that were selected because they represent just the high and low ends of a particular scale, and with no participants in the middle range. The third and fourth examples tend to inflate the correlation coefficient.

It is not uncommon to make incorrect inferences from correlation coefficients. We only can make inferences about causes if the design is a well-constructed, randomized experiment. Correlation coefficients are most common in associational, noncausal research approaches; hence, one should not infer causation even from a very strong correlation. Although correlations don't indicate causation, they can be strong, moderate, or weak.

In Chapter 22, we examine linear regression, used when the researcher wants to predict values of the dependent or outcome variable from the independent variable based on the strength of a correlation.

Associational Statistics for Nominal Variables

The Chi-Square Test and Accompanying Effect Size Indices

In the first part of this chapter, we described statistical methods used to test the statistical significance of a relationship between two variables that were either continuous or had many ordered categories or levels. Now we describe a statistical test, the *Pearson chi-square (χ^2) test for independence*, which examines the relationship between two variables that are dichotomous or nominal level, with a few nonordered categories. Nominal scale data provide less information than normally distributed or ordinal scale data. The finer the gradations on the measurement scale, the more information is transmitted, as long as there is evidence for reliability and validity. We recommend that ordered data not be divided into a few categories if the data are continuous or have a number of ordered levels, unless the measure to be divided has been validated against an external criterion that justifies using "cut points."

When there are more than two categories of at least one of the variables and these categories are ordered (i.e., ordinal scale), such as education level, which might vary from a little to a lot, power is lost if a χ^2 test is used to analyze the data. We recommend that such data be analyzed by using nonparametric statistics for ordinal data. Kendall's tau correlation could be used if both variables have more than two ordered levels, or a Mann-Whitney U test could be used if one of the two variables has only two levels and the other is ordered (see Chapter 19). Not discussed in this book is the *chi-square test*, for the *goodness of fit* of one sample of nominal data to some theoretical distribution or known distribution.

For the χ^2 test, the data to be considered are frequencies. Specifically, our interest is in how many people (the frequency count) fall into a particular category, relative to a different category. There are two major requirements of the χ^2 test. The first is that frequencies represent counts. The second is that each participant can be assigned to only one category or cell.

The χ^2 test for independence tests the association between two variables. Under the null hypothesis, the two variables are assumed to be independent of each other. First we discuss a χ^2 with only two categories of each variable, often referred to as a **two-by-two contingency table**, and then expand our discussion to χ^2 tests where there are more than two nonordered categories for at least one of the variables. Examples are provided for both situations. We also discuss effect size measures that describe the strength of relationship between two nominal scale variables.

The Chi-Square (χ^2) Test With One Degree of Freedom

The chi-square test with two categories of each variable is commonly used to test the impact of an intervention compared with a control group. In this design, participants in the intervention group are dichotomized into those who are successful and those who are not successful. The same is done for the comparison group. Thus, there are two levels of treatment (i.e., those who are treated and those who are not treated) and two levels of outcome (i.e., those who are successful and those who are not successful). A study by Walters (2005) demonstrates the use of the 2×2 chi-square, which is a chi-square test with one degree of freedom. Walters was interested in preventing recidivism in prisoners in a medium-security federal prison. The intervention in this study was the Lifestyle Change Program (LCP). The first phase was a 10-week psycho-educational class about lifestyle issues. The second phase consisted of three 20-week sessions titled "Advanced Group" examining the lifestyles of gambling, drugs, and crime, which were considered to be most relevant to offender populations. The third phase of the program was titled "Relapse Prevention" and lasted 40 weeks. For our purposes, we focus on Walters's first chi-square analysis, which categorized the intervention into those who completed at least the first phase of the LCP (intervention group) and those who also volunteered for the program but either were released or were transferred prior to undergoing any part of the program (control group). The outcome measure was arrest following the release from prison during a specified follow-up period (none versus one or more arrests). Table 21.2 shows the data for the first outcome in the Walters study. Walters reported the outcome as follows: "Data collected during the follow-up showed that 115 (39.5%) program participants and 49 (55.1%) control

TABLE 21.2

Frequency Data and Percentages

	One or more arrests	No arrests	Total
Control inmates	49 (55.1%)	40 (44.9%)	89 (100%)
Program participants	115 (39.5%)	176 (60.5%)	291 (100%)
Total	164	216	380

Source: Data are from Walters, G. D., *Criminal Justice and Behavior, 32,* 2005, 50–68.

inmates were arrested one or more times following their release from prison, a statistically significant difference, χ^2 (1, $N = 380$) = 6.71, $p < .01$ (p. 58).

The χ^2 statistic for these data was reported as $\chi^2 = 6.71$. The value of 6.71 is the computed χ^2 for this example. To arrive at this value, expected frequencies are generated for each cell in the contingency table by multiplying the corresponding row and column totals together and then dividing by the total sample. The *expected frequencies* are the frequencies we would expect if the two variables were not related. To obtain each cell value, the expected frequency is subtracted from the observed frequency (the actual cell frequencies), squared, and divided by the expected frequency. The four cell values are added to determine the χ^2 value.

There is one degree of freedom for this χ^2. In the previous statistical tests that we have discussed, such as the t test, F test, and correlation coefficient, degrees of freedom were associated with the sample size for either the whole study or specific groups. In the χ^2 test, degrees of freedom are associated with the number of categories within each variable. For any χ^2, the degrees of freedom are determined by multiplying the number of rows minus 1 times the number of columns minus 1. In the present example, the degrees of freedom are 2 rows minus 1 times 2 columns minus 1 equals 1.

The χ^2 value was reported, and it was statistically significant at $p < .01$. Statistical significance is determined by comparing the computed χ^2 value, 6.71, to a value in the χ^2 table associated with $p < .01$ and one degree of freedom.[3] This table value is referred to as the critical value. A critical value of 6.63 in the χ^2 table corresponds to the .01 level for one degree of freedom. Any χ^2 value that is as large as or larger than this critical value has a probability of occurrence of less than 1 in 100, assuming a true null hypothesis. Because the value of 6.71 exceeds 6.63, it is considered to be statistically significant ($p < .01$). A statement summarizing this result is that there was a statistically significant relationship between the variables of Lifestyle Change Program and outcome, subsequent arrests, with the program leading to fewer arrests.

Interpretation of the Chi-Square Test With One Degree of Freedom

Percentages

Perhaps the simplest method of interpreting the χ^2 test with one degree of freedom is to convert each cell frequency to a percentage and to examine the relationships among these cell percentages. For example, as mentioned earlier, Walters (2005) stated that only 39% of program participants compared with 55% of the control group were arrested after release. One could calculate percentages so that either the row or column percentages add to 100%. A general rule is to calculate row percentages so that they add to 100% if in the table, as here, the independent variable is a row variable, or vice versa if the independent variable is the column variable. Sometimes, as in the present study, the independent variable is obvious, such as when there is a treatment. Other times, however, when there has been no active independent variable, interpretation is not as obvious. When there is no active independent variable, one should determine the likely order of occurrence of the variables. A first variable that *precedes a second variable* in time is usually considered to be the independent variable.

Phi as an Effect Size

For a χ^2 test with one degree of freedom, a common effect size indicator of the strength of the relationship between the two variables is phi (φ). Phi is a nonparametric measure of association or correlation between two variables when both are dichotomous (i.e., have two levels). Like the Pearson product-moment correlation, discussed in the last section, a strong association would be indicated by a φ coefficient of +.5 or −.5 or greater from zero (Cohen, 1988). No association would be indicated by a coefficient near zero. The phi value for the chi-square test performed in the Walters (2005) study was .13, considered to be a small or smaller than typical effect size. One disadvantage of φ as an effect size is that the size of φ is restricted by the row and column percentages. The closer the two row percentages are to the two column percentages, the higher is the maximum upward limit of φ (Nunnally & Berstein, 1994). Thus phi, as in Walters, may underestimate the strength of the relationship and be hard to interpret as an effect size.

Strength of Association Measures Involving Risk

In addition to the effect size measure, φ, there are three measures of association often used in epidemiology and medical research with a two-by-two (2×2) contingency table. These fit in the *risk potency effect size* category discussed in Chapter 17. They express the risk of clinical-level outcomes. These measures are *relative risk, risk difference,* and *odds ratio.* The three measures can be understood from the Walters's (2005) example in Table 21.2.

The **relative risk** is determined by first computing a percentage by dividing those who are in the control condition and unsuccessful (49) by the total of the control condition (89). A second percentage is computed by dividing those who are in the intervention condition and unsuccessful (115) by the total of the intervention condition (291). In the Walters (2005) example, these two percentages are 55.1% for the control group and 39.5% for the intervention group. A ratio is then obtained by dividing the control percentage (55.1%) by the intervention percentage (39.5%). In the present example, the relative risk is 1.4. Thus, the relative risk of having an unsuccessful outcome (recidivism) is 1.4 times higher in the control condition compared with the intervention condition.

Risk difference is obtained with the same percentages as relative risk, except that instead of obtaining a ratio, a percentage difference is computed by subtracting the percent of unsuccessful cases in the intervention group from the percent of unsuccessful cases in the control group (55.1% minus 39.5%). Thus, there is an approximately 16% greater risk of having an unsuccessful outcome in the control group compared with the treatment group. The risk difference is very close to the phi coefficient for all 2×2 contingency tables. In the example, the risk difference (0.16) is close in magnitude to φ, which was 0.13.

Odds ratio, the most commonly reported of these measures, is determined by first computing the ratio of those in the control group who are unsuccessful to those in the control group who are successful (49/40). A second ratio is computed from those in the intervention group who were unsuccessful to those in the intervention group who were successful (115/176). In the Walters (2005) study, these two ratios are 1.23 for the control group and .65 for the intervention. The odds ratio is then obtained by dividing the control group ratio by the intervention group ratio. In our present example, the odds ratio is 1.9 (1.23/0.65), indicating that the odds of obtaining an unsuccessful outcome in the control group are 1.9 times higher than in the intervention group. It should be noted that odds ratios are often provided as a result of a logistic regression (Chapter 22). The major limitation of the odds ratio as an effect size index is that the upper limit may approach infinity if one of the cells is quite small relative to the other cells. Thus, it is difficult to decide what represents a large odds ratio compared with effect sizes that accompany parametric tests such as r and d. Although odds ratios intuitively seem to be meaningful to nonstatisticians, they can be quite misleading.

Which of the three measures of effect size involving risk presented here is the most appropriate? Rosenthal (2001) examined the three effect size measures and recommended risk difference. As stated earlier, the risk difference is very close to the φ coefficient, and partly, "For that reason, the risk difference index may be the one least likely to be quite misleading under special circumstances" (p. 135).

The Chi-Square Test With Greater Than One Degree of Freedom

Although a 2×2 contingency table analyzed by a χ^2 is commonly observed and relatively easy to interpret, there are many cases in which the number of rows, columns, or both exceeds 2. For example, a study published by Zeanah et al. (2001) compared an intervention group (IG) with a comparison group (CG) to examine outcomes for infants and toddlers in foster care. The four outcome categories for foster children were reunification with birth parents, termination of parental rights, surrender of parental rights, and placement with a relative. Table 21.3 shows the relationship between the treatment group and outcome type.

A statistically significant χ^2 was reported for these data (χ^2 [$df = 3$, $N = 240$] = 16.13, $p < .01$). The value 16.13 is the χ^2 for this example. There are three degrees of freedom for this χ^2 (4 rows minus 1 times 2 columns minus 1). Again, the relationship was statistically significant ($p < .01$).

TABLE 21.3

Frequency of Outcome Type by Group Membership

Outcome type	Group membership	
	Intervention group	Comparison group
Reunification	33 (34.7%)	71 (49.0%)
Termination	42 (44.2%)	30 (20.7%)
Surrender	8 (8.4%)	17 (11.7%)
Relative placement	12 (12.6%)	27 (18.6%)
Total	95 (100%)	145 (100%)

Source: Data are from Zeanah, C. H., Larrieu, J. A., Heller, S. S., Valliere, J., Hinshaw-Fuselier, S., Aoki, Y., et al., *Journal of the American Academy of Child and Adolescent Psychiatry, 40,* 2001, 214–221.

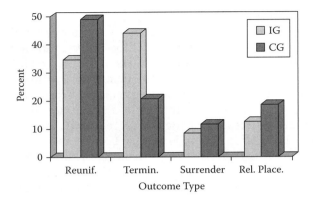

FIGURE 21.1

Frequency of outcome type by group membership, presented as a bar graph. (Data from Zeanah, C. H., Larrieu, J. A., Heller, S. S., Valliere, J., Hinshaw-Fuselier, S., Aoki, Y., et al., *Journal of the American Academy of Child and Adolescent Psychiatry, 40,* 2001, 214–221.)

Interpretation of the Chi-Square Test With More Than One Degree of Freedom

Percentages

Similar to the χ^2 with one degree of freedom, cell frequencies should be converted to percentages to detect patterns. The percentages following the frequencies for each cell this time are column percentages because the independent variable is group membership, a column variable (Table 21.3). When performing a χ^2 with more than one degree of freedom, a bar graph of the percentages is often a meaningful method to facilitate interpretation. Figure 21.1 displays the percentage data from Table 21.3.

The largest percentage discrepancies for the two groups were for reunification and termination; Zeanah et al. (2001) reported, "An examination of the frequency table indicated that this difference was due to the fact that the IG had more than twice as many terminations as the CG and the IG had significantly fewer reunifications" (p. 217). That is, "More children were freed for adoption … than before the intervention" (p. 214).

Two-by-Two Contingency Tables

A second method to facilitate interpretation of the chi-square test with more than one degree of freedom is to examine meaningful comparisons by setting up two-by-two contingency tables. In our present example, a two-by-two table could be established comparing the intervention group and the comparison group on reunification and termination. A phi value could be computed, or a measure of associated risk could be established. There are other methods to construct two-by-two contingency tables from larger tables, such as the chi-square corner test or combined category chi-square test (Rosenthal & Rosnow, 1991). We point out that the comparisons must be meaningful, usually established prior to the study, and related to the original hypotheses.

Summary

In this chapter we discussed the selection and application of appropriate statistical methods used to answer basic associational questions. These statistical methods are usually used in single-factor designs with many ordered levels of the independent variable. The most common correlation coefficient used to describe the relationship between a continuous independent and dependent variable is the Pearson product-moment correlation, r. The effect size of a correlation coefficient can be either the squared value of r or just the value or r. When the measurement of the independent variable is not at the interval level, or there are violations precluding the use of parametric statistics, the Spearman correlation is most often applied.

The chi-square (χ^2) test for independence is the appropriate statistical test for answering basic associational questions when both variables are nominal scale variables. The chi-square test with one degree of freedom (2 × 2 contingency table) is the most common. Interpretation of outcomes from this table is facilitated by converting frequencies to row or column percentages and calculating effect size measures such as the risk difference index or φ. Chi-square tests on contingency tables with more than two levels in the columns, rows, or both are often more difficult to interpret, but bar graphs are useful in conveying accurately and succinctly the relationship between two variables. Also, reduction to two-by-two contingency tables is recommended.

Key Concepts

Chi-square test (χ^2)

Correlation matrix

Kendall's tau (τ)

Odds ratio (*OR*)

Pearson product-moment correlation (*r*)

Phi (φ)

Relative risk (*RR*)

Risk difference (*RD*)

Spearman rank-order correlation (r_s)

Squared correlation coefficient (r^2)

Two-by-two contingency table (2 × 2)

Key Distinctions

Correlation coefficient versus squared correlation coefficient

Pearson product-moment correlation versus Spearman rank-order correlation

Odds ratio versus relative risk versus risk difference

Phi versus *r*

Application Problems

1. Using Table 21.1 and the text, write a sentence, including r, df, and p, interpreting the correlation between ACT score and lecture attendance. Also write such a sentence about the correlation of ACT score and exam performance.

2. A study was performed to determine if high school teaching performance in the classroom was related to scores on a licensure examination. Both measurement tools were normally distributed. What is the appropriate inferential statistic? Why? What is an appropriate measure of effect size?

3. There is a relationship between teaching evaluations and course grades. This hypothesis was tested in a graduate seminar with 10 students. The students' grades in the course ranged from C (2) to A (4). The course evaluations ranged from neutral (3) to very good (5). What analysis should be performed to test this relationship and why?

4. An investigator performs a study for an insurance company to determine the relationship, if any, between hand strength after surgery and length of time in treatment measured in hours from 1 to 15. The investigator measures each patient after surgery to determine hand strength from 0 to 100. Then she divides the patients into low (1–5 hours), medium (6–10 hours), and high (11–15 hours) length of time each patient spent in treatment. To determine if there are differences among the three groups, she performs a single-factor analysis of variance (ANOVA) with hand strength as the dependent variable. How could she use the associational approach in this study? What would be the advantages?

5. A therapist was interested in determining the effectiveness of a new treatment for children with cerebral palsy. The therapist had 40 such children in her clinic. She randomly assigned participants to one of two groups (20 in each group). The treatment group received the new treatment therapy. The control group received a traditional therapy. After 4 months, all 40 children performed a motor coordination task. If the child completed the task, treatment was considered to be successful. If the child was unable to complete the task, treatment was considered to be unsuccessful. What is the appropriate inferential statistic? Why? What effect size measure would you use? Why?

6. Given the following 2 × 2 cross-tabulation table, interpret the results.

	Fail	Pass	
Intervention	10 (26%)	29 (74%)	100%
Comparison	24 (67%)	12 (33%)	100%

$\chi^2 = 12.71$

φ (phi) = .41

Notes

1. In Chapter 10, we introduced the topic of correlation as a descriptive statistic. Here we expand that, in part, by discussing statistical significance and how to interpret effect size for correlation coefficients.
2. It is common for correlations in a matrix that are statistically significant to be identified with asterisks, as shown in Table 21.1. However, when space is available, it is best practice to include the exact p values, not just indicate whether a value is statistically significant.
3. When using a computer, the computer checks the table and gives the exact p value associated with the result.

22

Analysis and Interpretation
of Complex Research Questions

In this chapter we discuss the selection and application of appropriate statistical methods to answer complex research questions. When referring to complex research questions, we are discussing analyses that have more than one independent variable and sometimes more than one dependent variable. Although many different statistical analyses could be included in this category, we discuss the most common analyses in some detail, providing examples where appropriate. We focus on three analyses in particular: (1) the *two-factor between-groups analysis of variance*; (2) the *mixed analysis of variance* with reference to the analysis of designs that includes a pretest and posttest; and (3) *multiple regression*. We also touch on other analyses such as *analysis of covariance, two-factor within-subjects analysis of variance (ANOVA)*, linear or *bivariate regression, discriminant analysis,* and *logistic regression*. All of these complex difference and associational statistics have a dependent variable that should be approximately normally distributed or, for discriminant analysis and logistic regression, dichotomous. There are no common complex non-parametric inferential statistics for ordinal dependent variables. Data transformations or other statistical adjustments are necessary when the assumptions of these complex statistics are markedly violated.

Analysis and Interpretation of Complex Difference Questions

The Two-Factor Between-Groups Analysis of Variance

In Chapter 20 we discussed the single-factor between-groups ANOVA. Remember, in the single-factor ANOVA, there is one independent variable, a between-groups independent variable, with two or more levels. The dependent variable is assumed to be normally distributed without severe violations of homogeneity of variance. Now, we introduce an example of a study with a second between-groups independent variable and demonstrate how between-groups factorial designs are analyzed and interpreted.

There are two major reasons for adding a second independent variable in a study. The first reason is that it provides the researcher more information. When we have two independent variables in a single study, we can determine how each independent variable works by itself and determine how the two independent variables work together or interact. How an independent variable, by itself, affects the dependent variable is referred to as a **main effect**. How two independent variables interact on the dependent variable is referred to as an **interaction effect**. In a study with two independent variables, there will be two main effects (one for each independent variable) and an interaction effect. We would like to emphasize that the term *effect* can be misleading because it seems to imply a causal relationship. As noted in earlier chapters, this inference is not justified if the independent variable is an attribute (e.g., age or gender) and may not be justified with an active independent variable unless the study is a well-designed randomized experiment. Thus, one should be cautious about interpreting a significant main effect as meaning that the independent variable caused the difference in the dependent variable.

Consider a study by Conners et al. (2001), who were interested in the effects of two independent variables on an attention deficit hyperactivity disorder (ADHD) outcome assessment measured by a composite score. In one of their analyses, the two independent variables were treatment type and treatment site. In the analysis, there was one main effect for treatment and a second main effect for site. There also was an interaction effect between treatment and site.

The second reason for using a two-factor design instead of two single-factor designs is that *error variance* is more precisely estimated. Error variance is variability attributed to individual differences among participants. Often these differences are due to assessments not measuring a construct reliably. At other times these differences are due to age, gender, or site differences among participants. It is the latter type of error we are trying to reduce. If we introduce a second independent variable, such as site, then part of the error variance due to this variable could be removed and distributed as a second independent variable. Conners et al. (2001) were primarily interested in the active independent variable, type of treatment. The other independent variable, site, was not important by itself, but if it was statistically significant, it would reduce error variability in the study.

The study by Conners et al. (2001) had a 4 × 6 factorial design. Children aged 7 to 9 who met *Diagnostic and Statistical Manual of Mental Disorders*, 4th edition, text revision (*DSM-IV-TR*; American Psychiatric Association, 2000) criteria for ADHD combined type were randomly assigned to one of four treatments at each screening site. The four levels of the first independent variable were four types of treatment: (1) medication management; (2) behavior therapy; (3) a combination of these treatments; and (4) community comparison, which was composed of children who were assessed and then referred to local community care resources. The six levels of the second independent variable were six participating university sites.[1] The key dependent variable, the composite score, was converted to a standard score for each participant. This standard score was then compared with baseline scores, yielding a change score for each time period. Negative scores indicated a reduction in symptoms. The average change score for each treatment condition after 14 months can be seen in Table 22.1.

TABLE 22.1

Composite Outcome by Treatment 14 Months Postbaseline

Treatment	*n*	*M*	*SD*
Combined	145	−2.23	1.35
Medication management	144	−1.82	1.61
Behavior therapy	144	−1.42	1.47
Community comparison	146	−1.29	1.36

Source: Data are from Conners, C. K., Epstein, J. N., March, J. S., Angold, A., Wells, K. C., Klaric, J., et al., *Journal of the American Academy of Child and Adolescent Psychiatry, 40,* 2001, 159–167.

TABLE 22.2

Two-Factor ANOVA Source Table

Source	SS	df	MS	F
Treatment (A)	77.88	3	25.96	13.49*
Site (B)	83.02	5	16.60	8.63*
Treatment × site (A × B)	52.56	15	3.50	1.82
Within subjects (error)	1,067.76	555	1.92	

*$p < .01$.

Source: Data are from Conners, C. K., Epstein, J. N., March, J. S. Angold, A., Wells, K. C., Klaric, J., et al., *Journal of the American Academy of Child and Adolescent Psychiatry, 40,* 2001, 159–167.

Analysis of Two-Factor Designs

Two-factor designs are analyzed with a two-factor ANOVA if both independent variables are between-groups independent variables and the ANOVA assumptions of independence, homogeneity of variance, and normality are not markedly violated (see Chapter 19 for more discussion of these assumptions). For those studies with two independent variables and a dependent variable that is measured on an *ordinal* scale, there are no common statistics. These studies are sometimes analyzed with nonparametric techniques applied to one independent variable at a time, but the interaction effect is lost. There are sophisticated techniques such as log-linear analysis for categorical data that are beyond the scope of this book.

Source Table for a Two-Factor ANOVA

ANOVA procedures have an accompanying source table, which for the Conners et al. (2001) study is Table 22.2.

The two-factor ANOVA starts by dividing the sums of squares (*SS*) into a between-groups component and an error component. Next, as shown in Table 22.2, the between-groups component is divided into a *SS* for independent variable A (treatment), a *SS* for independent variable B (site), and the remainder is the interaction *SS*, A × B. The degrees of freedom (*df*) for independent variable A are the number of levels or types of treatment (four) minus 1. The *df* for independent variable B are the number of sites (six) minus 1. The interaction *df* are computed by multiplying the *df* for independent variable A (three) times the *df* of independent variable B (five). The *df* for the error term are computed by subtracting the sum of the *df* for independent variable A, independent variable B, and the interaction from the total *df*. The total *df* (not shown) is the number of participants minus 1. Each of the four *SS* is divided by its corresponding *df* to obtain mean squares (*MS*). Thus, there will be four *MS*.

Each of the three *F* values, seen in the last column in Table 22.2, is obtained by dividing the *MS* for that source of variation by the *MS* for error. As Table 22.2 shows, there are four *MS* and three *F* values in the source table. Thus, in a two-factor ANOVA, there are three *F* values and three questions that can be answered: one about each main effect and the interaction. To get a clearer picture of the role of the source table in a two-factor ANOVA, let's examine the data from the study by Conners et al. (2001).

Questions Answered in the Two-Factor ANOVA

In the single-factor design, one hypothesis is tested: the effect of that independent variable on the dependent variable. In the two-factor design, three null hypotheses are tested: (1) the means of the four conditions of independent variable A (treatment type) are equal; (2) the means of the six sites of independent variable B are equal; and (3) the interaction of independent variables A and B is zero.

Describing the Results in the Text

Although we have presented the data from the Conners et al. (2001) two-factor ANOVA in a source table, it is not uncommon to have authors report their results in the text to save space. The data from Table 22.2 might be reported as follows: There were statistically significant differences among four treatment conditions ($F_{3,555} = 13.49, p < .001$). There was also a statistically significant effect of site ($F_{5,555} = 8.63, p < .001$). The interaction was statistically significant at the .05 probability level but not the .01 probability level ($F_{15,555} = 1.82, p = .029$). When presenting the results in text form, the degrees of freedom for that effect and the error term are given as subscript numbers.

Interpretation of the Results From a Two-Factor ANOVA

A first step toward interpretation of the two-factor ANOVA could be to compute an overall eta^2 (η^2), which would determine how much of the variance in the dependent variable, composite score, was estimated by the treatment, the site, *and* the interaction between the two independent variables. However, in the Conners et al. (2001) publication, there was no discussion of the site differences or the interaction, probably because they were not the focus of their article, which was one of many from this large, multisite project. Like Conners et al., we start our interpretation of the results by focusing on the main effect of treatment type. Then we present simplified, hypothetical results to illustrate how to interpret a significant interaction.

Interpretation of Significant Main Effects

As noted there was a statistically significant main effect for treatment, which indicates that all of the means were not equal. Table 22.3 shows which pairs of means were statistically significantly different based on a *post hoc test* comparing each pair of treatments. Notice that the combined (medication management and behavior therapy) treatment was statistically significantly better than each of the other three at $p < .05$. Likewise, medication management was better than behavior therapy ($p = .015$) and community comparison ($p = .001$). However, behavior therapy was not significantly better than the community comparison ($p = .451$).

   Statistical significance does not tell us about the size or strength of the relationship (i.e., the effect size; ES) between the treatment group variable and the composite score. Conners et al. (2001) could have computed η^2 for the overall main effect of treatment. This would provide an estimate of the relationship of all of the treatments to the dependent variable, the composite score. This eta^2 value (computed from the data presented in Table 22.2) was .06, indicating that the treatment accounted for 6% of the variance of the dependent measure in the study, a medium effect size according to Cohen's (1988) guidelines. We think that best practice in this situation would be to compute effect sizes comparing individual

TABLE 22.3

Effect Sizes and Significance for Post Hoc Contrasts
Between Treatments

Contrast	p	ES
Combined > Med Management	.012	0.28
Combined > Behavioral	.000	0.58
Combined > Community	.000	0.70
Med Management > Behavioral	.015	0.26
Med Management > Community	.001	0.35
Behavioral ≈ Community	.451	0.09

Note: One-tailed hypothesis. ES = Cohen delta. Med Management = medication management. Behavioral = behavior therapy. Community = community comparison.

Source: Data are from Conners, C. K., Epstein, J. N., March, J. S. Angold, A., Wells, K. C., Klaric, J., et al., *Journal of the American Academy of Child and Adolescent Psychiatry, 40,* 2001, 159–167.

treatments, as Conners et al. did. They computed the Cohen delta (or *d*), which is presented in Table 22.3 in the ES column. Note that the ES for the statistically significant contrasts between the combined treatment and the other three vary from roughly small (0.28) to medium (0.58) to large (0.70) according to Cohen's general guidelines (see Table 17.1 for effect size interpretations). Conners et al. also discussed several ways, suggested by Kraemer (1992), of assessing the clinical importance of the findings. One index used to indicate a clinically meaningful effect, when comparing two types of psychotherapeutic treatments, is *d* ES of 0.2 or more. All of the statistically significant contrasts in this study are greater than 0.2 so appear to be clinically important.

Interpretation of an Interaction Effect

Table 22.2 showed that there were statistically significant main effects for treatment, site, and a statistically significant (at $p < .05$) interaction between treatment and site. Best practice is to interpret the interaction effect *first* because it provides a more accurate understanding of the results since the main effect may be misleading when there is a statistically significant interaction. To simplify the discussion of interaction effects, let us assume that the design had only two treatments (behavior therapy and community comparison) and three sites. The hypothetical findings for this 2 × 3 design are shown in Figure 22.1.

A first step in the examination of a statistically significant interaction is to plot the cell means. When setting up an interaction plot, the dependent variable is placed on the *y* (vertical) axis. When there are two independent variables, a guideline is to place the attribute independent variable (site) on the *x* axis and graph the active independent variable (type of treatment) with separate lines, as we have in Figure 22.1. In a *disordinal interaction,* the lines on the graph cross. An interaction is said to be *ordinal* if the lines are clearly not parallel but do not cross within the graph. When there is no interaction, the lines are approximately parallel to each other. Although a plot of the data is informative to guide interpretation, statistical significance can be determined only by follow-up statistical procedures.

One way to do these statistical procedures is referred to as *simple main effects* analyses with *post hoc comparisons.* Simple main effects analysis is a statistical procedure that takes advantage of the information already compiled from computing the two-factor ANOVA.

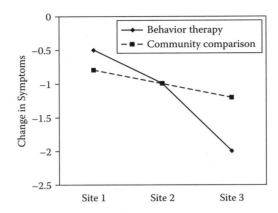

FIGURE 22.1
Hypothetical findings for a simplified 2 × 3 design showing a statistically significant interaction.

Performing simple main effects is similar to performing single-factor ANOVAs on each of the two independent variables in Figure 22.1, one level at a time. If simple main effects were performed for the independent variable of site, there would be three simple main effects, one for each site. Each simple main effect would be tested to determine whether there was a significant difference between behavior therapy and community comparison. In our hypothetical example, there was no significant simple main effect for site 1 or site 2, but there was a significant simple main effect for site 3. We might conclude that the statistically significant interaction resulted from site 3 children doing better (more reduction in symptoms) from behavior therapy than from community resources, whereas site 1 and site 2 students did not differ on the two treatments.

Simple main effects analysis could have been performed for the two treatment conditions instead of the three site conditions. However, if there were statistically significant differences for either of the treatment conditions, follow-up post hoc analyses would have to be performed, because there are three levels in each of the treatment conditions. These post hoc analyses would be similar to those discussed in Chapter 20 in the section about single-factor ANOVA.

Analysis of 2 × 2 Designs When Both Independent Variables Are Attributes

Caution should be exercised when there are two independent variables and both are attribute independent variables. The issue is one of interpretation of results if the choice of analysis is a two-way ANOVA. The underlying problem is that when both independent variables are attributes, there may be a correlation between the two variables, confounding the results. Since no manipulation of either independent variable is involved, this correlation could lead to a misinterpretation of the results (see Pedhazur and Schmelkin, 1991, pp. 537–538).

Studies examining two attribute independent variables with two-way ANOVAs are not uncommon. For example, Poole, Chiappisi, Cordova, and Sibbitt (2007) were interested in quality of life in American Indian women and White women with and without rheumatoid arthritis. The two independent variables, ethnicity and rheumatoid arthritis, are attribute independent variables. Two issues should be considered. First, is there a relationship between ethnicity and rheumatoid arthritis? Second, are there other underlying variables that could be accounting for the results of the study? Often, as in the present case, one is not sure of these possible relationships. Best practice is that one should be cautious about interpreting the results of the analysis, and avoid inferences about cause and effect.

The Two-Factor Within-Subjects (Repeated-Measures) Analysis of Variance

A design with two independent variables, where both variables are within-subjects (or repeated-measures) independent variables is much less common than the two-factor between-groups design. Since it is relatively rare we just touch on the design and analysis briefly. An example by Fuller, Thomas, and Rice (2006) demonstrates the use of the two-factor within-subjects design. These researchers were interested in return of movement of the affected arm in persons who had experienced a cerebral vascular accident (stroke). Specifically, the researchers wanted to observe arm movement under conditions of high and low *perceived* risk, with the affected and unaffected arm. There was just one group of participants who had experienced a cerebral vascular accident (CVA). There were two independent variables for this study. The first independent variable was perceived level of risk with two levels. The levels were high-risk (transporting a raw egg from an egg carton to a bowl with other eggs) and low-risk condition (transporting plastic eggs from the carton to the bowl). The second independent variable was extremity, affected and unaffected. One of the dependent variables was movement time (MT).

The analysis for this design is a two-factor analysis of variance with repeated measures on *both* factors. While the calculations and associated degrees of freedom are different from the two-factor between-groups ANOVA, the outcomes are the same; that is, there are two main effects and an interaction effect. Similar to interpreting the two-factor between-groups ANOVA, if there is a significant interaction effect, then that should be the focus. Fuller et al. (2006) found a statistically significant main effect for risk, with the high-risk condition yielding significantly slower movement time than the low-risk condition. They also found a statistically significant main effect for arm, with the affected arm yielding slower movement times than the unaffected arm. However, there was no statistically significant risk by arm interaction effect. The authors reported results as follows: "The change in the mean MT from the higher risk condition to the lower risk condition for the affected limb was not significantly different for the same comparison with the unaffected limb."

The Mixed Factorial (Split-Plot) Design

In this section and the next section, we discuss the analysis of designs that have at least one independent variable that is a between-groups independent variable and one independent variable that is a repeated-measures independent variable. The first design, the mixed factorial design, although relatively rare is often used in a crossover design situation (see Chapter 18). We provide an example of that situation. The second design, the pretest–posttest control group design, or its quasi-experimental counterpart, the pretest–posttest nonequivalent comparison groups design, are much more common, and we devote considerable detail in the next section to the analysis of these designs.

The mixed factorial design has one between-groups independent variable and one within-subjects or repeated-measures independent variable *that is not time*. Similar to the two-factor between-groups ANOVA and the two-factor within-subjects ANOVA, the mixed ANOVA provides an output that has two main effects and an interaction effect. While the calculations are different (the mixed ANOVA has two error terms), the method of interpreting the analysis focuses on the interaction effect first similar to the previously discussed two-way ANOVAs. Tebben and Jepsen (2004) used a crossover approach to examine wrist positioning with two different gardening tools (trowels): an ergonomically designed trowel and a standard designed trowel. In their study, participants were randomly assigned to one of two different groups. One group performed the task of filling flowerpots with soil using the ergonomically designed trowel first and then the standard design trowel second, whereas the other group did the task in the reverse order, using the standard design trowel first. Their dependent variables included measures of wrist movement and preference. The obvious focus of this design is the comparison of the two trowels, a within-subjects variable since all participants underwent both conditions. However, one cannot discount the order effect. In other words, is it possible that using one type of trowel first impacted the use of the other trowel? These types of results are referred to as asymmetrical transfer effects and need to be tested. Thus, a two-factor mixed ANOVA would provide that information in addition to the treatment effect. It should be noted that a Latin Square analysis also could be used to test the order effects with the two variables being sequence by order (see Rosenthal & Rosnow, 1991, pp. 400–401).

Pretest–Posttest Comparison Group Designs: Analysis and Interpretation

The Pretest–Posttest Comparison Group Design

This design is a *randomized experimental* design and one of the most extensively used methods to evaluate clinical research, but it is often overanalyzed with more than one analysis performed when one is sufficient. We discuss parametric approaches that are often used to analyze this design and the strengths and limitations of each approach. We then comment on common nonparametric approaches.

The simplest case of the pretest–posttest comparison group design has one treatment group and one comparison group. Prior to the pretest, participants are randomly assigned to groups or conditions. Random assignment is an important feature of the pretest–posttest comparison group design and separates it from nonequivalent (nonrandomized) group designs, which are quasi-experiments. Each group is measured prior to the intervention and after the intervention. Typically, one group receives a new treatment, and the other group receives the usual treatment or a placebo. The purpose of this design is to allow the investigator to evaluate a new treatment relative to the previously used treatment or no treatment at all.

The design is classified as a mixed design because there are two independent variables, a between-groups independent variable, the treatment, and a within-subjects or repeated-measures independent variable, change over time from pretest to posttest. Time is a within-subjects independent variable because two or more measures are recorded for each person. Although the simplest description of the design has two levels of treatment and two levels of time, it is not uncommon to have three levels of treatment, such as two treatments and a control group, or more than two repeated-measures. The number of levels of an independent variable makes a difference in the type of analysis selected, as does the scale of measurement of the dependent variable.

We start with the example of the study by Miller, Coll, and Schoen (2007). The objective of this study was to evaluate an occupational therapy treatment, sensory integration for children with sensory modulation disorder. To determine the effectiveness of the sensory integration approach, a pretest–posttest comparison group design was established. There were three levels of the between-groups independent variable: sensory integration therapy,

TABLE 22.4

Change Scores From Pretest to Posttest (10 Weeks)
on the Leiter-R Attention Measure

	N	Mean	SD
Sensory Integration	7	1.57	2.37
Activity	10	.10	1.10
No treatment difference	7	−.43	1.27

Source: Data are from Miller, L. J., Coll, J. R., & Schoen, S. A.,
American Journal of Occupational Therapy, 61, 2007, 228–238.

activity therapy, and no treatment. Time, the repeated-measures independent variable, was 10 weeks from pretest to posttest. While there were many dependent variables in this study, for our purposes, attention as measured by the Leiter International Performance Scale-Revised (Leiter-R) is examined. Participants were randomly assigned to one of the three groups, making this a pretest–posttest comparison group design. Best practice suggests three different approaches to the analysis of the pretest–posttest comparison group design: (1) the gain score approach; (2) the mixed ANOVA approach; and (3) the analysis of covariance (ANCOVA) approach.

Gain or Change Score Approach

This is the most straightforward approach for the analysis of this design. The gain score approach involves subtracting the pretest scores from the posttest scores within each group. Miller et al. (2007) used this approach, which changes the design from a mixed design to a single-factor design. Subtracting scores created just *one independent variable with three groups* or levels: the sensory integration (SI) group, the activity group, and the nontreatment group. The gain scores become the dependent variable. Table 22.4 shows the gain scores for the three groups. As reported in Figure 19.3 (Chapter 19), the proper analysis for this design is a single-factor analysis of variance, which tests whether the means of the gain scores for the three groups are equal. However, one should be cautious when using the gain score approach because the reliability of gain scores is often suspect, especially if there is not evidence for strong reliability of the measurement instrument. They found a significant difference among groups, with the SI group performing significantly better than the no treatment control group ($p < .03$) and the activity group ($p < .07$). It is presumed that these differences were evaluated with some form of post hoc test following a significant ANOVA.

Mixed Analysis of Variance Approach

The mixed ANOVA approach is a less common approach to the analysis of the pretest–posttest comparison group design. This analysis appears to be the proper analysis in this situation, because the design is a mixed design, but this is misleading. Since there are two independent variables in this design, the analysis yields three different F ratios: (1) between groups; (2) change over time; and (3) interaction between treatment and time. The only F of interest for this design is the treatment by time interaction. It has been demonstrated that the interaction F provides identical information to the gain score t (or F if there are more than two groups), which, as demonstrated in the previous paragraph, is a simpler approach. Therefore, we do not recommend the mixed ANOVA analysis of the pretest–posttest comparison design.

Analysis of Covariance

This approach, favored by many researchers, is a statistical method used to reduce error variance. When used in the analysis of the pretest–posttest comparison group design, the ANCOVA, like the gain score analysis, changes the design from a mixed design to a single-factor design. The ANCOVA makes use of differences in the pretest scores among conditions to reduce error variance by adjusting posttest scores. Once these adjustments have been made to the posttest scores, the analysis is applied only to the *posttest scores*. Use of ANCOVA in the pretest–posttest comparison group design allows the researcher to use the pretest as the covariate and to adjust posttest scores based on a significant linear relationship between the pretest scores (covariate) and posttest scores (variate). The rationale behind this approach is that there are usually pretest differences between the treatment and control groups prior to the intervention, even though participants were randomly assigned to groups.

Although the ANCOVA approach is common with the pretest–posttest comparison group design, two assumptions must be satisfied. The first is that the relationship between the pretest scores and the posttest scores must be linear. The second assumption is that the regression slopes for each pretest–posttest relationship must be homogeneous (regression lines must be parallel). This latter assumption is often not satisfied in the analysis of the pretest–posttest comparison group design, leading to two problems. First, research is often reported using ANCOVA without satisfying this assumption, making the conclusions invalid. Second, the researcher, after discovering the violation, must reanalyze the data using one of the other approaches previously mentioned. Note that a different solution using ANCOVA through multiple regression has been advocated (see Morgan, Gliner, & Harmon, 2006, p. 220).

All three approaches are acceptable (gain score, mixed ANOVA, and ANCOVA). However, the gain score approach used by Miller et al. (2007) seems the most appropriate for this example, especially considering the small sample size.

When the data to be analyzed in the pretest–posttest comparison group design are ordinal (and not normally distributed) or nominal/dichotomous, nonparametric analyses should be undertaken. With ordinal data, a gain score approach could be used. Then a Mann-Whitney U would be applied if there are just two conditions, or a Kruskal-Wallis test would be used for more than two conditions. ANCOVA cannot be used in this situation.

Often when clinical importance is being considered, posttest data are dichotomized based on a clinically relevant cut point, and then a statistical analysis is performed. It is recommended that if continuous data are to be dichotomized for clinical relevance, then risk potency effect size indices such as number needed to treat or absolute risk ratio be reported without significance testing.

Nonequivalent (Intact) Group Designs With a Pretest and Posttest

An essential feature of the pretest–posttest comparison group design just discussed is random assignment of participants to groups. When this feature cannot be accomplished (e.g., using different hospitals or classrooms as intact groups), the design is *quasi-experimental* and referred to as a nonequivalent groups design with a pretest and posttest. Penningroth, Despain, and Gray (2007) provide an example of this type of design. They were interested in the impact of a course designed to improve psychological critical thinking. The students in the new course called psychological science (PS) were those who had already taken a general psychology course or were currently enrolled in a general psychology course. The control group consisted of students who were currently enrolled in a general psychology course. Type of course with two levels was the between-groups independent variable. All students were measured at the beginning and end of the semester. Therefore, the second independent variable, a repeated-measures independent variable, was time. The dependent variable was a measure of critical thinking called the Psychological Critical Thinking Exam (PCTE), which was administered at the beginning and end of the semester to all students. Since participants were in intact groups, the design was a nonequivalent group design with a pretest and posttest.

Similar to analysis of the pretest–posttest control group design already described, there are three methods that sometimes are used to analyze this design. However, the ANCOVA should not be applied in this case because the population means on the covariate cannot be assumed to be equal since participants were not randomly assigned to groups (Huck, 2008). Thus the posttest-adjusted means could be biased. The gain score method also presents problems because it does not provide enough information about pretest scores. Again, since participants were *not* randomly assigned to groups, one cannot assume that differences in the pretest scores are unbiased. Therefore, the mixed ANOVA appears to yield the most information for analysis of this design. Penningroth et al. (2007) analyzed their design using a two-factor mixed ANOVA. There were two levels of groups and two levels of time. There was one between-groups independent variable and one dependent variable. While they found significant main effects for both group and time, the most important finding was the statistically *significant group by time interaction*. Planned comparisons revealed that there was no statistically significant difference between the two groups at the pretest but that there was a statistically significant difference at the posttest, with the PS group having higher scores.

One must be cautious when interpreting data from the nonequivalent group design with a pretest and posttest because of the possible confounds from intact groups. Stevens (1999) pointed out, "The fact is that inferring cause-effect from intact groups is treacherous, regardless of the type of statistical analysis. Therefore, the task is to do the best we can and exercise considerable caution …" (p. 324).

Analysis and Interpretation of Complex Associational Questions

Use and Interpretation of Multiple Regression

Multiple regression is a frequently used statistical method for analyzing data when there are several independent variables and one dependent variable. Although it can be used in place of analysis of variance, it is most commonly used in the associational approach. For example, Zamboanga, Padilla-Walker, Hardy, Thompson, and Wang (2007) were interested in prediction of examination performance based on students' academic background and course involvement. They hypothesized that course involvement based on class attendance would predict exam performance on lecture-based questions and that academic background would predict exam performance on text-based questions. In this example, the independent variables, which are referred to in multiple regression as predictor variables, are self-reported ACT score, grade point average (GPA), number of prior psychological courses taken, gender, school year, and lecture attendance. The dependent variable in multiple regression is called the criterion or outcome variable. In this study there were actually three dependent variables, performance on lecture-based questions, performance on text-based questions, and total exam performance. A separate multiple regression analysis was performed to predict each of these dependent variables. However, for our purposes, we focus on total exam performance as the dependent variable. Multiple regression was appropriate for this analysis because the variables are approximately normally distributed (some predictor variables could be dichotomous), and the research question asked how the many independent variables combined to predict the dependent variable.

Correlation and Bivariate Regression

In Chapter 20, we discussed how the strength of the relation between two continuous variables could be indicated with a Pearson product-moment correlation coefficient. For example, in the Zamboanga et al. (2007) study, the Pearson product-moment correlation between ACT score and exam performance was $r = .53$, $p < .01$. According to Cohen (1988), this indicates a large effect, somewhat larger than typical in the behavioral sciences. An additional step would be to form a *bivariate* (two variables) *regression equation* so that one could predict a student's examination performance from prior ACT scores. This is referred to as simple linear (or bivariate) regression. Therefore, if you knew students' ACT scores, you could predict their future examination performance. How well? The r^2 gives one indication, which in this example would be .28. How do we interpret r^2 in this situation?

The r^2 is the amount of shared variance between the two variables. We could say that there is some underlying relationship, which is common to both the ACT score and examination performance that explains about 28% of the variance. Another way of looking at the problem is to focus on the examination score, which in this case is the Y variable. We call the dependent variable Y or, in regression, the criterion variable. ACT score is referred to as the independent variable or predictor variable. From these data, we can conclude that the ACT score accounts for only 28% of the variance of the examination score. Looking at it from another direction, we could say that 72% of the variance in predicting a student's examination score is unexplained or could be explained by other variables. This leads to multiple regression, which includes adding independent variables to improve the prediction of the dependent or criterion variable.

Similar to the Pearson product-moment correlation, in multiple regression a multiple R is computed; it is a correlation of the combination of the independent variables with the dependent variable. The multiple R tells how strong a relationship exists between the predictor variables and the criterion variable. The goal is to find a linear combination of independent variables that explains the most variance in the dependent variable. Multiple regression is used to predict or explain the relationship between the linear combination of the independent variables and the dependent variable. As with correlation, even a high multiple regression coefficient does not mean that the independent variables *caused* the change in the dependent variable.

Computing Multiple Regression

The computation of multiple regression starts from a *correlation matrix* among all of the variables of interest, including the dependent variable. Then a linear combination of the variables is created so that the overall correlation, R, of the independent variables and the criterion variable is maximized, and the error in the prediction is minimized. For each of the independent variables a partial correlation is computed. This is a measure of the relationship between the independent variable and the criterion variable, keeping the other independent variables constant. From the partial correlations, *unstandardized coefficients* are calculated. These coefficients can then be used to create a formula that is a linear combination of independent variables to predict the criterion variable. Note that there are many possible linear combinations based on *different* sets of independent variables. Multiple linear regression finds the best linear combination of variables to predict the criterion variable using only those independent variables actually entered into the equation.

If the regression coefficients are converted to standardized or *z scores*, then comparisons can be made among the coefficients to determine the relative strength among each of the variables used in a particular analysis. A *t* test value is computed to examine the statistical significance of the relationship of each of the independent variables with the criterion variable. The *t* value tells whether the independent variable significantly contributes to the regression, assuming all the other independent variables are in the equation. Note that just because a predictor variable is not statistically significant in an analysis does not necessarily mean that variable should be dropped from the equation. The variable could still be making a contribution to the overall R^2. Furthermore, it is possible, but not common, to have a significant R^2, even if none of the individual predictor variables alone are statistically significant.

There are several assumptions related to multiple regression. As with other inferential statistics, if the assumptions are not met, there can be problems interpreting the results. One important assumption of multiple linear regression is that the independent variables are related to the dependent variable in a *linear* (straight-line) fashion. If the data do not meet this assumption (e.g., the independent variables are related in a *curvilinear* fashion to the dependent variable), then multiple regression is not appropriate. Another important condition is that the independent variables should be correlated with the dependent variable, but not highly correlated with each other. If the independent variables are highly correlated with each other, there will be the problem of *multicollinearity*. When there is multicollinearity in the data, methods such as transforming or combining variables might change the data to meet this assumption. Most of the other assumptions related to multiple regression concern error; errors should be independent, constant, and normally distributed. Residual plots can help in identifying problems with error not meeting the assumptions.

In multiple regression analysis, the criterion variable should be approximately *normally distributed*, having many ordered values. Two other statistical methods used to predict a criterion variable from several predictor variables, *discriminant analysis* and *logistic regression,* are discussed later in this chapter. In these latter two methods, the criterion variable has nominal categories; it is usually dichotomous.

There are several different forms or methods of analysis with multiple linear regression. Those discussed here are hierarchical multiple regression, simultaneous multiple regression, stepwise multiple regression, and all possible models.

Hierarchical Multiple Regression

Zamboanga et al. (2007) were interested in predicting overall examination performance from the predictor variables of gender, year, ACT, prior GPA, prior psychology courses, discussion section, and lecture attendance. Two of the variables, gender and year, were demographic variables and would be entered into the multiple regression as controls. The other variables were considered to be predictor variables. Thus, they used hierarchical multiple regression.

When using hierarchical multiple regression, variables are entered in steps, and the *change in R^2* is examined at each step. The decision of the order to enter each variable into the equation is decided ahead of time by the investigator. Usually these decisions are based on a careful conceptualization of the problem and result in the testing of particular

TABLE 22.5

Hierarchical Multiple Regression Model Predicting Total
Exam Performance (From Zamboanga et al., 2007)

Predictors	B	SE	Beta
Gender	−.35	.86	−.03
Year	.68	.50	.10
ACT	.57	.11	.40**
Prior GPA	1.76	.74	.21*
Prior psychology courses	.20	.58	.03
Discussion section	−.02	.50	−.01
Lecture attendance	.73	.20	.31**

$*p < .05$.
$**p < .01$.
Source: Data are from Zamboanga, B. L., Padilla-Walker, L. M.,
Hardy, S. A., Thompson, R. A., & Wang, S. C., *Teaching of
Psychology, 34*, 2007, 158–162.

hypotheses. In their 2007 study, Zamboanga et al. determined that the demographic variables, gender and class year, needed to be controlled, so they entered them first. This is considered the first step. In the second step, the independent/predictor variables of ACT, prior GPA, prior psychology courses, discussion section, and lecture attendance were added.

Table 22.5 shows the unstandardized (*B*) and standardized (β or beta) coefficients for each of the predictor variables. The level of significance for each of the predictors (indicated with asterisks) is also shown. To understand how much each predictor is contributing to the R^2, *standardized coefficients* (β weights) are computed for each predictor. The overall R^2 was .45. Three of the five predictor variables were considered to be statistically significant: prior GPA ($p < .05$), ACT ($p < .01$), and lecture attendance ($p < .01$).

Usually with multiple regression it is helpful to form a *regression equation*. This is done with the unstandardized coefficients. The equation then could be used in the future to predict student examination performance from these independent variables, assuming a similar sample of participants.

Simultaneous Multiple Regression

In this method, all of the predictor variables are entered simultaneously instead of in steps. As with the other methods, the best linear combination of variables is determined using a *least squares fit*, which is a method for maximizing the prediction accuracy. In least squares fit, the computer tries to fit the regression line so that the squared deviations (the distance between the scores and the prediction line) are minimized. Thus, the prediction line is as close as possible to all of the scores.

Stepwise Multiple Regression

The stepwise multiple regression approach is similar to hierarchical multiple regression, but the computer instead of the researcher decides the order and how many of the potential predictors are used. The stepwise regression procedure describes how much more each independent or predictor variable has contributed to the prediction from the predictor variables already used.

Although stepwise linear regression makes a lot of sense conceptually, several problems have been associated with this approach (see Thompson, 1995, for a critical review of this procedure). Researchers should probably use this approach only as an exploratory procedure. One of the basic problems with this approach is that because of the potentially large number of predictor variables that could be entered into the equation, the probability of a type I error is considerably larger than the usual alpha of .05. A second, and perhaps more important, objection with the stepwise approach is that the computer rather than the researcher is making the decision on which variables should be included in the equation. This is especially the case when one enters a large number of predictor variables into the stepwise analysis with little thought given to particular hypotheses or theories. Many statisticians associate this approach with the term *data mining* or *snooping*. Third, the approach takes advantage of possible small differences in correlations when entering variables and thus is not likely to be replicated in another sample.

Logistic Regression and Discriminant Analysis

Predicting the probability that an event will or will not occur, as well as identifying the variables useful in making the prediction, is important in the health sciences; it is central to risk research. Two statistical techniques can be used appropriately to predict a dichotomous dependent variable: discriminant analysis and logistic regression. These two statistical methods also can be used when the dependent variable has more than two categories, but the more common usage is with a dichotomous dependent variable. We previously discussed linear regression, used when the dependent variable is continuous. Discriminant analysis can be used with a dichotomous dependent variable, but the method requires several assumptions for the predictions to be optimal. Grimm and Yarnold (1995) provide more extensive, but still nontechnical, chapters on discriminant analysis and on logistic regression than we present here.

Discriminant Analysis

Discriminant analysis can be used to predict a dichotomous outcome variable from a combination of several independent variables (such as those listed in Table 22.5). A discriminant function prediction equation is a *linear* combination of the independent variables meant to discriminate between the two outcome groups. In discriminant analysis, the weights for each independent variable are selected based on how well they classify participants into the two groups.

Logistic Regression

Logistic regression requires fewer assumptions than discriminant analysis. Even when the assumptions required for discriminant analysis are satisfied, logistic regression still performs well so it is the more commonly used statistical test in clinical research. In logistic regression, the probability of an event occurring is estimated. Logistic regression models can include one or more independent (predictor) variables that may be either dichotomous or continuous. Logistic regression with one independent variable is called *bivariate logistic regression*; with two or more independent variables, logistic regression is called *multiple logistic regression*. These should not be confused with *multinomial logistic regression*, where the dependent variable has more than two categories. In this chapter, the focus is on dichotomous outcomes of the dependent variable with several independent variables. Thus, we focus on multiple logistic regression, often just called logistic regression.

In linear regression, the regression coefficient represents the amount of change in the dependent variable for one-unit change in the independent variable. Logistic regression coefficients are typically expressed as the *odds of an event* (outcome) occurring. The odds of an outcome is the ratio of the probability that the outcome occurs to the probability that it does not. Thus, if the probability of an event occurring is .8, the odds of the event is .8 divided by the probability of it not occurring (.2) or .8/.2 = 4.0. In everyday language, this means that the odds are 4 to 1. An *odds ratio* (*OR*) is simply the ratio of two odds. For example, if the odds of an event is 4 for boys (i.e., the risk is 4 of 5 = .80) and the odds of the same event is 3 for girls (i.e., the risk is 3 of 4 = .75), the *OR* relating gender to the event is 4/3 = 1.33.

Odds ratios are central to logistic regression, just as the correlation coefficient is central to linear regression. The null value of an *OR* is 1.0 (similar to a correlation coefficient of 0) and indicates random association. When a positive association increases, the correlation coefficient increases from 0 to 1 and the *OR* increases from 1 to infinity. As a negative association increases, the correlation coefficient decreases from 0 to –1 and the *OR* decreases from 1 to 0.

In logistic regression, significance tests are provided for each independent variable. As is the case with multiple regression, the contribution of individual variables in logistic regression is difficult to determine. The contribution of each variable depends on the other variables in the model. This is a problem particularly when independent variables are highly correlated.

A test for whether the combination of independent variables has a greater-than-chance ability to predict the status of people on the dependent variable in logistic regression is called a *goodness-of-fit test*. The goal is to identify a "good" set of independent variables (a model) that helps predict or explain group membership on the dependent variable.

Summary

In this chapter we discussed numerous analyses that are appropriate for complex designs. These are designs with more than one independent variable. The chapter was divided into two major sections: analyses applied to complex difference questions and analyses applied to complex associational questions. For the most part, the analyses that were covered were considered parametric statistics. The section on complex difference questions included two-factor between-groups ANOVA, two-factor within-subjects ANOVA, and mixed (between and within) ANOVA. We further divided the mixed ANOVA into the split-plot design and designs with a pretest and posttest. We focused attention on the latter design and described different methods of analysis depending on whether the design was randomized experimental or quasi-experimental.

In the second major section of this chapter we discussed analyses appropriate for answering complex associational questions. The primary analysis for this section was multiple regression. We discussed three common methods of multiple regression: hierarchical, simultaneous, and stepwise. We also mentioned two other methods for analyzing complex associational designs when the dependent variable is dichotomous: discriminant analysis and logistic regression. Examples from recent literature were provided throughout the chapter.

Key Concepts

Analysis of covariance (ANCOVA)

Discriminant analysis

Gain scores

Hierarchical multiple regression

Interaction effects

Logistic regression

Main effects

Mixed analysis of variance (ANOVA)

Simultaneous multiple regression

Stepwise multiple regression

Two-factor ANOVA

Two-factor within-subjects ANOVA

Key Distinctions

Discriminant analysis versus logistic regression versus multiple regression

Hierarchical regression versus stepwise regression

Gain scores versus mixed ANOVA versus ANCOVA

Main effects versus interaction effects

Two-factor ANOVA versus mixed ANOVA

Application Problems

1. A therapist was interested in predicting success on the job following therapy. The therapist felt that a good measure of therapy was the number of hours a person could spend in a simulated work task at discharge. The best measure of success on the actual job was number of months in current employment. The therapist gathered data from files of previous patients. What statistic is appropriate? Why? What type of evidence for measurement validity of the simulated work task could be obtained?

2. What is a factorial design? Why would you use a factorial design?

3. What is the difference between a main effect and an interaction effect?

4. Why would you do one analysis (factorial ANOVA) instead of two separate analyses (e.g., *t* tests) when you have two independent variables each with a few levels?

5. Why is it important to look first at interaction "effects"?

6. A faculty member conducted a study to determine who performed better in his research class: students in education or students in occupational therapy. In addition, he felt that gender could also make a contribution. Therefore, he conducted a retrospective study (i.e., went back into previous records) and formed the following four groups of 10 students in each group: male education (ME); female education (FE); male OT (MOT); and female OT (FOT). He then calculated the mean test scores for each group; the means were as follows:

   ME = 81

   FE = 93

   MOT = 89

   FOT = 84

   a. Plot the data to illustrate the interaction.
   b. The sums of squares for the results are in the following source table. Complete it.
   c. If an *F* of 4.11 is required for statistical significance, interpret the results.

Source table				
Source	**SS**	**df**	**MS**	**F**
Major	420			
Gender	250			
Major by gender	600			
Within-subjects (error)	5200			

7. An investigator was interested in the effect of teaching style on students' perception of credibility of their instructor. One style of interest was the participatory action style in which the students took responsibility for much of the class material. The other style of interest was labeled the traditional style, in which delivery of material was by lecture. Two instructors from the same department taught the same class; one instructor was skilled in the participatory learning style, whereas the other was skilled in the traditional style. The investigator also thought that the age of students might affect this research project due to different expectations among students. The investigator decided to select three different age groups for the project: young, middle, and older. The investigator performs a two-factor ANOVA. What additional analyses should the investigator do to interpret the results under each of the following situations?

   a. The investigator finds a significant main effect for teaching style but no significant main effect for age or for the teaching style by age interaction.
   b. The investigator finds a significant main effect for age but no significant main effect for teaching style and no teaching style by age interaction.
   c. The investigator finds no significant main effects for teaching style or age but a significant teaching style by age interaction.
   d. The investigator finds significant main effects for teaching style and age and a teaching style by age interaction.

8. Some researchers argue that ANCOVA is the most appropriate statistic to use with pretest–posttest data. Explain.

9. A researcher was interested in the effects of different treatments for back injury on return to work. Specifically, she was interested in whether those people who were treated for back injury noninvasively (e.g., rest and exercise) would perform differently from those who were treated through surgery. To model the back to work experience, a vibration machine was used to simulate driving of large machinery. A person who suffered a back injury might be able to sit for long periods of time if there was no vibration, but not under conditions of vibration. Therefore, each participant in the study underwent three conditions, driving with vibration, driving without vibration, and just sitting. There were eight patients in the exercise group and eight patients in the surgery group. The dependent variable was pain perception: a 10-point scale where 1 was no pain and 10 was intolerable pain. The means were as follows:

	Condition		
Treatment	Sitting	Driving without vibration	Driving with vibration
Exercise	.33	1.33	3.00
Surgery	.33	3.67	6.00

a. Describe the design (e.g., 2 × 2 factorial).

b. What type of statistical analysis would be performed?

c. Plot the data.

10. A physics professor was interested in demonstrating that his new method of teaching was superior to the traditional teaching method in changing the attitude of students toward physics. Prior to the start of the semester, students were randomly assigned to one of two beginning physics sections: the new method and the old method. During the first day of class, all students took the "Attitude Toward Physics" test. At the end of the semester the students took this test again. For each of the following analyses, explain what outcome/result would be used to support the professor's argument.

a. Mixed ANOVA

b. Gain score *t* test

c. Analysis of covariance

11. A consortium of researchers wants to look at some of the impacts of welfare reform on individuals/families who have not received public assistance for 2 years. They have a large multistate sample. For each participant, an "economic well-being" score from 1 to 10 was computed as the *outcome variable*. The researchers were interested in their ability to predict economic well-being from prior level of education, years of work experience, transportation availability, training received while on welfare, and the relative health of the local economy (all dichotomous or normally distributed measures).

a. What type of analysis would be appropriate? Explain.

b. If the researchers wanted to know what combination of the aforementioned factors predicted whether a former welfare recipient will have been employed *or not* since leaving welfare, what analytical approach should they use?

For questions 12–15, match the analysis with the particular question, and explain *why*.

    a. Factorial ANOVA

    b. Multiple regression

    c. Factor analysis (refer back to Chapter 15)

    d. Logistic regression

12. You have a pretest–posttest control group design. Your dependent variable is a 50-item questionnaire, which was given to 250 participants in the intervention group and 250 participants in the nonintervention group. Your next step is to reduce the number of questions to a smaller number of composite/summated variables.

13. You are interested in predicting if people are successful or unsuccessful when they return to work. Your predictor variables are strength, range of motion, IQ, and gender.

14. You have two independent variables each with three levels, and you have one normally distributed dependent variable.

15. You are trying to predict GPA in graduate school in an English department. Your predictor variables are undergraduate GPA, Graduate Record Examination (GRE) verbal scores, score on an interest inventory, and age.

Note

1. Note that there are six nominal levels of the site independent variable rather than the usual two to four levels for a difference statistic such as analysis of variance (ANOVA). Remember from Chapter 18 that a *nominal* independent variable with more than four levels would usually be analyzed with a difference inferential statistic.

Section V

Evaluating and Writing Research Reports

23

Evaluating Research Validity: Part I

A Framework for Evaluating Research Validity

This chapter summarizes and integrates many of the concepts from the preceding chapters (especially Chapters 8 and 9), leading to the evaluation of the quality of the design and analysis of a quantitative study (i.e., the *research validity* of a whole study). Our evaluation framework uses several research validity rating scales adapted from those developed by Gliner and Morgan (2000) and Morgan, Gliner, and Harmon (1999, 2006). Here we discuss key concepts and present several figures and tables that provide the information needed to make a comprehensive evaluation of the research validity of an empirical quantitative study. The studies described briefly in Chapter 1 are evaluated using this expanded framework in Chapter 25.

The Cook and Campbell Framework

Our framework is based on four research validity constructs originally proposed by Campbell and Stanley (1963/1966) and updated by Cook and Campbell (1979) and Shadish, Cook, and Campbell (2002). Our evaluation plan also was influenced by the What Works Clearinghouse (2006) framework called the Design and Implementation Device (DIAD) (http://ies.ed.gov/ncee/wwc/pdf/studydesignclass.pdf) endorsed by the Campbell Collaboration (n.d.; http://www.campbellcollaboration.org). The What Works system was designed specifically to evaluate intervention research. A major difference between our framework and the What Works framework (and most of Cook and Campbell's discussions) is that our framework is designed to be used with both experimental (i.e., intervention) and nonexperimental research approaches.

Several issues came up using Cook and Campbell's (1979) criteria for validity. Specifically, their terminology and their many "threats" to validity posed four types of problems. First, there was confusion about the uses of certain common research terms. For example, the term *validity* for Cook and Campbell refers to the design of the whole study, but a more common use in the research literature refers to the validity of a specific measurement or test. To make matters more confusing, they divided the validity of a study into four aspects now labeled *statistical validity, internal validity, construct validity*, and *external validity* (Shadish et. al., 2002).

Second, validity has sometimes been assumed to be all or nothing: a study or test was or was not valid. We think research validity should be assessed on a series of continua, from high to low, as discussed in this chapter and the next. Third, Cook and Campbell's (1979) specific threats to validity were hard to remember because many have peculiar names (e.g., history, interactions with selection, or mortality). Fourth, it was easy to lose track of the main issues because there were so many different threats to validity that deal with very specific, sometimes uncommon, situations. It was easy not to see the forest, only the trees.

Other Evaluation Frameworks

Many of the textbooks that discuss the evaluation of research studies have a broader or less focused framework than ours, emphasizing how completely, appropriately, or clearly the various parts (i.e., title, abstract, introduction, results, and discussion) of the article were written. Although we pose a few evaluation questions about how the study was written, the emphasis here is for the most part on the *method section* of an article, although the results section also comes into play. A study that is poorly written or inadequately justified may have less impact than if it was well written, but good writing should not substitute for a poor design. Thus, we emphasize the design, control of extraneous variables, quality of measurement, and the appropriateness of the data analysis and interpretation.

Of course, the importance or significance of the research problem is a key issue, but its evaluation is beyond the scope of this book and is best done by content experts in the area of study. (Indirect evaluation of the importance of the content is provided if the article is published in a peer-reviewed journal; see the evaluation of question 17 in Chapter 24.) A well-designed study on a trivial topic will not add much to the knowledge in a field. On the other hand, a poorly designed study, especially if convincingly written, may be accepted uncritically and even set the field back because the results are misleading.

Our Evaluation Framework

Our evaluation framework is based on 19 questions and eight rating scales. Some of the 19 questions request descriptive information about the design, and some ask for an evaluative rating. These questions are numbered and presented in bold throughout this chapter and Chapter 24.

The 19 questions are divided into three main groups. Questions 1 through 8 are about describing or naming key aspects of the design and methods, including the variables, research questions/hypotheses, approach, design, and support for the reliability and validity of each key measure.

The heart of the evaluation is questions 9 through 16, which use, in part, the answers to questions 1 through 8 to make eight evaluative ratings. These ratings fall under four main headings or aspects of research validity. We label these four key dimensions or aspects of research validity as follows: (1) *measurement reliability and statistics* (question 9); (2) *internal validity* (Q10 and Q11); (3) *measurement validity of the constructs* (Q12 and Q13); and (4) *external validity* (Q14 –Q16).

Questions 17 through 19 are general evaluation questions about peer review (Q17), the link between literature or theory and the research questions (Q18), and the clarity and accuracy of the authors' title, abstract, and discussion, given the evaluation of the aspects of research validity (Q19). These last three questions are intended to provide a general estimate of three aspects of the article that are not well covered by our evaluation of the design.

As mentioned earlier, our research evaluation framework maintains the four dimensions of research validity identified by Cook and Campbell (1979) but somewhat modifies the labels to help prevent the confusions already mentioned and to focus on the main issues. Before discussing these dimensions, we want to review reliability and validity in a broader context. Doing this also should help avoid some of the potential semantic confusion.

It is important to distinguish between the merit or worth of the study as a whole (**research validity**) as opposed to the quality of the measurement of each separate variable or test used in the study (**measurement validity**). As shown in Figure 23.1, measurement reliability and validity (top two boxes) are different from, but related to, aspects of research validity

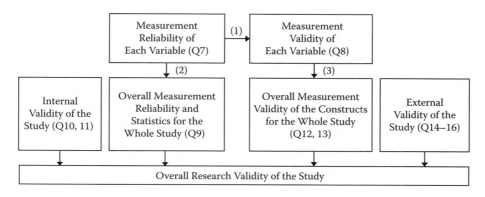

FIGURE 23.1
Schematic diagram showing how the overall research validity of a study depends on the four major aspects or dimensions of research validity and, in turn, on the measurement reliability and validity of the several variables.

(middle boxes), all four of which determine the overall research validity of a study (bottom box). Within each box, we list the number of the question we use to evaluate that aspect of validity. The horizontal arrow (1) from measurement reliability (Q7) to measurement validity (Q8) indicates that reliability or consistency is a necessary (but not sufficient) precursor for the validity of a measure. The vertical arrow (2) from measurement reliability (Q7) to overall measurement reliability and statistics (Q9) indicates that an important determinant of the quality of the statistical analysis is the amount of evidence for the reliability of the specific instruments used. Likewise the vertical arrow (3) from measurement validity (Q8) to overall measurement validity of the constructs (Q12 and Q13) indicates that this dimension is dependent on the evidence for the measurement validity of all of the variables.

Ideally a study should be rated high on each of the four main evaluation criteria or dimensions of research validity (shown in the middle row of boxes of Figure 23.1). However, there are always trade-offs, and few, if any, studies are high on all criteria. Furthermore, the weight that researchers give to each of the criteria varies. For example, experimental researchers, especially medical researchers who perform randomized clinical trials and meta-analyses for evidence-based practice, give more weight to internal validity. Survey researchers tend to value population external validity, and qualitative researchers value ecological external validity. Our experience indicates that studies usually compromise one or more aspects of external validity to achieve high internal validity or vice versa.

Analysis of the Design and Methods

Variables and Their Measurement Levels

Q1. What are the key independent/antecedent/predictor variables? For each:

    a. Is it an active, attribute, or change over time independent variable?

    b. What is the *number* of *levels*/categories of the independent variable?

    c. What is the level of *measurement* (nominal, dichotomous, ordinal, or approximately normal) of the independent variable?

TABLE 23.1

Traditional Measurement Terms and Our Recommended Terms

Our term	Our definition	Traditional term	Traditional definition
Nominal	Three or more *unordered* categories.	Nominal	Two or more *unordered* categories
Dichotomous	Two categories, either ordered or unordered.	N/A	N/A
Ordinal	Three or more *ordered* levels, but the frequency distribution of the scores is *not* normally distributed, probably markedly skewed.	Ordinal	*Ordered* levels, in which the difference in magnitude between levels is not equal.
Approximately normal	Many (at least five) *ordered* levels or scores, with the frequency distribution of the scores being approximately normally distributed.	Interval and ratio	**Interval:** *ordered* levels, in which the difference between levels is equal, but there is no true zero. **Ratio:** *ordered* levels; the difference between levels is equal, and there is a true zero.

In Chapter 3, we make an important distinction between *active* (sometimes called manipulated) *independent variables* and *attribute independent* or *predictor variables* that are characteristics of the participants. This distinction is important because it divides quantitative research studies into two main types: *experimental* (with one or more active independent variables) and *nonexperimental* (with only attribute variables). See Figure 4.1 and Figure 4.2 for more detail about this distinction and its implications.

Table 23.1 (which is the same as Table 10.1 and is based on Kraemer, personal communication, 1999) provides definitions for the traditional *measurement* terms and how they differ from ours. Chapter 10 provides more details about why we use these somewhat nontraditional measurement terms and also more information about variables and their measurement. In experiments, the level of measurement for the active independent variable is usually not stated but is often dichotomous or nominal, producing two or more groups to compare.

Q2. What are the key dependent or outcome variables? For each, what is the level of measurement?

Table 23.1 can be used to identify the level or scale of measurement. The level of measurement helps determine the appropriateness of the statistics used in the study. Again, refer to Chapter 10 for more details.

Research Hypotheses/Questions, Approaches, and Design

Q3. What are the main research questions or hypotheses?

Most studies have several questions or hypotheses, often spelled out in the introduction or method section of the article. Chapter 3 and Appendix D provide examples of descriptive, difference, and associational research questions and the types of statistics that are commonly used with each of them. Chapters 16 through 22 provide concrete examples of the research questions posed by a number of studies and discussions of how those questions were answered with the help of statistical tests.

Criteria	Randomized experimental	Quasi-experimental	Comparative	Associational	Descriptive
Random assignment of participants to groups by investigator	Yes	No	No	No (only one group)	No groups
Independent variable is active	Yes	Yes	No (attribute)	No (attribute)	No independent variable
Independent variable is controlled *by the investigator*[a]	Usually	Sometimes	No	No	No
Number of levels of the Independent variable[b]	Usually 2–4	Usually 2–4	Usually 2–4	Usually 5 or more ordered levels	No independent variable
Relationships between variables or comparison of groups	Yes (comparison)	Yes (comparison)	Yes (comparison)	Yes (relationship)	No

[a] Although the control of the delivery of the independent variable *by the investigator* is a desired quality of randomized experimental and quasi-experimental designs, it is not sufficient for distinguishing between them.

[b] This distinction is made for educational purposes and is only "usually" true.

FIGURE 23.2
A comparison of the five basic quantitative research approaches.

Q4. What is the research approach (i.e., descriptive, associational, comparative, quasi-experimental, or randomized experimental) for each question?

Remember that studies with a number of research questions may have more than one approach. Figure 23.2 and the answers to Q1 help one decide which approach was used for each research question. Some studies have one or several descriptive research questions, especially about the dependent variables. However, almost all quantitative studies published in peer-reviewed journals go beyond the purely descriptive approach to compare groups or associate/relate variables. Thus, most studies also will use one (or more) of the other four approaches. If a study has an active independent variable we would call it an experimental study even if the researcher also asks questions using attribute independent variables such as gender. Studies with no active independent variables are called nonexperimental or observational; they often have comparative, associational, and descriptive research questions.

Identifying the research approach is important because of its influence on the internal validity of a study and inferences about whether the independent variable *caused* any change in the dependent variable. In general, the randomized experimental approach produces the best evidence for causation. Neither the comparative nor the associational approaches are well suited to providing evidence about causes. Quasi-experimentation is usually in between the randomized experimental approach and the comparative or associational approaches.

Q5. What is the general design classification if the approach is randomized experimental, quasi-experimental, or comparative?

If the study has randomized experimental, quasi-experimental, or comparative research questions, the design classification can be identified using Chapter 18 and Table 18.1. This requires knowing (1) the number of *factors* (i.e., independent variables); (2) the number of *levels/values* of each factor; and (3) whether the *design* is *between groups, within subjects* (repeated measures), or *mixed*. For example, a design might be described as a 3 × 2 (mixed) factorial design with repeated measures on the second factor. This means that there are two independent variables, the first with three levels/groups and the second with two levels or, in this case, measured at two times because there are repeated measures. This classification of designs applies not only to the randomized experimental and quasi-experimental approaches (which is typical) but also to comparative approach questions, where there is no active/manipulated independent variable. Note that the mentioned 3 × 2 mixed design could be the typical experimental or quasi-experimental pretest–posttest design with three groups (e.g., two treatments and a control), or it could be a longitudinal (two ages) design comparing three types of participants (e.g., securely attached versus avoidant versus disorganized) over time.

Q6. What is the specific experimental design name if the approach is randomized experimental or quasi-experimental?

The names of specific randomized experimental or quasi-experimental designs are provided in Figure 5.1, an overview schematic diagram of most of the common designs and their names (see also Chapter 5). For example, randomized clinical trials (RCT) usually use *pretest–posttest control group designs.*

Note that if the specific research question/hypothesis and *approach* are *associational*, Q5 and Q6 are not applicable. In the associational approach, the analysis will usually be done with some type of correlation or multiple regression.

Measurement Reliability and Validity for Each Key Variable

Q7 and Q8 require an evaluation based on the principle that in a good study each key variable should be measured *reliably* and *validly*. Therefore, these aspects of *each* measured variable should be evaluated. Chapters 11 and 12 discuss measurement reliability and validity and point out that instruments are not valid or invalid per se. The data that an instrument produces are reliable and valid to some extent, for some purpose, and with some population, based on the evidence available.

Q7. Is the measurement reliability for each key variable acceptable?

    a. What types of evidence for reliability are presented?
    b. Is the evidence or support for *each* key variable acceptable?

Q7a. Were test–retest, parallel forms, internal consistency, or interrater reliability evidence cited or obtained? Table 23.2 and Chapter 11 help identify what types of reliability evidence were provided. Note that active independent variables (i.e., interventions) and demographic variables seldom have information about measurement reliability or validity, but it would be desirable to know if the treatment was delivered consistently (reliably) and validly. However, for most attribute independent variables and for dependent variables, the method section should report some evidence to support measurement reliability. This evidence could be based on literature using the instrument or on evidence gathered in this study. It is desirable to have at least some of the evidence come from the current population.

TABLE 23.2

Measurement Reliability and Validity (for Q7a and Q8a)

Measurement reliability: stability or consistency	Measurement validity: accuracy or correctness
The participants' scores are the same or very similar from one testing time to another. There is evidence for reliability of:	The score accurately reflects/measures what it was designed or intended to. Several sources of evidence can be used to support the validity of a measure:
Participants' responses	**Content evidence**
Test–retest reliability: Stability over time	All aspects of the construct are represented in appropriate proportions
Parallel forms reliability: Consistency across presumably equivalent versions of the instrument	**Evidence based on response processes**
Internal consistency: Items that are to be combined are related to each other	**Evidence based on internal structure**
	Factorial: Factor analysis yields a theoretically meaningful solution
Observers' responses	**Evidence based on relations to other variables**
Interrater reliability: Different observers or raters give similar scores	*Convergent:* Based on theory, variables predicted to be related are related
	Discriminant: Variables predicted not to be related are not
	Criterion-related evidence
	Predictive: The test predicts some criterion in the future
	Concurrent: Test and criterion are measured at the same time
	Validity generalization
	Evidence based on consequences of testing

Q7b. How strong is the *evidence* for the *reliability of the measurement* for each key variable? A reliability coefficient of .70 or higher is usually considered necessary for a variable to be measured with acceptable reliability, but in a complex study a few reliability coefficients between .60 and .69 are common and marginally acceptable. Table 23.3 provides a method to evaluate evidence for the measurement reliability of each measure.

Were reliability coefficients reported? It is desirable, but relatively uncommon, for researchers to report more than one type of reliability evidence (e.g., both test–retest and internal consistency) for each measure. If the instruments had been used before, the author only may refer to another study and not provide actual coefficients; in this case, it is probably reasonable to assume that the reliability was adequate. However, researchers who plan to use an instrument in their research should obtain the cited documents and personally check the evidence.

Q8. Is the evidence for measurement validity for each key variable acceptable?

    a. What types of evidence to support measurement validity are reported?

    b. Is the evidence or support for *each* key variable acceptable?

Q8a. Table 23.2 provides a summary of the types of evidence for measurement validity that were discussed in Chapter 12. In terms of the *validity of each measure*, authors often only cite previous studies that used the instrument without providing details about the numerical evidence for validity; it seems reasonable to assume that such published studies provided acceptable evidence, but it is prudent to be cautious when evaluating validity, especially of self-report measures.

TABLE 23.3

Evaluating Measurement Reliability
Coefficients (for Q7b)

Correlation coefficient	Support for reliability
+.90	Acceptable[a]
+.80	Acceptable[b]
+.70	Acceptable[b]
+.60	Marginally acceptable[b]
+.50	Not acceptable
+.30	Not acceptable
+.10	Not acceptable
−.10	Not acceptable[c]
−.30	Not acceptable[c]
−.50	Not acceptable[c]
>−.50	Not acceptable[c]

Note: Statistical significance is not enough for measurement reliability. Examine the size and direction of the correlation.

[a] Useful for decisions about individual selection, placement, etc.

[b] Useful for research but probably not for decisions about individuals.

[c] Check data for probable errors in coding or conceptualization.

Q8b. Table 23.4 provides a method to evaluate measurement validity when the evidence provided is a correlation coefficient (see also Chapter 12). Note that the coefficients for the validity of a measure do not need to be as high to be considered good as those supporting reliability.

In summary, for *each* key measure or variable, one should evaluate the evidence for measurement reliability and validity. Note that, as shown in Figure 23.1, measurement reliability is a necessary precursor of measurement validity, and both reliability and validity (top boxes of Figure 23.1) influence aspects of research validity.

Evaluation of the Four Key Dimensions of Research Validity

Now, we begin our discussion of the four key criteria and eight evaluative dimensions for the research validity of a study. A high-quality study should have moderate to high ratings on each of the four dimensions of research validity, as indicated by ratings on *each* of the eight scales shown in the figures in this chapter and the next, using the criteria listed in these figures. An evaluation can be made for each rating scale using the several issues listed on the scale and in the text to guide the evaluation rating for each of the eight research validity dimensions.

TABLE 23.4

Evaluating Measurement Validity Coefficients (for Q8b)

Correlation coefficient	Support for validity
+/−.60 or higher	Acceptable, but[a]
+/−.50	Acceptable[b,c]
+/−.30	Acceptable[b,c]
+/−.10	Maybe[b,c]

[a] If a validity coefficient is quite high (e.g., >.60), the same or very similar concepts probably are being measured, rather than two separate ones, so such high correlations may be more like measurement reliability than measurement validity.

[b] We base the strength or level of support for measurement validity on Cohen's (1988) effect size guidelines. For correlations: $r = .1$ is a small effect size so weak support for validity, $r = .3$ is a medium or typical effect size, and $r = .5$ is a large effect size and strong support. However, the correlation *must be statistically significant*. Thus, a correlation of +/−.20 would provide some support for validity only if r was significant but *no support* if r was not significant.

[c] Criterion and convergent evidence for validity would be expected to produce positive (+) correlations, unless the concepts are hypothesized to be negatively related (e.g., anxiety and grade point average).

Overall Measurement Reliability and Statistics

Q9. What is the overall rating of measurement reliability and statistics? Base the rating and comments on the following:

a. Is the overall measurement reliability of the variables acceptable?

b. Is the power appropriate?

c. Is the choice/use of statistics appropriate?

d. Is there adequate presentation of the statistical results, including effect size?

e. Is the interpretation of statistical results appropriate?

This first dimension of research validity emphasizes the importance of the overall measurement reliability as well as the use and interpretation of inferential statistics. Q9 requests an overall rating of the study from low through medium to high based on five issues (see Figure 23.3).

Q9a. First, there is the issue of whether the *variables as a group are measured reliably*. Q9 considers an overall rating of the measurement reliability of all the instruments. A principle often emphasized in measurement classes is that if a test does not consistently measure the construct, it cannot be accurately measuring it. Likewise, a study's validity is reduced if one or more of the key variables are unreliably measured (see also Chapter 11).

Q9b. Second, can a statistically significant relationship be detected, assuming that such a relationship exists? The ability to detect a statistically significant difference is most commonly referred to as **power**, or the ability to reject a false null hypothesis. Although adequate power is based, in part, on having enough participants in the study, there are other methods of increasing power (Lipsey, 1990). Some of these methods include decreasing variability and increasing reliability of the dependent variable or increasing the strength and consistency of administering the independent variable.

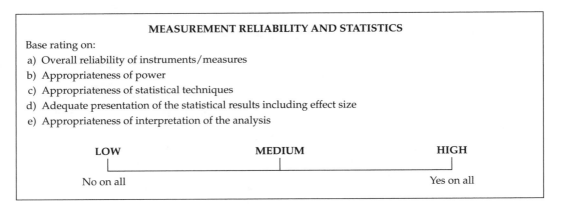

FIGURE 23.3
Evaluating the statistics and measurement reliability of the findings of a study.

Cook and Campbell (1979) brought up a second side to the issue of power, which involves having too much power, especially with respect to the number of participants in a study. For the most part, this problem arises when a very large sample size (e.g., several hundred participants) yields a statistically significant, but perhaps trivial, relationship. Thus, it is important to provide an estimate of the effect size (ES). See especially Chapters 16 and 17 for more about power and ES.

Q9c. A third issue to consider involves the *selection of the proper statistical method* to assess whether a relationship between the independent and dependent variable actually exists. Selection of appropriate statistics is discussed in more detail in Chapter 19. Sometimes researchers select the wrong statistic, such as a *t* test or correlation with a *nominal* dependent variable. However, more often problems involve violation of assumptions underlying statistical tests or problems in making several or many comparisons without adjusting the alpha level. Such problems often result in a Type I error. Our experience suggests that not adjusting the alpha level when multiple tests have been conducted is more common than selection of an inappropriate statistic.

Q9d. Fourth, were the statistical results presented adequately? Confidence intervals (Chapter 17) and effect sizes should be provided. If effect sizes are not provided, the necessary information (e.g., *M*, *SD*, *N*) should be presented so they can be computed. Discussion of several effect size measures is presented in Chapter 17 and in each of the chapters (20–22) on the interpretation statistics.

Q9e. The fifth issue to consider involves making the *proper interpretation* of the statistical analysis. Sometimes the correct statistic is selected, but the investigator misinterprets the findings, concluding more from the data than is actually provided. For example, if there is a significant interaction from the analysis of a factorial analysis of variance (ANOVA), one should examine first the interaction and the simple effects rather than the main effects, which may be misleading. Issues about interpretation of statistical results are discussed in more detail in Chapters 20 through 22.

Internal Validity

Internal validity is based on the strength or soundness of the design. This definition of internal validity allows us to evaluate nonexperimental as well as experimental research.

Randomized experimental designs are usually high on internal validity. We believe that one can and should judge the internal validity of any study on a continuum from low to high.

Internal validity is important because it indicates how confident we can be that the relationship between an independent and dependent variable is a cause-and-effect relationship. Although it is important to use the appropriate statistical analysis, the statistical method does not determine causation. Causation is inferred primarily from the research approach. Thus, although "correlation does not indicate causation," the same is true for *t* tests and ANOVA if the approach was comparative. In general, randomized experimental designs provide the best evidence for causation (high internal validity). The comparative and associational approaches, at best, provide suggestions about possible causes. The strength of a quasi-experiment affects how much confidence we can place in whether the independent variable is a cause of the dependent variable (see Chapters 4 and 5). Our evaluation framework divides internal validity into two dimensions: (1) *equivalence of the groups* on *participant characteristics* (Q10); and (2) *control of extraneous experience and environment variables* (Q11).

Q10. What is the evaluation of the equivalence of the groups on participant characteristics? Base the rating and comments on the following:

a. Was there random assignment of participants to the groups?

b. If no random assignment, were the participants in each group matched, made similar statistically, or found to be similar on a pretest? If random assignment was done, b and c should be scored as *yes*.

c. If no random assignment, were the participants in each group matched, made similar statistically, or found to be similar on other key participant characteristics (e.g., age, gender, IQ)?

d. Was the retention (low attrition) of subjects during the study high and similar across groups?

Equivalence of the Groups on Participant Characteristics

In the *randomized experimental, quasi-experimental,* and *comparative* approaches, a key question is whether the *groups* that are compared were *equivalent in all respects except the independent variable* or variables *before* the procedures of the study took place. There are a number of specific "threats" to internal validity, several of which are "participant" factors that could lead to a lack of equivalence of the participants in the two (or more) groups and thus influence the relationship with the dependent variable (see Chapter 8). This dimension is often called *selection bias*, because it should be rated low if the participants choose which group they will be in (i.e., if there is self-selection into groups). However, we think that the phrase *assignment bias* is less likely to be confusing because the key issue for internal validity is whether the participants were *randomly assigned* to the groups. Random *sampling* or *selection* of subjects is more *relevant* to population external validity, which is Q14. The top section of Figure 23.4 should be used to evaluate this aspect of internal validity.

Q10a. The best way to assure that the groups are unbiased and close to equivalent is by *randomly assigning the participants to adequately sized groups.*

Q10b and Q10c. However, if random assignment to groups is not possible, randomly assigning treatments to intact groups (strong quasi-experiments), matching, analysis of covariance (ANCOVA), or checking for demographic similarity of groups are methods of achieving a medium level of this aspect of internal validity. If the groups were known to be dissimilar and

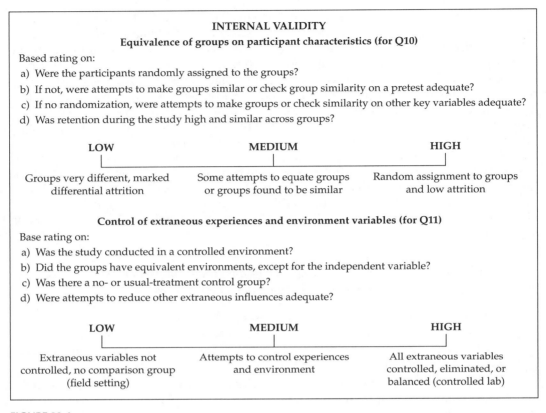

FIGURE 23.4
Rating scales to evaluate the internal validity of the findings of a study.

no attempts were made to confirm the similarity of the groups or make the groups similar with matching, ANCOVA, or other methods, the rating would be low. Associational approaches also would be rated low unless attempts were made to control for other key variables.

If the approach is *associational*, there is only one group. In that case, this aspect of internal validity comes down to the question of whether participants who score high on the independent or predictor variables of interest are equivalent to those who score low in terms of other attributes that may be correlated with the dependent or outcome variable. For example, it is likely that the persons who score high on an attribute independent variable such as anxiety are *not* equivalent to those who score low in terms of other variables such as age, social status, education, and especially other psychological characteristics. Thus, studies using an associational approach usually should be rated low on this dimension. Statistical controls may increase this aspect of internal validity to medium for the associational approach as well as the quasi-experimental and comparative approaches, by making the groups more similar, but such techniques cannot produce high internal validity.

Q10d. Thus, randomized experiments are rated high on this aspect of internal validity, *unless* there is markedly different attrition (dropouts) between groups or high overall attrition *during the study*. It is not good if too many people drop out during the study, especially if they are mostly in one group or the other. Attrition is also a potential problem for quasi-experiments and for comparative and associational studies that are longitudinal (i.e., last more than one time period).

Q11. What is the evaluation of the control of extraneous experience and environment variables?

a. Was the study conducted in a controlled environment?

b. Did the groups have equivalent environments?

c. Was there a no-treatment (placebo) or usual-treatment comparison group?

d. Were there adequate attempts to reduce other extraneous influences?

Control of Extraneous Experience and Environmental Variables

We use the issues listed in the lower half of Figure 23.4 to make the evaluation of this dimension of research validity. Several "threats" to internal validity have been grouped under a category that deals with the effects of *extraneous* (those variables not of interest in *this* study) experiences or environmental conditions during the study. This is also called **contamination**.

In general, well-controlled laboratory-type settings offer less contamination, and field or natural settings offer less control (more contamination) of extraneous variables. This dimension of validity is rated lower if extraneous variables or events, such as different environments or teachers, affect one group more than the others. In the *associational approach*, the issue is whether the experiences of the participants who score high on the independent or predictor variable are different from those who score low on the independent variable. In *experimental studies*, if participants know what group they are in, that may affect their motivation and contaminate the results. In experiments without a no-treatment (placebo) control group, any changes could be due to maturation or some other variable that the groups had in common.

Briefly, in laboratory experimental designs, these experiential and environmental variables are usually quite well controlled, but in *field experimental* designs, and especially in the comparative and associational approaches, such extraneous experiences may be inadequately controlled. In general, there is a trade-off between high control of extraneous variables and high ecological validity. It is difficult to have both.

If a study is rated low or medium on either or both of the two main dimensions of internal validity, the authors should not use terms such as *effect*, *impact*, and *determine* that imply cause and effect. Phrases such as *may affect*, *presumed cause*, or *possible determinant* are more cautious, but it is probably best to avoid causal terms and to just describe the results as indicating that there is a relationship or difference.

Summary

This chapter provides an integrated review of most of the important concepts related to the evaluation of measurement reliability and statistics and internal validity that were introduced in earlier chapters. Answers to the 11 questions discussed here and the 8 discussed in the next chapter provide a comprehensive evaluation of a research study, especially its methods. To perform this evaluation, one must identify the key variables and their characteristics (type and level of measurement). One must also identify the research questions, approaches, and design. Finally, we discussed the first two aspects of research validity, providing three rating scales and rubrics for using them to evaluate these dimensions of research validity. These first three key dimensions of research validity are as follows:

1. Measurement reliability and statistics.
2. Internal validity: equivalence of the groups on participant characteristics.
3. Internal validity: control of extraneous experience and environmental variables.

In the next chapter, we discuss five more dimensions, as follows:

1. Construct validity of the intervention or treatment.
2. Measurement or construct validity of the measured variables.
3. Population external validity.
4. Ecological external validity.
5. External validity: testing of subgroups.

The rating scales for these eight dimensions provide a comprehensive evaluation of the methods of a research study.

Key Concepts

Contamination
Control of extraneous experience and environment variables
Dependent or outcome variable
Effect size
General design classification
Independent or predictor variable
Internal validity
Level or scale of measurement
Levels or categories of a variable
Measurement reliability and statistics
Random assignment of participants to groups
Research approach
Research questions
Research validity
Retention of subjects (low attrition or dropout)
Specific experimental design name
Statistical power

Key Distinctions

Measurement reliability versus measurement validity
Measurement validity versus research validity

Application Problems

The application problems for Chapter 23 are presented at the end of Chapter 24.

24

Evaluating Research Validity: Part II

This chapter continues our discussion of how to evaluate the design and analysis of an empirical research study. The focus of our evaluation framework is quantitative research, but we think that most parts would apply to the evaluation of qualitative research studies as well; Q13 through Q19 discussed in this chapter would be especially applicable to the evaluation of qualitative and mixed methods research. Now, we continue our evaluation of the research validity of a study. First, we discuss the evaluation of overall measurement validity of the constructs, and then we evaluate three aspects of external validity.

Overall Measurement Validity of the Constructs

This dimension is sometimes labeled *construct validity,* but that may be confusing because the same phrase also has been used for *one specific* type of evidence for measurement validity (see Chapter 12). We began discussion of the issue of measurement validity with Q8 in the last chapter. Now, we make an *overall judgment* of the validity of the operational definitions of the several key variables in the study using Figure 24.1. This judgment has two main aspects: (1) the *construct validity of the intervention* or active independent variable (Q12); and (2) measurement or *construct validity of the outcomes* (or dependent variables) *and* any attribute independent variables (Q13).

Q12. What is the evaluation of the *construct validity of the intervention*? (If there is no active independent variable, this question is skipped as *not applicable*.)

a. Is the intervention (active independent variable) operationally defined and implemented appropriately based on an existing body of empirical or theoretical research?

b. Is the intervention described in enough detail for it to be replicated?

c. Is there a manipulation check or verification to be sure that the intervention was presented as planned?

This question is about the active independent variable (treatment or intervention) and its appropriate implementation—that is, whether it was based on commonly shared empirical or theoretical concepts and whether it was described in enough detail so that it could be replicated. The question also asks whether there was a **manipulation check** to see if the intervention was actually presented as planned and described in the study protocol. Such a check is important, especially with new curricula or programs, because it is common for instructors to slip back into old ways of doing things. Thus, the new techniques may not actually have been done consistently.

355

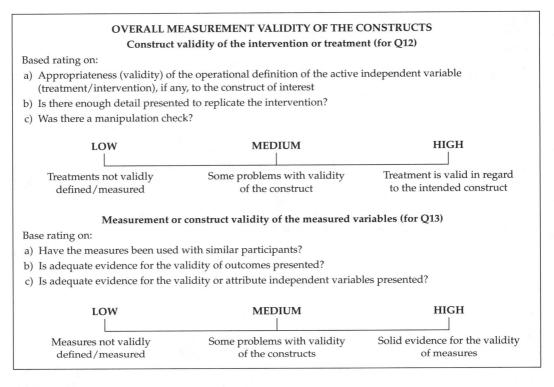

FIGURE 24.1
Evaluating the measurement validity of a study.

Furthermore, an intervention *could* be described in enough detail and have had a manipulation check so that it was implemented as *planned*, but the intervention might not be identified and labeled appropriately, given current theory and literature. For example, a curriculum could be said to use "constructivist" learning techniques, but a close examination of the program might indicate that the intervention as planned and implemented was not really constructivist. *If there is no active independent variable (intervention), this rating is not applicable.*

Q13. What is the *overall* evaluation of the construct validity *of the outcome measures* (dependent variables) *and any attribute independent variables*?

a. Have the measures been used with similar participants?

b. Is adequate evidence for the validity of the outcomes based on existing empirical or theoretical research presented?

c. Is adequate evidence for the validity of the attribute independent variables presented?

This question is about the attribute independent variables and dependent variables as a whole. Are they measured validly and appropriately defined so that they represent the concepts under investigation? The validity of the outcomes and measured (attribute) independent or predictor variables depends, in part, on whether the measures are appropriate for the types of participants in the study.

The issue for Q12 and Q13 is whether these operational definitions are representative of the intended concepts and constructs. Sometimes the intervention and outcomes are not based on commonly shared or theoretically derived ideas. If so, the overall ratings (Q12 and Q13) should be low.

External Validity

"External validity asks the question of generalizability: to what populations, settings, treatment variables, and measurement variables can this effect be generalized?" (Campbell & Stanley, 1963/1966, p. 5). In our evaluation framework, external validity has three aspects: (1) *population external validity* (Q14); (2) *ecological external validity* (Q15); and (3) *testing of subgroups* (Q16). The first two dimensions examine how representative the population and setting are of the target or theoretical population and of the procedures and setting. The third rating (Q16) evaluates whether the results are likely to generalize to diverse subgroups such as both genders.

Q14. What is the evaluation of the overall *population external validity*? Base the rating on answers to the following:

 a. Was the accessible population representative of the theoretical population?

 b. Was the selected sample representative of the accessible population?

 c. Was the actual sample representative vis-à-vis the selected sample? That is, was the response rate acceptable?

Population External Validity

This aspect of external validity is a participant *selection* or *sampling* issue that involves how participants were *selected to be in the study*. Were they randomly selected from a particular population, or were volunteers used? Most quantitative studies in the social sciences have not used random selection of participants, but the issue of population external validity is more complex than whether there was a random sample; as discussed in Chapter 9 (see Figure 24.2), external population validity depends on three steps in the sampling process.

To evaluate these three steps, we first *identify* the four components of the sampling process: (1) the *theoretical population*; (2) the *accessible population*; (3) the *sampling design* and *selected sample*; and (4) the *actual sample* of participants involved in the study. The three steps connect the four components of the process. It is possible that the researcher could use a random or other probability *sampling* technique (step 2) but have an actual sample that is not representative of the theoretical population, due either to a low response rate (step 3) or to the accessible population not being representative of the theoretical population (step 1). The latter problem seems almost universal, in part due to funding and travel limitations. Except in national survey research, researchers almost always start with an accessible population from the local school district, community, or clinic that is probably not fully representative of the target population of interest.

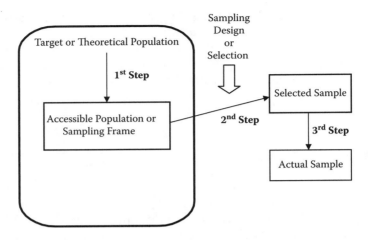

FIGURE 24.2
Schematic diagram of the sampling process.

Ratings now can be made for each subquestion (Q14a, Q14b, and Q14c) using the top section of Figure 24.3. Finally, an overall rating for Q14 can be made of whether the *actual sample of participants is representative of the theoretical or target population.* Examples of where and how the overall population external validity rating can be affected by problems at any of the three steps were discussed in Chapter 9.

There is an important distinction between *random sampling* (i.e., selection of subjects from the population), which influences population external validity, and *random assignment* (of participants to *groups*), which influences the participant equivalence aspect of internal validity. For Q14 we are considering random *sampling, not* random assignment to groups, which was evaluated in Q11 in Chapter 23.

Q15. What is the evaluation of the overall *ecological external validity*? The rating is based on the following:

   a. Is the setting (or conditions) natural and representative of the target setting?

   b. Is the rapport with testers or observers good?

   c. Are the procedures or tasks natural and representative of the behavioral concepts of interest?

   d. Is the timing and length of the treatment or intervention appropriate (not applicable [NA] if not an experiment because no intervention is done)?

   e. Will the results apply to more than the specific time in history that the study was done?

Ecological External Validity

This is an aspect of external validity that is about the conditions/settings, testers, procedures or tasks, and time in history. We evaluate each of these five aspects of ecological validity in terms of how representative they are of the target or intended settings and so on and, thus, whether the results can be generalized. Because the ecologically valid target settings, testers, procedures, and tasks are usually "natural," we use that term here. We

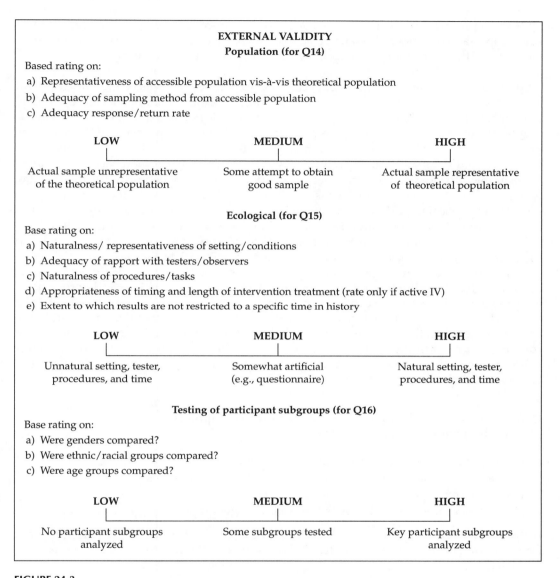

FIGURE 24.3
Rating scales to evaluate the external validity of the findings of a study.

rate each of the five aspects of ecological validity and then provide an overall judgment using the middle scale in Figure 24.3.

Q15a: Naturalness of the setting. A study in a field setting (e.g., home or school) is higher on this aspect of ecological external validity than one in a laboratory setting, especially if the lab conditions are highly artificial.

Q15b: Rapport with tester. The rapport or quality of the relationship between tester or observer and the participants is important. Differences between the participants and researcher or tester in personal style, ethnicity, gender, or age may reduce rapport. Skilled interviewers may be able to increase rapport by "getting to know" the interviewee, so that may help ecological validity.

Q15c: Naturalness of the procedures. Most of the procedures that use self-report measures, especially questionnaires, are at least somewhat artificial because they are not direct measures of the participant's actual behavior. Experimental tasks or tests are also typically at least somewhat unnatural.

Q15d: Length of intervention. In experiments, sometimes the intervention or treatment is too short to be representative of how the intervention would actually take place if widely implemented. (This rating is not applicable if the study is not an experiment.)

Q15e: When did the study take place? The topic of the study or phrasing of the questions may restrict its usefulness to approximately the time in history that it was conducted. Results related to topics about current events or trendy issues may soon become outdated. For example, attitudes about topics such as school vouchers, low-carbohydrate diets, or gay marriage may change over time. Thus, it is desirable that questions about such topics be repeated or replicated periodically. Remember that most surveys measure a specific "slice in time." Other topics are more timeless, and their results may stay relevant for decades.

Consider an example of a problem in ecological validity. If an educator is interested in the effect of a particular teaching style on student participation, the classroom should be similar to that of a normal classroom. Similarly, if the investigator asked students to come at night for the study but these students normally attended class during the day, then there is a problem with the setting aspect of ecological external validity. The question should be asked whether some representative method was used for selection of the setting and time or a convenience method was used. For high ecological validity, an intervention should be conducted by a culturally appropriate intervener (teacher, therapist, or tester) for an appropriate length of time. Finally, was this topic one that was trendy so that the results might be different depending on when the study was done?

Q16. What is the evaluation of the extent to which important participant *subgroups* were *tested or compared*?

   a. Are gender differences analyzed or compared?
   b. Are two or more ethnic or racial groups analyzed or compared?
   c. Are two or more age groups analyzed or compared?
   d. Are other important subgroups (e.g., cultures, geographic regions) compared?

If the study is experimental, how broadly was the *intervention* tested statistically across important subgroups of participants? Do the results of the intervention for one gender, ethnicity, or age group hold for the other gender, ethnicities, or ages?

If the focus of the study is on an attribute independent variable such as type of disability, the question becomes: Are differences on the dependent variable specific to a certain gender, age, or ethnicity (i.e., is there an interaction with gender, age, or ethnicity)? Or do the noted disability differences apply to both genders, all ages, and all ethnicities? Similar logic would apply to testing of these important subgroups for ordered or continuous attribute independent variables that were the focus of a nonexperimental study. However, if the focus of the study is on gender, age, or ethnicity as the main independent variable, that subquestion (Q16a, Q16b, or Q16c) would be considered not applicable for this rating.

Due to financial and time constraints, many research projects limit the participants to a few of the demographic groups, in part to have enough power to detect differences. Gender comparisons are quite common, but often a single age or ethnicity is used. Or there is a range of ages or ethnicities, but there are not enough participants in the smaller groups to analyze age or ethnic differences.

Other Issues

Q17. Was there adequate *peer review*?

Q17 is about the extent of peer review of the article or document. **Peer review** means that the article was evaluated by other experts (peers) in the field, usually without knowing who the author of the article was (i.e., masked or "blind" review). Although consumers of research often read newspaper or newsletter articles summarizing research studies, these sources are not peer-reviewed articles. Also, they may not give much detail about the methods used, but they usually provide some information about the source from which the article was written. Newspaper articles often are based on published peer-reviewed articles or presentations at professional meetings, which had some sort of peer review. However, the journalist may have left out important details.

If the source is a scholarly journal, the chances are that the peer review was at least moderately extensive and strict. One way to indirectly evaluate the quality of the peer review is to compare citation rankings of the journal that published the article to other journals in the same general discipline. For example, if many authors refer to articles in a specific journal, it would be considered to have high status; see ranks in *Journal Citation Reports. Social Sciences Ed.* (1994–present). Another common method of evaluating the quality of the journal is to obtain the percentage of articles that are accepted by the journal. The lower the percentage accepted, generally the higher the status of the journal.

If the association that publishes the journal is made up primarily of practitioners who are only secondarily interested in research, the peer review of the design and analysis is likely to be less strict because practitioner reviews focus more on the importance of the problem, application, and implications. Presentations at professional meetings, even research-oriented meetings, are usually less strictly reviewed, especially if the judgment to accept was based on a summary or abstract of the paper.

Furthermore, presentations to nonscholarly audiences or at events like press conferences are even less likely to be reviewed by independent scholars or researchers and thus do not have peer review. Finally, studies whose main or sole source is dissemination in a popular article or an article in a popular magazine or newspaper would not have had peer review.

If a study provides clinically significant results on an important topic, one would assume that it would be published in a peer-reviewed journal, at least within a few years of completion. It is not a good sign if a somewhat older study has *only* been presented at a conference, published in a book chapter, published in the trade or popular press, or posted on an Internet website. If the study was not published in a peer-reviewed journal, it may well indicate that there are serious flaws in the study or that the study lacked sufficient new, important findings to be published in a peer-reviewed source.

Q18. Do the authors adequately present the case for the theoretical importance or practical relevance of their research questions and design?

This question asks how well the research questions follow from the literature or theory used to support their importance. The theoretical background and rationale for the study are usually provided in the introduction of the study. Thus, does the introduction make a good case for the importance of the study and the relevance of the research questions to the problem of interest? This is obviously a very important criterion, but it is hard to evaluate if the reviewer is not thoroughly knowledgeable about the literature and theory on the topic.

Q19. Do the authors interpret their findings adequately? That is, were the title, abstract, and discussion clear and accurate (or overstated and misleading) given the evaluation of the several aspects of research validity?

Finally, Q19 is a summary question that evaluates the title abstract and especially the discussion and conclusions for indications of inaccuracy or misleading statements, given the previous analysis of the study. Often in popular articles the editor or writer will overstate the findings to make them seem more impressive or be more easily understood by the public. The author of a popular magazine or newspaper discussion of a study with relatively low internal validity (because of lack of proper control groups or lack of equivalence of groups) may report or imply that the independent variable *caused* the dependent variable, had an *impact* on, or *determined* the outcome. These overstatements may not have been made in the original article by the researcher, who may have presented the conclusions more cautiously and appropriately, given the relatively low internal validity of the study. Likewise, a study based on an unrepresentative sample of people or on one gender may be overgeneralized, perhaps without any mention of the types of participants used or without at least implying that there is no problem in making more general statements. The astute consumer should become aware of these possible overinterpretations and should evaluate the article appropriately.

Other questions could be asked about a research article, such as about its readability and clarity. However, we believe that we have discussed the major dimensions, and thus we have not tried to be overly exhaustive in our coverage.

In Chapter 25, we use this framework and the 19 questions from this chapter and Chapter 23 to provide narrative evaluations of the five sample research studies introduced in Chapter 1. Each of these studies is rated from low to high on the eight research validity dimensions (Q9–Q16).

The Relative Importance of Different Validity Dimensions

Another important consideration is how the eight research validity ratings should be weighted if one were required to provide an overall or composite score. We suggest that there *could be* equal weights for the eight dimensions to develop an average percentage score for Q9–Q16. Of course many researchers, especially those inclined to use experiments, would place more weight on internal validity, but other researchers emphasize external validity. Thus, it would be difficult to obtain agreed on differential weights for the eight research validity dimensions.

Furthermore, these eight research validity dimensions focus on the design and analysis of studies and deemphasize the importance and originality of the topic or research problem. These latter points obviously are key aspects of an overall rating of whether a research grant should be awarded or an article published. In a broader rating of the quality of an article, Q17–Q19 would have to be given substantial weight.

It is difficult for a single study to achieve high ratings for each of the dimensions of research validity. Typically, researchers sacrifice strength in one dimension to enhance another. Campbell and Stanley (1963/1966) discussed whether a study should be judged more harshly if it is weaker on certain validity dimensions than on others:

> Both types of criteria (internal and external validity) are obviously important, even though they are frequently at odds in that features increasing one may jeopardize the other … the selection of designs strong in both types of validity is obviously our ideal. (p. 5)

Cook and Campbell (1979) also addressed the issue in some depth. They suggested that if one is interested in testing a theory, then internal validity and measurement validity of the key constructs have the highest priority. Obviously, the constructs used in the study must represent those in the theory. Also, one would need to show a causal relationship (high internal validity) between or among variables when testing a theory.

Campbell and Stanley (1963/1966) made an oft quoted statement that "internal validity is the basic minimum without which any experiment is uninterpretable: Did in fact the experimental treatments make a difference in this specific experimental instance?" (p. 5). However, they followed that quote with the one we already examined about both internal validity and external validity being important and part of their ideal. And, they added a final sentence about external validity that has often been overlooked: "This is particularly the case for research on teaching, in which generalization to applied settings of known character is the desideratum" (p. 5). If one performs applied research, then emphasis should be placed on external validity, especially if the research involves comparing specific diagnostic groups.

We think that *all* of these dimensions are important for evaluating the quality of *all* types of research: experimental or nonexperimental, theory driven or applied. Furthermore, we believe that these dimensions can be evaluated separately even though there may well be some conceptual interdependence. Whether to weight internal or external validity higher probably depends on the purpose of the study. If one is interested in *evidence-based practice* (Chapter 26) (i.e., whether an intervention works), internal validity should probably be weighted more. However, as Cook and Campbell (1979) pointed out:

> There is also a circular justification for the primacy of internal validity…. The unique purpose of experiments is to provide stronger tests of causal hypotheses than is permitted by other forms of research, most of which were developed for other purposes…. Given that the unique original purpose of experiments is cause-related, internal validity has to assume a special importance in experimentation since it is concerned with how confident one can be that an observed relationship between variables is causal or that the absence of a relationship implies no cause. (p. 84)

Summary

This chapter completed our discussion, begun in Chapter 23, of the eight key dimensions that we use to evaluate the overall research validity of a study. In Chapter 23 we provided rating scales to evaluate three dimensions:

1. Measurement reliability and statistics.
2. Equivalence of the groups on participant characteristic.
3. Control of extraneous experience and environment variables.

In this chapter we provided rating scales to evaluate the following five dimensions:

4. Construct validity of the intervention.
5. Construct validity of the outcome measures and attribute independent variables.
6. Population external validity.
7. Ecological external validity.
8. External validity: Extent to which important participant subgroups were tested or compared.

In this chapter, we also discussed briefly three additional issues that are related to the quality of the written presentation of the research: (1) whether there was adequate peer review; (2) how well the research questions are justified and linked to the literature; and (3) how clearly and accurately the authors discuss the results. All 19 questions that we use to provide a comprehensive evaluation of a research study are presented in one place in Appendix E.

Key Concepts

Construct validity of the intervention (active independent variable)

External validity

Manipulation check

Overall measurement validity (of the outcome measures and attribute independent variables)

Peer review

Theoretical importance and practical relevance

Key Distinctions

External validity: population versus ecological versus comparison of subgroups

Overall construct validity of the variables (Q13) versus construct validity of a specific instrument (Chapter 12)

Application Problems

For each of the following problems, evaluate each of the eight key dimensions (Q9–Q16) of research validity. If not enough information is provided, state what you would need to know to make an evaluation.

1. Researchers in a large metropolitan school district with a diverse multiethnic student population have implemented a study regarding the possible effects of type of curriculum and type of counselor on student leadership levels measured with an instrument using a summated Likert scale. The researchers were able to choose a random sample from the entire senior class. These students were then randomly assigned to two groups, either the experimental multiethnic or traditional leadership curriculum, taught by a counselor with extensive training in multicultural issues and a traditionally trained counselor, respectively. In other regards, these individuals were very similar in education and experience.

2. A researcher is interested in studying the effect of sleep deprivation on teenagers' math performance. He has a limited research budget, so he decides to study students at the local college. He obtained a list of all the students for each level (freshman to senior). He randomly samples 10 students from each of the levels. All 40 agree to be in the study. They answer a questionnaire about the amount of sleep they had during finals week last semester and their SAT math scores.

3. A researcher plans to do a laboratory experimental study of sleep deprivation on math performance. He randomly assigns students from his sample to two groups of 20 each. Participants in one group are kept awake all night studying and given a math test in the morning. The participants in the other group are encouraged to sleep as long as they want before they take the math test in the morning.

4. A Ph.D. student asked a random sample of faculty at a college to answer a questionnaire; 50% responded. The faculty members classified their department heads as one of four types of leader (A, B, C, or D) based on answers to a brief leadership inventory. Faculty members were asked their own age, classified as younger (<35), middle (35–49), or older (50+). The researcher wanted to know if these characteristics seem to influence their job satisfaction, rated on a nine-point Likert scale.

5. A study was undertaken to determine the back-to-work effects of two types of treatment on postsurgical carpal tunnel syndrome patients. *Treatment Full* used splints on a full-time basis, whereas *Treatment Part* used splints on a part-time basis. In addition, the investigator also was interested in whether patients who scored high on the personality variable of codependency would do worse than patients who scored low on the variable of codependency. A total of 500 postsurgical patients from a large metropolitan area volunteered for this study. All 500 patients were given the Gliner Co-dependency Personality Inventory (test–retest reliability $r = .88$; predictive validity $r = 66$). From this sample of 500 carpal tunnel syndrome patients, the 20 patients with the highest codependency scores (H) and the 20 patients with the lowest codependency scores (L) were selected to continue in the study. From these two groups, H and L, half of the patients were randomly assigned to the full-time splint group F, and half of the patients were randomly assigned to the part-time splint group P. Prior to the interventions, all 40 participants were given the Gliner Carpal Tunnel Syndrome Pain Inventory (not currently found in the *Buros Mental Measurements Yearbooks*). A high score on this inventory meant much pain and little success. After 3 months of intervention, all 40 participants were tested again on the Gliner Carpal Tunnel Syndrome Pain Inventory.

25

Narrative Evaluations of the Five Sample Articles

To illustrate how to use the framework described in Chapters 23 and 24 to evaluate research validity, we now evaluate the five studies introduced in Chapter 1. They vary in the approach used but have a number of features in common: They all were published in peer-reviewed journals, made a reasonable case for the research questions and methods based on literature and theory, and interpreted the results with appropriate caution given the strengths and weaknesses of the methods used. Thus, Q17–Q19 (other issues) probably would not produce major differences in the evaluations for this set of peer-reviewed articles. However, there were differences in the strength of various aspects of the design and methods, as discussed next. We evaluate each of the studies in order using global judgments and narratives to rate each of the eight research validity scales (Q9–Q16) described in Chapters 23 and 24.[1]

There is, of course, some degree of subjective judgment involved both with the eight ratings used in this chapter and when using the 2006 numerical evaluation form. Thus, different knowledgeable evaluators might produce different ratings for the eight key dimensions (Q9–Q16). However, we believe that reliability would be quite high and that the mean difference in ratings would be small.

There are advantages and disadvantages to evaluations like the ones presented here. On the positive side, attention is given to all, or almost all, of the key factors of the research design and analysis that influence the research validity of a study. Doing such a comprehensive evaluation forces one to read the article carefully, especially the methods section, and encourages critical reading of not only what is said but what is implied and what is left out.

We think that an overall rating of each of the eight key ratings would be appropriate. However, we have found that such global ratings are hard to make for less experienced evaluators. Thus, the subquestions (e.g., Q9a, Q9b, Q9c, Q9d, and Q9e) are intended to facilitate consideration of the key issues for each of the eight key dimensions of research validity.

A comprehensive evaluation, using either narratives and global ratings of the eight key dimensions (such as in this chapter) or the 2006 numerical evaluation form, could be used for any empirical research study. However, such detailed evaluations are most appropriate for studies that are critical to some decision such as whether to fund a grant, publish a paper, use a design as a model for replication, or adopt a procedure or instrument for use in a planned study. In many cases, a briefer overview evaluation may be adequate.

We provide a narrative evaluation and eight ratings for each of the five sample studies that were introduced in Chapter 1. We have provided extensive narratives to explain the ratings of each of the eight dimensions. For many purposes such an extended narrative would probably not be necessary. A complete list of the 19 evaluation questions is provided in Appendix E.

Study 1: A Randomized Experiment

The purpose of this study (Schellenberg, 2004) was to test the hypothesis that music lessons enhance the intellectual abilities and educational achievement of 6-year-old children. The *active independent variable* or intervention in this study was the type of lesson. There were four *levels* of this independent variable: (1) standard keyboard music lessons; (2) Kodály voice music lessons; (3) drama lessons; or (4) no lessons. The two music lesson groups were considered *experimental* or intervention conditions, and the drama and no-lessons groups were considered the *comparison or control groups*. The 144 children were *randomly assigned* to one of the four groups. Because there was an active independent variable and the partici-pants were randomly assigned to each group, the approach was *randomized experimental*.

The *dependent* or *outcome variables* were IQ (measured by the Wechsler Intelligence Scale for Children-Third Edition [WISC-III] IQ scales; Wechsler, 1991), educational achieve-ment (measured by the Kaufman Test of Educational Achievement, K-TEA; Kaufman & Kaufman, 1985), and parent ratings of their child's behavior (measured by the Behavioral System for Children, BASC; Reynolds & Kamphaus, 1992). These are frequently used stan-dardized measures with considerable evidence to support their *measurement reliability* and *measurement validity*. However, in this short article this evidence is only implied by listing earlier publications and test manuals, so one would need to find and read these sources to learn the details.

The lessons (intervention) were given in small groups of six children each over a 36-week period by trained professionals at the Royal Conservatory in Toronto. All children were tested both before and after the intervention. Thus, this was a *pretest–posttest, comparison group design*. The general design classification was a *4 × 2 factorial design with repeated measures on the second factor* because there were two independent variables (the intervention with four levels) and change over time (two levels) from the pretest to the posttest. Because the author used the gain score approach to the data analysis, the design was reduced to one indepen-dent variable, type of lesson (see Chapter 22 for discussion of the gain score analysis).

Results indicated that the two music groups (combined) gained more on IQ than the two comparison groups combined ($t(130) = 1.99$, $p < .05$, $d = .35$), but they didn't gain statistically significantly more on educational achievement. The drama group improved significantly in adaptive social behavior, but the other three groups did not change on this variable.

Overall Measurement Reliability and Statistics (Q9)

Measurement reliability was not reported but, as already mentioned, should be good for these standardized instruments. *Power* was appropriate to detect a medium effect size; for statistical analyses the researchers were able to collapse/combine the two music groups and also to combine the two control groups because the two music groups were not signifi-cantly different on most measures. The *selection* and *interpretation* of the statistics seem to be appropriate, and *d* effect sizes were reported. Overall, we rated this dimension as high.

Internal Validity: Equivalence of Groups on Participant Characteristics (Q10)

The children were *randomly assigned* to the four groups, which were large enough ($n = 36$) that they should be and *were* very similar and unbiased on participant characteristics. Unfortunately, there was some *attrition* (about 14%) in the music groups between pretest and posttest, but there was little dropout in the control groups. Due to the differential attrition, this dimension was not rated as high as it would have been considering the random assignment to adequately sized groups, so it was rated medium high.

Control of Extraneous Experiences and Environment Variables (Q11)

The groups received their lessons at the conservatory, which appears to be a controlled environment. However, it is possible that there was some *contamination* if children or their parents were influenced by knowing what was happening in the other groups. The no-lesson group may have been somewhat disappointed because they didn't receive any lessons; this could possibly have affected their motivation to do well on the posttest. However, they were promised lessons the following year, which no doubt helped. The study was rated medium to high on this dimension.

Construct Validity of the Intervention (Q12)

The interventions seem appropriately related to the constructs (music and drama lessons) and well implemented. However, in this short article there was very little description of exactly how the lessons were implemented, and there was no direct evidence that a manipulation check was done to be sure the lessons were implemented as planned. Overall, this dimension was rated medium to high.

Construct Validity of the Dependent Variables (Q13)

The measures were standardized IQ, achievement, and behavioral assessment instruments that have been widely studied and used with typically developing children similar to those in this study. Thus, this dimension was rated as high.

External Population Validity (Q14)

The *theoretical or target population* appears to be 6-year-old children in developed, Western countries. The *accessible population* was Canadian children from the Toronto area whose parents read local newspaper advertisements for free arts lessons. Thus, the children were volunteers who were clearly a nonrandomly selected *convenience sample*. There was no mention of whether any of the volunteers in the *selected sample* were not included in the *actual sample*. We assume that these samples were the same. (Remember that there was some attrition *during* the study, which influenced internal validity, but that is less relevant for population external validity, the rating under consideration here).

Although the accessible population is different from many parts of the United States and Western Europe, Toronto is a large very diverse city, and in many ways 6-year-olds in Toronto are probably similar to the broader target population of 6-year-olds. However, the *selected sample* of volunteer parents and their children was probably quite different from all Toronto 6-year-olds. It probably was considerably more middle and upper-middle class with fewer minorities, and certainly it was biased toward parents and kids interested in the arts. Thus, the selected (and actual) sample is rated medium in terms of how well it represented the theoretical population.

Ecological External Validity (Q15)

The *setting* for the study, the conservatory, was a natural place for music and drama lessons to take place. *Rapport* was probably very good with the teachers and also was *probably* good with the IQ and achievement testers, but this is only speculation. However, the *tasks* and procedures for the testing were somewhat artificial, as is always the case with such standardized tests and inventories. The *timing and length of the intervention* seem appropriate: weekly for 36 weeks, essentially a school year. The intervention seems long enough to produce an effect if there would be one and is a natural length/intensity for beginning arts lessons. Finally, the topic and results do *not* seem to be restricted to a particular *time in history*. Similar music and drama lessons have been given for centuries and probably will be similar in the future, it seems likely that any result would be similar in the past and future. *Overall*, we rate *ecological external validity* high.

External Validity: Testing of Subgroups (Q16)

Finally, there does not seem to be any *testing of subgroups* to see if the intervention worked better with some than others. In fact, the article does not report the numbers of males and females overall or in each group. It may be that the children were mostly female so comparing genders might not have been feasible statistically. Probably there were relatively few ethnic minorities, again making it difficult to meaningfully compare ethnic groups. The age range was very narrow; all children were 6 so age comparisons would not be meaningful. Overall, *external validity: testing of subgroups* is rated low.

Study 2: A Quasi-Experiment

This study, titled "The Value of Time Limits on Internet Quizzes" (Brothen & Wambach, 2004), evaluated the effect of putting a time limit on "take-home" quizzes. Two sections of a psychology class were used as participants. The study is considered quasi-experimental because, although there was an active independent variable, the students were *not randomly assigned* to the two groups (timed quizzes versus untimed). The *active independent variable* was whether there was a time limit for students when they took a quiz. One section of the course had a 15-minute time limit, and the other section had no limit. The authors theorized that if students knew they would have a time limit, they were more likely to study the material before starting the quiz rather than starting the take-home quiz and *then* looking up the answers. The *dependent variables* were the students' scores on the regular exams and also how long they spent on the quizzes. Students who had a time limit on the quizzes did better on the monitored, closed-book unit exams ($t(44) = 2.44$, $p < .05$) and took less time on the quizzes ($t(44) = 3.88$, $p < .001$), which provided support for the main research hypothesis. The effect sizes were .75 and 1.4, respectively, based on our computations from their data. The *general design classification* was a single-factor (between-groups) design with two levels (timed versus untimed quizzes). The *specific experimental design* was a posttest-only design with nonequivalent groups, which without a pretest is a very weak quasi-experimental design. Under the evaluation of group equivalence, the authors did several things to improve, somewhat, this aspect of internal validity.

Overall Measurement Reliability and Statistics (Q9)

No evidence about *reliability* of the exam scores or other measures was reported. Interrater or interscorer reliability would be high because the four 1-hour exams were multiple choice and scored by the computer. However, whether students' scores would have been consistent over time or on parallel forms of the exams is unknown, but such reliability evidence probably would have been at least satisfactory. *Power* was low with only 21 and 25 students in the two sections; the *d* effect size would have to be large to find a significant difference between the groups (Table 16.1). An independent samples *t* test was an *appropriate statistic* to compare the two sections or groups. The *effect size* of the difference and tests of assumptions were not specifically reported, but means and standard deviations were reported, so *d* could be computed. The *interpretation* of the statistical results seemed to be appropriate. Overall, we rated measurement reliability and statistics as medium.

Internal Validity: Equivalence of Groups on Participant Characteristics (Q10)

As is true of all quasi-experiments, the participants were *not randomly assigned* to the groups, so this aspect of internal validity could not be high. However, it did not appear that students were aware of the independent variable in signing up for the classes. There was *no pretest*, so that could not be used to compare the groups or to adjust the posttest means. The groups were found to be "not significantly different" on number of previous credits, cumulative grade point average (GPA), high school percentile rank, and mean ACT score. These comparisons are helpful, but with the small numbers in each group (and, thus, low power) the groups could have been quite different even though not statistically significantly so. The authors of this short article do not provide descriptive statistics for these background variables separately for each group so it is possible that the experimental (timed quiz) group was somewhat higher on some or all of these background variables. On the other hand, one would not expect two sections of the same course to be very different, but they could be. Finally, overall there was pretty high (21%) *attrition*, mostly (14%) at the very beginning of the course, before completing any work, but four students (7%) did miss one or more exams and were excluded from the analysis, for a total of 21% attrition rate. It would not be good if most of the dropouts and excluded students were from the experimental group, especially if it was related to quizzes being timed. Equivalence of the groups on (other) participant characteristics was rated low to medium.

Control of Extraneous Experiences and Environment Variables (Q11)

The environment for the *quizzes* was *not controlled*; students in both groups took them online, whenever they felt ready, with books open if they wanted. However, the environment for the unit hour exams (the dependent variable) was controlled and the same for both groups. There was a "usual treatment" *comparison group*, the untimed quiz section. The researchers *assumed* that the timed quiz group would study and then take the quiz, whereas the untimed quiz group might take the quiz before studying the material, using a "quiz-to-learn" strategy. However, whether students really did study before taking the quizzes and what strategy they used were not really known or controlled. Thus, the experiences of the groups might have differed in ways other than those resulting directly from the independent variable. Also, there could have been some *contamination* (due to students in different groups discussing strategies), and other *extraneous influence* variables could have been different between the two groups. Overall, control of extraneous variables was rated low to medium.

Construct Validity of the Intervention (Q12)

In this quasi-experiment, the intervention was the introduction of a 15-minute time limit for quizzes. The purpose of the time limit was to encourage students to read and study before taking the quiz, but all students were told that this was the best way to use the quizzes.

The intervention was defined operationally and could easily be replicated. Because the time limit was implemented consistently by the WebCT system, no separate manipulation check was necessary. However, the researchers did assess how long students on the average spent to take the quizzes; as expected those who had timed quizzes spent significantly less time (about 4 minutes versus 7 minutes). Overall, the construct validity of this simple intervention was rated high.

Construct Validity of the Dependent Variables (Q13)

The dependent outcome variable was the total score on four computerized multiple-choice 1-hour exams. Although this score is probably a good measure of course "performance," one could question whether it is a valid measure of student "learning." It may be that some students do well and others do poorly due more to their skill in reading or their level of test anxiety than to what they *learned* in the course. Overall, the construct validity of the dependent variable was rated medium to high.

External Population Validity (Q14)

The *theoretical or target population* was probably American college undergraduate psychology students or maybe even college students more broadly. The *accessible population* was psychology of human development students at a large Midwestern state university. The *selected sample* was all 58 students registered for two sections of such a course. Because the research was part of the course requirements, all students in the course were initially in the *actual sample*, but there was 21% attrition.

   The accessible population was considerably narrower than the theoretical population because it included mostly female students in a specific (developmental) psychology course at one university. However, the students at this university may not be that different from students in psychology classes at many American universities. The selected sample was the total enrollment in the two classes, so it would be representative of the accessible population. However, the 21% attrition during the study means that the final actual sample was 79% of the accessible population. Overall, we rated the external population validity as medium.

Ecological External Validity (Q15)

The *setting* for the quizzes was natural (online, wherever, and whenever the student wanted to take them), but the setting for the 1-hour unit exams was artificial (proctored, in a computer lab) although typical for college exams. *Rapport* with the testers was probably medium at best. The *procedures* for the quizzes seemed to be natural, but, again, how the exams were administered was a typical but somewhat artificial way to assess student learning of the course material. The *length* of each of the 19 quizzes was very brief, but apparently the intervention was potent enough to have a significant effect. The topic of test-taking strategies is one that probably will persist across decades, even though the technologies for operationalizing it may be relatively new and may change some in the near future. Overall, ecological external validity was rated as medium.

External Validity: Testing of Subgroups (Q16)

There was no testing of subgroups, probably because the total sample was small, primarily female, and most likely had few minorities or nontraditional aged students. Overall, this dimension was rated low, as is usually the case with small sample studies.

Study 3: A Nonexperimental Study Using the Comparative Approach

DiLorenzo, Halper, and Picone (2004) compared older (60–85 years old) and younger (29–59 years old) persons with multiple sclerosis (MS) on physical functioning, mental health, and quality of life. The *independent variable*, age, is an *attribute* that for this study had two levels: older or younger. The duration of illness was another independent variable (covariate). There were many *dependent or outcome variables* that fell into the three broad categories of physical functioning, mental health, and quality of life. The approach was considered comparative because the main independent variable, age, was an attribute and had only a few levels or groups (younger and older) that were compared on each of the dependent variables. Although the older patients had poorer physical functioning ($F(1, 56) = 4.02$, $p < .05$), they were not different from the younger MS patients on mental health and perceived quality of life when length of illness was controlled.

The design was a single-factor design with two levels. There is no specific experimental design name because the study was nonexperimental.

Overall Measurement Reliability and Statistics (Q9)

The many dependent variables were assessed with published instruments, most or all of which had been used with persons with MS. However, no specific reliability coefficients for the instruments were reported, probably due to space limitations of the journal. Power was not high with 30 in each group, so the lack of significant difference on most variables could be due to lack of power. The choice of a statistic (analysis of covariance, ANCOVA) could have been appropriate, but there is little evidence from the article that covariance assumptions were not violated, which could have lead to inaccurate interpretations, especially with an attribute independent variable (see Kline, 2004, pp. 191–192). Effect sizes were not presented or discussed. Means and standard errors were provided, but the means were adjusted for duration of illness, making effect sizes calculated on these means difficult to interpret. If the researchers were to present effect sizes, they should have been computed on the unadjusted means. The results were interpreted appropriately, except more caution in interpreting the nonsignificant results as indicating "no difference" would have been better. We rated measurement reliability and statistics to be medium.

Internal Validity: Equivalence of Groups on Participant Characteristics (Q10)

This aspect of internal validity could *not* be high because this was a nonexperimental study using the comparative approach. However, the younger and older groups were matched in terms of gender and were quite similar in terms of race, marital status, and education (nearly 100% Caucasian in both groups, about two thirds married in both groups, and about one third in each group college graduates). The groups were different, not surprisingly, in duration of illness and in percentage currently employed. As noted earlier, duration of illness was used to adjust the means of the dependent variables so that statistically the groups would be more similar on that dimension. Because the study involved only a one-time interview, there was no attrition *during* the study. Overall, the equivalence of the groups was judged to be medium, which is good for a nonexperiment.

Control of Extraneous Experiences and Environment Variables (Q11)

This aspect of internal validity is unlikely to be high for a nonexperimental field study because the environment and experiences of the participants in the two groups (older and younger) were uncontrolled and could have been very different. For example, most of the older group experienced, as children, the Great Depression and World War II, whereas the participants in the younger group were postwar and baby boomers. Current friends and experiences also could be different. On the other hand, both groups had the same illness and went to the same MS center in the same city so they shared somewhat the same environment and experiences. We rated control of extraneous variables low to medium.

Construct Validity of the Intervention (Q12)

This is not applicable because there is no intervention in a nonexperimental study, which has only attribute independent variables.

Construct Validity of the Measured Variables (Q13)

Age was no doubt assessed accurately as was duration of illness, using the medical records. However, when an artificial cut point (in this case age of 60) is used to create groups in a comparative study, problems are created. The issue is whether many of the older participants and younger participants are close in age to the cut point. For example, how different is a 61-year-old from a 59-year-old on the dependent variables of interest? Yet they are in two different groups. There is probably considerably more difference between a 61-year-old and an 85-year-old, yet they are in the same group. Thus, the variable of age becomes less meaningful. A better method might have been to exclude anyone between the ages of 50 and 60 from the study. The validity of the dependent variables was probably acceptable because the researchers used published instruments that had been found to be appropriate for MS patients. However, no details about evidence for validity of these self-report measures were presented. This aspect of validity was rated as low to medium.

External Population Validity (Q14)

The accessible population was from one large comprehensive care center for MS in the Northeast, so it might not be fully representative of the national population of adults with MS, but subjects were randomly selected from the medical charts of all patients diagnosed with MS for at least 5 years. The response rates were slightly less than 50%, so not high. Overall, external population validity was rated medium to high.

External Ecological Validity (Q15)

The *setting* was the patients' homes using a telephone interview for efficiency and so that nonambulatory patients could easily participate. *Rapport* with the interviewer was probably okay, but the telephone and structured nature of the interview could have reduced rapport. The *self-report interview* ratings are an unnatural way to assess quality of life, physical health, and mental health. There is *no intervention* in a nonexperimental study so there was no rating of its appropriateness. Because this is a cross-sectional rather than longitudinal design, it is possible that the older patients might self-report less depression and better current quality of life than the younger cohort will when they get older.

However, the finding that older MS patients have more physical limitations but similar perceived quality of life will probably be applicable to future generations, so the study is *not* highly *bound to this time in history*. Overall, external ecological validity was rated medium high.

External Validity: Testing of Subgroups (Q16)

The study did not discuss gender or ethnic differences; there were very few racial minorities. Because age was the main independent variable, testing age differences is not applicable to the rating of this dimension. Thus, this aspect of external validity is rated as low.

Study 4: A Nonexperimental Study Using the Associational Approach

Zamboanga, Padilla-Walker, Hardy, Thompson, and Wang (2007) conducted a study about academic background and course involvement as predictors of exam performance in a university psychology class. The study is considered to be associational because there was no active independent variable or treatment, and both independent and dependent variable scores vary widely from low to high so they are essentially continuous. There were five key *attribute independent* or predictor variables: (1) ACT college entrance exam scores; (2) prior GPA in college; (3) number of prior psychology courses; (4) discussion section performance; and (5) frequency of attendance at the course lectures. The three key *dependent* or outcome variables were (1) overall exam performance (the average of the students' scores on the four exams); (2) performance on only lecture-based questions; and (3) performance on only text-based questions. The hypotheses were that background variables and course involvement (attendance) would predict both text-based and lecture-based exam performance. Only background variables would predict text-based performance.

ACT, prior GPA, and lecture attendance combined to significantly predict overall exam performance ($R^2 = .45$) and also lecture-based performance ($R^2 = .39$). ACT score was the only significant predictor ($R^2 = .33$) of text-based performance.

The research approach is associational because all five key predictor variables have many ordered levels as do the outcome (dependent) variables. There is no general design classification or specific design name because this is an associational approach.

Overall Measurement Reliability and Statistics (Q9)

The *internal consistency reliability* of the three outcome test measures was acceptable (alpha = .88, .77, and .73, respectively), and interrater reliability would be excellent because the items were objective. No information is provided in this short article about measurement reliability of the predictor variables, such as self-reported ACT or GPA, but consistency of such self-reports is likely to be good. With $N = 114$, power was adequate to find significant relationship when the effect sizes were medium to small. The *statistics* used (correlation and hierarchical multiple regression analyses) were appropriate and well presented (see Chapters 21 and 22 in this text for more about the interpretation of these results). Effect sizes (R^2) were presented and were large, but they were not specifically interpreted. Overall, the measurement reliability and statistics were rated high.

Internal Validity: Equivalence of Groups on Participant Characteristics (Q10)

This aspect of internal validity is rated low to medium. Although there are no groups in a purely associational study, we think that it is important to point out through this rating that one should *not infer* that the background variables (e.g., GPA, ACT score) or the course involvement variables (e.g., class attendance) *caused* higher (or lower) exam performance scores. In an associational study, this aspect of internal validity depends primarily on whether the persons who were high on the predictor variables (e.g., GPA, ACT score) were similar to participants who score low on such variables. There are almost always other important personal characteristics, such as reading skill or test anxiety, which could be the main cause of exam performance differences. There was, of course, *no random assignment* to groups. The researchers did measure gender and year in college and then entered them *first* into the multiple regression as demographic controls. This means that predictions of the exam scores controlled for these demographic variables. *Attrition* was quite high (41%) because many students had missing data for one or more of the 10 variables. (Multiple regression requires complete data on all variables.) The researchers did an analysis using what is called multiple imputation procedures to account for the missing data; the pattern of results did not differ from what they found with the smaller sample, which helps to control attrition problems. As stated earlier, overall the equivalence of groups was rated low to medium.

Control of Extraneous Experiences and Environment Variables (Q11)

The environment was quite well controlled in regard to the dependent/outcome exam variables. The predictor variables were gathered during class, so that was a relatively well-controlled environment. There were no groups, but the issue of equivalent environments for an associational approach has to do with whether participants who scored high on the independent/predictor variables had similar environments *during the study* to the persons who were low on these variables in this study. In this case, probably the environments were similar. There are lots of potential extraneous variables (e.g., parties, college adjustment issues) during the study that could affect some students more than others, but it is not clear how these kinds of variables would affect the results. Overall, the control of extraneous experiences/variables was rated as medium.

Construct Validity of the Intervention (Q12)

There is no intervention in an associational nonexperimental study so this dimension is not applicable.

Construct Validity of the Dependent Variables and Attribute Independent Variables (Q13)

The outcome measures and the predictor measures used within this study are common types of measures in studies of college student performance. However, there are some questions about the validity of the measures. Three of the five predictor variables (ACT, GPA, and prior psychology courses) were student self-report measures, whose validity could be questioned. The other two predictor variables, lecture attendance and discussion section performance, were probably valid measures of the intended concepts. As with study 2 on quiz time limits evaluated earlier, the course examinations here no doubt provide valid evidence of *performance* in the course, but one could question whether they are valid measures of student learning. The authors do cautiously and consistently describe these outcome variables as exam performance rather than as student learning. Overall, the construct validity of the dependent and attribute independent variables was rated as medium to high.

External Population Validity (Q14)

The target or *theoretical population* was probably all U.S. introductory psychology students or maybe even all U.S. undergraduates. The accessible population was introduction to psychology students at one large Midwestern state university. The *selected sample* was the 193 students who enrolled in this course. All these students were initially in the actual sample, but 79 (41%) had some missing data and thus were excluded from the regression analysis. Because most college students from all majors take an introductory psychology class and this state university's students are probably similar to the college population nationally, the accessible population was no doubt similar to the theoretical population. The selected sample was identical to the accessible population (all registered students). However, having a large percentage of students with missing data is troubling, even though the researchers demonstrated that the pattern of results did not change when the missing data were "inputted." Overall, the population external validity was rated medium to high.

Ecological External Validity (Q15)

The *setting* for the study, an introductory psychology course, is typical of course-related research but is a somewhat artificial setting for assessing learning of psychology. *Rapport* with the instructor was probably medium at best. The procedures and tasks, again, were typical for this type of research but somewhat artificial. There is *no treatment* in an associational study so that aspect of ecological validity is not applicable. Finally, the topic and results do not seem to be limited to the current decade. Overall, ecological external validity was rated as medium.

External Validity: Testing of Subgroups (Q16)

Subgroups were not assessed separately, but gender was used as a variable and found not to be significantly related to any of the three outcome variables. Likewise, year in college, which is probably related to age, was not related to the outcomes. Ethnicity was not assessed, and it may well be that there were only a small percentage of ethnic minorities, perhaps not enough to use as a variable. Overall, external validity testing of subgroups was rated low to medium.

Study 5: A Purely Descriptive Study

This study by Wolfe et al. (2006) described the results of 112 interviews about the use of antiretroviral therapy in HIV-positive persons in Botswana, Africa. There was *no independent variable* reported in this study because all of the participants had been offered the therapy and because its effects were not assessed in this report. Likewise, *no comparisons* or *associations* between variables were reported. Thus, there was no design classification or name. What was asked and reported were various aspects (variables) of the sample such as age, gender, and education. The key outcome variables were who, if anyone, the participants disclosed their illness to and what were the perceived social effects of the illness (i.e., how HIV had affected their social relationships, ability to work, and fear of loss of employment). Most of the participants had kept their illness secret from the community, and many felt that it affected their social relationships and ability to work. About 25% feared loss of employment. Although only the tabulated quantitative findings were reported in this article, the structured interview questions were supplemented by qualitative or open-ended questions for all 110 participants.

Overall Measurement Reliability and Statistics (Q9)

Reliability of the measure was not discussed in this short article, but the demographic measures (age, gender, and education) would no doubt be answered and scored consistently. Whether the disclosure and social effects variables would be stable/consistent even over a short time period is unknown. *Power* is not applicable because no hypotheses were tested. The cited *descriptive statistics* were simple and straightforward percentages, which are probably adequate for the purposes of this study. Effect sizes are not relevant here. Overall, measurement reliability and statistics were rated medium to high, given the basic purposes of the study.

Internal Validity: Equivalence of Groups on Participant Characteristics (Q10)

In this descriptive-only study, the sample was not divided in groups randomly or otherwise so equivalence is not applicable or relevant here. However, the sample could easily have been divided by age, gender, or education level, which was assessed, and then those groups could have been compared. In that case, the authors should not have implied (and they did not) that these demographic variables caused differences in disclosure or social effects. Overall, the equivalence of groups is rated as not applicable.

Control of Extraneous Experiences and Environment Variables (Q11)

The environment *during the study* was well controlled because patients were interviewed in a private setting at one of three clinics. The treatment (antiretroviral therapy) was given to all participants, but its effect was not studied in this article so a comparison group was not needed. There were many potential extraneous experiences that could and probably did affect the way the participants answered the interview questions, but they are unlikely to have occurred during the study. We think it is best to rate control of extraneous variables as medium.

Construct Validity of the Intervention (Q12)

This dimension is not applicable because there is no intervention in this purely descriptive study. The antiretroviral therapy is a constant, not a variable, *and* wasn't studied here.

Construct Validity of the Dependent Variables (Q13)

The outcome variables related to disclosure and social effects of being HIV positive appear to have been studied with other similar participants. It is hard to judge the validity of the responses because the topic was clearly a sensitive one that participants had concealed from their communities and even family members. In fact, 40% had delayed getting treatment even though they had access to medical insurance. In this situation, after deciding to get treatment, their responses were probably accurate (valid), but perhaps they overstated the degree of secrecy and the severity of social effects. Overall, the construct validity of the measure is rated as medium to high.

External Population Validity (Q14)

The *target population* was probably all HIV-positive adults in Botswana who were receiving antiretroviral therapy. The *accessible population* was the patients at three private clinics during a period of time in 2000. The *selected sample* was probably somewhat more than the 112 patients who were in the *actual sample*, but it is not clear how many of those who were asked to participate declined to be interviewed. Except on a few (<10%) busy days every patient at the clinics was recruited to be interviewed. The authors state that virtually all persons receiving therapy in Botswana at this time were treated at these three clinics. Thus, the accessible and target populations seem to be almost the same. We can also be fairly confident that the selected sample is representative of the accessible population at least for this time in history because almost all patients were selected. It also seems that almost all of those selected agreed to be interviewed or else the researchers would, hopefully, have noted the refusal rate. Overall, the population external validity was rated as high, assuming that the target population was those patients receiving therapy in 2000.

Ecological External Validity (Q15)

The *setting* for the study was a private room at the clinic, which though not a natural setting is appropriate for this type of interview. *Rapport* among the researchers is unclear but would be difficult to achieve given the stated sensitivity of the topic among the participants. The interviews were conducted by the principal investigator, apparently a medical doctor from a major U.S. medical school, and a locally trained field assistant. It is hard to know the effect that these persons had on rapport. The *procedures* (interviews) seemed to be pretty natural, but discussing the topic could have produced tension. The intervention (therapy) was not studied, so length and timing are not applicable. Finally, the topic and the results may be very time-bound. These interviews were performed just prior to a major new antiretroviral national program that was designed to reach a wide audience and to change attitudes. Overall, ecological external validity was rated as medium.

External Validity: Testing of Subgroups (Q16)

No testing or comparison of subgroups was done, even though the genders were split evenly so they could have been compared. This dimension was rated as low.

Summary

Each of the five sample studies first introduced in Chapter 1 was evaluated in depth on the eight dimensions of research validity. These narrative evaluations and ratings are summarized in Table 25.1.

TABLE 25.1

Comparative Evaluations of the Five Sample Studies

	Question	Evaluation ratings				
		Study 1	Study 2	Study 3	Study 4	Study 5
	Reliability and statistics					
9.	Overall measurement reliability and statistics	High	Medium	Medium	High	MH
	Internal validity					
10.	Equivalence of the groups on participant characteristics	MH	LM	Medium	LM	NA
11.	Control of extraneous experience and environment variables	MH	LM	LM	Medium	Medium
	Validity of constructs					
12.	Construct validity of the intervention (if any)	MH	High	NA	NA	NA
13.	Measurement or construct validity of outcomes and other measured variables	High	MH	LM	MH	MH
	External validity					
14.	Population external validity	Medium	Medium	MH	MH	High
15.	Ecological external validity	High	Medium	MH	Medium	Medium
16.	Testing of subgroups	Low	Low	Low	LM	NA

Note: LM = low to medium. MH = medium to high. NA = not applicable.

A side-by-side comparison indicates that in terms of overall research validity, based on these ratings, all five studies had some strengths. These somewhat similar ratings are not too surprising because all five were published in peer-reviewed journals. However, they all had areas of weakness, in part because they were applied studies.

Most of the studies had middling population external validity, with studies 3, 4, and 5 having somewhat better samples. The samples, as is often the case, may not be representative of the population of interest. On the other hand, measurement reliability and statistics, except for low power and lack of detail about reliability, was good for three of the five studies. The ecological external validity of, especially, studies 1 and 3 was quite good. Testing of participant subgroups was generally low, in part because the relatively small samples prevented adequate comparisons of gender, age, and ethnicity/racial subgroups.

The studies did vary considerably, as expected, on internal validity, which is considered to be the most important dimension by experimental researchers, including those who do randomized clinical trials, meta-analyses of what interventions work best, and evidence-based practice. The randomized experiment (study 1) was rated the highest on internal validity; the comparative and associational studies were rated the lowest. This particular quasi-experiment (study 2) was rated relatively low on internal validity because it did not include a pretest.

Key Concepts

See Chapters 23 and 24.

Key Distinctions

See Chapters 23 and 24.

Application Problems

See Chapter 24.

Note

1. In an earlier book, (Morgan, Gliner, & Harmon, 2006) we provided one possible method for making a more detailed *numerical* evaluation of the research validity of a study. However, using the 2006 evaluation form and assigning points to the scales made the evaluation somewhat mechanical, so we have not done that here.

26

Evaluating Research for Evidence-Based Practice

In previous chapters we discussed evaluation of the research process including statement of hypotheses, selection of an appropriate sample, formulation of an appropriate design, selection of measures with evidence of reliability and validity, choice of the appropriate data analysis, and interpretation of this analysis. Evaluation of research also compliments the process of using research as evidence to support a *new treatment method*, a *new community program*, a *new teaching approach*, or other applications of *new interventions*. Regardless of whether studies were carried out in clinical or applied settings, or whether they included an intervention, they provide evidence that may serve as a guide to practitioners, program directors or teachers. For the most part, using research as evidence has been a large part of the concept known as evidence-based practice (EBP). While evidence-based practice has been directed primarily toward those in clinical disciplines, it can and should be included everywhere that new programs are being offered.

Evidence-based practice, according to Law (2002), "is now part of every health care discipline and professional education program. While everyone agrees that it is important to use evidence in practice, the challenges of finding, evaluating, and using evidence are substantial" (p. xv). What is evidence-based practice? According to Sackett, Rosenberg, Gray, Haynes, and Richardson (1996), it is "explicit and judicious use of current best evidence in making decisions about the care of individual patients" (p. 71). The underlying idea behind EBP is that decisions about interventions in clinical areas should be based on the strength of the evidence. We feel that EBP need to apply not only to clinical practice but also to other situations such as teaching methods and community programs where new interventions are being considered.

Current best evidence is, however, not necessarily only research evidence: "This focus on research evidence can lead practitioners to misinterpret evidence-based practice to be a form of practice that is based solely on research study evidence and that is devoid of evidence based on clinical experience and the client's own needs and desires" (Tickle-Degnen, 1999, p. 538). On the other hand, information collected from clinical experience, expert testimony, and discussions with other professionals is subject to bias. Therefore, an important aspect of evidence-based practice is that it should be used to integrate research findings with these other, more subjective, pieces of evidence, rather than as the sole source of evidence.

Levels of Evidence

Evidence-based practice makes the assumption that not all evidence should be treated as having equal value or weight. There are several hierarchies or classifications provided to evaluate the levels of evidence from strong to weak (e.g., Holm, 2000; Sackett, 1989). Law

TABLE 26.1

Hierarchy of Levels of Evidence for Evidence-Based Practice

Level	Description
I	Evidence from at least one meta-analysis composed of studies using randomized controlled trials
II	Evidence from at least one randomized controlled trial with a large sample size
III	Evidence from quasi-experiments using designs such as cluster random assignment design, pretest–posttest nonequivalent group design, or interrupted time-series design
IV	Evidence from nonexperimental studies using either comparative or associational designs
V	Evidence from qualitative studies, case reports, and descriptive studies
VI	Evidence from expert opinion

(2002), in her book titled *Evidence-Based Rehabilitation,* described three different hierarchies or levels of classification. Table 26.1 provides a summary of these levels of evidence for evidence-based practice.

What do the various ways of rating levels of evidence have in common? First, quantitative research is viewed more positively than qualitative research. Second, internal validity is given more weight than external validity. Third, multiple studies on a topic are viewed more favorably than a single study. Last, studies with large sample sizes are rated higher than studies with small sample sizes. Each of these statements is viewed in more detail in the following sections.

Quantitative Versus Qualitative Evidence

Quantitative and qualitative research approaches represent two different paradigms or philosophies of how research should be conducted and interpreted. Although there are wide differences within each of these paradigms, there are also considerable consistencies among qualitative and quantitative researchers. However, the types of data, data collection methods, and data analyses are substantially different for the two paradigms.

Typically in these classifications of evidence schemes, qualitative research is seen near the bottom. One reason for this view is that most of these classification schemes come from the field of medicine, where objective data and randomized control trials are viewed as the gold standard. When participants are randomly assigned to groups, criticisms of bias in the study, although not totally removed, usually are reduced considerably. In qualitative research, random assignment into groups is rarely done. Data collection bias also is considered a problem because the researcher as observer is often the only instrument in the study. Not only does the researcher collect the data and code it into different categories, but the researcher also interprets the data. Because these are necessary parts of good qualitative research, they cannot help but give the appearance of strong subjective influence. Last, qualitative studies, due to their sampling methods, are low in external validity, not allowing for generalization to other situations.

Internal Validity Versus External Validity

Studies with strong internal validity usually are considered to provide more valuable evidence than studies with strong external validity in these classification schemes. What do we mean by strong *internal validity*? As discussed in Chapters 8 and 23, a requirement for strong internal validity is that participants have been randomly assigned to groups. This does not mean that the randomization process makes the groups exactly equal or equivalent, although the larger the number of participants, the greater is the possibility of equivalence. Random assignment of participants to groups means that there is no bias between the groups in the participant characteristics *prior to* introduction of the independent variable. Therefore, studies viewed as randomized experimental are given more weight than those that are quasi-experimental, where participants could not be randomly assigned to groups. Studies where the independent variable is an attribute, such as ones using the comparative or associational approaches, are viewed as having less internal validity and are given significantly less weight in the evidence-based practice evaluation schemes.

Strong population *external validity* means that the method of selection of participants should allow the researchers to generalize the results of the study to the population of interest. However, if one study is low in internal validity and a second is high in internal validity, the latter is viewed more favorably even if the low internal validity study has strong external validity (where participants were randomly selected to be in the study from the population of interest). Studies that are tightly controlled are viewed as higher, even though they may have less generalizability to the population. Qualitative studies are usually viewed as low in both internal validity and external validity, which is another reason that evidence from them is given lower weight.

A major reason that internal validity has been given more weight in these classification schemes than external validity is meta-analysis. Previously, studies with strong internal validity but relatively low external validity, due to convenience sampling, have been criticized. However, when large numbers of studies have been included in a meta-analysis, even though the majority of these studies might have used convenience sampling, the large number of participants with different demographic characteristics increases external validity substantially.

Multiple Studies Versus a Single Study

Evidence from a single, rigorously designed study, although persuasive, is still not nearly as convincing as a synthesis of multiple, well-designed studies on the same topic. Often, the problem with single studies is that they have not been replicated, or when replication is attempted the results do not hold up. Worse, many of the replication attempts that fail are not published in journals. To solve the problem of emphasis on single studies, a whole new methodology, meta-analysis, was developed. **Meta-analysis** (Chapter 17) is a method to synthesize research on a particular topic by combining the results of many studies dealing with the topic. These studies are combined by averaging an effect size index from each study. Recall from Chapter 17 that the **effect size** is an index of the strength of the relationship between the independent variable and dependent variable. Prior to the introduction of meta-analysis, one might read a review on a particular topic and see that some studies favor the treatment, whereas other studies suggest that the treatment was not effective. It was difficult to obtain an overall judgment about the effectiveness of the treatment. Meta-analysis solves this problem by obtaining an overall effect size average indicating the degree of success or lack thereof of the intervention. Meta-analyses have become more common in all fields, and collaborations have been formed such as the **Cochrane Collaboration** (for medical research) or the Campbell Collaboration (for social science research) that provide research syntheses on a wide range of topics.

Large Sample Size Versus Small Sample Size

Single studies that have a large sample size have been given more weight in the evidence-based practice evaluation schemes than studies with a small sample size. The reason for this is that, given appropriate sampling, there is less chance for error as we add more participants to a study. Not only is there less variability with larger numbers, but more importantly, there is more statistical power, the power to reject a false null hypothesis. Researchers hope to reject a hypothesis of no difference (the null hypothesis) and conclude that the intervention was successful. When the study has a small sample size, there could be greater variability. This means that the intervention could have worked, but because the sample size was relatively small, one might not have the statistical power to reject a false null hypothesis. Therefore, one might give up on the intervention, when it was actually not given a fair test. What constitutes a large compared with a small sample size is somewhat arbitrary, but statistical power can be determined for various sample sizes providing an estimate of the effect size (see Chapter 16).

In these evidence-based practice classification systems, studies that combine a large sample size with strong internal validity are most highly valued. It should be noted that, other things being equal, a large sample size is preferred to a small sample size. However, *many* studies with small sample sizes are preferred to one study with a large sample size. Better yet are many studies with large sample sizes.

Problems With the Use of Levels of Evidence Hierarchies

Failure to Focus on the Results of a Study

Levels of evidence hierarchies evaluate the rigor and design of a study but describe little about the specific results of the study. What exactly did the authors find about the intervention condition compared with the previously used intervention? This is usually what a clinician or program director would like to know from a single or multiple studies. What were the findings? When the investigator compared the two groups (or more than two in some situations), were there differences? Were these differences judged to be statistically significant? Even if the differences were statistically significant, what was the effect size, and were the results of practical importance? (Remember that in studies with large sample sizes, performing tests of statistical significance on the data is usually a trivial exercise because the statistical power is so great that any difference between the two groups will result in a statistically significant difference.) Without knowledge of how to evaluate research, it is difficult to make a judgment about these issues.

Special Populations

There is concern, especially among those in disciplines such as special education and occupational therapy, that too much weight is given to the use of randomized control trials as the gold standard for accumulating evidence. In an area where sample sizes typically are small and participants are not homogenous, not only is conducting randomized experiments difficult, but the results are also likely to be suspect. Often statistical power is low, resulting in type II errors. An alternative to randomized experiments with special populations is to use single-subject designs (Chapter 6). Although meta-analysis with these designs is somewhat problematic due to failure to agree on a representative effect size, still there have been a large number of published studies in reputable journals to allow for research syntheses that could be used as evidence for evidence-based practice.

Teaching Programs

New teaching methods provide excellent examples of situations that are in need of EBP. However, similar to research with special populations, randomized experiments often have not been carried out due, for the most part, to the problem of randomly assigning participants to groups prior to the intervention. When random experiments have been carried out in school situations, questions arise concerning the external validity of the studies. How realistic are these findings? Again, this does not mean that strong evidence has not been collected in the area of teaching methods. Best evidence here often has been gathered through the use of quasi-experimental designs (Chapter 5). Under the best situations, evidence of a new teaching method has been collected on multiple schools that can be compared to traditional teaching methods also carried out on multiple schools. In this approach, referred to as *cluster random designs*, the schools, instead of the students, are randomly assigned to the different teaching methods. Less optimal situations, but still considered good for EBP, are well-designed quasi-experimental designs where two different teaching methods are tried comparing differences between two schools or even between two classrooms within a school. As long as the assignment to groups (e.g., schools or classrooms) was not biased, good information can be obtained. This is especially true when multiple studies have been performed.

Community-Based Programs

Evidence-based practice also can be applied to the selection of a new intervention for community programs. For example, consider a program to get children to wear bicycle helmets. What might be the best method of intervention in this case? It is doubtful that one will find many randomized experiments that have been performed previously. A good place to start is the area of *single-group time-series designs*. It is possible that much of the evidence may be found in studies using a *single-group pretest–posttest design*. While this design is typically inadequate for making major decisions, there also might be studies investigating the same topic that have used a quasi-experimental single-group time-series design (Chapter 5). We feel that this type of design is much better than the single-group pretest–posttest design and is practical for evaluating these types of programs. Often, when a systematic review has been published on the topic, one might find, in addition to the two types of designs already mentioned, one or two studies using quasi-experimental two-group time-series designs. These designs, by offering both a comparison group and time, are even better for EBP.

Unfortunately, when practicing EBP, there is a tendency to reject all studies that do not provide evidence in the form of a randomized experimental design. We feel that this is being overly cautious and impractical. It is important to remember that not only is the quality of the design important, but when evidence has been provided from different designs, some better than others, one also must follow the trend or direction of the evidence to determine if it supports the intervention. Sometimes there are conflicts among evidence. Here, the higher-quality designs should be paid special attention. Overall, one must use the *best* evidence that has been provided, knowing that there may be flaws in those studies.

The Process of Evidence-Based Practice

Often when we think of evidence-based practice, we think of the clinician or program director becoming a researcher, using the current situation to collect evidence. Of particular interest is the view that good, systematic research practice makes one a better practitioner. Although training the practitioner/researcher might be the goal of every academic program, this expectation may not be realistic. What might be expected of the current practicing clinician or program director toward the use of evidence-based practice? The view taken here is that those persons seeking research evidence must be good consumers of research. That is, they must be able to understand the current research in the field to be able to evaluate interventions. It also means that there is a process to evidence-based practice. One purpose of this text is to help practitioners evaluate the research process through examples from articles selected from representative disciplines. Chapter 25 provided five examples of evaluations of individual studies based on the criteria and questions discussed in Chapters 23 and 24.

Sackett, Richardson, Rosenberg, and Haynes (2000) suggested five steps in the practice of evidence-based medicine:

Step 1. Converting the need for information into an answerable question.

Step 2. Tracking down the best evidence with which to answer the question.

Step 3. Critically appraising that evidence for its validity, impact, and applicability.

Step 4. Integrating the critical appraisal with clinical expertise and with the patient's unique biology, values, and circumstances.

Step 5. Evaluating our effectiveness and efficiency in executing steps 1–4 and seeking ways to improve them both for next time. (p. 4)

This process usually begins with asking a meaningful and answerable question, a question that is directly related to an issue of concern about practice. If the question is not one of concern, there will be little interest in pursuing evidence of support. This is not uncommon in research, for example, when students are attempting to select a thesis topic. Once this question has been defined, a search of the literature begins. This could include review of relevant journals, recent texts, and electronic databases. Once the literature is searched and relevant articles are retrieved, the next step is to systematically evaluate these articles. (It should be noted that although this seems like a horrendous task for the practicing clinician, there are certain shortcuts. For example, the Cochrane collaborative publishes meta-analyses on a wide range of topics. In addition, meta-analyses are published in most professional journals.) Not all published studies are of equal value; some are better designed than others, some have used improper statistical techniques, some have limited statistical power, and some have poor external validity that makes application to a specific population untenable. The task of the therapist or program director, as evidence-based practitioner, is to ask a question, collect the literature, and be able to evaluate both individual articles and *systematic reviews* toward answering the specific question. Even after all of these have been accomplished, the practitioner still must make a decision as to the usability of the information within the specific context of practice.

Summary

Because the "practice" in evidence-based practice is usually an intervention or treatment, the most relevant research to evaluate the effectiveness of that intervention is experimental research using the same or a very similar intervention. As discussed in Chapters 4 and 5, randomized experimental designs provide the best evidence for a causal relationship between the intervention and the outcome. However, randomized experiments are not always available and sometimes, when available, are low in external validity. In these situations quasi-experimental designs, especially those that use time-series designs, may be very effective in providing evidence. Qualitative and nonexperimental research also can provide some useful evidence, especially when experimental studies are not available or practical. For example, studies of the effectiveness of a treatment or practice that took place in the past, extended over a long period of time, or where an intervention would be unethical have to be nonexperimental. In these situations, the comparative (ex post facto) or associational approaches may provide the only relevant evidence. Clinical judgments and qualitative evidence also may supplement or enrich the data from quantitative studies, even data from randomized experiments.

In Chapters 23 and 24, we provided a framework for a comprehensive evaluation of research articles, including both experimental and nonexperimental studies. There we take a more balanced approach to the relative merits of internal and external validity because we recognize that there are several purposes or goals that a research study might have in addition to or instead of the "what works" goal of evidence-based practice. For some studies, the goal is description of a phenomenon or participants' views. In others the goal is prediction or the identification of relationships among variables. For those purposes internal validity is still important, but we don't think it is dominant.

Key Concepts

Cochrane Collaborative

Effect size

Evidence-based practice

Levels of evidence

Meta-analysis

Key Distinctions

Internal versus external validity

Large sample size versus small sample size

Quantitative research versus qualitative research

Application Problems

1. Why is the ability to evaluate research key to evidence-based practice?
2. What is the purpose of a hierarchy of levels of evidence?
3. What are the limitations of using a hierarchy of levels of evidence?
4. Select a quantitative article of interest to you and
   a. Evaluate it using the hierarchy of levels of evidence.
   b. Assess the value of using this hierarchy with your article.
5. List the steps in the practice of evidence-based medicine given in the chapter, and for each step explain how it might be applied to your field of practice.
6. Are all published studies valuable? Explain your answer.

27

Writing the Research Report

This chapter has three main sections that describe (1) typical contents of an empirical research article; (2) how to write about your results; and (3) ethical issues related to publishing and reviewing. In the first section, we describe the several parts of a typical journal article.

The Anatomy of a Research Article

There is no unique format that is used by all journals in disseminating research information. Each discipline has some peculiarity that is common to that discipline. This section provides an overview of what is usually found in each part of an *empirical* (i.e., data-based) *quantitative journal* article.[1] The format may differ when other types of research are reported. For example, the format for qualitative research studies such as ethnographies or case studies is often quite different from that described here for experimental, quasi-experimental, and nonexperimental (i.e., comparative, associational, or descriptive) quantitative research. The American Educational Research Association (AERA) (2006) article "Standards for Reporting on Empirical Social Science Research in AERA Publications" describes two overarching principles that they call "warranted" and "transparency"; the former means that "adequate evidence should be provided to justify the results and conclusions" (p. 33). Transparency means that the report should make explicit and clear the logic of the inquiry and also all the key decisions and actions from the problem development through data analysis and interpretation.

In this section we focus on the format for empirical, quantitative studies intended to be submitted in American Psychological Association (APA) format to a peer-reviewed journal. For the most part, APA format will be acceptable for research journals and is *required* for many journals in the behavioral sciences and education. The research format presented here has seven parts: (1) title; (2) abstract; (3) introduction; (4) method; (5) results; (6) discussion; and (7) references.

Title

The title should be brief (American Psychological Association, 2001, recommends a title length between 10 and 12 words) yet should describe what has been studied. The title is also a selling point for the article. Few researchers have the time or energy to read every article in journals to which they subscribe. Therefore, if they are like us, upon receiving the journal they turn to the table of contents and skim down to see if there are any articles they wish to pursue. Up to this point, the title is the only selling point for your article. There have been some memorable titles; for example, Cohen's (1994) "The Earth Is Round ($p < .05$)," was influential in motivating the APA Task Force (Wilkinson et al. & the Task Force on Statistical

Inference, 1999) whose report guided parts of this chapter. Our favorite is, "The Unicorn, the Normal Curve, and Other Improbable Creatures" (Micceri, 1989). For the most part, however, we suggest being brief and to the point, avoiding phrases and words such as *a study of, method,* and *results* that serve no useful purpose. It is important to point out that the words in the title are used in indexes and for computerized information services.

Abstract

Once the title catches the consumer's interest, the abstract is the next part, and often the only part, of the article that gets read. The abstract is especially important because, again, it is usually used by indexes for information services databases. The abstract follows the title and provides a summary of the article. Abstracts, like titles, are limited in length. American Psychological Association (2001) suggests an abstract of no more than 120 words in part because some abstracting services may truncate longer abstracts, possibly distorting the meaning. Usually an abstract describes briefly the purpose of the study, the methods, and a sentence or two about the results. Like the title, the abstract is also a selling point for the article. We have reviewed research studies that resulted in comments to the authors such as, "No one will read the paper because the abstract is not representative of what the study found," or "... The wrong content has been highlighted." It is critical to correctly represent the article in the abstract; it is the *most important paragraph* in the article.

Introduction/Literature Review

In this section we describe what should be in the introductory section of a research article. Notice that we have put a slash between Introduction and Literature Review. In most *journal* articles, the introduction and literature review are in one section, which, in APA format, is untitled. However, some of the journals you peruse have articles with separate sections for the introduction and the literature review. Most masters' theses and doctoral dissertations have separate chapters titled "Introduction" and "Literature Review." How one gets that information (e.g., from a library search) was discussed in Chapter 2 of this book. There are a number of good books on how to do a literature search, including Hart's (2001) *Doing a Literature Review: A Comprehensive Guide for the Social Sciences.*

What material should go into the introduction section of a journal article? *The first paragraph of the introduction section should be a general purpose statement of what is to be accomplished.* The American Psychological Association (2001) publication manual suggests that the first paragraph should introduce the problem. The problem statement should spell out the purpose and scope of the problem, making clear how the study contributed to knowledge. The AERA (2006) Standards for Reporting say that there should be a statement describing whether and how the study contributes to (1) enriching an established line of theory and research; (2) a new theory; (3) practical concerns; or (4) remedying lack of information about a problem.

After the introductory paragraph, the literature review begins. Although some degree of chronological order should be used, it should happen only after the literature is *organized,* for example, into studies that support your hypothesis and studies that contradict these findings. Suppose that we propose a general hypothesis that students who take a course in research design prior to a course in statistics will become better researchers than those students who take the courses in the reverse order. We would try to form two or three groups of articles. Articles that support our hypothesis would form one group; articles that oppose our hypothesis would form a second group. A third group might be articles that found no difference in their results. Within each group of studies, some articles might be quite relevant to the topic, and others may be only somewhat related to the topic. Articles that merely touch on the topic should be listed only as supporting or not supporting your hypothesis. Articles that are relevant to the topic should be explored in some depth, especially as to why they did or did not support your hypothesis. The purpose of the literature review is to lead up to a statement about why your study will make a difference with respect to the past literature. What is it about your study that is different from previous research? In summary, *one* good approach to a literature review in the introduction section of a journal article starts by categorizing studies (citing them) that do or do not support the research hypothesis and then describes in depth a few select studies that are relevant to the present study.

For studies on topics that are not well researched, some other organization would be used (e.g., chronological, by key variables, or by research question). In any case, what is to be avoided is a series of paragraphs each summarizing a single study without any clear transitions or organization. What is essentially an annotated bibliography is *not* desirable. There must be integration and synthesis. For example, there is nothing worse than reading that "Smith and Jones (2005) found one thing, then Up and Down (2007) found something else, and then Hill and Dale (2008) found something else." After several pages you wonder what the authors are up to, if you are still awake.

The last part of the Introduction section in many research journal articles is a formal statement of the hypotheses or research questions. These statements should be in operational terms so that the reader knows exactly what the researcher is attempting to study.

Method

The Method section for research articles usually is divided into several subsections. The ultimate purpose of the Method section is to instruct the reader exactly what was done in the study and to allow the reader to replicate the study under identical conditions. According to the American Psychological Association (2001) manual, these subsections are *Participants, Apparatus (or Instruments/Materials)*, and *Procedure*. We like to add *Design/ Analyses*. The APA Task Force (Wilkinson & the Task Force on Statistical Inference, 1999) recommends a more complete description of the method than has commonly been the case in published articles. Although it is doubtful that journals will allot sufficient space for authors to describe their methods in the detail recommended by the 1999 Task Force, dissertations *should* fully describe their methods as discussed in the following subsections.

Participants

This subsection should be composed of a thorough description of the participants. Where did the participants come from? How did you contact the sample? Did the participants volunteer for the project? A sentence or two referring to how informed consent was obtained should be included.

How were the participants selected? Were they a convenience sample, or was some recognized probability mode of selection (e.g., random, cluster, or stratified) used? Because the interpretation of the results depends on the characteristics of the population, it is important to define the population clearly. Unfortunately, this is not always done. The description of the sampling procedures should have inclusion or exclusion criteria, full information about how the sample was stratified (if it was), and the sample size for each subgroup. A convenience sample should be clearly identified as such. Sometimes the case for its representativeness can be strengthened by showing how your sample compares with the population on key variables.

Information should be provided about the process that led to your sample size decision. A *power analysis* (see Chapter 16) should be done *before* the data are collected.

After a description of how the sample was obtained, the Methods section deals with characteristics of the sample. These characteristics should include at least age (average and range/standard deviation) and gender. Ethnic grouping, type of disability, social/economic status, or level of education also should be included where appropriate. Remember, from our evaluations of articles in Chapter 25, that, unfortunately, some of the studies did not include complete descriptions of the sample. The AERA (2006) Standards for Reporting suggest that such relevant descriptive statistics, including those performed on each of the key variables as well as the sample, should be reported or available from the author on request.

Apparatus or Instrumentation or Materials

This section describes in detail all of the instruments or tests that will be used in the research. If an apparatus was involved, then the researcher must describe the type of equipment (including brand name), accuracy, specifications relative to the subject, and possible calibration information. If tests, questionnaires, or surveys were used in the study, information on measurement reliability and validity *must* be included. Was the instrument standardized, or was it developed for this study? If the instrument was standardized, was it used for purposes similar to those in this study and were the standardization samples similar to those in this study? If the instrument was developed for the present study, was a pilot study performed? If the instrument has many items, has it been factor analyzed? Have any sets or groups of items, which were summated or combined, been tested for internal consistency reliability as discussed in Chapters 11 and 15? Sample questions to demonstrate the content of the instrument should be included. Also, the level of measurement of the data should be given.

Each key variable should be carefully and explicitly defined. How such variables are related to the goals of the study and how they are measured should be demonstrated. The measurements should fit the language used in the Introduction and Discussion sections. Naming a conceptually abstract variable is almost as important as how it is measured, and these should be consistent. We discussed this topic in Chapters 12 and 24 as measurement validity.

Procedure

This section is a "blow-by-blow" description of how the study was carried out and is especially important for any replication to take place. Also included in this section is how participants were assigned to the different groups under study; that is, were they randomly assigned, or were they already in an intact group? It is especially important in this section to report any instructions that were given by the researcher to the participants.

The APA Task Force (Wilkinson & the Task Force on Statistical Inference, 1999) and this book emphasize the distinction between *random assignment* of participants to intervention and control (or comparison) groups and, on the other hand, the *random selection* or sampling of participants from the population. For research intended to make causal inferences, random *assignment* is critical because "it allows the strongest possible causal inferences…. If random assignment is planned, provide enough information to show that the process" for making the assignment is *actually* random, not haphazard (p. 595). The APA

Task Force recommends describing *how* randomization was performed, preferably using published tables of random numbers rather than trusting coin tosses, slips of paper in a hat, or physical devices.

If the participants cannot be randomly assigned to groups, a description should be provided of how initial group differences were controlled. Attempts should be made to determine the relevant covariates or confounds, and any methods used to adjust for them should be described. Also, methods used to attenuate sources of bias, including minimizing dropouts, noncompliance, missing data, and experimenter bias, need to be included.

Design and Analysis

We recommend that this section be the last subsection of the Method section; however, some texts place this section earlier in the Method section of the article, and sometimes the design is described in the Introduction. In the *Design* paragraph the researcher first spells out the independent variable or variables and the number of levels within each variable. The next piece of information, if the approach is experimental or comparative, is the type of design (between groups, within subjects, mixed, or associational). The third piece of information in the design section is whether the *independent variables* are active (manipulated) or attribute variables. The last part of the Design paragraph is the specification of the *dependent variables* and the level (scale) of measurement.

The Analysis paragraphs of this subsection specify the types of analyses that were carried out in the research. These analyses are determined by all of the information provided in the Design paragraph. The computer program (system) that was used to carry out the analyses may be specified (e.g., SPSS).

The APA Task Force report (Wilkinson & the Task Force on Statistical Inference, 1999) recommends using relatively simple statistical analyses, such as those described in Chapters 19–22 of this book, if they are reasonable for your research problem. The Task Force report goes on to state:

> The enormous variety of modern quantitative methods leaves researchers with a nontrivial task of matching analysis and design to the research question. Although complex designs and state-of-the-art methods are sometimes necessary to address research questions effectively, simpler classical approaches often can provide elegant and sufficient answers to important questions. Do not choose an analytic method to impress your readers or to deflect criticism. (p. 598)

A concluding comment in regard to the whole Methods section is that after data collection is completed, an *update* of the section or chapter should be provided. It needs to reflect accurately what was actually done. Any issues possibly compromising validity that arose during data collection or analysis such as attrition, missing data, or deviations from the planned procedures should be reported. Evidence from *your data* about the reliability and validity of your measures or instruments need to be added. Last, if any assumptions of the inferential statistics were markedly violated, how were adjustments made?

Results

The Results section is a summary of the analyses that were performed on the data collected in the study. A problem for most students in describing results is the level of description.

An editor once suggested, "Use the traumatic ocular test. If it hits you between the eyes, use it. Otherwise get rid of it." It is common for journal editors to require authors to condense their manuscripts, but key aspects of the Methods and Results, as described in this chapter, should be the last things to be deleted.

A problem in writing the Results section is whether to include material that might be more appropriate for the Discussion section. If the outcome pertains strictly to the analysis, then it belongs in the Results section. However, if you are explicitly relating your outcome to other studies previously discussed in the Introduction section, then this material belongs in the Discussion section.

More specifics (and an example) about writing the Results section are provided in the middle section of this chapter. That section follows our description of what to include in the Discussion section and References, and a brief discussion of how dissertations and research reports usually differ from manuscripts submitted to journals.

Discussion

We suggest starting the Discussion section with a brief review (no more than one paragraph in an article, probably a few pages in a thesis) of the hypotheses and whether they were confirmed. The major purpose of the Discussion section is to relate the results to the research hypotheses/questions within the context of the literature previously cited. Sometimes an outcome from the study is totally unexpected, and the Discussion section entails a whole new literature and hypothesis, indicating that the author forgot about the original intent of the study and the original hypotheses. Don't let this happen to you. Each hypothesis should be discussed with continued reference to previous findings from the literature review.

Researchers sometimes either overgeneralize their results or overparticularize them. A good approach to try is to explicitly compare the results of your study with the effect sizes reported in relevant previous studies.

As we have stressed throughout the book, caution should be instilled when inferring causation from approaches that are not randomized experimental. Even with randomized designs, one needs to make careful inferences. The APA Task Force (Wilkinson & the Task Force on Statistical Inference, 1999) supports our conclusion with a strong recommendation that "inferring causality from nonrandomized designs is a risky enterprise. Researchers using nonrandomized designs have an extra obligation … to alert the reader to plausible rival hypotheses" (p. 600). We think it is better to not make causal statements unless one has a randomized experimental design and, even then, be cautious.

Some Discussion sections have a separate heading called "Limitations." Our bias is that it is not the role of the researcher to attempt to review his or her own article (except in a thesis or dissertation). See also the section at the end of this chapter, "Misconduct and the Structure of Science." Reviewers may require some mention or discussion of limitations. Usually some of the limitations come out when discussing why hypotheses were confirmed or not confirmed. However, it may be useful to acknowledge limitations for the purpose of qualifying results and avoiding pitfalls in future research.

Although a Conclusion subsection is not usually required in a journal article, often the researcher attempts to describe, in the last paragraph or so of the Discussion section, what the next step in this line of research should be. Obviously, this next step will be contingent on what was found in the present study. However, a paragraph of this nature leaves the reader with a feeling about where the researcher thinks future research is headed and also may give the reader some research ideas.

References

The references should *uniformly* and *precisely* follow the specified format, which in psychology, education, and many, but not all, behavioral science journals is APA format. The APA publication manual provides examples of many kinds of publications and documents (see American Psychological Association, 2010). Every reference actually cited in the text—but only those cited—must be included in the reference list. This means that if material was read but *not* included in the text, it should not be cited. (However, it is a good idea to maintain such a complete *bibliography* separate from the manuscript.)

APA makes a distinction between a **"copy" manuscript**, which is one *submitted* to a journal for review and editing, and a **"final" document or manuscript**, such as a thesis, dissertation, or research project report for distribution to a library or consumers of the research. When *submitting* "copy" manuscripts to an APA journal editor, *everything needs to be double-spaced*, including references and tables, which might be partially single-spaced in a "final" manuscript to enhance readability. Note that references are listed in alphabetical order and use "hanging indents," as shown in the following examples. In the reference list, italics are used for the titles of books and for volume numbers (but not titles of articles or chapters). Examples of APA format for two journal articles and two books are as follows:

American Educational Research Association (2006, June). Standards for reporting on empirical social science research in AERA publications. *Educational Researcher, 35*(6), 33–40.
American Psychological Association (2010). Publication manual of the American Psychological Association (6th ed.). Washington, DC: Author.
Brothen, T., & Wambach, C. (2004). The value of time limits on internet quizzes. *Teaching of Psychology, 31*, 62–64.
Rudestam, K. E., & Newton, R. R. (2007). *Surviving your dissertation: A comprehensive guide to content and process* (3rd ed.). Newbury Park, CA: Sage.

The general format and punctuation for a reference starts with the author(s) surname, then initials followed by the publication year in parentheses. Note that there is a comma after each author's final initial, even before the ampersand. In some cases, as in examples 1 and 2, the author is a group such as a professional organization or task force.

The first and third examples are periodical or journal articles. The title of the article follows the author and date. If there is a colon in the article title, the subtitle begins with a capital letter; other words (except proper nouns) are not capitalized (i.e., use sentence case). Next is the *journal title*, which is italicized and *each* key word begins with a capital as shown in examples 1 and 3. Commas separate the journal title, volume number (both italicized), and pages (not italicized). The issue number is given in parentheses after the volume only if each issue starts on page 1, as in example 1. The pages are given last without pp. See the APA manual for more examples and exceptions. The first article is unusual because it is authored by a task force rather than one or several named authors.

The second and fourth references are books. The American Psychological Association is a group author, and is both author and publisher. In this case, the word "Author" is listed as the name of the publisher. After the author(s) and year of publication, comes the title, in italics, of a *non-periodical* (e.g., book, presentation, thesis, or document), but only the first word of the title is capitalized. Then the publication city, two letter postal code, a colon, and the publisher are listed. If the publisher's city is well known (e.g., New York or Boston), and not easily confused with another city with the same name, no two letter postal abbreviation is necessary.

The APA publication manual provides extensive annotated examples not only for references but also of the content and organization of a manuscript; writing style, grammar, and reducing bias in language; APA editorial style, including punctuation, spelling, capitalization, abbreviations, quotations, tables, and figures; reference lists; and manuscript preparation, including two complete and annotated sample articles. The APA publication manual also includes several additional technical chapters and appendixes.

References Cited in the Text

APA style (American Psychological Association, 2001) also specifies how references are cited in the text, using the author–date method of citation. In general, the *surname* (only) of the authors and the *year* (only) of publication are inserted at an appropriate place in the text. If the name of the authors is part of the narrative, only the date should be cited, in parentheses, for example, "Smith and Jones (1995) wrote ..." However, if the names of the authors are not part of the narrative, they should be included in the parentheses, for example, "Several studies (Smith & Jones, 1995; Wallace, May, & Fink, 1992) discuss ..." If there are three to five authors, all need to be listed in the text only the first time they are cited. After that, "et al." is used, for example, "Wallace et al., (1992) discuss..." More complex examples are discussed in the APA manual.

Theses and Dissertations

Theses and dissertations in education and the behavioral sciences are considered "final" documents, so they often use a somewhat modified version of APA format. The APA publications manual (2010) provides guidelines for "material other than journal articles" including theses, dissertations, student articles, and research reports. Basically, these guidelines say that you should do what your department (or the funding agency for grant reports) requires.

Dissertations and theses are almost always much longer than articles submitted to journals, in part because they usually have an extensive *separate* literature review chapter. Dissertations also usually do not limit the number of tables and figures. Most journals have limited space, which necessarily limits the number of tables and figures. Dissertations also usually have a longer abstract (up to 350 words), which is published in *Dissertation Abstract International.*

Writing About Your Results

One of the goals of this book is to help you write a research report, thesis, or dissertation. Thus, we provide an example at the end of this section of two paragraphs from a hypothetical research article. We have found four books and three journal articles, especially helpful for writing the results of a research study. Complete references are provided in Appendix A: Suggested Readings. The books are as follows:

1. *Publication Manual of the American Psychological Association* (2010).
2. Nicol and Pexman (1999), *Presenting Your Findings: A Practical Guide for Creating Tables.*
3. Morgan, Reichart, and Harrison (2002), *From Numbers to Words: Reporting Statistical Results for the Social Sciences*
4. Morgan, Leech, Gloeckner, and Barrett (2007), *SPSS for Introductory Statistics: Use and Interpretation*

The journal articles are:

1. AERA (2006), "Standards for Reporting on Empirical Research"
2. Wilkinson and the Task Force on Statistical Inference (1999), "Statistical Methods in Psychology Journals: Guidelines and Explanations"
3. APA Publications and Communications Board Working Group on Journal Article Reporting Standards (2008), "Reporting Standards for Research in Psychology: Why Do We Need Them? What Might They Be?"

Much of this section is adapted from the Morgan et al. (2007) book.

Before any inferential statistics are computed, an examination of your data should be undertaken by performing descriptive statistics. This is not the same as "data snooping" or an "opportunity to discard data or change values in order to favor your hypothesis. However, if you assess hypotheses without examining your data, you risk publishing nonsense" (Wilkinson & the Task Force on Statistical Inference, 1999, p. 597).

Any protocol violations, missing data, and attrition should be reported. Graphical inspection of data using scatterplots, boxplots, and other exploratory techniques to detect problems and errors in the data may be helpful to assure that the reported results are not due to anomalies in the data such as outliers, nonrandom missing data, sample selection bias, and attrition. However, due to space limitations, statistics such as exploratory analyses are usually omitted or highly condensed. It is desirable to present and discuss these issues in a thesis or dissertation.

This Results section includes a description (but not a discussion) of the findings in words, tables, and figures.[2] A picture is often worth a thousand words. We recommend putting a figure or a table near the beginning of the results, and then the significant results should be briefly described. The APA Task Force report (Wilkinson & the Task Force on Statistical Inference, 1999) states, "Figures attract the reader's eye and help convey global results…. It often helps to have both tables and figures" (p. 601). Figures should be kept relatively simple. The tables should have numbers rounded consistently to no more than two decimal places, except for p values, which are always less than 1.00 and often have three decimal places. A problem faced by persons attempting to publish articles is that for cost reasons editors historically have preferred to keep figures to a minimum. This possible restriction should not limit the use of figures in theses and dissertations to only those that provide valuable information.

The Results section should include the following numbers about each statistically significant finding (in a table or the text):

1. The value of the statistic (e.g., $t = 2.05$ or $r = .30$) to two decimals.
2. The degrees of freedom (often in parenthesis) and for chi-square the N (e.g., $\chi^2 = 5.26$, $df = 2$, $N = 49$).
3. The p value (e.g., $p = .048$). Preferably, the exact p value should be provided even when the statistic is not significantly significant (e.g., $p = .476$). A statement of $p < .001$ should be given when the computer output lists it as .000 because it is probably some truncated or rounded value such as .00075, not zero. The APA Task Force on Statistical Inference (Wilkinson & the Task Force on Statistical Inference, 1999) stated that it is almost always better to report the actual p value rather than merely saying whether the result was statistically significant. It is better still, they say, to report confidence intervals. Never use the expression "accept the null hypothesis."
4. An index of effect size from either the d family or the r family and, if the statistic is significant, a statement about the relative size of the "effect" (Table 17.1).

When not shown in a table, the preceding information (numbers 1–4) should be provided in the text as shown in the example at the end of this section.

In addition to the numerical information, *the significant results need to be described in words,* including the variables used, the direction of the finding, and an interpretive statement about the size/strength of the effect. The APA Task Force on Statistical Inference (Wilkinson & the Task Force on Statistical Inference, 1999) states that effect sizes *always* should be presented for primary outcomes and that it helps to add brief comments to put the effect sizes in context. In Table 17.1 we suggested the phrases *larger than typical, typical,* or *smaller than typical* depending on the results. Or, better still, the interpretation of effect size could be based on the effect sizes found in the research literature on your topic. It is important to realize that our effect size terms are only rough estimates of the magnitude of the "effect" based on what is typical in the behavioral sciences; they are not necessarily applicable to your topic. The AERA (2006) Standards for Reporting adds the following:

> … interpretation of the index of the effect that describes its meaningfulness in terms of the questions the study was intended to answer. This interpretation should include any qualifications that may be appropriate because of the uncertainty of the findings (e.g., the estimated effect is large enough to be educationally important but these data do not rule out the possibility that the true effect is actually quite small). (p. 37)

If your article has a table that includes the aforementioned statistics, it is usually *not* necessary or advisable to include all the details about the value of the statistic, degrees of freedom, and *p* in the text because they are in the table. If there is a table, it must be *referred to by number (e.g., Table 1) in the text* and *the main points described.* (Appendix F provides more information about and examples of tables and figures in APA format.) However, all of it does not need to be repeated, or the table is not necessary. Relationships that are not significant can be mentioned, the direction of the finding or *interpretation* of the effect size should not be discussed because the results could be due to chance. The effect size or the information (e.g., *n*s, means, and standard deviation) necessary for other researchers to compute the effect size needs to be included if your study is part of a meta-analysis.

Remember that the Discussion section puts the findings in context in regard to the research literature, theory, and the purposes of the study. An explanation of why the results turned out the way they did also should be attempted.

Steps in Interpreting Inferential Statistics

As a review for planning how to write about the interpretation of inferential statistics, we recommend the following:

1. *Decide whether to reject the null hypothesis.* However, that is not enough for a full interpretation. If the outcome is statistically significant, at least two *more* questions need to be answered. Figure 27.1 summarizes the steps described about how to more fully interpret the results of an inferential statistic.

2. *What is the direction of the effect?* Difference inferential statistics compare groups so it is necessary to state which group performed better. We discussed examples of how to do this in Chapters 20 and 22. For associational inferential statistics (e.g., correlation), the sign is very important, so an indication of whether the association or relationship is positive or negative must be included. We discuss how to interpret associational statistics in Chapters 21 and 22.

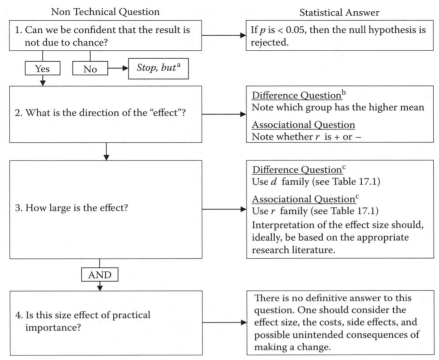

Non Technical Question | Statistical Answer

1. Can we be confident that the result is not due to chance? → If p is < 0.05, then the null hypothesis is rejected.

Yes | No → Stop, but[a]

2. What is the direction of the "effect"? → Difference Question[b]
Note which group has the higher mean

Associational Question
Note whether r is + or −

3. How large is the effect? → Difference Question[c]
Use d family (see Table 17.1)

Associational Question[c]
Use r family (see Table 17.1)
Interpretation of the effect size should, ideally, be based on the appropriate research literature.

AND

4. Is this size effect of practical importance? → There is no definitive answer to this question. One should consider the effect size, the costs, side effects, and possible unintended consequences of making a change.

[a]With a small sample (N), it is possible to have a nonsignificant result (it may be due to chance) and yet a large effect size. If so, replicating the study with a larger sample may be justified.

[b]If there are three or more means or a significant interaction a post hoc test (e.g., Tukey) will be necessary for complete interpretation.

[c]Interpretation of effect size is based on Cohen (1988) and Table 17.1. A "large" effect is one that Cohen states is "grossly perceptible." It is larger than typically found in the area, but does not necessarily explain a large amount of variance.

FIGURE 27.1
Steps in the interpretation of an inferential statistic.

3. *What is the size of the effect?* The effect size and confidence intervals or both should be included in the description of your results. Unfortunately, computer programs such as SPSS do not always provide effect sizes and confidence intervals, so for some statistics they must be computed or estimated by hand.

4. Ideally, the *researcher should make a judgment about whether the result has practical or clinical significance or importance.* To do so, they need to take into account the effect size, the costs of implementing change, and the probability and severity of any side effects or unintended consequences.

An Example of How to Write Results

The following example from Morgan et al. (2007) reports the results of a t test comparing male and female students, and it reports a Pearson correlation. Many other examples of how to write the results of statistical tests are provided in Morgan et al. (2007):

For research question 1, there was a statistically significant difference between male and female students on math achievement, $t(48) = 2.05$, $p = .04$, $d = .33$. Males ($M = 14.70$) scored higher than females ($M = 12.70$), and the effect size was small to medium according to Cohen's (1988) guidelines. The 95% confidence interval for the difference between the means was .50 to 6.50 indicating that the actual (population value) difference could be as little as half a point, which is probably not a practically important difference, but also could be as large as six and one half points.

For research question 2, there was a statistically significant positive correlation between math courses taken and math achievement $r(48) = .30$, $p = .03$. The positive correlation indicates that in general, students who took more math courses tended to score high on the math achievement test and students who did not take many math courses scored low on math achievement. The effect size of $r = .30$ is considered medium or typical. (p. 101)

Interpretation of Results

Authors need to be careful, in writing their results and Discussion sections, to avoid distorting the findings or their implications. For example, in earlier chapters we discussed several times the mistake of inferring causation from comparative, associational, or even quasi-experimental studies. Therefore, care should be taken not to state that the independent variable "caused," "determined," or "impacted" the dependent variable unless the study was a well-controlled randomized experiment. In discussing results from nonexperimental studies, these causal terms either should not be used or should be used with qualifiers such as *may cause* or *appear to influence*. Likewise, one should be careful about generalizations to broader populations from samples that may be unrepresentative of the population.

Ethical Issues Related to Publishing and Reviewing

Researchers should adhere to certain ethical principles when writing articles and reviewing the work of others. These ethical principles are no less real than those involving the protection of human subjects. The requirements for manuscripts submitted to biomedical journals (International Committee of Medical Journal Editors, 1997) and the American Psychological Association (2001) publication manual provide advice and discussion to supplement the issues raised in this chapter.

Integrity of Data Analysis

A portion of this book has been about appropriate use and interpretation of statistics. It is important to point out that there are many legitimate disagreements among statisticians and researchers. We have pointed out some of these differences in earlier chapters. Clearly, altering the data or deliberately reporting an incorrect p value is unethical. We also have pointed out a number of things a researcher might do in analysis or interpretation that are wrong but not unethical, unless done deliberately to deceive. For example, using an inappropriate statistic, such as a t test, with a three-or-more category nominal dependent variable is wrong but not unethical. Many other choices with regard to statistics are not the best practice, often because the researcher is relatively inexperienced or unknowledgeable about statistics. For example, not testing for assumptions could lead to the wrong conclusions if the assumptions were markedly violated.

In other cases, reports of data analysis may at least raise suspicions of unethical behavior. Meltzoff (1997) provided several examples. One is the case in which participants seem to be divided arbitrarily after the fact into groups (e.g., high and low) when there was a continuous independent variable. Did the researcher try many cutoff points until finally finding one that was statistically significant? This concern is one reason we recommend using a correlation when the independent variable is continuous or has many ordered categories.

Many statisticians think that null hypothesis significance testing (NHST) is appropriate only when the researcher has one or a few well thought out hypotheses to test. They are skeptical of a study with many significance tests. However, most would support exploratory data analysis, without NHST.

Dissemination of Results

The research process is not complete until the results are disseminated to the public and to interested researchers. Although oral presentations and publications in semipopular magazines have their place, publishing in refereed journals is key to the progress of science. As discussed earlier in this chapter, considerable detail should be provided about the procedures and data analyses so that the researcher's work is available for scrutiny by the scholarly community. Refereed publications also are used to evaluate performance of the researcher, and they are an important aspect of tenure and promotion at a university. Because there is considerable pressure, especially for young faculty, to produce refereed publications, a number of potential ethical problems arise. Similarly, graduate students are under considerable time pressures to complete articles and theses or dissertations.

Plagiarism

Plagiarism is presenting a portion of the work of another person without quotation or proper citation. Paraphrasing, which involves summarizing and rearranging sentences, is acceptable if credit is given in the text. Plagiarism refers not just to words but also to the data and ideas of another person. Because literature reviews and textbooks are based heavily on the work of others, there is conflict between providing appropriate credit to others and overusing quotations or impeding the flow of the text with citations.

Multiple Publications

Duplicate publication distorts the knowledge base and wastes scarce journal resources. However, pressures on authors to have a large number of publications and limitations by editors on space often lead to multiple publications from one study. Authors should not submit to a journal a manuscript that has already been published in substantially the same form. However, manuscripts previously published as an abstract or summary or in a limited-circulation document can be published in full later. There is always an issue about how similar the current manuscript is to the original and the similarity of the audience. It is not uncommon, but perhaps ethically questionable, for researchers to rewrite a research article for another journal with a different audience. Journal articles are sometimes revised for publication as a chapter in a book. This is acceptable as long as the original source is cited and permission to adapt or reprint is obtained from the copyright holder. Problems of duplicate publication also may arise if the material is first published on the Internet or through the mass media.

Articles must not be submitted to more than one journal at a time. Only after rejection or withdrawal of the manuscript is it appropriate to submit the same article to another journal.

It is common, but in some ways undesirable, for several substantively different articles to be published from the same study. However, for very large studies, multiple publications are unavoidable and may be necessary. The ethical issue is appropriate division into important pieces versus slicing into "just publishable units."

Authorship

There has been considerable discussion about who should be listed as an author and even whether the whole concept of authorship should be scrapped in favor of some other system. For example, Rennie, Yank, and Emanuel (1997) proposed that instead of authors, each article should provide a list of contributors, indicating their specific contributions (e.g., designed the statistical analyses, conceptualized the design, wrote the results and discussion). Part of the reason for this proposal was to identify responsibility or accountability for parts of the article.

A general, but not universally agreed on, policy is that authorship is reserved for those who make a substantial *professional* contribution to the study and that order of authorship be determined by the importance of such contribution. Substantial professional contributions may include formulating the problem or hypothesis, structuring the experimental design, planning and organizing the statistical analysis, interpreting the results, or writing a major portion of the article. Lesser contributions, which should be acknowledged but do not usually produce authorship, include supporting functions such as designing the apparatus, conducting the statistical analysis, collecting or entering data, and recruiting participants. Note that these latter contributions are often those of student volunteers or paid assistants, who may think that they deserve authorship.

Two types of problems result when determining authorship. On the one hand, there are *"guest" authors*, who have not made a significant professional contribution to the project but are given authorship as a favor or as a "right" due to their status in a department or laboratory or because their names on an article increase the probability of acceptance. On the other hand, there are *"ghost" authors*, who did make a significant professional contribution but are not included as authors.

Sometimes persons in power simply take advantage of less powerful or departed colleagues or students, who become "ghost" authors. However, the issues are not always clear. Often difficulties arise when a person loses interest or leaves the area after playing an important part in the initial aspects of the study. Perhaps the person even wrote a thesis or an early draft of the final article. The issue is what kind of credit should be given to such a person when an article is rejected, reanalyzed, and then fully rewritten without the assistance of the initial contributor.

A number of issues can arise when faculty and students collaborate on research. The situation is frequently similar to the example in the previous paragraph; that is, the student's thesis or draft article is not adequate for publication, so the faculty member must revise it extensively. In general, we think that if an article is based on a graduate student's thesis or dissertation, the student should definitely be an author, even if he or she does not participate in the revisions.[3] In most cases, we think the student should be the first author. However, another issue is whether the faculty advisor should be coauthor on a publication from a student's dissertation or thesis. The answer, it seems to us, is not unless the advisor funded the project or made a significant contribution to the *design* of the study or to the writing of the final article. Reading and providing extensive feedback *during* the thesis or dissertation process is what is expected of a faculty member and is not sufficient for authorship.

A good practice is for the collaborators to meet at the beginning of the project and agree on who should be authors and the order of authorship. It is also necessary for these authors to keep in contact and to renegotiate authorship if circumstances change. Each person's contribution should be documented and updated as necessary.

Finally, there are two other issues related to authorship. First, consent should always be obtained before someone is included as an author. Some editors even say one should obtain permission before including persons in an acknowledgment, especially if it is implied that the acknowledged person agrees with the conclusions. Second, all authors *should review the manuscript* before it is submitted because their names as authors imply that they take responsibility for the article. However, with multiple-authored articles it is probably unrealistic to assume that all authors are knowledgeable and should be responsible for *all* aspects of the article.

Citing Publications in Your Vita

Students sometimes ask when and how to cite research articles in their curriculum vitae (C.V.) or résumé. This is an important issue because incomplete citations can lead to concerns about sophistication, and inaccurate citations can lead to accusations of misconduct. For the exact format of citations, the publication manual used in your discipline (e.g., American Psychological Association, 2010) should be consulted. If there isn't such a manual, the format used by journals in your field is a good model to emulate. In all fields it is important to list *all* of the authors *in the order that they appear* in the publication, the date of publication, the exact title of the article, the publication's title (if the article appeared in a book or journal), the volume, if any, and the page numbers.

Reviews and Reviewers

Most grant proposals and manuscripts submitted to journals are reviewed by knowledgeable persons in the field; this is called **peer review** and was discussed in Chapter 24 as an important aspect of the evaluation of a study. Reviewers must be careful not to use the ideas of the authors until they are published and then give credit. Editors and reviewers must not quote from proposals they have reviewed unless given explicit permission by the author.

The process of reviewing requires a good deal of trust and integrity by the reviewers for the process to work fairly and not be exploitative. Problems related to fairness of reviews are relatively common, and most funding agencies and journals have specific policies to deal with them. Usually reviewers' identities are not revealed to the authors, on the assumption that this will make reviews more candid and negative reviews less open to reprisal. On the other hand, others have argued that reviews might be more responsible and balanced if the identity of the reviewer was known. In fact, in small fields, applicants can often guess the identity of the reviewer.

Masked review, formerly called *blind review*, occurs when the author's identity is not given to the reviewer. This type of review is common for manuscripts, but it is unusual for grant proposals. The argument for anonymous or masked review is that it gives a better chance to a new scholar because the work is judged solely on its merits rather than on the status of the authors. Again, in small fields, it may not be possible to disguise the manuscripts of well-known researchers.

Once an article or book is published, a different kind of review takes place, not just in published book reviews but also in literature reviews and meta-analyses, in which the reviewers exclude studies judged not to be of high quality. Or the reviewer may decide to weight studies in terms of their merit, so some count more than others. Although these practices are a necessary part of the scientific process, they provide the opportunity for potential abuse and, at the least, hurt feelings.

Conflicts of Interest

Although scholars do their research for a variety of reasons (e.g., curiosity, altruism), fame, tenure, and monetary gain are also motivators for doing research. A problem occurs when there is a real or apparent conflict between personal gain and obligations to the scientific community. One type of conflict is related to competition among scholars. This could lead to reviewers treating their competitors unfairly or withholding information from their colleagues. Because originality and priority are so important, there is often an inherent conflict of interest that may restrict collaboration and cooperation.

On the other hand, it is usually considered a conflict of interest to review grants or articles from close colleagues or persons from the same institution because of potential loyalty. In addition, if research on the value of a product is funded by the producer of that product, the funding should be acknowledged in the notes of the article.

Conflicts of interest are not the same as scientific misconduct, but the latter can result from unacknowledged conflicts, which need to be recognized and disclosed. Conflicts of interest are inevitable and not inherently bad, but *not* disclosing them and not managing actual conflicts are problems. Even the appearance of conflicts should be disclosed.

Misconduct and the Structure of Science

In a controversial article, Woodward and Goodstein (1996), professors of philosophy and physics, made the argument that "many plausible-sounding rules for defining ethical conduct might be destructive to the aims of scientific inquiry" (p. 479). They asked how fraud could be reduced without losing the positive effects of competition and reward. Woodward and Goodstein said that "an implicit code of conduct that encourages scientists to be a bit dogmatic and permits a certain measure of exaggeration" and limits discussion of its deficiencies may be perfectly sensible (p. 485). They argue that part of the responsibility of scientists is to provide the best possible case for their ideas. It is up to others to point out defects and limitations. They state that this is, in fact, what most scientists do. There are, of course, real limits here, and *exaggeration* is probably not the best word. Advocacy is appropriate, but any factual misstatement is unethical. The point is that what may seem like simple, obvious rules about misconduct are often less clear in the specific case.

How is the researcher to know what is acceptable advocacy and what crosses the line? Peer judgment is required to decide whether a researcher's procedures for selecting particular participants or selectively discarding data are appropriate or involve scientific misconduct. Junior researchers can learn about the complexities of appropriate behavior in their field best by observing and discussing issues with senior scholars/mentors in their field. However, care should be taken when emulating senior researchers because not all are good role models. We hope that this section of the chapter has conveyed not only the complexity of the issues presented but also some suggestions for action.

Summary

This chapter describes each of seven parts of an empirical (data-based) quantitative article: title, abstract, introduction/literature review, method, results, discussion, and references. Some differences between "copy" manuscripts to be submitted to journals and "final" documents (theses or dissertations) also were discussed. The middle section of this chapter presented a brief example of how to write about results and an extended discussion of what should be included. This chapter also extended the discussion in Chapter 14 of ethical problems and principles. We discussed ethical issues dealing with analyzing the data, writing the report, and issues about résumé citations, reviewers, conflicts of interest, and advocacy as contrasted with misconduct.

Key Concepts

Abstract

Authorship

Discussion section

Masked review

Method section

Multiple publications (the same study)

Peer review

Professional contribution (to a research project)

Results section

Scientific misconduct

Title (of an article)

Key Distinctions

"Copy" manuscript versus "final" document

Introduction (of an article) versus literature review (of a thesis)

Plagiarism versus paraphrasing

References versus bibliography

Results section versus Discussion section

Application Problems

1. If you were writing a article on data collection techniques and wanted to include the main idea from the following sentence from this text, what are two ways that you might do so appropriately?

   The concern about the filtering of participants' answers through perhaps faulty memories or in terms of socially desirable responses has led quantitative researchers, especially those who tend to use the randomized experimental and quasi-experimental approaches, to be suspicious about the validity of self-report instruments.

2. Bob has just completed a manuscript for publication. Although he had developed the rough outlines of the project on his own, he owes much to other individuals. The assistance he received includes the following:

   • A friend of his provided Bob with advice on how to obtain his sample.

   • The director of the stat lab gave Bob advice and also assisted in writing the Results section.

   • A graduate student collected most of the structured interview data and did the computer data entry.

   a. What kind of attribution should be given to each of these individuals? For example, who should be recognized as an author and who should receive an acknowledgment in the article? Who does not merit formal recognition? Explain.

   b. At what point in the process of one's research should decisions concerning authorship and acknowledgments be made?

3. List the different major sections of a journal article/research report, and briefly describe what goes into each.

4. The methods section of a journal article/research report often consists of four main subsections.

   a. Name each.

   b. Describe what goes into each.

5. Differentiate between the results section and the discussion section in a journal article/research report.

6. What is the purpose of data screening? Differentiate between data screening and data snooping.

7. What is the purpose of figures (i.e., graphs or charts) and tables in the results section?

8. What information in the results section is best included in figures or tables and what information is best included in the text of the article/research report?

9. You have conducted a study looking at the effectiveness of two types of therapeutic approaches with older teenage probationers. Your sample consists of 20 probationers, 10 in each group. Your t test yields a score of 1.648, which is *not* statistically significant at the .05 level. How would you report that in your results section?

Notes

1. The organization of this section is based on the *Publication Manual of the American Psychological Association* (American Psychological Association, 2001). We also drew heavily from an article by Wilkinson and the Task Force on Statistical Inference (1999) and the American Educational Research Association (2006) *Standards for Reporting on Empirical Social Science Research in AERA Publications*. The latter article (American Educational Research Association, 2006) covers, but is not limited to both qualitative and quantitative methods for doing empirical data-based research. Not covered well in any of these three sources (or in the present chapter) is the reporting of other forms of scholarship such as reviews of research, theoretical or methodological essays, or scholarship grounded in the humanities such as literary analysis. The 6th edition of the American Psychological Association (2010) publications manual is now available. It has been updated to acknowledge and incorporate advances in computer technology, including new guidelines for referencing electronic sources and expanded examples of online sources. The book also has been reorganized and streamlined for ease of use, and the focus has been broadened to include readers from other behavioral and social sciences and education.

2. Appendix F describes the components of tables and figures and provides some examples in APA format.

3. Note that the APA publication manual (American Psychological Association, 2001) states that all authors should read and approve the final manuscript and accept responsibility for it. This could be difficult if the professor has lost contact with the student.

References

Altman, E., & Hernon, P. (1997). *Research misconduct: Issues, implications, and strategies*. Greenwich, CN: Ablex.

American Educational Research Association. (2006). Standards for reporting on empirical social science research in AERA publications. *Educational Researcher, 35*(6), 33–40.

American Educational Research Association, American Psychological Association, & National Council on Measurement in Education. (1999). *Standards for educational and psychological testing*. Washington, DC: American Educational Research Association.

American Psychiatric Association. (2000). *Diagnostic and statistical manual of mental disorders* (4th ed. text revision). Washington, DC: Author.

American Psychological Association. (2001). *Publication manual of the American Psychological Association* (5th ed.). Washington, DC: Author.

American Psychological Association. (2010). *Publication manual of the American Psychological Association* (6th ed.). Washington, DC: Author.

Anastasi, A., & Urbina, S. (1997). *Psychological testing* (7th ed.). Upper Saddle River, NJ: Prentice Hall.

Antes, G., & Oxman, A. D. (2001). The Cochrane collaboration in the 20th century. In M. Egger, G. D. Smith, & D. G. Altman (Eds.), *Systematic reviews in health care* (2nd ed., pp. 447–458). London: BMJ.

APA Publications and Communications Board Working Group on Journal Article Reporting Standards. (2008). Reporting standards for research in psychology: Why do we need them? What might they be? *American Psychologist, 63,* 839–851.

Bambara, L., & Ager, C. (1992). Using self-scheduling to promote self-directed leisure activity in home and community settings. *The Journal of the Association for Persons with Severe Handicaps, 17,* 67–76.

Bartko, J. J., & Carpenter, W. T. (1976). On the methods and theory of reliability. *Journal of Nervous and Mental Diseases, 163,* 307–317.

Boote, D. N., & Beile, P. (2005). Scholars before researchers: On the centrality of the dissertation literature review in research preparation. *Educational Researcher, 34*(6), 3–15.

Brothen, T., & Wambach, C. (2004). The value of time limits on internet quizzes. *Teaching of Psychology, 31,* 62–64.

Bryze, K. A. (1991). *Functional assessment of adults with developmental disabilities*. Unpublished master's thesis, University of Illinois at Chicago.

Campbell Collaboration. (n.d.). *What helps? What harms? Based on what evidence?* Retrieved August 18, 2004, from http://www.campbellcollaboration.org

Campbell, J. M. (2004). Statistical comparison of four effect sizes for single-subject designs. *Behavior Modification, 28,* 234–246.

Campbell, D. T., & Kenny, D. A. (1999). *A primer on regression artifacts*. New York: Guilford Press.

Campbell, D. T., & Stanley, J. C. (1966). *Experimental and quasi-experimental designs for research*. Chicago: Rand McNally. (Originally published 1963)

Cohen, J. (1988). *Statistical power analysis for the behavioral sciences* (2nd ed.). Hillsdale, NJ: Lawrence Erlbaum Associates.

Cohen, J. (1994). The world is round ($p < .05$). *American Psychologist, 49,* 997–1003.

Conners, C. K., Epstein, J. N., March, J. S., Angold, A., Wells, K. C., Klaric, J., et al. (2001). Multimodal treatment of ADHD in the MTA: An alternative outcome analysis. *Journal of the American Academy of Child and Adolescent Psychiatry, 40,* 159–167.

Cook, T. D., & Campbell, D. T. (1979). *Quasi-experimentation: Design and analysis issues for field settings*. Boston: Houghton Mifflin.

Cooper, H., & Hedges, L. V. (Eds.). (1994). *The handbook of research synthesis*. New York: Russell Sage Foundation.

Corbin, J., & Strauss, A. (2008). *Basics of qualitative research: Techniques and procedures for developing grounded theory* (3rd ed.). Thousand Oaks, CA: Sage.

Cramer, K. M. (1999). Psychological antecedents to help-seeking behavior: A reanalysis using path modeling structures. *Journal of Counseling Psychology, 46*(3), 381–387.

Creswell, J. W. (2007). *Qualitative inquiry and research design: Choosing among five approaches* (2nd ed.). Thousand Oaks, CA: Sage.

Creswell, J. W. (2009). *Research design: Qualitative and quantiative approaches* (3rd ed.). Thousand Oaks, CA: Sage.

Crocker, L., & Algina, J. (2006). *Introduction to classical and modern test theory.* Belmont, CA: Wadsworth.

Cronbach, L. J. (1960). *Essentials of psychological testing* (2nd ed.). New York: Harper & Row.

Cronbach, L. J. (1990). *Essentials of psychological testing* (5th ed.). New York: HarperCollins.

Czaja, R., & Blair, J. (2005). *Designing surveys: A guide to decisions and procedures.* Thousand Oaks, CA: Sage.

Daniel, L. G., & Witta, E. L. (1997, March). *Implications for teaching graduate students correct terminology for discussing validity and reliability on a content analysis of three social science measurement journals.* Paper presented at the American Education Research Association, Chicago, IL.

Dellinger, A. (2005). Validity and the review of the literature. *Research in the Schools, 12*(2), 41–54.

Denzin, N. K., & Lincoln, Y. S. (1994). *Handbook of qualitative research.* Thousand Oaks, CA: Sage.

DeVellis, R. F. (2003). *Scale development: Theory and applications* (2nd ed.). Thousand Oaks, CA: Sage.

Dillman, D. A. (2007). *Mail and internet surveys: The tailored design method* (2nd ed.). Hoboken, NJ: Wiley.

DiLorenzo, T., Halper, J., & Picone, M. A. (2004). Comparison of older and younger individuals with multiple sclerosis: A preliminary investigation. *Rehabilitation Psychology, 49*, 123–125.

Dunlap, G., Foster-Johnson, L., Clarke, S., Kern, L., & Childs, K. (1995). Modifying activities to produce functional outcomes: Effects on the problem behaviors of students with disabilities. *The Journal of the Association for Persons with Severe Handicaps, 20*, 248–258.

Edgington, E. (1992). Nonparametric tests for single-case experiments. In T. Kratochwill & J. Levin (Eds.), *Single-case research design and analysis* (pp. 15–40). Hillsdale, NJ: Erlbaum.

Edutools. (2002). *Course management systems.* Retrieved September 17, 2008, from http://www.edutools.info/static.jsp?pj=4&page=HOME

Egger, M., Smith, G. D., & Schneider, M. (2001). Systematic reviews of observational studies. In M. Egger, G. D. Smith, & D. G. Altman (Eds.), *Systematic reviews in health care* (2nd ed., pp. 211–277). London: BMJ.

Finch, S., Thomason, N., & Cumming, G. (2002). Past and future American Psychological Association guidelines for statistical practice. *Theory & Psychology, 12*, 825–853.

Fink, A. (1998). *Conducting research literature reviews: From paper to the internet.* Thousand Oaks, CA: Sage.

Fink, A. (2009). *How to conduct surveys: A step-by-step guide* (4th ed.). Thousand Oaks, CA: Sage.

Fisher, A. G. (1995). *Assessment of motor and process skills.* Fort Collins, CO: Three Star Press.

Fowler, F. J., Jr. (2009). *Survey research methods* (3rd ed.). Thousand Oaks, CA: Sage.

Fowler, F. J., & Mangione, T. W. (1990). *Standardized survey interviewing: Minimizing interviewer-related error.* Newbury Park, CA: Sage.

Franklin, R. D., Gorman, B. S., Beasley, T. M., & Allison, D. B. (1997). Graphical display and visual analysis. In R. D. Franklin, D. B. Allison, & B. S. Gorman (Eds.), *Design and analysis of single-case research.* Mahwah, NJ: Lawrence Erlbaum Associates.

Fuller, H. M., Thomas, J. J., & Rice, M. S. (2006). Perceived risk: Effects on reaching and placing performance in persons with cerebrovascular accident. *American Journal of Occupational Therapy, 60*, 379–387.

Gaito, J. (1980). Measurement scales and statistics: Resurgence of an old misconception. *Psychological Bulletin, 87*, 564–567.

Gaito, J. (1986). Some issues in the measurement-statistics controversy. *Canadian Psychology, 27*, 63–68.

Ghiselli, E. E., Campbell, J. P., & Zedeck, S. (1981). *Measurement theory for the behavioral sciences.* San Francisco: W. H. Freeman.

Glaser, B. G. (1978). *Theoretical sensitivity.* Mill Valley, CA: Sociology Press.

Glaser, B. G., & Strauss, A. L. (1967). *The discovery of grounded theory: Strategies for qualitative research.* Chicago: Aldine.

Gliner, J. A., & Morgan, G. A. (2000). *Research design and analysis in applied settings: An integrated approach.* Mahwah, NJ: Lawrence Erlbaum Associates.

Gliner, J., Gliner, G., Cobb, B., Alwell, M., Winokur, M., Wolgemuth, J., et al. (2004). *Meta-analysis of single subject designs.* Technical Report, What Works in Transition. Ft. Collins: Colorado State University, School of Education.

Goddard, P. (2003). Implementing and evaluating a writing course for psychology majors. *Teaching of Psychology, 30,* 25–29.

Goodwin, L. D., & Leech, N. L. (2003). The meaning of validity in the new standards: Implications for measurement courses. *Measurement and Evaluation in Counseling and Development, 36,* 181–192.

Gorman, B. S., & Allison, D. B. (1997). Statistical alternatives for single-case designs. In R.D. Franklin, D. B. Allison, & B. S. Gorman (Eds.), *Design and analysis of single-case research.* Mahwah, NJ: Lawrence Erlbaum Associates.

Grimm, L. B., & Yarnold, P. R. (Eds.). (1995). *Reading and understanding multivariate statistics.* Washington, DC: American Psychological Association.

Grissom, R. J., & Kim, J. J. (2005). *Effect sizes for research: A broad practical approach.* Mahwah, NJ: Lawrence Erlbaum Associates.

Groves, R. M., Biemer, B. P., Lars, E. L., Massey, J. T., Nicholls, W. L., & Waksberg, J. (1988). *Telephone survey methodology.* New York: Wiley.

Harlow, L. L., Mulaik, S. A., & Steiger, J. H. (Eds.). (1997). *What if there were no significance tests?* Mahwah, NJ: Lawrence Erlbaum Associates.

Hart, C. (2001). *Doing a literature review: A comprehensive guide for sciences.* London: Publications Ltd.

Heller, J. (1972, July 26). Syphilis victims in U.S. study without therapy for 40 years. *The New York Times,* pp. 1, 8.

Herpertz, S. C., Wenning, B., Mueller, B., Qunaibi, M., Sass, H., & Herpertz-Dahlmann, B. (2001). Psychophysiological responses in ADHD boys with and without conduct disorder: Implications for adult antisocial behavior. *Journal of the American Academy of Child and Adolescent Psychiatry, 40,* 1222–1230.

Holm, M. B. (2000). Our mandate for the new millennium: Evidence-based practice, 2000 Eleanor Clarke Slagel lecture. *American Journal of Occupational Therapy, 54,* 575–585.

Huck, S. W. (2008). *Reading statistics and research* (5th ed.). Boston: Pearson.

Humphreys, L. (1970). *Tearoom trade: Impersonal sex in public places.* Chicago: Aldine.

International Committee of Medical Journal Editors. (1997). Uniform requirements for manuscripts submitted to biomedical journals. *Journal of the American Medical Association, 277,* 927–934.

Journal citation reports. Social science ed. (1994–present). (CD-ROM. Annual electronic resource). Philadelphia: Thompson/ISI.

Kaufman, A. S., & Kaufman, N. L. (1985). *Kaufman test of educational achievement.* Circle Pines, MN: American Guidance Service.

Kazdin, A. (1982). *Single-case research designs.* New York: Oxford University Press.

Keppel, G. (1991). *Design and analysis: A researcher's handbook* (3rd ed.). New York: Prentice Hall.

Keppel, G., & Zedeck, S. (1989). *Data analysis for research designs.* New York: W. H. Freeman.

Kerlinger, F. N. (1986). *Foundations of behavioral research* (3rd ed.). New York: Holt, Rinehart & Winston.

Kirk, R. E. (1982). *Experimental design: Procedures for the behavioral sciences* (2nd ed.). Belmont, CA: Wadsworth, Inc.

Kline, R. B. (2004). *Beyond significance testing.* Washington, DC: American Psychological Association.

Kraemer, H. C. (1992). Reporting the size of effects in research studies to facilitate assessment of practical or clinical importance. *Psychoneuroendocrinology, 17,* 524–536.

Kraemer, H. C., & Thiemann, S. (1987). *How many subjects? Statistical power analysis in research.* Newbury Park, CA: Sage.

Kraemer, H. C., Gardner, G., Brooks, J. O. III, & Yesavage, J. A. (1998). Advantages of excluding underpowered studies in meta-analysis: Inclusionist versus exclusionist viewpoints. *Psychological Methods, 3,* 23–31.

Kraemer, H. C., Morgan, G. A., Leech, N. L., Gliner, J. A., Vaske, J. J., & Harmon, R. J. (2003). Measures of clinical significance. *Journal of the American Academy of Child and Adolescent Psychiatry, 42,* 1524–1529.

Krueger, R. A., & Casey, M. A. (2000). *Focus groups: A practical guide for applied research* (3rd ed.). Thousand Oaks, CA: Sage.

Kuhn, T. S. (1970). *The structure of scientific revolutions* (2nd ed.). Chicago: University of Chicago Press.

Landrum, R. E., & Mulcock, S. D. (2007). Use of pre- and postcourse surveys to predict student outcomes. *Teaching of Psychology, 34,* 163–166.

Law, M. (Ed.). (2002). *Evidence-based rehabilitation*. Thorofare, NJ: Slack.

Leech, N. L., Barrett, K. C., & Morgan, G. A. (2008). *SPSS for intermediate statistics: Use and interpretation*. Mahwah, NJ: Lawrence Erlbaum Associates.

Levin, J., Marascuilo, L., & Hubert, L. (1978). N=1 nonparametric randomization tests. In T. Kratochwill (Ed.), *Single subject research: Strategies for evaluating change* (pp. 167–196). New York: Academic Press.

Likert, R. (1932). A technique for the measurement of attitudes. *Archives of Psychology,* No. 140.

Lipsey, M. W. (1990). *Design sensitivity: Statistical power for experimental research*. Newbury Park, CA: Sage.

Lipsey, M. W., & Wilson, D. B. (2000). *Practical meta-analysis*. Thousand Oaks, CA: Sage.

Locke, L. F., Spirduso, W. W., & Silverman, S. J. (2007). *Proposals that work: A guide for planning dissertations and grant proposals (Proposals that work: A guide for planning)*. Thousand Oaks, CA: Sage.

Loftus, G. R., & Loftus, E. F. (1982). *Essence of statistics*. Monterey, CA: Brooks/Cole.

McCleary, R., & Welsh, W. (1992). Philosophical and statistical foundations of time-series experiments. In T. Kratochwill & J. Levin (Eds.), *Single-case research design and analysis* (pp. 41–92). Hilsdale, NJ: Erlbaum.

Meltzoff, J. (1997). *Critical thinking about research: Psychology and related fields*. Washington, DC: American Psychological Association.

Mental measurements yearbooks. (1938–present). Lincoln, NE: Buros Institute of Mental Measurements, University of Nebraska.

Micceri, T. (1989). The unicorn, the normal curve, and other improbable creatures. *Psychological Bulletin, 105*(1), 156–166.

Milgram, S. (1974). *Obedience to authority: An experimental view*. New York: Harper & Row.

Miller, L. J., Coll, J. R., & Schoen, S. A. (2007). A randomized controlled pilot study of the effectiveness of occupational therapy for children with sensory modulation disorder. *American Journal of Occupational Therapy, 61,* 228–238.

Miller, W. L., & Crabtree, B. F. (1992). Primary care research: A multimethod typology and qualitative road map. In B. F. Crabtree & W. L. Miller (Eds.), *Doing qualitative research* (pp. 3–28). Newbury Park, CA: Sage.

Morgan, D. L. (2007). Paradigms lost and pragmatism regained: Methodological implications of combining qualitative and quantitative methods. *Journal of Mixed Methods Research, 1,* 48–76.

Morgan, G. A., Gliner, J. A., & Harmon, R. J. (1999). Evaluating the validity of a research study. *Journal of the American Academy of Child and Adolescent Psychiatry, 38,* 480–485.

Morgan, G. A., Gliner, J. A., & Harmon, R. J. (2006). *Understanding and evaluating research in applied and clinical settings*. Mahwah, NJ: Lawrence Erlbaum Associates.

Morgan, G. A., Leech, N. L., Gloeckner, G. W., & Barrett, K. C. (2007). *SPSS for introductory statistics: Use and interpretation*. Mahwah, NJ: Lawrence Erlbaum Associates.

Morgan, G. A., Maslin-Cole, C. A., Harmon, R. J., Busch-Rossnagel, N. A., Jennings, K. D., Hauser-Cram, P., & Brockman, L. (1993). Parent and teacher perceptions of young children's mastery motivation: Assessment and review of research. In D. Messer (Ed.), *Mastery motivation in early childhood: Development,* measurement and social processes (pp. 109–131). London: Routledge.

Morgan, S. E., Reichart, T., & Harrison, T. R. (2002). *From numbers to words: Reporting statistical results for the social sciences*. Boston: Allyn & Bacon.

National Commission for the Protection of Human Subjects of Biomedical and Behavioral Research. (1978). *The Belmont report: Ethical principles and guidelines for the protection of human subjects of research* (DHEW Publication [OS] 78-0012). Washington, DC: U.S. Government Printing Office.

Newton, R. R., & Rudestam, K. E. (1999). *Your statistical consultant: Answers to your data analysis questions.* Thousand Oaks, CA: Sage.

Nickerson, R. S. (2000). Null hypothesis significance testing: A review of an old and continuing controversy. *Psychological Methods, 5,* 241–301.

Nicol, A. A. M., & Pexman, P. M. (1999). *Presenting your findings: A practical guide for creating tables.* Washington, DC: American Psychological Association.

Nicol, A. A. M., & Pexman, P. M. (2003). *Displaying your findings: A practical guide for creating figures, posters, and presentations.* Washington, DC: American Psychological Association.

Nunnally, J. C., & Bernstein, I. H. (1994). *Psychometric theory* (3rd ed.). New York: McGraw-Hill.

Onwuegbuzie, A. J., Collins, K. M. T., Leech, N. L., Dellinger, A. B., & Jiao, Q. G. (2005). A. meta-framework for conducting and writing rigorous, comprehensive, and insightful literature reviews. In K. M. T. Collins, A. J. Onwuegbuzie, & Q. G. Jiao (Eds.), *Toward a broader understanding of stress and coping: Mixed methods approaches. The Research on Stress and Coping in Education Series* (Vol. 5). Greenway, CT: Information Age Publishing.

Onwuegbuzie, A. J., & Leech, N. L. (2005). On becoming a pragmatic researcher: The importance of combining quantitative and qualitative research methodologies. *International Journal of Social Research Methodology: Theory and Practice, 8,* 375–387.

Osgood, C. E., Suci, G. J., & Tannenbaum, P. H. (1957). *The measurement of meaning.* Urbana: University of Illinois Press.

Ottenbacher, K. (1986). *Evaluating clinical change.* Baltimore: Williams & Wilkins.

Parker, R. I., & Brossart, D. F. (2003). Evaluating single-case research data: A comparison of seven statistical methods. *Behavior Therapy, 34,* 189–211.

Parker, R. I., Brossart, D. F., Vannest, K. J., Long, J. R., De-Alba, R. G., Baugh, F. G., et al. (2005). Effect sizes in single case research: How large is large? *School Psychology Review, 34,* 116–132.

Parsonson, B., & Baer, D. (1992). The visual analysis of data, and current research into the stimuli controlling it. In T. Kratochwill & J. Levin (Eds.), *Single-case research design and analysis* (pp. 15–40). Hillsdale, NJ: Lawrence Erlbaum Associates.

Pedhazur, E. J., & Schmelkin, L. P. (1991). *Measurement, design, and analysis: An integrated approach.* Hillsdale, NJ: Lawrence Erlbaum Associates.

Penningroth, S. L., Despain, L. H., & Gray, M. J. (2007). A course designed to improve psychological critical thinking. *Teaching of Psychology, 34,* 153–157.

Phillips, D. C., & Burbules, N. C. (2000). *Postpositivism and educational research.* Lanham, MD: Rowman & Littlefield.

Poirier, C. R., & Feldman, R. S. (2007). Promoting active learning using individual response technology in large introductory psychology classes. *Teaching of Psychology, 34,* 194–196.

Poole, J. L., Chiappisi, H., Cordova, J. S., & Sibbitt, W., Jr. (2007). Participation by adults with physical dysfunction: Quality of life in American Indian and white women with and without Rheumatoid Arthritis. *American Journal of Occupational Therapy, 61,* 280–289.

Pross, C. (1992). Nazi doctors, German medicine, and historical truth. In G. J. Annas & M. A. Grodin (Eds.), *The Nazi doctors and the Nuremberg Code* (pp. 32–52). New York: Oxford University Press.

Rennie, D., Yank, V., & Emanuel, L. (1997). When authorship fails: A proposal to make contributors accountable. *Journal of the American Medical Association, 278,* 579–585.

Reynolds, C. R., & Kamphaus, R. W. (1992). *Behavior assessment system for children.* Circle Pines, MN: American Guidance Service.

Rosenthal, R. (2001). Effect sizes in behavioral and biomedical research. In L. Bickman (Ed.), *Validity and social experimentation* (pp. 121–139). Thousand Oaks, CA: Sage.

Rosenthal, R., & Rosnow, R. L. (1991). *Essentials of behavioral research: Methods and data analysis* (2nd ed.). Boston: McGraw-Hill.

Rudestam, K. E., & Newton, R. R. (2007). *Surviving your dissertation: A comprehensive guide to content and process* (3rd ed.). Newbury Park, CA: Sage.

Sackett, D. L. (1989). Rules of evidence and clinical recommendations on the use of antithrombotic agents. *Chest, 25,* 2S–3S.

Sackett, D. L., Richardson, W. S., Rosenberg, W., & Haynes, R. B. (Eds.). (2000). *Evidence-based medicine: How to practice and teach EBM*. New York: Churchill Livingstone.

Sackett, D. L., Rosenberg, W. M., Gray, J. A., Haynes, R. B., & Richardson, W. S. (1996). Evidence-based medicine: What is it and what isn't it. *British Medical Journal, 312*, 71–72.

Salant, P., & Dillman, D. A. (1994). *How to conduct your own survey*. New York: Wiley.

Schellenberg, E. G. (2004). Music lessons enhance IQ. *Psychological Science, 15*, 511–514.

Schmidt, F. L., & Hunter, J. E. (1997). Eight common but false objections to the discontinuation of significance testing in the analysis of research data. In L. L. Harlow, S. A. Mulaik, & J. H. Steiger (Eds.), *What if there were no significance tests?* (pp. 37–64). Mahwah, NJ: Erlbaum.

Schmitt, N. (1996). Uses and abuses of coefficient alpha. *Psychological Assessment, 8*, 350–353.

Scruggs, T. E., & Mastropieri, M. A. (1994). The effectiveness of generalization training: A quantitative synthesis of single subject research. In T. E. Scruggs & M. A. Mastropieri (Eds.), *Advances in learning and behavioral disabilities* (Vol. 8, pp. 259–280). Greenwich, CT: JAI.

Shadish, W. R., Cook, T. D., & Campbell, D. T. (2002). *Experimental and quasi-experimental designs for generalized causal inference*. Boston: Houghton Mifflin.

Shavelson, R. J. (1988). *Statistical reasoning for the behavioral sciences* (2nd ed.). Boston: Allyn and Bacon.

Shavelson, R. J. (1996). *Statistical reasoning for the behavioral sciences* (3rd ed.). Needham Heights, MA: Allyn & Bacon.

Sieber, J. E. (1992). *Planning ethically responsible research: A guide for students and internal review boards*. Newbury Park, CA: Sage.

Siegel, S., & Castellan, N. J. (1988). *Nonparametric statistics for the behavioral sciences* (2nd ed.). New York: McGraw-Hill.

Skinner, C. H. (Ed.). (2005). *Single subject designs for school psychologists*. Binghamton, NY: Haworth Press, Inc.

Smith, M. L. (1981). Naturalistic research. *Personnel and Guidance Journal, 59*, 585–589.

Spector, P. E. (1992). *Summated rating scale construction: An introduction*. Newbury Park, CA: Sage.

Stage, S. A., & Quiroz, D. R. (1997). A meta-analysis of interventions to decrease disruptive classroom behavior in public education settings. *School Psychology Review, 26*, 333–368.

Stake, R. E. (2005). Qualitative case studies. In N. K. Denzin & Y. S. Lincoln (Eds.), *The Sage handbook of qualitative research* (3rd ed., pp. 443–466). Thousand Oaks, CA: Sage.

Stark-Wroblewski, K., Wiggins, T., & Ryan, J. (2006). Assessing student interest and familiarity with professional psychology specialty areas. *Journal of Instructional Psychology, 33*, 273–277.

Stevens, J. P. (1999). *Intermediate statistics: A modern approach* (2nd ed.). Mahwah, NJ: Lawrence Erlbaum Associates.

Strauss, A. (1987). *Qualitative analysis for social scientists*. Cambridge, UK: University of Cambridge Press.

Strube, M. J. (2000). Reliability and generalizability theory. In L. G. Grimm & P. R. Yarnold (Eds.), *Reading and understanding more multivariate statistics* (pp. 23–66). Washington, DC: American Psychological Association.

Swanson, H. L., & Sachse-Lee, C. (2000). A meta-analysis of single-subject intervention research for students with LD. *Journal of Learning Disabilities, 33*, 114–136.

Tashakkori, A., & Teddlie, C. (Eds.). (2002). *Handbook of mixed methods in social and behavioral research*. Thousand Oaks, CA: Sage.

Tebben, A. B., & Jepsen, J. (2004). Trowels labeled ergonomic versus standard design: Preferences and effects on wrist range of motion during a gardening occupation. *American Journal of Occupational Therapy, 58*, 317–323.

Tesch, R. (1990). *Qualitative research: Analysis types and software tools*. New York: Falmer.

Test critiques (annually). Austin, TX: Pro-Ed.

Tests in print (VI). (2006). Lincoln, NE: Buros Institute for Mental Measurements.

Thompson, B. (1995). Stepwise regression and stepwise discriminant analysis need not apply here: A guideline editorial. *Educational and Psychological Measurement, 55*, 525–534.

Thompson, B. (2002). "Statistical," "practical," and "clinical": How many kinds of significance do counselors need to consider? *Journal of Counseling & Development, 80*, 64–71.

Thompson, B. (Ed). (2003). *Score reliability: Contemporary thinking about reliability issues.* Thousand Oaks, CA: Sage.

Thompson, B. (2004). *Exploratory and confirmatory factor analyses: Understanding concepts and applications.* Washington, DC: American Psychological Association.

Thorndike, R. L. (2004). *Measurement and evaluation in psychology and education* (7th ed.). New York: Upper Saddle River, NJ: Prentice Hall.

Tickle-Degnen, L. (1999). Evidence-based practice forum—Organizing, evaluating, and using evidence in occupational therapy practice. *American Journal of Occupational Therapy, 53,* 537–539.

Vaske, J. J., Gliner, J. A., & Morgan, G. A. (2002). Communicating judgments about practical significance: Effect size, confidence intervals and odds ratios. *Human Dimensions of Wildlife, 7,* 287–300.

Velleman, P. F., & Wilkinson, L. (1993). Nominal, ordinal, interval, and ratio typologies are misleading. *American Statistician, 47,* 65–72.

Walters, G. D. (2005). Recidivism in released Lifestyle Change Program participants. *Criminal Justice and Behavior, 32,* 50–68.

Wechsler, D. (1991). *Wechsler intelligence scale for children—third edition.* San Antonio: Psychological Corp.

What Works Clearinghouse. (2006 September). *What Works Clearinghouse Study Design Classification.* Retrieved March 28, 2008, from http://www.ies.ed.gov/ncee/wwc/pdf/studydesignclass.pdf

Wilkinson, L., & the Task Force on Statistical Inference. (1999). Statistical methods in psychology journals: Guidelines and explanations. *American Psychologist, 54,* 594–604.

Winer, B. J. (1962). *Statistical principles in experimental design* (2nd ed.). New York: McGraw-Hill.

Wolfe, W. R., Weiser, S. D., Bangsber, D. R., Thior, I., Makhema, J. M., Dickinson, D. B., et al. (2006). Effects of HIV-related stigma among an early sample of patients receiving antiretroviral therapy in Botswana. *AIDS Care, 18,* 931–933.

Woodward, J., & Goodstein, D. (1996). Conduct, misconduct and structure of science. *American Scientist, 84,* 479–490.

Yin, R. (2008). *Case study research: Design and methods* (4th ed.). Thousand Oaks, CA: Sage.

Young, E. D. (1999). *Research involving human subjects: Historical review, ethical theory, and Stanford guidelines.* Unpublished document. Stanford University School of Medicine, Stanford, CA.

Zamboanga, B. L., Padilla-Walker, L. M., Hardy, S. A., Thompson, R. A., & Wang, S. C. (2007). Academic background and course involvement as predictors of exam performance. *Teaching of Psychology, 34,* 158–162.

Zeanah, C. H., Larrieu, J. A., Heller, S. S., Valliere, J., Hinshaw-Fuselier, S., Aoki, Y., et al. (2001). Evaluation of a preventive intervention for maltreated infants and toddlers in foster care. *Journal of the American Academy of Child and Adolescent Psychiatry, 40,* 214–221.

Appendices

Appendix A: Suggested Readings

American Educational Research Association. (2006). Standards for reporting on empirical social science research in AERA publications. *Educational Researcher*, *35*(6), 33–40.

American Psychological Association (APA). (2010). *Publication manual of the American Psychological Association* (6th ed.). Washington, DC: Author.

APA Publications and Communications Board Working Group on Journal Article Reporting Standards. (2008). Reporting standards for research in psychology: Why do we need them? What might they be? *American Psychologist*, *63*, 839–851.

Creswell, J. W. (2009). *Research design: Qualitative, quantitative, and mixed* (3rd ed.). Thousand Oaks, CA: Sage.

Fink, A. (2009). *How to conduct surveys: A step-by-step guide* (4th ed.). Thousand Oaks, CA: Sage.

Hart, C. (2001). *Doing a literature search: A comprehensive guide for the social sciences*. London: Sage Publications Ltd.

Huck, S. J. (2008). *Reading statistics and research* (5th ed.). Boston: Allyn & Bacon.

Leech, N. L., Barrett, K. C., & Morgan, G. A. (2008). *SPSS for intermediate statistics: Use and interpretation*. New York: Erlbaum, Taylor and Francis Group.

Morgan, G. A., Gliner, J. A., & Harmon, R. J. (2006). *Understanding and evaluating research in applied and clinical settings*. Mahwah, NJ: Lawrence Erlbaum Associates.

Morgan, G. A., Leech, N. L., Gloeckner, G. W., & Barrett, K. A. (2007). *SPSS for introductory statistics: Use and interpretation*. Mahwah, NJ: Lawrence Erlbaum Associates.

Morgan, S. E., Reichart T., & Harrison T. R. (2002). *From numbers to words: Reporting statistical results for the social sciences*. Boston: Allyn & Bacon.

Newton, R. R., & Rudestam, K. E. (1999). *Your statistical consultant: Answers to your data analysis questions*. Thousand Oaks, CA: Sage.

Nicol, A. A. M., & Pexman, P. M. (1999). *Presenting your findings: A practical guide for creating tables*. Washington, DC: American Psychological Association.

Nicol, A. A. M., & Pexman, P. M. (2003). *Displaying your findings: A practical guide for creating figures, posters, and presentations*. Washington, DC: American Psychological Association.

Rudestam, K. E., & Newton, R. R. (2007). *Surviving your dissertation: A comprehensive guide to content and process* (3rd ed.). Thousand Oaks, CA: Sage.

Vogt, W. P. (2005). *Dictionary of statistics and methodology* (3rd ed.). Thousand Oaks, CA: Sage.

Wilkinson, L., & The Task Force on Statistical Inference. (1999). Statistical methods in psychology journals: Guidelines and explanations. *American Psychologist*, *54*, 594–604.

Appendix B: Confusing Terms

Partially Similar Terms for Different Concepts[1]

- Cronbach's *alpha* ≠ *alpha* (significance) level
- *Chi-square* for indepenence (two samples) ≠ *chi-square* for goodness of fit (one sample)
- *Dependent* variable ≠ *dependent* samples design or statistic
- *Discriminant* analysis ≠ *discriminant* evidence for measurement validity
- *Factor* (i.e., independent variable) ≠ *factor* analysis
- *Factorial* design ≠ *factorial* evidence for measurement validity
- *Independent* variable ≠ *independent* samples
- *Level*s (of a variable) ≠ *level* of measurement
- *Ordinal* scale of measurement ≠ *ordinal* interaction
- *Outcome* (dependent) variable ≠ *outcome* (results) of the study
- Research *question* ≠ questionnaire *question* or item
- *Random* assignment of participants to groups ≠ *random* assignment of treatments to groups
- *Random* assignment (of participants to groups) ≠ *random* selection (or sampling of participants to be included in the study) ≠ *random* order ≠ *random* selection of times to intervene
- *Related* samples design ≠ variables that are *related* (i.e., correlated)
- Random *samples* ≠ paired/related *samples* ≠ independent *samples*
- Measurement *scale* ≠ a rating *scale*
- *Single* subjects design ≠ *single* factor design
- *Theoretical* research ≠ *theoretical* population
- Measurement *validity* ≠ research *validity*

Different Terms for Similar Concepts[2]

Variables (Chapter 3)

- Active independent variable ≈ manipulated ≈ intervention ≈ treatment
- Attribute independent variable ≈ measured variable ≈ individual difference variable
- Change over time ≈ change between trials ≈ change between measures
- Dependent variable ≈ DV ≈ outcome variable ≈ criterion
- Independent variable ≈ IV ≈ antecedent ≈ predictor ≈ presumed cause ≈ factor ≈ *N*-way (e.g., 2-way)
- Levels (of a variable) ≈ categories ≈ values ≈ groups

Research Approaches and Questions (Chapter 4)

- Associational approach ≈ correlational ≈ survey ≈ descriptive
- Associational questions ≈ correlational questions
- Comparative approach ≈ causal comparative ≈ ex post facto
- Descriptive approach ≈ exploratory research
- Difference questions ≈ group comparisons

Designs (Chapters 5 and 18)

- Between groups ≈ independent samples ≈ uncorrelated samples
- Comparison group ≈ control group
- Factorial design ≈ two or more independent variables ≈ complex design
- Nonexperimental research (comparative, associational, and descriptive approaches) ≈ some writers call all three descriptive
- Quasi-experimental designs with major limitations ≈ preexperiments
- Random assignment to groups ≈ how subjects get into groups ≈ randomized design → high *internal* validity
- Randomized experiment ≈ true experiment ≈ randomized clinical trial ≈ randomized control trials ≈ RCT
- Single factor design ≈ one independent variable ≈ basic design
- Within subjects ≈ repeated measures ≈ related samples ≈ paired samples ≈ matched groups ≈ correlated samples ≈ within groups ≈ dependent samples

Validity (Chapters 8, 9, and 12)

- Measurement reliability and statistics ≈ statistical (conclusion) validity
- Measurement validity ≈ test, instrument, or score validity ≈ validity
- Measurement validity of the constructs ≈ construct validity
- Random assignment → internal validity
- Random sampling → external validity
- Research validity ≈ validity of the study

Threats to Internal Validity (Chapter 8)

- Additive and interactive threats ≈ combinations of two or more threats
- Attrition/mortality threat ≈ high dropout rate (from the study)
- Contamination ≈ low control of extraneous variables
- History threat ≈ extraneous environmental events
- Instrumentation threat ≈ observer or instrument inconsistency
- Maturation threat ≈ growth/developmental changes
- Nonequivalent groups ≈ biased groups ≈ intact groups ≈ nonrandomized assignment
- Placebo effect ≈ Hawthorne effect ≈ expectancy effect

- Regression (to the mean) threat ≈ use of extreme groups
- Selection threat ≈ self-assignment to groups ≈ biased groups ≈ nonrandomized assignment
- Testing threat ≈ carryover effects

Sampling (Chapter 9)

- Accessible population ≈ sampling frame
- Actual sample ≈ sample ≈ final sample
- Convenience sampling ≈ nonprobablility sampling ≈ biased sampling
- Random selection ≈ random sampling ≈ probability sampling → high *external* population validity
- Response rate ≈ return rate ≈ percent of selected sample consenting/participating
- Selected sample ≈ participants sampled
- Theoretical population ≈ target population ≈ population of interest

Measurement (Chapter 10)

- Categorical variable ≈ usually nominal, but many ordered variables that have discrete categories
- Continuous variable ≈ normally distributed ≈ interval scale
- Dichotomous ≈ binary ≈ dummy variable ≈ nominal with two categories
- Interval scale ≈ numeric ≈ continuous variable ≈ quantitative ≈ scale data
- Normal ≈ (approximately) normally distributed variable ≈ interval and ratio data
- Nominal scale ≈ unordered categorical variable ≈ qualitative ≈ discrete
- Ordered variable ≈ ordinal or interval scale
- Ordinal scale ≈ unequal-interval scale ≈ discrete ordered categorical variable
- Psychometric properties ≈ evidence for measurement reliability and validity

Measurement Reliability (Chapter 11)

- Alternate forms reliability ≈ equivalent forms ≈ parallel forms ≈ coefficient of equivalence
- Internal consistency reliability ≈ interitem reliability ≈ Cronbach's alpha
- Interrater reliability ≈ interobserver reliability
- Measurement reliability ≈ reliability ≈ test, instrument, or score reliability
- Test–retest reliability ≈ coefficient of stability

Data Collection Techniques (Chapter 13)

- Observer report ≈ researcher observation
- Participants ≈ subjects
- Questionnaire ≈ survey

- Self-report ≈ participant report or rating ≠ participant observation
- Summated scale ≈ aggregrated scale ≈ composite

Statistics (Chapters 16–21)

- Alternative hypothesis ≈ research hypothesis ≈ H_1
- Analysis of variance (ANOVA) ≈ F ≈ analysis of variance ≈ overall or omnubus F
- Associate variables ≈ relate ≈ predict → correlation or regression
- Basic inferential statistics ≈ univariate statistic (one independent variable [IV] and one dependent variable [DV]) ≈ also called bivarite statistics
- Chi-square for independence ≈ two-sample chi-square
- Chi-square for goodness of fit ≈ one-sample chi-square
- Compare groups ≈ test differences → t or ANOVA
- Complex inferential statistics ≈ multifactor statistics (more than one IV) ≈ multi-variate statistics (usually more than one DV)
- Data mining ≈ fishing ≈ snooping ≈ multiple significance tests (without clear hypotheses or theory)
- Mann-Whitney U test ≈ Wilcoxon Mann-Whitney test ≠ Wilcoxon matched pairs test
- Mixed ANOVA ≈ split-plot ANOVA ≈ sometimes called repeated measures ANOVA
- Multiple regression ≈ multiple linear regression
- Null hypothesis ≈ H_0
- Odds ratio ≈ OR
- Orthogonal ≈ independent ≈ perpendicular to
- Post hoc test ≈ follow-up ≈ multiple comparisons
- Relationship between variables ≈ relation between variables
- Repeated-measures ANOVA ≈ within-subjects ANOVA
- Significance level ≈ alpha level ≈ α
- Significance test ≈ null hypothesis significance test ≈ NHST
- Single-factor ANOVA ≈ one-way ANOVA

Notes

1. Italicized terms are listed alphabetically; ≠ means "not equal to."
2. Terms are listed alphabetically within the categories (e.g., Variables). The term we use most often is listed on the left. Similar terms (indicated by ≈) used by other researchers and/or us are listed to the right. In a few cases → is shown to indicate "leads to."

Appendix C: Glossary

Kathryn Kidd

Abstract: In a journal article, follows the title and provides a summary of the paper.

Accessible population: The group of participants to which the researcher has access; might also be an organization or group to which the researcher has entry; also called the survey population or sampling frame.

Accidental sampling: See *Convenience sampling*.

Active independent variable: A variable (e.g., a workshop, new curriculum, or other intervention) at least one level of which is given to a group of participants within a specified period of time during the study; experimental studies must have at least one active independent variable; also called a manipulated independent variable.

Actual sample: The participants that complete the study and whose data are actually used in the data analysis and report of the study's results.

Alternating treatment design: Design that compares the impact of two different treatments within the single subject design framework; also called multielement design.

Alternative hypothesis: Alternative to the null hypothesis; see also *Research hypothesis*.

Annotated bibliography: List of sources reviewed with accompanying summary of each source; not to be confused with a *Literature review* or *Reference list*.

Anonymity: The participant's name and other identifiers, such as Social Security or school ID number, are not known and cannot be deduced by the researcher or others.

Applied research: Research undertaken with the intent to apply the results to some particular practical problem.

Approximately normal level of measurement: Values of a variable where there are many (at least five) ordered levels or scores, with the frequency distribution of the scores being approximately normally distributed.

Associational approach to research: Approach in which two or more usually continuous variables, for the same group of participants, are related or associated; is also sometimes called correlational approach.

Attribute independent variable: An independent variable that cannot be manipulated but that is a major focus of the study; studies with only attribute independent variables are called nonexperimental studies; also called a characteristic or measured independent variable.

Attrition: See *Experimental mortality*.

Authorship: Those who make a substantial *professional* contribution to the study; order of authorship is determined by the importance of such contribution.

Bar graph: Chart of the frequency distribution.

Basic or single factor quantitative approach: Descriptive research approach in which only one variable is considered at a time, so that no statistical comparisons or relationships are made.

Behavioral observation: Observation of the participant's behavior; most common form of measurement in single subject designs.

Bell curve: See *Normal distribution*.

Between-groups design: Study design where each participant in the research is in one and only one condition or group.

Bibliography: List of references and resources, includes additional references not cited in the text of the literature review.

Box and whisker plot: Graphical representation of the distribution of scores; helpful in distinguishing between ordinal and normally distributed data.

Carryover effect: Effect on the dependent variable that comes from an earlier intervention phase (i.e., carry over from one intervention phase to another).

Cases: See *Participants*.

Case study qualitative approach: Qualitative research approach in which the goal is to develop a deep understanding of a case or cases; case(s) must be bounded by time, place, or context.

Categorical variable: A variable whose scores or values are measured by grouping into a limited number of levels or categories.

Causation: Evidence that the independent variable caused any observed change or difference in the dependent variable; the goal of random experimental and quasi-experimental studies.

Characteristic or characteristic variable: See *Attribute independent variable*.

Clinical observation: In research, practice observations that lead to a research problem or question.

Closed-ended question: Question in a survey or other research that provides all allowable responses to the question (participant must select from the provided list).

Clusters: Collections or groups of potential participants for a study that do not overlap.

Cluster sampling: A two-stage probability sampling procedure that is especially useful when the population is spread out geographically or when there is no single overall list of individuals in the accessible population; individual participants within a given cluster are usually geographically grouped together; basic strategy is to first select specific clusters from the list of all clusters using a probability sampling method and then to select all or randomly select a specific proportion of participants from the selected clusters.

Coding: Process of assigning numbers to the levels or values of each variable.

Comparative approach to research: Approach in which a comparison is made between/among a few groups based on an attribute independent variable.

Comparison group: Group in an experimental study that receives the usual treatment or a different treatment from the intervention group and whose results will be compared with those of the intervention group to determine the effect of the intervention on the dependent variables.

Conditional probability: The likelihood (chance) that an event will occur, given that another event has already occurred.

Confidence interval: Range of values within which the population mean (or other parameter of interest) may fall; 95% of the confidence intervals generated would contain the actual population mean.

Confidentiality: Private information about participants will remain private to the researcher, and the participant will not be identifiable in the reports or in conversations with persons outside of the research team.

Conflict of interest: Interests of the participants or the researcher are in conflict (or potentially in conflict) with interests of the study.

Consent: Agreement of the participant to join the study; fully informed voluntary consent must be obtained prior to beginning the study; see also *IRB*.

Constant: Measured characteristic that has only one value in the study.

Construct: Hypothetical concept that cannot be directly observed.

Construct validity: One aspect of measurement validity where the researcher demonstrates that the instrument (outcome measurement) is measuring a construct.

Constructivist paradigm/theoretical framework: Related ways of thinking about research where knowledge is constructed based on experiences; also called the naturalist or qualitative paradigm; see also *Paradigm*.

Contamination: See *Control of extraneous experience/environment variables.*

Continuous variable: A variable that has an infinite (or very large) number of scores or values within a range.

Control group: Group in an experimental study which receives no treatment and whose results will be compared with those of the intervention group to determine the effect of the intervention on the dependent variables; also called placebo group.

Control variable: See *Extraneous variable*.

Control of extraneous experience/environment variables: Dimension of internal validity that deals with the effects of extraneous (variables other than the independent or dependent variables) experiences or environmental conditions in the study; also called *contamination*.

Convenience sampling: Nonprobability sampling technique in which participants are selected on the basis of convenience or availability rather than attempting beforehand to select participants that are representative of the theoretical population; also called *accidental sampling*.

Correlation: A statistic that indicates the association or relationship between scores on two variables; may be positive (direct relationship: as one variable increases, so does the other), negative (inverse relationship: as one variable increases, the other decreases), or zero (no relationship).

Correlational approach: See *Associational approach to research*.

Covariates: See *Extraneous variable*.

Cross-tabulation: Table that gives frequencies (and often percentages) for values of two categorical variables; way of presenting data about two variables so their relationship is more evident.

Data fabrication: Unethical research activity in which data are not collected but fabricated (made up) by the researcher.

Data falsification: Unethical research activity in which the data are falsely manipulated or presented to show optimal results rather than those actually observed.

Debriefing: Process after the data collection where the researcher provides participants with the opportunity to share concerns or interests with the researcher and where the researcher provides the participants with additional information about the procedure, resources, or referrals.

Deception: Involves a misrepresentation of facts, by commission, that occurs when the researcher gives false information about the study; if the investigator does not fully inform the subjects about the important aspects of the study or its goals, omission or *concealment* has occurred.

Degrees of freedom: Refers to the number of independent pieces of information from the data collected in the study.

Dependent variable: A variable assumed to measure or assess the effect of the independent variable; thought of as the presumed outcome or criterion of the independent variable; also called outcome variable.

Descriptive approach to research: Approach that answers descriptive questions using only descriptive, not inferential, statistics; summarizes data from the current sample of participants without making inferences about the larger population of interest; no comparisons or associations are made; does not have an independent variable.

Dichotomous level of measurement: Values of a variable include two categories, either ordered or unordered.

Direct observation: The investigator trains observers to observe and record the behaviors of the participants in the study.

Directional hypothesis: Alternative research hypothesis that specifies the direction of the effect; see also *Nondirectional hypothesis*.

Disciplined inquiry: See *Research*.

Discussion section: In an article or research study, the section in which the major purpose is to discuss the results, relating them to the research hypothesis/question within the context of the literature previously cited.

Drop-outs: See *Experimental mortality*.

Ecological external validity: Extent to which the research may be generalized based on the degree to which the research environment is similar to the natural environment.

Effect size: The strength of the relationship between the independent variable and the dependent variable, or the magnitude of the difference between levels of the independent variable with respect to the dependent variable.

Elements: See *Participants*.

Equivalence of groups on participant characteristics: The degree to which the groups that are compared in a study are equivalent in all respects prior to the introduction of the independent variables; equivalence is assumed to be the case in experiments with random assignment to groups and where each group size is 30 or more.

Ethnographic qualitative approach: Qualitative research approach that describes a group of individuals who share the same culture.

Evidence-based practice: Use of evidence-based research to inform and enhance practice; decisions about interventions in clinical areas should be based on the strength of the evidence.

Existing literature: That which has already been written about the topic or question to be studied; provides the basis for the literature review section.

Experimental mortality: Refers to the phenomenon, generally with studies conducted over time, where participants leave the study; also called attrition or drop-out.

Experimental research approach: Research approach that has at least one active independent variable; may be randomized experimental or quasi-experimental.

External validity: Addresses the question of generalizability, to what populations, settings, treatment variables, and measurement variables can the observed effect be generalized; has three aspects: population external validity, ecological external validity, and testing of subgroups. The first two dimensions examine how representative the population and setting are of the target or theoretical population and of the procedures and setting. The third rating evaluates whether the results are likely to generalize to diverse subgroups such as both genders.

Extraneous variable: Variable that is not of interest in a particular study but that could influence the dependent variable; also called nuisance variables, control variables, or (in some designs) covariates.

Field research: Research conducted in settings where the participants live, work, or receive treatment.

Focus group: Relatively small groups of people interviewed together.

Frequency distribution: A graph that indicates how many participants are in each category.

Frequency table: Table that gives the number observed in the sample (frequency) for each value of the variable; often also includes the percentages for each value and the cumulative frequencies and cumulative percentages.

Grounded theory qualitative approach: Qualitative research approach in which the goal is to generate theory from data.

Histogram: A graph of a frequency distribution that connects the points between the categories; also called frequency polygons.

Homogeneity of variance: Assumption that the samples in the study have equal variation among their members.

Human subjects committee: See *IRB (Institutional Review Board)*.

Hypothesis: See *Research hypothesis*.

Independence assumption: Assumption that, within each sample, the scores for the variables are independent of each other (the performance of one participant does not affect the performance of any other).

Independent variable: A variable that is presumed to affect or predict the values of another variable; may be active or attribute; also called *predictor variable*.

Inferential process: Process of making an inference about the difference between two groups or the relationship between two variables.

Inferential statistics: Set of statistics that allow the researcher to make generalizations about the population from the sample studied.

Informed consent: See *Consent*.

Interaction effects: The differential effect that one independent variable has on a specific level of a second independent variable.

Internal validity: The degree to which the researcher can infer that a relationship between independent and dependent variables is causal.

Interval level of measurement: In traditional measurement approaches, values of a variable that are ordered levels in which the difference between levels is equal but there is no absolute zero.

Interview: Survey technique/instrument in which the researcher (or designee) verbally asks the questions of the participant; may be in person or via telephone.

Introduction (of an article): In an article or research study, provides a background and general purpose statement of what is to be accomplished by the study.

IRB (Institutional Review Board): A group that reviews proposals for studies with human participants *before* the research can begin; the committee is mandated by federal regulations to protect human subjects and to decide whether the research plan has adequately dealt with ethical issues related to the project; also called human subjects committee.

Knowledge (producing): Research that builds on or adds to the knowledge-base of the profession.

Laboratory research: Research conducted in a controlled, structured setting that is not where the subjects or participants usually live, work, or receive therapy.

Level: Gain or loss from phase to phase in time-series designs, including single-subject designs; also referred to as change in level.

Levels of measurement: Type of measurement of the values of variables important to the computation of certain statistics; traditional levels include nominal, ordinal, interval, and ratio; here called nominal, dichotomous, ordinal, and approximately normal (or normally distributed); *see each term.*

Levels of the variable: See *Values of the variable.*

Limited interest: Refers to the likely esoteric nature of the topic for a study, one that is of interest to a small and/or limited audience.

Literature review: An interpretation of a selection of documents (published or unpublished) on a specific topic that involves summarization, analysis, evaluation, and synthesis of the documents.

Manipulated independent variable: See *Active independent variable.*

Masked (blind) review: Review of a manuscript or proposal where the authors are unknown to the reviewers.

Matching: Process used to make groups equivalent based on some characteristics; the characteristics that are matched must be related to the dependent variable.

Mean: Measure of central tendency calculated by dividing the sum of the individual or raw scores in the sample by the number of observations in the sample; also referred to as the arithmetic average.

Measured independent variable: See *Attribute independent variable.*

Measurement: The assignment of numbers or symbols to the different levels or values of variables according to rules.

Measurement error: The difference between the true score and the observed score.

Measurement reliability: Consistency of a measure.

Measurement validity: Degree to which a measure or test measures what it was intended to measure.

Median: Measure of central tendency that is the midpoint of the individual or raw scores in the sample.

Measures of central tendency: Statistics that measure the center of distribution of the observed data; includes mean, median, and mode.

Measures of association: Statistical tests that describe the correlation between variables.

Measures of variability: Statistics that measure the dispersion (or spread) of the observed data; most common measure is the standard deviation.

Meta-analysis: A research synthesis of a set of studies that uses a quantitative measure, effect size, to indicate the strength of relationship between the treatment or other independent variable and the dependent variables.

Method section: In an article or research study, instructs the reader as to exactly what was done in the study and so allows the reader to replicate the study under identical conditions; generally divided into subsections of participants, instruments/materials, procedure, and design/analysis.

Mixed design: Study that has at least one between-groups independent variable and at least one within-subjects independent variable.

Mixed-methods study: Research study that uses both qualitative and quantitative methodologies. Common in program evaluation research.

Mode: Measure of central tendency that is equal to the individual or raw scores that are most frequent in the data.

Mortality: See *Experimental mortality.*

Multielement design: See *Alternating treatment design.*

Multiple baseline design: Single subject design where typically three baselines are recorded simultaneously (may be three different participants, three different behaviors of the same participant, or the same participant in three different settings).

Multiple group time-series design: Quasi-experimental design in which a baseline is determined to be stable prior to an intervention (via multiple pretests) so that the researcher can conclude that the change in the dependent variable is due to the intervention and not other environmental factors *and* there is a comparison group that receives the same number of measurements but does not receive the intervention.

Narrative qualitative approach: Qualitative research approach that explores the life of an individual; the goal is to identify and report stories from the participants.

Nominal level of measurement: Values of a variable include three or more unordered categories (traditional definitions require two or more categories; we use dichotomous for two).

Non-nil null hypothesis: A null hypothesis stated as some nonzero difference. In practical applications, where the null hypothesis could be stated as some amount of difference between the means of the two populations, to reject the null hypothesis, the treatment group would have to exceed the control group by an amount necessary to make a functional difference.

Nondirectional hypothesis: Alternative research hypothesis that states simply that there is a relationship between the active independent and dependent variables and does not specify the nature (direction) of that relationship; see also *Directional hypothesis.*

Nonexperimental research approaches: Research approaches with at least one attribute independent variable and no active independent variable.

Nonparametric statistical tests: Inferential statistics that are used when the data do not meet the assumption normality.

Nonprobability sampling: Selection of participants in which there is no way to estimate the probability that each participant has of being included in the sample; used when probability samples are not feasible.

Nonrandom assignment to groups: Assignment of participants to groups (i.e., experimental versus usual or no-treatment groups) by some process other than random assignment.

Normal curve: See *Normal distribution.*

Normal distribution: Probability distribution of the population; the normal distribution is unimodal; the mean, median, and mode are equal; the curve is symmetric; the range is infinite; the curve has no kurtosis; also called normal curve or bell curve.

Normality assumption: Assumes that the scores of the variable are normally distributed in each of the populations from which samples are drawn.

Normally distributed level of measurement: See *Approximately normal level of measurement.*

Null hypothesis: Hypothesis that states that the population means of the two or more samples are equal (e.g., the active independent variable has no impact on the dependent variable).

Null hypothesis significance testing: Utilization of inferential statistics to test whether to reject or not to reject the null hypothesis.

Nuisance variable: See *Extraneous variable.*

Observations: See *Participants.*

Observed score: Any score that is obtained from any participant on a particular instrument.

Open-ended question: Survey question that allows the participant to construct his or her own answer.

Operational definition of variable: Describes or defines a variable in terms of the operations or techniques used to make it happen or to measure it.

Ordered variable: Variable having a set of values that vary from low to high within a certain range, such that a larger value of the variable indicates more of it than a smaller value of the variable, and there is an assumption that there are or could be an infinite set of values within the range.

Ordinal level of measurement: Values of a variable include three or more ordered levels, but the frequency distribution of the scores is not normally distributed.

Outcome variable: See *Dependent variable*.

Outlier: Scores or values for a variable outside the expected range (generally extreme scores).

Paper–pencil test: A test given to participants where they are asked to use paper and pencil to answer the questions.

Paradigm: A way of thinking about and conducting research; it is a *philosophy* that guides how the research might be conducted.

Parametric statistical tests: Inferential statistics that assume the data are normally distributed and meet other assumptions.

Paraphrasing: Using another's ideas but rephrasing them in the writer's own words; the researcher must cite the source for paraphrased work.

Participants: Those who are the object of study in the research; generally individuals, but may be, for example, small groups, organizations, or communities; also called cases, observations, elements, or subjects.

Participant observation: The investigator observes those under study as a participant in the group.

Participant report: Information provided directly by the participants in the study.

Peer review: The article was evaluated by other experts (peers) in the field, usually without knowing who the author of the article was (i.e., masked or "blind" review).

Phenomenological qualitative approach: Qualitative research approach that helps researchers understand the meaning participants place onto, for example, events, phenomena, or activities.

Pie chart: Circular graphic representation of the groups (values) for a variable; especially effective with categorical data with a few categories.

Pilot study: Formal process of collecting data with a sample similar to the planned research study prior to actual data collection for the study; especially important to provide evidence about the reliability and validity of the outcome measures.

Pilot testing: See *Pilot study*.

Placebo group: See *Control group*.

Plagiarism: Using the words or ideas of another without citing the source.

Population: The larger group of interest for the study and from which the sample is drawn.

Population external validity: Examines how representative the population is of the target or theoretical population; answers the questions: Was the accessible population representative of the theoretical population? Was the selected sample representative of the accessible population? And was the actual sample representative vis-à-vis the selected sample?

Postpositivist paradigm/theoretical framework: A way of thinking about and conducting quantitative research; see also *Paradigm*.

Posttest: Measurement of the dependent variable taken subsequent to the intervention; used to determine change in the dependent variable due to the intervention (independent variable).

Practical relevance: The extent to which the study/research question has importance and practical applications for practitioners in the field.

Practical significance: See *Practical relevance*.

Predictor variable: See *Independent variable*.

Pretest: Measurement of the dependent variable taken prior to the intervention; used to establish a baseline.

Primary source: An original source of data, study results; preferred source for the literature review.

Privacy: Refers to participants' concern about controlling access to information about themselves; see also *Anonymity, Confidentiality,* and *Consent*.

Probability sampling: Involves selection of participants in a way that is nonbiased; in a probability sample every participant or element of the population has a known, nonzero probability of being chosen to be a member of the sample; relies on random or systematic selection of participants.

Purposeful sampling: A type of sampling strategy where the researcher defines how the cases are selected and includes a rationale for it; applies to both the selection of the cases to study and to the sampling of information used within the cases.

Purposive sampling: Nonprobability sampling technique in which participants are hand picked from the accessible population so that they presumably will be representative or typical of the population.

Qualitative data analysis: Involves various methods for coding, categorizing, and assigning meaning to the data, which are usually words or images.

Qualitative data and data collection: Data and data collection procedures that are more "subjective," in that they could be interpreted differently by different people; usually gathered from interviews, observations, or narrative documents.

Qualitative research: One of five main nonexperimental research approaches: phenomenological, grounded theory, ethnographic, case study, and narrative.

Quantitative data analysis: Involves various methods for coding, categorizing, and assigning meaning to the data, which are usually numeric and which usually involve the calculation of statistical measures.

Quantitative data and data collection: Data and data collection procedures usually gathered with some sort of instrument that can be scored numerically, reliably, and with relatively little training.

Quantitative research: Group of research approaches that can be analyzed numerically.

Quasi-experimental approach to research: Approach in which there is an active independent variable but without random assignment of participants to groups.

Questionnaire: Survey instrument that the participant completes by himself or herself; may be paper and pencil or online.

Quota sampling: Nonprobability sampling technique in which the researcher sets certain parameters for the selection of participants from which certain proportions must be obtained.

Random assignment: A random table of numbers (or other similarly random process) is used to assign each participant to a group.

Random assignment of participants to groups: See *Random assignment*.

Random assignment of treatments: Used in quasi-experimental studies where random assignment of participants to groups is not possible; instead, the treatment (experimental, usual, or none) is randomly assigned to groups.

Random sampling: Selection from the population of interest of study participants using a random selection technique so that the sample is representative of all the possible participants who fit the selection criteria.

Random selection of participants to be included in a study: See *Random sampling.*

Randomized experimental approach to research: Approach in which there is random assignment of participants to the intervention and comparison groups, and an active or manipulated independent variable.

Range: Distance between the lowest and highest observed values of a variable.

Ratio level of measurement: In traditional approaches, values of a variable that are ordered levels and that have an absolute zero.

Reference list: List, at the end of the article, that provides full citation information for each publication cited in the text of the article.

Repeated measures design: See *Within-subjects design.*

Representative sample: A sample that is a small replica of the population; has, on all of the key variables, the same proportions as in the whole population; is most likely obtained using techniques described as probability sampling.

Research: Disciplined method of gaining new information, building knowledge, or answering questions; also called disciplined inquiry; implies a systematic investigation with underlying guidelines regardless of the particular research paradigm.

Research hypothesis: Predictive statements about the relationship between variables.

Research problem: The research problem will set forth the phenomena to be studied, the curiosity as to "why something is as it is."

Research question: Similar to the research hypothesis but does not entail specific predictions about the relationship and is phrased in question format.

Research validity: The merit of the whole study (as distinguished from validity of the measurement of a variable); includes measurement reliability and statistics, internal validity, overall measurement validity of the constructs, and external validity.

Respect for persons: Ethical principle incorporating two ethical convictions: (1) that participants should be treated as autonomous agents, which means that the individual is capable of deliberating and making individual decisions and choices; and (2) that persons with diminished autonomy, such as children, the developmentally disabled, and persons with emotional disorders, are entitled to special protection.

Response rate: Proportion of selected potential participants who actually participate in the study; most frequently used with survey studies.

Results section: Section of an article or research study that provides a summary of the analyses that were performed on the data collected.

Reversal designs: The original and most common type of single subject design; often referred to as ABAB designs, where A refers to baseline periods and B refers to intervention periods.

Sample: General term for the selected part of a larger group of potential participants taken with the intent of generalizing from the smaller group or sample to the theoretical population.

Sampling: The process of selecting part of a larger group of subjects with the intent of generalizing from the sample to the population.

Sampling design: The procedure or process used to select the sample; there are two general types of sampling design, probability and nonprobability.

Sampling frame: See *Accessible population*.

Scientific misconduct: Unethical behavior on the part of the researchers.

Secondary source: Source that provides nonoriginal (i.e., secondhand) data or information.

Selected sample: The smaller group of participants who are selected from the larger accessible population by the researcher and asked to participate in the study.

Simple random sampling: Most basic of the probability sampling techniques; a sample in which all participants have an equal and independent chance of being included in the sample.

Single group time-series designs: Quasi-experimental designs involving only one group in which a baseline is determined to be stable (via multiple pretests) prior to an intervention so that the researcher can conclude that the change in the dependent variable is due to the intervention and not other environmental factors.

Single-subject designs: A subcategory of quasi-experimental time-series designs that can be used with one or a few participants.

Slope: The angle of the data points within a particular phase of a single-subject design; also referred to as change in slope.

Solomon four-group design: Experimental 2 × 2 factorial design where one intervention group receives the pretest while the other intervention group does not and one no intervention group receives the pretest while the other does not; interest is in the effects of taking a pretest on the posttest rather than the pretest scores themselves.

Source table: The table generated in analysis of variance that enumerates the sums of squared deviations from the mean of each group, the degrees of freedom for each group, the mean squares from each group and the *F* ratio.

Snowball sampling: A modification of convenience sampling that is used when the participants of interest are from a population that is rare or at least whose members are unknown to the researcher; a few participants are identified and then asked to refer additional potential participants who also fit into the same category.

Standard deviation: Measure of variability for normally distributed data.

Standard error of the mean: Standard deviation of the distribution of the sample means.

Standardized personality inventories: Standardized tests that measure some traits or characteristics of personality.

Standardized tests: Tests that follow specific guidelines. All participants take the test under the same circumstances. Most standardized tests have a manual.

Statistical significance: The probability that the difference between the population parameter and the sample statistic occurred by chance at a level less than the predetermined significance level, assuming a true null hypothesis.

Steps in planning research: Research process, includes steps: (a) identifying the research problem; (b) developing hypotheses or research questions; (c) developing a research design; (d) data collection and analysis; (e) making inferences or interpretations; and (f) deciding whether the hypotheses should be rejected or not rejected.

Strata: Variables that could be used to divide the population into segments (e.g., race, geographical region, age, or gender).

Stratified random sampling: Probability sampling technique in which the population is divided into segments based on key variables, sampling from each value of the key variable.

Subjects: See *Participants*.

Summated (Likert) attitude scales: Method developed by Likert as a way of measuring attitudes about particular groups, institutions, or concepts; the term *Likert scale* is used in two ways, for the summated scale and for the individual items or rating scales from which the summated scale is computed.

Survey: Research methodology in which generally large numbers of participants are asked to respond to a series of questions; may be interview or questionnaire, open-ended or closed-ended, or some combination.

Survey population: See *Accessible population*.

Systematic random sampling: Probability sampling technique in which a random number table is used to select the first participant in the study, then each subsequent participant is systematically selected at regular intervals; must consider whether the list of potential participants is ordered in some way (i.e., has some recurring pattern) that will have a differential effect on the resulting sample depending upon where the researcher started.

Target population: Includes all of the participants of theoretical interest to the researcher and to which he or she would like to generalize.

Theoretical importance: The extent to which the research questions follow from the literature or theory used to support their importance.

Theoretical population: See *Target population*.

Theory: A statement or group of statements that explains and predicts relationships among phenomena; a set of interrelated concepts, definitions, and postulations that present a systematic view of phenomena by specifying relations among variables.

Theory development: One purpose of research, to support the theoretical basis of the discipline.

Title (of an article): Titles of articles should be brief but should be a selling point for the article, should give an idea of the topic, and catch the reader's interest.

Type I error: Reject the null hypothesis when, in fact, it is true.

Type II error: Do not reject the null hypothesis when it is false.

Unordered categories or levels of a variable: Values of the variable are not ordered, that is, no value is more or less than another.

Unordered variables: Nominal variables whereby the values or levels of the variable are not ordered; see also *Nominal level of measurement*.

Validity: General term for the degree to which the measurement or study measures what it purports to measure.

Validity of the measure: See *Measurement validity*.

Value label: Titles or names given to the different values of a variable.

Values of the variable: Different possible characteristics, responses, and measurements for a given variable.

Variability: The spread of the data points within any particular phase of the study (i.e., baseline or intervention).

Variable: A characteristic of the participants or situation for a given study that has different values; a variable must have different values *in the study* or it is a *Constant*.

Variable label: Title or name given to a variable.

Widespread interest: A research question or hypothesis that is of interest to much of the profession or field of practice.

Within-subjects design: Study design in which each participant in the research receives or experiences all of the conditions or levels of the independent variable to complete the study; also called repeated measures designs.

Appendix D: Writing Research Problems and Questions

Frameworks for Stating Research Problems

A common definition of a *research problem* is a statement that asks what relationship exists between two or more variables, but most research problems are more complex than this definition implies. The research problem should be a broad statement, perhaps using summary terms that stand for several variables, that covers several more specific research hypotheses or questions. Several ways to state the research problem are provided in the next section.

Format

One way that you could phrase the problem is as follows:

> The research problem is to investigate whether (put independent variable 1 or group of variables here), (independent variable 2, if any, here), and (independent variable 3, if any) are related to (dependent variable 1, here), and (dependent variable 2, if any) in (population here).

All studies have several variables; except in a totally descriptive study, one or more usually are called independent or predictor variables and one or more are dependent or outcome variables. There can be two or more of each, and there often are. In the statement of the problem, in contrast to the research questions/hypotheses, it is desirable to use broad descriptors for groups of similar variables. For example, demographics might cover several variables such as gender, mother's education, and ethnicity. Course performance might include scores on lecture-based test items and on text-based items. Likewise, attitudes could refer to more than one variable. Concepts such as self-esteem or teaching style have several aspects that usually result in more than one variable.

Examples

If your study uses the randomized experimental approach, you could phrase the problem as follows:

> The research problem is to investigate the effect of music lessons on IQ and academic achievement in 6-year-olds (as in sample study 1, Schellenberg, 2004).

For studies that compare groups or associate/relate variables, you could phrase the problem as follows:

The problem is to investigate whether age is related to physical functioning, mental health, and quality of life in individuals with multiple sclerosis (as in sample study 3, DiLorenzo, Halper, and Picone, 2004).

If you have several *independent variables* and want to predict some outcome, you could say:

The problem is to investigate the background and course-related variables that predict or *seem* to influence exam performance in a college psychology course (as in study 4, Zamboanga et al., 2007).

This latter format is especially useful when the approach is a complex (several independent variables) associational one that will use multiple regression.

Framework for Stating Research Questions/Hypotheses

Although it is okay to phrase a randomized experimental research *problem* (in the format of the first example) as a "study of the effect of ...," we think it is generally best to phrase your research *questions or hypotheses* so that they do not appear to imply cause and effect (i.e., as *difference* or *associational* questions/hypotheses and/or as *descriptive* questions). The former are answered with inferential statistics, and descriptive questions are answered with descriptive statistics. There are several reasonable ways to state research questions. In the following sections, we show one way, which we have found useful, to state each type of question.

Descriptive Questions

Basic Descriptive Questions

These questions are about some aspect of one variable. Descriptive questions ask about the central tendency, frequency distribution, percentage in each category, variability, or shape of the distribution. Some descriptive questions are intended to test assumptions; some simply describe the sample demographics; others describe a dependent variable. A few *examples* are as follows:

1. Is course test performance distributed approximately normally?
2. What percentage of participants is of each gender?
3. What are the mean and standard deviation of the achievement scores?
4. What percentage of participants kept their HIV status secret from their family? (as in study 5)

Complex Descriptive Questions

These questions deal with two or more variables at a time but do not involve inferential statistics. Cross-tabulations of two categorical variables, factor analysis, and measures of reliability (e.g., Cronbach's alpha) are examples. An *example* is as follows:

What is the internal consistency reliability of the lecture based exam items? (see study 4, Zamboanga et al., 2007)

Difference Questions/Hypotheses

Basic Difference Questions

The *format* is as follows:

> Are there differences between the (insert number) levels of (put the independent variable name here) (you could name the levels here in parentheses) in regard to the average (put the dependent variable(s) name here) scores?

An *example* is as follows:

> Are there differences between the four levels of lessons (piano, voice, drama, and no lessons) in regard to the average IQ and achievement scores of the children? (see study 1, Schellenberg, 2004)

> *Appropriate analyses*: One-way analysis of variance (ANOVA) or a *t*-test could be used if there were only two levels of the independent variable (see Chapter 20).

Complex Difference and Interaction Questions

When you have two categorical independent variables considered together, you will have *three* research questions or hypotheses. There are advantages of considering two or three independent variables at a time. See Chapter 21 for an introduction about how to interpret the *interaction* question. Sample *formats* for a *set* of three questions answered by *one* two-way ANOVA are as follows:

1. Is there a difference between (insert the levels of independent variable 1) in regard to the average (put dependent variable 1 here) scores?
2. Is there a difference between (insert the levels of independent variable 2) in regard to the average (dependent variable 1) scores?
3. Is there an interaction of (independent variable 1) and (independent variable 2) in regard to the (dependent variable 1)?

(Repeat these three questions, for the second dependent variable, if there is more than one.) A few *examples* follow:

1. Is there a difference between students who have music lessons versus the control children in regard to their IQ scores? (see study 1, Schellenberg, 2004)
2. Is there a difference between pretest and posttest scores in regard to children's average IQ?
3. Is there an interaction between type of lessons and time (pre versus post) in regard to IQ?

Note that the first question states the *levels* or categories of the first independent variable; that is, it states the groups that are to be compared (music lessons versus control students). The second question does the same for the second independent variable; that is, it states the *levels* (pretest and posttest) to be compared. However, the third question (the interaction) asks whether the first *variable* overall (type of lessons) interacts with the second variable (time). No mention is made *in the interaction question* of the levels of the variables.

> *An appropriate analysis*: Factorial ANOVA (see Chapter 22).

Associational/Relationship Questions/Hypotheses

Basic Associational Questions

When both variables are ordered and essentially continuous (i.e., have five or more ordered categories), we consider the approach and research question to be associational. There are two main types of basic associational statistics: correlation and regression. The *format* for a correlation is as follows:

> Is there an association (or relationship) between (variable 1) and (variable 2)?

In this case, it is arbitrary which variable is independent (or antecedent) and which is dependent or outcome. An *example* for a single association or relationship is as follows:

> Is there an association between prior GPA and number of prior psychology courses (as in study 4)?

If there are more than two variables, which is common, and each pair of variables is associated separately, you can have a series of questions asking whether there is an association between *each* variable and every other variable. This would produce a *correlation matrix* (see Chapter 21).

An *example* that would produce a correlation matrix is as follows:

> Are there associations among ACT scores, prior GPA, and number of prior psychology courses? (see study 4, Zamboanga et al., 2007)

Note that what is said to be associated in these questions is the variable itself; no mention is made of the levels or values here.

If one variable is clearly the independent or predictor, you would phrase the question as follows and use *bivariate regression* analyses:

> In study 2, can we predict total exam points (the dependent variable) from time spent on quizzes (the independent variable)?

> *Appropriate analyses*: Bivariate regression, if there is a clear independent or antecedent variable and you want to make a prediction (see Chapter 22); correlation if there is no clear independent variable (see Chapter 21).

Complex Associational Questions

In the associational approach, when two or more *independent* variables are considered together, rather than separately, as in the previous *basic* associational format, you get a complex associational question. The *format* can be phrased something like:

> How well does the combination of (list the several specific independent variables here) predict (put dependent variable here)?

An *example* is as follows:

> How well does the combination of ACT scores, prior GPA, and number of prior psychology courses predict exam performance? (see Zamboanga et al., 2007)

> *An appropriate analysis*: Multiple regression (see Chapter 22).

Appendix E: Questions for Evaluating Research Validity

Listed below are the 19 questions that we use to (a) describe the design and methods of a study (questions 1–8); (b) evaluate the eight key dimensions of research validity (questions 9–16); and (c) evaluate three other broad, important issues about the study (questions 17–19).

Analysis of the Design and Methods

Variables and Their Measurement Levels

1. What are the key *independent*/antecedent/predictor *variables*? For *each*:
   (a) Is it an active, attribute, or change over time independent variable?
   (b) What is the *number* of *levels*/categories of the independent variable?
   (c) What is the level of *measurement* (nominal, dichotomous, ordinal, or approximately normal) of the independent variable?
2. What are the key *dependent* or outcome *variables*? For *each*, what is the level of *measurement?*
3. What are the main *research questions* or hypotheses?
4. What is the *research approach* (i.e., descriptive, associational, comparative, quasi-experimental, and/or randomized experimental) *for each question?*
5. What is the *general design classification if* the approach is randomized experimental, quasi-experimental, or comparative?
6. What is the *specific experimental design* name *if* the approach is randomized experimental or quasi-experimental?

Measurement Reliability and Validity for Each Key Variable

7. Is the *measurement reliability* for *each* key variable acceptable?
   (a) What types of evidence for reliability are presented?
   (b) Is the evidence or support for *each* key variable acceptable?
8. Is the evidence for *measurement validity* for *each* key variable acceptable?
   (a) What types of evidence to support measurement validity are reported?
   (b) Is the evidence or support for *each* key variable acceptable?

Evaluation of the Four Key Dimensions of Research Validity

Overall Measurement Reliability and Statistics

9. What is the overall rating of measurement reliability and statistics? Base the rating and comments on the following:

   (a) Is the overall measurement reliability of the variables acceptable?

   (b) Is the power appropriate?

   (c) Is the choice/use of statistics appropriate?

   (d) Is there adequate presentation of the statistical results, including effect size?

   (e) Is the interpretation of statistical results appropriate?

Internal Validity

10. What is the evaluation of the equivalence of the groups on participant characteristics? Base the rating and comments on:

    (a) Was there random assignment of participants to the groups?

    (b) If no random assignment, were the participants in each group matched, made similar statistically, or found to be similar on a pretest? If random assignment was done, (b) and (c) should be scored as yes.

    (c) If no random assignment, were the participants in each group matched, made similar statistically, or found to be similar on other key participant characteristics (e.g., age, gender, or IQ)?

    (d) Was the retention (low attrition) of subjects during the study high and similar across groups?

11. What is the evaluation of the control of extraneous experience and environment variables?

    (a) Was the study conducted in a controlled environment?

    (b) Did the groups have equivalent environments?

    (c) Was there a no treatment (placebo) or usual treatment comparison group?

    (d) Were there adequate attempts to reduce other extraneous influences?

Overall Measurement Validity of the Constructs

12. What is the evaluation of the construct validity of the intervention? If there is no active independent variable, this question is skipped as not applicable.

    (a) Is the intervention (active independent variable) operationally defined and implemented appropriately, based on an existing body of empirical or theoretical research?

    (b) Is the intervention described in enough detail for it to be replicated?

    (c) Is there a manipulation check or verification to be sure that the intervention was presented as planned?

13. What is the overall evaluation of the construct validity of the outcome measures (dependent variables) and any attribute independent variables?

    (a) Have the measures been used with similar participants?

    (b) Is adequate evidence for the validity of the outcomes based on existing empirical or theoretical research presented?

    (c) Is adequate evidence for the validity of the attribute independent variables presented?

External Validity

14. What is the evaluation of the overall population external validity? Base the rating on answers to the following:

    (a) Was the accessible population representative of the theoretical population?

    (b) Was the selected sample representative of the accessible population?

    (c) Was the actual sample representative vis-à-vis the selected sample? That is, was the response rate acceptable?

15. What is the evaluation of the overall ecological external validity? The rating is based on:

    (a) Is the setting (or conditions) natural and representative of the target setting?

    (b) Is the rapport with testers or observers good?

    (c) Are the procedures or tasks natural and representative of the behavioral concepts of interest?

    (d) Is the timing and length of the treatment or intervention appropriate? (NA if not an experiment because no intervention is done)

    (e) Will the results apply to more than the specific time in history that the study was done?

16. What is the evaluation of the extent to which important participant subgroups were tested or compared?

    (a) Are gender differences analyzed or compared?

    (b) Are two or more ethnic or racial groups analyzed or compared?

    (c) Are two or more age groups analyzed or compared?

    (d) Are other important subgroups (e.g., cultures or geographic regions) compared?

Other Issues

17. Was there adequate *peer review*?

18. Do the authors adequately present the case for the theoretical importance or practical relevance of their research questions and design?

19. Do the authors interpret their findings adequately? That is, were the title, abstract, and discussion clear and accurate (or overstated and misleading) given the evaluation of the several aspects of research validity?

Appendix F: Making American Psychological Association Tables and Figures

Don Quick

Tables and figures are used in most fields of study to provide a visual presentation of important information. They are used to organize the statistical results of a study, to list important tabulated information, and to allow the reader a visual method of comparing related items. Tables offer a way to display information that would be difficult to describe briefly in the text.

A figure may be just about anything that is not a table, such as a chart, graph, photograph, or line drawing. These figures may include pie charts, line charts, bar charts, organizational charts, flow charts, diagrams, blueprints, or maps. Unless the figure can clearly illustrate a comparison that a table cannot, use a table. A good rule is to use a table when there are only numbers and words, and use figures for other visual presentations.

The meaning and major focus of the table or figure should be evident to the readers without them having to make a thorough study of it. A glance should be all it takes to convey to the reader the idea of what the table or figure represents. By reading only the text itself, the reader may have difficulty understanding the data; by constructing tables and figures that are well presented, the readers will be able to understand the study results more easily.

The purpose of this appendix is to provide guidelines that will enhance the presentation of research findings and other information by using tables and figures. It will highlight the important aspects of constructing tables and figures using the *Publication Manual of the American Psychological Association, Fifth Edition* (2001) as the guide for formatting.

General Considerations Concerning Tables

Be selective as to how many tables are included in the total document. Determine how much data the reader needs to comprehend the material, and then decide if the information would be better presented in the text or as a table. A table containing only a few numbers is unnecessary, whereas a table containing too much information may not be understandable. Tables should be easy to read and interpret. If at all possible, combine tables that repeat data.

Keep a consistency to all of your tables throughout your document. All tables and figures in your document should use a similar format, with the results organized in a comparable fashion. Use the same designation measure or scale in all tables, figures, and the text. Each table and figure must be discussed in the text. An informative table will supplement but will not duplicate the text. In the text, discuss only the most important parts of the table. Make sure the table can be understood by itself without the accompanying text; however, it is never independent of the text. There must be a reference in the text to the table.

In a final manuscript such as a thesis or dissertation, adjust the column headings or spacing between columns so the width of the table fits appropriately between the margins. Fit all of each table on one page. Reduce the data, change the type size, or decrease line spacing to make it fit. A short table may be on a page with text, as long as it follows the first mention of it. Each long table should fit on one page as near as possible to where it is mentioned in the text. If the fit and appearance would be improved, turn the table sideways (landscape orientation, with the top of table toward the spine) on the page.

Construction of the Table

Table F.1 is an example of an American Psychological Association (APA) table for displaying simple descriptive data collected in a study. It also appears in correct relation to the text of the document; that is, it is inserted below the place that the table is first mentioned either on the same page, if it will fit, or the next page. (Figure F.1 shows the same table with the table parts identified.) The major parts of a table are the number, the title, the headings, the body, and the notes.

Table Numbering

Arabic numerals are used to number tables in the order in which they appear in the text. Do not write in the text "the table on page 17" or "the table above or below." The correct method would be to refer to the table number like this: (Table 1) or "Table 1 shows..." Left-justify the table number (see Table F.1). In an article, each table should be numbered sequentially in the order of appearance. Do not use suffix letters with the table numbers in articles. However, in a book, tables may be numbered within chapters—for example, Table 7.1. If the table appears in an appendix, identify it with the letter of the appendix capitalized, followed by the table number; for instance, Table F.3 is the third table in Appendix F.

Table Titles

Include the variables, the groups on whom the data were collected, the subgroups, and the nature of the statistic reported. The table title and headings should concisely describe what is contained in the table. Abbreviations that appear in the body of the table can sometimes

TABLE F.1

Means and Standard Deviations on the Measure of Self-Direction in Learning as a Function of Age in Adult Students

Age group	n	Self-directed learning inventory score	
		M	SD
20–34	15	65.05	3.50
35–49	22	88.13	6.31
50–64	14	79.33	5.63
65–79	7	56.67	7.15
80+	—[a]	—	—

Note: The maximum score is 100.

[a] No participants were found for the over 80 group.

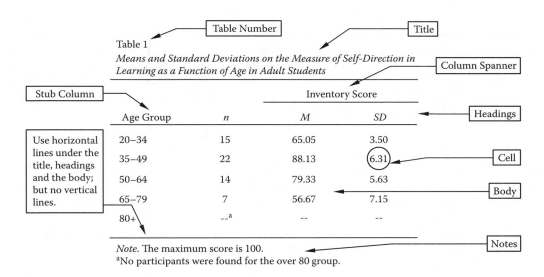

FIGURE F.1
The major parts of an APA table.

be explained in the title; however, it may be more appropriate to use a general note (see also comments on *Table Headings*). The title must be italicized. Standard APA format for journal submission requires double spacing throughout. However, tables in student papers and theses may be partially single spaced for better presentation.

Table Headings

Headings are used to explain the organization of the table. You may use abbreviations in the headings; however, include a note as to their meaning if you use mnemonics, variable names, and scale acronyms. Standard abbreviations and symbols for nontechnical terms can be used without explanation (e.g., *no.* for *number* or % for *percent*). Have precise title, column headings, and row labels that are accurate and brief. Each column must have a heading, including the *stub column*, or leftmost column. Its heading is referred to as the *stubhead*. The stub column usually lists the significant independent variables or the levels of the variable, as in Table F.1.

The *column heads* cover one column, and the *column spanners* cover two or more columns—each with its own column head (Table F.1 and Figure F.1). Headings stacked in this manner are called *decked heads*. This is a good way to eliminate repetition in column headings, but try to avoid using more than two levels of decked heads. **Column heads, column spanners**, and **stubheads** should all be singular, unless referring to a group (e.g., children). Table spanners, which cover the entire table, may be plural. Use sentence capitalization in all headings.

Notice that there are no vertical lines in an APA style table. The horizontal lines can be added by using a "draw" feature or a "borders" feature for tables in the computer word processor.

The Body of the Table

The body contains the actual data being displayed. Round numbers improve the readability and clarity more than precise numbers with several decimal places. A good guideline is to report two digits more than the raw data. A reader can compare numbers down a column more easily than across a row. Column and row averages can provide a visual focus that allows the reader to inspect the data easily without cluttering the table. If a cell cannot be filled because the information is not applicable, then leave it blank. If it cannot be filled because the information could not be obtained or was not reported, then insert a dash and explain the dash with a note to the table.

Notes to a Table

Notes are often used with tables. There are three different forms of notes used with tables: (1) to eliminate repetition in the body of the table; (2) to elaborate on the information contained in a particular cell; or (3) to indicate statistical significance:

- A *general note* provides information relating to the table as a whole, including explanations of abbreviations used:

  Note: This could be used to indicate if the table came from another source.

- A *specific note* makes a reference to a specific row or column or cell of the table and is given a superscript lowercase letter, beginning with the letter "a":
- [a]$n = 50$. Specific notes are identified in the body with the corresponding superscript.
- A *probability note* is to be included when one or more inferential statistic has been computed and there isn't a column showing the probability, p. Asterisks indicate the statistical significance of findings presented within the table. Try to be consistent across all tables in a paper. The important thing is to use the fewest asterisks for the largest p value. It is common to use one asterisk for .05 and two for .01. For example:

  *$p < .05$.
  **$p < .01$.

Notes should be listed with general notes first and then specific notes and should conclude with probability notes, without indentation. They may be single spaced for better presentation. Explain all uses of dashes and parentheses. Abbreviations for technical terms, group names, and those of a similar nature must be explained in a note to the table.

Examples of a Few Tables in APA Format

Tables F.2–F.5 and Figure F.2 are adapted from *SPSS for Introductory Statistics* (Morgan et al., 2007).

Using Figures

Generally, the same concepts apply to figures that have been previously stated concerning tables: They should be easy to read and interpret, consistent throughout the document when presenting the same type of figure, kept on one page if possible, and supplement the

TABLE F.2

Chi-Square Analysis of Prevalence of Taking Geometry Among Males and Females

	Geometry				
Variable	Not taken	Taken	Totals	χ^2	p
Gender				12.71	<.001
Males	10 (29%)	24 (71%)	34 (100%)		
Females	29 (71%)	12 (29%)	41 (100%)		

TABLE F.3

Intercorrelations, Means, and Standard Deviations for Four Achievement Variables ($N = 75$)

Variable	1	2	3	4	M	SD
1. Visualization	—	.36**	.13	.42**	5.24	3.91
2. SAT math	—	—	.37**	.79**	490.53	94.55
3. Grades	—	—	—	.50**	5.68	1.57
4. Math achievement	—	—	—	—	12.56	6.67

*p < .05.
**p < .01.

TABLE F.4

Comparison of Male and Female High School Students on a Math Achievement Test, Grades, and a Visualization Test ($n = 34$ males and 41 females)

Variable	M	SD	t	df	p
Math achievement			2.70	73	.009
Males	14.76	6.03			
Females	10.75	6.70			
Grades			−.90	73	.369
Males	5.50	1.64			
Females	5.83	1.52			
Visualization			2.39[a]	57.2[a]	.020
Males	6.43	4.47			
Females	4.26	3.11			

[a] The t and df were adjusted because variances were not equal.

TABLE F.5

One-Way Analysis of Variance of Grades in High School by Father's Education

Source	df	SS	MS	F	p
Between groups	2	18.14	9.07	4.09	.02
Within groups	70	155.23	2.22		
Total	72	173.37			

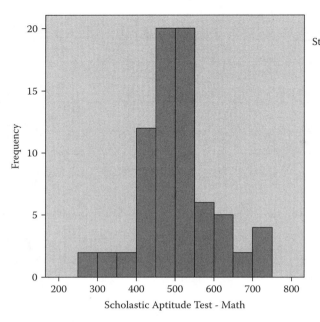

Mean = 490.53
Std. Dev. = 94.553
N = 75

Note: The figure number is italicized but the caption text is not. Also, the caption text is sentence case. In APA the captions are all listed on a separate page but for student papers and theses place them below the figure.

FIGURE F.2
Frequency bar chart of the Scholastic Aptitude Test math scores.

accompanying text or table. There are numerous types of figures; however, a few things are consistent with all figures. The figure number and caption description are located *below* the figure, and the description, similar to that of the title of a table, is detailed enough so that the figure can be understood without the accompanying text. Also, like tables, figures must be mentioned by number in the text before the figure is presented, and key points must be described briefly in the text (Figure F.2). Some cautions in using figures are as follows:

1. Make it simple. Complex diagrams that require lengthy explanation should be avoided unless it is an integral part of the research.
2. Use a minimum number of figures for just important points. If too many figures are used, important points may be lost.
3. Integrate text and figure. Make sure the figure compliments and enhances the accompanying text.

Subject Index

Author Index

A

Ager, C., 77
Algina, J., 161
Allison, D. B., 73
Altman, E., 204
Alwell, M., 83
Anastasi, A., 156, 177
Angold, A., 320–323
Antes, G., 254
Aoki, Y., 313–314

B

Baer, D., 82
Bambara, L., 77
Bangsber, D. R., 13, 21, 91, 186, 377
Bartko, J. J., 160
Barrett, K. C., 209, 218, 220–221, 223, 398, 399, 401, 421, 450
Baugh, F. G., 84
Beasley, T. M., 73
Beile, P., 25
Bernstein, I. H., 156, 161
Biemer, B. P., 186
Blair, J., 177, 185
Boote, D. N., 25
Brockman, L., 171
Brossart, D. F., 84
Brothen, T., 12, 24, 58, 184, 370, 397
Brooks, J. O. III, 255
Bryze, K. A., 170
Burbules, N. C., 17,
Busch-Rossnagel, N. A., 171

C

Campbell, D. T., 57, 62, 68, 103, 105–106, 107, 341, 342, 350, 357, 362–363
Campbell, J. M., 84,
Campbell, J. P., 155
Carpenter, W. T., 160
Casey, M. A., 186
Castellan, N.J., 295
Chiappisi, H., 324

Childs, K., 76
Clarke, S., 76
Cobb, B., 83
Cohen, J., 128, 171–172, 173, 238–239, 241, 243, 252, 253, 308, 312, 322–323, 330, 349, 391, 401, 402
Coll, J. R., 326–328
Collins, K. M. T., 26
Conners, C. K. 320–323
Cook, T. D., 57, 62, 68, 103, 105–106, 107, 341, 342, 350, 363
Cooper, H., 255
Corbin, J., 97
Cordova, J. S., 324
Crabtree, B. F., 96
Cramer, K. M., 22
Creswell, J. W., 21, 96, 98, 421
Crocker, L., 161
Cronbach, L. J., 153, 157, 161, 168, 169
Cumming, G., 240
Czaja, R., 177

D

Daniel, L.G., 157, 159
De-Alba, R. G., 84
Dellinger, A. B., 25, 26
Denzin, N. K., 96
Despain, L. H., 160, 328, 329
DeVellis, R. F., 185
Dickinson, D. B., 13, 21, 91, 186, 377
Dillman, D. A., 177, 184, 185, 210
DiLorenzo, T., 12, 40, 92, 104, 186, 373, 440
Dunlap, G., 76

E

Edgington, E., 83
Egger, M., 255
Emanuel, L., 404
Epstein, J. N., 320–323

F

Feldman, R. S., 289–292
Finch, S., 240
Fink, A., 27, 115, 398, 421
Fisher, A. G., 166–167, 169
Foster-Johnson, L., 76
Fowler, F. J., Jr., 115, 177
Fowler, F. J., 186
Franklin, R. D., 73
Fuller, H. M., 325

G

Gaito, J., 137
Gardner, G., 255
Ghiselli, E. E., 155
Glaser, B. G., 97
Gliner, G., 83
Gliner, J. A., 83, 251, 308, 328, 341, 381, 421
Gloeckner, G. W., 209, 398, 399, 401, 421, 450
Goddard, P., 296, 298, 299
Goodstein, D., 406
Goodwin, L. D., 166, 167, 171
Gorman, B. S., 73
Gray, J. A., 383
Gray, M. J., 160, 328, 329
Grimm, L. B., 333
Grissom, R. J., 251
Groves, R. M., 186

H

Halper, J., 12, 40, 92, 104, 186, 373, 440
Hardy, S. A., 12, 27, 40, 91–92, 159, 306–308, 329–332, 375, 440, 442
Harlow, L. L., 240
Harmon, R. J., 171, 251, 328, 341, 381, 421
Harrison T. R., 398, 421
Hart, C., 27, 392, 421
Hauser-Cram, P., 171
Haynes, R. B., 383, 388
Hedges, L. V., 255, 294